CANADIAN EDITION

LAUER

LAUER

ABRAMSON

AUGER

SOCIAL PROBLEMS
AND THE QUALITY OF LIFE

ROBERT H. LAUER
Alliant International University

JEANETTE C. LAUER
Alliant International University

ZELDA ABRAMSON
York University

JEANETTE A. AUGER
Acadia University

 **McGraw-Hill
Ryerson**

Toronto   Montréal   Boston   Burr Ridge, IL   Dubuque, IA
Madison, WI   New York   San Francisco   St. Louis   Bangkok   Bogotá
Caracas   Kuala Lumpur   Lisbon   London   Madrid   Mexico City   Milan
New Delhi   Santiago   Seoul   Singapore   Sydney   Taipei

Social Problems & The Quality of Life
Canadian Edition

ISBN: 0-07-093991-8

1 2 3 4 5 6 7 8 9 10 TCP 0 9 8 7 6

Printed and bound in the Canada

Statistics Canada information is used with the permission of the Minister of Industry, as Minister responsible for Statistics Canada. Information on the availability of the wide range of data from Statistics Canada can be obtained from Statistics Canada's Regional Offices, its World Wide Web site at <http://www.statcan.ca>, and its toll-free access number 1-800-263-1136.

Care has been taken to trace ownership of copyright material contained in this text; however, the publisher will welcome any information that enables them to rectify any reference or credit for subsequent editions.

Executive Sponsoring Editor: James Buchanan
Developmental Editor: Christine Gilbert
Director of Marketing: Jo-Ann DeLuca
Director of Sales: Jeff MacLean
Supervising Editor: Jaime Smith
Copy Editor: Kelli Howey
Senior Production Coordinator: Jennifer Wilkie
Page Layout: Michelle Losier
Cover Design: Sharon Lucas
Cover Image: © Bryan Mullennix/Photodisc
Printer: Transcontinental Printing Group

Library and Archives Canada Cataloguing in Publication
      Social problems & the quality of life / Robert H. Lauer ... [et al.]. —Canadian ed.

Includes bibliographical references and index.
ISBN 0-07-093991-8

      1. Social problems—Textbooks. 2. Quality of life—Textbooks. I. Lauer, Robert H. II. Title: Social problems and the quality of life.

HN106.S63 2005   361.1   C2005-904030-0

BRIEF CONTENTS

CONTENTS

▪▪ Chapter 6   Gender Inequality 157

▪▪ Chapter 7   Race, Ethnic Groups, and Racism 186

▪▪ PART 4   PROBLEMS OF SOCIAL INSTITUTIONS 215

▪▪ Chapter 8   Government and Politics 216

▪▪ Chapter 9   Work and the Economy 244

▪▪ Chapter 10   Education 272

■■ Chapter 11   Family Problems 299

■■ Chapter 12   Health Care and Illness: Physical and Mental 328

■■ PART 5   GLOBAL SOCIAL PROBLEMS 361

■■ Chapter 13   Peace and Conflict 362

▪▪ Chapter 14   The Environment 387

LIST OF FIGURES

LIST OF TABLES

People everywhere want to maximize their quality of life. There is widespread agreement that a high quality of life requires such things as a good education, freedom from fear of crime, good housing, meaningful work, and good health. A high quality of life, then, can be attained only if people deal with the social problems that detract from that quality. As the authors point out in the first chapter of this text, a social problem is, by definition, a condition or pattern of behaviour that is incompatible with people's desired quality of life.

To deal with a problem, you must understand it—how it affects the quality of life, what causes it, what tends to maintain it. Sociologists have used three theoretical perspectives to answer these questions, to analyze and deal with social problems. The authors discuss the three major perspectives in chapter 1, and show how elements from each are used to analyze individual problems and to talk about how the problems can be attacked.

The authors do not mean to give the impression here that either understanding a problem or attacking it is a simple matter. Even experts disagree on such things. The factors that combine to cause and perpetuate any particular problem are many and complex.

■■ Overview of the Canadian Edition

The Canadian Edition of *Social Problems & The Quality of Life* has a unique focus of "social solutions for social change." Each chapter has either a section or a pedagogical element addressing how various social problems can be addressed and how social action has made a difference to the quality of life. No other Canadian social problems text has this focus. In the first part of the text, the authors lay the groundwork by establishing key approaches to social problems. In the remaining sections, they discuss the social problems that most acutely influence our lives, and examine each problem for its impact on the quality of our lives.

■■ Organization

This book is divided into five parts and 14 chapters. Part 1 introduces students to social problems. Chapter 1 discusses the various tools needed, including the difference between social problems and personal problems and a discussion of sociological theories and methods and fallacious ways of thinking.

In part 2, the authors look at a cluster of problems that involve behaviour that is diverse. Chapters 2 through 4 cover the problems of sexual diversity, alcohol and other drugs, and crime and social control.

Part 3 provides examples of problems that involve social inequality. Poverty (chapter 5) is inequality in income and wealth. Gender inequality (chapter 6) and racial and ethnic inequality (chapter 7) include the multiple ways in which there is disparity in valued things between genders and among the various multicultural groups across the country.

Part 4 focuses on problems of social institutions. Chapters 8 through 12 cover the institutions of government and politics, work and the economy, education, family, and health care. These institutions are factors in other kinds of social problems, but are also problematic in themselves.

Finally, part 5 covers two global social problems: peace and conflict (chapter 13) and the environment (chapter 14). These problems pose a concern to civilization itself, and cannot be understood apart from their global context.

▪▪ Features

Social Problems & The Quality of Life, Canadian Edition, is

- organized around the *quality of life* theme, giving the book a sense of continuity and keeping it grounded in the fact that human beings are the chief victims of social problems and also the chief beneficiaries of their solutions.
- unique "from social problems to solutions" approach
- based on a Socratic framework for defining and understanding social problems
- cognizant of different theoretical perspectives in the analysis of social problems
- focused on social solutions throughout the text
- part of a technology and solutions package

▪▪ Pedagogical Features

- **"From Social Problems to Solutions"**—Unique sections throughout the text that suggest ways for improving each problem discussed and provide suggestions for what can be done; this approach goes beyond the mere analysis of a problem and encourages students to seek solutions themselves.
- **Global Comparison boxes**—Provide fascinating cross-cultural discussions that add dimension to students' understanding of social problems by giving them a glimpse into how other countries address their social problems.
- **Involvement boxes**—Describe various scenarios for activities students can participate in that will help them to obtain a greater understanding of the social problem and get them thinking about ways they can help bring about social change.
- **Public Policy and Private Action boxes**—Provide students with examples of how legislation and government are dealing with a particular social problem, and asks them to "think outside the public policy box."
- **Fallacy icons**—Marginal icons identify how people use the fallacies detailed in chapter 1 to draw erroneous conclusions about social problems.

▪▪ WHAT'S NEW FOR THE CANADIAN EDITION?

Chapter 1—Understanding Social Problems

- Thorough Canadian content
- Updated Canadian statistics and data
- Section on fallacies revised and condensed for ease of reading
- End of chapter material revised and updated

Chapter 2—Sexual Diversity

- Revised title to better reflect Canadian attitudes and values
- Thorough Canadian content including data, statistics, and examples
- Information on legislation regarding youth prostitution, child pornography, and same-sex marriage
- End of chapter material revised and updated

Chapter 3—Alcohol and Other Drugs

- Completely revised and updated with Canadian data and statistics on such topics as alcohol abuse and drug use
- Section on Aboriginal substance abuse problems
- Information on tobacco consumption and health care costs
- Section on decriminalization of marijuana
- End of chapter material revised and updated

Chapter 4—Crime and Social Control

- Revised chapter title to better reflect movement away from the concept of "delinquency" in sociology
- Entire chapter extensively revised to include current Canadian statistics and data
- Complex relationship among the state, family, and the individual in understanding crime is emphasized
- End of chapter material completely revised and updated

Chapter 5—Poverty

- Revised and updated to include current Canadian data and statistics
- Information on food banks added as an Involvement Box, encouraging students to take an active role in their society
- Discussion on poverty and minority groups
- Various Canadian examples of how citizens can organize and effect change, such as the Out of the Cold program in Toronto
- End of chapter material revised and updated

Chapter 6—Gender Inequality

- Chapter revised and updated to include current Canadian statistics and data
- Discussion of the White Ribbon Campaign—the men's movement to end violence against women
- Section on Canadian pay equity legislation
- Discussion of the growing concern in Canadian schools about gender inequalities between male and female students
- End of chapter material revised and updated

Chapter 7—Race, Ethnic Groups, and Racism

- Entire chapter thoroughly revised to better reflect Canadian multicultural values and culture
- Current Canadian data and statistics added throughout the chapter
- Discussion on housing discrimination, including that against Aboriginals
- Discussion of racial profiling issue with regard to various police forces
- End of chapter material revised and updated

Chapter 8—Government and Politics

- Includes a section on government scandals (with the Liberal Sponsorship Scandal as an example)
- Chapter completely revised to reflect the Canadian system of government, including discussion of federal, provincial, and municipal government systems
- Current data and statistics on demographics of voting
- Discussion of the *War Measures Act* and The October Crisis in 1970 to provide historical background with regard to government powers

- Discussion of government legislation to fight terrorism and its impact on civil liberties
- End of chapter material revised and updated

Chapter 9—Work and the Economy

- Chapter revised to include current Canadian data and statistics on the workforce and economy
- Sections on women's participation in the workforce and on unionization in Canada
- Discussions of workplace stress and workplace health and safety
- Discussion of workplace discrimination (race, gender, pay equity)
- End of chapter material revised and updated

Chapter 10—Education

- Chapter completely revised to reflect the Canadian system of education, including primary, secondary, and post-secondary systems
- Discussion of private and public schools in Canada
- Chapter revised to include current Canadian data and statistics
- Student debt in post-secondary education is discussed
- Discussion on educational attainment in Canada and how it compares to other countries
- Section on government spending on education
- Discussion of problems of racism and bullying in Canadian schools
- End of chapter material revised and updated

Chapter 11—Family Problems

- Chapter revised with current Canadian data and statistics, such as divorce and birth rates
- Discussion of child abuse, including information on the "spanking law" legislation
- Section on same-sex marriage and the changing face of the family
- Section on spousal/family violence and its effects on the quality of life
- End of chapter material revised and updated

Chapter 12—Health Care and Illness: Physical and Mental

- Chapter completely revised to include discussion of Canadian health care system and its problems
- Current Canadian data and statistics included throughout, such as on health care spending
- *From Social Problems to Solutions* feature includes discussion of the Romanow report
- Section on health status of First Nations people
- Discussion of genetic testing
- Section on history of medicare in the Canadian health care system
- Discussion of health care spending on drugs
- End of chapter material revised and updated

Chapter 13—Peace and Conflict

- Focus of the chapter is on war as it pertains to other conflictual situations (*i.e.*, not just the war in Iraq, but the war against cancer, AIDS, hunger, terrorism)
- The ways in which terrorism impacts Canadian life is also discussed (*i.e.*, Canadian anti-terrorism legislation)

- Canada's role as a peacekeeper is emphasized throughout the chapter
- Canadian peacekeeping missions such as Rwanda and Afghanistan are included as examples
- Current Canadian data and statistics on such topics as military spending are included
- End of chapter material revised and updated

Chapter 14—The Environment

- Discussion of Canadian environmental law and on the Kyoto Accord
- Chapter revised to include current Canadian data and statistics, such as air quality and pollution and their effects on the health care system
- Discussion of Canada's energy consumption and its effects on our natural resources
- Sections on contamination of water supply (*i.e.*, Walkerton, Ontario and Sydney, Nova Scotia) and its effects on Canadians
- End of chapter material revised and updated

▪▪ Supplements

Instructor's Supplements

Your **Integrated Learning (*i*Learning) Sales Specialist** is a McGraw-Hill Ryerson representative who has the experience, product knowledge, training, and support to help you assess and integrate any of the below-noted products, technology, and services into your course for optimum teaching and learning performance. Whether it's using our test bank software, helping your students improve their grades, or putting your entire course online, your *i*Learning Sales Specialist is there to help you do it. Contact your local *i*Learning Sales Specialist today to learn how to maximize all of McGraw-Hill Ryerson's resources!

McGraw-Hill Ryerson offers a unique *i*Services program designed for Canadian faculty. For additional information visit http://www.mcgrawhill.ca/highereducation/iservices.

Instructor's Online Learning Centre (OLC)
The OLC at **www.mcgrawhill.ca/college/lauer** includes a password-protected Web site for Instructors. The site offers a downloadable Instructor's Manual and access to PageOut, the McGraw-Hill Ryerson Web site development centre.

Instructor's CD-ROM contains the Instructor's Manual, Computerized Test Bank, and PowerPoint Presentation.

Instructor's Manual The Instructor's Manual contains (for each chapter of the text) chapter outlines, learning objectives, key terms, section summaries, lecture/discussion topics, class and student activities, suggestions for term research projects, and essay questions.

EZ Test McGraw-Hill's EZ Test is a flexible and easy-to-use electronic testing program. The program allows instructors to create tests from book-specific items. It accommodates a wide range of question types and instructors may add their own questions. Multiple versions of the test can be created and any test can be exported to use with course management systems such as WebCT, BlackBoard, or PageOut. The program is available for Windows and Macintosh environments.

PowerPoint® Presentation   This presentation system offers visual presentations that may be edited and manipulated to fit a particular course format. These slides contain useful outlines, summaries, and exhibits from the text.

Student Supplements

Student Online Learning Centre   This powerful electronic learning aid, located at **www.mcgrawhill.ca/college/lauer**, offers a wealth of materials including quizzes, flashcards, crossword puzzles, learning objectives, chapter outlines, chapter summaries, Internet exercises, annotated Weblinks, bonus material, *Globe and Mail* news feeds, access to E-Stat, and much more.

PowerWeb   A unique online tool that gives you access to course-related journal articles, weekly updates, timely world news, Weblinks, a discipline-specific search engine, study tools, and interactive exercises.

■■ Acknowledgments

Extensive feedback from numerous reviews and the valuable suggestions provided by that process helped us to develop this Canadian Edition. Thank you to the following colleagues for their invaluable advice:

Kimberley Ducey, Brock University
Leonard Friesen, Wilfrid Laurier University
Lindsay Harris, Algonquin College
Andrew D. Hathaway, McMaster University
Kelly Little, St. Clair College
Beverly Matthews, Mount Royal College
Keith Nickson, George Brown College
Vappu Tyyska, Ryerson University
Marni Westerman, Douglas College

We would like to thank Sarah Jacobs, Kate Rossiter, Miranda Snow, and Myka Tucker-Abramson for their invaluable research assistance. Ron Jourard and Hugh Benevides provided invaluable expertise in criminal law and the environment, respectively. Box 12.2—Canada's Health Care System, was compiled and written by Kate Rossiter; box 14.2—Canada's Environmental Law Regime and box 14.3—The Kyoto Accord, were compiled and written by Sarah Jacobs.

At McGraw-Hill Ryerson, we would like to thank James Buchanan, Executive Sponsoring Editor; Jaime Smith, Supervising Editor; Kelli Howey, Copy Editor; and a very special thanks to Christine Gilbert, our Developmental Editor, for their support and assistance throughout this process.

And finally, we are grateful to our families and friends for all of their support and encouragement. Of note, Zelda would like to thank Myka and Zak for their intellectual curiosity and enthusiasm, and John for his gentle presence. Jeanette thanks Susan for sharing her sabbatical with this manuscript preparation and writing.

Zelda Abramson
York University

Jeanette A. Auger
Acadia University

Chapter Opener

Chapter Previews: Chapter-opening vignettes personalize the various problems presented in the text and chapter objectives keep students on track as they work through the chapters.

Global Comparison box

Fascinating cross-cultural discussions that add dimension to students' understanding of social problems by giving them a glimpse into how other countries address their social problems.

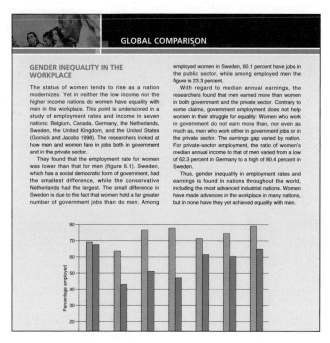

Involvement box

These boxes describe various scenarios for activities students can participate in that will help them to obtain a greater understanding of the social problem and get them thinking about ways they can help bring about social change.

LEGALIZING MARIJUANA?

Recall from chapter 3 that in the early part of the 1900s the use of marijuana and other opiates was not a criminal offence. More than 70 percent of Canadians now believe that marijuana should be legalized. Marijuana is neither addictive nor harmful when used occasionally. Further, others have argued that the legalization of marijuana can financially benefit the state: "If we treat marijuana like any other commodity we can tax it, regulate it, and use the resources the industry generates rather than continue a war against consumption and production that has long since been lost" (Easton 2004; reported on CTV.ca). In the meantime, drug offence rates continue to increase: in 2002 three-quarters of all drug offences involved marijuana; of these, 72 percent were for possession of less than 30 grams (Wallace 2004).

Write an informed letter to your member of Parliament either recommending or opposing the legalization of marijuana. Your letter should include arguments regarding the costs and benefits of legalization and what effect it would have on crime rates in Canada.

Public Policy and Private Action box

These features provide students with examples of how legislation and government are dealing with a particular social problem, and asks them to "think outside the public policy box."

PUBLIC POLICY & PRIVATE ACTION

Tobacco consumption is by far the most important risk factor for lung cancer and is also a significant risk factor for other diseases including heart diseases, chronic obstructive pulmonary diseases (COPD), and cancer of the mouth. Decreasing tobacco consumption could therefore reduce healthcare costs, and increase the quality of life of those who stop smoking or decide not to start.

... [A] 1-percent reduction in smoking prevalence in Canada may be associated with a decrease of 4.85 cases of heart disease per 100,000 people and 0.44 cases of lung cancer per 100,000 people. Moreover, a decrease of one cigarette smoked per day for daily smokers may be linked to a 3.2 per 100,000 decrease in lung cancer. For the country as a whole, this implies that in 1999, every combined decrease of 1 percent in smoking prevalence and of one smoked cigarette per

reduction in cases of heart disease cases and 1,108 in cases of lung cancer. These translate into healthcare cost savings of $39.5 million. Since these two conditions represent 28.9 percent of tobacco-related hospital days, the maximum healthcare cost savings could amount to $39.5 million / 28.9 percent = $136.7 million following a decrease of 1 percent in smoking prevalence and of one smoked cigarette per day among daily smokers. Such calculations assume that the unit costs of treatment for other tobacco-related diseases are similar to that of heart disease and lung cancer. A more conservative estimate may fall between $40 million and $80 million.

SOURCE:
"Impact of an anti-tobacco campaign on direct health care costs in Canada," A Study by Analysis Group / Economics Commissioned by the Canadian Council for Tobacco Control, May 2002.

Myth Buster icon

Marginal icons identify how people use the fallacies detailed in chapter 1 to draw erroneous conclusions about social problems.

no of wives who did not bear him a son (Ironically, it is now known that the male chromosome, not the female, determines the sex of the child), to the unfaithful husband of today who blames his wife for the affair *he* is having.

In the 1980s and 1990s, as Carol Tavris (1990) pointed out, a number of books were published with the ostensible purpose of helping women. Many of them, however, basically fell into the trap of blaming the victim, the *fallacy of personal attack*. One book discusses the "Cinderella complex," a hidden fear of independence. Another tells women that they tend to "love too much." A number of books have looked at the problem of "codependency," which included an addiction to men who abuse or who are addicted to drugs or alcohol. Many women joined recovery groups to overcome their "disease" of codependency. The women learn that they are as responsible for their spouses' problems as the spouses themselves, because they "enable" the spouse to continue the problem behaviour. (Of course, men also can be codependent, but books and articles seem to focus on it as a problem of women.)

From Social Problems to Solutions section

Unique sections throughout the text that suggest ways for improving each problem discussed and provide suggestions for what can be done.

 From Social Problems to Solutions

Our analysis suggests a variety of ways to attack the various problems of education. Clearly, it must be a multifaceted attack. Undoubtedly, parental involvement is one of the crucial factors in children's educational attainment. Among other things, having high expectations for the children's education, creating an educationally rich environment in the home, and helping with homework will make a difference in how much children achieve academically (Bibby 2001).

Another obvious need is reform of school financing. The inequities between school boards must be addressed. In addition, a variety of other efforts and proposals exist that hold promise: quality enhancement measures, efforts to reduce racial and ethnic inequality, and compensatory and other innovative programs. Some are quite controversial.

End of chapter material

Chapter reviews, end of chapter summaries, key terms lists, and study questions provide students with ample review and study materials.

■■ SUMMARY

Good health is a primary value of Canadians. Some advances have been made, as indicated by the increasing life expectancy. The main problem of physical health today is chronic diseases rather than the infectious diseases that plagued society in earlier times. Millions of Canadians are limited in their activities because of chronic conditions. There is general agreement about the classification of mental disorders, which are found in all societies. It is difficult to predict the exact percentage of the Canadian population that suffers from some kind of mental disorder. It has been estimated that approximately 20 percent of Canadians will be affected by mental illness in any year.

Illness affects the quality of life in many ways. The illness itself and the inadequate care that many Canadians receive cause stress and suffering. Interpersonal relationships are adversely affected. Individual freedom is threatened by certain medical advances. Often, heavy economic costs are involved for the nation and for individuals. Both physical and mental illnesses cause fears and anxiety. There is, in fact, a close relationship between physical and mental illness; each can be a factor in bringing about the other, so the individual can be caught in a vicious circle.

Structural factors contribute to the problem. Certain stress-inducing roles have been associated with illness,

especially the female role and certain occupational roles. Patterns of interaction and socialization in the family can promote or inhibit good physical and mental health. The industrial economy exposes people to carcinogenic materials and to various pollutants. Fluctuations in the economy generate stress. Political decisions reflect economic interests rather than health needs.

Health care problems are more serious for those in the lower than the higher socioeconomic strata. People in the lower strata suffer higher rates of mental and physical illness and receive less adequate care for both. Also, different kinds of illness characterize the various socioeconomic strata.

Among social psychological factors, attitudes and values are related to illness. The ill person's attitudes about the illness and his or her prospects for recovery are important. Negative attitudes toward one's work and certain attitudes rooted in traditional values increase the probability of illness. Once a person is ill, negative attitudes of others can inhibit recovery—a problem stressed by labelling theory. Finally, the deterioration of Canada's health care system over the last 15 years has contributed to the maldistribution of care. But most Canadians, including the economically secure, value and are committed to a universal health care system.

■■ KEY TERMS

AIDS 332	Incidence 329	Neurosis 336	Schizophrenia 337
Carcinogenic 349	Life Expectancy 330	Pica 351	Socialization 349
Deinstitutionalization 337	Manic-Depressive	Prevalence 329	Stigma 340
Epidemiology 329	Reaction 337	Psychosis 336	
Etiology 348	Medicalization 341	Psychosomatic Disorder	
Iatrogenic Problems 340	Morbidity 348	336	

■■ STUDY QUESTIONS

1. What are the various kinds of physical and mental illness, and how prevalent are they?
2. What kinds of suffering are associated with illness?

7. How do gender and occupational roles contribute to health and illness?
8. In what ways is the health problem affected by the

Foundations

A Chinese philosopher remarked that one should not attempt to open clams with a crowbar. In other words, any task demands the proper tools. Part I of this book is about the proper tools for the study of social problems. What kind of perspective should you bring to the study? What kind of information do you need, and what are the proper ways to gather it? Unless you answer such questions appropriately, you cannot answer the vexing question of how to deal with social problems. This part, then, prepares you to delve into particular problems. It shows you how to use the proper tools to open the "clams."

UNDERSTANDING SOCIAL PROBLEMS

LEARNING OBJECTIVES

1. Explain the difference between personal and social problems.

2. Understand how to address social problems using sociological approaches.

3. Understand three of the different theoretical perspectives used to explain and analyze social problems.

4. Explain the meaning of social research.

5. Give examples of different kinds of social research and describe how they have been used to study social problems.

"WHY IS IT MY FAULT?"

Marie, her husband, Jim, and their two children had a good life until Jim lost his job. Stress built up, their marriage fell apart, and he moved to another province. Marie's life has never been the same:

> I've never gotten any financial help from Jim since we were divorced. I went to work. It was really hard, raising two kids by myself and working full-time. But we were making it. And I enjoyed working—having people tell me I was doing a good job. Then the company downsized and I was laid off. It's been awful since then. My son dropped out of school, started hanging out with a bad group of kids, and started using and selling drugs. My daughter moved in with her boyfriend and is now pregnant. There is no-one I can turn to in the community.
>
> For the first time in my life, I know what it's like to be poor. I know what it's like to try to get help from the government. And you know one of the worst things? It's feeling ashamed. It's feeling like for some reason it's my fault, like there's something I could have done to avoid it. Why is this my fault? I keep telling myself I shouldn't feel that way, but I can't help it. ■

▪▪ INTRODUCTION

Who is at fault if you are poor? Are you responsible because you are lazy and unwilling to work or because you are a spendthrift and refuse to properly manage your finances? If so, you have a personal problem. Or are there other factors such as the state of the economy that are responsible for your situation? If so, you are caught up in a social problem. Later in this chapter we will define social problems precisely. As a preliminary definition, however, think of social problems as behaviours or conditions that are caused by factors external to individuals and that detract from the quality of life.

Actually, "we are all part of some social problem" (Lopata 1984:249). In fact, we are all part of the biggest social problem of all—the race to save the planet (Brown 2000). These assertions will become increasingly clear in subsequent chapters. In addition, many individuals are wrestling with several problems at once. For example, the stress of poverty may lead to health problems, both mental and physical. If the impoverished individual is a woman or a minority, the stress may be intensified. The individual also may have to deal with unemployment or underemployment, poor performance at school by a child, and the threat of victimization by criminals. Indeed, social workers deal with families who are coping simultaneously with the majority of problems discussed in this book!

It is important, therefore, to understand the difference between social and personal problems. Canadians tend to turn social problems into personal problems and to deal with them by trying to identify *who is at fault*. So your first task in this chapter is to understand the distinction between personal and social problems as well as the difference it makes when a particular problem is defined as personal or as social.

We also look at the sociological approach and explain a model for understanding problems as *social* rather than *personal*. Finally, we discuss two important tools of analysis for social problems—critical thinking skills and methods of research.

▪▪ PERSONAL VERSUS SOCIAL PROBLEMS

personal problem
a problem that can be explained in terms of the qualities of the individual

social problem
a condition or pattern of behaviour that contradicts some other condition or pattern of behaviour; is defined as incompatible with the desired quality of life; is caused, facilitated, or prolonged by social factors; involves intergroup conflict; and requires social action for resolution

institution
a collective pattern of dealing with a basic social function; typical institutions identified by sociologists are the government, economy, education, family and marriage, and religion

We define a **personal problem** as one whose causes and solutions lie within the individual and his or her immediate environment. A **social problem,** on the other hand, is one whose causes and solutions lie outside the individual and the immediate environment. This distinction is not based on the individual's experience of suffering, because a certain amount of suffering may occur in either case.

C. Wright Mills (1959:8–9) made a similar distinction, calling personal problems the "personal troubles of milieu" and social problems the "public issues of social structure." He offered many illustrations of the difference between the two. If one individual in a city is unemployed, that individual has a personal trouble. The person may have personality problems, may lack skills, or may have family difficulties that consume all of his or her energy. But if there are 100 million jobs in a society and 150 million people are available for work, this is a public issue. Even without personal problems, a third of the people will be unemployed. Such a problem, thus, cannot be resolved solely by dealing with individual personalities or motivations.

Similarly, a man and woman may have personal troubles in their relationship. They may agonize over their troubles and ultimately separate or divorce. If theirs is one of few marriages that experience such problems, you may conclude that they have personal problems and their marriage broke up because of some flaw in their personalities or in their relationship. But when the divorce rate soars and millions of families are broken up, you must look for causes and solutions beyond the personalities of individuals. The question is no longer "What is wrong with those people?" but "What has happened to the **institution** of marriage and the family in our society?"

Whether you define a problem as social or as personal, then, is crucial. The distinction determines how you perceive the causes of the problem, the consequences of the problem, and *appropriate ways* to cope with the problem.

■■ The Causes of Problems

When asked why there is poverty in affluent North America, a 31-year-old female bank teller said the poor themselves are to blame because most of them "are lazy and unreliable . . . and the little money they do make is spent on liquor and nonnecessities rather than for their economic advancement" (Lauer 1971:8). This is a common approach; namely, that problems are personal. *The victim is blamed as both the source and the solution of the problem.*

Similarly, Aboriginal and some ethnic minorities are said to have problems because they don't work to advance themselves. Individualistic explanations, like this, are held even among many whites who otherwise seem to show little or no prejudice. Such "reasoning" can influence whites' attitude about government policies designed to raise the status of blacks and others (Kluegel 1990). Thus, the way problems are defined— as social or personal—has important consequences for identifying causes. In turn, the kinds of causes identified affect the way problems are handled.

A word of caution is in order here. We are not arguing that *all* problems are social problems, nor that personal problems have no social factors, nor that social problems are free of any personal elements. There are certainly psychological and, in some cases, physiological factors at work. The point is that if you do not look beyond such factors, you will have a distorted view about the causes of problems.

■■ The Consequences of Problems

Viewing a problem as either personal or social leads you to identify very different consequences as well as different causes. Consider, for example, a father who can obtain only occasional work and whose family, therefore, lives in poverty. If the man defines his problem as the result of his own inadequacies, he likely will despise himself and passively accept his poverty. Sennett and Cobb (1972:96) told of a nearly illiterate garbage collector who placed the blame for his lowly position entirely on himself: "Look, I know it's nobody's fault but mine that I got stuck here where I am, I mean . . . if I wasn't such a dumb— . . . no, it ain't that neither . . . if I'd applied myself, I know I got it in me to be different, can't say anyone did it to me." This man defined his problem as personal and, consequently, viewed himself as inadequate.

The *sense of inadequacy*—blaming or downgrading oneself—is not uncommon among those victimized by social problems. Some children who grow up in impoverished homes view themselves unfavourably, believing that their impoverishment is proof of their inferiority. Some women who are beaten by their husbands feel they have done something to deserve the abuse. Some people who lose their jobs during an economic crunch believe they are failures, even though they had no control over what happened.

If a problem is defined as personal, *individual strategies* are employed to cope with the problem. Thus, the individual looks inward for a solution. Sometimes that solution is found in an *escape mechanism,* such as neurosis, physical illness, heavy drinking, or self-destructive behaviour. At other times a solution is sought from specialists such as psychotherapists or religious advisers who help the person to change. These specialists may facilitate adjustment to the problem but not ultimately resolve it. If Canada's troubled families sought the help of counsellors, they might learn to cope with or endure their troubles. But troubled families would continue to appear just as frequently.

Helping individuals deal with personal problems is important; however, it is only a stopgap approach to social problems. Identifying something as a social problem views it from a much different perspective and leads to far different conclusions and actions. Thus, if a man defines his poverty as the result of a declining economy, he may join in collective action such as a social movement, a rent strike group, or an organization set up to relieve the plight of the poor. Rather than blame himself for his poverty, he sees it as a *social* problem and takes action to redress it.

Or consider the problem of rape. Whether rape is defined as a social or personal problem makes a great deal of difference (see figure 1.1). Defining it as a personal problem either *blames the victim* or *castigates the offender*. Defining it as a social problem recognizes the need for *collective action* that attacks factors outside the individual.

Several cases of rape (as reported in *Time,* September 5, 1983, pp. 28–29) illustrate the need to consider it a social rather than a purely personal problem. A physician, 39 years old, married, and the father of two children, confessed to raping 22 women and sexually attacking at least 10 other women, one of whom was a nun. The doctor was a respected member of his community by day but an attacker of women by night. A teenage girl, who decided to follow others and cool off in a park fountain on a hot July day, was raped by two young men while at least three adults ignored her screams for help. Another young woman met a man at a New Year's Eve party. The man's sister, whom the young woman knew, introduced them. The man drove the two women home, dropped his sister off first, then asked if he could come up to the young woman's apartment for coffee. He was a genial, polite man and, since she had no reason to suspect him, she agreed. Once in her apartment, however, the man forced her to participate in various sex acts. When she prosecuted, she discovered that the man was on parole for a prior rape conviction. Yet people who had been at the party testified on the man's behalf, claiming that they had seen the couple talking and that the woman had been drinking. The man was acquitted. Subsequently he was brought to trial again for the alleged rape of a 13-year-old girl.

FIGURE 1.1 ■ ■ ■

Some possible differences when a problem—in this case, rape—is defined as social or personal.

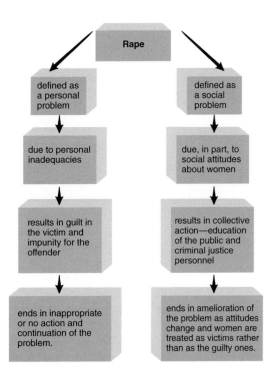

How can we account for these rapes? Were the victims at fault in the preceding cases? Did they bring it on themselves by luring their attackers? A female student told us, "My father always said that if a woman was raped, it was her fault, that she somehow provoked the guy to do it." Or can the rapes be attributed to mentally ill or evil males? Are the rapists "sick" individuals who need therapy? Or are they evil men who ought to be castrated? You can blame the victims and say that they have personal problems—their wayward behaviour. Or you can accuse the rapists of having personal problems—disturbed or evil natures. Neither will resolve the problem. Women who fight, scream, and risk their physical well-being (and even their lives) to ward off an attacker can hardly be said to be luring the man—and there was no evidence that the attackers were mentally ill.

Nor would castration solve the problem. Contrary to popular belief, castration does not prevent a man from having sexual relations. Castration has been used in a number of European countries to punish sex offenders; but of 39 offenders in West Germany who had voluntarily agreed to castration, 11 could still have sexual relations a number of years afterward, and four of the men had sex one to three times a week (Heim 1981).

Rape, in sum, is not a personal problem that can be solved by individual efforts. Like other social problems, rape requires collective action to attack such things as the social attitudes that legitimate exploiting women and a legal system that may treat the victim as harshly as the rapist does. Important differences, thus, result from defining a problem as social rather than personal. Unless problems like rape are defined as social, causes may not be identified nor solutions found.

■■ A MODEL FOR UNDERSTANDING

structural functionalism
a sociological theory that focuses on social systems and how their interdependent parts maintain order

conflict theory
a sociological theory that focuses on contradictory interests, inequalities between social groups, and the resulting conflict and change

symbolic interactionism
a sociological theory that focuses on the interaction between individuals, the individual's perception of situations, and the ways in which social life is constructed through interaction

interaction
reciprocally influenced behaviour on the part of two or more people

Given that problems are social and not merely personal, how do we go about understanding them? First let's define precisely what we mean by a *social problem:* It is *a condition or pattern of behaviour that (1) contradicts some other condition or pattern of behaviour and is defined as incompatible with the desired quality of life; (2) is caused, facilitated, or prolonged by factors that operate at multiple levels of social life; (3) involves intergroup conflict; and (4) requires social action to be resolved.* We explain this definition in the following pages. It uses major insights of sociological theories and is the basis for the model we use in discussing each of the problems in this book.

■■ A Theory-based Model

There are three major theoretical perspectives in sociology: **structural functionalism, conflict theory,** and **symbolic interactionism.** Each theory has distinctive emphases that are useful for understanding social phenomena. Structural functionalism focuses on social systems and the way in which their interdependent parts maintain order. Conflict theory focuses on contradictory interests of groups, inequalities in society, and the resulting conflict and change. Symbolic interactionism focuses on the **interaction** between individuals, the importance of knowing individuals' perspectives to understand their behaviour, and the ways in which social life is constructed through interaction.

To illustrate these three approaches, consider the problem of crime. A structural functional approach would point out the way that rapid change has weakened social solidarity and social institutions like the family, so that insufficient order is maintained. A conflict approach would note that the powerful groups in society define the kind of behaviour that is crime (resulting in higher rates among the poor), and that much crime results from the lack of opportunities for the poor and for racial or ethnic minorities. A symbolic interactionist approach would stress the fact that people learn criminal behaviour by interacting with, and accepting for themselves the perspective of, others who approve of such behaviour.

Some sociologists use only one of the theoretical approaches to analyze social problems. We believe that all three approaches are necessary. Each of the theoretical approaches to crime noted above is valid. Our model, therefore, incorporates emphases of each perspective (figure 1.2). In essence, the model posits mutual influence between social structural factors, social psychological/cognitive factors, and social interaction. Social problems arise when people define **contradictions** among these various elements as incompatible with their quality of life.

Each of the three theories contributes to this model. In structural functionalism, a problem involves a system of interdependent parts, including **norms** (shared expectations about behaviour), **roles** (behaviour associated with particular positions in the social structure), **institutions** (collective means of dealing with basic social functions, e.g., government, the family, and the economy), and **values** (things preferred because they are defined as having worth). The parts are interrelated and exert pressure to maintain the system.

According to conflict theory, however, contradictions and inequalities exist between the parts of the system that generate conflict between groups. This is manifested in the **stratification system,** the pattern of inequality of wealth, power, and prestige that exists in all societies.

And according to symbolic interactionism, social interaction and the perspectives of individuals, including their **attitudes** (predispositions of individuals toward something) and **ideologies** (sets of ideas that explain or justify some aspect of social life) are important components of the system. Only as you understand how an individual perceives his or her social world can you understand that individual's behaviour.

The pairs of arrows in the model indicate *mutual influence.* For example, social structural factors affect the way people interact. Norms and roles may lead a white person and a black person to treat each other as equals at the factory but not in other settings. The influence can go both ways: patterns of social interaction can alter the social structural factors. In recent years, for instance, women have interacted with men in ways that have altered the female role. Similarly, Aboriginal Canadians and non-whites have persisted in interacting with whites in ways that have changed traditional roles. An ideology of white supremacy and colonialism can help to create and main-

contradiction
opposing phenomena within the same social system

norm
shared expectations about behaviour

role
the behaviour associated with a particular position in the social structure

values
things preferred because they are defined as having worth

stratification system
arrangement of society into groups that are unequal with regard to such valued resources as wealth, power, and prestige

attitude
a predisposition about something in one's environment

ideology
a set of ideas that explain or justify some aspect of social reality

FIGURE 1.2 ■ ■ ■

A model for analyzing social problems.

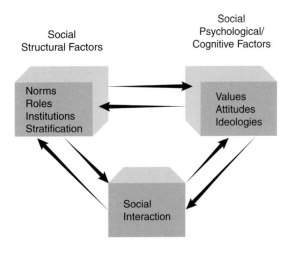

tain other races in a subservient role; but as minorities refuse to accept the role and assume instead the same kinds of roles as whites, the ideology will be rejected by increasing numbers of people.

By the very nature of social life, there are numerous *contradictions* among the elements in figure 1.2. This means that opposing phenomena exist within the same social system. The phenomena are opposed in the sense that both cannot be true or operative. When the contradictions are defined as incompatible with the *desired quality of life,* you have a social problem. For example, the limited opportunities available in the economy are a contradiction to the ideology that all people should support themselves by working. The contradiction, as we shall see in chapter 6, is incompatible with the desired quality of life of the poor.

By our definition, not all societal contradictions signal social problems, only those defined as detracting from the quality of life. In other words, objective data alone do not compose a problem. In accord with symbolic interactionism, only when people define a situation as problematic and persuade others to view it in the same way is there a social problem (Fine 2000).

Whether people generally define something as detracting from their quality of life depends upon such things as how the problem is presented in the media, how the problem squares with people's experiences, how readily people can understand the various facets of the problem, and how political leaders shape public opinion on issues (Hawden 2001). Such factors help explain why ozone depletion, for example, is more widely accepted as a problem than is global warming (Ungar 1998).

Finally, consider gender equality as another example of the usefulness of the model. Among the opposing phenomena involved in the problem are:

1. The *ideology* of equal opportunity versus the *reality* of limited opportunities for female participation in the economy.
2. The *value* of the pursuit of happiness versus the *narrowness* of the traditional female *role.*
3. The *value* of human dignity versus male–female *interaction* in which females are treated as intellectual inferiors.

Each of these oppositions has consequences that are incompatible with the desired quality of life of many women.

■■ Quality of Life

What is this *quality of life* that plays so prominent a role in determining whether a contradiction is defined as a social problem? Thoreau captured its meaning in his desire to avoid discovering, at the point of death, that

> I had not lived. I did not wish to live what was not life, living is so dear; nor did I wish to practise resignation, unless it was quite necessary. I wanted to live deep and suck out all the marrow of life . . . (Thoreau 1968:113)

The desire to "live deep," to maximize the quality of life, is reflected in a proliferation of studies in recent decades. In quality-of-life studies, cities and provinces and towns are evaluated in terms of such things as equality of opportunity, agriculture, crime rates, technology, education, climate, the economy, cultural opportunities, and health and welfare. They are then ranked according to their overall "quality of life."

After decades of these studies, there is considerable agreement about what Canadians define as important to the quality of their lives (Ferriss 2000). In essence, they evaluate their quality of life according to how well they are doing financially, physically, emotionally, socially, and culturally. Canadians want well-paying and meaningful work and financial security. They want good health, access to good health care facilities, opportunity for a good education, opportunity to participate in cultural activities, and opportunity to live and work in areas with minimal crime. Canadians also want respect from others, self-respect, and a sense of personal worth. Finally, they want to live without fear and with reasonable freedom from stress.

To the extent that these things are missing, Canadians perceive the quality of life to be diminished. Thus, the quality of life is reduced by such things as personal health problems (Woodruff and Conway 1992), work demands that interfere with nonworking time (Rice, Frone, and McFarlin 1992), and environmental problems (Tickell 1992).

Quality of life, then, involves far more than income. You may be able to purchase security devices for your home, but you can't buy total peace of mind when the newspapers regularly remind you of the pervasiveness of crime. You may be able to afford the best seats in the house, but that's meaningless if your community lacks cultural opportunities. You may live in the most expensive area available, but you can't shut out the polluted air that engulfs your property.

Moreover, undesirable conditions that diminish the quality of life affect you both directly and indirectly. For example, some people are the direct victims of criminal activity: assaults, muggings, robberies, rapes, swindles, and so forth. But everyone has some *fear of criminal victimization,* even people who have never been directly victimized. This fear may put limits on where they go or what they do or how secure they feel—limits that reduce the quality of their lives. In Canada, victimization surveys are conducted to ask people whether they have been victims of crime, and if so whether they reported it to the police. Various surveys have found that only 55 percent of crimes are reported to police (Besserer 2002). Unfortunately, like other crime statistics victimization surveys have limitations in that they require victims to understand what has happened to them and to be willing to disclose such information to interviewers and researchers conducting surveys (Johnson 1996). Where this situation is especially problematic is regarding older persons, who sometimes feel that they are to blame for violence against them, especially in the case of elder abuse (Auger and Tedford Little 2002).

In sum, there are numerous contradictions in society that create conditions incompatible with the desired quality of life. Everyone is affected, though some suffer far more than others. Because of the diminished quality of life, we define these contradictions and the conditions they create as social problems.

▪▪ From Social Problems to Solutions

Many individuals and groups are involved with attempts to create solutions to social problems. You are probably reading this book as a requirement for a university or college course—many academics are interested in conducting research in order to explain how social problems are created and maintained, by whom, where, and when. As well, academic researchers are involved in the search for solutions to social problems.

But academics are not the only people involved in this search: individuals and groups within the community at large are also engaged in this important work. Community groups in neighbourhoods across Canada are examining the social problems within their area. The concerns range from Neighborhood Watch programs to antipoverty groups, childcare programs for single-parent families, rape crisis centres, environmental action groups, and so on. For every social problem in Canada there are local groups seeking to more clearly understand the issue, who or what is involved, who can help, and where to find solutions.

Sometimes academics and community groups work together, sometimes not. Researchers working within academic settings can provide a great deal of experience, support, and assistance to community-based groups trying to bring about social change. Increasingly, funding agencies that provide money to academic researchers are requiring that they conduct *participatory research*, which includes the group attempting to find social solutions to social problems, in the research design and implementation as well as in the role of data providers. When we conduct participatory research we help individuals and groups create social change by encouraging and facilitating their participation in the process. In this approach, the people who experience the problem, or who are members of the community, have ownership of the research process. This type of research is also known as *action research*, *community development*, *action for social change*, and *public-interest research*.

When academic researchers conduct participatory research, we see our efforts as attempting to build a bridge between the academic world—seen by some as an "ivory tower"—to the world of community action where people in need may sometimes fall through the cracks; the challenge is to bridge this gap.

One author of this text has been involved in conducting participatory research for the past 25 years, working predominantly with older persons and those who are dying (and their important ones) in their attempts to improve services and programs as well as to raise awareness of the problems they have in accessing them.

Even though being older and having a life-threatening illness are not social problems *per se*, not having enough—or the right types of—programs and services available to meet needs is viewed by many to be a social problem. In addition, as the population of most parts of the world continues to grow older so too grows the need for social and health-related services, and the costs of these programs must be provided by all citizens. In these ways, the needs of the old and the dying, and their ability (or inability) to meet them, can be seen as social problems not just in Canada, but everywhere in the world. To know what those needs are, and who might be able to meet them, and at what cultural, social, and financial cost, it is important to ask not only the individuals most affected but also those who plan, provide, and pay for these programs and services.

Throughout Canada, various individuals and groups work to address and provide social solutions to meet the needs of older persons and the dying. Every province has a number of senior citizens' councils, old-age pensioner organizations, Royal Canadian Legions, Canadian pensioner concern branches, and provincial government–run advisory councils on the needs of elders, to name but a few. There are also federal governmental organizations such as the National Advisory Council on Aging (NACA) and the Division of Aging and Seniors.

In terms of the needs of the dying, especially regarding whether they are able to choose to die at home or in a hospital, nursing home, or hospice, agencies like the Canadian Hospice/Palliative Care Association, the Canadian Cancer Society, the Alzheimer's Society of Canada, and other community-based or government-assisted groups are there to address some of the problems encountered by these individuals and their families, friends, and communities.

In our quest for solutions to social problems it is important to recognize that what may be viewed as a problem for some is not necessarily the case for others. For example, although some Canadians, because of their religious or moral beliefs, may see being a lesbian or gay man as a social problem, for the individual who is a lesbian or gay man their sexual preference may feel normal and natural. While some may see the smoking of marijuana as a social problem (except in the case of those allowed to use it for medical purposes), for those who use this illegal drug this behaviour is seen as a pleasant and social activity similar to going out for a beer with friends.

It is important to recognize that not all social problems and their solutions are viewed the same way by all Canadians, which makes the search for solutions even more challenging and interesting.

▪▪ The Changing Nature of Social Problems

One additional factor adds to the difficulty of resolving social problems—both the definition and the objective aspects of a particular problem change over time. Sometimes the change may be so rapid that an issue barely has time to be a problem. Until the exceptionally hot and dry summer of 1988, the public did not respond much to the warnings of scientists about global warming (Ungar 1992). That summer brought the problem to the public's attention. In 1999, the National Oceanic and Atmospheric Administration (NOAA) noted that 1998 had been the hottest year on record, and the twentieth consecutive year that a global mean temperature exceeded the long-term average (cited in Mooney, Knox, Schacht, Nelson et al. 2001:471).

Thus, problems may *rise and decline in perceived importance* and rise again, as illustrated by the problem of poverty. Views of poverty have changed over time. A 1952 edition of a social problems text omitted the two chapters on poverty that had appeared in the original 1942 edition (Reinhardt, Meadows, and Gillette 1952). The omission reflected the belief in the 1950s that poverty was largely a problem of the past. (Even the 1942 edition reflected more the opinion of sociologists than that of the public.) Gallup opinion polls conducted in the U.S. since 1935 about the most important problems facing the nation show that the public did not consider poverty an important problem until 1965 (Lauer 1976). Concerns about poverty peaked in the 1960s and 1970s. By 1999, only 12 percent of Americans considered poverty the nation's most important problem (Polling Report 1999).

According to the *Canadian Fact Book on Poverty in Canada* (Forster 2002), while Canada routinely ranks among the top three countries in the world for overall living standards, UNICEF (United Nations Children's Fund) has criticized the Canadian government for maintaining disproportionately high levels of child poverty.

In 2001, the Organisation for Economic Co-operation and Development (OECD) conducted a study looking at poverty rates in all 29 of its member states and found that 47 million children in these countries live below the poverty line. The report primarily examined inequality using the OECD's own methodology of after-tax relative measurements (i.e., total income is half or less of the average national income). Table 1.1 compares the poverty rates of 20 of these countries.

One of the largest social problems facing Canadians is how to eradicate child poverty. Table 1.2 compares Canada with other OECD countries. The U.S. has one of the highest rates of child poverty relative to all OECD members: 22.4 percent of its children live in poverty, second of those countries listed in Table 1.2.

When examining child poverty rates, the Canadian Council on Social Development found an overall correlation between higher levels of public expenditures and lower relative poverty measures (Forster 2002). In other words, the more funds governments spent on eradicating child poverty, the less likely it was to find poor people living in those countries. Clearly, for a country with a wealth of economic and natural resources Canada has a long way to go in dealing with the social problem of poverty.

The objective conditions of poverty also have changed over time: the amount of poverty has changed (as measured by some standard such as family income); the composition of the poor has changed (such as the relative proportions of racial, ethnic, and age groups); and the organization of antipoverty efforts has changed (such as the vigour and focus of protest groups and official attitudes and programs).

TABLE 1.1 ■ ■ ▪

OECD Poverty Rates

Country	Mid 1980s	Most Recent
Australia	12.2	9.3
Austria	6.1	7.4
Belgium	10.5	7.8
Canada	11.6	10.3
Denmark	7.0	5.0
Finland	Not measured	4.9
France	8.0	7.5
Germany	6.4	9.4
Greece	13.4	13.8
Hungary	Not measured	7.3
Ireland	11.0	11.0
Italy	10.3	14.2
Mexico	21.3	21.9
Netherlands	3.4	6.3
Norway	6.9	10.0
Sweden	5.3	6.4
Switzerland	Not measured	6.2
Turkey	16.4	16.2
United Kingdom	6.9	10.9
United States	18.3	17.0

Source: M. Forster (2002). "Trends and driving factors in income distribution and poverty in the OECD area," *Labour Market and Social Policy Occasional Paper, No. 42*, Paris: OECD. Cited in *The Canadian Fact Book on Poverty: 2000*. Ottawa: Canadian Council on Social Development, 17.

TABLE 1.2 ■ ■ ▪

OECD Poverty Rates Compared to Canada

Country	Percentage
Mexico	26.2
United States	22.4
Italy	20.5
United Kingdom	19.8
Turkey	19.7
Canada	**15.5**
Australia	12.6
Germany	10.7
Hungary	10.3
France	7.9
Finland	4.4
Sweden	2.6

Source: M. Forster (2002). "Trends and driving factors in income distribution and poverty in the OECD area," *Labour Market and Social Policy Occasional Paper, No. 42*, Paris: OECD. Cited in *The Canadian Fact Book on Poverty: 2000*. Ottawa: Canadian Council on Social Development, 17.

Recognizing such changes in problems is important for both understanding and action. For example, many people continue to identify poverty as essentially a problem of work—the poor are unemployed. As you will see, the problem of poverty would be little changed even if every able-bodied person in Canada had a job. It is true that during the depression of the 1930s a considerable number of the impoverished were unemployed. Many people who lived through that period continue to associate poverty with unemployment, failing to recognize the changed nature of the problem. Today, a large number of poor people are working but still live in poverty. Therefore, to continue associating the two concepts is to misunderstand the contemporary problem and thereby fail to take appropriate action.

As you study the various problems, you will see fluctuations in all of them. Some appear to be getting better, and some appear to be getting worse. It is important to remember that improvement does not mean that the problem is resolved (gains can be quickly lost in the ongoing struggle for justice and equality), nor does deterioration mean that the problem is hopeless (lost ground may be regained and new ground may be gained dramatically when appropriate social action is taken).

▪▪▪ Analyzing Social Problems

The definition given earlier shapes our approach to each problem considered in this book. First, we "get the feel" of the problem by seeing how it affects people's lives and examining how the problem involves a contradiction and is defined as incompatible with the desired quality of life. Second, we analyze the multiple-level factors involved in the problem. We do not relate every factor identified in figure 1.2 to each problem: Research has not yet identified the components of every problem. Yet in each we see the multiple-level components that show how the problem arises and is perpetuated. Third, we consider various ways to attack the problem. Our examination is sketchy (any adequate treatment would require a book in itself), but we do discuss some kinds of both public policy and private action that can ameliorate each problem.

Before we turn to specific problems, we need to address an additional issue. Seemingly reasonable statements are made about every social problem. For example, following a series of highly publicized killings by preteens and teenagers in the 1990s, explanations ranged from the pampering of criminals by the legal system to violence in video games and movies to mental illness. How do you know which of these, if any, are correct? Or to put it another way, how do you distinguish opinion from valid analysis?

critical thinking
the analysis and evaluation of information

First, you need to *develop critical thinking skills*. **Critical thinking** is the process of carefully attending to spoken or written information in order to evaluate its validity. Make sure you understand the information, then evaluate it by asking such questions as whether it is logical and reasonable. One important way to evaluate information is to look for *any fallacies of thinking*. These fallacies are commonly used when people analyze social problems. You will find illustrations throughout this book on how fallacies lead to misunderstandings.

Second, you need to examine how sociologists research social problems by gathering data to test various explanations. The data may lead you to revise your explanations. Remember, the study of social problems is not an exercise in speculation; it needs explanations that are supported by evidence. Let's look, then, at fallacious ways of thinking and at methods of social research.

■■ CRITICAL THINKING: RECOGNIZING FALLACIES

Nine different fallacies have been used to analyze social problems. An important aspect of critical thinking is the ability to recognize these fallacies. This enables you not only to assess the validity of information and arguments presented by others but also to make your own analyses with logic and clarity.

■■ Fallacy of Dramatic Instance

fallacy of dramatic instance
overgeneralizing

The **fallacy of dramatic instance** refers to the tendency to *overgeneralize,* to use one, two, or three cases to support an entire argument. This is a common mistake among those who discuss social problems. It may be difficult to counter because the limited number of cases often are a part of an *individual's personal experience.* In a 2004 social problems class where students were asked to discuss the issue of Aboriginal rights and land claims, one student remarked that "I am not responsible for the status of Indians today; I know several who live near me in the Northwest Territories who just live off welfare all the time and don't even look for work. They need to get jobs like the rest of Canadians" (Auger 2004).

This student, along with some of his peers, did not consider the impact of the systemic racism that exists in Canada toward Aboriginal people (and others) and affects their self-esteem, level of education and work experience, access to employment, and so on. The fallacy of dramatic instance mistakes a few cases for a general situation.

This fallacy is difficult to deal with because the argument is based partly on fact. There are, after all, black Canadians who are millionaires. Does this mean there is no discrimination and that any black person can attain success? To use another example, many Canadians believe that welfare recipients are "ripping off" the rest of us, that we are subsidizing their unwillingness to work and supporting them at a higher standard of living than we ourselves enjoy. Is this true? Yes, in a few cases. Occasionally, newspapers report instances of individuals making fraudulent use of welfare. But does this mean that most welfare recipients are doing the same? Do people on welfare really live better than people who work for a living?

The point is, in studying social problems, you must recognize that exceptions always exist. To use such cases in support of one's argument is to fall into the trap of the fallacy of dramatic instance, because social problems deal with general situations rather than with individual exceptions.

Systematic studies are needed to determine whether the one or two cases you know represent the norm or the exception. This does not mean that individual examples or cases are unimportant or unusable. At various points throughout this book (including the chapter-opening vignettes) we use examples of people's experiences. These examples are not given as proof or even as evidence. Rather, we use them to *illustrate the impact of social problems on people's quality of life.* These examples may dramatize better than statistics the ways in which people's lives are adversely affected by social problems.

■■ Fallacy of Retrospective Determinism

fallacy of retrospective determinism
the argument that things could not have worked out any other way than they did

The **fallacy of retrospective determinism** is the argument that things could not have worked out any other way than the way they did. It is a *deterministic* position, but the determinism is aimed at the past rather than the future. The fallacy asserts that what happened historically *had* to happen, and it had to happen just the way it did. If you accept this fallacy, the present social problems are inevitable. Whether racial discrimination, poverty, war, or the well-being of the family, the fallacy of retrospective determinism makes them unavoidable.

This fallacy is unfortunate for a number of reasons. History is more than a tale of *inevitable tragedies.* History is important for understanding social problems. You cannot fully understand the tensions between Canada's minority groups and the white majority unless you know about the decades of exploitation and humiliation preceding the emergence of the modern civil rights movement. Your understanding will remain clouded if you regard those events as nothing more than an inevitable process. Similarly, you cannot fully understand the tension between the People's Republic of China and the West if you view it only as a battle of economic ideologies. It is vital to know that the tension is based in the pillage and humiliation to which China was subjected by the West. Yet your understanding will not be enhanced by the study of history if you regard the Western oppression of China in the 19th century as inevitable.

If you view the past in terms of determinism, you have little reason to study it and are deprived of an important source of understanding. Furthermore, the fallacy of retrospective determinism is but a small step from the stoic *acceptance of the inevitable.* That is, if things are the way they have to be, why worry about them? Assuming that the future also is determined by forces beyond your control, you are left in a position of apathy: There is little point in trying to contest the inevitable.

The social problem of increasing tuition fees at Canadian universities is often invoked by students using this fallacy, who say that they feel powerless in the face of such increases and that they do not know *who* is increasing their tuition fees (e.g., the university administration, or provincial or federal governments), and *why* (e.g., as a result of reduced transfer credits from the federal to provincial governments, or as a result of universities needing to increase spending on programs). This lack of information and awareness as to the process of increased tuition costs causes a sense of the inevitability of the number of students who will be unable to pursue (or access) university education due to increasing costs. As one author's student commented, "Every year I worry about whether or not I shall be able to continue my degree in terms of finding the money. Tuition fees just seem to be here to stay."

This fallacy is probably less common in discussions about social problems than the fallacy of dramatic instance, but it does appear in everyday discussions. For example, during a classroom discussion on the topic of poverty in Canada, one author's student said, "If you look at the history of Canada we have always had poor people, especially in the marginalized provinces. It's just the way it is and I don't think it will change. We shall always have poverty in Canada." A businessman expressed a similar fatalism: "I don't actually know the cause of poverty, but it's here to stay and we must learn to live with it. We have to take the good with the bad."

An individual might view social problems in deterministic terms for reasons other than intellectual conviction. Determinism can relieve you of responsibility and can legitimate a lack of concern with efforts to effect changes you do not want. Whatever the basis for affirming determinism, the outcome is the same: You may as well accept the problem and learn to live with it, because it is inevitably and inextricably with you.

■■ Fallacy of Misplaced Concreteness

reification
defining what is abstract as
something concrete

There is a tendency to explain some social problems by resorting to **reification**—making what is abstract into something concrete. "Society," for example, is an abstraction. It is not like a person, an animal, or an object that can be touched. It is an idea, a way of thinking about a particular collectivity of people. Yet we often hear people assert that something is the fault of "society" or that "society" caused a certain problem. This

fallacy of misplaced concreteness
making something abstract into something concrete

is the **fallacy of misplaced concreteness.** In what sense can society "make" or "cause" or "do" anything? To say that society caused a problem leaves you helpless to correct the situation because you haven't the faintest notion where to begin. If, for example, society is the cause of juvenile delinquency, how do you tackle the problem? Must you change society? If so, how?

The point is that "society" is an abstraction, a concept that refers to a group of people who interact in particular ways. To *attribute social problems to an abstraction* like "society" does not help resolve the problems. Sometimes people who attribute the cause of a particular problem to society intend to *deny individual responsibility.* To say that society causes delinquency may be a way of saying that the delinquent child is not responsible for his or her behaviour.

You can recognize the social causes of problems without either attributing them to an abstraction like society or relieving the individual of responsibility for his or her behaviour. For instance, you could talk about the family's role in delinquency. A family is a concrete phenomenon. Furthermore, you could say that the family itself is a victim of some kind of societal arrangement, such as government regulations that tend to perpetuate poverty, cause stress, and create disruption in many families. You could say that families can be helped by changing the government regulations that keep some of them in poverty and, thereby, facilitate delinquent behaviour. As well, individual family members may perceive the delinquency in different ways than do others within the family. For example, a teenager may experience the smoking of marijuana as normal within his or her peer group, whereas parents may define this behaviour as delinquent.

Society, in short, does not cause anything. Rather, problems are caused by that which the concept of society represents—people acting in accord with certain social arrangements and within a particular cultural system.

■■ Fallacy of Personal Attack

fallacy of personal attack
argument by attacking the opponent personally rather than dealing with the issue

A tactic among debaters is to attack the opponent *personally* when you can't support your position by reason, logic, or facts. This diverts attention from the issue and focuses it on personality. We call this the **fallacy of personal attack** (philosophers call it *ad hominem*). It is remarkably effective in avoiding the use of reason or the consideration of evidence in discussing a social problem. In analyzing social problems, this fallacy can be used either to attack an opponent in a debate about a problem or to *attack the people who are the victims of the problem.* Ryan (1971) called this "blaming the victim" and said it involves nearly every problem in North America. In the case of persons living with HIV/AIDS in Canada there is often the suggestion that some with the virus "deserve" to have it, whereas others don't. What exists, then, is a dichotomy between those defined as "innocent" victims of the virus, who acquired it through tainted blood transfusions, and the "guilty" individuals who acquired the disease through intravenous drug use, or more than one sexual partner, or as the result of sexual orientation. In this example, rather than a focus on care for an individual regardless of how they acquired HIV/AIDS, the attention is on how they contracted it; this is another example of blaming the victim (Auger 2004).

Historically, the poor have suffered from this approach. Instead of offering sympathy or being concerned for the poor, people may label them as disreputable and, consequently, deserving of or responsible for their plight. This means that those who are not poor are relieved of any responsibility.

The meaning and seriousness of any social problem may be sidestepped by attacking the intelligence or character of the victims or of those who call attention to the problem. A few of the labels that have been used illustrate how common this approach is: deadbeats, draft dodgers, niggers, kikes, bums, traitors, perverts, queers, homos, and so on.

■■ Fallacy of Appeal to Prejudice

fallacy of appeal to prejudice
argument by appealing to popular prejudices or passions

In addition to attacking the opponent, a debater may try to support an unreasonable position by using another technique: **fallacy of appeal to prejudice.** (Philosophers call it argument *ad populum.*) It involves using popular prejudices or passions to convince others of the correctness of your position. When the topic is social problems, this means using *popular slogans* or *popular myths* to sway people emotionally rather than using reasoning from systematic studies. In a recent class discussion dealing with gambling, drugs, and alcohol addiction (Sociology 1033: Introduction to Social Problems, Auger 2004), students spoke about their assumptions that such addicts were "probably working-class people and those from the lower strata of society" rather than the facts showing that individuals in *all* social classes can be addicted to gambling, drugs, and alcohol.

In another discussion, on the topic of the provincial governments' stated need for new immigrants in the Maritime provinces, one female first-year Arts student remarked that, "I don't think we should allow any more of these people into Nova Scotia, they just take away jobs from Canadians."

Some slogans or phrases persist for decades and are employed to oppose efforts to resolve social problems. "Creeping socialism" has been used to describe many government programs designed to aid the underdogs of society. The term is not used when the programs are designed to help business or industry, or when the affluent benefit from the programs. As someone remarked, "What the government does for me is progress; what it does for you is socialism."

In some cases, the slogans use general terms that reflect *traditional values.* Thus, the various advances made in civil rights legislation—voting, public accommodations, open housing—have been resisted in the name of the "rights of the individual." These slogans help to perpetuate the myth that legislation that benefits minority Canadians infringes on the constitutional rights of the white majority.

Myths, in turn, help to perpetuate social problems. In the absence of other evidence, people tend to rely upon popular notions. Many Canadians continue to assume that rape is often the woman's fault because she has sexually provoked the man. These Canadians either have seen no evidence to the contrary or have dismissed the evidence as invalid. Unfortunately, myths tend to become so deeply rooted in people's thinking that, when they are confronted by new evidence, they have difficulty accepting it.

Myths are hard to break down; but, if you want to understand social problems, you must abandon popular ideas and assumptions and resist popular slogans and prejudices that cloud your thinking. Instead, you must make judgments based on evidence.

■■ Fallacy of Circular Reasoning

fallacy of circular reasoning
the practice of assuming something in order to prove the very thing that you assumed

In a response similar to the one noted above, some students also expressed the opinion that they couldn't get jobs when they graduate because Canada lets in "too many" immigrants. The idea was also suggested that "immigrants take away jobs that rightly belong to Canadians" (second-year male Arts student). In this circular argument, the student provides a reason for his potential unemployment (Canada lets in too many immigrants) which is the same as his conclusion (I won't get a job because immigrants will take it). This is an example of the **fallacy of circular reasoning:** using conclusions to support the assumptions that were necessary to draw the conclusions. This form of fallacy is also known as *begging the question*, as it can be used to "prove" anything without providing evidence to support the assertions given.

Circular reasoning creeps into analyses of social problems. Someone might argue that black Canadians are inherently inferior and assert that their inferiority is evident because they "hold only menial jobs and do not do intellectual work." In reply, you might point out that some black Canadians are not doing more intellectual work because of discriminatory hiring practices. The person might then counter that black Canadians could not be hired for such jobs anyway because they are inferior.

Similarly, you might argue that lesbians and gay men are sex perverts because they commonly have remained secretive about their sexual preference. But, we counter, the secrecy is due to the general disapproval of homosexuality. No, you reply, homosexuality is kept secret because it is a perversion. Thus, in circular reasoning people bounce *back and forth between assumptions and conclusions.* Circular reasoning leads nowhere in the search for an understanding of social problems.

■■ Fallacy of Authority

Virtually everything you know is based on some authority. You know comparatively little from personal experience or personal research. The authority you necessarily rely on is someone else's experience, research, or belief. You accept notions of everything from the nature of the universe to the structure of the atom, from the state of international relationships to the doctrines of religion—all on the basis of some authority. Most people accept a war as legitimate on the authority of their political leaders. Many accept the validity of capital punishment on the authority of law-enforcement officers. Some accept that use of contraceptives is morally wrong on religious authority. Most rely on the authority of the news media about the extent and severity of various problems.

fallacy of authority
argument by an illegitimate appeal to authority

The knowledge that you acquire through authority can be inaccurate and can exacerbate rather than resolve or ameliorate social problems. The **fallacy of authority** means an *illegitimate appeal to authority.* Such an appeal obtrudes into thinking about social problems in at least three ways.

We rely on authorities for information, but authorities are not always right.

First, *the authority may be ambiguous.* Thus, appeal is made to the Bible by both those who support and those who oppose capital punishment. Supporters of capital punishment point out that the Bible, particularly the Old Testament, decreed death for certain offences. Opponents counter that the death penalty contradicts New Testament notions of Christian love. An appeal to this kind of authority, then, is really an appeal to a particular interpretation of the authority. Because the interpretations are contradictory, you must find other bases for making judgments.

Second, *the authority may be irrelevant to the problem.* The fact that a man is a first-rate physicist does not mean he can speak with legitimate authority about race relations. Most of us are impressed by people who have significant accomplishments in some area, but their accomplishments should not overwhelm us if those people speak about a problem outside their area of expertise.

Third, *the authority may be pursuing a bias* rather than studying a problem. To say that someone is pursuing a bias is not necessarily to disparage that person, because pursuing it may be part of a job. For example, military officers are likely to analyze the problem of war from a military rather than a moral, political, or economic perspective. This is their job—and this is why decisions about armaments, defence, and war should not be left solely to the military. From a military point of view, one way to prevent war is to be prepared to counter an enemy attack. The nation must be militarily strong, according to this argument, so that other nations will hesitate to attack—and military strength requires the most sophisticated technology, a stockpile of weaponry, and a large, standing military force.

The shortcomings of this line of reasoning were dramatically illustrated by the incidents of September 11, 2001, when terrorists seized jet liners and crashed them into the World Trade Center towers in New York City and the Pentagon in Washington, D.C. At the time, the United States was clearly the strongest military power in the world. Nevertheless, the terrorists struck and they struck effectively. As we discuss in chapter 13, the notion of defending against enemies must now be reexamined in the light of a new face of war in the world.

While some people pursue a bias as a normal part of their work, others pursue it because of *vested interests.* That is, the authority may deliberately or unconsciously allow biases to affect what he or she says because it is personally advantageous. The head of a corporation that builds private prisons and argues that the private sector can deal with prisoners more effectively than can the government will obviously benefit from public policy that privatizes provincial and federal prisons. The corporate executive who talks about federal overregulation would clearly benefit if the government withdrew from consumer protection programs. Political leaders credit their own policies when crime rates fall and point to uncontrollable circumstances when crime rates rise. Their policies may have no effect on crime rates, but they benefit if they can persuade people that their actions have lowered the rate or will do so in the future.

▪▪ Fallacy of Composition

fallacy of composition
the assertion that what is true of the part is necessarily true of the whole

That the whole is equal to the sum of its parts appears obvious. That what is true of the part is also true of the whole likewise seems to be a reasonable statement, but the former is debatable and the latter is the **fallacy of composition.** As economists have illustrated, the notion that *what is valid for the part is also valid for the whole* is not necessarily true. Consider, for example, the relationship between work and income. If a farmer works hard and the weather is not adverse, his income may rise; but if every farmer works hard and the weather is favourable, and a bumper crop results, the total farm income may fall. The latter case is based upon supply and demand, while the former assumes that a particular farmer outperforms other farmers.

In thinking about social problems, *you cannot assume that what is true for the individual is also true for the group.* An individual may be able to resolve a problem insofar as it affects him or her, but that resolution is not available to all members of the group. For example, a man who is unemployed and living in poverty may find work that enables him to escape poverty. The work may require him to move or to work for less pay than someone else, but still he is able to rise above poverty. As you will see in our discussion of poverty, however, that solution is not possible for most of the nation's poor. Thus, something may be true for a particular individual or even a few individuals and yet be inapplicable or counterproductive for the entire group of which the individuals are members.

■■ Fallacy of Non Sequitur

fallacy of non sequitur
something that does not
follow logically from what
has preceded it

A number of the fallacies already discussed involve non sequitur, but we look at this way of thinking separately because of its importance. Literally, *non sequitur* means "*it does not follow.*" This **fallacy of non sequitur** is commonly found when people interpret statistical data.

For example, data may show that the amount of welfare payments by provincial governments has increased dramatically over the past few decades. What is the meaning of such data? You might conclude that the number of those unwilling to work has increased, that more and more "freeloaders" are living off the public treasury, but there are other explanations. The increase may reflect adjustments due to inflation, better efforts to get welfare money to eligible recipients, or a rise in unemployment due to governmental action to control inflation.

As Curtis and Tepperman (2004) note, contrary to the picture presented by the news media in Canada, which give violent crime far more airtime than it deserves numerically, violent crimes in 2000 accounted for about 12 percent of total crime reported. Taking into account the larger numbers of "hidden," unreported crimes committed by white-collar and organized criminals, they are probably only a fraction of the total crimes committed (2004:103). An increase in reported crime rates can mean different things, but it does not necessarily signify an actual increase in the amount of crime.

One other example involves studies of women who work. Some employers believe that women are not desirable workers because they are less committed to the job than men, as indicated by their higher turnover rate. Women do indeed have a higher rate of turnover than men. But what does this mean? Are women truly less committed to their jobs?

When you look at the situation more closely, you find that the real problem is that women tend to be concentrated in lower-level jobs. Also, women who quit a job tend to find another one quickly. Thus, women may be uncommitted to a particular low-level job but strongly committed to work. Furthermore, if you look at jobs with the same status, the turnover rate is no higher for women than men.

These illustrations are not meant to discourage you from drawing conclusions. Instead, they are a reminder of the need for thorough study and the need to avoid quick conclusions, even when those conclusions seem logical on the surface. Contrary to popular opinion, *"facts" do not necessarily speak for themselves.* They must be interpreted in the light of the complexities of social life and with the awareness that a number of different conclusions can usually be drawn from any set of data.

When examining the effectiveness of a fallacy of thinking, and when we attempt to formulate an opinion on a social problem, it is important to ask ourselves this question: *Is it our task to find what we are looking for, or is it our job to look at what we*

HOW, AND HOW NOT, TO THINK

"Use it or lose it" is a common saying. We might paraphrase that and say "Use it and learn it." That is, one of the best ways to learn something is to use it and not simply to memorize it. For this involvement, therefore, we are asking you to learn the fallacies by using them.

Select any social problem in which you are interested. Show how people could use each of the fallacies to "explain" that problem. Construct nine different explanations that are one or two sentences long. Try to make your explanations sound reasonable. Test them by sharing them with someone and seeing how many you can get the other person to accept. If the entire class participates in this project, gather in small groups and have each member share his or her explanations. Group members should then try to identify the fallacy in each of the explanations. Be sure not to present the fallacies in the order in which they appear in the book.

Take a problem that can be analyzed with the sociological imagination; it should be a topic that is often seen as a personal problem but is actually related to social factors. Some examples are unemployment, distress, rape, murder, AIDS, homophobia, racism or prejudice, poverty, dissatisfaction (with school or a job), pollution, good health and well-being, and so on. Almost all problems have a social component, so you might pick something that you are personally interested in (like grades, test-taking anxiety, returning to school) and try exploring it.

As an alternative, use simple observation to test the accuracy of common (or your own) notions about people involved in particular social problems. For instance, attend a meeting of gay activists, a feminist group, Alcoholics Anonymous, or an ecology group. Ask a number of people to describe the typical member of the group you visit, and compare their responses (and your own preconceptions) with your observations.

find? In the first instance, the researcher sets out to prove her own assumptions; in the second, she relies on the data—the bits and pieces of collected information, descriptions, and facts to tell a story. In our roles as detectives of social problems we systematically observe, record, and analyze what we see, hear, and experience before drawing conclusions to support or refute our assumptions.

▪▪ THE SOURCES OF DATA: SOCIAL RESEARCH

The various "intellectual blind alleys" we have described create and help to perpetuate myths about social problems. *Social research* is designed to gain information about social problems so that you can have a valid understanding of them and employ realistic efforts in resolving them.

Not everything called research is scientifically valid. Therefore, you need to use critical thinking skills as well as information and arguments to evaluate research. Some so-called social research aims to shape rather than gain information. If you want to gain information and discover the nature of social reality, you must use scientific social research. Scientific research is both rational and *empirical.* That is, it is logical and comes to conclusions based on evidence rather than speculation or feelings. The stages of such research typically include a clear statement of the problem or issue to be researched; formulation of *hypotheses* so that the problem or issue is in researchable form; selection of the appropriate method, including the sample; collection of the data; analysis of the data; and interpretation and reporting of the conclusions (see figure 1.3). A guiding principle throughout the foregoing stages is the desire to discover evidence, not to confirm preconceptions.

qualitative methods
methods of data collection that are used to obtain specific information on individuals and small groups at the micro level

Sociological research can be broken down into two main approaches: **qualitative methods** of data collection—such as focus groups, observation, case studies, and face-

FIGURE 1.3 ■ ■ ■

The research cycle.

Source: Created by J. Auger

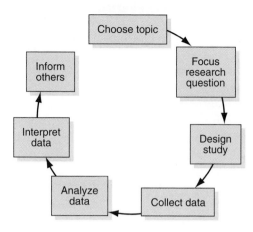

to-face interviews—are used to obtain specific information on individuals and small groups at the micro level. On the other hand, surveys and statistical analyses rely on **quantitative methods** of data collection, which give a macro perspective on social life that can provide explanations about how the social problem is created, maintained, and constructed at the more complex institutional level.

The types of data we seek to answer our research questions are affected by the methods of data collection we choose. For example, if we wanted to find out how members of a specific group of university students were reacting to their first year of courses, we might choose to use qualitative research methods such as face-to-face interviews, observation, or focus groups. However, if we wanted to know about the experiences of a large number of students we might choose to conduct a survey. There is, then, a direct relationship between the research question and the methods we choose to collect data to inform our work.

Many different methods are used in social research. We look below at four methods that have yielded important information about social problems: survey research, statistical analysis of official records (particularly of government data), experiments, and participant observation.

■ ■ Survey Research

The **survey** uses interviews and/or questionnaires to gain data about some phenomenon. The people from whom the information is gathered are normally a *sample* (a small number of people selected by various methods from a larger population) of a *population* (a group that is the focus of the study). The data include everything from attitudes about various matters to information such as gender, age, and **socioeconomic status.** You can learn two important aspects of social reality from surveys. First, you can discover the *distribution of people along some dimension.* For example, you can learn the proportion of people who say they will vote Liberal, Conservative, New Democratic, or for some other political party in an election; the proportion of people who favour, oppose, or are neutral about capital punishment; or the proportion of people who believe that lesbians and gay men should be allowed to marry. Second, you can discover *relationships among* **variables.** (A *variable* is any trait or characteristic that varies in value or magnitude.) For instance, you can investigate the relationship between people's positions in the stratification system (socioeconomic status) and their attitudes toward the race problem, gender inequality, or the plight of the poor.

quantitative methods
methods of data collection that give a macro perspective on social life

survey
a method of research in which a sample of people are interviewed or given questionnaires in order to get data on some phenomenon

socioeconomic status
position in the social system based on economic resources, power, education, prestige, and lifestyle

variable
any trait or characteristic that varies in value or magnitude

Survey research is one of the most common methods used in sociology. Let's examine one piece of such research that deals with the problem of spousal assault. It illustrates both the technique of survey research and the kind of information it can yield about a social problem.

At present, Canada has no rape laws on the books but it does have a series of sexual assault categories. According to Clarke and Lewis (1997), before 1983 and the introduction of Canada's sexual assault laws it was legally impossible for a man in Canada to rape his wife, because the rape law contained a marital exemption. A man could be found guilty of rape on his own wife only if he were party to someone else raping her (e.g., if he forcibly restrained his wife while another man raped her).

In 2001, researchers Holly Johnson and Valerie Pottie Bunge used **secondary data sources** obtained from Statistics Canada's 1999 General Social Survey on Victimization to examine if the rates of spousal assault had increased in the past ten years. In this survey, 9,178 women and 7,827 men who were living with a marital partner (whether married or common-law) were invited to participate. Participants were initially asked to complete a telephone survey and later a telephone interview that asked them a series of questions regarding whether they experienced sexual assault within their relationship, the incidence and types of such assaults, from whom they sought support for their victimization, whether they reported an assault, and other related questions. The research sample was selected using the random dialing technique. Each province was divided into broad geographic strata and telephone numbers within each stratum had the same chance of being selected randomly. The response rate was relatively high, at 81.3 percent.

The findings of this research showed that 7.9 percent of respondents stated that they had experienced some form of marital violence. Rates of violence for women and men were 8.7 and 7 percent, respectively.

Even though there was not a high statistical difference between the experiences of women and men in terms of spousal assault, there was a marked difference in the types of violence each sex encountered. Women were more likely to be subject to threats of violence; pushing, grabbing, or shoving; being beaten or choked; having a gun or knife used against them; or sexually assaulted. Higher percentages of men were slapped or kicked, bitten, or hit. As a result of these responses the researchers noted that women are almost four times more likely than men to fall into the most serious and potentially injurious category of assaults: 3.8 percent of female as compared to 1.1 percent of male victims.

From their data analysis the researchers were able to conclude that the social problem of spousal violence results in a high cost to society in terms of medical, social, and criminal justice services, as well as psychological problems for the individual and his or her family and community. Further, they noted that women victims were more than five times as likely to require medical attention for their injuries and to spend time in hospital. This survey utilized **secondary data analysis** of existing research, a common technique when dealing with large data sets such as those produced by Statistics Canada and other government and private agencies.

Another survey also produced and distributed by Statistics Canada is worthy of mention here in that it too addresses a Canadian social problem and illustrates the secondary use of existing material.

In the 2001 Aboriginal Peoples Survey (APS) conducted by Statistics Canada, 117,000 Aboriginal people from across the country were asked to provide information about their living conditions and lifestyles. The survey concluded that non-reserve Aboriginal people were less likely than other Canadians to complete their education; 45 percent reported chronic health conditions such as arthritis and rheumatism and

secondary data sources sources of data not compiled or analyzed personally by the researcher

secondary data analysis analysis of existing research

high rates of diabetes and tuberculosis. Concerns were also raised by respondents to the survey about overcrowded living conditions. Although the report outlines some concerns among Aboriginal peoples, it also noted that some gains had been made since the 1996 census, especially regarding the revitalization of Aboriginal languages, the improved health among younger Aboriginal people, and the recognition of the necessity for culturally appropriate education for younger Aboriginal families. However, while there were some positive responses to this survey, it nonetheless also identified the need for more government and social recognition, understanding, and attention to the social problems that Aboriginal peoples experience in their struggle for equality with other Canadians.

▪▪ Statistical Analysis of Official Records

Suppose you want to see how *self-esteem* enters into various social problems. For instance, you might want to see whether prejudice and discrimination affect the self-esteem of minorities, whether negative attitudes about growing old affect the self-esteem of the aged, or whether rapists or other offenders have low self-esteem. You could use a questionnaire to measure self-esteem, then compute the **mean** (average) scores of your respondents.

mean
the average

Let's say that the mean score of a random sample of offenders was 8.9 and the mean score of a random sample of average citizens of the same age, gender, and socioeconomic status was 10.2. The offenders have lower self-esteem. But is the difference between 8.9 and 10.2 a significant one? If not, how much difference would be required before you could say that it was significant—that is, before you could say with some confidence that the two groups differ in level of self-esteem?

test of significance
a statistical method for determining the probability that research findings occurred by chance

The question can be answered by using a **test of significance,** which is a technical way of determining the probability that your findings occurred by chance. That is, if the difference is not significant statistically, then you cannot say that offenders have a lower self-esteem than nonoffenders. A different set of samples might yield scores of 9.4 for both groups, or a slightly higher mean for offenders than for nonoffenders. If the difference is statistically significant, however, you can say with some confidence that offenders generally have lower self-esteem than nonoffenders.

We will not examine details of tests of significance; they require greater knowledge of statistics. Note, however, that many of the findings about social problems discussed in this book—whether gathered through survey research, experiment, or official records—have been subjected to statistical tests. This gives you confidence that the results reflect significant differences between the groups and, if the samples were adequate, that the results apply to more groups than the ones tested. Thus, you can make general statements about, say, women in Canada without having surveyed the majority of Canadian women.

frequency distribution
the organization of data to show the number of times each item occurs

There are some other questions that can be asked about data gathered in research. For example, you might want to know how many of the offenders scored high, medium, and low in self-esteem. To get this information, you need a **frequency distribution,** which we use in subsequent chapters. The frequency distribution provides information not available in the mean.

As table 1.3 shows, you can have different frequency distributions with the same number of cases and the same mean. If the scores in the table represented thousands of income dollars of women in an organization, you would draw different conclusions about the women's economic well-being in the two cases even though the means were the same.

median
the score below which are half of the scores and above which are the other half

Another question that can be asked is, "What is the **median** score?" The median is the score below which half the scores fall and above which the other half fall. This fur-

TABLE 1.3 ■ ■ ▪

Frequency Distribution of Two Sets of Hypothetical Data

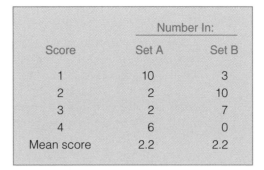

| | Number In: | |
Score	Set A	Set B
1	10	3
2	2	10
3	2	7
4	6	0
Mean score	2.2	2.2

TABLE 1.4 ■ ■ ▪

Frequency Distribution, Mean, and Median of Two Sets of Hypothetical Income Data

| | Number of Families | |
Income level	Set A	Set B
$ 1,000	2	1
2,000	1	2
3,000	1	1
4,000	1	0
5,000	2	1
10,000	0	2
Mean	$ 3,000	$ 4,714
Median	3,000	3,000

nishes important information for dealing with things such as income distribution. For instance, if A and B represent two communities in table 1.4, the mean incomes of the two are quite different. You might conclude that the people in community B are better off than those in community A. Actually, the median income is the same for both A and B, and the higher mean for B is due to the two families with very high incomes. Thus, *extreme figures* will affect the mean but not the median. When you find a big difference between the mean and the median, you know extremes are involved.

Statistical analysis is useful for several types of research. Suppose you want to see whether women are discriminated against with respect to income. You will need a frequency distribution of male and female incomes as well as mean and median income for the two groups. This information can be obtained from government census data: the analysis has already been made, and you need only interpret it. You do not need to make a test of significance because census data involve the entire population; tests of significance are used only when you want to know the probability that your findings about a sample are true for the population.

■■ Experiments

In essence, the *experimental method* involves manipulation of one or more variables, control of other variables, and measurement of the consequences in still other variables. The manipulated variables are called the **independent variables,** while those that are measured to see the ways they have been affected are called the **dependent variables.** To see whether the independent variables cause change in the dependent variables, the experimenter uses *both an experimental group and a control group.*

independent variable
the variable in an experiment that is manipulated to see how it effects changes in the dependent variable

dependent variable
the variable in an experiment that is influenced by an independent variable

Measurements are taken in both groups, but the control group is not exposed to the treatment (the independent variable).

Suppose you want to set up an experiment to test the hypothesis that prejudice is increased by negative interpersonal encounters with those of other races. You get a group of white volunteers, test them on their level of prejudice, and select 20 who score about the same (that is, you control for level of prejudice). You then divide them into two groups and give each group the same brief lecture by a black Canadian. One group is treated kindly by the lecturer, while the other group is treated in an abusive manner. Following the lecture, you again test the 20 subjects for their level of prejudice.

If the 10 who hear the abusive lecturer increase their level of prejudice, while the 10 who listen to the kindly lecturer show no increase, the hypothesis is clearly supported. In practice, experiments never come out this neatly. Some people who listen to the abusive speaker will not increase their level of prejudice, and some who listen to the kindly speaker will show more prejudice afterward. In other words, factors other than just the interpersonal contact are at work. The experimenter tries to control the setting and the subjects in order to minimize the effect of these other factors.

Canadian sociology has several subfields. One of these is social psychology, and it is within this academic perspective that most experiments are conducted—usually within a small-group laboratory, which many sociology departments do not have (most are situated within psychology departments).

While a graduate student at the University of British Columbia, one author of this textbook was fortunate to work with two of the leading Canadian researchers in this field, the late Reginald A. H. Robson, and Dr. Martha Foschi. Dr. Foschi is interested in status characteristics such as gender, age, race and ethnicity, and so on, and their relationships to expectation states—the expectations we have of others based on their status characteristics. Essentially, Dr. Foschi is interested in the cause-and-effect relationships that can be observed and measured in a laboratory setting, normally to test theories and hypotheses.

Other uses of the experimental approach to the understanding of social problems include susceptibility to influence studies in which subjects (the experimental group) are placed in small-group laboratory situations with others (the control group) who have been given a script ahead of time by the researcher. What is being measured is the amount of influence needed, and by whom, to cause members of the experimental group to change their opinions on an issue.

What people do in a laboratory setting does not necessarily predict what they will do outside the laboratory, because controlling all variables is impossible. For this reason, experimenters often take pains to make their settings as "natural" as possible.

■■ Participant Observation

participant observation
a method of research in which one directly participates in and observes the social reality being studied

Participant observation, the last method we consider, involves a number of elements, including interaction with subjects, participation in and observation of pertinent activities of the subjects, interviews, and use of documents and artifacts. In participant observation, then, the researcher directly participates in and observes the social reality being studied. The researcher is both a part of and detached from the social reality being studied.

However, there are differences in the extent to which the researcher is involved in the social reality being studied. The relative emphasis on participation versus observation, and whether the researcher reveals his or her identity to the subjects, are decisions that must be made (and are matters of ethical debate). For instance, if a researcher uses observation to study poverty, he or she might live in an impoverished community and pretend to be a poor person. Or the researcher might acknowledge that research is being conducted while he or she participates in community activities. The researcher might decide to participate only in selective community activities that he or she specifically wants to observe. Or the researcher could choose to be primarily an observer, watching poor children in a schoolroom behind a one-way mirror. Which will yield the best information? Which, if any, would be considered unethical? Researchers must answer such questions.

Canadian sociologist Rod Michalko is interested in and concerned with the ways that issues of disability are commonly presented in Canada. As a blind person, he has observed how he and his peers accomplish the "sighted world" (2002, 1998).

Through his lived experiences as a blind man, and his shared experiences with others who are blind, he was able to write about the ways in which blind individuals and other disabled persons discuss how their disability is constructed, labelled, and socially controlled. Using an auto-ethnographic approach, he examines his own experiences with blindness and analyzes societal notions of identity as they affect disabled people. He argues that disabled people "live disabilities" based on social and cultural representations of disability.

Michalko places disability and the concept of suffering at the centre of his analysis. He rejects person-first language—"a person with a disability"—and argues for placing disability at the centre of one's identity: in other words, "a disabled person." The first phrase strips away important aspects of identity that characterize an individual. It dilutes one's identity and diminishes the fact that disabled persons are often excluded from social and public life. This is a collective, not an individual, issue that includes disabled and non-disabled people in public life; often, he points out, efforts to include disabled people actually reinforce stereotypes about disability, are defined through the lens of ability, and end up being exclusionary in nature. His analysis of suffering, in which he critiques the ways in which suffering is viewed as individual rather than as culturally constructed, is also a unique contribution to the literature. In the end, he challenges the reader to rethink these notions as they shape our understanding of ability and disability (2002:43).

Another new Canadian researcher who has used this method of research to examine a topic in which she is also a participant is April Wiles, an honours student in the sociology department at Acadia University (2004–5). April is a learning-disabled student who is interested in learning more about the ways in which she and other learning-disabled students are dealt with in the university, at all levels. Using focus group discussions with learning-disabled students and asking for their experiences, she was able to conclude that more services and programs are needed for this group of students. Further, she concluded that faculty, staff, and other students also need to be educated as to the types of learning disabilities students may have, the areas in which they need help and support, and the important consequences for those who do not get what they need (2005).

▪▪ SUMMARY

You need to distinguish between personal and social problems. For the former, the causes and solutions lie within the individual and his or her immediate environment. For the latter, the causes and solutions lie outside the individual and his or her immediate environment. Defining a particular problem as personal or social is important because the definition determines the causes you identify, the consequences of the problem, and how you cope with the problem.

The model we use to analyze social problems treats them as contradictions. It emphasizes that multiple-level factors cause and help perpetuate problems. You must understand social problems in terms of the mutual influence between social structural factors, social psychological or cognitive factors, and social interaction.

In addition to attending to the multiple factors involved, two additional tools are necessary for an adequate understanding of social problems. One is to use critical-thinking skills to identify fallacious ways of thinking that have been used to analyze social problems and that create and perpetuate myths about those problems. The other is to understand the methods of social research. An adequate understanding of social problems is based on research and not merely on what seems to be reasonable.

Nine different fallacies have been used to analyze social problems. The fallacy of dramatic instance refers to the tendency to overgeneralize, to use a single case or a few cases to support an entire argument. The fallacy of retrospective determinism is the argument that things could not have worked out differently. The fallacy of misplaced concreteness is the tendency to resort to reification, to make something abstract into something concrete. The fallacy of personal attack is a form of debate or argument in which an attack is made on the opponent rather than on the issues. Appeal to prejudice is the exploitation of popular prejudices or passions. Circular reasoning involves the use of conclusions supporting assumptions necessary to make those conclusions. The fallacy of authority is an illegitimate appeal to authority. The fallacy of composition is the idea that what is true of the part is also true of the whole. Finally, non sequitur is drawing the wrong conclusions from premises even though the premises themselves are valid.

Four methods of social research that are useful for understanding social problems are survey research, statistical analysis of official records, experiment, and participant observation. Survey research employs interviews and questionnaires on a sample of people in order to get data. Statistical analysis of official records may be simple (computing means, medians, and frequency distributions) or relatively complex (computing tests of significance). Experiment involves manipulation of one or more variables, control of other variables, and measurement of consequences in still other variables. Experiments frequently take place in a laboratory setting, where the researcher has a high degree of control over what happens. Finally, participant observation involves both participation and observation on the part of the researcher; the researcher is both a part of and detached from the social reality being studied.

▪▪ KEY TERMS

Attitude 7
Conflict Theory 6
Contradiction 7
Critical Thinking 13
Dependent Variable 25
Fallacy of Appeal to Prejudice 17
Fallacy of Authority 18
Fallacy of Circular Reasoning 17
Fallacy of Composition 19
Fallacy of Dramatic Instance 14
Fallacy of Misplaced Concreteness 16
Fallacy of Non Sequitur 20
Fallacy of Personal Attack 16
Fallacy of Retrospective Determinism 14
Frequency Distribution 24
Ideology 7
Independent Variable 25
Institution 3
Interaction 6
Mean 24
Median 24
Norm 7
Participant Observation 26
Personal Problem 3
Qualitative Methods 21
Quantitative Methods 22
Reification 15
Role 7
Secondary Data Analysis 23
Secondary Data Sources 23
Social Problem 3
Socioeconomic Status 22
Stratification System 7
Structural Functionalism 6
Survey 22
Symbolic Interactionism 6
Test of Significance 24
Values 7
Variable 22

▪▪ STUDY QUESTIONS

1. Using homelessness or some other problem as an example, how would you distinguish between a personal and a social problem?

2. What difference does the distinction between personal and social problems make in understanding the causes and consequences of problems?

3. Going back to the chapter-opening vignette, formulate some questions and decide which research methods might most appropriately address this social problem.

4. What is meant by "quality of life," and in what way is it a part of social problems?

5. Illustrate each of the nine fallacies of thinking by showing how each can be used to "explain" a social problem.

6. How is survey research used to study social problems?

7. In what ways are official records useful for the study of social problems?

8. How do you set up a scientific experiment to research a social problem?

9. What did participant observation teach you about a program designed to help the homeless, and how did the researcher go about being a participant observer?

10. When we talk about social problems there are some key questions we want to address. They are as follows:

   a. What is the problem?

   b. For whom is it a problem?

   c. How is the problem defined?

   d. Who is involved with the problem?

   e. How is the problem made visible; for example, through the media, on the streets, in people's homes, in religious settings, in universities, in the workplace, and so on?

   f. What techniques or evidence do people present to show that the problem is "real"?

   g. Who has the solutions?

   h. Who can help with the solutions?

   i. Whom do we need to talk to, read, and observe to help create solutions?

   j. Who should be involved in the search for solutions?

   k. How can we approach the people who may have the solutions?

   l. How will we know the best steps to take to research the problem and solution?

There are many other steps to take to try to achieve social solutions to social problems; can you think of some of them?

▪▪ FOR FURTHER READING

Gilbert, Nigel, ed. *Researching Social Life*. 2nd ed. Thousand Oaks, CA: Sage, 2001. Shows how qualitative and quantitative methods can be used to research social phenomena.

Huff, Darrell. *How to Lie with Statistics*. New York: W. W. Norton, 1993. A readable, fascinating exposition of proper and improper use of statistical data. Shows how statistics as well as myths can impart incorrect information.

Kingdon, John W. *Agendas, Alternatives and Public Policies*. 2nd ed. New York: Longman, 1995. Explores the ways that agendas are set and public policy is formulated in the government. Underscores the complexity of dealing with social problems.

Lindblom, Charles Edward. *Inquiry and Change: The Troubled Attempt to Understand and Shape Society*. New Haven, CT: Yale University Press, 1990. A discussion of the ways people gather and analyze information as they deal with social problems.

Nussbaum, Martha C., and Amartya Sen, eds. *The Quality of Life*. New York: Oxford University Press, 1993. Various authors discuss how to measure the quality of life and compare differing societies on quality-of-life scores.

Shreve, Susan Richards, Porter Shreve, and James Reston. *How We Want To Live: Narratives on Progress*. Boston: Beacon Press, 1998. Essays on the notion of progress and how the pursuit of progress affects the quality of life.

Problems of Behavioural Variance

What do such things as prostitution, homosexuality, body piercing, tattoos, drug addiction, and arson have in common? They all involve behaviour that deviates from social norms. As such, most Canadians view the behaviour as within the individual's control and responsibility. That is, if a person engages in prostitution, has their body pierced, uses drugs, or robs a store, it is a matter of his or her free choice. Further, because it is a choice that violates social norms, the person who engages in any kind of behavioural variance is likely to be (1) condemned and punished, (2) defined as "sick" and given therapy, or (3) both.

As you will see, the matter is not as simple as this view suggests. If, for example, you define crime as any infraction of the law—including such things as speeding or failing to report income on tax returns—few if any Canadians are innocent of crime. Or if you believe that homosexuals could just as freely choose to be heterosexual as homosexual, then you ignore the growing evidence that homosexuality has a genetic basis and is as natural for some people as heterosexuality is for others. Like all problems discussed in this book, problems of behavioural variance are complex issues that involve social contradictions, are defined as having adverse effects on the quality of life, and have multilevel causes.

SEXUAL DIVERSITY

LEARNING OBJECTIVES

1. Learn the meaning and some of the types of sexual diversity.

2. Show how prostitution affects an individual's way of life.

3. Understand factors that make prostitution, pornography, and homophobia social problems.

4. Know how pornography affects people's behaviour.

5. Learn various explanations of homosexuality.

6. Identify ways to address the problems of prostitution, pornography, and homophobia.

7. Understand the various terms that describe a person's sexual preferences and possible behaviour.

"I DIDN'T UNDERSTAND"

Wanda is in her 60s. She is part of a crusade because of her son, Dale. Her crusade is to get people to understand homosexuality, because for many years she couldn't understand her gay son and it caused a great deal of pain in her family:

> If I had understood homosexuality 20 years ago, Dale wouldn't have had to spend the first half of his life feeling isolated and alone. He wouldn't have had to struggle with his guilt and anger. He wouldn't have had all those arguments with me and his father. But I didn't understand.

Dale told us about himself when he was a teenager. I grew up at a time when homosexuality was hardly mentioned, and then only to ridicule and reject it. When Dale admitted he was gay, we felt everything from panic to hysteria to rage. We tried to talk him out of it. We tried to convince him to just keep dating girls and he would find one who would change his mind. We sent him to a psychiatrist, expecting that soon Dale would change. It didn't happen. And of course all of our efforts only led to heated arguments and feelings of rejection by both Dale and us.

My husband and I are both well educated. You'd think we would have been able to handle it better than we did. But we struggled with Dale for years before we found a book that gave us a different perspective. Then we talked to some of Dale's gay friends. And finally, we sat down and tried to talk calmly with Dale—not just once, but many times over a period of many months.

Eventually, we realized that our son is not perverse and that he is not sick. Dale did not choose to be homosexual; he just is homosexual. Why would he have chosen to be rejected rather than accepted by us? Dale told us that he knew he was different when he was a kid, but he didn't know why. He preferred to be like other boys, but he didn't know how. As he grew older, he dated girls. As a young man, he had sexual relations with a couple of young women. But he hated it.

We have no problems with Dale's homosexuality now. We accept it as part of his nature, of who he is. What I do have problems with is my awareness of the amount of gay bashing that goes on. I have nightmares about homophobes. How can we make them understand our son?

As part of the social solution to dealing with homophobia, Wanda has joined a local chapter of PFLAG (Parents, Families, and Friends of Lesbians and Gays) to fight homophobia, and to educate the public about lesbian, gay, bisexual, and transgender issues. PFLAG chapters exist across Canada, the U.S., and Europe. ■

▪▪ INTRODUCTION

There is an old story about an expert who was scheduled to give an after-dinner speech on sex. At the appointed time, he arose and said: "Ladies and gentlemen. Sex. It gives me great pleasure." Then he sat down.

Clearly, sex is a source of great pleasure to humans. It is also a source of pain and controversy. Whether it is one or the other depends on whom you're talking to and what kind of sex you're talking about. In this chapter, we look at what is meant by sexual diversity. Then we focus on three kinds of sexual diversity: prostitution; the use of pornography, erotica, and obscenity; and homosexuality.

▪▪ EXAMPLES OF SEXUAL DIVERSITY

What is sexual diversity? The answer depends on which society you are talking about. All societies regulate sex, but not all regulate it in the same way. In their study of 190 different societies, Ford and Beach (1951) concluded there are wide variations in normative sexual behaviour and considerable permissiveness for some kinds of sexual behaviour that North Americans have historically considered deviant (such as extramarital sex and homosexuality). More recently, in her 2001 book *The No-Nonsense Guide to Sexual Diversity*, Vanessa Baird noted that global change in sexual diversity issues is "happening fast—and so is reaction to it. In a rapidly globalizing and fundamentalizing world rapid shifts in the sexual and gender landscape are giving repercussion that go around the world" (9).

Sexuality is not merely about sex, but it also involves our emotional, physical, cultural, social, and spiritual selves. There is a great diversity in sexual behaviour; the following table briefly outlines some forms of sexual expression.

Sex and Gender

Sex represents our biological makeup and is based on sex characteristics such as genitalia and chromosomal, hormonal, and reproductive attributes.

Gender is socially constructed—we are not born into a specific gender; rather, we are socialized to behave and present ourselves in ways that are deemed appropriate for our sex.

Sexuality refers to our desire and sexual orientation.

Sexual orientation refers to our attraction to someone of the same or a different gender, including identities such as gay, lesbian, bisexual, and heterosexual.

Lesbians are women who are emotionally, physically, and sexually attracted to other women.

Gays are men who are emotionally, physically, and sexually attracted to other men.

Heterosexuals are individuals who are emotionally, physically, and sexually attracted to members of the opposite sex.

Bisexual individuals are emotionally, physically, and sexually attracted to both men and women.

Transgendered persons are those whose gender identity or sexual expression differs from societal expectations of their physical sex, so that we hear people say they feel as though they were born into the wrong body. Transgendered people can be lesbian, gay, bisexual, or heterosexual. Transgendered persons include the following:

> **Transsexuals**: Whether male to female or female to male, and whether pre or post surgical intervention to alter their bodies.
>
> **Transvestites** (also known as cross-dressers): This category would also include people who identify as drag kings and drag queens.
>
> **Intersexed** individuals are born with both sets of genitals. They were formerly referred to as hermaphrodites but this medical term is rejected by intersexed persons.
>
> **Eunuchs** are individuals who have no genitals due to birth defects, surgical errors, or genital mutilation.

Twin spirited is the Aboriginal term for persons who are lesbian or gay.

We choose whether to act on our sexual attractions, and for some people sexual orientation changes throughout life. Of course, people everywhere take their own norms seriously, but the point is that sexual behaviour, like all other behaviour, is social. No particular type of sexual behaviour is "natural" or "normal" in contrast to other types.

Consider two types of sexual behaviour that some North Americans tend to regard as deviant: sex between an unmarried individual and an excessive number of partners, and sex between a married individual and someone who is not his or her mate. **Promiscuity,** indiscriminate casual relations with many partners, is not acceptable to most North Americans. Both men and women say that they prefer sex within the context of a caring relationship, and women say that they enjoy intercourse most in a committed as well as a caring relationship (McCabe 1987).

promiscuity
undiscriminating, casual sexual relationships with many people

By the mid-1980s, another factor leading people to avoid promiscuity emerged—AIDS, or acquired immune deficiency syndrome (see chapter 12). Historically, few people have abstained from sexual relations due to fear of disease. Many think that AIDS is changing, or will change, this. So far, despite the widespread dissemination of information, it appears that only a minority of people have altered their sexual behaviour; many continue to engage in high-risk behaviour (see, e.g., Feinleib and Michael 1998; Hillis et al. 2001; Fierros-Gonzalez and Brown 2002). If concern over AIDS diminishes, North Americans may continue to devalue promiscuity but for reasons other than fear of disease.

Let's look in greater detail at prostitution, pornography, and homosexuality. All three have been both strongly condemned and vigorously defended by some—and all three continue to survive every attempt to completely suppress them.

Prostitution, while seen by some as a serious social problem, is seen by others as a matter of a trade agreement between a buyer and a seller (except in the cases of children and others who cannot make informed choices). In a 1995 survey of Canadian attitudes toward social problems, sociologist Reginald Bibby noted that prostitution was not an issue most Canadians see as particularly problematic. He found that fewer than one percent of his extensive sample found it to be a pressing social problem (1998:143).

Criminologist John Lowman (1992 and 1995) has conducted extensive research on prostitution in Canada. He has found that most street prostitutes are women and men who come from lower socioeconomic backgrounds and are immensely dissatisfied with their family life. He, along with others (see for example Lautt 1993, Gomme 1993, and Sacco 1992), has found that Canadian prostitutes join the profession for three main reasons. They are 1) economic necessity, 2) exploitation and recruitment, and 3) "big sisters" (1992:49).

Economic necessity: In the first instance, Lowman found that 67 percent of prostitutes in Canada enter that line of work between the ages of 12 and 18, and so are without financial resources, education, or work-related skills. Due to physical, emotional, or sexual abuse in the family, they leave home and work on the streets. They normally have no other access to shelter, food, or an income.

Exploitation: Lautt (1993) conducted research into the lives of prostitutes in Canada's Prairie provinces. She found that many girls, in particular those between the ages of 12 and 18, some from Aboriginal communities, were recruited by "new friends" whom they met at bus terminals, train stations, airports, and gas stations when running away from home. These "new friends" force them into the sex trade in exchange for shelter, food, clothing, and sometimes drugs and alcohol.

Some women enter prostitution because they are emotionally attached to someone—a lover, friend, or relative who exploits their relationship by coercing them into the profession as a test of their emotional commitment. In a report by Gomme on Vancouver prostitutes, 50 to 60 percent claimed they were introduced to the life by other people (1993:294).

Big sister recruitment: Close friends who are sexually active or professional prostitutes will influence younger girls to join them on the streets. Older prostitutes will often take the role of "big sister" by introducing the new girls to the trade, educating them about the best places to work (without taking over the territory of others), how to protect themselves physically and sexually, how to select the "best" pimps, and how to avoid trouble with the law. In exchange for the training, "big sisters" usually share a percentage of the new recruits' earnings (Gomme 1998:294).

▪▪ PROSTITUTION

prostitution
having sexual relations for remuneration, usually to provide part or all of one's livelihood

Prostitution, or *sex-trade work*, is a paid sexual relation between the prostitute and his or her client. Male prostitutes are often young boys—mostly from impoverished homes. They have run away or been thrown out of their homes and offer themselves as sexual partners to gay men. The boys often consider themselves to be a bisexual or heterosexual who are only engaging in homosexual prostitution temporarily in order to survive. Since research on male prostitution is sparse, our focus here is on the female prostitute and her clientele.

However, in 1999 Doreen Duchesne reported that between 1986 and 1995 just less than half (47 percent) of all persons charged with communicating for the purpose of prostitution in Canada were male. In 1996, while men (mostly clients) accounted for slightly more than half (56 percent) of those convicted of prostitution-related offences, they were much less likely to receive jail terms than women convicted of the same offences (3 percent versus 39 percent).

In Canada prostitution is not illegal, although activities closely related to it are—such as running a bawdy house or brothel, communicating for the purposes of prostitution, soliciting, and living off the avails of prostitution (Library of Parliament 1994:67). In 2002, Statistics Canada reported that the rate of prostitution offences had increased by 12 percent (The Daily, July 24, 2003; Crime Statistics 2002).

In this country, prostitution is often viewed as a victimless crime where adults engage in a supply-and-demand economic transaction. This is also the case in countries such as Holland, Thailand, Singapore, and others where prostitution is legal, and indeed a source of revenue for governments that receive taxes from this profession.

Who uses the services of a prostitute? It is impossible to give exact figures. Yet considering the number of prostitutes available and the number of times they have sex each day, it is clear that a substantial portion of the male population has sex with prostitutes. The *typical customer,* or "john," is a married, middle-aged white male (National Victims Resource Center 1991; Lowman, Atchison, and Fraser 1997). Only a small proportion of the men limit their use of prostitutes to one time. In a survey of 120 customers in the U.S., one-quarter of the men reported using prostitutes 51 or more times, and 16 percent said they had purchased sex more than 100 times (Lowman, Atchison, and Fraser 1997).

Those who use prostitutes tend to do so over an extended period of time rather than having a single encounter. A study of 101 clients of street prostitutes found that they had used prostitutes an average of 5.3 years (Freund, Lee, and Leonard 1991). Nearly two-thirds of the men reported using a prostitute once a week or more, and over half said they had sex with the same prostitute or the same small group of prostitutes.

▪▪ Prostitution and the Quality of Life

Prostitutes typically prefer their profession to other perceived options. This is not so much evidence of the high quality of life for prostitutes as it is testimony to the *low quality of life endured by the women before they decided to become prostitutes.*

Physical Problems.   In the first place, *prostitution contradicts our value of physical well-being.* Canadians cherish good health and value the youthful physique. Most prostitutes, however, face certain occupational hazards that may lead to physical problems. In the past, *venereal disease* was a prominent problem. Today it is less frequent because many prostitutes get regular medical checkups and also carefully examine each customer for signs of venereal disease. Juvenile prostitutes, however, rarely seek medical help because they are afraid of attracting the attention of authorities (National Victims Resource Center 1991).

Finally, prostitutes face the hazard of contracting acquired immune deficiency syndrome (AIDS) (Quadagno et al. 1991). They run the risk both from their clients and from the tendency of some to become intravenous drug users. In the United States, prostitutes not only contract but also help spread AIDS (Stine 1998). Rates of infection are particularly high among male prostitutes. A survey of 224 male street prostitutes found rates of infection to be 50 percent for homosexuals, 36.5 percent for bisexuals, and 18.5 percent for heterosexuals (Boles and Elifson 1994). In nations where AIDS is more rampant, even higher rates of infection are found. A study of 426 female prostitutes in West Africa, for instance, reported that 58.2 percent were infected with the AIDS virus (Lankoande et al. 1998), while a survey of Cambodian prostitutes reported an infection rate of 54 percent (Ohshige et al. 2000).

A different problem is the *physical abuse that threatens the prostitute.* Abuse may come from a customer or from the **pimp** (one who earns all or part of his living by

pimp
one who earns all or part of his living by acting as a manager or procurer for a prostitute

There are different kinds of prostitution, with differing consequences for the prostitutes.

acting as a manager for the prostitute) (Dalla 2000). The highly paid call girl, who serves an affluent clientele, is not likely to endure physical abuse, but the streetwalker must be constantly alert. As one former prostitute said to U.S. writer and broadcaster Studs Terkel (1972:98), "I remember having knives pulled on me, broken bottles held over my head, being raped, having my money stolen back from me, having to jump out of a second-storey window, having a gun pointed at me." Miller and Schwartz (1995) interviewed 16 street prostitutes and found that 15 had been victims of sexual assault, including rape. The violence was justified on a number of grounds, including that prostitutes can't be raped or that they "deserve" to be raped.

The constant threat of abuse is one reason a prostitute needs a pimp: "if you're gonna whore you need protection: a man's protection from other men. All men are in the protection business. . . . If men didn't beat us up we wouldn't need half the husbands we got" (Millett 1971:95). At the same time, the pimp himself inflicts physical abuse (Williamson and Cluse-Tolar 2002). Sometimes the pimp will beat a prostitute when he begins his relationship with her in order to establish his dominance and ensure the woman's loyalty. If the prostitute does not behave in a way the pimp deems appropriate, he may continue to abuse her. One prostitute explained the pimp's behaviour in terms of the master–slave relationship. The master seems to have total power but lives in fear because of the uncertainty of how the slave will react to his or her bondage. Like the master with his slave, the pimp fears the loss of his property. In addition, the pimp may feel compelled to maintain his ideal of masculinity before other men:

> Pimps do rotten things. I guess they have to. You've got to prove everything all over every day, right? You've got all the guys watching you. What do they do? . . . I saw a girl walk into a bar and hand the pimp a $100 bill. He took it and burned it in her face and knocked her down on the floor and kicked her and said, "I told you, bitch, $200. I want $200, not $100." Now she's gotta go out again and make not another hundred, but two hundred. I know of some pimps who killed a whore with an overdose of heroin and then fucked her dead body. They're sick. (Millett 1971:101–3)

We do not know how frequently prostitutes endure physical abuse from customers or their pimps, but the threat of abuse is constant. It is unlikely that any prostitute can ply her trade for many years without suffering abuse (Nixon et al. 2002). According to Lautt, who has conducted extensive research in the Prairie provinces, exploitation is most frequent in the recruitment of girls between the ages of 12 and 16. Pimps scout for young, naïve-looking girls around bus depots, airports, train stations, and other places of access to the city. The pimp will follow an appropriate target until dusk, then try to befriend the girl, perhaps offering her a place to stay. Soon the young woman becomes emotionally dependent on her new "friend"; at this point, the teen is asked to prostitute herself. Should she refuse, threats of violence or violence itself will be employed by the pimp.

A few women enter the profession because they are emotionally attached to someone, a lover or friend, who coerces them to take up the trade. In the report based on the findings of the Fraser Committee, it was stated that in Vancouver between 50 and 60 percent of prostitutes claimed that they were introduced to "the life" by other people (Gomme 1993:294, cited in Sturdy 1997).

Amnesty International (1995) has also reported on violence against women in war-torn countries such as Kubuye, Rwanda, and Bosnia-Herzegovina, where women are not only raped and tortured, but also forced into prostitution with the proceeds going to their captors.

Psychological and Emotional Problems.

A psychological problem reported by prostitutes arises from the contradiction between the value of sexual fulfillment and the role of the prostitute. Far from achieving sexual fulfillment, the prostitute often becomes *virtually asexual* with respect to her own sexual functioning (Dalla 2001). Again, however, we have to distinguish between different kinds of prostitutes. Prince (1986) found that two-thirds of the streetwalkers agreed that they should avoid orgasms, but only a little over a third of the brothel workers and 4 percent of the call girls agreed.

There is also a contradiction between the value of *human dignity* and the prostitute's role. The former prostitute interviewed by Studs Terkel was first a call girl and then a streetwalker. Both activities were *dehumanizing*.

> As a streetwalker, I didn't have to act. I let myself show the contempt I felt for the tricks. They weren't paying enough to make it worth performing for them. As a call girl, I pretended I enjoyed it sexually. You have to act as if you had an orgasm. As a streetwalker, I didn't. I used to lie there with my hands behind my head and do mathematics equations in my head or memorize the typewriter keyboard. (Terkel 1972:98)

A sense of alienation and isolation, drug use, and attempted suicide may all express a prostitute's sense of lost dignity and dehumanization. Prostitutes generally do not form a cohesive group among themselves because they are competing for customers. They often cannot form close relationships with people not connected with "the life" because of the stigma attached to their role. Therefore, prostitutes are barred from a sense of community.

One way prostitutes cope with this problem is to seek *refuge in drugs* (Gunn et al. 1995; Dalla 2000). A considerable number of prostitutes need help with addiction (Valera, Sawyer, and Schiarldi 2001). The rate of *attempted suicide* is also high among prostitutes. In Prince's (1986) study, 68 percent of the streetwalkers, 25 percent of the call girls, and 19 percent of the brothel workers admitted trying to kill themselves.

Finally, there is a *higher rate of emotional problems among prostitutes.* Research shows that about two-thirds of prostitutes suffer serious emotional problems, including anxiety, hostility, depression, and guilt (Farley and Barkan 1998; Zuger 1998).

There is, then, ample evidence of psychological and emotional problems among prostitutes. Moreover, these problems are built into the role of the prostitute, making escape difficult. For some women, prostitution seems to be more desirable than other available options, but the psychological and emotional quality of the prostitute's life is low.

Exploitation.

Quality of life is further diminished by the *contradiction between the roles of the prostitute and the people with whom she must deal and the ideal of "I–Thou" relationships* where people relate to each other as person to person and not as person to thing. The role of prostitute involves *exploitation*. Pimps, madams, bellboys, taxi drivers, lawyers, disreputable medical examiners, abortionists, police officers receiving hush money—the prostitute must deal with them all, and they all treat her as a "thing" rather than as a person by using her to make or to supplement their own living. Silbert and Pines (1981) noted that 88 percent of the 200 prostitutes they studied reported themselves as poor. Nearly half of them said they were victimized by an unfair split of money with their pimps, and 41 percent reported victimization by the police (including forced unpaid sex with a policeman).

CHILD PROSTITUTES

Women may become prostitutes because, among other things, they come from impoverished backgrounds. In some other countries, the relationship between poverty and prostitution takes a different twist—children sell themselves, or are sold by their parents, into prostitution in order to survive. For instance, a 17-year-old Chilean prostitute said that the first effort she and her brothers made to get food was to go out and beg, or pick up leftovers at the market. Then they started selling celery, but when they couldn't sell enough to get the food needed by the family, "my mom almost beat us to death." After that, the girl began to sell herself. A Chilean sociologist has estimated that as many as 50,000 children in Chile engage in prostitution in order to survive.

Southeast Asia is another area with child prostitutes. No one knows just how many, but estimates run into the hundreds of thousands and as high as a million. One-fifth of prostitutes in Thailand begin their work between the ages of 13 and 15, and girls as young as eight are in the brothels of Thailand, Cambodia, India, China, Taiwan, and the Philippines. Many of the girls were sold to the brothel owners by their parents in order to get money for food or other essentials for their families. Once sold, the girls are considered the property of the brothel owners and must work until they pay off their purchase price—or until they get AIDS.

In some cases, the family may run its own prostitution business. A mother with four daughters in Manila looked for clients for the two youngest daughters, ages eight and 12. When the 12-year-old resisted, the mother held her down while the men raped her.

The clients of child prostitutes come from many different nations, including North America. Why do they want children? No doubt they have various motivations, but one seems to be the fear of AIDS. The AIDS virus is spreading rapidly among prostitutes in Asia. The younger the prostitute, so the reasoning goes, the less likely she is to have AIDS. As a result, hundreds of thousands of Asian girls are living in sexual slavery.

Child prostitution is not only a global social problem; surveys have identified up to 3,000 child prostitutes in Montreal alone (Dorman 2001:203). In the same study, it was noted that there were 2,930 child prostitutes in Athens, Greece and up to 300,000 in the United States. Child prostitution occurs throughout the world and is particularly prevalent in Asia and Central America. In poor countries, families often sell the sexual services of their children in an attempt to get money. Some children are kidnapped or lured by traffickers with promises of employment, only to end up in a brothel. An estimated one-quarter of all visitors using child prostitutes in Asia are North American businessmen and military personnel (Kennedy 1996:1–6).

SOURCES
Chicago Tribune, March 17, 1996; *New York Times*, April 14, 1996; Kuo (2000).

Thus, the women offer their sexual services to men, pay their fines to men, and return to the streets only to be arrested again by men—all to satisfy the public's sense of "decorum." Arresting prostitutes satisfies the public because the appearance of police safeguarding morality is maintained. The prostitute is exploited by many different people, all of whom regard her as an object to serve their own interests.

■■ Contributing Factors

If the quality of life for the prostitute is so low, and if some Canadians believe the very presence of prostitutes offends traditional morals, why does prostitution continue?

Social Structural Factors. Social structural factors help explain both why men seek prostitutes and why women enter into the life. Canadian society has traditionally held to the norm of sex only within marriage. In addition, sex has not been openly discussed through much of the nation's history. These two factors—*rejection of nonmarital* *sex and no open discussion of sex*—were set forth by Winick and Kinsie (1971) as crucial determinants of the amount of prostitution in a society. They pointed out that among the Tokopia of the Solomon Islands, both nonmarital sex and open discussion of sex are accepted, and there is practically no prostitution. They hypothesize that where social norms forbid either or both of these conditions, there will probably be prostitution. This line of reasoning is supported by the fact that open discussions about sex have become more acceptable, and nonmarital sex (especially premarital) has become more widely accepted in Canadian society. At the same time, while roughly the same number of men appear to use the services of prostitutes, fewer are young men, and the number of visits by each man may have declined.

In addition to traditional norms about nonmarital sex and discussion of sex, the *institution of marriage* does not provide sufficient sexual gratification for some males. Married men may go to prostitutes to experience variety, to compensate for a lack of gratification with their mates, or to avoid concern about pregnancy (Weiss 1990; McKeganey 1994; Lowman, Atchison, and Fraser 1997). Married men who give and receive oral sex report they are happier with their sex lives and their marriages, but wives are more likely than their husbands to be embarrassed and inhibited about oral sex (Blumstein and Schwartz 1983). Desire for fellatio is an important reason men go to prostitutes (Monto 2001).

Men may also go to prostitutes because their wives do not desire sexual relations as often as they do. The prostitute then provides a sexual outlet that does not require the time and emotion that would be involved in an extramarital affair.

The nature of the economy also facilitates male use of prostitution (Davis 1993). Workers such as male truck drivers and salesmen must spend a considerable amount of time away from home. Symanski (1974) reported that tourists, travelling salesmen, and truck drivers were among the major sources of business for the brothels in Nevada. To the extent that *the economy requires travel,* there will likely be clientele for the prostitute.

Structural factors help explain why women enter the life. They tend to come from a *low position in the stratification system.* They usually have little education and few job skills, and resort to prostitution out of what they regard as economic necessity (Dalla 2000).

They also frequently come from backgrounds of *disturbed family experiences and participation in groups with norms that accept prostitution.* Prince (1986) reported that the prostitute's relationship with her father seems to be the most important family factor. In particular, the prostitutes tended to describe a father who abandoned the family, who lost contact after a divorce, or who treated the girl abusively or with indifference. About nine out of 10 of the streetwalkers said that they did not have a close or happy relationship with either their mother or father while growing up. The call girls tended to have a good relationship with their mother, but fewer than half had one with their father. Among the brothel workers, the proportions reporting good relationships were 43 percent with their mother and 39 percent with their father.

Similarly, interviews with 33 parents of teenage prostitutes reported that the parents were stressed from a history of failed intimate relationships and financial hardships (Longres 1991). They also raised their daughters in neighbourhoods conducive to easy entry into prostitution.

In many cases, the disturbed family experiences go beyond mere deprivation. Prostitutes come disproportionately from families where there is physical and/or sexual abuse, alcoholism, and use of other drugs (Davis 1993; Widom and Ames 1994; Farley and Barkan 1998; Dalla 2001; Nixon et al. 2002). Prince (1986) found abuse, including incest, particularly common among the streetwalkers. Abuse, exploitation, and deprivation combine to lead many young women to run away from home. Faced with the urgency of getting food and shelter, and possessing little or no money, they are lured into prostitution in an effort to survive. Even if they do not run away, early sexual abuse increases the chances of becoming a prostitute (Simons and Whitbeck 1991).

Social Psychological Factors. Although "respectable" people are frequently thought to abhor prostitution, the bulk of the prostitute's clientele are so-called respectable men. Both the tolerant attitudes of officials and public acceptance of the ideology that male sexuality needs the outlet help to maintain prostitution.

It is often said that prostitution could not continue if the authorities were determined to eliminate it. While this is an overstatement, it is true that police seldom make a determined effort to stop all prostitution. Of course, as long as there is a demand for the services of prostitutes, it is unlikely that the police can eliminate the practice even if they wished to do so.

The topic of youth prostitution has witnessed fundamental changes in Canada over the last 15 years. During this period, there has been growing recognition that young prostitutes should be treated as victims in need of protection, not deviants requiring punishment. As Bittle (2002) notes, secure care legislation has been enacted in Alberta, British Columbia, and Ontario, the intention of which is to assist youth prostitutes to remain off the street through supportive care programs. Although there is controversy around such programs, which some see as a source of social regulation and control over prostitutes and their families in that it places responsibility on them and not the johns who exploit them (Bittle 1999, Brannigan and Fleishman 1989, Brock and Kinsman 1996, among others), this debate nonetheless can be seen as part of the solution to youth prostitution in Canada.

Prostitution is one of the oldest professions in history; it is unlikely that it will disappear anytime soon. The major cause for the existence of the trade is that men have been socialized to view sex as a commodity that they can buy, and women as objects whose sole purpose is to provide this sexual gratification. So long as there are men who are willing to pay for sex there will be women willing, or forced through necessity, to provide it.

▪▪ PORNOGRAPHY, EROTICA, AND OBSCENITY

One person's pornography is another person's literature. It is no surprise, then, that this is a subject that generates strong feelings and great disagreement. What exactly are we talking about when we speak of pornography and how extensively does it penetrate society?

▪▪ Nature and Extent of the Problem

What comes to mind when you see or hear the word *pornography?* What, if anything, do you think should be done about materials that you would personally label as pornographic? Read the following discussion, then return to these questions and see whether your answers have changed in any way.

Definitions. People tend to label as pornographic any kind of *sexual materials that they find personally offensive;* but a finer distinction is required, one that differentiates between pornography, erotica, and obscenity (Hyde 1986). Generally, social scientists define **pornography** as *literature, art, films, or Internet materials that are sexually arousing.* You can further distinguish between so-called soft-core pornogra-

pornography
literature, art, Internet materials, or films that are sexually arousing

phy, which is suggestive but does not depict actual intercourse or genitals, and hard-core pornography, in which sexual acts and/or genitals are explicitly depicted.

Some people are aroused by sexual acts that others would consider degrading, such as forced sex or sex involving children. **Erotica** refers to *sexually arousing materials that are not degrading or demeaning to adults or children.* Erotica, for example, may involve a depiction of a couple engaged in sex play and sexual activity. To be sure, some will find this offensive and degrading. Yet for many, including scholars who research this area, there is an important distinction between erotica and pornography. A woman being raped is pornographic. Two mutually consenting adults engaged in sexual activity is erotica, not pornography.

Section 163 of the Criminal Code of Canada provides this country's legal definition of **obscenity** as follows:

erotica
sexually arousing materials that are not degrading or demeaning to adults or children

obscenity
material that is offensive by generally accepted standards of decency

163. (1) Every one commits an offence who

a) makes, prints, publishes, distributes, sells or has in his possession for the purpose of publication, distribution or circulation any obscene written matter, picture, model, phonograph record or other thing whatever; or

b) makes, prints, published, distributes, sells or has in his possession for the purposes of publication, distribution or circulation a crime comic.

(2) Every one commits an offence who knowingly, without lawful justification or excuse,

a) sells, exposes to public view or has in his possession for such a purpose any obscene written material, picture, model, phonograph record or other thing whatever;

b) Publicly exhibits a disgusting object or an indecent show;

c) offers to sell, advertise or publishes an advertisement of, or has for sale or disposal, any means, instructions, medicine, drug or article intended or represented as a method of causing abortion or miscarriage; or

d) advertises or publishes an advertisement of any means, instructions, medicine, drug or article intended or represented as a method for restoring sexual virility or curing venereal diseases or diseases of the generative organs.

(3) No person shall be convicted of an offence under this section if the public good was served by the acts that are alleged to constitute the offence and if the acts alleged did not extend beyond what serves the public good.

(4) For the purposes of this section, it is a question of law whether an act served the public good and whether there is evidence that the alleged act went beyond what served the public good, but it is a question of fact whether the acts did not extend beyond what served the [public good].

(5) For the purposes of this section, the motives of the accused are irrelevant.

In Canada, obscenity laws were enacted to ensure that materials are not distributed that are considered offensive by generally accepted standards of decency. However, such laws also raise a number of questions, such as: Who decides what is a prurient interest? What is the "community" whose standards must be followed? Who decides whether something has literary, artistic, political, or scientific value? What about the Internet? Should governments regulate Internet content to protect children from pornographic materials? The struggle between opposing positions continues in both public forums and the courts.

In 1993 the law on child pornography in Canada was passed and it is considered to have some of the harshest penalties in the world. Under the *Criminal Code*, offenders who possess images of children under the age of 18 engaging in sexual activity may now be sentenced to up to five years in jail.

The Internet has brought with it a need for Canadian laws specifically designed to deal with online activity. While child pornography laws pre-date the growth of the World Wide Web, it has been only recently that laws have evolved to keep up with new issues associated with this technology. Bill C-15A became law in July 2002. It deals specifically with child pornography and the exploitation of children on the Internet and it specifically bans cyber-luring, using the Internet to communicate with children for the purposes of sex. It is now illegal to use the Internet to communicate with a child for the purposes of committing a sexual act, and this offence carries a maximum five-year prison sentence. Under a child sex tourism section, Bill C-15A also protects children from other countries who are exploited by Canadians who are visiting or working abroad (Department of Justice 2002).

One of the challenges facing lawmakers is the fact that with the Internet international boundaries become blurred; this was the case in what is known as "Operation Snowball."

From 1997 until August 2001 Thomas and Janice Reedy, a Fort Worth, Texas couple, provided a gateway for paying subscribers to access child pornography via Web sites. The Reedys were making as much as US$1.4 million per month via a database called "Landslide"; hundreds of thousands of credit card numbers from suspected clients in North America and Europe were ultimately investigated by the U.S. Postal Inspection Service and the International Internet Crimes Against Children Task Force. The Federal Bureau of Investigation in the United States has since passed on the names of subscribers to various international authorities, including the Royal Canadian Mounted Police, and their investigations have led to more than 1,300 suspects in the United Kingdom and 2,329 in Canada, as well as many thousands in the United States.

The very nature of the Internet and the lack of appropriate international child pornography laws and police personnel make it very difficult to track down perpetrators of this crime.

In "Landslide," a *Fifth Estate* television special aired on November 5, 2003, reporters noted that, "of the 2,329 Canadian leads in the Landslide database, almost 2,000 have never been looked at by the police. That is because most communities simply do not have the will or the resources or the officers who are trained to do the job."

The Internet makes erotic and pornographic materials easily accessible, including the violent pornography that increases male aggression.

Further, "'There [are] an awful lot of them. That's the worst part, we worked really hard in Toronto to try and address this issue and the harder we work it just feels like we're scraping the tip of the iceberg' [said] Detective Sgt. Paul Gillespie of the Toronto Child Exploitation unit, one of the few such units in Canada that actually investigates child porn on the Internet" (*Fifth Estate* 2003).

Extent of the Problem. Erotica, pornography, and obscenity appear in many places—books, magazines, videos, telephone messages, and the Internet. It's difficult to know just how much is available, but pornography, including child pornography, is clearly present on the Internet (Durkin and Bryant 1995). Video stores usually have a section of "adult" films, which range from the erotic to the sexually violent and degrading (Duncan 1991). A study of magazines and videos available in a New York township reported that one-quarter of the magazines and 26.9 percent of the videos contained some kind of sexual violence (Barron and Kimmel 2000). Estimates of the number of pornographic videos rented each year range as high as 800 million (Oliver 1995).

Lebeque (1991) reviewed the 3,050 magazine and book titles surveyed in the 1986 U.S. Attorney General's Commission on Pornography to see whether the titles themselves fulfilled the criteria for an act of **paraphilia** (the need for a socially unacceptable stimulus in order to be sexually aroused and satisfied). Paraphilia is a disorder listed and described by the American Psychiatric Association. Using their criteria, Lebeque found that 746 (one-quarter of all the titles) fit the definition of paraphilia. **Sadomasochism** is the most common kind of paraphilia. It includes such behaviour as being tied up, gagged, whipped, or beaten and using verbal abuse as part of a sexual encounter.

We cannot say exactly how much of this type of material is consumed by North Americans. Much child pornography used by **pedophiles** (adults who depend on children for sexual stimulation) is underground. We do know that Canadians spend hundreds of millions of dollars every year to buy erotic and pornographic magazines and billions of dollars to rent or buy hundreds of millions of X-rated videos, and that a substantial number subscribe to porn television stations (Schlosser 1997; Paige 1998).

paraphilia
the need for a socially unacceptable stimulus in order to be sexually aroused and satisfied
sadomasochism
the practice of deriving sexual pleasure from the infliction of pain
pedophile
an adult who depends on children for sexual stimulation

▪▪ Pornography, Erotica, Obscenity, and the Quality of Life

With most social problems, there is some consensus about the ways in which a particular problem affects the quality of life. Researchers in the area of pornography, erotica, and obscenity, however, proceed from different premises (Francoeur 1991). Some assume that pornographic materials provide people with an outlet for sexual feelings and needs. The materials are like a safety valve, allowing people to reduce sexual tension without harming others. A different premise is that the materials do just the opposite: They offer models of behaviour that lead people to act in sexually aggressive and offensive ways which are harmful to others. Thus, researchers, like the general population, are divided in their assumption about and approaches to the problem.

It is our position that pornography and obscenity do have adverse effects on the quality of life, including some not yet known because there is no supporting research. For example, there is no research that addresses such questions as how the use of pornographic materials affects an individual's day-to-day intimate relationships, including those with friends, spouse, and children. There is evidence that extensive use of pornography produces negative attitudes about the value of marriage, and that wives who discover such use by their husbands struggle with the meaning of their marriage and their own worth and desirability (Linz and Malamuth 1993; Bergner and

Bridges 2002). There is also evidence that exposure to televised pornography has potential negative effects on children, including the modelling of the behaviour; interference with normal sexual development; emotional problems such as anxiety, guilt, confusion, and shame; stimulation of premature sexual activity; and the development of harmful attitudes and beliefs about sex and sexual relationships (Benedek and Brown 1999). Consider a few other consequences.

Exploitation of Children. On one point, at least, there is consensus—child pornography is exploitation. Films and pictures that depict sexual acts with children clearly victimize the children: "Children, by virtue of their developmental level, cannot give true informed consent to participate in such activities, and the potential for doing psychological damage to them is great" (Hyde 1986:514).

Such exploitation is a contradiction with the value of *a child's right to dignity and protection.* A study of 66 children who had been in sex rings found various kinds of psychological damage, including being conditioned to use sex to get attention in the future and/or to boost low self-esteem (Burgess 1984).

Children are caught up in pornography in various ways, but *frequently the exploiter is a relative, even a parent.* When a porn magazine ran an ad for young girl-child models, dozens of parents responded. An 11-year-old girl was accepted and told to have sex with a 40-year-old man. She ran to her mother and said she couldn't do it, but her mother told her she had to do it because they needed the money (Hyde 1986:514).

A recent ABC Television poll suggested that there are more than 100,000 Web sites involved in the global child pornography market. The International Watch Foundation (IWF), a non-profit organization whose objectives include eradicating child pornography online, noted that it received information about 400 new child pornography sites every week in 2003 (ABC News 2001).

Degradation of Women. Canadian ideology says that all people should be treated with dignity and respect, but much pornography contradicts that ideal. This seems clear in the case of obscenity or pornography that portrays such things as rape and men urinating on women. Many women feel that pornography generally is degrading because, even if there is no violence, there is a depiction of women as sex objects whose bodies can be purchased and used for male pleasure.

Pornography also reinforces certain **stereotypes.** Mayall and Russell (1993) analyzed pornographic magazines, books, films, videos, games, and cards to see how women of various ethnic groups were portrayed. Generally, they found Asian women appeared as pliant dolls, Latin women as sexually voracious but also completely submissive, and African American women as dangerous sexual animals.

Since most pornography and obscenity involves male dominance and female subordination, it is not surprising that women would react negatively even if no violence were involved. When erotic and pornographic slides were shown to a group of female undergraduates, they reacted positively to the erotica (Senn and Radtke 1990), but they disliked the pornography and strongly disliked the pornography that included violence. Measures of mood before and after watching the slides showed that the pornography led to significant mood disturbance.

Many feminist scholars locate the use of pornography that denigrates women and children within the realm of *patriarchy*, a social system in which males dominate females and in which males are more highly valued than females (see, for example, the works of Burstyn 1985, Jolin 1994, Leuchtag 1995, and many others).

Violence. One of the more controversial aspects of the problem is whether the use of pornographic and obscene materials leads to violent behaviour. Some researchers

stereotype
an image of members of a group that standardizes them and exaggerates certain qualities

SEXY OR DISGUSTING?

Looking at an erotic picture of a scantily clad young woman, a man responded: "That is the sexiest thing I've ever seen." A woman evaluated the same picture with: "I think it's disgusting." Do men and women always react so differently to erotic materials? Take a survey of a number of students in your class. Enlist the aid of at least one other student of the opposite sex.

Interviewers should interview a minimum of 10 subjects of their own gender. Ask the following three questions:

1. Do you see any positive value to magazines like *Playboy* and *Playgirl*? What? (List as many as respondents can think of.)

2. Do you see any negative consequences from such magazines? What? (Again, list as many as possible.)

3. Have you ever looked at, or do you now look at, such magazines? Why or why not?

Analyze your results. What positive values do students see in such materials? What negative consequences? Do men and women differ in their opinions? If so, how? Did nonreaders have very strong opinions? Did nonreaders differ from readers? How? Finally, if the positive values and negative consequences identified by your respondents represented the thinking of all Americans, including researchers, what recommendations would you make about the availability of such materials?

find no relationship between the use of pornography and sexual violence (Gentry 1991; Becker and Stein 1991). Others argue that there is a significant relationship between the use of pornography, hatred of women, and rape (Russell 1998). Research supporting the latter includes the work of Boeringer (1994), who distinguished between different types of pornography in his testing of 477 college men in the United States. Those who watched pornography that included violence and rape were more likely to be sexually aggressive. Those who watched "soft-core" pornography were less likely to approve of or engage in rape, but more likely to use sexual force and other kinds of coercion.

Boeringer's research is consistent with that of others who have found an association between violent pornography and men's aggressive attitudes and behaviour (Donnerstein 1984; Golde et al. 2000; Malamuth, Addison, and Koss 2000). In fact, two researchers who gathered data from 100 female victims of sexual violence reported that 28 percent of the victims said the abuser used pornography and 12 percent said that the abuser imitated the pornography during the abusive incident (Bergen and Bogle 2000).

Violent pornography, then, *contradicts our value on human well-being as well as the norm that sexual behaviour should be voluntary and not coerced.* It is not only the women who are directly involved who are affected. The existence of violent pornography is a threat to all women. Every time a woman sees a store that sells such materials, she is reminded that she is a potential victim.

■■ Contributing Factors

Clearly one of the big factors in maintaining the supply of pornographic and obscene materials is the demand. By the nature of the industry, it is not easy to know who the customers are. Studies show that the typical customer is an educated, middle-class man in his 20s or early 30s (Hyde 1986). Some women also are consumers of pornography, but the majority of consumers are men. Social structural factors help guarantee a continuing supply of materials for those men.

Social Structural Factors. From an institutional perspective, *the economy and the legal system both work to maintain the supply of materials.* Economically, the porn business is extremely profitable. The profit margin on magazines is high; a store with a brisk business can bring in hundreds of thousands of dollars in gross sales a year. Overall, Canadians spend billions of dollars on pornographic materials each year, and it has been estimated that about 40 percent of the money is spent on child pornography (Hyde 1986:515). Even telephone sex is a multimillion-dollar business. In one year, Pacific Bell earned nearly US$25 million from the 1-900 porn lines (Francoeur 1991:641).

The legal system presents an extremely difficult issue: *Does any effort to suppress materials, to exercise censorship, violate Charter rights?* The reason for ongoing legal issues is that the battle over pornography and obscenity involves a *conflict of values.* Some people value openness in sexual matters. They believe that the worst thing that could happen would be to pass any laws infringing on the constitutional right of free speech, and they point out some of the extremes to which people go as they try to guard their own version of morality—such as the removal of a copy of Goya's masterpiece, *The Nude Maja,* from a classroom wall at Pennsylvania State University on the grounds that it made some of the female students uncomfortable (Strossen 1995), or the order of U.S. Attorney General John Ashcroft in 2002 to cover the bare breast of the statue *Spirit of Justice,* in the Justice Department's Great Hall.

Others contend that society must be responsible and responsive to the needs of people whose quality of life is depressed by the materials. They argue, for instance, that to protect the right of pornographers in the name of free speech is a violation of the more basic right of women to freedom from exploitation and inequality (Leidholdt and Raymond 1990).

In June 1993 Parliament passed legislation outlawing child pornography in Canada. However, in 1995 an Ontario judge in the Eli Langer case (Langer is an artist who draws naked children engaging in sex with each other and sexually aroused adults) ruled that such work was "artistic" and did not violate the child pornography law. In 1998, a Vancouver judge ruled that Robin Sharpe, a convicted pedophile, was not guilty of possessing child pornography because it was part of his freedom of expression and privacy. In January 2001 the Supreme Court of Canada overturned this ruling, arguing that freedom of expression which resulted in the exploitation and abuse of children, whether in writings, drawings, videos, photographs, or films (as well as via the Internet), was in fact a violation of the 1993 law (CBC News 2003; see also CBNC News Online 2004).

Each side tends to use the *fallacies of dramatic instance* and *personal attack.* For example, those who argue for regulation may cite a newspaper article about sexual violence by someone who read pornographic magazines and call their opponents the destroyers of personal and social morality. Those who stand for openness, on the other hand, may offer Nazi Germany as an example of a repressive society and argue that Canadians are heading in the same direction when they suppress materials simply because some people find them offensive. They may call their opponents prudes or narrow-minded people who are willing to sacrifice the basic rights of all Canadians to alleviate their own fears.

In essence, *the legal system has helped both sides.* By its ongoing effort to specify what is obscene, the Supreme Court has made the production and distribution of some offensive materials a criminal matter. In the effort to maintain the right of free speech, on the other hand, the courts have allowed the continued production and distribution of materials that women find offensive and degrading, as well as some (violent pornography) that increase the aggressiveness of men against women.

▪▪ HOMOSEXUALITY, HOMOPHOBIA, AND HETEROSEXISM

In North American society, fulfilling sexual love is often conceived as *heterosexual—male–female* relationships. Yet people gain sexual satisfaction in a variety of ways. In this section we discuss **homosexuals,** those who have a sexual preference for individuals of the same sex. We examine the problems they encounter because of **homophobia,** an irrational fear of lesbians, bisexuals, and gay men, and **heterosexism,** the erroneous assumption that everyone is heterosexual. We also look at the factors that perpetuate these problems.

homosexual
having sexual preference for persons of the same sex; someone who privately or overtly considers himself or herself a homosexual

homophobia
an unnatural fear and dislike of lesbians, bisexuals, and gay men

heterosexism
the erroneous assumption that everyone is heterosexual

▪▪ Homosexuality: Definitions and Numbers

Not everyone who engages in a homosexual act can be considered a homosexual. Boys and girls may commonly engage in homosexual activity during adolescence, but most of them become exclusively heterosexual. We define a homosexual as an individual who both has a sexual preference for those of the same sex and who also defines himself or herself as lesbian or gay.

Some people are *bisexual,* finding gratification with both sexes and having no strong preference for either, but bisexuals are not as common as those who are exclusively heterosexual or homosexual. The terms *homosexual* and *gay* refer to both males and females. In addition, *lesbian* is used for females, and *gay men* (or *gay males*) is used for males. Most studies in the past focused on gay males rather than lesbians.

Homosexuality is found throughout the world. Research into various societies finds homosexuals in all of them and in roughly the same proportion of the population (Whitam 1983). Moreover, that proportion tends to remain relatively stable over time in each society.

What is the proportion? How many homosexuals are there in North America? In the United States, one of the most comprehensive and most recent studies of sexual behaviour was the National Health and Social Life Survey conducted by researchers at the University of Chicago (Laumann et al. 1994). Using a sample of 3,432 American men

Many lesbians and gay men lead well-adjusted lives even when faced with negative societal reaction.

and women between the ages of 18 and 59, the researchers found that 2.7 percent of sexually active men and 1.3 percent of sexually active women had had a homosexual experience in the past year. Further, they reported that 9.1 percent of men and 4.3 percent of women have had a homosexual experience since puberty, and 7.7 percent of men and 7.4 percent of women said they felt some degree of same-sex *attraction* or interest.

The above figures are consistent with those reported by researchers in other nations. For example, researchers reported that 4.5 and 8.5 percent of males, and 2.1 and 3.3 percent of females in the United Kingdom and France, respectively, had had a homosexual experience in the previous five years (Sell, Wells, and Wypij 1995). The figures for homosexual attraction (as opposed to homosexual behaviour) were 7.9 and 10.7 percent for males and 8.6 and 11.7 percent for females in the two nations.

It is commonly believed that the number of lesbians and gay men in the Canadian population is one in ten (see, for example, Compas Opinion and Market Research 2000, Michael et al. 1994). Although we doubt that this figure will ever be truly known, as sexual preference is not necessarily a fixed entity and people's self-identity may not correspond with their behaviour, studies asking people about sexual orientation consistently show that individuals who identify themselves as heterosexual also admit to having same-sex fantasies, attractions, and relationships (e.g., Michael et al. 1994; Faulkner and Cranston 1998; Kinsey, Pomeroy, and Martin 1948; Bohan 1996; and Money 1988, among others).

The 2001 census was the first in Canada to include a question regarding same-sex relationships. At that time, only 34,200 same-sex couples were counted. Gay-rights advocates argue that many lesbians and gay men did not truthfully answer this question, especially in rural areas, because they do not trust government with such details of their lives (Thompson 2002). The only other countries to include a question on same-sex common-law relationships in their census information have been New Zealand in 1996 and the United States in 1990 and 2000 (ibid).

On January 30, 2003, Statistics Canada announced that it would conduct a national survey to ask people if they are gay, lesbian, or bisexual. The Canadian Community Health Study will survey 130,000 Canadians over the telephone. However, John Fisher, Executive Director of EGALE Canada, suggested that many will not truthfully respond to the survey because "if it's a teenager living at home with his or her parents who has not yet disclosed their sexual orientation to their family, it is unlikely that they're going to disclose it to a government statistician" (Sui 2003).

Gay activists argue that it is important for lesbians and gay men to register relationships both in the census and in provincial jurisdictions so that they are recognized and counted as fully functioning families with the same rights, obligations, and needs as heterosexual cohabiting couples.

▪▪ Why Are Some People Lesbian or Gay?

Enormous pressures exist in most societies for people to be heterosexual. In her excellent book *The Trouble with Normal: Postwar Youth and the Making of Heterosexuality* (1999), Mary Louise Adams notes that sexuality is socially constructed, and that it changes across time and place. Some thoughts we ought to ponder when thinking about sexuality are how is it organized, normalized, and regulated, and by whom? As well, we might wonder why it is that we categorize ourselves and others by our sexual behaviours and identities.

Sociologists interested in the social regulation of sexualities are interested in examining what social practices normalize heterosexuality and view other forms of sexual expression and desire as deviant (see, for example, Fone 2000, Foucault 1980, Kinsman 1996 and 2003, and Weeks 2000, among others).

In a similar view to Adams, Kinsman argues that biological determinism and a positivistic approach to sexuality, which suggests that heterosexuality is normal, intrinsic, and natural, does not take into account the ways in which gender, sexualities, and sexual identifications are socially constructed practices of everyday life (2003:263). Among other things, few readers of this book have grown up without hearing the word "homosexual," or another slang term, applied to someone in a disparaging way. Moreover, books, movies, popular music, advertisements, television, and observation all reinforce the expectation of heterosexual relations.

As Barry Adam (1995, 1999, and 2002) has noted, in the past 20 years there has been a tremendous increase in the development of global movements for social change regarding the status of lesbians and gay men worldwide. This continued acceptance of lesbians and gay men in every aspect of society is most notable in the struggle for marriage rights. Please go to this text's Online Learning Centre at **www.mcgrawhill. ca/college/lauer** for a brief overview of this legislation.

Canada is one of the countries that has also moved forward regarding same-sex marriage, as illustrated by the following table:

A Review of the History of Same-Sex Legislation in Canada

The following Canadian provinces have passed legislation granting benefits to same-sex partners:

British Columbia	1992
Manitoba	2001
New Brunswick	2000
Newfoundland and Labrador	2000
Nova Scotia	2000
Ontario	1999
Prince Edward Island	2002
Quebec	1998
Saskatchewan	2001
Yukon	1998

As of December 9, 2004, the following provinces and territories have granted same-sex marriage rights to lesbians and gay men in Canada:

British Columbia	Nunavut
Manitoba	Ontario
Newfoundland and Labrador	Quebec
Northwest Territories	Saskatchewan
Nova Scotia	Yukon

On December 9, 2004, the Supreme Court of Canada ruled that lesbians and gay men were entitled to marry as their constitutional right, and on June 28, 2005, Canada became the fourth country in the world to affirm equal marriage for same-sex couples. (For more information on the specific pieces of legislation, see Department of Justice Canada, *Backgrounder: Modernization of Benefits and Obligations*. Available on the

World Wide Web at http://canada.justice.gc.ca/en/news/nr/2000/doc25021.html; or Gordon 2001).

Clearly, the issue of granting equal rights and obligations to same-sex partners will remain controversial for some time to come; gay rights activists and their supporters worldwide are confident, however, that they will achieve equality.

■■ Homosexuality and the Quality of Life

Homosexuality is a pattern of behaviour involving social contradictions that both homosexuals and heterosexuals define as incompatible with the desired quality of life. Homosexuals point to two contradictions in particular. One is that the *North American ideology of equality contradicts North American attitudes and behaviour toward homosexuals.* The other is that the stereotyped homosexual role (see the discussion of myths in the following section) contradicts the actual homosexual role. Those who condemn homosexuals are frequently condemning the stereotyped rather than the actual role.

In other words, homosexuals argue that their behaviour is a problem detracting from quality of life not because something is intrinsically wrong or damaging about it, but because of the *societal reaction.* In the following paragraphs we look at some ways in which the quality of life is diminished for homosexuals by such things as restricted opportunities, ridicule, being labelled sick or perverted, and stress.

Myths about Homosexuality.   There is a contradiction between the ideal of the *dignity of human beings and the prevalent ideology about homosexuals.* This contradiction is manifested in *a number of myths about homosexuality,* myths that involve the *fallacies of personal attack* and *appeal to prejudice.* Perhaps the most common myth is that homosexuals have characteristics that are normal for the opposite sex—males are "effeminate" and females are "masculine." Actually, as Bell, Weinberg, and Hammersmith (1981) reported in their large-scale study, such traits characterize only a minority of homosexuals.

A second myth about homosexuals is that they fear, and are incapable of, having heterosexual relationships. Homosexuality is commonly attributed to unsatisfactory heterosexual experiences that cause fear of relationships with the opposite sex.

Michael Stark, left, and Michael Leshner kiss after their marriage in Superior Court in Toronto, June 2003.

While experiences with those of the opposite sex may be a factor in the development of homosexuality, there does not seem to be any evidence that homosexuals are incapable of relating to the opposite sex. By definition, a homosexual prefers sexual relations with those of his or her own sex exclusively. However, homosexuals do make and maintain good relationships with people of the opposite sex. Research by the Institute for Sex Research, founded by Kinsey, showed that about one-fifth of homosexuals in the sample had been married at one time and about half of them had intercourse from two to four times a week during the first year of marriage (Bell and Weinberg 1978). Bell, Weinberg, and Hammersmith

(1981) reported that the lesbians in their sample had early histories of heterosexual experiences that were virtually identical to those of straight women.

Finally, Kehoe (1989) reported that 27 of the 100 older lesbians she studied had been married and had children. Such studies, combined with the fact that many people are homosexuals for only a part of their lives, suggest that homosexuals are capable of all kinds of heterosexual relationships and that preference rather than fear is the critical factor.

A third myth is that people typically become homosexual by being seduced by a homosexual. No evidence supports this.

Still another myth is that a homosexual is attracted to, and will make advances to, anyone of his or her own sex, children as well as adults. The homosexual, however, is as selective as anyone else and is unlikely to be a pedophile. A study of erotic age preference reported that gay males who prefer mature partners respond no more to male children than do heterosexual males, who also prefer mature partners to children (Freund, Watson, and Rienzo 1989).

Finally, there is the myth that homosexuals do not form the same kinds of long-term attachments as heterosexuals. It is true that gay males tend to be promiscuous. About half of the white males studied by Bell and Weinberg (1978) in San Francisco reported that they had had more than 500 partners. The lesbians tended to prefer a more stable relationship with a partner.

In the Kehoe (1989) study of older lesbians, 20 of the 100 women reported a relationship that lasted 20 years or more (four had relationships of 40 or more years). On the average, the women reported relationships that averaged around 14 years. Many males also have long-lasting relationships (Silverstein 1981), and, in contrast to most heterosexual couples, their relationships tend to be ones of equality (McWhirter and Mattison 1984).

Long-term homosexual relationships are indistinguishable from their heterosexual counterparts in terms of what the partners want—being able to talk about feelings, being able to laugh together, giving and receiving support, and so on (Peplau 1981). In other words, *homosexual couples have the same hopes, the same needs, the same desires, and, indeed, the same problems as heterosexual couples* (Patterson 2000). The problems include instances of verbal and physical abuse (Lockhart et al. 1994).

Homosexuals may want, like heterosexuals, to be parents and may find great satisfaction in parenting. Of 47 lesbian couples studied by Koepke, Hare, and Moran (1992), 40 percent had children and were more satisfied with their relationship and their sexual relations than were the childless couples. Gay men who are fathers are similar to heterosexual fathers in both parenting style and attitudes (Bigner and Jacobsen 1992).

Independent of desire and satisfaction is the question of the *well-being of children raised in a homosexual family*. Researchers who compared children ages three to nine raised in 15 lesbian families with those raised in 15 heterosexual families found no differences in cognitive functioning or behavioural adjustment (Flaks et al. 1995). The lesbian couples, however, appeared to have more parenting awareness skills than did the heterosexual couples. In sum, research indicates that the overall well-being of children raised in a homosexual family is as high as that of children raised in heterosexual families (Strickland 1995; Patterson 2000). Most of the children raised in a homosexual family do not themselves become homosexuals. In a comprehensive examination of research materials on same-sex couples, families, parenting, and relationship status for the Vanier Institute of the Family, Canadian sociologist Ann-Marie Ambert (2003) could find no differences between gay and lesbian couples and their heterosexual counterparts with respect to any of these issues.

Gay couples, then, are like heterosexual couples in important ways. Yet because of the social stigma attached to homosexuality in the past, gay couples have found it difficult to establish a long-term relationship with a single partner. Depending upon what happens to public attitudes, there will be many more such relationships in the future.

Equality of Opportunity.

The Canadian *ideology of equality of opportunity contradicts the norms and laws about the hiring of homosexuals.* But homosexuals and lesbians have had to contend with a number of legal barriers to equal opportunity within both the government and the business sectors.

The lack of equal opportunity is not based on any lack of ability or inferior performance by homosexuals. In fact, homosexuals may *suffer discrimination in spite of proven adequate or even superior performance.* They may experience harassment, stalled careers, and even termination if their sexual orientation is known. In one case in the United States, the Pennsylvania Superior court upheld the right of a business owner to dismiss an employee for homosexuality and then collect damages from the ex-employee for opening a competing business (Dunlap 1995). And 1,250 Americans (the highest number since 1987) were dismissed from the military in 2001 for being homosexual (Zuckerbrod 2002).

Thus, it is still true that homosexuals may have to choose between making their sexual orientation known ("coming out") and thereby risking their jobs, or remaining secretive and retaining their jobs. Unlike others who are defined as criminals, the homosexual poses no threat to life or property.

Negative Sanctions.

Sanctions are rewards (positive sanctions) or punishments (negative sanctions) designed to influence behaviour. Homosexuals are subjected to *numerous negative sanctions,* including ridicule, suppression, physical abuse, and ostracism. This contradicts the Canadian ideology that every citizen has a right to live freely. All the sanctions, of course, are aimed at changing the homosexual into a heterosexual.

sanctions
mechanisms of social control for enforcing a society's standards

One negative sanction is likely to be the reaction of family members to disclosure of homosexuality. Parents and even siblings may resent the homosexual and try to pressure him or her to change. Guilt, anger, frustration, and grief may characterize family relationships. A lesbian in her 70s recalled strained relationships with her siblings:

> I regret that not once in my adult life could I ever establish rapport with my brother and my twin sister . . . vis-a-vis my lesbianism, and our family relationship was and is one of total lack of communication on this entire subject. A blank wall stands between me and them and all three of us in growing old are unlikely to penetrate the wall. (Kehoe 1989:30)

Many homosexuals have endured being *labelled perverts* or *called mentally ill* and treated as such by their family or others. Some young gays who roam the streets and survive by engaging in homosexual prostitution were forced out of their homes because of their sexual orientation (Kruks 1991). Those who label and treat homosexuals as perverted or ill, whether from a misguided effort to help gay persons change or because of their own sexual insecurities, only add to the difficulties of homosexuals.

Finally, many homosexuals—both youths and adults—have been verbally and physically attacked (Herek et al. 1997; Franklin 2000; Thurlow 2001). Thousands of these attacks occur each year, resulting in injuries or even, in a few cases, in murder (Lacayo 1998; D'Augelli and Grossman 2001).

Fear.

It is little wonder that *homosexuals live with a certain amount of fear,* including the fear of making their sexual identity known to physicians because of possible negative reactions (Lehmann, Lehmann, and Kelly 1998). One of the freedoms cherished by Canadians is the freedom from fear. For the homosexual, this ideal is contradicted by the norms and laws that apply to gay people as well as by the experience of being abused.

In other words, the homosexual is subject to fear of exposure if he or she decides to remain secretive and to fear of negative sanctions if he or she decides to "come out." This is not to say that every homosexual goes around constantly haunted by fear. Nevertheless, all homosexuals must come to terms with realistic fears. These fears are realistic because all homosexuals are familiar with stories of harassment and attacks. For example, imagine what it must be like to be a homosexual and read in a national magazine of a gay man who, because he led a campaign against an antigay resolution passed by the local government in the area where he and his partner lived, received anonymous telephone calls that threatened to "slit your throat and watch your faggot blood run in the street" (Henry 1994:57). Gays know that such incidents are neither rare nor confined to isolated areas of the nation.

Psychological and Emotional Problems.   You might expect that it is difficult for homosexuals to avoid psychological and emotional problems as they wrestle with the contradictions that impinge upon their lives. In fact, a number of studies have identified problems that result from the *stress generated by the societal reaction to an individual's homosexuality* (Radkowsky and Siegel 1997; Hershberger, Pilkington, and D'Augelli 1997). In brief, homosexuals have higher rates than heterosexuals of isolation, depression, low self-esteem, attempted suicide, and alcohol abuse (Grossman and Kerner 1998; Cochran and Mays 2000; Diaz et al. 2001).

For example, among a sample of middle-aged lesbians, 73 percent had sought counselling for emotional problems and 16 percent had tried to commit suicide (Sang, Warshow, and Smith 1991). In the National Lesbian Health Care Survey conducted in the United States, more than half the sample acknowledged having had thoughts about suicide at some time and 18 percent had attempted suicide (Bradford, Ryan, and Rothblum 1994). About three-fourths had been in counselling, and half of those had sought counselling for sadness and depression. On the other hand, there are no significant differences between homosexuals and heterosexuals in the incidence of neurotic disorders, and homosexuals generally function adequately in society (Latorre and Wendenburg 1983; Strickland 1995).

What does all this mean? First, there is no basis for claiming that a homosexual orientation is associated with clinical symptoms of mental illness. As the American Psychiatric Association has underscored by removing homosexuality from its list of mental disorders, the notion that gays are inherently disturbed individuals who need therapy in order to change their sexual preference is no longer tenable. Second, the stress induced by societal reaction to the individual's homosexuality creates emotional and psychological problems. Third, many homosexuals come to terms with the societal reaction, cope with the problems, and lead well-adjusted and productive lives.

■■ Contributing Factors

Without the societal reaction to homosexuality among Canadians, we could not speak of homosexual behaviour as a social problem. In this section we look at some of the multiple-level factors that account for this societal reaction and that create stress for homosexuals.

Social Structure Factors.   In the United States and Canada, *normative sexual behaviour* is heterosexual. The norms of society define homosexuality as deviant, but such norms do not reflect universal standards or innate biological imperatives. In fact, even when heterosexual relations are dominant, a society may not disapprove of or *punish homosexuality*. In her study of a variety of primitive societies, Brown (1952) found that 14 of 44 of the societies for which data were available did not punish male homosexuality, and 8 of 12 did not punish female homosexuality.

Many modern societies refrain from formally punishing homosexual acts that are conducted in private between consenting adults. These acts, for example, are not considered a crime in Japan, Korea, Mexico, Argentina, Uruguay, Egypt, and the Sudan.

In a recent poll (July 1, 2004), the Canadian Centre for Research Statistics and Information reported that 57 percent of Canadians support same-sex marriage.

Has the fear of AIDS affected attitudes toward gays? According to polls, most North Americans say no. Still, a great many feel that homosexuals should be barred from being food handlers, doctors, or day care nurses, or should be tested for AIDS before taking those jobs. The strong feelings of those with negative attitudes because of AIDS may affect others. A student reported his own experience in disquieting words:

> With the growing fear of AIDS, people are talking more about heterosexuality. And the people I talk to talk about gays as if they are animals. "Kill them all" or a variation of that attitude seems to prevail. It scares me. Not because I'm gay, but because it reminds me of Nazi Germany. Hate is a disease. It spreads.

The negative societal reaction to homosexuality is also legitimated by the ideology that homosexuals are "sick." For the professional, this means that people who prefer homosexual relations suffer from an emotional disorder and need to be treated in the same way as any other emotionally disturbed individual. We heard a therapist analyze homosexuals as people who can never be happy because heterosexual relations are basic to human development and well-being. This view implies that *those who prefer homosexual relations should be identified, treated, and cured.* We do not know the number of therapists who view homosexuals as sick despite the 1973 American Psychiatric Association vote to remove homosexuality from its list of mental disorders. Most members of the American Psychiatric Association believe homosexuality to have biological rather than psychological causes (Gallagher, McFalls, and Vreeland 1993). Still, there are therapists who insist that at least some homosexuals can become heterosexual after treatment (Berger 1994).

Many nonprofessionals view homosexuals as not only sick, but perverse as well (the *fallacy of personal attack*). Just as many Canadians believe that alcoholics could stop drinking "if they only wanted to," they also believe that homosexuals could change their sexual behaviour "if they only wanted to." In other words, many Canadians view homosexuality as a personal problem, not a social one. They believe that the norms, institutional arrangements, attitudes, values, and ideology that work together to condemn and oppress homosexuals are legitimate.

■■ From Social Problems to Solutions

In this chapter we discussed the social problem of homophobia and some of its consequences for those who are discriminated against on the basis of their sexual orientation. Across Canada, various groups and organizations are working together to eliminate heterosexism and homophobia in all aspects of social life, in institutions ranging from the law to education, religion, family, schools, workplaces, and the playground.

Some of the key consequences for victims of heterosexism and homophobia are feelings of shame and guilt, self-hate, depression, anxiety, family rejection, alcohol and drug abuse, homelessness, violence and hate crimes, dropping out of school, eating disorders, HIV infection, sexually transmitted diseases, and youth suicide (Lesbian, Gay & Bisexual Youth Project 2001:4).

It has been documented by many authors (D'Augelli, Hershberger, and Pilkington 2001; Bagley and Tremblay 1996; Garofalo 1998; Grossman 1997; Mallon 1998; Ryan and Futterman 1997, among others) that suicide among lesbian and gay youth is up to 40 percent more prevalent than among heterosexual youth.

In a Canadian study by Bagley and Tremblay (1996) at the University of Calgary, it was found that lesbian and gay youth were 13.9 times more likely to commit suicide than their heterosexual counterparts. When gay youth in particular were asked about their suicidal ideation, most claimed that it was due to homophobic behaviours from their parents, peers, and from classmates and others in their school environment.

In a recent study conducted in California, the researchers found that 46 percent of lesbian, gay, bisexual, and transgendered students experienced repeated harassment at school on the basis of their sexual orientation (Youth Suicide Problems 2004). The study's Website also includes the results of research conducted in Trinidad, various U.S. states, South Africa, Australia, New Zealand, India/South Asia, Norway, and the United Kingdom. All share similar findings: that the most serious consequence of homophobia and heterosexism when directed toward young people is youth suicide. The Website also provides a thorough overview of the published research on this topic over the past 20 years.

In another study conducted by Peters, also in the United States, it was found that 94 percent of high school students heard anti-gay comments "frequently" or "sometimes" in their school environments; 86 percent of those students reported that school officials "rarely" or "never" challenged this type of harassment. (2003:332). As a correlate to these experiences, one of the authors of this textbook also found that gay and bisexual youth were two to five times more likely to drop out of school than their heterosexual peers.

In a survey conducted in the United States, Canada, and Australia, D'Augelli et al. (2001) concluded that the main support systems needed by these youth were peer and individual counselling sessions, opportunities to meet and socialize with other youth who have similar needs, and community support.

According to Cato and Canetto, the U.S. National Center for Health Statistics (1990) has indicated that youth suicide is the second leading cause of death for persons aged 15 to 24 and accounts for 11 percent of all deaths in this age group. From 18.5 to 42 percent of youth who self-identified as lesbian, gay, or bisexual reported attempting suicide (2003:39).

According to the above authors, 35,000 to 3,000,000 youth attempt suicide every year in the United States. Lesbian, gay, and bisexual youth are four times more likely to attempt suicide, five times more likely to have used cocaine as a way to deal with their depression and anxiety, and five times more likely to miss school for fear of feeling unsafe (2003:40).

In 2003, Health Canada organized a workshop dealing with suicide-related research in this country. At that time, sexual identity was seen as one of the major determinants of suicide ideation among Canadians, especially youth. Again, the issue of the provision of supportive services to encourage and assist lesbian, gay, bisexual, and transgendered youth was suggested. In many Canadian provinces such services exist (see, for example, www.youthnet.on.ca, a mental health project run for and by youth and funded through Health Canada); www.pinktriangle.org provides a wide range of services for youth living in the Ottawa area. Services for youth in every province and territory in Canada can be found at www.gay.canada.com/index/php, which provides a breakdown of various programs and services in individual towns, cities, and rural areas. One of the first such services to exist in Atlantic Canada to provide support services to lesbian, gay, transgendered, and questioning youth is the Lesbian, Gay & Bisexual Youth Project (which shall be referred to from here on as the Youth Project) in Halifax, Nova Scotia; we will use it as a case study for what can be done to create solutions to the social problem of youth suicide based on sexual preference and gender identity.

The Youth Project was started in 1993 by a social work student who needed to conduct a practicum placement in her community as part of her degree program. This young woman, herself a lesbian, was extremely concerned about the needs of lesbian, gay, and bisexual youth under age 25 and the high rate of suicide among this cohort. With some others, she decided to create the Youth Project with the objective to "Make Nova Scotia a safer, healthier, and happier place for lesbian, gay, bisexual, and transgendered youth both through support, education, resource expansion and community development." The Youth Project provides free services to all youth, regardless of ethnicity or race, religion, ability, or economic class background.

Since it began, the project has provided services and programs to thousands of young people—not only directly in its Halifax main office, but also via the Internet using Website and e-mail, over the telephone, and through workshops, retreats, social events, and educational sessions with health care and other social service providers. The project also provides speakers for educational sessions of all types, ranging from primary through high schools, colleges, and universities across Nova Scotia. As well, project staff travel throughout North America sharing the success of their endeavours. The Youth Project is run by a board of directors comprising youth; the board is responsible for all aspects of the agency including budget and policy development, service implementation, hiring, and personnel and volunteer issues.

Specifically, the project provides the following services: facilitated youth groups; social events (dances, movie nights, barbecues, Pride Week activities, pot-luck meals); weekend and week-long retreats (one in summer as a camp, the other in winter for recreational activities such as skiing, snowboarding, and hiking); counselling (on a face-to-face basis or within groups); peer support; a "safe house" program where youth who have been asked to leave their family homes because of their sexual orientation are taken in by those supportive of them; a "safe classroom" where youth who have dropped out of school due to persecution, bullying, and physical and emotional taunting can complete high school and other academic qualifications; a tutoring program to assist youth to complete school when their academic skills are threatened; access to computers and the Internet for study or personal use; HIV testing and counselling; an ally program where supportive individuals from all walks of life can volunteer to be an ally to a young person in their community, school, place of work, or church; a lending library; and individual and community consultations.

The project also provides specific groups for young women age 25 and under who prefer to meet without men; likewise, they hold a young men's group for the same reasons. Rural groups are also provided, and the project staff are helpful and supportive of those in rural areas who want to start up groups in their own community. The project also works closely with local PFLAG (Parents, Families, and Friends of Lesbians and Gays) groups to provide support and assistance to those who have a difficult time dealing with the sexual preferences of their children and friends. The project also works closely with NSRAP (The Nova Scotia Rainbow Action Project), which holds similar interests as well as theme-focused groups such as same-sex marriage legislation, health coverage for sexual realignment surgery, and the spiritual needs of the community.

In 2004, the project was asked to extend its programs and services to individuals over age 25 who have challenges similar to those of their younger counterparts. The project also facilitates the creation of gay/straight alliances in high schools, colleges, and universities across the province where students approach them for assistance. Many of the youth who attend the Youth Project programs originally did so because they had suicidal thoughts, and some had even attempted suicide; however, because of their activity with the project, they no longer held such thoughts or attempted such actions.

In one of the authors of this textbook's Lesbian and Gay Studies classes, youth from the project who have shared their experiences with students say that the most successful component of the project is the opportunity to socialize with others like themselves—and all claim to have found heightened self-esteem and pride as a result of their involvement. Many have contemplated suicide at some point in their lives, but since joining the project and taking an instrumental role in what it provides they no longer entertain such thoughts. In addition, they now feel proud, accepted, and content with their choices of intimate partners, and say that they learned vital coping techniques to deal with the challenges facing them in adulthood.

The Lesbian, Gay & Bisexual Youth Project is an excellent example of a group of individuals who, when faced with a serious social problem affecting themselves and their community, attempted to create social solutions—and succeeded very well. The Youth Project can be reached at www.youthproject.ns.ca.

▪▪ SUMMARY

Sexual gratification is an important part of Canadian life. Prostitution and pornography are two ways of gaining sexual gratification that deviate from the norm. Both involve contradictions and incompatibility with the desired quality of life, and both are sustained by multiple-level factors. At any one time, thousands of prostitutes are at work in the nation. The prostitute's quality of life is diminished by physical problems inherent in "the life," as well as by psychological, emotional, and economic problems, including fear, alienation, isolation, and exploitation.

Prostitution is maintained because of (1) norms about nonmarital sex and open discussion of sex; (2) lack of sexual gratification in marriage; and (3) characteristics of the economy, such as jobs that require men to travel and women being discriminated against in job opportunities and income. The tolerance of prostitution on the part of both the public and officials is rooted in Canadian ideology about sexuality—the notion that male sexuality, in contrast to female sexuality, must find expression.

It is important to distinguish among pornography, erotica, and obscenity. Such materials are available in multiple forms and are widely consumed in Canada. Pornographic and obscene materials have a negative impact on the quality of life by exploiting children; degrading women; and, in the case of violent pornography, increasing aggressive attitudes and behaviour of men toward women.

The materials continue to be widely available for a number of reasons. They are extremely profitable, and public attitudes are divided, perhaps reflecting concern over censorship.

Sexual orientation such as homosexuality is the third type of behavioural variance. Both biological and sociocultural explanations are offered in the chapter about why some people are homosexual in the face of strong pressures to be heterosexual. Studies of brain structure and of twins suggest a biological basis for homosexuality. Findings on family and peer group relationships and on patterns of sexual behaviour over the life span suggest that sociocultural factors underlie homosexual behaviour. Both viewpoints probably have some validity.

The quality of life for non-heterosexuals is diminished by various factors. A number of myths detract from their dignity. The quality of life is also diminished by the lack of equality of opportunity, by negative sanctions, and by the fear and the psychological and emotional problems that result from societal rejection and oppression.

Social structural factors that tend to perpetuate prejudice and discrimination against non-heterosexuals include societal norms and the legal and religious policies and practices that support those norms. Social psychological factors include attitudes toward extending full rights to non-heterosexuals, and ideologies about the morality and healthiness of alternative forms of sexual expression, desire, and ways of life.

▪▪ KEY TERMS

Bisexual 34	Homophobia 48	Pimp 36	Sexual Orientation 33
Erotica 42	Homosexual 48	Pornography 41	Sexuality 33
Eunuch 34	Intersexed 34	Promiscuity 34	Stereotype 45
Gay 34	Lesbian 34	Prostitution 35	Transgendered 34
Gender 33	Obscenity 42	Sadomasochism 44	Transsexual 34
Heterosexism 48	Paraphilia 44	Sanctions 53	Transvestite 34
Heterosexual 34	Pedophile 44	Sex 33	Twin Spirited 34

▪▪ STUDY QUESTIONS

1. What is meant by sexual diversity?

2. What problems do prostitutes face?

3. Why do women and men become prostitutes?

4. How would you distinguish among pornography, erotica, and obscenity?

5. How do pornographic and obscene materials affect men? women? children?

6. What is meant by homosexuality and homophobia?

7. How do the law and religion support negative sanctions against non-heterosexuals?

8. What attitudes and ideologies help you understand the problems non-heterosexuals face?

9. Do bisexuals suffer double discrimination?

10. Why is Canada moving to support same-sex marriages?

11. What role does organized religion play in discussions of sexual diversity?

12. Why do we seldom ask the question, What causes heterosexuality?

For more questions to consider on the topics of heterosexism and homophobia, please go to the text's Online Learning Centre at **www.mcgrawhill.ca/college/ lauer**.

■■ FOR FURTHER READING

Albert, Alexa. *Brothel: Mustang Ranch and Its Women.* New York: Random House, 2001. Interviews with prostitutes at a legal house of prostitution in Nevada, telling how they came to be there and how they feel about what they do.

Barry, Kathleen. *The Prostitution of Sexuality: The Global Exploitation of Women.* New York: New York University Press, 1995. A discussion of the abuse suffered by prostitutes and an argument that the only appropriate response is to be outraged and to punish men who use prostitutes.

Comstock, David Gary. *Violence against Lesbians and Gay Men.* New York: Columbia University Press, 1991. Discusses the sources of hostility toward homosexuals and acts of violence against homosexuals and examines the way in which religion enters into the issue.

Juffer, Jane. *At Home with Pornography: Women, Sex, and Everyday Life.* New York: New York University Press, 1998. A study of the use by women of pornographic and pseudopornographic materials (such as the Victoria's Secret catalog).

Kantor, Martin. *Homophobia.* New York: Praeger, 1998. Argues that homophobia is an emotional disorder and discusses the sources and characteristics of the disorder.

Sang, Barbara, Joyce Warshow, and Andrienne J. Smith, eds. *Lesbians at Midlife: The Creative Transition.* San Francisco: Spinsters Book Company, 1991. Covers all aspects of the life of lesbians, from intimate relations to religion to menopause, including the experiences of lesbians from various racial and ethnic groups.

Stiers, Gretchen A. *From This Day Forward: Commitment, Marriage, and Family in Lesbian and Gay Relationships.* New York: St. Martin's Press, 2000. Interviews with 90 gay men and lesbians offer their perspectives on making a commitment, getting married, and having a family in a homosexual relationship.

Williams, Linda. *Hard Core: Power, Pleasure, and the Frenzy of the Visible.* Berkeley: University of California Press, 1999. New edition of a groundbreaking study of the nature and effects of hard-core film pornography.

ALCOHOL AND OTHER DRUGS

LEARNING
OBJECTIVES

1. Learn the types and effects of alcohol and various other drugs.

2. Identify the patterns of use in Canada.

3. Explain the personal, interpersonal, and societal consequences of the use and abuse of alcohol and other drugs.

4. Understand the varied social structural factors that facilitate and help perpetuate the problem.

5. Describe the kinds of attitudes and ideologies that underlie Canada's problem of alcohol and other drugs.

DESPAIR AND HOPE

Jeremy became addicted to alcohol and drugs at a young age. His story illustrates the multi-layering of personal and social factors that contribute to addictions.

I grew up in an affluent neighbourhood outside of Toronto. In spite of all the privileges afforded to me, I never appeared to be at peace; I was a very fearful child. I was restless in school and had difficulty focusing in the classroom. I was quiet and withdrawn. The few friends I had, according to my parents, were "negative influences, from the wrong side of town." I began experimenting with alcohol and drugs at age 13. By age 15 I drank heavily and regularly.

On my 16th birthday I left home and moved to Toronto. I could not find work, did not have a permanent place to live, and was not eligible for welfare. The nights were spent on the street or in shelters. My dependency on drugs increased and I would deal drugs to afford my addiction. My health was rapidly deteriorating; I was so thin and malnourished. After a long and serious bout of illness I decided to live in a group home until I got my strength back. In the group home, however, I connected with a youth street worker. I slowly began to trust this worker and, with her support, began my long journey of rehabilitation. This was not easy because I had to confront my past family life, which I resisted doing. At first I thought I was betraying my family by talking about them, even though I had nothing to do with them for years. I do not feel this way anymore. My father was an alcoholic who was verbally and physically abusive. This was my big secret that I could not share with anyone growing up. Who would believe me? My dad was a successful professional making big money. I had no other choice but to run. I now know that being a "difficult" child was a symptom, not a problem.

I am now 25, and have just finished university. I am optimistic that I have conquered my addictions. But, being straight takes a lot of inner strength. I really know how lucky I am to be where I am today. I know that my story is somewhat exceptional. Most kids on the street do not end up in university but are trapped in poverty. My goal now is to become a youth street worker and maybe I too can make a difference in someone's life. ■

▪▪ INTRODUCTION

North Americans have had ambivalent feelings about alcohol and other drugs throughout their history. In general, the colonists regarded alcoholic beverages as one of God's gifts to mankind. As Furnas (1965:18) noted, our forebears "clung long to the late medieval notion that alcohol deserved its splendid name, *aqua vitae,* water of life." Drunkenness was punished, but drinking was generally considered one of life's pleasures. Yet by the 19th century a growing temperance movement began urging its members to abstain from all alcoholic beverages (Furnas 1965:67).

Until the beginning of the 19th century, the use of opium and its derivatives was less offensive to North Americans than smoking cigarettes or drinking. At the turn of the 20th century, the *Opium Narcotic Act* of 1908 was legislated to outlaw importing, manufacturing, and selling non-medical opiates. Although the law was enacted to target opium use among Chinese workers living in poverty in British Columbia, warnings were issued about the dangers of addictions, especially to white women. The *Opium and Narcotic Act* of 1929, which included the banning of cocaine and marijuana, shaped Canada's drug policy.

No legislation has ever been successful in stopping drug use. Hundreds of thousands of Canadians use drugs, and more than one-quarter of Canadians believe that marijuana use should be legalized (CCSA 1999).

The controversy about drugs is based partly on the distinctions among use, **abuse,** and addiction. The abuse of alcohol and other drugs, not the use, creates the problem. We define *abuse* as the *improper use of alcohol and other drugs to the degree that the consequences are defined as detrimental to the user or to society.* Addiction is a form of abuse. Addiction has been called a "brain disease" because continued abuse of a drug causes changes in brain function that drive the addict to compulsive seeking and use of the drug (Leshner 1998).

Not every case of abuse involves addiction. A man may not be an alcoholic, but he may get drunk and kill someone while driving his car. A woman may not be hooked on any drugs, but she may be persuaded to try LSD, have a "bad trip," and commit suicide.

Our focus in this chapter is on abuse, including addiction. We look at alcohol and other drugs, discussing their effects on users, patterns of use, effects on the quality of life, multiple-level factors that create and perpetuate the problems, and ways people have attempted to cope.

abuse
improper use of drugs or alcohol to the degree that the consequences are defined as detrimental to the user or society

▪▪ ALCOHOL

The use and abuse of alcohol can lead to serious health problems. We examine first the effects of alcohol use.

▪▪ Effects

All alcoholic beverages contain the same drug, ethyl alcohol or ethanol, but the proportion varies in different beverages. An individual can consume about the same amount of alcohol by drinking a pint of beer, a glass of wine, or a shot (1.5 ounces) of whiskey. What happens when that alcohol is ingested? The alcohol is burned and broken down in the body at a relatively constant rate. If an individual drinks slowly, there is little or no accumulation of alcohol in the blood; but if an individual consumes alcohol more quickly than it can be burned in the body, the *concentration of alcohol in the blood increases.*

A small amount of alcohol can result in changes in an individual's mood and behaviour, and the effects become more serious as the concentration of alcohol in the blood increases (National Institute on Alcohol Abuse and Alcoholism 2001). A blood alcohol level of about 0.05 percent (one part alcohol to 2,000 parts blood) can make the individual feel a sense of release from tensions and inhibitions. This mild euphoria is the aim of many people who drink moderately. As the alcohol level increases, however, there is an increasing loss of control because alcohol acts as a depressant on brain functions. At the 0.10-percent level, the individual's motor control is affected—hands, arms, and legs become clumsy. At 0.20 percent, both the motor and the emotional functions of the brain are impaired, and the individual staggers and becomes intensely emotional. This is the level at which someone is defined as drunk.

At 0.30 percent, an individual is incapable of adequately perceiving and responding to the environment and may go into a stupor. At 0.40 or a higher percentage, the individual lapses into a coma and may die.

What does this mean in actual drinks? Suppose you are a 150-pound individual who drinks on an empty stomach. After drinking two bottles of beer or the equivalent (11 ounces of wine, two highballs, or two cocktails), you will feel warm and relaxed. After three bottles of beer or the equivalent, you will start experiencing more intense emotions and are likely to become talkative, noisy, or morose. Four bottles of beer or its equivalent produces clumsiness and unsteady walking and standing. At this point, you are legally drunk in most jurisdictions. If you drink four bottles of beer or the equivalent on an empty stomach, it takes about eight hours for all the alcohol to leave your body.

The damaging effects of alcohol abuse are most obvious in the *alcoholic*—the individual who is addicted to alcohol. Alcoholism is defined in terms of four symptoms (National Institute on Alcohol Abuse and Alcoholism 2001): (1) a craving or compulsion to drink; (2) loss of control to limit drinking on any particular occasion; (3) physical dependence, so that withdrawal symptoms (nausea, sweating, shakiness, anxiety) are experienced if alcohol use ceases; and (4) tolerance, the need to drink increasingly greater amounts in order to get "high." Because the effects can be so deleterious and the use of alcohol is so widespread, many experts consider alcohol abuse the major drug problem in North America today.

▪▪ Patterns of Use

According to the 2002 Canadian Community Health Survey (CCHS 2004), 77 percent of Canadians who are 15 years and older had a drink in the past year, 35 percent of adults drink heavily (more than five drinks during on occasion), and just under half of heavy drinkers say that heavy drinking happens once a month (see figure 3.1). The CCAS (2004) survey on alcohol use reported that 7.2 percent of Canadians do not drink and 13.5 percent were once drinkers.

Proportionately more men (82 percent) than women (72.5 percent) not only drink alcohol, but also are heavier drinkers (35.3 and 24.3 percent, respectively). Heavy drinking is most common among the early twenties crowd (60 percent of the age 20 to 24 cohort) and decreases substantially thereafter (16 percent of individuals who are older than age 55) (see figure 3.2). Heavy alcohol use is also prevalent among teenagers between the ages of 15 and 19: 42 percent of teenagers said they had at least one incident of heavy drinking in the past 12 months.

FIGURE 3.1 ■ ■ ■

Alcohol use in past 12 months, by sex.

Source: Adapted from *Canadian Community Health Survey—Mental Health and Well-being, 2002.* Statistics Canada, Catalogue No. 82-617-XIE.

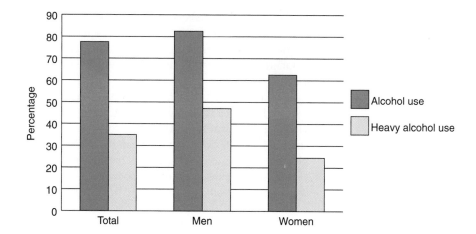

FIGURE 3.2 ■ ■ ■

Percentage of people reporting heavy drinking in past 12 months, by age group.

Source: Adapted from *Canadian Community Health Survey—Mental Health and Well-being, 2002.* Statistics Canada, Catalogue No. 82-617-XIE.

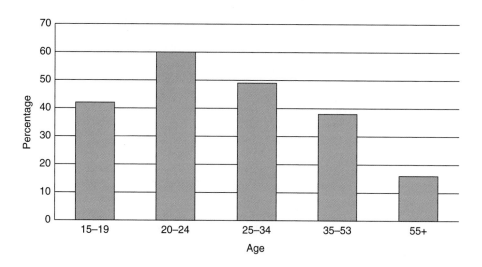

Alcohol use also varies among provinces. PEI and Newfoundland and Labrador had the lowest percentage of drinkers, while Quebec had the highest percentage. But when we look at percentages of heavy drinking by province, a different picture emerges. Newfoundland and Labrador has the highest rate of heavy drinking, and Quebec has the lowest (CCSA 2004).

Drinking patterns vary across different groups, though all groups are affected to some extent. Canadian First Nations probably have the highest rates of use and abuse of alcohol. Compared to the general population, drinking begins at an earlier age and is more frequent and in greater amounts (CCSA 1999).

An Aboriginal Peoples Survey in 1991 reported that 73 percent of First Nations respondents believe that alcohol is a problem within their community. But, we have very few current statistics on First Nations people and alcohol use (see box 3.1: An Overview of Aboriginal Peoples).

Gender differences are decreasing, but *alcohol abuse and alcoholism are primarily male problems.* Overall, proportionately more men (78.1 percent) than women (66.7 percent) drink, and men consume more alcohol than women (CCHS 2000–1).

Alcohol abuse is also more common among the young, especially binge drinking. A Canadian Campus Survey in 1998 found that 62.7 percent of students said they had had five or more drinks on a single occasion since the academic year began (Gliksman

Box 3.1

An Overview of Aboriginal Peoples

There is currently little clear information describing substance-use problems among Canadian Aboriginal peoples. Statistics on violent death (including suicide, homicide, poisoning/overdose, accidents, and drownings) provide some indication, and as a population, Aboriginal peoples have rates of violent death much greater than the Canadian population as a whole. Aboriginal adolescent suicide rates are much higher than the national adolescent rate. It appears that *Fetal Alcohol Spectrum disorders* (FASD) are more prevalent among Aboriginal people. Use of solvents for intoxication among children in some Aboriginal communities is a serious concern. In some remote Indigenous communities, gasoline sniffing, primarily by young people, is said to have contributed to a systemic breakdown of community and family relationships. Among Aboriginal people in Canada's territories, indications are that while a smaller percentage identify themselves as drinkers than their non-Aboriginal counterparts, those that do drink are more likely to drink heavily. There are indications that tobacco and injecting drug use are also particular concerns among Aboriginal populations—with, for example, one in five Indigenous street youth in seven major Canadian cities reporting they had injected drugs.

Issues of poverty, low education, unstable family structure, unemployment, physical abuse, poor social support networks, and involvement with the law are precipitated or aggravated by discrimination, the effects of residential schools, and barriers to health care such as language and the lack of culturally sensitive services. While these issues present a considerable challenge for which substance use is identified as a coping mechanism, many Aboriginal communities have succeeded in preventing or reducing substance-use problems among their people. These communities are successfully applying community-wide, culturally based solutions to problems that are largely socially determined.

The Royal Commission on Aboriginal Peoples had identified the dimensions of community health that need to be addressed for the improved health and well-being of Aboriginal peoples:

- Poverty and social assistance,
- Shelter, water, and sanitation facilities, both at the individual and community levels,
- Environmental conditions, including pollution and regeneration of land and habitat.

Source: Canadian Centre on Substance Abuse (CCSA): http://www.ccsa.ca/CCSAIEN/Topics/Populations/AboriginalPeoplesOverview.htm

et al. 2000). Binge drinkers are far more likely than others to have unprotected sex, to drive after drinking, to fall behind in school, to be aggressive, and to be involved in property damage. But, according to a U.S. study at the University of Wisconsin–Madison, relatively few students—only 6 to 8 percent—binge more than once a week. Most students binge only occasionally. Further, binge drinking in university does not necessarily translate into drinking problems in later life; in fact, many students after graduation "move on" (Brower 2002:253).

A substantial portion of adolescents drink. An Ontario study that examined drug abuse among students found that 68.3 percent of males and 64.3 percent of females in Grades 7 to 12 drink alcohol, increasing significantly each grade (see table 3.1).

	Total	Males	Females		G7	G8	G9	G10	G11	G12	
Alcohol	66.2	68.3	64.3	*	39.1	48.9	65.1	75.1	79.9	82.5	*
Cannabis	29.6	30.9	28.3		6.2	10.7	27.9	35.9	45.0	44.8	*
Binge Drinking	26.5	29.4	23.8	*	5.8	7.7	23.5	29.8	40.9	45.2	*
Cigarettes	19.2	18.0	20.3		4.4	10.2	17.0	21.8	28.3	30.2	*
Hallucinogens	10.0	12.1	8.0	*	1.8	2.6	7.8	12.5	17.4	15.3	*
Solvents	6.1	5.9	6.3		10.2	9.5	6.5	4.2	3.6	3.9	*
Stimulants (NM)	5.8	4.7	6.7	*	1.6	3.7	5.6	6.6	8.2	7.8	*
Cocaine	4.8	5.4	4.3		3.1	1.9	4.9	4.6	6.9	6.7	*
Ecstasy (MDMA)	4.1	4.2	3.9		0.5	0.8	3.7	4.6	6.6	7.2	*
Methamphetamine	3.3	3.8	2.9		1.0	0.9	3.8	4.2	5.4	3.6	*
LSD	2.9	3.5	2.3	*	0.7	1.1	3.7	4.2	4.0	2.7	*
Ritalin (NM)	2.9	3.4	2.5		1.2	1.2	3.0	3.3	5.0	3.1	*
Glue	2.8	3.0	2.6		5.2	3.2	2.4	2.4	2.3	1.8	*
Crack	2.7	2.8	2.6		1.7	1.7	3.1	3.0	3.6	2.5	
Barbiturates (NM)	2.5	2.6	2.5		1.8	2.2	3.0	2.8	3.1	1.8	
PCP	2.2	2.9	1.6	*	1.3	0.8	2.1	3.6	2.6	2.7	*
Tranquillizers (NM)	2.2	2.7	1.8	*	0.6	1.2	1.8	2.4	4.1	2.7	*
Ketamine	2.2	3.0	1.6	*	1.0	s	1.7	1.6	4.7	3.7	*
Rohypnol	1.6	1.7	1.5		1.2	1.2	1.4	2.0	2.3	1.3	
Heroin	1.4	1.9	0.9	*	1.4	0.8	1.5	2.0	1.3	1.1	
Ice	1.2	1.3	1.0		1.2	0.8	1.3	1.0	1.1	1.5	
GHB	0.7	0.8	0.6		s	s	s	0.9	1.7	s	
Any Illicit, including cannabis	32.2	33.1	31.3		10.1	13.9	29.6	38.6	47.5	47.1	*
Any Illicit, excluding cannabis	15.3	16.6	14.2	*	6.6	8.0	13.0	18.0	21.7	22.3	*
Steroids (lifetime)	3.0	4.4	1.7	*	0.7	1.8	1.6	3.8	4.6	5.3	*

Notes: binge drinking (5+ drinks on one occasion) refers to the past 4 weeks time period; NM=non-medical use; s=estimate suppressed; * indicates a significant sex difference, or grade differences (p<.05), *not* controlling for other factors.
Source: The 2003 OSDUS Drug Report.

TABLE 3.1   ▪ ▪ ▪

Past Year Drug Use (%) by Total, Sex, and Grade, 2003 Ontario Student Drug Use Survey (OSDUS)

Although 12 percent of students drink at least once a week, very few—less than 1 percent—drink every day (Adlaf and Paglia 2003).

Thus, the skid-row image of the alcohol abuser is false. Those most likely to drink frequently and to consume higher quantities of alcohol per drinking session are young, white, male, and comparatively well-to-do.

▪▪ Alcohol and the Quality of Life

Alcohol, like other drugs, has some medical benefits when used in moderation. In fact, there is evidence that moderate drinkers, compared to both abstainers and heavy

Alcohol use and abuse
is most likely to take
place in groups.

drinkers, have a lower rate of coronary heart disease and are less likely to have a heart attack (Mukamal and Rimm 2001). Alcohol abuse, on the other hand, is highly deleterious to the quality of life.

Physical Health. The physical consequences of alcohol abuse contradict the North American *value of physical well-being.* As mentioned earlier, the immediate effects of intoxicating levels of alcohol include impaired motor performance. The long-range effects of heavy drinking involve impairment of the major organs of the body, including the heart, brain, and liver (National Institute on Alcohol Abuse and Alcoholism 2001). Cirrhosis of the liver, one of the more widely known effects of heavy drinking, is an occupational disease of the alcoholic. A lesser-known effect is the premature aging of the brain (Noonberg, Goldstein, and Page 1985). At any given time, the neuropsychological functioning of the alcoholic—as measured by such things as eye–hand coordination and spatial ability—will be equivalent to that of someone about 10 years older. *In terms of cognitive ability,* in other words, alcoholism costs the user about 10 years of life.

Heavy drinking also may result in muscle diseases and tremors. Heart functioning and the gastrointestinal and respiratory systems may be impaired by prolonged heavy drinking. The ills of the gastrointestinal system range from nausea, vomiting, and diarrhea to gastritis, ulcers, and pancreatitis. Problems of the respiratory system include lowered resistance to pneumonia and other infectious diseases. Among women, alcohol abuse can result in menstrual cycle irregularity, inability to conceive, and early onset of menopause (Gavaler 1991). Among men, alcohol can lead to impotence and sterility (Wright, Gavaler, and Van Thiel 1991).

Alcohol abuse can lead to early death. A study of male veterans found that the death rate among alcoholics was 2.5 higher than that of nonalcoholics, and that alcoholics in the 35- to 44-year-old age group were 5.5 times as likely to die as were nonalcoholics of the same age (Liskow et al. 2000).

Alcohol plays a role in various kinds of physical trauma. Consider the following (Rivara et al. 1997; Thun et al. 1997; Greenfeld 1998; Addiction Research Foundation,

1994; Single et al. 1996; Xie et al. 1998; also Xie et al. 1996; Norström 2001, 2002; Ramstedt 2002b; Rossow 2001, 2002; Skog 2003):

- Alcohol use is associated with an increased risk of violent death (suicide or homicide) in the home.
- Alcohol abuse leads to higher rates of death from heart disease, cirrhosis, injuries, traffic accidents, suicides, and various kinds of cancer.
- More than 50 percent of offenders who were convicted of assault, murder, or attempted murder in Ontario used alcohol before committing the crime.
- In Ontario, alcohol use is also implicated in half the cases of spousal abuse, and in 38 percent of child abuse cases.
- Two-thirds of the victims of intimate violence report that alcohol was a factor in the attack.
- Nearly a third of fatal accidents involve an intoxicated driver or pedestrian (mostly a driver).

As in the case of other drugs, the health problems of alcohol include effects on the unborn children of pregnant women who drink. The most severe cases are called *fetal alcohol syndrome* (FAS) (Dorfman 1989). Some children have less obvious or milder fetal alcohol damage; this is referred to as *fetal alcohol effects* (FAE). There is no safe level of alcohol consumption during pregnancy. Exact occurrences of FAS are not known. Recent research shows that the prevalence of FAS in Canada is between 2.8 and 4.8 per 1,000 live births (Canadian Paediatric Society 2002).

Among the health problems of children born with fetal alcohol syndrome are head and face deformities; major organ problems that result in heart defects, ear infections, hearing loss, poor eyesight, and bad teeth; and problems with the central nervous system, leading to such things as mental retardation, hyperactivity, learning disabilities, attention and/or memory deficits, difficulty managing anger, limited problem solving ability, and stunted growth (Streissguth 1992; Aronson and Hagberg 1998; Health Canada 2004).

Alcohol abuse generally, and the fetal alcohol syndrome in particular, illustrate an important point—social problems have consequences at the community level as well as the individual level. In a real sense, a community can become the victim of a problem, for social problems can strain the community's resources and deprive it of the positive contributions that could otherwise be made by people caught up in the problems.

Although FAS occurs across all races and ethnic and socioeconomic groups, it is believed to be disproportionately higher among First Nations children. An examination of children at birth in a northern Manitoba community estimated that 7.2 per 1,000 children are born with FAS (Williams et al. 1998). The authors note that this may be a very conservative estimate, as FAS often is under-recognized in newborns. However, a report on fetal alcohol syndrome published by the Aboriginal Healing Foundation (2003) calls for a cautious approach in how the data are interpreted: "The study does not have a sample group of either non-Native women or Native women from a different region of Canada to use for comparison purposes as part of the research design" (106).

Alcohol and drug problems among First Nations communities may be rooted, according to Storm (1994), in the history of threatened loss of culture—children uprooted from their communities and relocated in residential schools. As well, alcohol and drug use "takes place within a complex social mosaic of problems, including poverty, poor housing, isolation, child and spousal abuse, violence and suicide" (Storm 1994:61). Thus, FAS among First Nations communities may be a manifestation of political, social, economic, and possibly biological factors. Some people believe that First Nations people metabolize alcohol at a faster rate compared to the general population and this may explain the higher rates of babies born with FAS.

Spousal Violence and Alcohol Use.   The issue of spousal violence and alcohol use is contentious. What we do know is that there is a correlation between wife abuse and alcohol consumption. According to the 1999 General Social Survey, there is almost a three-times greater likelihood of spouse abuse occurring in households where one spouse is a heavy drinker compared to those who drink moderately or do not drink at all (Family Violence in Canada 2004:9). However, the exact nature of the relationship between alcohol and spousal abuse is not straightforward. Alcohol abuse and spousal abuse each on their own are rooted in similar causes, such as a history of childhood violence and powerlessness. Thus, alcohol use may be a catalyst, not the cause of spouse abuse (Family Violence in Canada 2004).

Psychological Health.   The *desire for psychological well-being* is contradicted by the various degrees of impairment that result from alcohol abuse. Even a small amount of alcohol can reduce the individual's sensitivity to taste, smell, and pain. Vision can be affected by large amounts of alcohol (one factor in the dangers of driving while drinking). Such things occur because alcohol adversely affects the brain. In the alcoholic, the adverse effects are severe (National Institute on Alcohol Abuse and Alcoholism 2001). At least half of all alcoholics may have difficulty with problem solving, abstract thinking, memory tasks, and psychomotor performance. Severe alcoholics may succumb to *alcohol amnestic disorder* (short-term memory impairments) or *dementia* (general loss of intellectual abilities, impaired memory, and possible personality change). Some alcohol abusers take the final solution to their despair: Alcohol abuse is associated with a substantial proportion of suicides (Norstrom 1995).

One popular belief is that alcohol "releases inhibitions," so that the person who drinks "loosens up" and may, for example, be more motivated toward sexual activity. Actually, heavy drinking inhibits sexual performance, and alcoholics report a deficient sex life or even impotence (Peugh and Belenko 2001). Another belief is that a drink in the evening helps the individual to relax and thereby to sleep better. Whatever the value of a drink, having several drinks before going to sleep decreases the amount of dreaming, which can impair concentration and memory, and increase anxiety, irritability, and a sense of tiredness.

Interpersonal Problems.   Alcohol abuse leads to *problems of interaction* both within and outside the family. Early use of alcohol by children is likely to lead to early sexual activity, with all its potential hazards, including pregnancy and disease (Rosenbaum and Kandel 1990). Alcohol use is also associated with risky sexual behaviour, and is more of a risk factor for sexually transmitted diseases than are other drugs (Ericksen and Trocki 1994). Adult alcoholics have poorer relationships generally with friends, co-workers, spouses, and children (McFarlin et al. 2001). Many adolescents and adults get increasingly aggressive as they become intoxicated. This can lead to ill will and conflict with others (Bachman and Peralta 2002), and the conflict can take a violent turn. There is a higher rate of both verbal and physical abuse in homes where one or both spouses are alcoholic (Miller, Downs, and Gondoli 1989; Kantor and Straus 1989). Even if a person who is drinking is not an alcoholic and is not intoxicated, there can be serious violence. A study of homicides in the state of New York reported that alcohol use was likely in homicides that arose spontaneously from personal disputes, and in some cases the alcohol was probably a causal factor in the killing (Welte and Abel 1989).

Even if an alcoholic does not become abusive, his or her behaviour is certain to cause *stress* within the family. Partners and children of alcoholics tend to develop physical and psychological problems of their own. Couples endure painful frustration (trying to cope) and guilt (blaming themselves for their partner's problems) and may require treatment themselves (Wiseman 1991; Asher 1992). Children tend to develop

behaviour disorders and, as compared to those from nonalcoholic homes, are more likely to have poorer self-concepts; higher rates of drug use; and higher rates of anxiety,
depression, alcoholism, and other disorders when they become adults, as well as lower
rates of coupling—and when they do couple the quality of the relationship is poorer.
(Rearden and Markwell 1989; Tween and Ryff 1991; Tubman 1993; Obot, Wagner, and
Anthony 2001; Watt 2002). Often there is enormous relief when the alcoholic partner
moves out of the home, illustrating the intensity of stress under which the family lived.

Alcohol abuse is costly to the individual, the family, the community, and the state.
In 1995, approximately 81,000 hospitalizations and 6,500 deaths (motor vehicle accidents and liver cirrhosis) in Canada were due to alcohol use. More than 60 percent of
all provincial offences are alcohol-related. Heavy alcohol use has deleterious effects in
the workplace. It is the primary reason why workers are unemployed or absent from
work. A substantial number of workplace accidents are caused by alcohol consumption.
Overall, the approximate costs of alcoholism to industry are $4.1 billion (CCSA 1999).

▪▪ Contributing Factors

The factors that contribute to the alcohol problem both maintain demand and guarantee
supply. The problem is embedded in the Canadian way of life.

Social Structural Factors

Being a part of a *group whose norms and behaviour
condone drinking* is the most powerful *predicting factor* of an individual's drinking
(Flannery et al. 1994; Ames, Grube, and Moore 2000; Olds and Thombs 2001). Males,
in fact, use alcohol to bond with each other and to enhance their sense of importance
and power (Liu and Kaplan 1996). The situation is particularly hazardous when the
norms allow drinking at very early ages, for those who take up drinking before the age
of 15 are four times more likely than others to become alcohol-dependent (Grant and
Dawson 1998).

Integration into a group where the use of alcohol is approved does not mean the individual will abuse it. Many people use alcohol without becoming addicted. A lower rate
of alcoholism is correlated with the following characteristics (National Institute on
Alcohol Abuse and Alcoholism 2001):

1. Children are given alcohol early in life in the context of strong family life or
   religious orientation.
2. Low-alcohol-content beverages—wines and beers—are most commonly used.
3. The alcoholic beverage is ordinarily consumed at meals.
4. Parents typically provide an example of moderation in drinking.
5. Drinking is not a moral question, merely one of custom.
6. Drinking is not defined as a symbol of manhood or adulthood.
7. Abstinence is as acceptable as drinking.
8. Drunkenness is not socially acceptable.
9. Alcohol is not a central element in activities (like a cocktail party).
10. There is general agreement on what is proper and what is improper in drinking.

Under such conditions, a group or an entire society could have high per capita rates
of alcohol consumption and relatively low rates of alcoholism. Group norms are an
important factor in alcohol use and abuse, but they need not demand abstinence to prevent abuse. Both Jews and Italians use alcohol as part of a traditional way of life, but
alcoholism in those groups is extremely low. The norms of many religious groups
also make abuse less likely; in three samples of American college students, those high
on religiosity were less likely to use or abuse alcohol (Free 1994).

"I'D KILL BEFORE I'D DRINK"

Two of the authors once attended a meeting of Alcoholics Anonymous with a friend who had been "dry" for a short time. As they drove through the countryside to the small town where the group met, the friend kept commenting on the beauty of the scenery. He was enchanted by what they thought was a fairly common view on a warm spring evening. But his years as an alcoholic had been a living hell, and in the course of rediscovering what life can be like when you are free of addiction, he was finding beauty in the commonplace. "I really think," he told them, "that if someone tried to force me to take a drink I would kill them." The thought of ever returning to alcohol terrified him.

One of the best ways to understand the impact of addiction on an individual is to talk with an ex-addict. If you do not know an ex-alcoholic, contact Alcoholics Anonymous and attend one of their open meetings. Ask one of two members if they would be willing to discuss their understanding of why they became addicted, what their life was like when they were addicted, and what finally led them to seek the help of AA.

List the adverse effects on the quality of life discussed in this chapter that apply to your informants. Based on your interviews, make a report, oral or written, of your recommendations for dealing with the problem of alcoholism.

Role problems that generate emotional distress can lead to alcohol abuse (Holahan et al. 2001). People trying to cope with role conflict may resort to alcohol for relief. Those under stress at work and those who believe that alcohol relieves stress are more likely to drink (Rohrlich 1990). Undesirable role changes also may lead to alcohol abuse. A major loss (for example, divorce or death of a spouse) or separation can result in alcohol abuse, particularly for men (Horwitz and Davies 1994). Furthermore, the loneliness that accompanies moving or loss of intimate relationships is associated with alcohol abuse (Akerlind and Hornquist 1992).

Three kinds of *family experiences* are involved in alcohol abuse. First, alcohol abusers are more likely to come from *homes where other family members are abusers* (Jennison and Johnson 1998; Chermack et al. 2000). Second, alcohol abusers are more likely to come from *broken homes* (Flewelling and Bauman 1990; Wolfinger 1998). Third, alcohol abuse is associated with various *problematic relationships within the family* (Tubman 1993; Clark et al. 1998). Problem drinking among adolescents is associated with homes where the parents express hostility to the adolescents or where there is severe family conflict (Conger et al. 1991; Smith, Rivers, and Stahl 1992). Father–daughter verbal aggression is an important factor in women's developing alcohol problems (Downs et al. 1992). Students with drinking problems report less positive regard from parents, and parents who deny or ignore their children's feelings (Jones and Houts 1992).

Social Structural Problems.   Finally, any social–structural factors that can increase stress levels are likely to affect alcohol consumption. Throughout the 1960s and 1970s alcohol consumption increased, according to Rorabaugh (1979), because of stresses induced by a rapidly changing society. An overall sense of powerlessness can lead to heavy drinking and alcohol problems (Seeman, Seeman, and Budros 1988). Your sense of powerlessness can be affected by the world situation, such as war, national economic and social problems, your work, and, as stated above, your family life. One Canadian study of high school students found that alcohol and drug problems were associated with low socioeconomic neighbourhoods (Smart et al. 1994). These neighbourhoods are "characterized by low-cost substandard housing, social and racial problems and delinquency" (37). American researchers have shown that experiencing discrimination can lead to escapist drinking, which in turn can lead to a drinking problem (Martin et al. 2003).

Social Psychological Factors. *Attitudes* toward drinking and drunkenness tend to be different from attitudes toward use and abuse of other drugs. Although alcoholism is a major factor in death and disease, there is little public outcry. Parents who would be horrified to find their children smoking marijuana have allowed them to drink spiked punch or other alcoholic beverages at parties.

The importance of attitudes is underscored by the fact that adolescents who are moderate to heavy drinkers have more positive and more liberal attitudes about the use of alcohol. The attitudes are formed or reinforced by the treatment of drinking on television. There is a great deal of drinking without any negative consequences. Adolescents who watch such portrayals of drinking are more likely to decide to drink (Pinkleton, Fujioka, and Austin 2000).

The problem of alcoholism is further complicated by *an ideology that essentially transforms it into a personal rather than a social problem.* Many Canadians believe the alcoholic can recover if he or she "really wants to change"—that alcoholism is basically a problem of individual self-control.

■■ From Social Problems to Solutions

There is a growing recognition that instead of asking what can be done for an alcoholic, you need to ask first what kind of alcoholic you are dealing with. Experts are attempting to sort out the special needs of the alcoholic with psychiatric problems, the chronically relapsing alcoholic, the alcoholic's family members who may be both victims of and contributors to the problem, and addicted adolescents and women (Abbott 1987). Special programs are being developed for these special needs. For example, the chronically relapsing alcoholic may be placed in a group with other relapsers and undergo group therapy that focuses on ways to confront and overcome the tendency to relapse.

Whatever the special needs may be, of course, the alcoholic is likely to need one or more of the following: individual therapy, drug therapy, behaviour therapy, or group therapy. Drug therapies involve administration of either a nausea-producing agent along with an alcoholic beverage or a "deterrent agent" that causes intense headaches and nausea when alcohol is consumed. Obviously, drug therapy requires close supervision by a physician.

In group therapy, the alcoholic is in a group with other alcoholics and with a therapist as facilitator. The task of the group members is to attain insight into their individual reasons for drinking and to get control over drinking. The task is achieved by frank and open discussion of each alcoholic's life, feelings, and thoughts. A form of group therapy that is quite successful and does not utilize a professional therapist is Alcoholics Anonymous (AA), which was started by alcoholics. Members gather regularly in small groups to share their experiences and to sustain each other in sobriety. Each member is available to every other member at any time help is needed—when, for example, a member needs to talk to someone in order to resist the urge to drink. Those who join AA begin by admitting they are powerless over alcohol and lack control of their own lives. This is a significant admission because it opposes the ideology discussed earlier (an ideology, incidentally, held by alcoholics as well as by others). New members also agree to surrender to a Higher Power (as they understand it), to make amends to those harmed by their drinking, and to help other alcoholics become sober.

Thousands of alcoholics have sought help through AA, which is still one of the most effective ways to deal with alcoholism (Vaillant 1983; Connors, Tonigan, and Miller 2001). Of course, not everyone who turns to AA will break the habit; no form of help can claim 100-percent success rates.

Two spin-offs of AA that are designed to help family members of the alcoholic are Al-Anon and Alateen. Al-Anon is for the alcoholic's spouse or significant other. It helps the person to both deal with the problems caused by the alcoholic and to see his or her own contribution to the interpersonal problems that may be a factor in the alcoholism. Members of Al-Anon learn to take care of their own needs and to stop focusing their lives around the alcoholic's problems. Alateen uses the same principles to help the teenaged children of alcoholics. Frequently, the sponsor of an Alateen group is a member of Al-Anon.

The problem of alcoholism also has been attacked through various other programs and facilities. Among these are community care programs, which allow alcoholics to remain in their homes and communities while undergoing treatment. Other programs remove alcoholics from their environments. Throughout the nation, there are hundreds of halfway houses for alcoholics, places where they can function in a relatively normal way while receiving therapy. Most of these make Alcoholics Anonymous groups, counselling, and other services available to the alcoholics. Alcoholics who are acutely ill may have to be hospitalized for a period of time before going to a halfway house or returning to their homes.

Ultimately, to resolve the problem, the social bases of alcoholism must be attacked through public policy. Prevention and education programs face difficulty because group norms and alternative means of coping with stress are involved. Nevertheless, there is evidence that educational programs can help reduce the negative effects of alcohol (Flynn and Brown 1991).

Educational programs must help people understand not only the dangers of alcohol but also ways they can deal with the pressure to drink. For instance, adolescents, who are most likely to give in to peer pressure, can resist drinking even in high-pressure situations by using a number of cognitive and behavioural techniques (Brown, Stetson, and Beatty 1989). These techniques include defining themselves as nondrinkers and defining drinkers in negative terms (e.g., drinkers are weak), developing strong refusal skills, finding alternative activities (such as volunteering or religious activities), and limiting direct exposure to high-risk situations (such as not going to a party where heavy drinking will occur and may even be expected) (Weitzman and Kawachi 2000; Brown et al. 2001; Guo et al. 2001).

Finally, both informal and formal measures can be taken to help those victimized by alcohol-impaired driving and to ameliorate or prevent further victimization. At an informal level, peer intervention—trying to stop a friend or acquaintance from driving drunk—has been shown to be effective in the bulk of cases (Collins and Frey 1992).

At a formal level, campaigns against alcohol-impaired drivers began in the 1980s when a California woman founded Mothers Against Drunk Drivers (MADD). She took action after her teenaged daughter was killed by a man who was not only drunk but also out on bail from a hit-and-run arrest for drunken driving just two days prior to the accident. The first chapter of MADD Canada was formed in 1990, and there are more than 70 chapters throughout Canada (MADD 2004). Other groups formed as well: Students Against Driving Drunk (SADD) and Remove Intoxicated Drivers (RID). As a result of the work of these organizations, a number of provinces have taken measures to reduce the risks to citizens from alcohol-impaired drivers, including graduated licensing, roadside sobriety tests, vehicle impoundment, licence suspensions, and licence reinstatement fees (MADD 2004). As a result of these varied formal and informal measures, the proportion of fatal crashes involving an intoxicated driver has dropped sharply: in 1982 there were 2,501 alcohol-related fatalities (60 percent of all motor vehicle accidents); in 2003 there were 1,042 (37.5 percent) (MADD 2004).

■■ OTHER DRUGS

Although alcohol abuse is the major drug problem, the use and abuse of other drugs affects nearly all Canadians directly or indirectly. We begin our examination of the problem by looking at the different kinds of drugs and their effects.

■■ Types and Effects

Five main types of nonalcoholic drugs are narcotics, depressants, stimulants, hallucinogens, and cannabis. For a detailed table describing these and their effects, please go to the text's Online Learning Centre at **www.mcgrawhill.ca/college/lauer**. In addition, we need to note that new *designer drugs* continue to appear. In recent years, concern emerged about "ecstasy" and flunitrazepam (marketed under the brand name Rohypnol). Ecstasy is a stimulant that has psychedelic effects lasting between four and six hours (Spiess 2002). Initially it was used mainly at all-night dance parties known as "raves." Ecstasy can cause confusion, depression, anxiety, paranoia, and serious damage to the kidneys, heart, and brain. Rohypnol is the so-called date-rape drug. It is also referred to as "roofies," "Rocies," "R2," and "forget pill" (Gorin 2000). It is a powerful sedative that can cause partial amnesia.

Legal drugs can harm or kill you just as effectively as illicit ones. A study in the *Journal of the American Medical Association* (Temple and Himmel 2002) reported that serious adverse and previously unrecognized side effects are found in 20 percent of new drugs. Adverse or *iatrogenic* effects include liver, bone marrow, and heart damage, as well as increased pregnancy risks (see also chapter 12 on health).

In addition to alcohol, tobacco is one of the deadliest drugs in North American society. In 1997 the Liggett Group, the U.S. maker of Chesterfield cigarettes, openly acknowledged that smoking is both addictive and deadly (Vedantam, Epstine and Geiger 1997). Being legal does not mean that a drug is harmless.

■■ Patterns of Use

It is difficult to know the number of drug users in Canada. Not all users are addicts, and not all addicts are known to the authorities. There is wide variation in use, depending on such things as the type of drug and the age, sex, and place of residence of the user (CAS 2004). With regard to age, drug use tends to be higher among the young. The highest usage rates of marijuana, cocaine, crack, and hallucinogens occur among those 18 to 25 years of age.

A 1998 survey examining illicit drug use among Canadian undergraduate students found that approximately 30 percent of men and 28 percent of women use marijuana (for further information, see the Public Policy and Private Action box on decriminalizing marijuana). The Senate Special Committee on Illegal Drugs (2002) reported that Canadians between the ages of 12 and 17 "would appear to have one of the highest rates of cannabis use among youths." Marijuana is typically first tried at age 15. Aside from marijuana, approximately 10 percent of students reported illicit drug use (LSD, speed, cocaine, heroin). Patterns of illicit drug use among high school students are similar to those of undergraduates (refer to table 3.1 on page 66). The Ontario Drug Use Survey (2003) studied 6,616 high school students and found that one-third of high school students use drugs. In all but two drug categories, proportionately more males than females use drugs. The one exception is cigarette smoking: female youth smoke more than do their male counterparts.

Drug use also varies by province (see table 3.2). Whereas British Columbia has the highest rate of drug use in all of Canada, Newfoundland and Labrador has the lowest.

Medicinal Use of Marijuana

Canadian law has traditionally criminalized the possession, production, and trafficking of marijuana. *The Controlled Drugs and Substances Act* (CDSA) has been criticized for imposing harsh criminal penalties for possession. A series of court decisions and government committee reports prompted the government to decriminalize the possession and, to an extent, the cultivation of marijuana.

In a 2000 Ontario Court of Appeal case, a man who was charged with possessing and cultivating marijuana claimed that he used marijuana to control his epilepsy, and that due to the lack of a legal source of the drug he was forced to cultivate his own *(R. v. Parker 2000)*. The court held that banning marijuana possession and cultivation for medicinal purposes violated the *Charter of Rights and Freedoms*, and consequently Parliament created a medical exemption for possessing and cultivating marijuana.

Canada introduced the *Marijuana Medical Access Regulations* in 2002, making it the first country to regulate the use of marijuana for medical purposes. The regulations were appealed to the Ontario Court of Appeal in 2003, on the basis that they did not provide a legal source for obtaining marijuana; users were forced to purchase the drug on the black market. Some of the restrictions on growers were removed, as the court held that the prohibitions violated the *Charter* rights of "life, liberty and security of person." In the same decision, the court confirmed the recreational use of marijuana to be a criminal act (Jaffey 2003). The Supreme Court of Canada further noted that the prohibition of the recreational use of marijuana does not violate the *Charter*, and that it is up to Parliament—not the courts—to decriminalize recreational use.

Decriminalizing Recreational Use of Marijuana

Two government committees were established to make recommendations on non-medical use of marijuana. The House of Commons Special Committee on Non-Medical Use of Drugs recommended that possession and trafficking should continue to be illegal, but that Canada should remove its criminal penalties for possession and cultivation of less than 30 grams of the drug for personal use. The Senate Committee on Illegal Drugs assumed a more liberal view, finding that marijuana use is actually less harmful than alcohol use and so should be treated and regulated as a social and public health issue, not a criminal one (Khoo 2004).

The debate over decriminalization of marijuana extends beyond government. Politicians and groups in favour of decriminalization generally argue that it is unfair for people who possess small amounts of marijuana to have criminal records, which may bar them from jobs and educational opportunities. The Canadian Association of Chiefs of Police has also pointed out that prosecuting people for small amounts of marijuana is a significant strain on resources. Those against decriminalization, such as the Canadian Police Association, are concerned that it may lead to increased use of harder drugs (Khoo 2004). There is even a third side to the debate, which advances the position that marijuana use should be completely legalized (i.e., no fines or penalties).

Bill C-17

In 2003 the Liberal government introduced a bill to decriminalize recreational use of marijuana, but the bill died when Paul Martin was sworn in as prime minister. It was reintroduced in November 2004 as Bill C-17, which decriminalizes possession of small amounts of marijuana for personal use. If passed, both adults and youths found to possess less than 15 grams of marijuana, or less than one gram of cannabis resin (hashish) will be fined, but will not face criminal charges. If a person possesses between 15 and 30 grams of marijuana, it will be left to an officer's discretion whether to issue a ticket or to lay criminal charges for a summary offence. The law also replaces criminal penalties with fines for growing between one and three marijuana plants for personal use. However, the criminal penalties for growing more than four plants carry increased fines and/or jail terms (Schmitz 2004).

More than half of British Columbia's population (52.1 percent) has used marijuana in their lifetime, compared to 38.5 percent of Newfoundlanders. The proportion of current drug users is of course much smaller than the percentage of lifetime users. For example, 44.5 percent of Canadians have used marijuana in their lifetime, compared to 14.1 percent in the past year. Marijuana, after alcohol, is the most commonly used drug, followed by hallucinogens (11.4 percent), and crack and cocaine (10.6 percent).

TABLE 3.2 ■ ■ ■

Use of Selected Drugs by Province, Canada, 2004

	Canada	NL	PE	NS	NB	QC	ON	MB	SK	AB	BC
Marijuana, past year	14.1	11.6	10.7	14.4	11.1	15.8	12.4	13.4	11.4	15.4	16.8
Marijuana, lifetime	44.5	38.5	36.5	43.4	42.1	46.4	40.4	44.6	41.0	48.7	52.1
Cocaine/crack, past year	1.9	0.9	1.1	1.1		2.5	1.3	2.0	1.7	2.4	2.6
Speed, lifetime	6.4	1.2	3.3	3.2	4.5	8.9	5.5	4.5	4.0	6.1	7.3
Ecstasy, lifetime	4.1	1.5	2.6	3.4	1.9	3.7	3.7	2.6	3.1	5.1	6.5
Hallucinogens, lifetime	11.4	6.2	9.1	10.6	7.3	11.0	10.5	10.6	9.3	12.3	16.5
Inhalants, lifetime	1.3	0.7	1.4	1.1	1.0	2.1		1.6	1.6	1.6	1.7

Source: Adapted from *Canadian Addiction Survey*, Health Canada 2004.

In general, drug use is higher among males than females, the young rather than the elderly, and the lower rather than the middle or upper social classes (CAS 2004). Alcohol is the most widely used drug, followed by tobacco and marijuana. First Nations people have comparatively high rates of illicit drug use. Tobacco smoking is widespread, and there is a two to six times greater risk of alcohol abuse among youth compared to other Canadians (CCSA 1999).

It appears that drug-use trends in Canada are declining, unlike those in the United States, where drug use increased somewhat in 2001 (U.S. Department of Health and Human Services 2002). A 2003 study of drug use among Ontario youth between 2001 and 2003 found that use of illicit drugs—particularly ecstasy, barbiturates, and LSD—is declining; cigarette smoking, as well, decreased significantly. Marijuana use in girls has increased, and cocaine use—which declined throughout the 1980s and 1990s—appears to be on the rise (Adlaf and Paglia 2003). The reason offered to explain why ecstasy use is declining is that, unlike in previous time periods, youth now believe there are greater risks associated with ecstasy use.

A relatively recent form of drug abuse is the use of *steroids,* compounds that include hormones. Hundreds of thousands of athletes use steroids to increase muscle strength and improve performance. A study of weight lifters reported that those who used steroids had significantly more fights, verbal aggression, and violence against wives and girlfriends (Choi and Pope 1994). Steroids also pose physical health problems. Large doses may damage the liver, increase cardiovascular disease, reduce sperm production and sex drive, and increase aggressiveness.

A question often raised is whether the use of one drug leads to the use of others. A number of studies have investigated the question, and in general they support the conclusion that there is a *tendency for multiple use* (Martin, Clifford, and Clapper 1992; National Center on Addiction and Substance Abuse at Columbia University 1998). The likelihood of using marijuana, for instance, is 65 times higher for those who have ever smoked or drank than for those who have done neither, and the likelihood of using cocaine is 104 times higher for those who have smoked marijuana than for persons who have not (Leshner 1998:4).

Nevertheless, we cannot say that the use of one drug causes the individual to experiment with another drug. To do so would be the *fallacy of non sequitur.* At this point, we can say only that whatever leads an individual to experiment with one substance may lead that individual to experiment with others.

Who are the users of drugs? For some people, drug use and, particularly, drug addiction conjure up images of skid row and the ghetto. However, the problem extends far beyond such places.

In North America, drug use is beginning at an increasingly earlier age (Johnson and Gerstein 1998). Among those born in the 1930s, for example, only alcohol, cigarettes, and marijuana were used by more than one percent of people before the age of 35. For those born between 1951 and 1955, 10 drugs were used by more than 5 percent of people before the age of 35.

In both rural and urban areas, children begin experimenting with drugs as early as the third grade (McBroom 1992). A dramatic change occurs, however, between ages 12 and 13 (National Center on Addition and Substance Abuse at Columbia University 1998). The proportion of those who say they can buy marijuana if they want more than triples (from 14 to 50 percent), and the proportion who say they know a student at their school who sells illegal drugs almost triples (from 8 to 22 percent).

Throughout the teen years, then, young people have increasing exposure to, and opportunities for, drug use. Few users begin experimenting as adults. Adults who smoke, for example, typically become daily smokers before the age of 20 (Centers for Disease Control 1995b). Similarly, adults who use other kinds of drugs, including heroin, typically begin at an early age (Epstein and Groerer 1997).

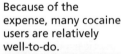

Because of the expense, many cocaine users are relatively well-to-do.

■■ Drugs and the Quality of Life

Drug abuse affects both abusers and nonabusers. Residents in drug-trafficking neighbourhoods are often terrorized by and fearful of dealers and users. As we discuss the effects of *abuse on the quality of life of individuals,* keep in mind how whole communities are impacted.

Physical Health. A person may experiment with drugs because they seem to hold the promise of fulfillment, but the fulfillment is elusive; greater and greater quantities are consumed, and ultimately the person suffers physical and psychological deterioration.

The *physical harm resulting from the use of illegal drugs includes* (U.S. Department of Justice 1992:10):

1. Death.
2. Medical emergencies from acute reactions to drugs or toxic adulterants.
3. Exposure to HIV infection, hepatitis, and other diseases resulting from intravenous drug use.
4. Injury from accidents caused by drug-related impairment.
5. Injuries from violence while obtaining drugs in the drug distribution network.
6. Dependence or addiction.
7. Chronic physical problems.

Drug abuse is now the main preventable cause of illness and premature death in North America. Each year hundreds of thousands die from smoking, alcohol abuse, and the use of illicit drugs. Early death from illegal drugs is often associated with an overdose of the drug. Heroin slows the vital functions of the body, and if a sufficient amount of the drug is ingested, those vital functions will completely stop. The addict can never be sure how much of the drug constitutes an overdose, nor can he or she be sure about the purity of the drug. Also, the *addict's tolerance level can vary* from one day to another, depending on how much of the drug has been used. If the addict manages to avoid death by overdose, he or she still may die from infections carried by the needle. Thus, the user *is at risk not merely from the drug itself but from other factors associated with drug use.* Crack cocaine use, for example, is spreading the AIDS virus as addicts sell sex for drugs (Edlin et al. 1994).

The health consequences go beyond the addict herself in the case of a pregnant woman. Cocaine and tobacco use are both associated with a significant risk of spontaneous abortion (Ness et al. 1999). Children who survive the risk and are born to addicted mothers have a significant number of perinatal medical problems, behavioural problems in early infancy, and developmental deficiencies in their cognitive and psychomotor skills (Singer et al. 2002). In later childhood, the children may exhibit disturbances in their activity levels, attention spans, and sleep patterns (Householder et al. 1982). Cocaine addiction has a devastating effect, including "strokes while the baby is still in the womb, physical malformations, and an increased risk of death during infancy" (Revkin 1989:63).

Tobacco causes more physiological damage among North Americans than any other nonalcoholic drug and is the leading cause of preventable death (Fellows et al. 2002; Canadian Council for Tobacco Control 2002). The effect of smoking on morbidity and mortality is well documented in the literature (The Daily, June 22, 2001). Smoking adversely affects both longevity and quality of life (for further information, see the Public Policy and Private Action box on tobacco consumption and healthcare costs). Among the known consequences of smoking are increased probability of lung cancer and other respiratory diseases, increased risk of heart disease, and increased probability of complications during childbirth. *Mortality rates of older adults from all causes are highest among current smokers* (LaCroix et al. 1991). As many as 85 percent of lung cancer deaths and a third or more of deaths from heart and blood vessel disease are directly related to smoking.

The most recent Canadian Tobacco Use Monitoring Survey (December 2003) reported that more than 5 million Canadians over the age of 15 smoke (CTUMS 2003)—a substantial decline from 1985, when 35 percent of Canadians smoked. Overall, proportionately more men (23 percent) than women (18 percent) smoke, but the trend has shifted among youth. Although proportionately fewer youth between the ages of 15 and 19 smoked in 2003 than in 2002 (18 and 22 percent, respectively), relatively more girls (22 percent) than boys (17 percent) smoke. However, on a daily average, boys smoke more cigarettes than girls (13 and 11.7, respectively). Smoking continues to be most prevalent among young adults between the ages of 20 and 24. In recent years, not only are fewer Canadians smoking, but also those who do smoke smoke less daily.

Women's smoking history is different from men's. At the beginning of the 20th century, women who smoked were socially frowned upon. However, after the Second World War, women smoking were no longer seen as unusual or rebellious. By the mid 1960s, 38 percent of women over the age of 15 smoked, compared to 61 percent of men (see figure 3.3). Smoking rates among men and women have steadily declined since the 1960s, but dramatically more for men than women. In turn, rates of lung cancer in men have steadily dropped (figure 3.4), whereas rates for women have increased. Why have lung cancer rates increased among women even though proportionately fewer women

Tobacco consumption is by far the most important risk factor for lung cancer and is also a significant risk factor for other diseases including heart diseases, chronic obstructive pulmonary diseases (COPD), and cancer of the mouth. Decreasing tobacco consumption could therefore reduce healthcare costs, and increase the quality of life of those who stop smoking or decide not to start.

… [A] 1-percent reduction in smoking prevalence in Canada may be associated with a decrease of 4.85 cases of heart disease per 100,000 people and 0.44 cases of lung cancer per 100,000 people. Moreover, a decrease of one cigarette smoked per day for daily smokers may be linked to a 3.2 per 100,000 decrease in lung cancer. For the country as a whole, this implies that in 1999, every combined decrease of 1 percent in smoking prevalence and of one smoked cigarette per day for daily smokers could be associated with a 1,479 reduction in cases of heart disease cases and 1,108 in cases of lung cancer. These translate into healthcare cost savings of $39.5 million. Since these two conditions represent 28.9 percent of tobacco-related hospital days, the maximum healthcare cost savings could amount to $39.5 million / 28.9 percent = $136.7 million following a decrease of 1 percent in smoking prevalence and of one smoked cigarette per day among daily smokers. Such calculations assume that the unit costs of treatment for other tobacco-related diseases are similar to that of heart disease and lung cancer. A more conservative estimate may fall between $40 million and $80 million.

SOURCE:
"Impact of an anti-tobacco campaign on direct health care costs in Canada," A Study by Analysis Group / Economics Commissioned by the Canadian Council for Tobacco Control, May 2002.

FIGURE 3.3 ■ ■ ■

Smoking rates by sex, Canada, 1965–2003

Source: Adapted from Physicians for a Smoke-Free Canada (http://www.smoke-free.ca) and Canadian Tobacco Use Monitoring Survey (December 2003).

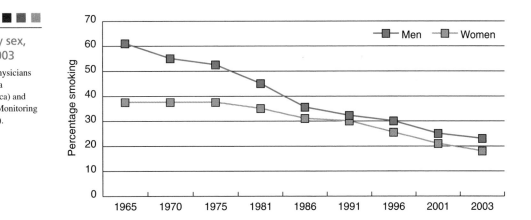

FIGURE 3.4 ■ ■ ■

Incidence of lung cancer by sex, Canada, 1980–2004.

Source: Adapted from CANSIM Table 103-0004, Statistics Canada.

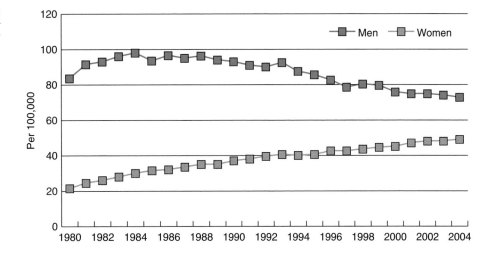

are smoking? Lung cancer does have a latency period. That is, you may smoke for 30 years before lung cancer appears. Simply put, "the men had a head start … When women and men have the same smoking patterns (number of years smoked, number of cigarettes per day, etc.), the risks of illness are likely to be similar … When women smoke like men, they die like men" (Cunningham 1996). Women's rates of smoking are indeed declining, but much more slowly.

There are, of course, people who smoke regularly and live to a "ripe old age," but using them to counter the systematic evidence is the *fallacy of dramatic instance.* What matters is not the few exceptions, but the great numbers who support the conclusions.

Moreover, nonsmokers who are exposed to a smoking environment also may suffer. Nonsmokers who live or work in a smoking environment are more likely than those not in such an environment to develop coronary heart disease (Howard et al. 1998; He et al. 1999). Thus, thousands of nonsmokers die each year as a result of inhaling secondhand smoke. Researchers also have found that babies are more likely to die of sudden infant death syndrome when they are exposed to smoke (Pollack 2001). Parents who smoke may double the chances of their children developing lung cancer in later life (Scott 1990b). Consequently, smoke-free environments at work and in public places are becoming the norm.

Let us examine more closely the effects of marijuana, which have been a matter of considerable controversy. Some believe that marijuana causes only slight physiological changes in the user and that it is not as dangerous a drug as alcohol, but numerous studies underscore the fact that there are both acute (brief and severe) and chronic, and both physiological and psychological, consequences of marijuana that are undesirable (Petersen 1984; National Institute on Drug Abuse 1998).

According to Canada's Senate Special Committee on illegal drugs, most marijuana users "are not at-risk users insofar as their use is regulated, irregular and temporary, rarely beyond 30 years of age" (2002). As well, the committee noted that heavy marijuana use might cause adverse psychological effects such as impaired concentration and learning. Further, heavy use can lead to dependence and in turn treatment. But, compared to alcohol and other psychotropic drugs, marijuana dependence occurs less often and is less severe.

Although more research on marijuana is needed to understand its full physiological and psychological effect, there is anecdotal evidence suggesting that marijuana may have more medical uses than previously thought—including treating glaucoma patients, relieving the pain of cancer patients, ameliorating the side effects of chemotherapy, and relieving the suffering of asthmatics. Undoubtedly, research on the effects of marijuana will continue (for more information, refer to the Public Policy and Private Action box on decriminalizing marijuana on p. 75).

Psychological Health. North Americans value psychological as well as physical health. The search for "happiness," "peace of mind," or "contentment" is common. The short-range euphoria that follows drug use is misleading because the long-range effects of drug abuse contradict the *quest for psychological well-being.* For example, the high that is produced by a drug like crack can be followed by severe depression. You need only listen to the stories of addicts or ex-addicts to realize the devastation to psychological health that results from drug abuse (Engel 1989). You also should note that, in contrast to the common belief that people turn to drugs for relief from distress, a study of adolescents found that users did not start drugs because of preexisting psychological distress; rather, the drug use led to both physical and psychological impairments (Hansell and White 1991).

The greater the use, the more intense the problems. A study of 161 adolescents reported that increased drug use was associated with increased depression, decreased self-esteem, and a deterioration of purpose in life (Kinnier et al. 1994). Even smoking is associated with psychological problems. Nicotine-dependent individuals are more likely to have serious depression and anxiety (Breslau, Kilbey, and Andreski 1994). The mother who smokes while pregnant can decrease her baby's IQ by as many as four points (Olds, Henderson, and Tatelbaum 1994).

Disagreement exists about the psychological consequences of marijuana usage. The underlying motive for marijuana use is the experience of being "high," which is associated with such positive characteristics as euphoria, feelings of relaxation, and heightened sensory feelings and perceptions (Jaffe 1985). However, some marijuana users experience adverse psychological effects; they may experience panic attacks or feelings of depression (Thomas 1993). "Psychotic symptoms such as delusions and hallucinations," according to a report prepared for the National Task Force on Cannabis, "are very rare experiences that occur at very high doses of THC [tetrahydrocannabinol], and perhaps in susceptible individuals at lower doses (Hall et al. undated).

Interpersonal Difficulties.

In addition to a sense of physical and psychological well-being, the desired quality of life for North Americans demands harmonious relationships. That is, they value the ability to "get along well" with others. This value is contradicted by relationship problems that tend to result from drug abuse.

A variety of interpersonal problems are associated with drug use and abuse (U.S. Department of Justice 1992). They include arguing with family and friends, feeling suspicious and distrustful of people, encountering troubles at school or work, and getting into trouble with the police. Among adolescents, the greater the involvement with drugs, the higher the rate of delinquent behaviour, including felony crimes (Johnson et al. 1991). Young adults who are heavy marijuana users have unstable lives and work histories (Bourque et al. 1991). Married men who abuse drugs have higher rates of wife abuse (Kantor and Straus 1989). Children whose parents abuse drugs are almost three times more likely to be abused and more than four times more likely to be neglected than are children of nonabusing parents, and they are also likely to have emotional, academic, and interpersonal problems (Reid, Macchetto, and Foster 1999; Wilens et al. 2002).

Interpersonal problems may continue for addicts even after they no longer abuse drugs. The ex-addict may attempt to compensate for past failures and assume a role of leadership. The outcome may be a power struggle between the ex-addict and his or her mate. In other cases, there may be unrealistic expectations about the outcome of treatment. The mate of an ex-addict may expect immediate and dramatic changes, and when such changes do not appear, the result can be disillusionment or bitterness. Also, the ex-addict may find that long-term or permanent damage has been done to his or her relationships. The fear and resentment built up over years of coping with an addicted individual may preclude healthy interpersonal relationships.

Economic Costs.

All social problems involve certain *economic costs,* and these affect the quality of life. The more money required to deal with a social problem, the less money there is for other desired services and programs.

Determining the exact dollar cost of any social problem is difficult. The costs of the drug problem include some that can be measured and some that can only be estimated. There is, of course, a cost to the user: the expense of maintaining the habit (for some, hundreds of dollars a week or more) and the loss of earnings over the life span (Kandel, Chen, and Gill 1995).

The measurable costs to the nation are staggering. Table 3.3 identifies the individual and public costs of drug abuse. The effect of drug abuse on the individual is staggering and is reported as "productivity loss," the loss of earnings and wages due to drug-induced illness or death. The remaining items listed are costs carried by govern-

TABLE 3.3 ■ ■ ■

Estimated Costs of Illicit Drug Abuse in Canada, 1992

SOURCE	$M	%
Productivity losses	823.1	60.0
Law-enforcement costs	400.3	29.2
Health care costs	88.0	6.4
Prevention and research	41.9	3.1
Other direct costs	10.7	0.8
Direct losses in the workplace	5.5	0.4
Administrative costs for transfer payments	1.5	0.1
TOTAL	**1371.0**	**100.0**

Source: Single and Robson et al. 1996 in Jackson 2002.

ment, other agencies, and employers (Jackson 2002). What is of particular note is that, "Canada spends nearly ten times as much on law enforcement for drug offences as on prevention and research" (Jackson 2002:4).

The way in which the drug problem and the crime problem intersect is underscored by the fact that in 2001–2, 9 percent of all adult criminal court cases and 7 percent of youth court cases were drug offences (Desjardins and Hotton 2004). Clearly, the economic and social costs of the drug problem are enormous.

■■ Contributing Factors

The various contributing factors have a double-barrelled effect: They maintain demand by encouraging use of drugs, and they guarantee a supply.

Social Structural Factors.   As with alcohol, *group norms* are one of the most important factors in the problem of other drugs, creating *peer pressure* that leads individuals to drug use. For the most part, young people do not take drugs to relieve emotional distress, but to be accepted by their peers—and the pressure begins in elementary school.

Group norms are important for adults as well. Being *integrated into a group in which drug use is approved* is one of the strongest factors associated with drug use at all ages. The "group" may be your family as well as your friends. In fact, a survey of 1,802 fourth- and fifth-grade pupils in the United States found that perceived family use was a stronger influence at that age than peer use (Bush, Weinfurt, and Iannotti 1994). Further, a study of employees who abused drugs reported that they tended to come from families with substance abuse problems and that they, in turn, associated with substance-abusing friends (Lehman et al. 1995).

Some North Americans who regard themselves as respectable citizens find it difficult to imagine following group norms when those norms are illegal. They need to realize that people all follow the norms of their groups and follow them for basically the same reasons. The respectable citizen who abides by the norm that the appearance of one's house and yard should be neat and clean derives satisfaction and a sense of acceptance from that normative behaviour. Similarly, the youth who uses drugs finds certain *rewards*—including admiration, respect, and acceptance—in that usage when it is the norm of his or her group.

Role problems are a second social structural factor in the drug problem. *Role problems create stress* in the individual, who may then use drugs to deal with the problems and their consequent stress. Indeed, when you consider that the first use of a drug like tobacco is likely to be a highly unpleasant experience, it is reasonable that strong forces are at work to develop the habit. Once a youth tries a cigarette, either peer pressure or stress can lead to subsequent tries, but stress seems to lead the individual more quickly to develop the habit (Hirschman, Leventhal, and Glynn 1984).

What kinds of role problems create such stress? One type of role problem is **role conflict.** Two or more roles may be contradictory—as, for example, when a woman experiences a contradiction between her role as a physician and her role as a wife because she does not have time to meet the expectations of both her patients and her husband. Contradictory expectations may impinge upon a single role, as when a physician's patients demand the right of abortion and his or her peers and friends define abortion as illegal and immoral. An individual may define the expectations of a role as somehow unacceptable or excessive, as when a physician feels overwhelmed by the multiple demands made upon his or her time and professional skills.

Physicians have been deliberately used in the examples here because of the high rate of drug addiction among doctors. The actual cause of addiction is not known, but it probably is rooted in a combination of easy access to drugs and the stresses of the role. Drug abuse is a symptom of stress, and role problems do generate stress in the individual. To the extent that particular roles are especially likely to create problems, people who occupy those roles will be particularly vulnerable to stress and perhaps to using drugs to deal with stress.

An important point here is that role conflict is a social phenomenon, not an individual phenomenon. It is not a particular doctor who is oppressed by the demands of the role; rather, all doctors must come to terms with the role of a physician in Canadian society. The expectations attached to the role tend to create the same problems for everyone who occupies the role.

Another role problem that can generate stress and increase the likelihood of drug abuse is a *role change that is defined as undesirable.* Such a role change occurs when a spouse dies. Suddenly a person is no longer a husband or a wife—that role has been lost. After the loss (which may be the result of separation or divorce as well as death), the individual must work through the grief process. A person copes with a significant loss by passing through a series of emotional phases. The process may take as long as two or more years. Typically, the initial phase is shock, followed by a period of numbness, or lack of intense emotion. In the next phase, the individual wavers between fantasy and reality, overcomes fantasies, and then experiences the full impact of the loss. A period of increasing adjustment follows, punctuated sporadically by episodes of painful memories. Finally, if the full grief process has been experienced, the individual accepts the loss and reaffirms his or her life. The grief process is painful, and some individuals may resort to drugs.

Family experiences also are involved in the use and abuse of drugs. Families that are strong, healthy, and highly cohesive tend to inhibit the use and abuse of drugs (Wilens et al. 2002). Family values and practices such as eating dinner together are associated with less likelihood of drug abuse (Hardesty and Kirby 1995; National Center on Addiction and Substance Abuse at Columbia University 1998).

However, the three kinds of family experiences that contribute to the alcohol problem also are involved in the abuse of other drugs. First, as noted above, drug abusers are more likely to come from homes where other family members are abusers (Petoskey, Van Stelle, and DeJong 1998; Kilpatrick et al. 2000).

Second, drug abusers are more likely to come from broken homes than are nonabusers. Adolescents who grow up in single-parent homes are more likely to use tobacco and illegal drugs than those who live with both parents (Flewelling and Bauman 1990). Looking at overall drug involvement (including alcohol), rates are higher among those whose homes are disrupted by divorce than those who grow up in

---

role conflict

a person's perception that two or more of his or her roles are contradictory, or that the same role has contradictory expectations, or that the expectations of the role are unacceptable or excessive

intact homes (Wolfinger 1998). This trend, however, may be explained by the fact that more than 80 percent of single-parent families are headed by women and more than half of these families live in poverty (Statistics Canada 2000). What we may in fact be observing is the effect of poverty, and not that of living in a single-parent family, on drug abuse.

Third, drug abuse is associated with various problematic relationships within the family. The problems may be severe, such as sexual abuse (Kang, Magura, and Shapiro 1994). For example, Freeman, Collier, and Parillo (2002) found that among female crack users, a high percentage experienced childhood sexual abuse. A similar relationship is noted with alcohol abuse (Galaif et al. 2001). Even parental conflict and *alienation between youth and their parents* can lead both to the use and abuse of drugs (Simcha-Fagan et al. 1986). Of course, the sense of rejection and alienation from parents can follow from drug use rather than precede it. Even if it is true, for instance, that a young person first uses drugs because of his or her group's norms and then becomes alienated from his or her parents, this alienation is likely to perpetuate the drug use. Thus, even if alienation is not one of the causes of initial use, it is likely to be a cause of continuing use.

A fourth structural factor is the government, and especially the *government's definition of drug use as illegal*. For some drugs, the illegal status is the consequence of social and political processes rather than of scientific evidence. Why, for example, is tobacco legal while other drugs are not? Once a drug is declared illegal, criminal elements enter the drug traffic in order to profit from black-market dealings. In essence, illegality raises the cost of maintaining the drug habit, deeply involves criminals in the drug traffic, strains the criminal justice system, and leads the addict to undesirable behaviour. Criminal involvement results from the potential for high profits. For example, the street value of heroin may be 50 times or more its wholesale cost and 10,000 times the amount paid to the farmer who supplies the opium! Similar profits are realized in the sale of other illicit drugs and is one reason why pushers risk prison to ply their trade.

A fifth structural factor is the *economy*. The economy supports the drug problem in at least two ways. First, many who get involved in the distribution, sale, and/or use and abuse of drugs come from the margins of the economy. That is, they are from the more impoverished families and have little hope of achieving any kind of financial success apart from that which drugs appear to offer them. Second, the legal drugs—alcohol and tobacco—are marketed freely and openly, and the industries are so profitable that they exert enormous pressure on the government to remain a legitimate part of the economy. The success of the marketing efforts is underscored by the fact that ads are more influential than peers on adolescents' decisions to start smoking (Evans et al. 1995). Research

Young girls often smoke because of peer pressure.

over a three-year period in California concluded that a third of all experimentation with smoking resulted from advertising (Pierce et al. 1998).

Finally, while structural factors that create the *demand for drugs* are crucial, there is also a *powerful organization of supply.* For instance, thousands of tonnes of coca, marijuana, and opium are grown in Latin America, processed in refineries, and smuggled into Canada every year. In addition, smugglers exploit the massive corruption that exists at all layers of government (including law enforcement agencies) and among businesspeople (who may "launder" drug money).

The supply network in Latin America and elsewhere is so powerful and the potential profits are so enormous that efforts to cut off supplies have been fruitless. Cut off at one point, smugglers find alternatives. This is not to say that efforts to stop the supply should be abandoned, but many experts agree that as long as there is demand and profits are high, the suppliers will find a way to provide drugs.

Social Psychological Factors. Among those who reach a crisis, a number of different *motivations for drug abuse* are reported. Some abusers seek certain psychic effects—euphoria, pleasure, and change of mood. Some are dependent upon the drug, and some intend to commit suicide. The quest for psychic effects may be rooted in problems of low self-esteem, low self-confidence, and lack of purpose in life (Dukes and Lorch 1989). Depression is linked to alcohol dependence and illicit drug use (see figure 3.5) (Tjepkema 2004). According to the 2002 Canadian Community Health Survey, 15 percent of heavy drinkers experienced a major depressive episode in the past year, compared to 4.4 percent of non-drinkers. The effect was much stronger for illicit drug users: 26.1 percent of drug users experienced depression compared to 4.1 percent of non-users. However, Tjepkema believes that the results underestimate substance dependence rates for two reasons (16). First, there may be a tendency to underreport alcohol and drug dependence; and second, the study excluded institutionalized populations and the homeless, "both of whom are known to have higher rates of substance dependence than the household population" (16). In other words, for some users it isn't just a matter of seeking quick gratification through drugs, but of grasping at one source of symptom relief.

Motivations for drug abuse may change over the years. A study of 60 clients of a clinic reported that most said they began drug use because of its popularity during their school years (Johnson and Friedman 1993). Once they reached the point of using heroin, however, the motivation became mainly physiological survival.

The attitudes that support drug use may themselves find support in popular movies and music. A study of 200 popular movies and 2,000 popular songs reported that illic-

FIGURE 3.5 ▪ ▪ ▪

Prevalence of depression, by frequency of heavy drinking and illicit drug use in past year.

Source: 2002 Canadian Community Health Survey: Mental Health Survey: Mental Health and Well-being; and M. Tjepkema (2004, p. 16).

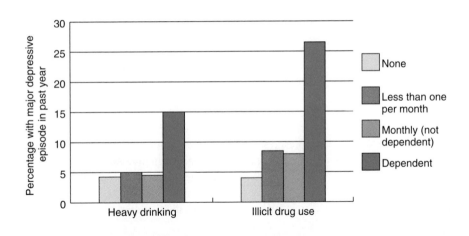

it drugs appeared in 22 percent and alcohol and tobacco appeared in more than 90 percent of the movies (Roberts, Henriksen, and Christenson 1999). One-quarter of the movies that included illicit drugs had explicit information about the preparation and use of the drugs. Illicit drugs or alcohol were mentioned in 27 percent of the songs. References to drugs were particularly heavy in rap lyrics: 63 percent mentioned illicit drugs and almost half mentioned alcohol.

The researchers did not look at the effects the movies and music had on actual drug usage, but you have seen in other chapters that the mass media do influence people's behaviour. It seems highly probable, therefore, that at least some experimentation with drugs stems from popular movies and music.

From Social Problems to Solutions

Is it possible to eliminate the drug problem? No society we know of has completely solved the problem. Even China, which seemed to have eradicated the problem, has experienced renewed drug trafficking (Tyler 1995).

Still, progress can be made, and the severity of the problem can be lessened. For that to happen, you must attack the social bases as well as treat individual addicts and also focus on *reducing demand rather than stopping the supply*. For example, as noted earlier, demand and use are highest in the lower social classes. Public policy that enables those in the lower strata to better their lot will also reduce the demand for illegal drugs. This is not to say that enforcement is useless, but only that treatment as well as programs of education and prevention must be given at least as much, and perhaps more, attention and support.

The purpose of treating an addict is to reduce or eliminate his or her dependence on the drug. Because there is no single cause for all addictions, however, there is no single treatment that will work for everyone (Rodgers 1994). One method that has claimed some success with cocaine addicts is a form of behavioural therapy—contingency contracting (Petry and Martin 2002). In *contingency contracting*, the addicts make an agreement with the therapist to pay a severe penalty if urine tests reveal that they have ingested any of the drug during the week. For instance, a nurse signed a contract in which she agreed that she would write a letter to her parents confessing her drug habit and asking that they no longer give her any financial support. She would write a second letter to the provincial board of nursing in which she would confess her habit and turn in her licence. Some cocaine addicts have broken the habit through such contracts.

detoxification
supervised withdrawal from dependence on a drug

With heroin addicts, a first step is **detoxification**, the *elimination of dependence* through supervised withdrawal. One of the more common methods of treating heroin addiction is methadone maintenance. In *methadone maintenance*, the addict orally ingests the drug methadone, which is considered less dangerous than heroin and has a number of properties that allows the addict to lead a more normal life than is possible with heroin. Methadone may also be used in the detoxification program, but detoxification involves the elimination of all drug use—including the methadone after it helps mitigate withdrawal symptoms.

While there is some disagreement as to whether methadone maintenance is more effective than drug-free treatment programs, it is clear that the methadone program reduces the use of heroin (Marsch 1998). In the United States, methadone cannot be prescribed by a physician but must be dispensed at a licensed clinic (Wren 1997); in Canada, physicians have been given permission by the Office of Controlled Substances to prescribe methadone (Health Canada 2003).

A more recent form of treatment is *brief intervention therapy* (Rodgers 1994). In a relatively few sessions, the therapist seeks to establish a warm and supportive relationship with the addict, while giving advice, exploring various ways to deal with the addiction, and helping the addict to see that he or she must take responsibility for getting free of the addiction. The therapist also instills a sense of empowerment in the addict—not only "I *have* to do this," but "I *can* do this."

Addiction is more than physiological, of course. Relationships are involved. Consequently, successful treatment must enable the individual to cope with the conditions that led to the addiction. For many, this involves treatment through group therapy.

One type of group therapy is *family therapy*. Since, for example, adolescent drug abuse may be a symptom of family problems in many cases, family therapy may be the most effective mode of treatment (Reilly 1984). For adults, small-group therapy may be helpful. Cocaine Anonymous emerged in the 1980s (Cohen 1984). It is run by former addicts and provides group support to the addict as a means of breaking the habit.

Another variation of group therapy that may be combined with individual therapy is the *drug-treatment centre*. The efficacy of the centres is a matter of debate. However, one study showed that 80 percent of the treated addicts were off hard drugs after completing a program at an inpatient or an outpatient centre (Biden 1990).

Finally, a more recent form of group therapy involves the use of peer support (Levy, Gallmeier, and Wiebel 1995). Peer support is not new, of course, but the program—"Outreach-Assisted Peer-Support"—is unique in that it targets active addicts who are not in treatment and who may decide to continue drug use while in the group. Whether they opt for total abstinence, or for reduced or controlled usage, addicts may join the group.

Most of the money allocated to the drug problem goes into enforcement, but many people believe that education and prevention are as important—if not more so—because they reduce the demand. Significant declines in tobacco use have occurred in U.S. states that have implemented statewide tobacco prevention and education programs, including an increase in the tax on cigarettes (Centers for Disease Control 1999). Programs in schools, of course, must begin early because drugs are available even in elementary schools. Among other things, building self-esteem and teaching youth how to resist peer pressure can reduce rates of drug usage (Botvin et al. 1995).

Harm reduction is a non-judgmental approach to illicit drug use. It recognizes the complexity surrounding drug use and promotes programs that minimize harm. One example of a harm-reduction program is a *supervised injection facility* (SIF). The first government-sponsored SIF, referred to as "Insite," was opened in the Vancouver lower east side, which is known for its high rates of poverty and intravenous drug users (approximately 5,000), in September 2003 (Wood et al. 2004). At Insite, drug users inject their drugs under the supervision of qualified medical personnel. Other services available include primary health care, counselling services, and referral to detoxification centres. There also is space to "chill out": drink coffee or watch television (Johal 2004). A primary goal of the program is to reduce the number of intravenous drug overdoses. The one-year evaluation of the program has noted many successes (BC Centre for Excellence in HIV/AIDS 2004). Insite has been used by 600 people. There have been no fatalities recorded since Insite's opening. Overall, public-injection drug use and discarded syringes have been significantly reduced, and "measurable improvements [have been made] in the public order, which in turn may improve the liveability of communities and benefit tourism while reducing community concerns stemming from public drug use and discarded syringes" (Wood et al. 2004:733). Finally, there is no evidence of increased numbers of drug dealers surrounding Insite.

Decriminalization of drug use is an additional step that can be taken to attack the social bases of the problem. Although decriminalization would reduce the demand for illegal drugs, it is a controversial issue. Advocates claim that it would resolve many aspects of the problem: drug traffic would no longer be profitable (making it useless for

MARIJUANA USE IN THE NETHERLANDS

In the first rigorous study comparing marijuana use in the Netherlands and the United States, researchers have found no evidence that decriminalization of marijuana leads to increased drug use. The results suggest that drug policies may have less impact on marijuana use than is currently thought. […]

The study compared the cannabis (marijuana and hashish) habits of users in Amsterdam and San Francisco to test the premise that punishment for cannabis use deters use and thereby benefits public health. […]

Highlights of the study include:

- The mean age at onset of use was 16.95 years in Amsterdam and 16.43 years in San Francisco.
- The mean age at which respondents began using marijuana more than once per month was 19.11 years in Amsterdam and 18.81 years in San Francisco.
- In both cities, users began their periods of maximum use about 2 years after they began regular use: 21.46 years in Amsterdam and 21.98 years in San Francisco.

- About 75 percent in both cities had used cannabis less than once per week or not at all in the year before the interview.
- Majorities of experienced users in both cities never used marijuana daily or in large amounts even during their periods of peak use, and use declined after those peak periods.

The Netherlands effectively decriminalized marijuana use in 1976, and it is available for purchase in small quantities by adults in licensed coffee shops; in the United States, marijuana use carries stiff criminal penalties, and more than 720,000 people were arrested for marijuana offenses in 2001. […]

Despite widespread lawful availability of cannabis in Amsterdam, there were no differences between the two cities in age at onset of use, age at first regular use, or age at the start of maximum use.

The study found no evidence that lawfully regulated cannabis provides a "gateway" to other illicit drug use. In fact, marijuana users in San Francisco were far more likely to have used other illicit drugs—cocaine, crack, amphetamines, ecstasy, and opiates—than users in Amsterdam. […]

SOURCE:
Excerpts from News-Medical.Net: Medical News from Around the World, *Medical Study News*, Published Monday, 3 May 2004: http://www.news-medical.net/?id=1164.

organized crime), the courts would not be overwhelmed with cases of drug violators, addicts would not be required to engage in criminal activity to support their habits, and the money now spent on enforcement could be used for better purposes. Opponents claim that decriminalization would only exacerbate the problem: cheap, readily available drugs would increase the rate of addiction; the health costs of dealing with abuse would skyrocket; and the citizenry would get the wrong message (namely, that drug use is okay).

In The Netherlands, marijuana has been decriminalized since 1976. There was no difference in patterns of youth drug use—age of first use, age of regular use, and age of maximum use—between the two countries (see the Global Comparison box).

▪▪ SUMMARY

The problem of alcohol and other drugs is one of abuse and not merely of use. Various drugs have various effects, and the effects depend on the method of administration, the amount taken, and the social situation as well as the chemical composition of the drug. Alcohol is the most widely used drug, and its effects can be extremely deleterious. Many experts consider alcohol abuse much more serious than abuse of other drugs.

Around 1980, drug use of all kinds began to decline for the first time in two decades. In the 1990s, patterns of use fluctuated. Although less than in the peak years, use and abuse are still quite high. More than three-quarters of Canadians drink, and more than a third say that drinking has been a source of trouble in their families. Millions of Canadians indicate that they are current users of marijuana. There is a tendency for multiple drug use. Most alcohol users are young and male but not poor, whereas other drug addicts tend to be young, male, and poor.

The meaning of the drug problem for the quality of life is seen in the consequences for physical health, psychological health, interpersonal relationships, and economic costs. Abusers suffer various undesirable effects in all areas. The nation as a whole also suffers great economic cost because billions of dollars per year are involved in lost services and in efforts to combat the deleterious effects of abuse.

Various structural factors contribute to the problem. An important one is group norms. Integration into a group that approves drug use is one of the most reliable predictors of use. Role problems, including role conflict and undesirable role change, create stress in the individual and that stress can lead to abuse. Abusers are more likely to come from homes where family members are abusers, from broken homes, or from homes where there are problematic relationships. The government's definition of many drugs as illegal has several implications: More people are classified as criminal; previously classified criminals become deeply involved in the drug traffic; the criminal justice system is strained; and users and abusers are led into various kinds of undesirable behaviour. Finally, the suppliers of illegal drugs are organized effectively and take advantage of corruption, so that there always will be a supply available when there is a demand and profits are high.

Among social psychological factors is the alienation of users from the larger society. Many people believe drug use produces desirable psychic effects.

In treating the problem, efforts to help the individual abuser or reduce the supply available to users have far exceeded efforts to get at the social roots of the problem. If it is to be dealt with effectively, both approaches are needed—attacks on the social factors as well as treatment of individual abusers.

▪▪ KEY TERMS

Abuse 62   Detoxification 86   Role Conflict 83

▪▪ STUDY QUESTIONS

1. What is meant by the fact that Canadians have had ambivalent feelings about alcohol and other drugs throughout their history?

2. Identify the various types of drugs and briefly note their effects on people.

3. Who are the most likely users and abusers of alcohol and other drugs?

4. How do the use and abuse of alcohol and other drugs affect physical health?

5. What are the consequences of alcohol and other drugs for psychological health?

6. How does alcohol affect interpersonal relationships?

7. Indicate the economic costs of drug use and abuse.

8. Why are women's rates of lung cancer increasing, while men's are decreasing?

9. In what ways do group norms affect patterns of drug use?

10. What kind of role problems enter into drug use and abuse?

11. How do social institutions contribute to the problem?

12. What are the attitudes and ideologies that are important in understanding the drug problem?

13. Name some steps that can be taken to alleviate the problem of alcohol and other drugs.

■■ FOR FURTHER READING

Akers, Ronald L. *Drugs, Alcohol, and Society: Social Structure, Process, and Policy.* Belmont, CA: Wadsworth, 1992. An examination of differing kinds of drug use, each of which is looked at from three perspectives—social structure, social process, and social policy.

Clark, Walter B., and Michael E. Hilton, eds. *Alcohol in America: Drinking Practices and Problems.* Albany: State University of New York Press, 1991. A collection of articles on practices, problems, and patterns of drinking, including minority drinking patterns.

Clawson, Patrick L., Rensselaer W. Lee III, and Rensselaer W. Lee. *The Andean Cocaine Industry.* New York: St. Martin's, 1998. An examination of cocaine, beginning with its cultivation in South America to its sale on American streets. Includes an analysis of the economic and political effects of the drug business on Andean nations.

Dodes, Lance M. *The Heart of Addiction: A New Approach to Understanding and Managing Alcoholism and Other Addictive Behaviours.* New York: HarperCollins, 2002. Identifies myths about addiction and discusses the common elements in addictions of all types. Includes addiction problems of particular groups and ways to get help.

Engel, Joel. *Addicted: Kids Talking about Drugs in Their Own Words.* New York: Tom Doherty Associates, 1989. Ten young people tell in their own words how drugs overtook their lives and controlled them. Most began with alcohol and marijuana before they were 13 years old.

Erdmann, Jack. *Whiskey's Children.* New York: Kensington, 1997. An account of the personal trauma endured by a man whose drinking resulted in both personal and professional disasters.

Heron, Craig. *Booze: A Distilled History.* Toronto: Between the Lines, 2003. A critical history of drinking in Canada over four centuries.

Kluger, Richard. *Ashes to Ashes: America's Hundred-Year Cigarette War, the Public Health, and the Unabashed Triumph of Philip Morris.* New York: Vintage Books, 1997. A comprehensive examination of the American tobacco industry and the complex social, medical, economic, and psychological factors in the industry's growth and the current controversies and legal battles.

CRIME AND SOCIAL CONTROL

LEARNING OBJECTIVES

1. Know the different kinds of crime.

2. Explain the ways in which crime data are obtained, and describe the problems inherent in official records.

3. Discuss the amount and distribution of crime in Canada.

4. Explain the factors that contribute to the problem of crime.

5. Discuss the varied and sometimes contradictory suggestions for reducing crime.

6. Understand youth crime and explain the factors that contribute to youth crime.

TARGETED

I don't know why they arrested me. Whenever my buddies got caught, the cops would just take their weed and let them go, probably go smoke it behind the station. The guy was just a hardass, I guess. So me and my buddy got caught, with like, barely a gram. We'd just smoked a bowl and were leaving the park when these cops pull up to us and start shining a flashlight in our eyes.

They take us to the station and put us in separate rooms. After 15 minutes, a cop comes in and starts acting like he's my best friend: "We know he was the dealer. You were just at the wrong place at the wrong time," he says, 'cause my buddy had the pipe on him. I mean, I'm not gonna kid you, I thought about it. You ever been in a police station? The cop said no charges would be pressed and they wouldn't tell anyone if I ratted him out and I knew my parents weren't gonna be impressed if I came home in the back of a cruiser, but I didn't tell. So then another cop comes in and starts acting like I've been busted with a boatful of cocaine. He starts telling me my buddy's turned me and they know everything and if I don't start talking they're gonna charge me for dealing, tell my parents that I'm running a big operation and get me in Juvi. At first I was totally pissed off at my friend for lying about me, but then I realized they were probably giving him the same lines so I just kept quiet. Anyway, I guess they got bored and let me go with a minor possession charge and a court date.

When we showed up for our trial date, there were more kids my age in the courtroom than in homeroom, but I felt like we were the only white guys there. We took our seats and the judge started calling up cases. They were all possession and minor trafficking charges. She seemed pretty anal, most of these guys were just smoking weed. She gave out a lot of fines, long periods of probation, and some guys weren't gonna be allowed to leave their house except for school, until June. The last thing I need is more time at home with my parents and house calls from cops. But our lawyer kept telling us not to worry.

When she called us up, our lawyer said it was our first offence and we were good kids, got good grades, and how my buddy was on the team. Pretty much, he told the judge that we didn't smoke weed a lot and were just trying to fit in. Luckily no one knew us there. I couldn't look any of the other guys in the eye. It seemed to work though, 'cause the judge let us off easy. She gave us 10 hours bagging clothes at the Sally Ann. ■

■■ INTRODUCTION

A small child is killed, a mother is strangled by her estranged husband, or a business-man cheats people out of their retirement. In contrast to major crimes like murder, robbery, and theft, historian Herbert Butterfield suggested that a society can be destroyed by crimes involving "petty breaches of faith" of "very nice people" (Butterfield 1949:54). Such crimes enrage people and can lead to an increased demand for law and order.

In U.S. polls taken during 2001, Americans identified crime and violence as second only to education as important problems facing their community—even in face of declining crime rates (Bureau of Justice Statistics 2001:101). Canadians, however, are less concerned about crime than our American neighbours are. Numerous surveys in recent years have shown that Canadians are increasingly less concerned about crime (Roberts 2001). A poll taken in 2001 showed that 29 percent of Canadians were "very concerned" about crime as a pressing social issue compared to health (69 percent), child poverty (58 percent), education (52 percent), environment (45 percent), and homelessness (43 percent) (Perspectives Canada 2001).

In this chapter, we look at the varieties of crime and define crime. We then examine the extent of crime in Canada, the effects that crime has on the quality of life, and the kinds of sociocultural factors that contribute to the problem. Finally, we discuss measures that can be taken and have been taken to resolve the problem.

■■ THE TYPES OF CRIME

Technically, crime is any violation of the criminal law. However, as you will see when we examine "white-collar" crime, this is an inadequate definition. Nevertheless, we begin with a discussion of the kinds of acts embodied in the criminal law—acts that are defined as threatening to the state or to citizens whom the state is obligated to protect.

■■ *Criminal Code* Crime

According to Canada's *Criminal Code*, crime is often categorized into "violent crime," "property crime," and "other *Criminal Code*." *Violent crime* includes assault, robbery, sexual assault, homicide and attempted murder, and abductions. *Property crime* (without intent of violence) includes theft ($5,000 and under, and over $5,000), breaking and entering, motor vehicle theft, fraud (for example, illegal use of debit/credit cards or cheques), and possession of stolen goods. Most other crimes that do not involve violence or property are categorized under "other *Criminal Code*" and include mischief, bail violations, disturbing the peace, counterfeiting, offensive weapons, arson, obstruction of a public/peace officer, indecent acts, prostitution, and trespassing at night. Offences such as mischief and arson are often associated with youth (Wallace 2002). Traffic offences—impaired driving, failure to stop and/or remain at the scene of an accident, dangerous driving, driving when prohibited—and drug offences (under federal statute)—possession, trafficking, and importation and production—are reported separately from *Criminal Code* offences.

▪▪ Computer Crime

Computer crime is growing rapidly. In the workplace alone, computer crime costs businesses more than a billion dollars each year (Goodman 2001). In essence, computer crime is "any illegal act for which knowledge of computer technology is used to commit the offence" (Conly and McEwen 1990:3).

There are five basic types of computer crime (Conly and McEwen 1990:3): *Internal computer crimes* are alterations to computer programs to change the outcome in some way. For example, financial records can be systematically changed or even deleted. *Telecommunication crimes* involve the use of telephone lines to gain illegal access to computer systems or to misuse the telephone system. In one case, a man found a way to avoid the tracking system for long-distance calls. He sold time to friends and made international calls for them. The company lost more than US$100,000 before the man was caught.

Computer manipulation crimes involve changing data or creating records in a system for the purpose of engaging in some illegal activity. Embezzlers use this technique; they create false accounts or modify the data in existing accounts. *Support of criminal enterprises* involves the use of databases for drug trafficking, money laundering, or other activities. A prostitution ring with at least US$3 million yearly income used a microcomputer system to monitor its operations in a metropolitan area. Prostitutes and clients could call the central office, which checked the names and arranged the meetings. Client information on file included name, credit card number, and preferred type of prostitute. Finally, *hardware and software theft* includes such things as software piracy (making a copy of software rather than paying for it) and thefts of microprocessor chips and trade secrets.

▪▪ White-Collar Crime

white-collar crime
crimes committed by respectable citizens in the course of their work

White-collar crime is the crime of "respectable" people. The term was coined by Edwin Sutherland (Sutherland and Cressey 1955), who said that white-collar crimes are *committed by respectable people in the course of their work*. According to the RCMP, white-collar crime includes "fraud and false pretences, theft, breach of trust, secret commissions, offences against the Government of Canada, the corruption of public officials, offences relating to property rights, [and] crimes involving computers, the insolvency process, securities fraud, and counterfeiting on an interprovincial, national, and international scale" (RCMP 2004).

Edelhertz (1983:115–17) has suggested four different types of white-collar crimes. First, there are "personal," or "ad hoc" crimes. The individual in this case generally does not have a face-to-face confrontation with the victim. Cheating on federal income taxes and credit card fraud are examples of personal crimes. Then there are "abuses of trust," which are crimes committed by those who have custody of someone else's wealth (e.g., embezzlement) or who have the power to make decisions (e.g., accepting a bribe to make a favourable decision). Third, there are crimes that are "incidental to and in furtherance of organizational operations," though they are not part of the purpose of the organization. Violations of antitrust laws fit in here. Or on a smaller scale, Edelhertz says that this "most troublesome" of the four categories involves such things as fraudulent medicare claims (physicians billing the health care system for services not rendered).

Edelhertz said that the third category is most troublesome because the offenders do not think of themselves as criminals and generally have high status in their communities. Nevertheless, the outcome is victimization of people. Consider, for instance, the problem of deceptive advertising. The advertising agency and the corporate executives who pay for ads do not think of themselves as engaging in criminal activity. Yet millions of Canadians buy products based on this deceptive advertising.

The fourth category is white-collar crime carried on as a business by full-time con artists. This includes things from stock swindles to street games in which people are cheated out of their money.

Examples of white-collar crime abound. Individuals, small businesses, large corporations, and governmental agencies are all involved. Examples of individuals include computer criminals, some of whom work out of their homes to defraud companies. At the small-business level, an example is insurance fraud in auto body repair shops. A study in the United States found that estimates of the shops were significantly higher with insurance coverage than without, independently of the type of car or extent of the damage (Tracy and Fox 1989). Nor are large corporations immune. In January 2004, Conrad Black was forced to step down as the chief executive officer of Hollinger International, which controlled 60 percent of Canada's newspapers, because it was reported that he, along with other senior executives, had received more than $32 million in unauthorized payments. Hollinger has slapped Black with a $200-million lawsuit.

Corporations also get involved in white-collar crime, including Bre-X, a Calgary-based mining company that created the largest gold discovery scam in the world's history. Overnight, the stock's value went from pennies to more than $280 a share—only to return to pennies when it was discovered that there was in fact no gold. The samples were "salted": gold dust was added to the rock before it was sent to the testing laboratory. In 2002, the Enron corporation's "creative" accounting practices and manipulation of energy markets came to light (Eichenwald 2002); the Enron case is being prosecuted as of this writing. At this point, however, it appears fairly certain that among the outcomes of the corporate practices were soaring energy costs when markets were manipulated, hurting countless individuals and businesses that could not afford the higher rates; investors losing huge sums of money and many, including Enron employees, losing their life savings and retirement when the corporation collapsed; and many innocent Enron employees losing their jobs.

In each case of crime committed by a large corporation (except perhaps the Enron situation, which has not yet been settled), the only punishment endured was fines. No corporate officers had to spend time in jail. No charges were laid in the Bre-X case because, according to an RCMP spokesperson, "[t]here is no doubt that a fraud took place, but we have no evidence" (*The Globe and Mail*, May 12, 1999).

Some practices of respectable people are not

Conrad Black is an example of a high-profile Canadian charged with committing a white-collar crime.

defined by the law as crimes but should be treated as crimes, Sutherland argued. He asserted that businesspeople were more criminalistic than people of the ghettoes. A major difference is that criminal law distinguishes between the two groups, so that some acts that logically could be defined as crime are not in the criminal law. Further, some acts involving businesses and corporations are handled by governmental commissions rather than the criminal justice system. You can reasonably argue that when a company advertises a 6-percent interest rate on instalment payments and actually collects 11.5 percent, it is committing fraud. The executives of the company will not be charged with fraud; the company will merely be ordered to stop advertising the false rate.

Even when the offence is covered by the criminal law, white-collar criminals may receive less severe punishment. One reason why white-collar criminals may receive less severe treatment is the perception that they are normally decent citizens who are one-shot offenders. A study of more than 1,000 cases, however, found that, except for antitrust violations, the offenders were more likely than not to have records of prior criminality (Weisburd, Chayet, and Waring 1990). Thus, white-collar crime is at least as serious as—and, some would argue, is even more serious than—the violent acts of street criminals. Street criminals tax the patience and resources of society, but white-collar criminals are like an insidious corrosion that slowly but surely destroys.

▪▪ Organized Crime

The term *organized crime* brings up American images of Al Capone, machine guns, the Mafia, the Mob, La Cosa Nostra, the Syndicate, and films like *The Untouchables* and *The Godfather*. Is there such a phenomenon in Canada? Are there groups that control the criminal activities of cities, regions, or even the entire nation? Criminologists themselves do not agree on the exact nature of organized crime, but there is some consensus on five characteristics of **organized crime:** the determination of a group of people to make money by any means necessary; the provision of illegal goods and services to people who want them or can be coerced into taking them; the use of political corruption to maintain and extend the activities; the persistence of the activities by the same organizations over successive generations of people; and a code of conduct for members (Barlow 1996:244–45; see, e.g., Berger 1999). There is also likely to be some involvement in legitimate business, which is used to launder illegal funds or stolen merchandise. For instance, profits from drug sales may be claimed as legitimate profits of a legitimate business by manipulating its accounting records.

The activities of organized crime include gambling, prostitution, drugs, extortion, loan-sharking, bookmaking, and various legitimate enterprises (such as restaurants) that are used to launder money received from the illegal activities. There is, however, no single organization that controls all organized crime at the international or national level. Rather, there are numerous and diverse groups.

Canada houses many of the major international organized crime groups, including Asian, Eastern European, Italian, and Latin American organizations and outlaw motorcycle gangs that deal in drugs, weapons, extortion, prostitution, and contract murder (RCMP 2004). Asian organized crime, particularly the numerous Chinese gangs, tends to specialize in drugs. Chinese criminal gangs have taken over some of the heroin trafficking from the Mafia. Colombian cartels specialize in cocaine. Jamaican posses control a portion of the traffic in crack and have been implicated in thousands of drug-related murders. Some of the groups originated in Canada, while others involve immigrants who may still have ties to foreign-based criminal organizations. Organized crime is no longer the province of any particular racial or ethnic group. Rather, it involves diverse groups who use it to gain economic and social mobility.

organized crime
any group of five or more people engaged in a continuing pattern of serious criminal activity where the primary motive is profit (RCMP 2004)

▪▪ Youth Crime

The American concept of juvenile delinquency is a modern one. Until the late 19th century, juvenile offenders were regarded as incapable of certain crimes or were treated as adults in the criminal justice system. This concept changed in the 19th century when a group of reformers set out to redeem the nation's wayward youth (Platt 1969). These "child savers" helped to establish the juvenile court system in the United States. As a result, juveniles were treated differently from adults, and certain behaviour that was once ignored or handled in an informal way came under the jurisdiction of a government agency. Thus, the *concept of delinquency* was "invented" in America in the 19th century.

The history of youth justice in Canada predates Confederation. In the early 1800s, youths who broke the law were viewed as "little adults." In 1892, the minimum age of 7 for charging a child with a criminal offence was established. The *Youthful Offenders Act* was passed in 1894, mandating that youth trials and incarceration be separate from adults. At their discretion, judges could choose foster care or reform schools; instead, youth offenders often received sentences similar to those of adults and were incarcerated in adult prisons.

The *Juvenile Delinquents Act* (JDA) of 1908 guaranteed a separate justice system for youth. Youth were not viewed as offenders but rather as delinquents needing guidance and supervision. Youth court judges were assigned the role of *parens patriae* (pseudo-parent), thus having vast discretion in sentencing. Sentencing focused on rehabilitation, not incarceration. Thus, delinquent youth were either fined, placed on probation, or taken into custody with Children's Aid Society.

Many concerns were raised. Foremost, given the discretionary powers of judges there were substantial variations in sentencing for similar crimes. Further, children had no legal rights and their cases were not bound by the laws of evidence. What this meant is that a judge had the discretion to hold a youth in custody until the age of 21, regardless of innocence. Youth who were placed in custody had little protection from staff abuse. However, for many Canadians, the biggest concern was that youth crime rates were increasing and the public believed that youth, in similar fashion to adults, must be responsible for their behaviour. In short, the punishment must fit the crime (see mapleleafweb.com).

In 1982, the *Juvenile Delinquents Act* was replaced with the *Young Offenders Act* (YOA). The underlying philosophy of the YOA was that youth need to be responsible for their actions but they should not be held accountable in the same way adults are. Incarceration should be avoided whenever possible. Finally, children's legal rights and freedoms would be protected by the *Canadian Charter of Rights and Freedoms* or the *Canadian Bill of Rights* (Young Offender Act, Declaration of Principal 1985). The Act did not allow the publication of names and photographs of offenders between the ages of 12 and 17. The YOA did not allow any term of incarceration longer than three years—even for murder—and furthermore, five years after sentencing the criminal record would be destroyed. From very early on, the YOA came under much criticism. Every case that involved a murder by a youth was followed by a public outcry that violence among youth was on the rise and that Canada was moving in the same direction as the United States (Parker 1996).

Other critiques were put forth by the police, who claimed that the Act made it difficult for them to apprehend offenders because they were not able to publicly identify young suspects unless they were considered dangerous. For their part, lawyers and social workers involved with young offenders expressed concern that the Act removed the discretionary sentencing powers that the correctional authorities were able to exercise under the old *Juvenile Delinquents Act*, which allowed more lenient treatment for youngsters who showed signs of being capable of rehabilitation. Under the new Act,

DECLARATION OF PRINCIPLE—Youth Criminal Justice Act (2002, c.1)

a) the youth criminal justice system is intended to
   (i) prevent crime by addressing the circumstances underlying a young person's offending behaviour,
   (ii) rehabilitate young persons who commit offences and reintegrate them into society, and
   (iii) ensure that a young person is subject to meaningful consequences for his or her offence in order to promote the long-term protection of the public;

c) within the limits of fair and proportionate accountability, the measures taken against young persons who commit offences should
   (i) reinforce respect for societal values,
   (ii) encourage the repair of harm done to victims and the community,
   (iii) be meaningful for the individual young person given his or her needs and level of development and, where appropriate, involve the parents, the extended family, the community and social or other agencies in the young person's rehabilitation and reintegration, and

   (iv) respect gender, ethnic, cultural and linguistic differences and respond to the needs of aboriginal young persons and of young persons with special requirements; and

d) special considerations apply in respect of proceedings against young persons and, in particular,
   (i) young persons have rights and freedoms in their own right, such as a right to be heard in the course of and to participate in the processes, other than the decision to prosecute, that lead to decisions that affect them, and young persons have special guarantees of their rights and freedoms,
   (ii) victims should be treated with courtesy, compassion and respect for their dignity and privacy and should suffer the minimum degree of inconvenience as a result of their involvement with the youth criminal justice system,
   (iii) victims should be provided with information about the proceedings and given an opportunity to participate and be heard, and
   (iv) parents should be informed of measures or proceedings involving their children and encouraged to support them in addressing their offending behaviour.

said Peter Jaffe, director of the family court clinic in London, Ontario, courts are now "focusing on the offence and not the offender," with the result that more young offenders are being sent to jail—though often for shorter terms than under the old law (Dolphin, 1989:43).

The *Youth Criminal Justice Act* (YCJA), a new law replacing the YOA, was passed in February 2002. Excerpts from its Declaration of Principle are stated in the Public Policy and Private Action box. The purpose of the new Act in part was to lower the incarceration rate among Canadian youth (which was the highest in the world); to settle more cases outside of court by reintroducing the youth justice committees; to eliminate differences among judges in sentencing; to effectively reintroduce an offender after he or she is released from custody into society; and to differentiate between serious and less serious violent crimes (Department of Justice Canada 2003). Overall, the Act underscores the importance of rehabilitation, believing that treatment will ultimately better serve the individual and the larger community.

■■ Youth Violence and Youth Gangs

Part, but not all, of the problem of youth violence stems from youth gangs. *The proliferation of gangs, along with involvement in drugs and the ready availability of guns, has exacerbated the problem of violent crime by youths* (Howell 1998; Moore and

Terrett 1999). A substantial percentage of youth violence in Canada involves male youth gangs (National Clearinghouse 2003).

Canadians have been increasingly concerned about youth gangs since the early 1990s. Youth gangs are no longer viewed as an urban phenomenon; their presence has also been reported in many smaller communities (Youth Violence 2002:10). That said, the extent of participation in organized crime, or the degree of gang activity, is not known. This is because charges reported in crime statistics are against individuals, not groups. A study by the Federation of Canadian Municipalities (FCM 2002) reported that there is an increasing amount of group-related violence in many Canadian schools. Because the attacks seem to be more vicious and drawn-out, "this pattern suggests an increase in the presence of informal gangs. While not necessarily engaging in violent or criminal activity, these gangs often intimidate other students." (4–5). In recent years, *swarming* (threatening acts of harassment and intimidation or actual violence by a group against one or more persons) has become so common that the Toronto police have claimed there are an average of 6.7 swarmings every day (CBC News Online 2005). Swarming is not necessarily a gang-related activity; many occur spontaneously outside of a gang structure.

One other reason why we do not know the extent of youth gangs in Canada is because there is no uniform definition of what constitutes a youth gang. The media, the public, the government, and police officials all use different definitions. The definition of youth gangs ranges from kids hanging out to groups as small as two people (Totten 1999). The FCM (2002) suggests that youth gang activity should be viewed as a continuum, starting with loosely based friendship groups and ending with highly organized criminal youth gangs. Friendship groups are loosely organized, have no leadership, engage in violence spontaneously, and are generally not interested in crime for profit. Criminal youth gangs, in contrast, are highly organized, have a defined leadership structure in place, are systematically involved in violence, and engage in crime for profit, which often is a major activity (7). According to the FCM, there are very few highly organized youth gangs in Canada (10).

Totten (1999), an Ottawa journalist, also argues that our understanding of the term "youth gang" is not only problematic but also overstates the prevalence of gangs:

> A group of two or more youths, especially if they are black, would appear to warrant the label of gang. Cases in point: the *Citizen*'s headline "Teen to serve 17 months for gang attacks" last Saturday. Apparently swarming a stranger with several other teenagers, irrespective of the seriousness of violence, constitutes a gang activity. Likewise the *Toronto Star*'s conclusion that there are more than 180 youth gangs across greater Toronto is grossly inaccurate. Included in the *Star*'s definition are youths who band together, think up a name, and try to act tough and commit offences ranging from shoplifting to assault to murder.

The following definition of gangs is helpful in clarifying the difference between groups and gangs of youth. Most youths belong to a group of friends, which is a positive, healthy influence upon their social and emotional development. Groups can provide acceptance, identity, self-affirmation, and support young people in their transition from dependent childhood, through the difficult stage of adolescence, into independent adulthood. Fewer than one percent of youth in Canada belong to hard-core criminal youth gangs (Totten 1999).

One reason why youths join gangs is that the conditions that spawn the gangs—poverty, discrimination, and lack of legitimate opportunities—continue to exist throughout the nation. Once gangs appear in an area, they *tend to perpetuate themselves by setting models for each succeeding generation.* They also are perpetuated by a small number of members who stay in the gangs into adulthood and even parenthood.

Youths join gangs for a variety of reasons, among them being the desire to gain status and escape poverty.

Youths tend to join gangs for a variety of reasons, including the desire to gain status and income—two goals that otherwise may be very elusive to those in impoverished areas. There are also gangs in middle-class areas; youths may join them for status or for security against other gangs in their neighbourhood or school. Once in a gang, their rates of drug use and delinquent behaviour tend to rise dramatically (Fagan 1990; Thornberry et al. 1993). Among those involved in criminal behaviour prior to gang membership, then, involvement is even higher while they are members of the gang (Esbensen and Huizinga 1993).

How pervasive is youth violence in Canada? Over the past five years (since 1998–9), youth violent crimes have steadily declined (–3.1 percent). In 2002–3, 48 youth were charged with homicide and 76 with attempted murder, representing fewer than .1 percent of all youth offences. Totten (1999) asks, "[w]hy, then, do the media insist on fanning the flames of the most atypical, albeit serious, form of youth violence?" He blames the media for feeding the public's fear of rising youth crime. This is problematic on two fronts: first, youth violence rates are declining; and second, the vast majority of youth are "generally law-abiding, respectful [and] vibrant."

■■ THE EXTENT OF CRIME

How widespread is crime in Canada? The question is difficult to answer because of certain problems with official statistics. Here, we examine ways to gather data, look at problems with official records, and then draw conclusions about the extent of crime in Canada.

■■ Sources of Data

Records of crime have been made available to the Canadian public since 1962. Police agencies throughout the country are obliged to report criminal incidents "according to a nationally approved set of common crime categories and definitions," to the Canadian Centre for Justice Statistics (CCJS) through the Uniform Crime Reporting (UCR) Survey (Wallace 2003:2).

In contrast to the UCR, the Victimization Survey includes crimes never *officially reported*. The General Social Survey (GSS)—administered every five years, the most recent being 1999—asks Canadians whether they have been victims of crime. Six crime categories are examined: sexual assault, robbery, assault, break and enter, theft of motor vehicle/parts, and vandalism. The survey also includes a series of questions to determine whether spousal abuse (physical or sexual) has occurred.

■■ Problems with Official Records

If you attempt to estimate the crime rate from official records, you encounter a number of problems. First, quite a number of crimes are *undetected*. There are two ways to get an estimate of the amount of undetected crime. One is by asking people whether they have ever committed various crimes. When allowed to respond anonymously, people will often admit to a number of felonies for which they were never convicted as a criminal. The other way is to ask people whether they have been victims of the various crimes and then compare their responses with official records.

Second, according to the 1999 GSS, only 37 percent of crimes are reported to the police; 59 percent are not. More than 70 percent of reports are made by the victim, while the rest are reported by friends, family members, or witnesses to the crime (Besserer and Trainor 2000:10). Although reporting patterns throughout Canada more or less reflect the average of 37 percent, Newfoundland has the lowest reporting rate at 30 percent and Manitoba has the highest at 44 percent. Reporting victimization increases with age: 13 percent of victims between the ages of 15 and 24 reported victimization, compared to 30 percent over age 45. The rate of reporting varies with the type of crime (see figure 4.1), and the reasons for not reporting also vary (see figure 4.2).

Thus, when a crime is not reported to the police or the police do not believe that further criminal investigation is warranted, it goes unrecorded in the crime statistics

FIGURE 4.1   ■ ■ ■

Reporting victimization to police.

Source: Adapted from Statistics Canada, General Social Survey, 1999.

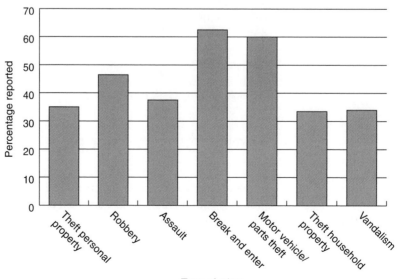

Percentage reported

Type of crime

FIGURE 4.2   ■ ■ ■

Reasons for not
reporting crime to
police.

Source: Statistics Canada, General
Social Survey, 1999.

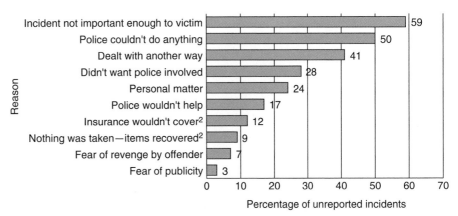

Notes:
[1]Total exceeds 100 percent due to multiple responses. Excludes incidents that were not
classified by crime type and incidents of spousal sexual and physical assault.
[2]Excludes incidents involving sexual assault or a physical attack.

(Besserer and Trainor 2000). Official figures, then, underreport nearly every kind of crime.

Crime reporting is not an objective exercise, as there are many influential factors that may affect crime statistics. They are, according to Wallace (2002:2), "reporting by the public to the police; reporting by police to the CCJS; the impact of new initiatives such as legislation; policies of enforcement practices; and social, economic, and demographic changes." A problem with official records is that *definitions of crime change* and the *methods of reporting crime change*. Because a crime is a violation of the criminal law, any change in the law changes the amount of crime. In the early 1930s a considerable number of inmates in U.S. federal prisons were there for crimes that would not have been crimes a few years earlier. They were serving time for violating laws related to the Prohibition of alcohol.

Another problem with official records involves *police procedures*. Whether or not some behaviour is defined officially by the police as criminal depends on factors other than the behaviour itself. For instance, the police may be caught in political cross-pressures when they decide whether to report offences (Selke and Pepinsky 1982). If they report offences, they may be blamed for failing to stem the rising tide of crime. If they fail to report them, they may be blamed for being unresponsive. There also may be pressure to keep reported offences low in order to make areas more attractive to business, residents, and tourists.

The trend in recent years has been for an overall significant decrease in reporting crime (Besserer and Trainor 2000), particularly theft of personal and household property. The declining reporting rates may be due in part to an increase in the amount deductible for insurance claims. In the early 1990s, $200 was the typical deductible amount; by the end of the decade, most homeowner policies required a $500 deductible (Besserer and Trainor 2000).

These qualifications to the reliability of official records suggest that the amount of crime in the nation is considerably greater than official records indicate. They also suggest that caution must be exercised when comparing rates across time and drawing a quick conclusion that a "crime wave" is in process. However, when official records are used in conjunction with victimization studies and other evidence, the conclusions are more reliable.

Hate Crimes

When a crime happens to an individual because of race/ethnicity, religion, or sexual orientation, it is referred to as a *hate crime*.

Pilot Survey of Hate Crime (2001–2)

Twelve major Canadian police forces reported a total of 928 hate crime incidents during 2001 and 2002. While the majority of these incidents involved one hate motivation, in some cases more than one motivation was recorded. Overall, more than half of these hate crimes (57 percent) were motivated by race or ethnicity. The second most common hate motivation of incidents was religion (43 percent). Sexual orientation was the motivation in about one-tenth of incidents.

Blacks and South Asians were among those most frequently targeted in hate crime incidents motivated by race or ethnicity. The majority of incidents motivated by religion involved anti-Semitism, followed by those targeting Muslims.

The largest single group identified in the pilot survey was Jewish people or institutions. One-quarter of the 928 hate crime incidents reported by the 12 participating police services was anti-Semitic in nature.

The most common types of hate crime violations included mischief or vandalism (29 percent), assault (25 percent), uttering threats (20 percent), and hate propaganda (13 percent). These offence types varied based on the hate crime motivation.

Just over half (53 percent) of hate crimes based on race/ethnicity were against the person, including assault and uttering threats, criminal harassment, and robbery. In the case of anti-religion hate crimes, about two-thirds included acts of vandalism, arson, other property offences, and hate propaganda.

Individuals targeted because of their sexual orientation were more likely than other groups to suffer violent crimes, including assault and uttering threats.

Offence Types Vary Depending on Hate Crime Motive

Types of offences varied according to the nature of the motivation. Hate crimes based on race/ethnicity were most likely to involve physical assaults (29 percent), mischief or vandalism (26 percent), uttering threats (17 percent), and hate propaganda (17 percent).

In the case of anti-religious hate crimes, more than one-third involved acts of mischief or vandalism (36 percent) followed by hate propaganda and uttering threats, where each accounted for 23 percent of incidents.

Individuals targeted because of their sexual orientation were more likely than other hate crime victims to suffer violent crimes. Victims of sexual-

▪▪ The Amount of Crime

What do the data reveal about the amount of crime in Canada? The amount differs depending upon whether you look at UCR or victimization data. According to UCR data, rates of serious crime fluctuate over time; Canada's crime rate since 2000 has been relatively stable, and there has been a noticeable decline since the early 1990s (see figure 4.3). In fact, the rates are similar to those in 1979.

Violent crime rates have been steadily declining since 1999 (see table 4.1). In 2002, the rate declined 2 percent, largely due to the declining rates of robbery and assaults (Wallace 2003). Although most crime rates dropped, there were increases in homicides, frauds, and drug offences (table 4.1). Homicide rates were up,

> driven by a large increase in British Columbia, up from 84 homicides in 2001 to 126 in 2002. Part of this increase is a result of homicide investigations undertaken by the Missing Women's Task Force in Port Coquitlam, B.C., which resulted in 15 homicides being reported by police in 2002. (Wallace 2003:7)

For the ninth year in a row drug crime rates have increased, up 42 percent since 1992. Three-quarters of all drug offences are marijuana-related, and of those, 72 percent are for possession of less than 30 grams (Wallace 2003:1).

orientation hate crimes experienced assaults in 41 percent of incidents, followed by slightly more than one-quarter with mischief or vandalism (27 percent), and uttering threats (14 percent).

Hate Crimes More Likely to Be Reported to Police

Nearly half (45 percent) of self-reported hate crime victimizations were brought to the attention of police, according to the 1999 General Social Survey. Hate-motivated incidents were more likely than non–hate crimes to be reported; only 37 percent of self-reported victimizations in which the victim did not believe the incident was motivated by hate came to the attention of police.

The difference in reporting rates may be partly because of the fact that in almost one-half of all hate crime incidents the perpetrator was a stranger, and victims are more likely to report to police if the offender is not known.

In addition, a greater proportion of hate crimes are violent in nature. The degree of severity of an offence influences whether the victim reports it to police.

The Events of September 11, 2001 Increased Hate Crimes for a Short Period

The 12 police forces that participated in the pilot survey found a short-lived increase in the number of hate crimes reported following the September 11, 2001 terrorist attacks in the United States.

Overall, police associated 15 percent of the hate crimes following the attacks during the pilot survey period with the events of September 11, 2001. Almost three-quarters of these incidents occurred within two months of the attacks.

Police reported 232 hate crimes recorded during these two months, more than three times the level of 67 during the same two-month period in 2000.

Two-thirds (68 percent) of the hate crime incidents police associated with the events were violent in nature, including assault, criminal harassment, and uttering threats. Another 23 percent involved violations against property. Fully 92 percent of acts against property involved vandalism.

The remaining 9 percent of hate crime incidents associated with September 11 involved "other" criminal incidents, such as hate propaganda. Religion and race/ethnicity were almost equally likely to be the target of these offences. About 30 percent of incidents involved Muslims, 27 percent Jewish people, 15 percent Americans, and 13 percent Arabs/West Asians.

SOURCES:
   The Daily, Tuesday, June 1, 2004 (Statistics Canada); *Juristat: Hate Crime in Canada*, Vol. 24, no. 4, 85-002-XIE, 85-002-XPE.

Obtaining information about white-collar crime is difficult, but evidence indicates that such crime is extensive. *Unethical and illegal behaviour abound in business and industry.* According to one estimate, fraud and other employee crimes cost employers more than US$400 billion a year (Gray 1997). Overall, organizations lose about 6 percent of their revenues to fraud and abuse (Gips 1998). The median loss caused by owners and executives is 16 times greater than that caused by rank-and-file employees. Bank employees steal more from banks than do robbers. Businesses are offenders as well as victims, engaging in criminal activity against consumers and customers. Indictments for criminal activity and fines for serious misbehaviour occur regularly among both small businesses and the nation's largest corporations. For statistics on the rate of fraud in Canada, see table 4.2.

Finally, according to statistics, there is an enormous amount of crime as a result of some relatively trivial kinds of behaviour. Youths may be arrested for conduct that would not be defined as criminal on the part of an adult (e.g.,violation of curfew, running away from home, and possession of an alcoholic beverage). Youths also are involved in serious crimes, and rates for some kinds of youth offenders are decreasing. In 2002, there were 5 percent fewer police charges against youth than during the previous years, continuing a decade-long trend of reduced crime. Violent crimes decreased by 2 percent and property crimes by 5 percent, the lowest level in more than 25 years

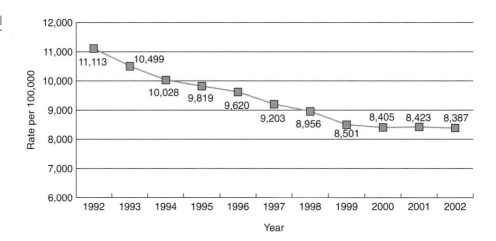

FIGURE 4.3 ▪ ▪ ▪

Total federal statute incidents.

Source: M. Wallace (2003), Canadian Crime Statistics, *Juristat*, Vol. 24, No. 6, Catalogue No. 85-002-XPE-24-06, Statistics Canada.

(Wallace 2003:1). The pattern of youth crime in Canada is different from that in the United States, where crime charges against youth increased throughout the 1990s. In Canada, however, youth are responsible for 16 percent of violent crimes, 26 percent of property crimes, 20 percent of *Criminal Code* crimes (mischief, arson, prostitution, offensive weapons), and 18 percent and 5 percent of marijuana and cocaine offences, respectively. As in the United States, youth crime is gendered: more than three-quarters of all youth charged are male (Statistics Canada 2003). Youth in the U.S., especially males (three-fourths of delinquency cases involve males), commit a disproportionate amount of crime.

▪▪ The Distribution of Crime

Crime is unequally distributed in Canada. There are variations by region, by province, and by population size. One study showed the highest rate of crime in Canada for the fourth consecutive year in Saskatchewan—the only province where crime increased over the past decade—followed by Manitoba (see figure 4.4). Quebec had the lowest rate of crime, and Ontario was close behind. Crime rates were down in all the major cities, with the exception of Edmonton and Ottawa, where crime was up by 5 percent and 3 percent, respectively (Wallace 2003).

Canadian black and First Nations people are overrepresented in the justice system (Carriere 2003; Wortley and McCalla 2003). Aboriginal people (see figure 4.5), who comprise 2 percent of the adult Canadian population, represented 20 percent of populations in provincial and territorial correction facilities, and 17 percent in federal facilities (Carriere 2003). Canadian blacks, who account for 2 percent of the Canadian population, represent 6 percent of the prison population; their custody rate is approximately five times greater than that of whites (Wortley and McCalla 2003). First Nations people were also more likely to be victims of violent and personal crime compared to the general Canadian population (Canadian Centre for Justice Statistics Profile 2001). Compared to other Canadians, visible minorities were less likely to be victims of violent crimes but more likely to be victims of personal crimes and theft (Canadian Centre for Justice Statistics Profile 2001).

▪▪ The Politics of Gun Control

Gun control is a highly controversial subject, with strong arguments on both sides. Let us first examine some data. More than one million Canadians (26 percent) own guns.

	Rate per 100,000					
	1997	1998	1999	2000	2001	2002
All incidents	**9,203.0**	**8,956.0**	**8,500.9**	**8,404.7**	**8,429.5**	**8,386.6**
Crimes of violence	980.0	979.1	954.9	981.1	981.0	965.5
Homicide	2.0	1.8	1.8	1.8	1.8	1.9
Attempted murder	3.0	2.5	2.3	2.5	2.3	2.2
Assaults (level 1 to 3)[1]	734.0	740.3	725.5	759.1	761.7	748.9
Sexual assault	86.0	84.5	78.2	78.0	77.3	77.5
Other sexual offences	12.0	11.4	10.8	10.1	8.6	8.7
Robbery	98.0	95.8	94.2	87.8	87.7	85.0
Property crimes	**4,817.0**	**4,555.3**	**4,260.9**	**4,067.4**	**3,992.0**	**3,959.8**
Breaking and entering	1,233.0	1,160.0	1,043.0	952.7	898.3	875.1
Motor vehicle theft	585.0	548.5	529.0	520.7	541.9	514.1
Theft over $5,000	79.0	78.0	73.7	69.4	67.0	63.3
Theft $5,000 and under	2,503.0	2,359.2	2,223.5	2,153.4	2,120.1	2,128.3
Possession of stolen goods	98.0	96.4	96.1	92.7	86.7	88.6
Frauds	319.0	313.5	296.2	278.6	278.0	290.4
Other *Criminal Code* offences	**2,558.0**	**2,602.1**	**2,509.1**	**2,592.6**	**2,660.5**	**2,664.4**
***Criminal Code* offences (traffic offences)**	513.0	466.7	385.6	365.2	386.5	374.5
Impaired driving	297.0	289.8	281.9	257.3	265.9	257.2
Other traffic offences[3]	215.0	123.5	120.0	119.4	117.6	117.3
Drugs	220.0	234.5	262.7	286.1	287.4	294.7

Source: Canadian Crime Statistics, 2002, *Juristat*, Vol. 23, No. 5, Catalogue No. 85-002-XIE, Statistics Canada.

TABLE 4.1 ▪ ▪ ▪

Crime Rates in Canada, 1997–2002

TABLE 4.2 ▪ ▪ ▪

Rate of Fraud by Province, 2002

Province	Number of Frauds, 2002 (rate per 100,000 population)
Ontario	276.8
Quebec	249.0
Alberta	415.0
B.C.	313.3
Saskatchewan	409.1
Nova Scotia	254.9
New Brunswick	312.4
Manitoba	223.4
Newfoundland and Labrador	207.1
P.E.I.	308.1
Yukon Territory	477.9
Northwest Territories	314.0
Nunavut	303.0
Canada	**290.4**

Source: Canadian Crime Statistics, 2002, *Juristat*, Vol. 23, No. 5, Catalogue No. 85-002-XIE, Statistics Canada.

FIGURE 4.4 ■ ■ ■

Crime incident rate by province, 2002.

Source: Canadian Crime Statistics, 2002, *Juristat*, Vol. 23, No. 5, Catalogue No. 85-002-XIE, Statistics Canada.

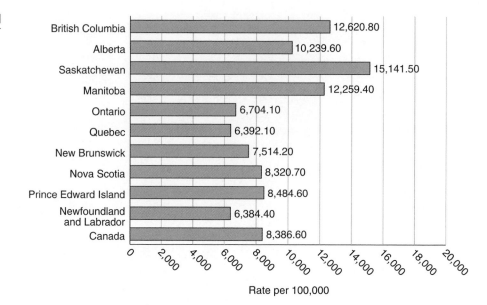

FIGURE 4.5 ■ ■ ■

Aboriginal people in sentenced custody.

Source: Statistics Canada, Canadian Centre for Justice Statistics, Adult Correctional Services Survey, 2001/02.

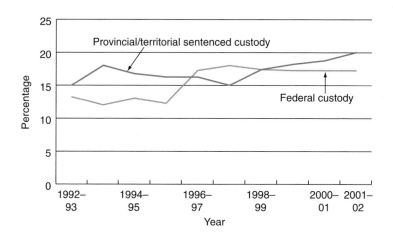

The rates of firearm ownership vary dramatically by province and territory (table 4.3). Gun ownership in the territories (67 percent) is considerably more prevalent than in any province. Approximately 40 percent of Albertans own guns, compared to 15 percent of Ontarians.

The above data vary substantially from those in the United States, where 40 percent of Americans (more than 100 million) have guns (Bureau of Justice Statistics 2001:148–49). Firearm regulations in Canada, at least since the 1930s, have always been tougher than in the United States. In 1995 Parliament passed the *Firearms Act*, and gun ownership became even more restricted: all firearms must be registered into a national information system; semi-automatic and military assault rifles are banned; there are stricter penalties for the misuse of firearms; and there are more controls on the export and import of weapons (Coalition for Gun Control 2001). All Canadian owners of shotguns and hunting rifles must purchase licences (which are subject to eligibility checks), and the weapons must be stored in a locked cabinet, separate from any ammunition. Finally, police have the right to search the homes of people they suspect of owning unlicensed guns (Carter 2000). In summary, gun ownership in Canada "has never

	Nfld	PEI	NS	NB	Que.	Ont.	Man.	Sask.	Alb.	B.C.	Yuk.	NWT	CAN
Firearm suicide*	3.0	3.1	4.8	5.9	4.0	2.2	3.5	4.8	4.7	3.4	8.7	13.3	3.4
Firearm homicide*	0.1	0.0	0.6	0.6	0.9	0.5	0.6	0.5	0.8	0.8	0.8	0.4	0.6
Firearm accidental deaths*	0.5	0.1	0.1	0.3	0.2	0.1	0.4	0.3	0.2	0.2	0.8	1.9	0.2
Total firearm deaths	3.8	3.2	5.7	6.9	5.2	2.7	4.8	5.8	5.8	4.4	11.1	16.6	4.3
% households with firearms	32%	20%	31%	35%	23%	15%	28%	32%	39%	24%	67%	67%	26%

Source: Kwing Hung. Firearm Statistics (Supplementary Tables). Research and Statistics Division, Department of Justice. March 2000 and Angus Reid Survey, 1991 and Coalition for Gun Control (2004). http://www.guncontrol.ca/Content/TheCaseForGunControl.html.

TABLE 4.3 ■ ■ ■

Firearm Deaths and Ownership in Canada, Average 1990–1998 (*Rate per 100,000)

been regarded as a right and several court rulings have reaffirmed the right of the government to protect citizens from guns" (Coalition for Gun Control 2001).

Gun control is supported by the majority of Canadians (70 percent), but support is weaker in the Western provinces (54 percent), where much opposition has been voiced from farmers and rural residents who are more closely impacted by these laws. In fact, in 1996 the Province of Alberta launched a Supreme Court challenge, arguing that the legislation "encroached on provincial jurisdiction" over property and civil rights (CBC 2000). The Supreme Court upheld the gun control law in June 2000. Alberta and the Prairie provinces have refused to enforce gun control, and Albertans continue to actively lobby against gun control through organized groups such as the Law-abiding Unregistered Firearms Association.

The overall effectiveness of Canada's gun control is yet to be determined. That is, does gun control reduce violent crimes? More than one-quarter of all homicides committed in 2002 (figure 4.6) were with a firearm (Savoie 2004). The decreasing trend of firearm homicides in Canada since the 1970s may indeed be due to stricter gun control laws. Figure 4.7 traces both homicides from firearms between 1961 and 2001 and times of legislative changes to gun control laws. These data do indicate a cause-and-effect relationship between gun control and decreased homicide rates. Further, there appears to be a positive relationship between the number of firearm deaths and the percentage of households with firearms (refer to table 4.3). For example, Ontario has the lowest rate of households with firearms (15 percent), and at the same time has the lowest firearm death rate (2.7 per 100,000). Alberta, in contrast, has the highest percentage among provinces of households with firearms (39 percent), and the second highest rate of deaths by firearms (5.8 per 100,000).

Many people insist that the widespread existence of guns does not contribute to the amount of violence in the nation. One argument is that it is people, not guns, that kill; if a gun is not available, a person will find a different weapon. Professionals dispute the relationship between the number of guns and the amount of violence. Some argue that this is a violent society and that violence will not be reduced simply by controlling the sale and possession of guns. As a popular slogan puts it, when guns are outlawed, only outlaws will have guns. This is the *fallacy of appeal to prejudice.* It taps into popular

FIGURE 4.6 ■ ■ ■

Homicide causes of
death, Canada, 2002.

Source: Homicide Survey,
Canadian Centre for Justice
Statistics, Statistics Canada.

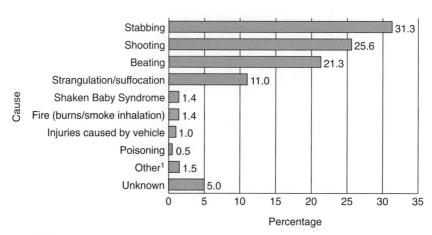

Note: [1]Other includes exposure, hypothermia, and heart attack.

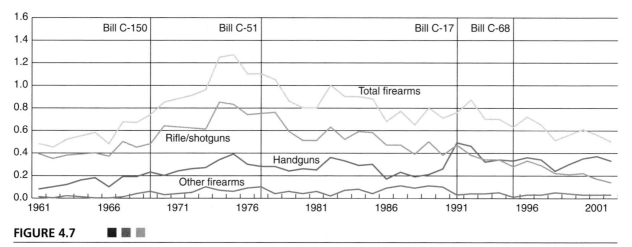

FIGURE 4.7 ■ ■ ■

Rate of firearm homicides, 1961–2002.

Source: Homicide Survey, Canadian Centre for Justice Statistics, Statistics Canada.

passions in this country about citizens' right to defend themselves. However, evidence, not emotional slogans, is needed to make a reasonable decision about the issue.

In the first place, guns are the weapon most frequently used in homicides. Contrary to the argument that killers would simply find alternative weapons, the gun is the deadliest of weapons; the fatality rate for shootings is about five times higher than the rate for stabbings. Moreover, murder frequently is an act of passion that the killer himself or herself might later regret. At least in some cases, without the gun there would be no murder.

Second, guns are the most frequent weapons used in armed robberies. A gun often seems essential for armed robbery, because without it the offender is unable to produce the necessary threat of force. The fatality rate in armed robberies involving guns is about four times as high as the rate involving other weapons.

Some citizens believe firearms are necessary to defend their home. This argument has little substance. Many murders occur in homes, but seldom do they involve strangers. The most frequent kind of offender–victim relationship in homicide in homes is that of husband and wife. There is also the possibility of accidental injury or death because of a gun in the home. Ironically, you may face greater danger from a weapon purchased for defence against intruders than from an actual intruder.

▪▪ THE CRIMINAL JUSTICE PROCESS

To understand the problem of crime in the nation, it is important to know about the criminal justice process. What happens when you report a crime to the police? The path from the reporting to the final settlement is long and complex. Here we can only give you a sketch of the process to illustrate its complexity.

After a crime is reported and police verify that it has indeed been committed, police will try to identify a suspect. Frequently, extensive investigation is required. After investigation, police will decide whether to lay a charge. If they decide to do so, they will make an arrest. Once a charge has been laid, the suspect becomes an "accused." Police may release the accused with a requirement to attend court at a later date or hold the accused for a bail hearing.

If the accused is detained for a bail hearing, he or she must be brought before a Justice without unreasonable delay and within 24 hours or as soon as possible. The Crown may consent to the release of the accused or ask the court to order his or her detention pending trial. Where an accused opposes a Crown request for detention, a bail hearing must be held. Generally, the onus is on the Crown to show why the accused should be kept in custody. An accused may be ordered detained for a number of grounds including concerns that he or she will not attend court, will endanger the safety of witnesses, or very likely will commit other offences if released.

After a charge is laid, the Crown has a constitutional obligation to provide disclosure to the accused. Disclosure includes all of the evidence collected by police in the course of investigating the charges against the accused. At a minimum it will include witness statements and police notebook notes. After the accused has obtained disclosure, a meeting known as a pretrial is generally conducted between Crown counsel and counsel for the accused. The meeting is designed to facilitate plea bargaining in cases where an accused inclines toward a plea of guilty. Alternatively, the pretrial may be used to narrow trial issues and determine the amount of time required for a trial.

Often, an accused will take advantage of plea bargaining and plead guilty. Generally, plea bargaining means that the Crown and defence agree to a lesser offence or, where several charges have been laid, to only one of the original charges. Plea bargaining generally allows the offender to get a lighter sentence, assures the Crown that the offender will not be totally acquitted, and saves everyone the time and expense of a court trial. However, a guilty plea may be rejected by the court if the judge finds that the plea was coerced.

If the case proceeds to trial, the trial may be before a judge or, for very serious charges, before a judge and a jury. If the trial results in conviction, the accused may appeal to a higher court. If no appeal is made, or if the appeals are rejected, the offender must submit to the sentence imposed by the court. A sentence is handed down only after a sentencing hearing, in which the defence may present mitigating circumstances or other evidence to help minimize the severity of the sentence. The median elapsed time from when a case is first heard to its last appearance was 92 days in 2001/2. Offences such as sexual assault and homicide take much longer to resolve; the median elapsed time is more than 200 days (Robinson 2003).

The youth justice system differs in a number of important ways. Yet this explanation outlines the basic process. The system reflects the Canadian belief that the accused is presumed innocent until proven guilty. For more on provincial and federal case processing, see figure 4.8.

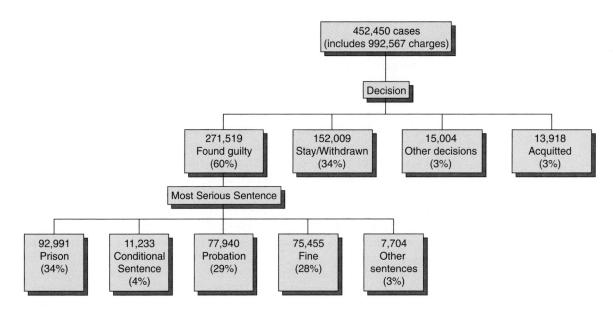

Notes:
Found guilty decisions include absolute and conditional discharges. Stay/Withdrawn includes cases stayed, withdrawn, dismissed and discharges at preliminary inquiry. Other decisions includes final decisions of found not criminally responsible, waived in province/territory, and waived out of province/territory. This category also includes any order where a conviction was not recorded, the court's acceptance of a special plea, cases which raise Charter arguments and cases where the accused was found unfit to stand trial. The sentence was not known in approximately 2% of convicted cases in 2001/02. Conditional sentencing data was not collected in Québec for 2001/02, resulting in an undercount of conditional sentences. Probation totals include mandatory probation for cases given a conditional discharge (approximately 5% of cases with a guilty finding) or a suspended sentence (approximately 10% of cases with a guilty finding). Adult Criminal Court Survey data are not reported by Manitoba, Northwest Territories, and Nunavut.

FIGURE 4.8 ■ ■ ■

Provincial and federal case processing.

Source: Adult Criminal Court Survey, Canadian Centre for Justice Statistics, Statistics Canada.

▪▪ THE COSTS OF CRIME

Crime, by definition, often involves exploitive or violent relationships and thereby diminishes the quality of life by exacting high physical, psychological, and economic costs.

▪▪ Physical and Psychological Costs of Crime

Crime causes physical and psychological suffering. Although it is difficult to measure, there is evidence that this suffering is considerable. Crime affects physical and emotional health, increases fear, and fosters alienation.

trauma
physical or emotional injury

Physical and Mental Health.   The victim of a crime experiences **trauma.** The victim may be temporarily or permanently injured (either physically or emotionally) or even killed. One-quarter of all violent crime victims, and half of rape victims, are injured (Simon, Mercy, and Perkins 2001). Emotional trauma such as anxiety, depression, shame, humiliation, or despair is also likely. As a result, many Canadians who have been victimized receive mental health counselling or therapy every year (Cohen and Miller 1998). Crime victims represent between one-quarter and one-fifth of all clients of mental health care professionals.

White-collar crime also takes its toll on North Americans' physical and mental health. Some people have lost their businesses or life savings because of fraud.

Decisions in Adult Criminal Court

The decision categories in this report are as follows:

- *Guilty* includes guilty of the charged offence, of an included offence, of an attempt of the charged offence, or of an attempt of an included offence. This category also includes cases where an absolute or conditional discharge has been granted.
- *Stay/Withdrawn/Dismissed* includes stay of proceedings, and withdrawn/dismissed/discharged at preliminary inquiry. These decisions all refer to the court stopping criminal proceedings against the accused.
- *Acquittal* means that the accused has been found not guilty of the charges presented before the court.

- *Other decisions* includes final decisions of found not criminally responsible, waived in province/territory, and waived out of province/territory. This category also includes any order where a conviction was not recorded, the court's acceptance of a special plea, cases that raise *Charter* arguments, and cases where the accused was found unfit to stand trial. In jurisdictions not providing superior court data (i.e., Newfoundland and Labrador, Nova Scotia, Quebec, Ontario, Saskatchewan), the "other decision" category includes charges having a committal for trial in superior court as the decision on the final appearance in provincial court.

Consumers have suffered financial and health losses because of corporate practices. For example, the suppression of negative information about the defects and dangers of silicone breast implants resulted in health problems and emotional trauma for many women who had implants (Chapple 1997).

Fear and Its Consequences. Widespread crime can produce pervasive fear in a society. With the falling crime rates since the early 1990s, the fear of crime also diminished. Perceptions of personal safety have steadily increased over the last decade. Still, 31 percent of adult Canadians describe themselves as fearful. Not surprisingly, substantially more women (41 percent) than men (12 percent) report fear. There are also geographical differences in fear; the Atlantic provinces have the lowest rates while British Columbia has the highest; 14 percent and 39 percent, respectively. Generally, however, the majority of Canadians feel safe in their neighbourhoods (Roberts 2001:1). Because they fear being victimized, some people will abstain from what they would otherwise like to do (Keane 1998). The fear generated by crime means that everyone loses—victims, people who are afraid they might be victims, and residents and businesspeople in high-crime areas.

Alienation. Sutherland (1968) argued that white-collar crime has a psychological impact that cannot be measured in monetary terms alone. He pointed out that such crimes create an atmosphere of distrust in a society, lowering social morale and creating widespread social disorganization. People become cynical about social institutions (illustrated by the common belief that all politicians are crooked), and there is a tendency to develop a social Darwinist approach to life ("It's a dog-eat-dog world and you have to look out for yourself above all else"). In a sense, then, white-collar crime may be more damaging to a society than predatory crime. It indicates that the whole society is corrupt—that fraud, theft, and exploitation pervade the panelled offices of professionals as well as the littered streets of the slums. White-collar crime, thus, produces a pervasive sense of distrust and **alienation** and suggests that the society is sick.

alienation
a sense of estrangement from one's social environment, typically measured by one's feelings of powerlessness, normlessness, isolation, meaninglessness, and self-estrangement

■■ Economic Costs of Crime

A great many factors must be taken into account when we try to assess the economic losses due to crime. These factors include the personal loss of property; expense of insurance; cost of loan sharks, false advertising, and shoddy workmanship on consumer goods; work absences and lost wages resulting from physical and emotional trauma; medical cost for treating injuries; cost of maintaining security systems and other crime-prevention measures; and cost of maintaining the criminal justice system. The criminal justice system alone (including local, provincial, and federal levels of government) costs more than $100 billion per year. Allowing one youth to leave high school for a life of crime and drug abuse costs society from US$1.7 to US$2.3 million over that person's lifetime (Snyder and Sickmund 1999:82). Losses of victims add tens of billions more to the total cost.

Some costs cannot even be measured. Consumers pay higher prices because of organized crime's involvement in legitimate business and because of business losses from crimes (including employee theft). Shoplifting adds to the cost of retail items. Many crimes of fraud, embezzlement, and arson-for-profit are never detected. Some crimes go unreported because the victims are afraid (blackmail or retaliation), embarrassed (con games), or involved in illegal activity (gambling).

When the costs are added, including direct losses due to personal and household crime and the cost of maintaining the criminal justice system, crime costs billions of dollars every year.

▪▪ CONTRIBUTING FACTORS

Like crime itself, the factors that generate and sustain crime involve both respectable and nonrespectable elements of society.

Social Structural Factors

Age Structure of the Population.
As noted earlier, crime has decreased over the last decade. This trend is similar in the United States and Britain. One possible explanation is that there is an inverse relationship between crime and age; the older the population the less crime there is. Crime historically is more prevalent among young persons ages 15 to 24 than any other age group. In 2002, for example, young persons between 15 and 24 years (13 percent of the population) accounted for 46 percent of property crime and 31 percent of violent crime charges (see figure 4.9) (Wallace 2003). With age, crime rates drop dramatically. In fact, Canada's population is aging; that is, there are proportionately fewer persons in the high-crime-risk age group. Thus, an aging population may explain the trend for lower crime rates.

But age can not fully explain decreasing crime rates, because crime is decreasing at a faster rate than the population is aging (Gartner and Dawson 2003:506). There may be a number of factors that play a role in crime rates. One other explanation is that lower unemployment rates and changes in collective values may influence declining crime rates (Ouimet 2002 in Gartner and Dawson 2003).

Hot Spots.
Cohen and Felson (1979) developed a "routine activities" approach to crime. Rather than the characteristics of offenders, they focused on circumstances. In particular, they emphasized the importance of *likely offenders, suitable targets,* and *a lack of capable guardians* occurring at a particular place and time. "Capable guardians" can include anything from the presence of police to alarm systems. The convergence, or lack of convergence, of these three factors can explain changing crime rates, and why certain areas become "hot spots," or locales of high crime rates (Weisburd and Mazerolle 2000).

Van Koppen and Jansen (1999) used this approach to explain daily, weekly, and seasonal variations in robbery rates. Robbers' expectations of the amount of money available at a particular time and place comprise the suitable target, while the increased number of dark hours during the winter means less adequate guardianship. Bryjak

Rate per 100,000 population

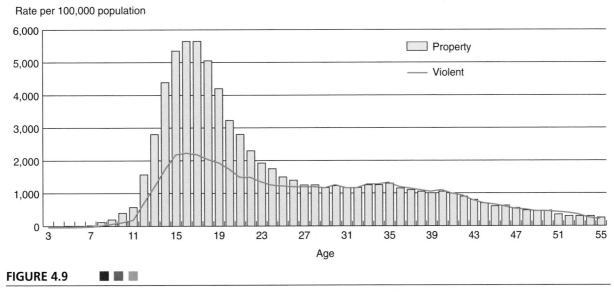

FIGURE 4.9 ■ ■ ■

Age-specific rates of persons accused of violent and property crimes, 2002.

Source: Incident-Based Uniformed Crime Reporting Survey, CCJS.

(1999) explained the drop in burglary rates in the 1990s in terms of increased guardianship of suitable targets; namely, the fact that more people are spending time in their homes because of personal computers, cable television, VCRs, and video games.

Other research, covering 52 nations over a 25-year period, suggests that this approach may apply more to property crime than to personal crime (Bennett 1991). At any rate, the convergence of offenders, suitable targets, and inadequate guardianship helps explain a certain amount of crime. It follows that changing any one of the three factors may alter crime rates. For example, convenience stores are targets for robbery. Some local governments have passed ordinances requiring convenience stores to have at least two clerks on duty at all times. These additional clerks may reduce the amount of armed robbery by increasing the number of capable guardians.

differential association theory
the theory that illegal behaviour is due to a preponderance of definitions favourable to such behaviour

Norms. The **differential association theory** of criminal behaviour was developed by Sutherland (1947) to identify those conditions that cause crime. The theory states that most criminal behaviour is learned from interactions with intimate social groups (family, friends) and the prevailing values or norms of the group. What this means is that if the values of a peer group sanction criminal behaviour, there is a strong likelihood that the group members will engage in criminal behaviour. In other words, deviance is viewed as socialization. Sutherland recognized that crime is overrepresented in communities where minorities and poor people live. He points out that not everyone engages in criminal behaviour; most individuals respect the law. At the same time, there are wealthy and powerful people who engage in criminal behaviour. Certain practices in business and industry may be justified on the basis that everyone does them, that they are necessary for continuing one's enterprise, or that they are acceptable by those in authority. News accounts have reported corporate executives justifying illegal behaviour on the grounds that their competitors engaged in the behaviour; so, if they did not, they would lose business and profits.

Sutherland's theory underscores that social influences and learning experiences (depending on frequency, duration, priority, and intensity) are powerful factors in determining criminal behaviour. In general, Sutherland's theory is designed only to understand the individual, irrespective of economic or ethno-racial background.

The Politics of Control: The Prison.

How should society respond to crime? The nature of the response is a political decision. There are alternative ways of dealing with criminals (see the Global Comparison box). Some people believe that **rehabilitation** should be the focus of the criminal justice system, while others believe criminals should be put into prisons for *punishment* and *isolation from society*. Still others believe that rehabilitation should be combined with the punishment of imprisonment. To address the issue, we examine what happens in the nation's prisons and jails. (A jail is a locally administered institution that has authority to retain adults for 48 hours or longer. A prison is a provincially or federally administered facility for correction only.)

Not all prisoners have *access to rehabilitation programs.* This is particularly true in the nation's jails, where only a fraction of the total jail population have access to any programs other than religious services. The need for programs of support and rehabilitation is underscored by the fact that the *suicide rate in jails is far higher than that in prisons and in the larger society* (Snell 1995). On the average, a prisoner stays in jail about 17 days, though some may remain for a year or more because of the shortage of prison space. The prisoner, who may be frightened, confused, or emotionally disturbed, has no one to talk with except other prisoners.

Among those jails that do have rehabilitation programs, basic adult education is the most common, followed by vocational training. Only the larger jails (those with 250 or more inmates) are likely to have such programs.

The *nature of prison life* also makes rehabilitation unlikely. In fact, *longer time spent in prison can increase the likelihood of* **recidivism** (repeated criminal activity and incarceration) (Orsagh and Chen 1988). For one thing, jails and prisons are *seriously overcrowded* (Gilliard 1999). For example, a man awaiting trial for car theft spent seven months in a Toronto jail. The conditions were substandard, raising many health, safety, and human rights concerns (John Howard Society of Toronto 2002:1); for example, three inmates shared a cell (4 by 2.5 metres) that was originally designed to house one person. Typically, they were restricted to their cells for 12 to 14 hours a day.

Conditions in provincial prisons are not better. During 2001–2, the Ontario Ombudsman received 7,697 complaints by prisoners "related to: staff conduct, health (adequacy, medications delay) and living conditions (food and diet, clothing size and condition, cleanliness, hygiene and sanitation, heating, ventilation and air, overcrowding and lockup" (John Howard Society 2002:2). Such conditions are *stressful* and make any efforts at rehabilitation difficult.

Far from serving as a deterrent to further crime or as a place of rehabilitation, the jail or prison at best keeps criminals away from the public for a period of time. At worst, the prison becomes a *training ground* for making criminals more competent and more committed to a life of crime. If the abnormal circumstances of the prison, including extended, close association with hardened offenders, does not ensure continued criminal behaviour, the stigma of having been in prison probably will. The prison itself is a *dehumanizing institution,* and those who enter it are unlikely to escape being brutalized, hardened, and better trained in criminal behaviour. Moreover, the *culture of prisons may be getting worse.* Interviews with a sample of California ex-prisoners suggest that prison life has become more volatile, more unpredictable, and more dangerous (Hunt et al. 1993). The respondents talked about newly formed gangs that continue gang activities prisoners engaged in before imprisonment. The number of gangs has increased, pitting inmates of the same race and ethnic background against each other. The ex-prisoners also saw more recent prisoners as being more violent and indifferent to existing prison culture.

Normal behaviour and feelings are impossible in prison. The prison is a **total institution,** a place where the totality of the individual's existence is controlled by various

rehabilitation
resocializing a criminal and returning him or her to full participation in society

recidivism
repeated criminal activity and incarceration

total institution
a place in which the totality of the individual's existence is controlled by external forces

ALTERNATIVES TO IMPRISONMENT: GERMANY AND ISRAEL

Would alternatives to imprisonment be beneficial for both the criminal and society? The fact that the United States has a higher proportion of its population in jails and prisons than any other country in the world does not mean that the nation also has higher crime rates or more effective policing (which would catch greater numbers of criminals). The high incarceration rate reflects the American societal attitude that criminals should be removed from society and punished. Evidence from Germany and Israel suggests otherwise.

German courts make use of suspensions, probation, fines, and community service. Judges have lifetime appointments and sole authority to sentence offenders who are 18 to 20 years old. "Hard-line" judges continue to use imprisonment, while liberal judges try to use alternatives. Researchers found that those sent to prison had higher rates of recidivism than those given alternative sanctions. Even if the imprisonment included job training, offenders had a harder time getting a job after release than those who had an alternative sanction. A study of regions reported the proportion of offenders increased over a period of four years by 7 percent where imprisonment was the norm, and fell by 13 percent where alternative sanctions were the norm.

In Israel, the Kibbutz Resocialization Program is an effort to put offenders into a close-knit society that will change them into respectable citizens. The offenders are placed with an adoptive family, put into a cohesive work group, and expected to become productive members of the kibbutz.

A study of 27 long-term offenders assigned to a kibbutz found that, three years after being assigned, three-quarters of them had no additional criminal activity: nine were working full-time, five served in the army, five were engaged or married, and eight remained in the kibbutz as members.

Thus, programs in both nations offer evidence that alternatives to imprisonment may be a more effective way to deal with some kinds of criminals. If the goal is to rehabilitate, alternatives may work better than imprisonment.

SOURCES
National Institute of Justice 1996a; Fischer and Geiger 1996.

---

external forces. Those who enter the maximum security prison are immediately deprived of valuable things: freedom, goods and services, heterosexual relationships, autonomy, and security (from attacks of other prisoners). Moreover, they are in place with a high proportion of disturbed individuals: from 10 to 15 percent of jail and prison inmates have severe mental illness (Lamb and Weinberger 1998). The constraints of prison life are so severe that an individual must focus on survival rather than personal development or change.

The combination of the inmate code and the demands of the authorities virtually eliminates any possibility of individual growth or personal lifestyle. There is a popular notion that "stone walls do not a prison make," and that even in a cell the individual's mind is free to roam and explore; but only a rare individual can transcend the forces that impinge upon him or her and thereby avoid the dehumanization of the prison.

dehumanization
the process by which an individual is deprived of the qualities or traits of a human being

The *inmate code* contributes to the **dehumanization.** The code requires that an inmate must never report infractions of rules by another inmate and must never notice anything. For example, an inmate walking down a prison corridor saw a fellow inmate lying on the floor, bleeding. He had an impulse to help the man on the floor but went to his cell instead. Other inmates who discussed the incident with the prison psychiatrist agreed with the behaviour. They pointed out that if the man had called a guard, the guard would have suspected him of having struck the man on the floor or would have intensely questioned him. Further, any other inmate who saw him call the guard would have accused him of "snitching." Had he stopped to help the fallen man, he might have been beaten by the man's attacker. Also, to personally help would suggest a homosexual relationship between the two inmates.

CODDLING CRIMINALS

Many Canadians believe that one way to deal with the problem of crime is to stop "coddling" criminals. Actually, it is true that some criminals are coddled. Consider, for example, the following cases:

Item: The portfolio manager of two mutual funds cheated investors out of almost $10 million. He was sentenced to six months in prison and put on five years' probation.

Item: A manufacturer of drugs watered down an antidote for poisoned children with a useless substance. He was given one year's probation and a $10,000 fine.

Item: A methane gas explosion in a coal mine in Westray, Nova Scotia caused the deaths of 26 miners. The mine was managed by a private company that did not comply with the necessary health and safety procedures. Although the mine managers were charged with criminal negligence and manslaughter, the Crown eventually stayed the proceeding.

These are just a few examples of the numerous white-collar crimes in which the offenders received very light punishment.

In this chapter we have stressed the seriousness of white-collar crime. How aware are the people in your area of the extent and corrosiveness of this crime? For one week, note any articles in your local newspaper that talk about crime. Assuming that the newspaper gave an accurate picture of the problem of crime in your area, how much and what kind of a crime problem exists? Do you think your paper is sensitive to the significance of white-collar crime? Make a list of various crimes, including street crimes and white-collar crimes (Al Eagleson and Conrad Black are two examples of public figures in Canada who have committed white-collar crimes that have been extensively covered by the media). Ask some people in your community to rank them by seriousness, and ask them why they ranked them as they did. How do they feel about the different kinds of crime?

Finally, to survive in such an inhuman context, inmates practise and hone the same skills they used in their criminal careers. The most likely outcome of a prison sentence, then, is an improvement of criminal skills and thus the high probability of a continued criminal career and an eventual return to prison.

The Family Background of Offenders.   Because the *family plays a significant role in the socialization of children,* much attention is focused on family background to discover why young people become delinquents. Many family factors have been associated with criminal behaviour, but the most important is the *quality of the relationships between parents and children.*

Rates of delinquency are higher among youths in abusive, troubled, or disrupted families (Kobayashi et al. 1995; Ge, Donnellan, and Wenk 2001; Scaramella et al. 2002). When there are poor relationships among family members, parental moral and emotional authority is weakened. The diminished authority tends to weaken children's bonds to the social order and increases the likelihood of criminal behaviour (Browning and Loeber 1999).

Virtually all criminal careers (other than white-collar crime) begin before the age of 18. A large number of those who engage in serious criminal behaviour will continue their criminal activities as adults. In a follow-up study of 99 formerly incarcerated persons, researchers found that 89 had adult criminal records (Lewis et al. 1989). The average number of their offences as adults was 11.6.

Social Stratification and Crime.   Crime and delinquency are related to the social stratification system in three ways: (1) The kind of behaviour considered criminal is defined by those who have power within the system. (2) The type of crime com-

Prison life is dehumanizing and frequently violent.

mitted varies by socioeconomic position. (3) Disproportionate numbers of persons charged with criminal offences come from lower socioeconomic backgrounds.

Behaviour of people who are poor and powerless is more likely to be defined as criminal compared to similar behaviour of people with power and money. This is true especially when the behaviour involves monetary exploitation. A corporate executive might support the definition of employee theft as criminal but would not define false advertising and exploitation of consumers as theft or crime. A physician might deplore abuses of the welfare system, labelling them criminal fraud, but think little about prescribing expensive brand-name drugs rather than less expensive generic counterparts because, in part, his or her retirement plan rests on investments in the pharmaceutical industry, or prescribing laboratory tests that are not necessary. In both cases, those who influence the defining process are the *holders or wielders of power in society,* and they *do not define their own behaviour as criminal.*

The second way in which social stratification and crime intersect involves the kinds of crime committed. Whereas crime and delinquency is often associated with poorer people, white-collar crime is largely coupled with wealth—Martha Stewart, who served a prison sentence for insider trading on the New York Stock Exchange, is a recent example.

Delinquency, violence, and property crime are, and always have been, more characteristic of those struggling to survive the deprivations of a seriously unequal society. A study of youths concluded that hunger leads to theft of food, problems of hunger and shelter result in serious theft, and problems of unemployment and shelter foster prostitution (McCarthy and Hagan 1992). Basically, the more impoverished an area and the fewer opportunities there are for dealing with economic deprivation, the higher the rates of crime (Hannon and Defronzo 1998, Shihadch and Ousey 1998; Lee and Ousey 2001).

Thus, the third way the stratification system is related to crime is in the disproportionate number of criminals who come from the lower socioeconomic strata (Thornberry and Farnworth 1982). Poor people, and in particular black Canadians and First Nations persons, are overrepresented in the criminal justice system (see table 4.4). How are race and crime connected? One explanation is that a disproportionate number of blacks and First Nations persons come from dysfunctional families, and confront high rates of unemployment and poverty (La Prairie 1996; Satzewich 1998)—factors that predict greater participation in crime. While poverty is a factor, it provides only a partial explanation. One other explanation may be that the criminal justice system discriminates against visible minorities: they are more closely scrutinized by police, they have more hostile relationships with police, they are held overnight awaiting bail more often, and they have more difficulty getting bail thus spending longer periods in detention while awaiting trial (Rankin et al. 2003). Consequently, they have a greater likelihood of being convicted and placed in custody (Gartner and Dawson 2003:1). Further, relatively more black drivers receive tickets following a traffic stop: "civil libertarians, community leaders, and criminologists suggest police use racial profiling in deciding whom to pull over" (Rankin et al. 2003). **Racial profiling**, according to the Ontario Human Rights Commission (OHRC), includes "any action undertaken for reasons of safety, security or public pro-

racial profiling
police targeting racialized groups

LEGALIZING MARIJUANA?

Recall from chapter 3 that in the early part of the 1900s the use of marijuana and other opiates was not a criminal offence. More than 70 percent of Canadians now believe that marijuana should be legalized. Marijuana is neither addictive nor harmful when used occasionally. Further, others have argued that the legalization of marijuana can financially benefit the state: "If we treat marijuana like any other commodity we can tax it, regulate it, and use the resources the industry generates rather than continue a war against consumption and production that has long since been lost" (Easton 2004; reported on CTV.ca). In the meantime, drug offence rates continue to increase: in 2002 three-quarters of all drug offences involved marijuana; of these, 72 percent were for possession of less than 30 grams (Wallace 2004).

Write an informed letter to your member of Parliament either recommending or opposing the legalization of marijuana. Your letter should include arguments regarding the costs and benefits of legalization and what effect it would have on crime rates in Canada.

tection that relies on stereotypes about race, colour, ethnicity, ancestry, religion, or place of origin rather than on reasonable suspicion, to single out an individual for greater scrutiny or different treatment" (Human Rights Commission 2003:6). Thus, a police officer may—consciously or unconsciously—assume that a black Canadian or First Nations person is more likely to engage in a criminal offence (see box 4.1). Racial profiling in itself may lead to crime. One lawyer who wrote to the OHRC Inquiry describes this potential vicious circle (2003:28):

> I cannot count the number of times when young Black clients have said to me in frustration, 'If the police are going to arrest me anyway (when I haven't done anything wrong), I might as well do something bad, so least I would deserve it.' This is a most insidious damage being wreaked on our youth by racial profiling. It perpetuates a cycle whereby youths lose respect for the law; this in turn leads a small number of them to act out.

In fact, youth themselves who testified for the inquiry reported feelings of impotence, powerlessness, helplessness, and emasculation after having contact with the police. Note that not all individuals who have a run-in with police pursue a life of crime—most don't. But they are left with low self-esteem, which in turn can adversely affect many future education and career choices.

Offence Categories	% Black Offenders	% Blacks in Population	Ratio of Black Offenders/ Black Population	% White Offenders	% Whites in Population	Ratio of White Offenders/ White Population
Out-of-sight traffic charges	34.30	8.10	4.24	51.80	62.70	0.83
Drug possession	24.30	8.10	3.00	63.30	62.70	1.01
Cocaine possession	29.60	8.10	3.65	61.20	62.70	0.98
Prostitution	11.90	8.10	1.50	68.10	62.70	1.09
Impaired driving	7.00	8.10	0.86	73.60	62.70	1.17

Source: Wortley S., and Tanner, J. (2003) "Data, Denials, and Confusion: The Racial Profiling Debate in Toronto." *Canadian Journal of Criminology and Criminal Justice*, 45(3), pp. 367–388.

TABLE 4.4 ■ ■ ■

Selected Arrest Statistics for All Police Divisions (Toronto 2002), by Race of Offenders

In sum, *the powerless are more likely to be defined as criminals throughout the criminal justice system.* They are more likely to be suspects and more likely to be arrested. The criminal justice system does not treat equally people who commit the same kinds of crime; those in the lower strata are treated more severely.

■■ From Social Problems to Solutions

In this chapter we have posited theories that explain crime rates. Now we can suggest some strategies that may reduce crime rates. For example, whatever ameliorates economic deprivation reduces crime rates (Hannon and Defronzo 1998; Rosenfeld 2002). Finding employment for older offenders reduces recidivism (Uggen 2000). Prevention programs that help youths by fostering a healthy family life, making communities safe, encouraging the young to stay in school, and developing skills and healthy lifestyle choices can reduce the number who begin a life of crime (Coolbaugh and Hansel 2000). In addition, a variety of other programs hold promise; but first we examine the issue of punishment versus rehabilitation.

Will crime be reduced by punishing or by rehabilitating criminals? Should criminals be required to reimburse their victims? Are criminals themselves victims, people who can be rehabilitated with the proper methods, or are their offences unjustified acts that demand punishment? Can you trust a criminal to become a law-abiding citizen again? Such questions are behind the various solutions proposed for the problem of crime.

For many centuries the societal reaction to crime was simply one of punishment in order to deter others who might consider the same acts. Now more people advocate *rehabilitation instead of punishment.* In this view, the criminal has the same potential as anyone else to become a law-abiding citizen and should be given the opportunity to do so. Even if this is true, some would argue that *criminals should make restitution* to their victims, and in recent years some courts have required offenders to do so. Usually the restitution is a cash payment large enough to offset the loss, and the payment may be reduced to fit the earning capacity of the offender. But what kind of payment can be made to compensate for emotional trauma? Sometimes services that benefit the victim directly or indirectly also may be required or substituted for the cash payment.

Box 4.1

Social Stratification of First Nations People

The following quotation is a good example of the type of [First Nations] story that the Commission heard during the inquiry (Ontario Human Right Commission Inquiry 2003: 57).

There was three of us, and we decided we were going to walk to the park just over here and go and sit down on the park bench. And the park was full of people.... It was warm, it was nice. And as I walked into the park, there was a policeman and a policewoman, and the policeman came up to greet us and he asked me for my ID. And I just said to him, 'Is there a reason why you want my ID?' And he said, 'Well, we have to check everybody's ID.' I don't know what he said, but I said, 'Why don't you ask that woman over there? Have you asked that woman over there for her ID? ... If you give me a good reason to give you my ID, then you know, I could do that for you. But until you do that, I can't do that for you. ... Why didn't you ask those other women over there?' He said, 'Well, we are trying to establish good community relations.' That was his answer to me. And that was it.

Those who advocate rehabilitation face the problem of the offender's *reintegration* into the community. How can offenders be reintegrated into society? Since many offenders got in trouble because of the environment in which they lived, reintegration requires community resources such as vocational counselling and employment to restructure the offender's life. The goal is to help the offender find a legitimate role in the community. Halfway houses and work-release programs are two ways of trying to achieve this aim.

In recent decades, pressures have mounted for a *get-tough* policy—of more and longer prison terms. Canada's crime rate has been steadily decreasing since 1994–5 (down 13 percent). That said, in 2000 Canada had the fourth highest incarceration rate (118 per 100,000) among Western countries; only the United States, New Zealand, and England are higher (Carriere 2003). It should be noted that these countries score high on the human poverty index for industrialized countries, which means a very high level of poverty.

Parliament abolished the death penalty in Canada in 1976, by a narrow vote. Historically Canadians have supported the death penalty, but this trend is beginning to change. Whereas in 1973, 73 percent of Canadians supported the death penalty, its popularity has been steadily declining—to 69 percent in 1987, and 53 percent in 2001 (Ipsos-Reid/Globe and Mail/CTV Poll 2001). The shift in public opinion away from support for the death penalty is explained by the exoneration—due to new DNA testing evidence—of Donald Marshall, David Milgaard, and Guy Paul Morin, all innocent men who were falsely accused of murder and consequently spent many years in prison. As such, there has been much publicity surrounding wrongful convictions in both Canada and the United States.

From the criminal justice point of view, is capital punishment an effective deterrent for murder? Experts disagree. Stack (1990) found a 17.5-percent drop in homicide rates in South Carolina in months with publicized executions. In contrast, Bailey (1990) examined national monthly rates over a 12-year period. He found no drop in homicide rates in months with nationally publicized executions. Sorenson, Wrinkle, Brewer, and Marquart (1999) found no evidence of deterrence in Texas (the most active execution state in recent times) from 1984 through 1997. A *New York Times* survey reported no higher rates of homicide between states with and without capital punishment (Bonner and Fessenden 2000).

In Canada, the abolition of capital punishment is viewed as a "principle of fundamental justice" (Department of Justice Canada 2003). On the international front, Canada has been vocal in denouncing the death penalty as a method of punishment. Further, Canada will not extradite an individual who committed a capital offence without assurance that there will be no death penalty.

Thus, two questions linger: 1) how can we reduce crime, and 2) how can we revamp the Canadian criminal justice system? We can not reasonably answer these questions apart from the larger social context. Indeed, efforts must be made, through reform of prisons or through innovative alternatives, to establish effective rehabilitation programs such as prison-based vocational education programs and drug treatment (Sherman et al. 1998). More effective rehabilitation programs hopefully will effect change in others and help them to live socially useful lives. Such solutions may be a way forward for individuals in the correction system. But according to the theory of differential association discussed earlier, the peer environment that offenders face daily would reinforce a criminal mindset. In this light, rehabilitation within a prison framework becomes unfeasible (Macionis et al. 2002). The question that needs to be asked now is this: With the exception of dangerous offenders, is incarceration a reasonable solution? On a somewhat different note, public policy should focus on ways to prevent incarceration in the first place.

Some solutions to the present system, including some that are popular with citizens and law-enforcement officials, are ineffective in reducing crime. In a comprehensive study of crime-prevention programs, researchers concluded that the following are among the programs that do not lower crime: gun "buyback" programs, drug prevention classes that focus on fear or on building self-esteem, increased arrests or raids on drug market locations, correctional boot camps using military basic training, "Scared Straight" programs in which juvenile offenders visit adult prisons, intensive supervision on parole or probation, and community mobilization against crime in high-crime poverty areas (Sherman et al. 1998).

According to Allen Benson, director of a Native healing centre, "there is an attitude within our society that influences government to punish, to police, but not to prevent. There are prevention dollars, but they've put this bureaucratic structure in place that has this philosophy that crime prevention can only occur in partnership with the police." His solution is to train "good community workers, working with Elders to set up opportunities for healing work within the community, solid recreation ... to get young people involved in developing a healthy lifestyle, role models, leadership camps. All these things have proven to have an impact, a positive impact, yet there are limited resources" (Hutchinson 2001). Yet, "the average inmate costs Canadian taxpayers $68,000 a year. Currently there are approximately 4,500 Aboriginal offenders in the federal system, costing taxpayers an estimated $306,000,000 per year" (Hutchinson 2001).

Fighting crime is fighting poverty. To this end, programs must include subsidies for decent housing, healthy food, clothing, accessible daycare, neighbourhood groups, education, and employment opportunities. Finally, recall that crime is disproportionately distributed among visible minorities, specifically First Nations persons and black Canadians. To this end, social policies need to be implemented that will address racial profiling in the criminal justice system.

An important public-policy effort involves *compensation to the victims*. Compensation to victims is provided by governments to prevent a double victimization—once by the offender and again by the criminal justice system. Some problems faced by the victim of a crime include a lack of transportation to court, difficulty in retrieving stolen property from the police, threats by defendants if the victim testifies, and the amount of time consumed by the various procedures in the criminal justice system. A compensation program can counterbalance for some of these losses incurred by the victims.

Most provinces now have compensation programs to help the victims of violent crime; to be eligible, the crime must be reported to the police. Awards vary from small amounts to tens of thousands of dollars. The compensation programs provide for the recovery of medical expenses, lost earnings, and pain and suffering.

▪▪ SUMMARY

Crime is one of the problems about which Canadians are very concerned. Technically, crime is any violation of the *Criminal Code*. Therefore, the acts defined by law as crime vary over time. The *Criminal Code* classifies crime into three broad categories: violent crime, property crime, and "other *Criminal Code*." Computer crime may be either predatory or illegal service, while white-collar crime is primarily predatory. Organized crime involves groups of people in an ongoing organization who provide illegal goods and services and who use predatory crime and political corruption to maintain their activities. Youth gangs may get involved in a range of criminal activities, from predatory crime to illegal goods and services.

Crime is widespread, as measured by various indexes—official records or victimization surveys. It is estimated that approximately 60 percent of crimes are not reported to the police. Break and enter offences are more often reported than are crimes of assault. Crime rates have been steadily decreasing since the 1990s. Crime is not uniformly distributed, however: the likelihood of being a victim depends on the kind of crime, where the person lives, and his or her sex, race, age, education, and income.

Crime diminishes the quality of life and exacts physical, psychological, and economic costs. Crime threatens physical and mental health. It generates fear, which restricts people's activities. White-collar crime can lead to pervasive cynicism and alienation. Crime costs the nation billions of dollars yearly, and the costs are increasing because the amount of crime is increasing.

Norms are an important sociocultural factor contributing to the problem of crime and delinquency because they encourage members of certain groups to engage in criminal behaviour. In particular, norms that are counter to the law have developed among lower-class youths and groups of businesspeople and professionals.

The political aspects of crime control contribute to the problem, especially through the nation's prison system. Prisons make rehabilitation unlikely because they tend to dehumanize offenders, remove them further from noncriminal social control, and make them more competent in criminal activity.

Gun control seems to be an effective measure in reducing homicide rates. Even though there is vocal opposition to gun control in the Western provinces, the majority of Canadians (70 percent) support the government's stance on gun control.

The family may be a factor in crime. A disproportionate number of "criminals" come from families with poor relationships between parents and children or from broken homes. Adult offenders are likely to have had troubled family backgrounds.

The stratification system also relates to crime. Monetary exploitation of others is more likely to be defined as crime among lower-class people than among middle- and upper-class people. The lower class has a greater proportion of violent crime and delinquency, while middle and upper classes have more white-collar crime. A lower-class individual is more likely to be defined as a criminal by the processes of the criminal justice system. Finally, visible minorities have more encounters with the criminal system because of racial profiling by the police.

▪▪ KEY TERMS

Alienation 111	Differential Association	Racial Profiling 117	Total Institution 114
Dehumanization 115	Theory 113	Recidivism 114	Trauma 110
	Organized Crime 95	Rehabilitation 114	White-collar Crime 93

▪▪ STUDY QUESTIONS

1. Define and describe the various types of crime.

2. What are the problems in obtaining accurate data on the amount of crime?

3. How much crime is there in Canada, and where is a person most likely to be a victim?

4. How does crime affect physical and psychological well-being?

5. What is the cost of crime in economic terms?

6. How is the amount of crime affected by the age structure of the population?

7. What is the role of norms in criminal activity?

8. How do prisons help or worsen the problem of crime?

9. In what ways do the family and the social stratification system contribute to the problem of crime?

10. What is racial profiling?

11. What can be done to reduce crime?

12. Do you think that non-dangerous offenders should be punished by going to prison? Based on your answer, design the "perfect" punishment.

▪▪ FOR FURTHER READING

Benson, Michael L., and Francis T. Cullen. *Combating Corporate Crime*. Boston: Northeastern University Press, 1998. A U.S.-based study of what prosecutors are doing about corporate crime in local jurisdictions, including the influence of voters and federal agencies on the local efforts.

Bouza, Anthony V. *The Police Mystique: An Insider's Look at Cops, Crime, and the Criminal Justice System*. New York: Plenum, 1990. A retired police chief looks at the daily work of the police, the criminals with whom they deal, and the criminal justice system. Based on 36 years as a police officer.

Boyd, Neil. *The Last Dance: Murder in Canada*. Scarborough, ON: Prentice Hall Canada, 1988. A study of murder and punishment in Canada.

Brock, Deborah R. *Making Work, Making Trouble: Prostitution as a Social Problem*. Toronto: University of Toronto Press, 1998. A social history of prostitution, arguing that social problems are socially constructed.

Muncie, John, and Eugene McLaughlin, eds. *The Problem of Crime*. Newbury Park, CA: Sage, 1996. An interdisciplinary examination of such topics as changing conceptions of crime, white-collar crime, crime and the family, and politics and crime.

Ross, Jeffrey Ian, ed. *Varieties of State Crime and Its Control*. Monsey, NY: Criminal Justice Press, 2000. Case studies of government crimes in the United States and other nations, including political corruption and various kinds of violence and repression by governments against their citizens.

Sanders, W. B. *Gangbangs and Drive-bys: Grounded Culture and Juvenile Gang Violence*. New York: Aldine De Gruyter, 1994. Analysis of patterns of gang violence, based on data over a 12-year period. Also discusses lifestyles and perspectives of gang members.

Walters, Glenn D. *The Criminal Lifestyle*. Newbury Park, CA: Sage, 1990. Addresses the issue of why some individuals pursue crime as a lifestyle and shows how biological, psychological, and sociological factors all contribute to the problem.

Weisburd, David, Stanton Wheeler, Elm Waring, and Nancy Bode. *Crimes of the Middle Classes: White-Collar Offenders in the Federal Courts*. New Haven, CT: Yale University Press, 1991. Details the variety of crimes committed by white-collar criminals, most of whom are average people in financial trouble who see actions like fraud as a way to resolve their problems.

Problems of Inequality

The next three chapters are concerned with inequalities in the distribution of things Canadians value. These inequalities are so significant that major segments of the population suffer from serious deprivations. We look first at the unequal distribution of wealth in Canada and discuss the problems of the poor in some detail. Then we examine inequalities experienced by two major segments of the population—women and various minority groups.

The people we focus on in this part are victims of inequality because of the circumstances of their birth. That is, they did not choose their sex or race. These groups face inequitable treatment by a society whose norms and values they generally affirm and strive to follow.

POVERTY

■ "WE FEEL LIKE DEADBEATS"

Marlene is in her late 30s, married, the mother of two, and poor. Poverty is something new in her life. For some years, her married life resembled the middle-class home in which she was raised. Then an accident forced her to go on long-term disability leave, her husband's business failed, and for the past three years they have lived deep in poverty. Savings, credit, friends, and relatives helped for a while, but now they have reached "the year I lost 25 pounds without even trying":

We've hit bottom. We have no insurance. We are continually harassed by collection agents. They tell us we're deadbeats. Actually we feel like deadbeats. The first time I really got angry was a few months ago when I saw a guy with a toy attached to his car window. I knew that toy cost around $15, and I could feel the anger rising in me as I thought about how much food I could buy with $15.

I thought about my kids, who now are getting used to strange combinations of vegetables and rice or noodles, and how much they would enjoy the meal I could buy. And all of a sudden I was enraged at someone I didn't even know for spending so much money on a joke. Then it made me mad that $15 seemed like so much money. Then it made me mad that I had gotten mad.

I started watching the expensive cars go by when I was walking or taking a bus. It's like they were advertising the fact that they made it and I haven't. I've never had that kind of car, but it bothered me that other people did. Suddenly I began to take their arrogance personally. And when I read about a guy paying $20,000 for a watch, I wondered if he was part of the human race. How could he do that when there were hungry kids living just a few kilometres away?

I've gotten to the point where I see that without money, a person just doesn't matter. I thought I was a pretty knowledgeable person, but I had no idea of the violent, demoralizing effect of poverty. I had no idea how it would feel to have no food in the house, no gas to drive to buy food, no money to buy gas, and no prospect of money. My husband and I believe we'll pull out of this. But I have a dread in my bones that the worst is not over yet, and that even when it is over, it will never be altogether in the past for any of us. ■

▪▪ INTRODUCTION

"I was jogging through my neighbourhood park one early winter morning. As my run was coming to an end I saw, on a bench, a young woman, not older than 18, desperately trying to keep warm while she was sleeping. Next to her was a loaf of bread. I slowed down for that moment before returning home."

Canada has been consistently ranked by the United Nations as one of the 10 best countries in which to live. This is because, on average, incomes are high, the population is healthy, there is a long life expectancy, and communities are vibrant and safe. That said, there is a part of the population who spend their entire lives at the edge of desperation, barely able to gather sufficient money to exist.

In this chapter we discuss what is meant by poverty, identify who the poor are and how many there are, and examine how poverty affects the quality of life. To understand why the poor are poor, it is important to understand why the rich are rich. After we identify the structural and social psychological factors that contribute to poverty, we consider what has been done and what might be done to address the problem.

▪▪ WHAT IS POVERTY?

Poverty in Canada is old and new. It is old in the sense that it has always existed, and it is new in the sense that it was not *commonly defined* as a problem until more recently. As late as the 1950s, economists assumed that, economically, North Americans were consistently improving. They were producing more, and incomes were increasing. The question about poverty was not *whether* but when it would be eliminated. Although sociologists have always identified poverty as a problem, polls showed that not until the 1960s did the public begin to identify poverty as a serious problem (Lauer 1976).

Today, however, poverty is a concern for many Canadians. The Perspectives of Canada Survey in 2000 asked Canadians to rank their concerns on various social issues. More than half of Canadians (58 percent) expressed strong concern about child poverty, and 43 percent about homelessness. At the same time, only 8 percent and 14 percent of Canadians said they were "unconcerned" about child poverty and homelessness, respectively. Canada has no government-mandated poverty line, although Statistics Canada since the 1960s has "unofficially" used the Low Income Cutoff (LICO). In the last five years the debate over how to define poverty has reopened. The following are the four main poverty measures currently being debated in Canada.

▪▪ LICO (Low Income Cutoff)

The Low Income Cutoff (LICO) is calculated using both pre- and post-tax income. It is based on the size of a family and the size of the community, and measures the average percentage of income spent on necessities—mainly food, clothing, and shelter. According to Statistics Canada, the average family spends 35 percent of its pre-tax income on necessities. People who spend 20 percent more than the average—that is,

TABLE 5.1 ■ ■ ▪

**After-Tax Low-Income
Cutoffs (LICOs), 2003**

Family Size	Population of Community of Residence				
	500,000+	100,000–499,999	30,000–99,999	Less than 30,000*	Rural
1	$16,348	$13,771	$13,558	$12,389	$10,718
2	$19,948	$16,803	$16,544	$15,118	$13,079
3	$25,230	$21,252	$20,924	$19,120	$16,542
4	$31,424	$26,469	$26,061	$23,814	$20,603
5	$35,122	$29,584	$29,127	$26,616	$23,028
6	$38,820	$32,699	$32,193	$29,418	$25,453
7 +	$42,519	$35,814	$35,259	$32,220	$27,878

Source: Canadian Council on Social Development and Statistics Canada, 2004

any family that spends 55 percent of its income on necessities—are considered to fall below the poverty line by LICO. Table 5.1 shows the pre-tax income poverty line according to family size and size of community. According to LICO, if you live in a family of four in a large city like Montreal, Toronto, or Vancouver the poverty line is raised to $31,424. On the other hand, if you live in a rural community, the poverty line is $20,603.

▪▪ LIM (Low Income Measure)

A Low Income Measure (LIM), frequently used internationally to measure poverty, defines poverty as being "much poorer than average." The LIM is based on family size and the nation's median adjusted family income (50th percentile). According to the LIM, a Canadian family of two adults and two children whose income fell below $31,000 in 2001 is poor (table 5.2).

▪▪ BNI (Basic Needs Index)

The Basic Needs Index (BNI) was created by Christopher Sarlo, whose work is supported by the Fraser Institute, a right-wing think tank. The BNI uses the subsistence notion definition of poverty; that is, the idea that poverty is the lack of items required to maintain basic physical well-being (table 5.3). BNI is based on Sarlo's calculations of the income needed for a family to buy these basic necessities (2001). Thus, according to Sarlo, to be poor in Canada means that the family's income must be below $18,856.

TABLE 5.2 ■ ■ ▪

**Before-Tax Low Income
Measures (LIMs) by
Family Type, 2001**

Number of Adults	Number of Children					
	0	1	2	3	4	5
1	$15,470	$21,658	$24,752	$29,393	$34,034	$38,675
2	$21,658	$26,299	$30,940	$35,581	$40,222	$44,863
3	$27,846	$32,487	$37,128	$41,769	$46,410	
4	$34,034	$38,675	$43,316			
5	$40,222	$44,863				
6	$46,410					

Source: Canadian Council on Social Development and Statistics Canada, 2004

TABLE 5.3 ▪ ▪ ▪

**Looking at Basic Needs
for Canada (1997); All
Values for Family of
Four**

Basic Need	Actual Expenditures: Famex (1996)			Sarlo 1997
	Average	Bottom Quintile	Bottom Decile	
Food	$8,028	$5,868	$5,436	$5,306
Shelter	$10,122	$7,538	$7,471	$8,051
Clothing	$3,128	$1,624	$1,333	$2,012
Local telephone service	$286	$263	$253	$297
Cleaning supplies	$339	$267	$240	$159
Household insurance	$381	$221	$198	$200
Furniture and equipment	$1,735	$904	$873	$299
Laundry	$114	$81	$80	$481
Public transportation*	$838	$678	$767	$648
Personal care	$1,148	$757	$660	$457
Health care (direct costs to household)	$833	$533	$425	$846
Miscellaneous	$100			
Taxes	$15,805	$2,169	$792	$0
Total	**$42,757**	**$20,903**	**$18,528**	**$18,856**
Total after taxes	**$26,952**	**$18,734**	**$17,736**	**$18,856**

* for those who use public transportation only

Source: Sarlo 2001 and FAMEX 1996

▪▪ MBM (Market Basket Measure)

Introduced in May 2003, the Market Basket Measure (MBM) was created largely by the National Council of Welfare through the HRDC (Human Resources and Development Canada) as an attempt to mediate the differences between definitions based on subsistence (BNI) and social inclusion (LICO). The calculations are based on 29 community sizes in 10 provinces and a family of four (two adults, two children); calculations are modified according to changes in family size. The MBM creates a "basket" containing five categories: food that is nutritious, clothing and footwear, housing based on the average costs for a two or three-bedroom apartment, transportation (a monthly transit pass), and a small allowance for recreation and entertainment.

▪▪ Evaluating Poverty in Canada

Why did Canadians generally fail to identify poverty as a social problem until the 1960s? One reason is that the poor were largely invisible to many Canadians. Another reason is many people failed to make the distinction between absolute and relative poverty; they insisted that even the lowest-income groups in Canada were not really poor because they fared better than the starving people in other countries.

To be sure, many of Canada's poor have more food, more clothing, better shelter, and so on than the poor in other nations, but the standard for evaluating Canada's poor cannot be those who are starving in other nations. Rather, poverty in Canada must be evaluated in terms of the *standard of living* attained by the majority of Canadians. To tell a poor Canadian whose family suffers from malnutrition that there are people in other nations who are starving to death is not consoling, particularly when the poor person knows that millions of Canadians throw away more food every day than that person's family consumes.

poverty
a state in which income is insufficient to provide basic necessities such as food, shelter, and clothing

What then, exactly, is poverty? **Poverty** is a state in which income is insufficient to provide basic necessities such as food, shelter, and clothing. *Absolute poverty* means that the insufficiency is so severe that it is life-threatening. *Relative poverty* means that the insufficiency is substantially greater than that of most others in the society.

All these methods of defining poverty are considered woefully inadequate by many social scientists. They do not reflect regional differences or business cycles, and do not take into account whether families whose incomes fall above the poverty line can afford necessary goods and services. Critics of the BNI measure add that the definition of necessities is unrealistic. First, how realistic is it for a family of four in any major urban community to find adequate housing for $670 a month, or to feed a family of four nutritious food on a budget of $442 a month (refer to table 5.3)? Second, the BNI does not include basic goods such books, toys, dentist appointments, school supplies, and so on (Canadian Council of Social Development 2001). Similarly, National Anti-Poverty Alliance policy analyst Christopher Shillington argues that the MBM approach limits governmental obligations to a "basket of goods" rather than to a share of Canada's wealth.

▪▪ Extent of Poverty

The proportion of Canadians officially defined as poor has fluctuated over time. Poverty rates were high in the early 1980s and gradually declined to a low of 13.9 percent in 1989 (see figure 5.1). Rates rose again in the first half of the 1990s and peaked at 18.5 percent in 1996. Poverty rates then steadily declined until 2001 (13.3 percent). These low rates of poverty can be explained by an upswing in the Canadian economy that saw higher employment rates and wage growth. In turn, rates of poverty declined. That said, rates are now similar to those of 1989. Further, in 2002 poverty rates *increased* slightly. Does this mean that we are about to enter a trend reversal, as we saw in the early 1990s? According to Scott and Lessard (2004), Canada "is not growing its way out of poverty."

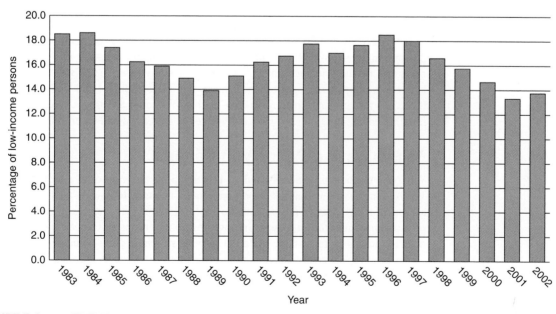

FIGURE 5.1 ▪ ▪ ▪

Percentages of low-income persons, before taxes, 1983–2002.

Source: Adapted from Statistics Canada, 2004.

A caution—one dealt with in the previous section—is that the official figures minimize the number of poor. Many of you would probably consider yourselves poor if your income were just above the poverty level. In addition, there are people who are not now poor but will be, and there are people who are not now poor but have been. In other words, there is always movement into and out of poverty, so the number of poor at any given time does not reveal the total number of people who will be affected by the problem during their lifetime.

■■ Who Are the Poor?

Wealth and poverty are not *distributed equally* among various social groups. Most Canadians are neither wealthy nor impoverished, but the chances of being in one of these categories are greater for certain social groups. For example, the probability of being poor is greater for females, persons over the age of 65, persons not living in economic households, and children living in female single-parent families (see figure 5.2). Females in all categories are poorer than men.

Other factors that may contribute to low income are education and unemployment. Families whose main wage earner did not graduate from high school were more than twice as likely to live in poverty compared to those with college diplomas or university degrees. Canadians who work full time and all year long have a much lesser likelihood of low income. Only 5 percent of Canadians who work full-time live in poverty, compared to 28 percent of part-time and occasional workers (Canadians with Low Incomes 2001).

Poverty is linked to race and ethnicity in a troubling fashion (see figure 5.3). Just over 70 percent of all Canadians in 1998 with low income were represented by First Nations persons (28.9 percent), immigrants (18.6 percent), and visible minorities (24.3 percent). First Nations persons' wages are 34 percent below the national average, and almost half (44 percent) of the population on reserves live below the low-income rate. Newly arrived immigrants living in large cities are twice as likely to live in poverty. Approximately 35 percent of new immigrants in 2002 have a low-income rate, compared to 23 percent in 1980 (Heisz and McLeod 2004). Visible minority groups are among the poorest: more than half live in poverty, compared to 10 percent of Canadians who are of white British or European origin (Ornstein 2000). Poverty rates are high for Central Americans, Jamaicans, West Indians, and people with multiple South Asian backgrounds. Ornstein believes that racism in large part explains poverty among these

FIGURE 5.2 ■ ■ ■

Characteristics of people with low incomes.

Source: Adapted from Statistics Canada, 2004.

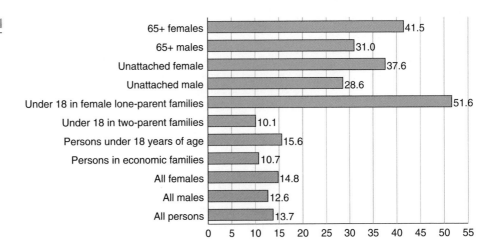

FIGURE 5.3 ▪ ▪ ▪

Canadian groups with low incomes.

Source: Adapted from Statistics Canada, Survey of Labour and Income Dynamics, 1998.

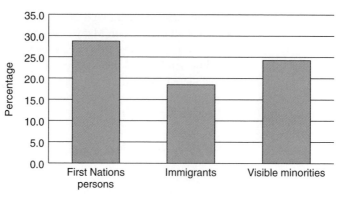

groups; although most are employed, they are trapped in low-paying jobs. For example, black Canadians should have higher incomes according to their education qualifications, but they confront job discrimination at every level, from securing employment to progressing through the ranks.

Finally, the rate of poverty is higher in rural areas than in urban centres (Vera-Toscano et al. 2001), but the characteristics of those living with low income are similar: "female working age, unattached individuals in one-person households, married/with children under 25 years old, and female lone parents with children under 25 are the dominant characteristics in both low income sub-samples" (17). One substantive difference between rural and urban low-income characteristics is that pay levels on average are lower in rural areas. As well, seasonal and temporary work is more common in rural communities. Extensive rural poverty is one reason why many Canadians are unaware of the seriousness of the problem; the rural poor are even less visible than those in urban **ghettoes.**

ghetto

an area in which a certain group is segregated from the rest of society; often used today to refer to the impoverished area of the inner city

An additional fact about the identity of the poor is important: Contrary to popular opinion, people are not poor primarily because of their *unwillingness to work*. The research of Vera-Toscano et al. indeed suggests that low pay and low-income rates are linked. The unemployed do not make up the bulk of Canada's poor. Many Canadians on welfare would prefer to work if they had their choice. When employment rates are high, welfare rates are down (see figure 5.4). That said, working does not preclude poverty. One-quarter (25.3 percent) or 2 million Canadian workers in 2002 had low-paying jobs. This rate was virtually unchanged from the mid 1990s, which was the beginning of the most recent economic boom (figure 5.4). According to Campaign 2000, an information and advocacy group to end child poverty:

> A good pay cheque is one of the best cures for poverty, but good jobs are scarce. Significant changes to the labour market include the growth of jobs in the small business sector and self-employment, as well as the move to non-standardized forms of employment. Full-time jobs increased 13 percent between 1990 and 2000 while part-time employment grew 21 percent. And while permanent jobs during the recovery years of 1997 through 2000 grew 8 percent, temporary employment grew by 21 percent.

> As the employment earnings of poor families declined and transfer benefits failed to offset falling incomes, the number of poor children in working families grew. Among working poor families child poverty increased 57 percent during the 1990s, totalling almost 600,000 children.

We noted earlier that there is movement into and out of poverty; but there is also a core of people who remain in poverty, *an underclass that experiences chronic hunger*

FIGURE 5.4 ■ ■ ■

Number of Canadians employed and on welfare in Canada, in millions, 1997–2003.

Source: Adapted from Statistics Canada, 2004, and National Council of Welfare

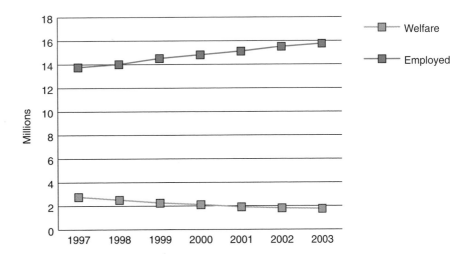

malnutrition

inadequate food, in amount or type

and **malnutrition,** *unemployment, and substandard housing.* Insufficient food, in turn, increases depression and suicide attempts and it inhibits cognitive and psychosocial development (Alaimo, Olson, and Frongillo 2001, 2002). The underclass is only a minority of the nation's poor, but it presents poverty's most serious challenge—how to deal with those who seem caught in the throes of poverty on a more or less permanent basis (Devine, Plunkett, and Wright 1992; Jencks 1992).

Finally, there are the *homeless.* The Canada Housing and Mortgage Corporation (CMHC) defines homelessness in three ways: those for whom, literally, there is no home; those who are chronically homeless, in and out of temporary housing; and those who are at risk of becoming homeless or are in precarious living situations (CMHC 1995). The very lack of a stable, identifiable residence makes it difficult to know exactly how many Canadians are homeless. However, the numbers run into the hundreds of thousands in any given year and the numbers may be increasing as the demand for emergency shelters has increased (Swift et al. 2003).

The homeless are a diverse group of people. Only a minority of homeless people fit the stereotypes of the substance abuser or the mentally ill individual. The homeless include both sexes, all age groups, all races, people of every marital status (married, separated, divorced, widowed, never married), and single mothers with children (Government of Canada 2004). Moreover, many have worked half or more of the time since they were 18. A survey of the poor in the United States reported that out of 1,440 people who were working, 45.3 percent were homeless because their income was too low for them to afford any kind of housing (National Coalition for the Homeless 2000:23). In Toronto, 15 percent of hostel residents are immigrants and refugees. Families are "the fastest growing group among the homeless … because some landlords refuse to rent apartments to families with children, [to] single mothers, or to people on social assistance" (Swift et al. 2003:29)

Youth who are homeless did not seek out life on the streets; they have run from somewhere else. Almost all youth homelessness can be traced back to their family life: 70 percent of street youth experienced some form of sexual, physical, or emotional abuse. Other factors that contribute to "at risk" categories include First Nations youth (in Ottawa, Aboriginal youth make up 18 percent of the homeless population, but represent only 1.5 percent of the population) (Environment Scan on Youth Homelessness); queer youth (20 to 40 percent, versus 10 percent of the general population); youth with mental health and drug-addiction problems; and youth who come from single-parent

Box 5.1

Life of the Homeless

Nancy describes the routine of sleeping in the rough, securing food, panhandling, the camaraderie among long-term street people, and where she sleeps outdoors:

It is not always safe. Sometimes you can get robbed. Sometimes you can get knocked out even before you wake up. It is not that safe but when you have somebody around you we can protect each other. I have learned to make street friends. Sometimes, like most people, we get sick of each other so we have to look for other friends. If you are panhandling sometimes people go by and give you money. Sometimes they just go by. Mostly we eat at soup kitchens. We go to the missions. Sometimes when you are panhandling, people will give you food. In their minds, it is better to give me food than money because money, I might spend on alcohol or drugs. So they buy the food and give it to me. I think these people are smart. Sometimes the police harass you. Sometimes they can be very nice. I had one bring me a sandwich and ask me how I was feeling. I said "I'm ok and I'm going to be out of here soon. I am about $1.50 short of a sub sandwich." He says "Come with me, I'll buy you one." Sometimes restaurants won't even serve you. They won't let you pass through the door. That is how we learn to get food from fast food chains. We can order it out and eat outside without having everyone stare at you or whisper about you under their breath. When there is drinking, there is a lot of promiscuous sex. When you are half-loaded or you are smoking pot, you don't realize what you are doing until the next morning. A lot of unsafe sex has caused people to contract the disease that is going around. If we have enough money after the drinking, we will buy food—if we have enough money. And if we are too hung over, we just go in a never-ending circle. We talk, we walk, and we console each other. Sometimes we argue. Sometimes we laugh about it the next day. We take care of each other. I sleep in the park, underneath the overpass or behind the library or downtown beneath the restaurant... as long as you find a spot where the cops won't bother you or people won't bother you...

Sometimes you have to walk miles just to find a spot where you can sleep. I find good clean cardboard and I always carry my own sleeping bag. The most important thing is to have blankets. We learn to carry those blankets. We learn to because this is our home.

Excerpt from *Voices: Women, Poverty and Homelessness in Canada* by Rusty Neal

families. As well, almost 50 percent of street youth have had past involvement with the child welfare system (CBC, *Fifth Estate*). One possible explanation for high rates of homelessness among youth is that there are gaps in social services. Child welfare protects youth up to the age of 16, but in many provinces youth have to be 18 in order to collect income assistance (ESYH).

On the street, youth face many challenges (see box 5.1 discussing the life of the homeless). In addition to their precarious working situations (primarily panning, squeegeeing, drug trafficking, or working in the sex industry), they have to manage street gangs and police harassment. Further problems arise because many "at risk" youth also avoid shelters and other social assistance for fear of harassment or abuse.

INVOLVEMENT

FROM SUPERMARKET TO FOOD BANKS

Food banks were first introduced in 1981 to address the problem of hunger in Canada. Since then, more than 2000 food banks have opened. Food banks are a phenomenon not only of urban living, but also exist in rural communities. Most food-bank users are welfare recipients, many who are single-mothers and persons on disability income. The institutionalization of charitable food services may in fact be a poor solution to addressing hunger in Canada. Food supplies are often limited and inconsistent, as they rely on donations from community members and local businesses. As such, the food quality may be low. When food resources are low, food banks may be limited in the amount of food distributed and, in the worst-case scenario, people may be forced to leave without any food, thus having little control over what and how much they eat. Finally, going to a food bank may be viewed as degrading and disempowering. Food banks are, in essence, charity. They do not address the larger social and structural issues of eliminating poverty so that people will never go hungry.

Volunteer for a food bank in your community. While helping out, think about the people who depend on the food bank for nourishment. Imagine how they feel when they ask for food. Take note of what food they receive (and how much). Is the food adequate for a well-balanced diet according to Canada's Food Guide? Based on your observations, write a policy report—"Are Food Banks a Solution to Hunger in Canada?"—and send it to your local politicians.

Women are especially vulnerable to abuse by pimps and the danger of sexual harassment, and almost half of all young women on the street will become pregnant (ESYH).

Like poverty generally, homelessness may be short-term, episodic, or long-term. Those who are chronically homeless, compared to the temporarily homeless, are more likely to be male, have less education, have never married, and have a disability (Morris 1997).

Homelessness emerged as an issue of national concern in the 1980s. It was also a matter of national concern during the Great Depression, but after the Second World War most people simply assumed that the homeless were worthless people unwilling to work and addicted to alcohol or drugs. As noted earlier, however, some do work. Homelessness is inextricably linked to government policy. In Toronto, for example, 60 percent of people in homeless shelters would have qualified for Employment Insurance, disability, or other social assistance programs that existed 10 years ago (Ornstein in Salvo 2003).

 ## ■■ From Social Problems to Solutions

Politics and policy are the largest determiners of who become homeless. In Ontario in 1995, the provincial Conservative government under Premier Mike Harris cut 21.6 percent in welfare benefits, which pushed almost 67,000 Ontario families out of their rental housing (Ornstein, in Salvo 2003). At the same time (between 1995 and 1998), the number of rental dwellings being built in Canada averaged 7,000 per year versus 38,000 per year, as had been the case between 1986 and 1990 (Swift et al. 2003). Those who become homeless are almost always those who are excluded from policy and politics: women in poverty, visible minorities, Aboriginals (the number of Aboriginals in core housing need are double their non-Aboriginal counterparts), immigrants, the disabled, and single mothers (Salvo 2003). As well, whereas men's poverty and homeless rates are linked to the job market, women's poverty is often linked to the ending of a heterosexual relationship in which they are financially dependent on a man (Voices 2002); also a factor is the job market, which discriminates against women both in terms of opportunity and wages.

Affordable housing is a must, but Canada has no housing policy (Swift et al. 2003). Under the Conservative government led by Brian Mulroney, Parliament placed the responsibility for housing on the provinces and municipalities. But affordable housing needs an initial government subsidy, which only the federal tax base can provide. Although in recent years some money has been put into housing, overall a comprehensive federal policy remains elusive.

National Affordable Housing Strategy (NAHS). The Federation of Canadian Municipalities created the NAHS in response to the mayors of Canada's major cities calling homelessness a national disaster. It is a three-part plan consisting of a flexible 10-year federal capital grant program, GST breaks on housing and other tax measures to encourage private investment, and provincial/territorial rental and shelter allowance initiative programs. Since it is cheaper to house someone in an apartment—let's say $22 to $30 per night, compared to the $30 to $43 a night it costs to stay in a shelter, such initiative programs would actually save the province money in both the short and the long term (Salvo 2003).

One-Percent Solution. The "one-percent solution" was launched by the Toronto Disaster Relief Committee in 1998; it calls for every level of government to allocate one percent of its budget to affordable housing initiatives.

Squats. In protest against government inaction on the issue of affordable housing, activist groups across the country have been leading actions called squats. Squats occur when people reclaim buildings that are deserted or no longer in use for people in need. The most famous squat, Pope Squat (named for Pope John Paul II's arrival in Toronto for World Youth Day)—was organized by the Ontario Coalition Against Poverty (OCAP) and lasted from July 25, 2003 until early November when the squatters were evicted.

■■ The Changing Nature of Poverty

Certainly the proportion of Canadians who are poor is lower than it was in the past—but are those who are poor now in better or worse condition than the poor of other generations? Although we have no systematic evidence on the question, it seems reasonable that poverty is more difficult when the proportion becomes smaller. It is one thing to be poor when the majority of people, or even a substantial minority, share your poverty. It is another thing to be poor when most people are living comfortably or in affluence.

Still, if the poor are making gains relative to the rich, poverty might be less stressful than in the past. Unfortunately, this is not the case. According to the latest Census (2001), the gap between rich and poor in Canada is increasing. Whereas the richest 10 percent of Canadians have witnessed an incredible 14.6-percent increase in income, there has been less than a one-percent increase for the bottom 10 percent (figure 5.5). What is even more worrisome is that many areas, incomes of working families who are just under the 50th percentile have in fact decreased. The top 10 percent of families in 2001, whose incomes were higher than $117,850, comprised 28 percent of all Canadian families' total income, compared to 26 percent in 1990. In contrast, those Canadians whose family income fell below $18,900 (the lowest 10 percent) represented only 1.6 percent of the total income of all Canadian families, a similar percentage to that of 1990 (see table 5.4).

The 1990s represent one of the most prosperous decades in Canada's history, yet more people lived in poverty in 2000 (4.72 million) than in 1990 (4.28 million) (CCSD 2004). Canada is increasingly becoming a polarized society (figure 5.6). Income and wealth continue to grow for the top 10 percent of the income ladder (Morissette, Zhang, and Drolet 2002). At the same time, Canadians at the lower rungs of the income ladder

FIGURE 5.5 ■ ■ ▦

Change in average income by income details, census families, Canada, 1990–2000.

Source: Statistics Canada, 2004.

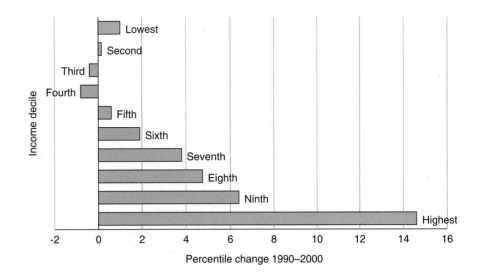

TABLE 5.4 ■ ■ ▦

Average Income and Share of All Census Families' Income, by Income Decile, Canada, 2000

Income Decile	Income Decile Range	Share of All Census Family Income (%)
Lowest decile	Less than $18,991	1.6
Second decile	$18,991–$28,211	3.6
Third decile	$28,212–$37,216	5.0
Fourth decile	$37,217–$45,859	6.3
Fifth decile	$45,860–$55,015	7.6
Sixth decile	$55,016–$65,018	9.1
Seventh decile	$65,019–$76,661	10.7
Eighth decile	$76,662–$91,971	12.6
Ninth decile	$91,972–$117,849	15.6
Highest decile	More than $117,849	28.0

Source: Adapted from Statistics Canada, 2004.

FIGURE 5.6 ■ ■ ▦

GNI per capita for selected countries, 2002.

Source: World Bank World Development Indicators 2004.

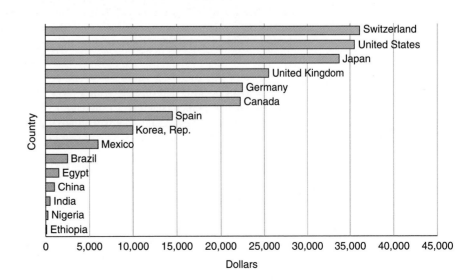

have experienced whopping cuts throughout the 1990s to social service programs. Consider the following cuts (Scott and Lessard 2004):

- The new Employment Insurance program in 1996 has adversely limited income support for many groups of workers, including women and young people.
- Social assistance reforms have made eligibility more difficult and reduced benefit levels.
- Programs that supported working families, such as childcare, have been eliminated in many provinces.

In sum, there has been a redistribution of income in this country during the 20th century, but it has not benefitted the poor. Rather, the upper-middle and upper income groups are the beneficiaries of income redistribution. The lower 5 percentile have lost ground to the upper 20 percent in income as well as in total wealth. When you try to assess the extent of poverty in Canada, you must, therefore, recognize that while the proportion of the poor is less than it was in earlier time periods, the lot of the poor is worse when compared with the rest of society.

■■ POVERTY AND THE QUALITY OF LIFE

Some sense of the trauma of living in poverty, even if you assume that it is only a temporary state, may be seen in the account of Marlene (see "We Feel Like Deadbeats" at the beginning of the chapter). In essence, the trauma arises from the fact that the poor get less of everything considered important and necessary for a decent life (less money, food, clothing, shelter). The *deprivation of the poor is pervasive* (Corcoran 2000; Mullahy and Wolfe 2000; Samaan 2000; Rank 2001). Compared to infants of the non-poor, infants of the poor are more likely to die. Their children are more likely to fail in school even when they are intelligent. Their children are more likely to drop out of school. They are more likely to become mentally ill. They are more likely to lose their jobs and to drop out of the labour force. They are more likely to experience hostility and distrust rather than neighbourliness with those around them. They are less likely to participate in meaningful groups and associations. They are more likely to get chronic illnesses. In the ultimate deprivation, they are likely to die at a younger age. Thus, poverty diminishes the quality of a person's life in many ways.

The *ravages of poverty* and the way in which *poverty intersects with other social problems* are illustrated in the plight of the homeless. A number of the homeless are former mental patients who were put out onto the streets as a result of deinstitutionalization (see chapter 12) (King 1989). Life on the streets only intensifies their emotional problems. Homelessness can also create mental health problems among those who had no disorders before living on the streets (Hall 1987). Moreover, the homeless face a whole array of hazards and threats to their physical well-being. For example, homeless youths, such as Nancy (see box 5.1 on page 134), report more exposure to violence and sexual victimization than do youths who are not homeless (Kipke et al. 1997).

■■ The Right to Life and Happiness

The inadequacy of their financial resources deprives the poor of freedom to pursue a full and happy life. Some people argue that lack of money should not be equated with lack of happiness, that many of the poor are carefree, spontaneous, and even better off without the worries that accompany possession of money. It's generally only people with money who use this argument. There is, in fact, a positive correlation between income

POVERTY IN THE WORLD SYSTEM

Gross inequalities exist not only within most nations but also between the nations of the world. There are various ways in which we could characterize the inequalities: average family income, average life span, expenditures for health care or education, and so on. Figure 5.6 shows one measure—the **gross national income (GNI)** per capita for a number of countries. The gross national income is the total value of goods and services produced by a nation during a year. To a large extent, people's standard of living is related to the gross national income per capita.

As figure 5.6 illustrates, there are enormous differences in the gross national income per capita of various nations. Switzerland's per capita GNI is 361 times higher than Ethiopia's! People in the richer nations have seven or more times as many physicians per capita as those in the poorer nations. The infant mortality rates in the poorer nations are five or more times higher than those in the richer nations. At least 1.2 billion people suffer from hunger and malnutrition in the poorer nations, and the life expectancy of people in the richer nations is, on the average, 15 to 20 years higher than in the poorer nations. A child born in Canada in 2001 could expect to live to 79; a child born the same year in Afghanistan, Angola, Haiti, or a number of other poor countries could expect to live less than 50 years.

In other words, the people of poorer nations suffer the kinds of deprivations that afflict the very poorest people in Canada. The number of the poor throughout the world is staggering—more than a billion people, or one out of every five persons on earth. At least 100 million of those people live without any kind of shelter. Hundreds of millions of people do not get enough food or the kind of food needed for an active and healthy life.

Even the poorest nations, of course, have a small number of well-to-do people. Yet with few exceptions, the well-to-do of the poor nations have a living standard far below the well-to-do of the richer nations.

SOURCES
Lauer 1991; World Bank 2004; Gardner and Halweil 2000.

---

gross national income (GNI)
the total value, usually in dollars, of all goods and services produced by a nation during a year

and *perceived happiness.* Surveys of attitudes worldwide show that the proportion of people who describe themselves as very happy is lower among those in the lower-income than those in the middle- and upper-income groups (Mitchell 1983; Diener, Diener, and Diener 1995). Poverty brings more *despair* than happiness and more *fear* than fullness of life.

Discontent and Despair. When deprivation was widespread during the Great Depression of the 1930s, unrest was also widespread. People marched and demonstrated, demanding food and expressing a willingness to fight rather than starve. In one demonstration there were "no bands" and "no quickstep," only "rank after rank of sodden men, their worn coat collars turned up, their caps . . . pulled down to give as much protection as possible" as they marched in driving rain (Hutchinson 1962:274).

The multitude of problems and frustrations of poverty—crowded, dilapidated housing in crime-ridden neighbourhoods; inadequate health care; constant financial strain; poor-quality and inadequate food; lack of opportunities for betterment; and so on—are so overwhelming that the impoverished individual may suffer from chronic depression. Low-income mothers, for example, are likely to be depressed, and this adversely affects the development of their children (Petterson and Albers 2001).

Despair is not the lot of all the poor, but it is much more frequent among the poor than among the nonpoor. When despair comes, it can be devastating, and it can strike even the young. Consider Elaine, a teenager whose mother is a chronic alcoholic. Elaine lives in poverty with her grandmother in an urban apartment. She watches television 10 or more hours a day, even though the television only increases her depression

CONSTRUCTING POVERTY

Music has always been one way that people have voiced hardships, injustices, and frustrations. Hip-hop and rap, as an example, is rooted in African-American culture. It was introduced in New York City in the early 1970s and quickly became a political platform for disenfranchised black youth. Today, hip-hop has become globalized and has been adopted by various different social and political groups or communities to deliver their message. The lyrics below—"Final Notice"—were written by Eric McIntyre, a Nova Scotian hip-hop musician who writes about the relationship between poverty and capitalism.

Final Notice

The so called rational international language of money is louder than the screams of the impoverished masses as the free market passes those from which the benefits were extracted They said prosperity is like water it's going to trickle down well it must have evaporated before it hit the ground take a walk down south and visit a shanty town nothing but poverty and neglect to be found the exception was for these global rulers controlling the fields the factories the slaves the consumers they were high on power like they were drug abusers it's a two class system that's winners and losers in the new class war that's justified and indorsed from their text books to their business reports there is only one way and this is the course it's their vision of the world and it's an endless resource this is the mission they can never abort exploitation called progress perpetuated by force morals and money went through a divorce the only union here is a marriage of wealth and force.

Think about poverty in your community—for example, who are the poor, why are they poor, how are poor people viewed, and even what you have learned about food banks. Write a song or a poem. You may also want to create a poster that captures the key themes of your work. At the same time, it is a good idea to keep a journal in order to record your impressions, feelings, and insights.

because it continually reminds her of how much she lacks. Despite her superior intelligence, Elaine has always felt extremely ashamed in school:

> "If I only had some clothes." Today Elaine . . . [is] dressed in neatly ironed jeans that are badly frayed at the cuffs and worn thin. On top she wears a stained cheerleader's sweater, out in one elbow, which she has had since she was thirteen. Despite its holes and stains, Elaine wears the sweater every day. It reminds her, she says, of a time when she was happy. (Williams and Kornblum 1985:8)

The despair that always threatens to overcome the poor is manifested in what Rainwater (1967) called *survival strategies*—ways of living that enable the poor to adapt to their "punishing and depriving milieu." The *expressive strategy* involves manipulating others and making oneself appealing through means such as bettering someone in a rap battle, gaining the affection of a female, wearing dramatic clothes, or winning a gambling bet. The expressive strategy leads some nonpoor to define the poor as natural, spontaneous, and carefree; but, as Rainwater pointed out, this strategy, like the others, enables the individual to gain some measure of status and retain some degree of stability and sanity in the midst of an oppressive situation. The *violent strategy* involves things such as fighting, shoplifting, or making threats. It is a dangerous strategy for everyone, and not many of the poor adopt it. The *depressive strategy,* which involves withdrawal and isolation, characterizes a great number of the poor as they grow older. An individual may alternate among the strategies as he or she grows older, but all three strategies have the same purpose—to enable the individual to cope with a punitive situation. As such, they dramatize the despair that always hovers near the poor.

Freedom from Fear.   The poor live in a *capricious world.* The chronic uncertainty of their lives means they have much to fear. We discuss this topic further under

FIGURE 5.7 ■ ■ ▪

Risk of personal property and violent crimes by household income, 1999.

Source: Adapted from Statistics Canada, General Social Survey, 1999

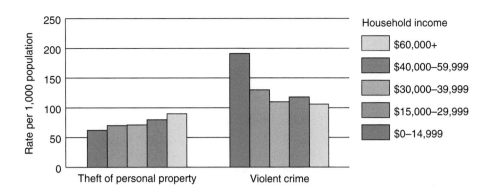

the subheading "Dilemmas of Poverty" later in this chapter. Here we will look at a specific fear that affects the poor more than others—the *fear of being the victim of a crime.*

The poor are more likely to be victims of crimes of violence and less likely to be victims of theft to personal property (see figure 5.7). Persons with a household income of less than $15,000 a year are more than three times as likely to be victims of violent crime than are persons whose household income is greater than $60,000 a year. Crimes of personal property increase every income bracket. In all likeliness, high-income households are attractive targets for property crime because of valuable material goods, jewellery, and the greater likelihood of available cash.

Approximately 60 percent of Canadian families know someone who has experienced family violence (NSACSW 2002). Young women between the ages of 18 and 24 are five times more likely to experience violence than are women over the age of 45. More than half of female victims of homicide are killed by their present or former partner or boyfriend. Low-income women (income of less than $30,000 a year) experience relatively more violence than women whose household income is greater than $60,000—3 percent and 1 percent, respectively.

Overall, fear of neighbourhood crime is linked to income. Although most Canadians believe that crime in recent years is stable, in contrast to those from high-income households, low-income Canadians are twice as likely to think that crime is more prevalent in their neighbourhood than in other areas (Canadians with Low Income 2001:7). As well, household income has an effect on feelings of personal safety. Persons from lower-income households are more fearful about walking alone at night, using public transportation alone at night, being alone at night in their home, and generally feeling safe from crime (Canadians with Low Income 2001).

■ ■ The Right to Dignity as a Human Being

For the poor, the *right to dignity as human beings* is violated by the *contradiction between the Canadian ideal of the worth of every individual and the pattern of interaction between the poor and the nonpoor.* At best, the poor tend to be treated paternalistically. At worst, they tend to be subjected to contempt and rejection, and blamed for their plight (Cozzarelli, Wilkinson, and Tagler 2001). The loss of dignity is manifested in a number of myths about the poor, myths that employ the *fallacy of personal attack* to discredit the poor and legitimate an unwillingness to support programs to help them.

"The Poor Are Lazy." It's a myth that the poor are lazy; they are willing to work and, in fact, most male heads of poor families do work. To say that the poor are lazy justifies the nonpoor's contempt and disavowal of personal or societal responsibility for dealing with poverty. No evidence supports the myth, but it is still prevalent, and it robs the poor of human dignity.

"People on Welfare Have It Good."   The expressive style of coping that we discussed earlier may have helped create the myth that those on welfare often live at higher standards than do people who work. A few "con artists" may manage to get a substantial living by *welfare fraud,* but the majority of people on welfare (and the majority of the poor in general) live in circumstances that would be repugnant to most Americans. What dignity is there, for instance, in not being able to buy adequate food for your children, or in living in a rat-infested apartment, or in huddling inside your apartment at night in fear of thieves and drug addicts?

And what kind of dignity is there in trying to survive on welfare payments that may mean an income far below the poverty level? According to table 5.5, single parents (mostly mothers) on welfare live well below Canada's low-income cutoff level (refer to table 5.1). For example, according to Statistics Canada, the LICO level for a one-child, one-parent household in a large urban centre is $19,948. Yet the same family type on social assistance—in, for example, British Columbia, which pays the highest social assistance dollars—receives only $10,300. Basically, a family on welfare can barely cover housing and grocery costs. Whatever else may be said of welfare, it is clearly not true that those on welfare "have it good."

"Welfare Is Draining Us."   One myth by which the poor are humiliated is that they are social leeches. This myth asserts that the cost of maintaining the poor is depriving the nonpoor by raising taxes and reducing their standard of living. As we noted, however, the poor receive a lower share of national income now than they did earlier in the 20th century. Historically, welfare payments have done little to reduce the inequity, and the standard of living for upper middle- and upper-class Canadians is higher than ever. A large number of Canadians now possess two or more automobiles, television sets, and computers, items that were luxuries in the not-too-distant past.

"Welfare Turns People into Lazy, Dependent Deadbeats."   "Welfare bums" is the term used by some Canadians to show their contempt for those who rely on welfare rather than on their own earnings. Even with the change to "workfare" (discussed later in this chapter), some continue to view those who receive government aid as lazy and unmotivated, preferring a "free ride" at the expense of those who work (Seccombe, Walters, and James 1999).

TABLE 5.5 ■ ■ ■

Estimated 2002 Annual Basic Social Assistance Income by Single Parent, One-Child Household

Province	Basic Social Assistance Income (Single-Parent, One Child)
Newfoundland and Labrador	$11,436.00
Prince Edward Island	$9,814.00
Nova Scotia	$8,760.00
New Brunswick	$8,772.00
Quebec	$8,712.00
Ontario	$10,210.00
Manitoba	$9,636.00
Saskatchewan	$9,036.00
Alberta	$8,505.00
British Columbia	$10,300.00

Source: Adapted from Canadian Council on Social Development, and data from *Welfare Incomes 2002.*

The problems and frustrations faced by the poor can be so overwhelming that the poor individual suffers from chronic depression.

This myth ignores certain important facts. First, most of the people on welfare are not able-bodied workers. Well over half of welfare recipients are children, the aged, the disabled, or mothers of small children (some of whom work). Second, as shown by a number of studies, those who are able-bodied workers generally prefer to work rather than to be on welfare. Third, there is very little long-term dependency among welfare recipients. In fact, as we pointed out earlier, there is a *good deal of movement in and out of poverty.* Only one of four children who spend most of their growing-up years in poverty is still poor in the middle to late twenties (Corcoran 2000). Edin (1995) found that 86 percent of the welfare mothers planned to leave welfare for work. Their plans were tempered, however, by their previous work experience in the low-paying labour market. This experience taught them two things: They were no better off financially by working than by being on welfare; and no matter how long or diligently they worked, their low-paying jobs did not lead to better jobs.

■■ Poverty and Health

The circumstances under which the poor are required to live cause higher rates of mental and physical illness among the poor than among the rest of the population (Jackson and Mustillo 2001; Chen, Matthews, and Boyce 2002). The *homeless are particularly prone to ill health.* A substantial proportion of the homeless suffer from various physical ailments, drug addiction, and mental illness (Jencks 1994; Menke and Wagner 1998).

Even the poor who are not homeless suffer a disproportionate amount of ill health. Compared to the nonpoor, the health problems of the poor are manifested in higher rates of clinical depression and far more difficulty with such daily living tasks as cooking, shopping, managing money, walking, eating, and dressing (Lynch, Kaplan, and Shema 1997). Mortality and morbidity (death and illness) rates are much higher among low-income Canadians, irrespective of age, sex, race, or place of residence (Toward a Healthy Future 1999). Chronic illnesses are particularly a problem to First Nations people, both men and women (see table 5.6). For example, First Nations women are five times more likely and men are three times more likely to develop diabetes. Overall, Canadians from lower-income households are less likely to report excellent or very good health than those from higher-income households (see figure 5.8). Psychological health may also be affected by income, as low self-esteem is substantially more prevalent in low-income than high-income households. Women living in poverty have infant mortality rates that are 60 percent higher than those not in poverty (Centers for Disease Control 1995c). If they survive infancy, poor children are more likely to suffer from mental as well as physical illnesses (McLeod and Edwards 1995; Alaimo et al. 2001).

Some of the health problems of the poor result from poor nutrition, which, in turn, is related to inadequate income. Fourteen percent of people in the low-income brackets

TABLE 5.6   ■ ■ ■

Age-Adjusted Ratio of Prevalence for Selected Chronic Disease for First Nations/Canada, 1997

Disease	Ratio: Men	Ratio: Women
Diabetes	3:1	5:1
Heart problems	3:1	3:1
Cancer	2:1	2:1
Hypertension	3:1	3:1
Arthritis/rheumatism	2:1	2:1

Source: *First Nations and Inuit Regional Health Survey 1997*, and *Toward a Healthy Future 1999*.

FIGURE 5.8   ■ ■ ■

Self-rated health (1996–97) and reporting of low self-esteem (1994–95) of Canadians, by income level.

Source: Adapted from Statistics Canada—*National Population Health Survey, 1996–97* and *1994–95; Toward a Healthy Future, 1999*.

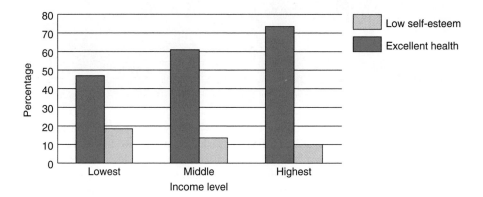

don't have enough to eat (National Center for Health Statistics 1998). More than half of those who don't have enough to eat are in families where at least one member is employed. In fact, the greatest risk of insufficient food among the poor is found in families of married couples with children!

The consequences of inadequate food or of malnutrition are serious (Alaimo et al. 2001). In recent decades, North American children have suffered from pellagra, scurvy, rickets, parasitic worms, and mental retardation as a result of prolonged malnutrition. Children who receive an inadequate amount of protein in the first year of life can develop problems of various kinds, including an inability to concentrate in school (Galler and Ramsey 1989). Even mild undernutrition can have long-term adverse effects on children's development. Opponents of the welfare system sometimes ask how many children have starved to death in Canada. The answer is few, if any; but this is little solace to the mother who watches her child grow up with mental or physical deficiencies because of inadequate diet.

Clearly, poverty contradicts the value of good health. The relationship between poverty and health, in fact, is another of the *vicious circles* that often characterize social problems. Because health problems put additional strains on a family's meagre financial resources, illness can be perpetuated. Poverty can generate stress that leads to illness that intensifies the stress, and the circle continues.

■ ■ Dilemmas of Poverty

autonomy

the ability or opportunity to govern oneself

Canadians want **autonomy**—the ability to control their own destiny—and they want opportunities for advancement. These values are *contradicted* by the realities of poverty. People at the lower end of the stratification system have little control over their lives and have few, if any, opportunities compared to people at the upper end. Poverty is an ongoing series of *dilemmas*. Even when a poor person can choose among options, all of the options may have undesirable aspects.

Consider the problem of existing on a poverty budget. What kind of a diet would you have if you existed on the food budget allocated to the poor? Keep in mind that this budget is for those who are just above the poverty scale. Since most of the poor are not at the top, most have even less money for food. How much of what you like to eat now would you be able to have? Another way to look at it is that the poor person's food budget for a whole day could be spent on one meal at a fast-food hamburger restaurant. For some of the poor, the choice may be between adequate nutrition and clothes, or between adequate nutrition and medical care. Most students do not face such limited choices.

One of the key dilemmas of the poor is the *choice between security and change*. Should a poor individual maintain whatever security he or she has, or take some risks in order to change his or her lot? For instance, children may be told that the only way to escape poverty is to stay in school and with education they can get a good job; but the only security the child's family may have against utter deprivation is for the child to drop out of school and earn money to add to the family income. At the same time, perhaps the only way children can be *psychologically secure* is to accept the negative judgments of their peers about school. The low value that many of the poor place on intellectual achievement threatens ostracism to any young person who is serious about education. Furthermore, these children have grown up in an unpredictable world, where they have felt powerless to change their life circumstances. Why should one risk years of schooling (which involves a loss of income) when the payoff is vague and uncertain?

Adults also face dilemmas and the *frustrations of powerlessness*. A woman who grew up in a housing project related an incident in her life: "When I was a girl, I was given a part in the school play. I was as happy as I could be, and proud to think of my parents watching me perform. But on the night of the play my father got drunk instead of coming to school. I was terribly upset at the time, but later on I realized why he had gotten drunk. He was ashamed to come to the play in the clothes he had, and he didn't have enough money to buy anything new. He didn't know what to do; so he got drunk."

It is easy enough to condemn the man, but remember the poor live with an agonizing mixture of ambition and powerlessness, of the need for security and the need for change. The security is meagre, but the risk of change may appear to be great.

▪▪ CONTRIBUTING FACTORS

It is true that there always have been poor people. It is also true that poverty is a global problem and that the poor of other nations are worse off in absolute terms than the poor in Canada. But why is there any poverty in affluent Canada? Canada has sufficient resources to eliminate poverty. Of course the elimination of poverty would require some shift in public policy (see "From Social Problems to Solutions," page 152). Nevertheless, poverty in Canada is not an inevitable outcome of something like overpopulation or inadequate resources. Why, then, do millions of Canadians continue to suffer an impoverished existence? Because, in part, a number of structural and social psychological factors operate not only to create poverty but also to perpetuate it.

▪▪ Social Structural Factors

The structural factors that bear upon the problem of poverty include the institutional arrangements of government, the economy, and education. We examine each in turn.

The Politics of Poverty.   The problem of poverty is the problem of wealth turned inside out. Poverty continues in Canada, in large part, because of the *distribution of power*. Those who control the wealth are among the most powerful, while the poor are among the most powerless. Governmental decisions typically reflect the interests of the well-to-do rather than of the poor.

In particular, the political structure is detrimental to the poor because of the combination of *multiple decision-making centres, the middle-class composition of the bureaucracy, and the complexities of obtaining government aid.* The term *multiple decision-making centres* refers to the federal, provincial, and local governmental levels and also multiple branches—legislative and judicial—at each level. All these facets of government have certain decision-making powers, and all have different constituencies. This means that most categories or organizations of citizens can exercise influence at some point, but it also means that there are many points at which a program or a policy initiative can be stopped. However, some categories of the population have little influence at any point in this complex, and one such category is the poor.

The political arrangements, therefore, mean that programs designed to help the poor are particularly vulnerable to variation, veto, sabotage, or atrophy through neglect. One such example is the serious shortage of affordable housing in Canada. The CMHC projects that for the next 10 years there will be a need for 45,000 new rental units each year (Swift et al. 2003:32). There is very little incentive for developers to build low-income housing, because profits are low. The federal government has abandoned its responsibility to provide affordable housing; all federally sponsored housing programs since the mid 1980s have been dismantled, and the responsibility of housing has been put onto provincial and municipal governments, which do not have the financial means to adequately address affordable housing needs.

There are many other programs that have been set up to help the poor. Unfortunately, most of these programs have been eliminated. Prior to the recession of the 1990s, the federal government covered 50 percent of welfare costs, while the provincial governments covered 30 percent and the municipalities were responsible for the remaining 20 percent. Between 1991 and 1993, under the Conservative government and Prime Minister Brian Mulroney, welfare grants from Ottawa to the provinces were cut from 50 percent to 30 percent. The Conservatives were ousted from power and the Liberal government under Prime Minister Jean Chrétien continued the cuts. Transfer payments to provinces between 1994 and 1998 were cut by more than $10 billion. Many health, education, and social assistance programs either were eliminated or saw their services privatized. Canada's social spending has been severely reduced over the last decade, comprising only 11.5 percent of the **gross domestic product (GDP)**, the standard measure of the size of Canada's economy (consumer and government spending, and the difference in the values of exports and imports). Compared to other countries, Canada ranks very poorly (see figure 5.9). Thus, the purchasing power of social assistance benefits was dramatically lower in 2001 than in 1986. For example, in 1986 a couple from British Columbia, with two children and on welfare, received—in constant 2001 dollars—$15,891; in 2001, the same family's welfare benefit was $13,534 (National Council of Welfare 2002; Hulchanski 2002).

Regardless of the intentions of the various programs and policies, the work of interest groups and the middle-class composition of government make it unlikely that the poor will greatly benefit or that the upper-middle strata will be greatly hurt by governmental action. The largest tax-cut in Canada's history was introduced in 2000 to be implemented over a five-year period. Then–finance minister Paul Martin boasted that this tax cut was a reward to Canadians for the hardships they endured in eliminating the federal deficit. But McKenzie points out that this may be:

gross domestic product (GDP)

the standard measure of the size of Canada's economy (consumer and government spending, and the difference in the values of exports and imports)

FIGURE 5.9 ■ ■ ■

Net social expenditure as a percentage of the GDP, 1997.

Source: Willem Adema, *Net Social Expenditure*, 2nd Edition, Labour Market and Social Policy—Occasional Papers No. 52, Paris: OECD, August 2001.

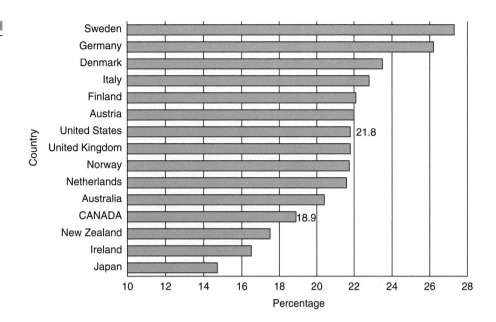

Fine-sounding rhetoric, except that the Canadians who were rewarded were not the Canadians who had suffered the sacrifices imposed on them through federal budget cuts. The burden of the cuts had fallen disproportionately on the poor and disabled … on the unemployed (as a result of substantial cuts in unemployment insurance benefits); on students (through the cuts in federal transfers to the provinces for higher education and as a result of changes to the Canada Student Loans Program); on the under-housed and homeless (as a result of the elimination of the co-operative and non-profit housing program); and on Canadians who depend on our health care system (as a consequence of a reduction of the federal share of provincial Medicare costs). The benefits went disproportionately to the highest-income individuals in Canada. More than 30 percent of the benefit from the Martin tax package went to the highest-income 5.3 percent of taxpayers. The highest-income 30 percent of taxpayers received 70 percent of the benefit, and the middle 50 percent of taxpayers received 31 percent of the benefit. (McKenzie 2004:61)

Another fact that underscores the *class composition of the government* is that the nonpoor generally benefit as much from the programs designed to help the poor as the poor themselves do. Programs that would help the poor at the expense of other groups are unlikely to be implemented or even proposed. Job-training programs help some of the poor, but they also provide high-salaried positions for a number of upper-middle-class administrators.

The *complexities of getting government aid* is the third aspect of the detrimental combination of political realities. One reason for this is the cumbersome application process. Similarly, other kinds of programs never reach the intended recipients because of inadequate staffing of governmental offices, complex application processes, and inadequate communication of the availability of the programs. In a survey of low-income parents, half the respondents said they were never informed about childcare services for which they were eligible, and 52 percent said that the lack of childcare caused them to lose a job (National Coalition for the Homeless 2000).

Some benefits do filter down to the poor, but the primary beneficiaries of governmental decisions and programs are (and always have been) the well-to-do. It is ironic that the people on welfare are castigated as "freeloaders," whereas the well-to-do have used their power to secure handouts from the federal government; but the handouts that

subsidy
a government grant to a private person or company to assist an enterprise deemed advantageous to the public

the well-to-do secure are referred to as **subsidies,** or tax benefits to stimulate business. From extensive gifts of land, to guaranteed prices for various farm products, to tax concessions and research money for industry, the federal government has been engaged in a long history of acts that have benefited the well-to-do. In many cases the benefits received by the well-to-do are not as obvious as those given to the poor, even though they are greater.

Finally, *subsidies to profit-making businesses* is the fourth area of abuse. The federal government has subsidized everything from private golf clubs to farm crops to giant corporations. Other areas of corporate welfare abuse have been identified by Ralph Nader (1990), an American consumer advocate: he calls them *bailouts, taxpayer-funded research and development,* and *subsidies to profit-making business.* Bailouts occur when the federal government guarantees loans to large corporations. To avoid bankruptcy in the 1990s, Canadian Airlines received hundreds of millions of dollars from the federal government. In the end, the airline declared bankruptcy and merged with Air Canada. Now Air Canada is in a similar position, demanding financial assistance from to government to stave off bankruptcy.

Between 1971 and 1999, the powerful and highly profitable oil industry received an average of $1.4 billion a year from the Canadian government. In addition, the industry pays low tax and royalty rates provincially. According to Dobbin (2004), "[g]overnments feel real pressure from manufacturers for financial breaks of all kinds because they can threaten to move their operations offshore." Using information from Canada Revenue Agency, Dobbin points out that between 1995 and 1998 the average amount of income tax paid by 80 percent of Canada's largest and most powerful corporations (revenues greater than $250 million) was less than $25,000 a year. Further, many of these corporations (ranging from 29 to 41 percent) did not pay any taxes.

In sum, millions in corporate welfare come from the federal government alone each year. Provincial and local governments also contribute to the welfare, which takes the form of such things as tax exemptions and tax reduction, training grants, investment credits, infrastructure (roads, water and sewer lines, etc.) improvements, and low-rate loans.

Why is it immoral to feed the hungry and moral to pay for private golf clubs? Is the president of an airline, whose high salary is possible partly because of government subsidies, more moral than the child who has no father and receives paltry sums of money through welfare? If the government can pay millions of dollars to rescue a corporation from bankruptcy, why is it wrong to rescue people from poverty? The answer is that the poor are powerless to secure what the well-to-do secure with relatively little difficulty. Ironically, through the structure and functioning of government, the well-to-do and powerful give to each other that which they say is immoral to give to the poor.

Probably few people in the middle class are aware of how many benefits they receive from government programs. For example, a young man attends a public school, rides on a free school bus, and then possibly attends a university, where his education is heavily subsidized. The average Canadian university tuition was $4,025 for the 2003/04 academic year; Nova Scotia had the highest tuition at $5,557, and Newfoundland and Labrador the lowest at $2,606 (The Daily, August 12, 2003). (Compare these numbers to those in the United States, where a four-year private college costs $19,710 a year (College Board 2004).) Once the young man is working he can put money into a registered retirement savings plan (RRSP), which can be used to reduce his taxes. He does not have to worry about healthcare costs, as they are all covered by the federal and provincial governments. Nor does he have to worry about his aging parents should they need nursing home care, as these homes are also government subsidized. His community may benefit economically from an industrial project underwritten by the government, and his children may be able to go to a college because of financial assistance from the government. Then the man, like many good Canadians, may rebel against federal programs and high taxes and assert that this country was built on rugged individualism, unaware that his whole existence is enriched and subsidized by various government programs.

The interests of the upper middle and upper strata are also reflected in the *tax structure*. Ostensibly, the tax structure is an equalizing mechanism that takes disproportionately from the rich in order to benefit the poor. This has not happened. Certain other taxes, such as the sales tax and the G.S.T., work to the detriment of the poor. Adding 15 percent to the cost of purchases is considerably more burdensome to the family whose income is only $15,000 per year or less than it is to the family with $80,000 or more per year income.

Although the wealthy enjoy advantages, we do not mean to imply that they pay no taxes. Most do, in fact, pay a considerable amount in taxes. The question is whether they have paid a proportionately larger amount of their income than the nonwealthy. The answer depends on whether only federal taxes or the total taxes paid—federal, provincial, and local taxes—are included. When all taxes are considered, the poor have paid as high a proportion of their income as the nonpoor, or even higher.

Poverty and the Economy. The Canadian economy works for the rich and against the poor in various ways. A capitalist economy that is supported by government policies allows *concentration of wealth*. Recall that income continues to grow for the top 10 percent of income earners; however, it should also be recognized that a large part of the wealth of the very rich does not come from personal income. *Stocks, bonds, and real estate are important sources of wealth* for those at the top of the socioeconomic ladder. This is why it is important to consider wealth and not merely income when assessing the amount of inequality.

A second way the economy works against the poor is by *entrapping them in a vicious circle*. Consider, for example, a woman whose job pays her only poverty-level wages. She cannot get a better-paying job because she lacks education or skills. She cannot afford to quit to gain the skills or advance her education because she has a family to support. There is no union, and she is unwilling to risk her job and perhaps her physical well-being to try and organize her fellow workers or even to support a move to unionization. Meanwhile, her debts mount, and the rate of inflation may far surpass any wage increase she gets. As she sinks more deeply into debt, she is less and less able to risk the loss of the income she has. Ultimately, she may reach the point of despair we described earlier. Perhaps she will cling to the hope that at least some of her children can escape the poverty that has wrung the vigour out of her own life.

A third way the economy hurts the poor is by *guaranteeing that a certain proportion of the population will be unable to find employment or unable to find jobs that pay more than poverty-level wages*. While most of the poor are not unemployed, a substantial number of families are poor because the family head is squeezed out of the job market or can find only low-paying jobs. This "squeezing out" can occur when companies close down or downsize, recessions occur, and technological changes make jobs obsolete (Rinehart 2001). Some of these people will spend time on welfare as they struggle against economic forces that are beyond their control.

The low-paying jobs that keep the working poor impoverished are most likely to be found in the retail and service industries (Kim 2000). Such jobs are widespread, namely service industry and clerical jobs. Women are more likely than men to be employed in low-paying jobs. Low earners also tend to have less education than other workers. Economists posit that education not only increases future earning potential, it also "may open up a more varied and interesting set of career opportunities, in which case job satisfaction would be higher among those with more education" (Benjamin et al. 1998:310).

Immigrants are prime targets for those who pay low wages. A New York reporter went into a Brooklyn garment factory that had a sign posted in Chinese: "Earnestly, urgently looking for workers" (Lii 1995). Because she spoke Chinese, the owner assumed the reporter was an immigrant seeking her fortune in America. She accepted the job and took her place in a long line of Chinese women bending over sewing machines and working diligently in silence. At the end of seven days and 84 hours of work, she was told that in three weeks she would be paid $54.24—which came to 65 cents an hour! She walked away "from the lint-filled factory with aching shoulders, a stiff back, a dry cough and a burning sore throat."

Similar stories could be told of immigrants in Canada. The reality for many visible minorities and immigrant groups is that they tend to be concentrated in low-paying industries such as services (food, accommodation, nursing attendants, domestics) and clothing manufacturing that offer no job security and are highly volatile (Das Gupta 1996). The clothing industry has been particularly unstable over this past decade since the advent of the free trade movement (Pierson and Cohen 1996). More than three-quarters of all Canadian garment workers are women. Of those, 50 percent are immigrants, and about 30 percent are visible minorities (Yanz et al., 1999), mostly of Asian origin[1] (Das Gupta 1996). Das Gupta believes that, forced into difficult and unstable working conditions, "working class women of colour and Black women are subordinated by an interplay of racist, sexist and classist ideologies" (1996:10).

One way to deal with low-paying jobs is to *unionize* the workers. Unfortunately, as we point out in chapter 9, unions have had their own problems in recent years in organizing the workforce. The problem of low-paying jobs is likely to continue for some time.

The same economy that allows low-paying labour furthers the disadvantage of the poor in regard to the purchase of consumer goods. For example, one company sold $500 vacuum cleaners door to door in poorer neighbourhoods. The poor residents, generally with low education, were relatively "easy targets" for salespeople:

> The sales tactics were those often used in poor neighborhoods: salesmen concealed the purpose of their visit, concealed the total cost of the equipment they were selling, concealed the interest and late-payment charges, and concealed the customers' legal right to terminate or cancel the contracts. (Blumberg 1989:52)

When poor people shop in stores in their neighbourhoods, they may pay more than the well-to-do who shop in other areas. Many supermarket chains, for example, have moved out of poor neighbourhoods. The small, independent stores that remain charge higher prices, in part because of higher operating costs (including the cost of insurance in areas with high crime rates). To be sure, it is more costly to do business in ghetto neighbourhoods than elsewhere because of greater losses through theft and higher insurance premiums. Although such practices may be legitimate from the perspective of the businessperson, they do contribute to keeping the poor impoverished. Even worse than higher prices is the interest that may be charged. Rent-to-own stores, which often target poor people who have no credit cards, may finance purchases at exorbitant interest rates. For example, an investigation into the charges of an appliance store in an impoverished neighbourhood found that the cash-and-carry price for a washing machine was $295; the same machine financed by the store for two years would cost the consumer $828 (Green 1997).

The Education of the Poor.

In general, the lower the income, the lower the educational achievement of children (Duncan et al. 1998). The poor have, on average, the least amount of education. In times of growing economic inequality (which, as table 5.1 shows, has occurred in recent decades), children from the higher social classes attain more education while those from the lower social classes attain less (Mayer 2001). This low level of attainment in turn exacerbates the worst aspects of poverty, for it depresses physical and psychological well-being and shuts people off from many economic opportunities (Reynolds and Ross 1998).

Unfortunately, the educational environment itself contributes in a number of ways to the low academic achievement of the poor. Chapter 10 considers the problem of the inequitable distribution of quality education and shows that schools in poor neighbourhoods tend to have meagre facilities and inexperienced or inadequate teachers. Here, we focus on the ways *school personnel affect poverty-level students* at the interpersonal level.

discrimination
arbitrary, unfavourable treatment of the members of some social group

Children of poor families may experience **discrimination** when they attend school with children of nonpoor families. In a classic study, Hollingshead (1949) found that high school students in a small midwestern U.S. town were treated differently by teachers and administrators, depending on the social-class level of the students' parents. Students from the lower levels received less consideration and harsher punishments. Becker (1952) also identified social-class variations in aspects of the teacher–pupil relationship such as teaching techniques, discipline, and moral acceptability of the pupils.

Other studies have corroborated these findings and extended them to show that *teachers have different expectations for students from different socioeconomic backgrounds* (Kozol 1967; McLoyd 1998). Expectations can significantly retard or stimulate intellectual growth (Rosenthal and Jacobson 1968). Hence, when middle-class teachers expect students from poor families not to perform well, this expectation can lead the children to perform below their capabilities.

In essence, the poor are less likely than the nonpoor to have gratifying and encouraging experiences in school. They are, therefore, more likely to drop out. Children from lower socioeconomic levels, compared to those from the middle and upper strata, also tend to be more dissatisfied with school, report more interpersonal problems (such as not being popular), feel more difficulty in expressing themselves well, and are more likely to express difficulties concentrating and studying. It is not surprising, then, that the majority of school dropouts are from the lower strata.

In sum, the poor are less likely than the nonpoor to perform well in school or to seek more than minimal education—not necessarily because of innate ability, but because of sociocultural factors. Even when ability levels of poor and nonpoor are equated, the poor are less likely to pursue higher education.

■■ Social Psychological Factors

Some attitudes and values held by both the nonpoor and the poor help to perpetuate poverty (Rogers-Dillon 1995). For example, many of those among the nonpoor accept the *fallacy of retrospective determinism* with regard to poverty: They believe that poverty is inevitable—"There have always been poor people, and there always will be poor people." This kind of attitude may manifest itself as opposition to governmental antipoverty programs, pitting the nonpoor against the poor as various interest groups vie for funds.

Disparagement and Discrimination.   As we pointed out earlier, *the nonpoor tend to disparage the poor.* Through history, and in virtually all societies, the poor have been considered disreputable in some sense. Such attitudes seriously undermine self-respect among the poor and at the same time perpetuate the political and economic processes that maintain poverty. You might think that people's disparagement of the poor would lessen during times of more general economic hardship; but beliefs about the causes of poverty and attitudes toward welfare change little—even when the entire society is in an economic recession (Kluegel 1987).

Basically, many Canadians believe that each person is responsible for his or her own status in a system that allows opportunities to all. Poverty is due wholly or at least partly to the lack of individual effort. More important, the belief that the poor are blameworthy is stronger among the well-to-do than among those in the lower income brackets—and those in the higher brackets have the greatest influence on governmental policies and practices.

self-fulfilling prophecy
a belief that has consequences (and may become true) simply because it is believed

Negative attitudes toward the poor may become **self-fulfilling prophecies.** If a man is poor because he is out of work, he may find that when he secures work, hostility is directed toward him because he comes from an impoverished background. In a community where two of the authors once lived, a manufacturing company placed a full-page advertisement in the local newspaper, pointing out that a program to bus inner-city workers to the plant had failed. The ad asked what was wrong with the workers. Why were the jobs still open? The company implied that what many people think is actually true: The poor are too lazy to work and will not accept an opportunity even if it is offered to them. A subsequent investigation showed that the chronically unemployed, who were all black, were unwilling to work because of pressures, hostility, and racial bias.

The Ideology of Wealth and Poverty.   The Canadian *ideology of wealth and poverty* has two elements: a belief that there are *opportunities for advancement* for all and a belief that particular characteristics enable people to seize the opportunities. This ideology is longstanding and includes the idea that wealth comes from a combination of "hard work, ability, motivation, and other favorable personal traits" (Huber and Form 1973:100). A poll conducted in November 1999 by the Angus Reid Group asked Canadians their views on poverty:

- Half of Canadians believe that people are poor "mainly through no fault of their own."
- Just under one-third of Canadian believe that poverty occurs "mainly because of their own choices and actions."
- 50 percent said that the government should be "primarily responsible for helping the poor." Other groups and institutions that should bear responsibility are:
    - poor people and their families (14%)
    - charitable organizations and community associations (11%)
    - the business sector (6%)
    - church and religious groups (2%)
    - all of these parties equally responsible (15%)

Finally, the poor and the unemployed are "the most likely to hold Canada's governments responsible for helping the poor." Thus, the well-to-do are more likely than the poor to accept such an ideology, but some of the poor also agree with it. The ideology of wealth and poverty inhibits the nonpoor and at least some of the poor from action that could alleviate poverty.

■■ From Social Problems to Solutions

There have, of course, been attempts to resolve the problem of poverty. In spite of these efforts, the prevalence of poverty in Canada has not really changed. The Canadian poor fared slightly better in the first part of 2000 due to six consecutive years of economic growth. Child poverty, for example, went down from 16.4 percent in 2000 to 15.6 percent in 2001. But this rate is still higher than 14.9 percent in 1989. Child poverty rates vary across Canada: the lowest is in Prince Edward Island, at 12.5 percent, and the highest is in Manitoba at 22.5 percent.

The cutbacks in social welfare programs throughout the 1990s had a particularly adverse effect on those families that have historically been disadvantaged: First Nations, immigrants, and visible minorities (2003 Report Card on Child Poverty in Canada). Child poverty rates in 2001 among these groups are 34 percent, 41 percent, and 42.4 percent, respectively. According to the 2003 Report Card on Child Poverty in Canada, there are three lessons to take from the trend of child poverty in Canada:

> Lesson 1: We cannot rely on economic growth alone to have a major effect on reducing the rate of child poverty—social investments are crucial; Lesson 2: The structural sources underlying child poverty remained the same for 30 years: a higher labour market that does not deliver the jobs or the wages to allow parents to raise their children in dignity, and an income security system that does not provide an adequate income floor to protect children from the vagaries of the economic cycle; Lesson 3: A job is no longer a guaranteed escape from poverty for families with children. (2)

To eliminate poverty, some attitudes and ideologies among the political leadership must be altered. The commitment of the federal government is essential. Past programs of the federal government have been inadequate, and a commitment to new policies and programs is needed.

Since single mothers have the highest rate of poverty in the nation, strategies to help them must have priority. The Report Card on Child Poverty suggests that policies—if implemented—can have a positive long-term effect in reducing poverty (2003:10). It calls for an enhanced Child Tax Benefit of at least $4,400 per child. Families on social assistance should have increased benefit levels, and funding for these programs must trickle down from the federal government. Strategies are needed to address the issues of bad jobs and low wages. An individual worker can not support his or her family working at minimum wage. Jobs pay so low that even full-time work cannot move the workers out of poverty. In fact, the income of the poorest single mother has worsened, because what she gains through earnings is less than what she received in benefits (dental and drug plans) on social assistance. Thus is necessary the availability of jobs that pay well and provide good working conditions. In order to enable parents to work, a national system of early childhood education and care is needed. Finally, all persons have a right to decent and affordable housing. To address the shortage of affordable housing in Canada, a housing strategy is necessary that will see to the development of no fewer than 25,000 units each year.

Rates of poverty have declined in recent years. As stated above, this trend is in large part due to an economy that has steadily grown over the last six years. That said, the decrease in poverty has been slight and in no way has matched the growth of income of Canada's most wealthy. And, should there be another downturn in the economy, the conditions under which the poor live could worsen considerably.

Finally, various forms of social action can help the poor. One example is the "Out of the Cold" program, run by a multi-faith alliance on the coldest weeks of the year, that provides food, showers, clean clothes, basic nursing care, and overnight shelter to the homeless.

Tent City is another example of how citizens can organize and effect change. In the early 1990s, the Canadian government cancelled its national housing program. Soon thereafter, the provincial government in Ontario followed suit, and cut its subsidized housing program. To make matters worse, welfare rates were cut by more than 20 percent, and the *Landlord and Tenant Act* was amended to be more sympathetic to the needs of landlords than of tenants (Crowe 2004). In 1998, a group of "homeless people striving for a healthier existence outside of the shelter system initiated Tent City … a squatter's camp of 140 people—the largest and longest act of civil disobedience by homeless people in Canadian history" (Crowe 2004). Many Toronto organizations such as the Toronto Disaster Relief Fund (comprising street nurses, primary health care, and social service workers) became involved, and Tent City became equipped with portable toilets, wood stoves for heat and food, and even prefabricated or mobile homes (Crowe 2004). Tent City, for many of Toronto's homeless, was viewed as an improvement from overcrowded shelters (Hardell 2002).

In September 2002, security guards removed the squatters. Since the eviction and numerous protests, some municipal federal housing changes have occurred. There are more beds available to the homeless, and rent supplements to former occupants of Tent City have been implemented—more than 100 of them are now living in their own apartments. The federal government has responded to the national housing crisis with its "Affordable Housing Framework." These programs are only one step forward in addressing the affordable housing crisis in Canada.

Other programs include the work of various civic and religious groups in repairing and renovating homes, providing food for the hungry, offering health care to the poor, and giving scholarships to poor children. Such programs reach a portion of the poor, but they cannot replace the broader public policies that are needed to help the millions of poor Canadians.

▪▪ SUMMARY

Poverty may not be as bad in Canada as it is in some parts of the world, but Canada's poverty must be evaluated in terms of the standard of living attained by the majority of Canadians. Although Canada has no government-mandated poverty line, Statistics Canada unofficially uses the Low Income Cutoff (LICO). The poverty line for a family of four (two children, two adults) is $31,424 in large urban centres and $20,603 in rural communities. This unofficial definition is challenged as inadequate or unrealistic by some groups because it sets the poverty level either quite low (Canadian Council of Social Development) or too high and generous (Fraser Institute). Poverty rates have rollercoastered since the 1980s. The latest trend is toward declining poverty rates, in large part due to an upswing in the economy during the late 1990s.

Poverty is not equally distributed among the population, however. Your chances of being poor are greater if you are in a female-headed family, are a member of a minority group, are under 18 years of age, and are living in a rural area. Contrary to popular opinion, poverty is not basically a problem of unemployment. Many of the poor work, and some work full time. Some of the poor are homeless. Homelessness is associated with many other problems, such as mental and physical health.

The quality of life for the poor can be characterized as pervasive deprivation: The poor get less of everything that is valued in Canadian society. Poverty brings despair and fear, including the fear of being victimized by crime. Various myths that disparage the poor diminish their dignity as human beings. Their health is poorer than that of most Canadians, and their poverty and ill health can become a vicious circle. The individual living in poverty is forced to choose between limited, undesirable alternatives.

Among the structural factors that contribute to poverty, the distribution of power is of prime importance. Those who control the wealth are the most powerful, and their interests are typically reflected in governmental decisions. Both the structure and the functioning of Canadian government tend to work to the detriment of the poor. Multiple decision-making centres, the middle-class composition of the bureaucracy, and the complexities of getting aid work to the detriment of the poor. Ironically, the well-to-do are highly critical of welfare recipients for living off the state, yet they too largely depend on government handouts—for example, in the form of tax breaks. The economy works against the poor in three ways: by allowing the concentration of wealth, by entrapping the poor in a vicious circle, and by guaranteeing that a certain proportion of the population will be unable to find employment or jobs that pay more than poverty-level wages.

The family environment tends to perpetuate poverty when there are many children in the family. Even when there are few children, poverty is perpetuated because of an array of factors such as inconsistent parenting, delayed development of language skills, and living in single-parent families. Disrupted families are an important source of poverty, since many widows and divorced women spend a part of the time in poverty. Educational arrangements themselves contribute to the problem because quality education is much less likely to be available to poor children than to nonpoor children. Also, poor children tend not to have gratifying and encouraging experiences in school or to pursue higher education even when they have the ability to do so.

Attitudes and values of both the poor and the nonpoor contribute to the poverty problem. The ideology of wealth and poverty asserts that opportunities are available to all and that certain personal qualities such as hard work and ability enable the individual to seize opportunities. This ideology legitimates blaming the poor for their problem and resisting programs designed to alleviate poverty.

▪▪ KEY TERMS

Autonomy 144	Gross Domestic Product	Malnutrition 133	Subsidy 148
Discrimination 151	(GDP) 146	Poverty 130	
Ghetto 132	Gross National Income	Self-Fulfilling Prophecy	
	(GNI) 139	152	

■■ STUDY QUESTIONS

1. How is poverty defined in Canada? How many Canadians are poor?

2. Who is most likely to be poor in Canada?

3. How have the problems of poverty and the lot of the poor changed over time in our country?

4. Explain the various ways in which poverty affects the basic rights and needs of people.

5. What is meant by the "dilemmas of poverty"?

6. How do social institutions contribute to the problem of poverty?

7. How do attitudes and ideologies help perpetuate poverty?

8. What are some steps that could be taken to eliminate or at least minimize poverty?

■■ FOR FURTHER READING

Belle, Deborah, ed. *Lives in Stress: Women and Depression.* Beverly Hills, CA: Sage, 1982. Observations and interviews with 43 low-income mothers and their children, showing the way in which poverty creates depression. Underscores the helplessness of people in the face of overwhelming circumstances.

Danziger, Sheldon H., and Robert H. Haveman, eds. *Understanding Poverty.* Cambridge, MA: Harvard University Press, 2002. Various experts address the causes and consequences of poverty, antipoverty policies, and efforts by local communities and neighbourhoods to ameliorate the problem.

Ehrenreich B. *Nickel and Dimed: On (Not) Getting By in America.* New York: Metropolitan Books, 2001. Ehrenreich sets out to the southern states, rents the cheapest lodging, and plays the part of an inexperienced homemaker, taking whatever job she can find. This book examines the life of an individual living on minimum wage.

Fine, Michelle, and Lois Weis. *The Unknown City: The Lives of Poor and Working-Class Young Adults.* Boston: Beacon Press, 1998. An in-depth examination of the lives of poor and working-class men and women as explained by the people themselves as they talk about their struggles with work, school, family life, and sexuality.

Kotlowitz, Alex. *There Are No Children Here: The Story of Two Boys Growing Up in the Other America.* New York: Anchor, 1991. A graphic look at the dilemmas and stresses of poverty through the eyes of two boys and their mother in a Chicago housing project.

Noble, Charles. *Welfare as We Knew It: A Political History of the American Welfare State.* New York: Oxford University Press, 1997. Discusses various factors about U.S. culture and institutions that account for the fact that the United States is the least generous welfare state among Western industrial nations.

Schram, Sanford F. *After Welfare: The Culture of Postindustrial Social Policy.* New York: New York University Press, 2000. Analyzes the welfare reform legislation of 1996 that created TANF, showing how the thrust of the program is to get people to work regardless of the consequences for their families or even of the amelioration of their poverty.

Sherraden, Michael. *Assets and the Poor: A New American Welfare Policy.* New York: M.E. Sharpe, 1991. A proposal for a radical new approach to welfare—focusing not merely on income, but on helping the poor to accumulate assets.

Swanson J. *Poor-Bashing: the Politics of Exclusion.* Toronto: Between the Lines, 2001. This book examines how the language of "poor bashing" individualizes poverty, thus hiding the underlying determinants of poverty.

■■ NOTE

1. There are virtually no black women working in the clothing industry, as black women are stereotyped as "rebellious," a characteristic that is not suited to "the meticulous, precise and repetitive work garment making entails" (Das Gupta 1996:57).

GENDER INEQUALITY

LEARNING OBJECTIVES

1. Discuss the issue of biological versus social bases for gender differences.

2. Show how inequalities between the sexes affect the lives of women and men.

3. In terms of gender inequality, explain the significance of traditional sex roles and socialization, and their place in social institutions such as the family, religion, education, the professions, sports, and so on.

4. Identify the kinds of attitudes, values, and ideologies that contribute to gender inequality.

5. Reflect upon the ways in which sex role socialization has affected the choices you have made thus far in your life.

NATURE OR NURTURE?

In a typical first-year sociology class, Professor Jane Smith and her students were discussing family life, parenting issues, and gender inequality. Professor Smith asked the students (most in their late teens and early twenties) how many planned to be parents. Of the 60-odd people present, approximately 75 percent raised their hands (the class was about 70-percent female). Professor Smith then asked how many intended to interrupt their careers in order to raise their children. After some thinking and looking around the class at their peers, approximately 50 percent of the original group who said that they planned to parent raised their hands: all but one were female. When Professor Smith asked the students who had originally raised their hands why they had not this time, they mainly responded by saying things like, "I hadn't thought about it," or "I just assumed I would have to, isn't it a woman's job?"

As they pursued the topic, Professor Smith asked the males in the class if they had planned for career interruptions to parent, and all but one said no. Further, they found the question humorous—as one said, "Weird question; everyone knows guys don't stay home taking care of kids." The reasons most often raised as to why the social expectations of Canadians are that women take the primary responsibility for raising children were that a) caring for others, children in particular, is "natural" to women and not to men; that women have a "maternal instinct" which makes them the "obvious" caretakers of children, and b) that because men normally earn more money than women it makes sense for women to stay at home. The one male in the class who said that he would like to stay home and parent said that he couldn't see the difference in who stayed home, and that he would be "willing" to do it if his wife earned as much money as he. This example from everyday life provides an illustration of gender inequality at a primary level. It is subtle and implicit rather than explicit, but it nonetheless creates interesting decisions for women and men who want to challenge prevailing stereotypes of gender-appropriate behaviour. ■

▪▪ INTRODUCTION

All things considered, do you think there are more advantages in being a man or in being a woman in society today? In the United States, a nationwide CBS News poll found that men and women differed in their responses to the question (The Polling Report 2002). Forty-one percent of men and 57 percent of women agreed that men have more advantages, while 14 percent of men and 6 percent of women agreed that women have more advantages. Most of the remaining believed that neither has more advantages.

Why would the majority of women and four out of 10 men agree that men have more advantages? After all, most Canadians affirm the ideal of equality of opportunity. Yet as you will see, the ideal has been elusive for women.

Because women suffer from inequality as a result of an **innate** characteristic (their sex), as do minorities, women are called the *largest minority* in North America. Actually, females are in a slight majority because although more male than female babies are born in Canada, the mortality rate is higher among males. The female population was 51 percent of the total in 2000 (Canadian Census 2001: A Profile of the Canadian Population by Age and Sex).

As we discuss inequality between the sexes, we use certain important terms. The terminology is not yet standardized, but the following definitions are consistent with usage adopted by most social scientists. **Sex** refers to an individual's biological identity as male or female. **Gender** is the meaning of being male or female in a particular society, and **gender role** refers to the attitudes and behaviours that are expected of men and women in a society. Whereas *sex* refers to genital differences and biological ones determined by chromosomal makeup (females have XX and males XY chromosomes), *gender* is socially constructed and maintained by all cultures through sex-role socialization throughout the life cycle.

The terminology indicates that *some aspects of men and women are determined by social rather than biological factors.* This is the first issue we examine. Contrary to the argument that gender inequalities are the necessary outcome of biological differences, we show that the problems are sociocultural in origin and how they affect the quality of life for women. Finally, we look at structural and social psychological factors that contribute to gender inequality and suggest some ways to address the problems.

innate
existing in a person from birth

sex
an individual's identity as male or female

gender
the meaning of being male or female in a particular society

gender role
the attitudes and behaviour that are expected of men and women in a society

▪▪ BIOLOGY OR SOCIETY?

Unquestionably, there are numerous differences in the attitudes and behaviours of the sexes. Men and women do not perceive in the same way (Herlitz and Yonker 2002). They do not have the same kinds of aspirations or use the same strategies in competitive games. The question we want to examine here is, what accounts for those differences? Are they rooted in biology or in society? The questions are important because those who hold to a strong biological position are likely to fall into the *fallacy of retrospective determinism,* arguing that whatever has happened to women in North American society is inevitable because people are determined by their own biological makeup to behave and function in certain ways.

▪▪ Gender and Biology

The "damsel in distress" and "white knight" of folklore illustrate the longstanding notion that men are the independent and women the dependent creatures. This notion was given a pseudoscientific legitimacy in the writings of Sigmund Freud, who argued that biology is critically important in sex-related behaviour. Freud's arguments were

Nurturing is a significant part of the traditional role of women. But men can also nurture—remember that there is no gene for nurturing!

summed up in his famous idea that *anatomy is destiny*. Freud claimed that girls reach a point in their development at which they recognize that they are anatomically different from boys. They lack a penis and therefore feel shortchanged. They develop "penis envy." According to Freud, only in the act of conceiving and giving birth to a child can a woman find fulfillment for her desire to have a penis. He also concluded from his observations that women are naturally more passive, submissive, and neurotic than men (Freud 1949).

Freud's arguments are based on questionable evidence at best. Essentially, he developed his psychoanalytic theories by observing middle-class behaviour of his day and then explained the relationships between the sexes in terms of his theories. There is a high degree of circularity involved, so that those who use his arguments often fall into the *fallacy of circular reasoning*.

A more empirical basis for asserting the natural subservience of women is claimed by those who draw on research in the areas of sociobiology, also known as essentialism and evolutionary psychology (the use of biological factors to explain social phenomena), the brain, and human hormones (Wilson 2000; Pfaff 2002). These researchers claim, on the basis of various kinds of evidence, that human behaviour must be understood in terms of *innate biological differences between the sexes*. Some stress humans' continuity with other animals and argue that male and female behaviour reflects the imperatives of the evolutionary process—the struggle to survive and to perpetuate one's kind.

Those who draw on research on the brain and hormones also stress the biological differences but do not necessarily talk about them in terms of evolutionary imperatives. Rather, the differences are used to explain such things as the higher levels of aggression among males, the greater verbal abilities of females, and the greater mathematical, visual, and spatial skills of males (Kolata 1995; Pratarelli and Steitz 1995).

Clearly, there are differences between males and females in both the structure and the functioning of the brain (Kolata 1995; Kreeger 2002), but the implications of these differences are unclear and controversial. First, many of the differences are relatively small or even trivial (Hyde and Plant 1995). For example, while women are more cooperative than men in group tasks, the difference is very small and women are pressured more than are men to conform to the group (Doherty 1998). Second, new research continues to modify some of the conclusions about differences. For example, while boys are more aggressive than girls, researchers who took into account differing forms of aggression found that girls were significantly more *relationally aggressive* than boys (Crick and Grotpeter 1995).

Thus, while male and female brains differ in some ways and while the two sexes have differing hormonal structures, the implications for behaviour are still controversial. A biologist, Anne Fausto-Sterling (1985), looked in detail at the implications for sex differences in research on the brain and on sex hormones. She pointed out deficiencies in the research and concluded that there are definite limitations in the extent to which humans are shaped by biological factors. With respect to brain structure, genetic factors are important but "extensive development of nervous connections occurs after birth, influenced profoundly by individual experience" (Fausto-Sterling 1985:77). Rather than a simplistic causal relationship between biological factors and behaviour, she argued that mind, body, and culture interact with each other in human development. No human behaviour can be explained merely in terms of either biological or social factors. Behaviour is always a function of multiple factors, and we cannot say how much of any particular behaviour is biological and how much is social.

This is not to deny the importance of biological factors, but rather to recognize that *humans are not driven inexorably in a particular direction by their genetic makeup.*

■■ Men's Issues

In the late 1980s, a *men's movement rapidly gained momentum* in the United States, and some U.S. organizations have now formed Canadian chapters. In the University of California reference system, the number of books related to men and masculinity increased sevenfold between 1989 and 1995 (Newton 1998). During the period, the number of scholarly essays in the area tripled and the number of popular magazine articles increased tenfold.

We look briefly at this movement for two reasons. First, we don't want to give the impression that men have all the advantages and none of the problems. Men's issues are as legitimate as women's. Second, the men's movement illustrates our point that gender behaviour is sociocultural and not merely biological.

Issues of concern to men include (Throop 1997; Newton 1998; Schwolbe 1996):

- The meaning of masculinity in a time of changing gender roles (Kaufman 1993, 1997).
- The meaning of being a father and a husband in the face of feminist assertions and cultural expectations.
- The rights of divorced and single fathers.
- Perceived discriminatory treatment by lawyers and the courts in divorce and child custody hearings.
- Reverse bias in hiring and promotions when women are chosen over men who are more qualified.
- Eradicating violence against women.

In 1991, a handful of Canadian men in Toronto began a campaign to end violence against women—in Canada, especially, but also globally. As of January 2005, hundreds of thousands of men have joined this campaign. The men sell and wear white ribbons to show their support for women and actively participate in pro-feminist activities aimed at eradicating violence of all types against women and children. This is an example of individuals and groups creating social solutions to social problems (www.whiteribbon.ca 2005).

Some segments of the men's movement take the position that men, not women, are the truly oppressed group today (Ferber 2000). They argue that men have been "demasculinized," that women and the women's movement are responsible, and that men must reclaim their masculinity and their rightful authority.

Others in the movement are concerned with more specific issues such as fatherhood (Ranson 2001). In the past, fathers were thought of as breadwinners who had limited time to spend with their children. Today, fathers are expected to be much more involved in their children's lives; but they are also expected to be successful in the workplace. How can they meet the competing demands? What do they do when parenting and work requirements contradict each other? What is the role of the wife and mother in all this?

Clearly, such questions arise not out of biology but out of the social milieu. Men's issues, like women's, are a reflection of the sociocultural context—or, to put it another way, gender roles result from sociocultural, not merely biological, factors.

An issue that the men's movement (as well as the women's movement) highlights is that strict, socially constructed gender scripts hinder rather than assist women and men to behave and react in ways that suit their temperament, upbringing, social conditioning, and desires. The concepts of *femininity* and *masculinity* need to be broadened to reflect the myriad ways in which the genders can present and be accepted as somewhat representative of these sex-typed categories. Some authors (Brooks 1996, Courtney 2000, Fox 2001, Salamon and Robinson, 1987, among others) argue that within the categories of femininity and masculinity exist hierarchies of behaviours that identify some individuals as more feminine or masculine than others. Some lesbians and gay men are often found at the bottom of these stratification systems, and "macho" men and "sexy" women are found at the top. As well, the societal expectations of who is "most" masculine or feminine are usually restricted to younger individuals, especially those in their teen years and early twenties. It is seldom that we read about—or see—older women and men presented as "typically" masculine or feminine after the age of 50.

Having said that, though, de Beauvoir (1977), Sontag (1973), and many others have noted that when it comes to older persons and gender inequality, there is a "double standard of aging." This double standard refers to the fact that, whereas older women are thought to become less sexually desirable or attractive as they age, men are seen to become more so because the lines on their faces (called "wrinkles" when they occur in the faces of women) are thought to represent signs of maturity and thus handsomeness! As well, the highest rates of poverty, globally, are among older women; this situation contributes to what is known as the "feminization" of poverty. Further, older women are more often widowed and living alone, and more are institutionalized (Auger and Tedford Little 2002).

The same sex-role socialization that begins even before we are born—when decisions are made about what colour of clothes to put us in, names to call us, or what we might be when we grow up—continues throughout the life cycle and even into our dying days. In one author of this text's work with the dying and their important ones (Auger 2001 and 2003), especially among those who chose to die at home or in hospices, it is noted that assumptions are made by health care providers, and individuals and their families, about how women and men will deal with their impending death and grief based upon stereotypical assumptions that women are better at displaying their emotions than men and that men have trouble being open and honest about their feelings. As with all stereotypical expectations, these too limit individuals' rights to express themselves in their own unique ways.

▪▪ GENDER INEQUALITY AND THE QUALITY OF LIFE

Although men as well as women have problems and complaints, our focus is on the inequality faced by women. As noted earlier, the majority of women and four of 10 men agree that men have more advantages. In this section, we examine those advantages. In essence, they are *contradictions between the ideology of equal opportunities and the reality of life for women.*

▪▪ The Right to Equal Economic Opportunities

Trends in Participation. A growing percentage of women are participating in the paid labour force. As table 6.1 shows, the proportion of employed women in the Canadian labour force continues to rise. In 1976 there were 42 percent; in 1999, 55 percent. However, according to the Statistics Canada report *Women in Canada 2000*, 55 percent of all employed women in Canada aged 15 and over had jobs in 1995, up from 42 percent in 1976. In that same year, 28 percent of employed women worked fewer than 30 hours per week, compared with just 10 percent of employed men. As well, the majority of employed women continue to work in occupations in which they have traditionally been concentrated.

In 1999, according to the same report, unemployment rates were slightly lower among women than men: 522,000 women or 7.3 percent of female labour force participants were unemployed, compared with 7.8 percent of male labour force participants.

TABLE 6.1 ▪ ▪ ▪

Labour Force and Participation Rates, 1999–2003

	1999	2000	2001	2002	2003
	Thousand				
Labour Force	**15,721.2**	**15,999.2**	**16,246.3**	**16,689.4**	**17,046.8**
Men	8,534.0	8,649.2	8,769.2	8,989.8	9,135.9
Women	7,187.2	7,350.0	7,477.1	7,699.6	7,910.9
Participation Rates	Percentage				
15 years and over	65.6	65.9	66.0	66.9	67.5
Men	72.5	72.5	72.5	73.3	73.6
Women	58.9	59.5	59.7	60.7	61.6
15–24 years	63.5	64.4	64.7	66.3	67.0
Men	65.3	65.9	66.1	67.7	68.0
Women	61.7	62.9	63.3	64.9	66.0
25–44 years	85.8	86.0	86.3	86.8	87.1
Men	92.1	92.1	92.1	92.4	92.5
Women	79.6	80.0	80.4	81.2	81.6
45 years and over	47.8	48.5	48.9	50.3	51.7
Men	56.6	56.9	57.1	58.6	59.6
Women	39.9	40.9	41.5	42.8	44.6
65 years and over	6.2	6.0	6.0	6.7	7.3
Men	9.8	9.5	9.4	10.5	11.5
Women	3.4	3.3	3.4	3.7	4.1

Source: Statistics Canada, CANSIM, table 282-0002.

This report also noted that even when employed, women are still largely responsible for looking after their homes and families, and often also caring for elders and other relatives who live nearby.

The average earnings of employed women in 1999 were still substantially lower than those of men. Even when employed full time, the earnings of women were only 73 percent of what men made in that same year. Women made up a disproportionate share of the population in Canada with low incomes. In 1999, 2.8 million women, who comprised 19 percent of the total female population, were living in low-income situations, compared with 16 percent of the male population.

The income situation of women in Canada varies greatly depending on their family status. In 1997, 56 percent of lone-parent families headed by women had incomes below the low-income cutoffs, as did 49 percent of elderly women who lived alone. It might appear from this evidence that economic discrimination against women is diminishing and that women are increasingly free to enter the labour force even when they have small children at home.

Such a conclusion is reasonable in the light of *unemployment rates*. The rates give us a measure of the number of people who desire employment but who are out of work. From the end of the Second World War to the 1990s, the rates were nearly always higher for women than for men, a contradiction of the *ideology of equal opportunity*. Since 1990, the rate for women has been about the same as that for men, at times a little lower and at times a little higher.

The right to equal economic opportunities begins only at the point of gaining employment, however. Once in a job, are a woman's opportunities for advancement as good as those of a man? Will she earn as much as a man? It is to these critical questions that we now turn.

Career Inequality.   According to Canadian ideology, if you have the ability and the determination, you are on your way to success in a career. This ideology, however, is *contradicted by the discriminatory treatment of women in various occupations*. Women experience discrimination in hiring, in on-the-job training, in promotions, and in the way they are treated by supervisors and co-workers (Cohen, Fast, and Da Pont 1997; Neft and Levine 1997; Broschak and Haveman 1998; Knoke and Ishio 1998; Haynie and Gorman 1999; Yoder and Berendsen 2001). There is also discrimination in the sense that women may be discouraged from entering certain occupations. Consider the following facts. In many occupational categories, women are found disproportionately in the lower-echelon jobs such as the services-producing sector (see table 6.2). Even though women make up the majority of those in the educational sector of the economy (as table 6.2 indicates), at the university level there is a gender gap of $8,500 per year. According to Canadian researchers Ornstein and Stewart (1996), discriminatory processes of promotion account for much of the discrimination against female faculty in terms of salary issues. As these authors note, even when female faculty have similar experiences—including research productivity, years of teaching, publications, and so on—they are still likely to receive less than their male counterparts with similar qualifications (Ornstein and Stewart 1996). Although far more women than men are teachers, the proportion of women in top administrative jobs in education (superintendents, assistant superintendents, principals, and assistant principals) is low. At the college and university level in the U.S., women compose more than half of the student body but only 16 percent of presidents, 3 percent of chief business officers, and 25 percent of chief academic officers are women (Chliwniak 1997). Increasing proportions of admissions to medical schools are female, but women may be encouraged to pursue the traditional "female" specialties such as pediatrics, psychiatry, and preventive medicine. Moreover, although women comprise 43 percent of all medical students in the U.S.,

TABLE 6.2 ■ ■ ■

**Employment by
Industry and Sex, 2003**

	Number Employed 2003 (%)		
	Both Sexes	Men	Women
All industries	**100.0**	**100.0**	**100.0**
Goods-producing sector	25.3	36.3	12.8
Agriculture	2.2	2.9	1.4
Forestry, fishing, mining, oil and gas	1.8	2.9	0.6
Utilities	0.8	1.2	0.4
Construction	5.9	9.9	1.4
Manufacturing	14.6	19.4	9.1
Services-producing sector	74.7	63.7	87.2
Trade	15.6	15.1	16.2
Transportation and warehousing	4.9	6.9	2.5
Finance, insurance, real estate, and leasing	5.9	4.6	7.5
Professional, scientific, and technical services	6.3	6.8	5.9
Business, building, and other support services[1]	3.9	3.9	3.9
Educational services	6.7	4.5	9.2
Health care and social assistance	10.7	3.5	18.9
Information, culture, and recreation	4.5	4.4	4.6
Accommodation and food services	6.5	5.0	8.3
Other services	4.5	4.1	5.0
Public administration	5.2	5.1	5.3

[1]Formerly management of companies, administrative, and other support services.
Source: Statistics Canada, CANSIM, table 282-0008.

only 27 percent of full-time medical faculty are women and fewer than 11 percent of women faculty are full professors (compared to 31 percent of men) (Bickel 2000).

Although women have been notably absent from the sciences and engineering, the proportion of engineers who are women has increased considerably in recent decades— from less than 1 to nearly 10 percent. Yet female students majoring in math, science, or engineering still report discriminatory practices and gender-based obstacles in the pursuit of their chosen careers (Steele, James, and Barnett 2002).

As Tomislava (2002) has noted, even though Canadian society has undergone many transformations regarding the equality of women with men, there are still areas where women's success has been impeded. Writing in the *Canadian Women's Studies* journal, Tomislava discusses the involvement of female faculty in physical education programs in schools and universities across the country. She notes that women are highly underrepresented in these fields. She suggests that within the field of physical education gendered methods of teaching and administration establish sport and recreation as essentially male-dominated entities of competition, domination, and power. As a result, "female students do not benefit from the physical, social, mental and emotional components of health that are attributed to regular physical activity" (2002:100). As this study illustrates, the issue of equality for women with men covers every aspect of an individual's life.

As women attempt to achieve a greater degree of equality in career advancement, they may face yet another problem: The tendency for people to evaluate jobs and careers in terms of the gender of the workers as well as the education required of and the income received by the workers. Work that is done primarily by women tends to be valued lower than that done primarily by men (Status of Women Canada 2003). Nor do women gain the same prestige as men when they enter predominantly male occupations. Many women in male-dominated careers feel that they not only must prove their competence but must also do so by performing their job even better than a man would. Yet when men enter predominantly female occupations, their competence is more likely assumed (Neft and Levine 1997). Ironically, a study of 404 medical technologists in the U.S., a female-dominated occupation, found that the women reported more gender discrimination than did the men (Blau and Tatum 2000).

▪▪ Canadian Pay Equity Legislation

In the opening vignette for this chapter, we discussed the opinions of some first-year university students who implied that the reason why women are paid less than men is because the latter are the real breadwinners in the family. However, recent (2000) statistics show that one of the largest increases in the Canadian labour market has been the participation of mothers. One breadwinner in the family is not always enough to support a two-parent household (Almey et al. 2000:43).

pay equity
equal pay for work of equal value

In Canada, all provinces and territories have legislation aimed at providing **pay equity**, or equal pay for work of equal value (also called *comparable worth legislation*), to all citizens regardless of gender. Generally, three types of legislation deal with pay equity: human rights legislation, employment standards laws, and pay equity legislation. Table 6.3 identifies the laws in each province and territory as of 2002.

TABLE 6.3 ▪ ▪ ▪

Canadian Pay Equity Laws

Province	Type of Legislation
Alberta	*Human Rights, Citizenship and Multicultural Act*
British Columbia	*Human Rights Code*
Manitoba	*Employment Standards Act Pt. IV; Human Rights Code Pt. 11; Pay Equity Act*
New Brunswick	*Human Rights Act, Employment Standards Act, Pay Equity Act*
Newfoundland and Labrador	*Human Rights Code*
Nova Scotia	*Labour Standards Code, Human Rights Act, Pay Equity Act*
Northwest Territories	*Fair Practices Act*
Nunavut	Has yet to decide on an act
Ontario	*Employment Standards Act, Human Rights Code, Pay Equity Act*
Prince Edward Island	*Human Rights Act, Pay Equity Act*
Quebec	*Pay Equity Act, Charter of Human Rights and Freedoms*
Saskatchewan	*Human Rights Code; Labour Standards Act Pt. 111*
Yukon	*Employment Standards Act, Human Rights Act*
Federal	*Canadian Human Rights Act, Equal Wages Guidelines 1986*

Source: Adapted from *Pay Equity: A Fundamental Human Right, 2002*, Canadian Status of Women; available online at http://www.swc-cfc.gc.ca.

Because pay equity laws differ from province to province and generally require the worker to pursue legal recourse if he or she feels discriminated against on the basis of gender (or race, ethnicity, or age), and because the various pieces of legislation themselves are often contradictory and difficult for the lay person to understand, Canada still has a long way to go in terms of wage parity between women and men. According to Dahinten (2003), who examined the Survey of Labour and Income Dynamics together with Statistics Canada demographic projections, a substantial wage gap will continue in Canada until at least 2031.

Finally, women face career discrimination because they may be allowed certain privileges that men have only if they make sacrifices not required of men. In particular, women may find that their careers will suffer if they have children, or even that they must choose between a career and a family (Long 1990; Lichter and Landry 1991; Drolet 2002). A study of 51 women faculty members reported that a higher proportion of younger faculty women chose to remain childless or to have fewer children than older faculty women, primarily because of the requirements of getting tenure and promotion (Montgomery 1989). As we noted at the beginning of this chapter, men do not have to sacrifice their careers to family life; why should women?

Income Inequality.   Slower advancement means that women tend to cluster in the lower levels of virtually all occupational categories and are, therefore, accorded less prestige and lower salaries than men. The demand of the women's movement for *equal pay for work of equivalent value* reflects the fact that women are not rewarded equally with men even when they are equally prepared, equally qualified, and equally competent. There is a "glass ceiling," a term used to refer to the arbitrary and often invisible barriers that limit women's advancement. The glass ceiling on income exists in all occupational categories (Cotter et al. 2001; Schaefer 2000; Yamagata et al. 1997).

Statistics Canada first began collecting data on the income distribution of women and men in 1967. At that time women earned 58.4 percent of what men earned. Since that time the gender-based wage gap has diminished, but it is still by no means equal (see table 6.4).

TABLE 6.4 ▪ ▪ ▪

Average Earnings by Sex and Work Pattern, 1993–2002

Year	All Earners		Earnings Ratio
	Women	Men	
	$ constant 2002		%
1993	22,300	34,700	64.1
1994	22,500	36,200	62.0
1995	23,000	35,400	64.8
1996	22,700	35,300	64.5
1997	22,900	36,200	63.3
1998	23,900	37,400	64.0
1999	24,200	37,800	64.0
2000	24,900	39,000	64.0
2001	25,100	39,100	64.1
2002	25,300	38,900	65.2

Note: Data before 1996 are drawn from Survey of Consumer Finances (SCF) and data since 1996 are taken from the Survey of Labour and Income Dynamics (SLID). The surveys use different definitions, and as a result the number of people working full-year full-time in the SLID is smaller than in the SCF.
Source: Statistics Canada, CANSIM, table 202-0102.

Why is there such inequality? There could be many reasons. For example, we know that income is closely related to education, occupational category, and proportion of time worked. Are the differences between men and women accounted for by some of these factors? Do women earn less because they have less education, because they work fewer hours, or because they obtain lower-paying jobs?

Some of the difference in median income can be explained by such factors, but when all the factors are taken into account, there is still a substantial wage gap that is not explained. In 2001, Dr. Karen Hadley authored a report entitled *And We Still Ain't Satisfied—Gender Inequality in Canada: A Status Report for 2001*. This research was a joint endeavour between the National Action Committee on the Status of Women Canada and the Canadian Social Justice Foundation. In it, Dr. Hadley noted that the gender gap in Canada is much wider than commonly believed. At the time the report was written, women's incomes were 61 percent of those of men, and an overwhelming number of women lived in poverty. Hadley estimated that 20 percent of women in Canada lived below the poverty line. Among the poorest were women of colour (37 percent) and Aboriginal women (43 percent). Women aged 45 to 64 made only 51 percent of the earnings of their male counterparts; of this situation, Dr. Hadley said that, "We've got to pay attention to these issues. It is unacceptable for so many women to live in poverty and for women to continually bear the weight of system-wide failure." The data for this study were collected from a special run of Statistics Canada's Survey of Labour and Income Dynamics, a monthly survey of 20,000 income earners across Canada.

One positive result that Dr. Hadley found from her research is that women who work in unionized settings make up to 82 percent of the earnings of their male counterparts—indicating that unionized settings are doing more to promote women's equality, at least in the paid labour force, than non-unionized ones. For example, Tsui (1998) examined the income gap among business managers and concluded that women still received lower pay than men even after controlling for such things as number of hours worked, educational background, and self-confidence. Indeed, the inequality exists at career entry, when women tend to begin at lower salaries than men and find themselves steered into jobs that are defined as more suitable for women (which means less likelihood of getting equal pay) (Marini and Fan 1997). Looking at young (ages 25 to 34) wage and salary earners, the median annual earnings of men is 1.39 times that of women, ranging from 1.66 for those with less than a high school education to 1.31 for those with four or more years of college (Wirt et al. 2002:156). Women now attain more education than do men, according to Statistics Canada's publication *The Daily* on September 14, 2000. Yet this has not translated into higher or even equal incomes.

The Daily also notes that Canadian women have made tremendous strides in their educational attainment in the past several decades. In 1996, 12 percent of all women aged 15 and over had a university degree—double the figure in 1981 (6 percent), and four times that in 1971 (3 percent). However, women are still less likely than men to have a university degree. The overall difference in the proportions of women and men with a university degree is likely to narrow further in the future, since women currently make up the majority of full-time students in universities. However, women's share of full-time university enrolment declines at higher levels of study, with fewer women continuing on to receive graduate degrees. While they make up the majority of full-time students in most university departments, women continue to account for a minority of full-time enrolment in mathematics and science faculties. In 1999, 55 percent of all women aged 15 and over had jobs, up from 42 percent in 1976. As a result, women accounted for 46 percent of the workforce in 1999, up from 37 percent in 1976.

GENDER INEQUALITY IN THE WORKPLACE

The status of women tends to rise as a nation modernizes. Yet in neither the low income nor the higher income nations do women have equality with men in the workplace. This point is underscored in a study of employment rates and income in seven nations: Belgium, Canada, Germany, the Netherlands, Sweden, the United Kingdom, and the United States (Gornick and Jacobs 1998). The researchers looked at how men and women fare in jobs both in government and in the private sector.

They found that the employment rate for women was lower than that for men (figure 6.1). Sweden, which has a social democratic form of government, had the smallest difference, while the conservative Netherlands had the largest. The small difference in Sweden is due to the fact that women hold a far greater number of government jobs than do men. Among employed women in Sweden, 60.1 percent have jobs in the public sector, while among employed men the figure is 23.3 percent.

With regard to median annual earnings, the researchers found that men earned more than women in both government and the private sector. Contrary to some claims, government employment does not help women in their struggle for equality: Women who work in government do not earn more than, nor even as much as, men who work either in government jobs or in the private sector. The earnings gap varied by nation. For private-sector employment, the ratio of women's median annual income to that of men varied from a low of 62.3 percent in Germany to a high of 80.4 percent in Sweden.

Thus, gender inequality in employment rates and earnings is found in nations throughout the world, including the most advanced industrial nations. Women have made advances in the workplace in many nations, but in none have they yet achieved equality with men.

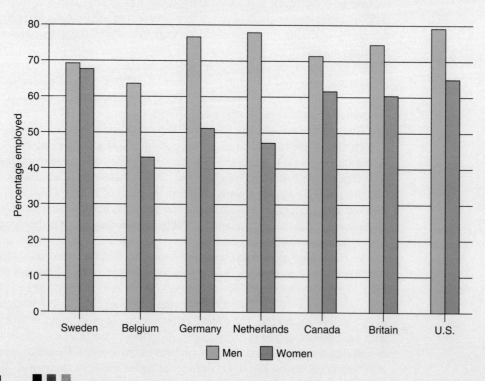

FIGURE 6.1

Employment rates, selected countries.

Source: Gornick and Jacobs 1998.

▪▪ Political Participation

According to North American ideology, all citizens can and should *participate in the political processes* of the nation. Voter apathy is considered cause for alarm. It is believed that only through maximum citizen participation will you have the kind of nation that provides freedom and opportunity for all. In the case of women, this ideology *contradicts norms and the female role.* That women were so long denied their right to vote is the most blatant example of the contradiction.

Political participation includes more than voting. Historically, the number of women holding appointed or elected governmental offices has been small at every level (municipal, provincial, and national). Some gains have been made in recent decades. In May 2004 (one month prior to the federal election on June 28), the Nova Scotia Advisory Council on the Status of Women compiled a chart listing the then-latest figures regarding the involvement of women in politics. Table 6.5 provides figures up to and including May 12, 2004. Tables 6.6 and 6.7 show world and regional averages for women in parliament. Clearly, women do not participate equally with men in the political process and are still a long way from being equally represented in government. Moreover, when women do participate, they tend to be deprived of the more prestigious positions (Riccucci and Saidel 1997).

▪▪ The Right to Dignity as a Human Being

Certain beliefs about women and certain patterns of interaction between men and women are an affront to the dignity of women as human beings. Here again we encounter a *contradiction between the belief in the dignity of human beings,* on the one hand, and the *ideology about a particular group and interaction with members of that group,* on the other hand. We examine three manifestations of the contradiction: the beauty myth, belief in female inferiority, and harassment and violence against women.

TABLE 6.5 ▪ ▪ ▪

Women's Political Representation in Canada, 2004

This chart last updated: May 12, 2004.

Parliament/Legislature	Number of Seats	Number of Women	Number of Men	Percentage Women
Newfoundland and Labrador	48	10	38	21%
Prince Edward Island	27	6	21	22%
Nova Scotia	52	6	46	12%
New Brunswick	55*	7	47	13%
Quebec	125	38	87	30%
Ontario	103*	22	80	21%
Manitoba	57	14	43	25%
Saskatchewan	58	10	48	17%
Alberta	83	17	66	24%
British Columbia	79	19	60	24%
Yukon	18	3	15	17%
Northwest Territories	19	2	18	11%
Nunavut	19	2	17	11%

*one seat currently vacant
Source: http://www.gov.ns.ca/staw/politicalwomen.htm.

	Both Houses Combined	Single House or Lower House	Upper House or Senate
Total MPs	42,605	36,273	6,332
Gender breakdown known for	40,868	34,560	6,308
Men	34,566	29,156	5,410
Women	6,302	5,404	898
Percentage of women	**15.4%**	**15.6%**	**14.2%**

Source: http://www.gov.ns.ca/staw/politicalwomen.htm.

	Single House or Lower House	Upper House or Senate	Both Houses Combined
Nordic countries	39.7%	—	39.7%
Americas	18.5%	18.2%	18.5%
Europe—OSCE member countries including Nordic countries	18.1%	15.3%	17.6%
Europe—OSCE member countries excluding Nordic countries	16.0%	15.3%	15.9%
Asia	15.5%	13.6%	15.3%
Sub-Saharan Africa	14.6%	12.8%	14.4%
Pacific	10.9%	20.5%	12.2%
Arab States	6.0%	7.5%	6.4%

Source: http://www.gov.ns.ca/staw/politicalwomen.htm.

The Beauty Myth.   According to the "beauty myth," a woman must be beautiful to be acceptable and attractive (Wolf 1991; Sullivan 2001). It's a destructive myth. Women spend billions of dollars a year on cosmetics and cosmetic surgery in an effort to appear more beautiful. Teenage girls use a variety of surgical procedures to enhance their beauty, including breast augmentation, eyelid surgery, liposuction (to remove fat), reshaping of the nose, and the "tummy tuck" to tighten the abdomen (Gross 1998). Beauty is a trap. Women who feel homely cannot enjoy their accomplishments because they are haunted by their failure to be beautiful, and women who are beautiful and successful may attribute their success to their beauty rather than to their abilities.

A particularly destructive aspect of the beauty myth is the current ideal of a slender figure for women. In their effort to attain the requisite slimness, some women have succumbed to eating disorders: *anorexia nervosa; self-starvation; and bulimia, repeated binge eating followed by vomiting or laxatives* (Hesse-Biber 1996). The disorders are associated with both physical and emotional health problems, including depression (Stice and Bearman 2001). In Canada, in 1997, nine out of ten persons diagnosed with eating disorders were young women. It is estimated that 15 to 25 percent of Canadian women experience eating disorders (Vanin 1997).

In extreme cases, some young women have died from these eating disorders. A woman can go to such an extreme because the disorders involve a disturbed body image (Mazzeo 1999). That is, the woman does not see herself as thin even when others see her as emaciated. Unfortunately, the number of women with poor and distorted body images has been increasing in recent decades (Feingold and Mazzella 1998).

Body image is an issue for men also (Grogan and Richards 2002). For men, a well-toned, muscular body provides confidence and a sense of power in social situations; but the concern is greater among women, who express more dissatisfaction than do men about their body shape (Demarest and Allen 2000).

The Belief in Inferiority.
Another belief that assaults women's dignity is one that has pervaded human societies; namely, the belief that women are inferior to men. You can see the disparagement in everything from Confucius's statement that women and those of low birth are alike in being difficult to deal with, to Aristotle's contention that a woman is an unfinished man and stands on a lower plane of development, to the American Puritan conviction that women are less intelligent than men. Until recent times, it was widely believed that the presumed inferior intellect of woman was related to her smaller brain. In the 1830s, when Oberlin College in the U.S. offered women a course of study similar to the men's, it shortened the literary work because of the belief that women could not assimilate as much material as men.

The belief in female inferiority is seen clearly in the *differing standards of evaluation of men and women.* For example, people tend to judge performance differently, depending upon whether the person being judged is male or female. One researcher had undergraduates read an essay that, to some of the students, appeared to have been written by a male, and to the other students appeared to have been written by a female (Gallivan 1991). Although they rated the writing skill of the author the same, the students who thought the author was male tended to rate the essay as less biased and more knowledgeable than did those who thought the author was female.

Certain patterns of interaction also reflect the belief in male dominance and female inferiority. For instance, a good deal of research has shown that men interrupt women in conversation much more than the reverse. Such interruptions are interpreted as an exercise of power and dominance over the conversational partner. Thus, physicians will interrupt patients far more than the reverse, *except,* as Candace West (1984) discovered by videotaping physician–patient conversations, when the doctor is a woman. In the tapes, patients interrupt a female doctor as much as or more often than male doctors interrupt their patients. Similarly, researchers found that male doctoral students in marriage and family therapy interrupted women clients three times more than men clients (Werner-Wilson et al. 1997). In all kinds of settings, men tend to interact with women in a dominant–subservient frame of mind.

Women also tend to be *victims of the Eve syndrome.* In the biblical account in Genesis, Adam blamed Eve for his sin of disobedience to God. Throughout human history, men have blamed women for problems and troubles, from Henry VIII, who got rid of wives who did not bear him a son (ironically, it is now known that the male chromosome, not the female, determines the sex of the child), to the unfaithful husband of today who blames his wife for the affair *he* is having.

In the 1980s and 1990s, as Carol Tavris (1990) pointed out, a number of books were published with the ostensible purpose of helping women. Many of them, however, basically fell into the trap of blaming the victim, the *fallacy of personal attack.* One book discusses the "Cinderella complex," a hidden fear of independence. Another tells women that they tend to "love too much." A number of books have looked at the problem of "codependency," which included an addiction to men who abuse or who are addicted to drugs or alcohol. Many women joined recovery groups to overcome their "disease" of codependency. The women learn that they are as responsible for their spouses' problems as the spouses themselves, because they "enable" the spouse to continue the problem behaviour. (Of course, men also can be codependent, but books and articles seem to focus on it as a problem of women.)

Women take their work as seriously as men do.

sexual harassment
unwelcome sexual advances, requests for sexual favours, and other sexual behaviour that either results in punishment when the victim resists or creates a hostile environment or both

Thus, "once again, whatever's wrong is women's fault" (Tavris 1990). Instead of looking at their powerlessness, at the role expectations and financial realities that may keep them in a bad relationship, women in the codependency movement are likely to identify and work on personal faults and failings. Such an approach tends to lower self-esteem and is thereby an assault on the dignity of women as human beings.

Harassment and Violence. A different form of assault on dignity is the **sexual harassment** to which so many women have been subjected. Sexual harassment refers to unwelcome sexual advances, requests for sexual favours, and other verbal or physical conduct of a sexual nature that results in some kind of punishment when the victim resists or that creates a hostile environment. Although both men and women may be sexually harassed, the proportion of women who experience it is far higher. For example, a survey of U.S. military personnel found that 70.9 percent of the women who participated in the survey and 35 percent of the men said they had experienced sexually harassing behaviour during the previous 12 months (Antecol and Cobb-Clark 2001).

Sexual harassment occurs in diverse settings. According to Dranoff (2001:73), in 1998 complaints of sexual harassment accounted for one-fifth of new complaints presented to the Canadian Human Rights Commission.

Perhaps the most destructive harassment occurs in the *sexual exploitation of women by men in power positions* (Rutter 1989). Male power figures include psychiatrists and other therapists, physicians, lawyers, clergymen, and teachers or mentors. Women are particularly vulnerable to sexual pressures in dealing with such power figures. A therapist, for example, may convince a woman that he can provide her with the kind of sexual experience she needs to work through her problems. A clergyman may convince a woman that there is some kind of divine sanction to their relationship. Although we don't know the number of women exploited in this way, increasing attention is being paid to the problem. Indeed, some professional organizations have explicitly condemned such behaviour in their codes of ethics.

The National Day of Remembrance and Action on Violence against Women has occurred every December 6 since Marc Lepine systematically shot and killed 14 female engineering students at the Ecole Polytechnique in Montreal in 1989. This event, which came to be known as the Montreal Massacre, was partly responsible for stricter gun control laws in this country. On December 6, 2003 the Status of Women produced a fact sheet to raise awareness of violence against women. The report was based on data collected in 2000 from 166 police departments across the country representing 53 percent of the national volume of reported crimes. Some of the highlights included the following facts:

- Half of Canadian women (51 percent) have been victims of at least one act of physical or sexual violence since the age of 16.
- In 2000, there were 27,154 sexual offences reported in Canada, including 24,049 sexual assaults and 4,105 other types of sexual offence (such as sexual touching, invitation to sexual touching, sexual exploitation, incest, and sodomy

and bestiality). Women made up the vast majority of victims of sexual assault (86 percent) and other types of sexual offences.

The report also noted that in 2001 the number of spousal homicides in Canada rose, accounting for one out of every five solved homicides. In that year, 86 persons were killed by a current or ex-spouse, up by 18 victims from 2000. The rise over the single year can largely be attributed to the increase in homicide committed by legally married husbands. Four out of five victims of spousal homicide were female.

Finally, violence is the ultimate assault on the dignity of women. Hundreds of thousands of violent acts are committed against women every year, and about a fifth of all violence against women comes from an intimate partner (Johnson 1996:11). The problem is worldwide. According to United Nations data, one in every three women in the world has been beaten, abused, or sexually assaulted, usually by someone known to the victim (United Nations Population Fund 2001).

■■ CONTRIBUTING FACTORS

As with all social problems, many factors contribute to gender inequality. As we examine these factors, it will be clear that the problem is not simply one of men versus women but of a plexus of factors that together create and maintain this inequality.

■■ Social Structural Factors

The Normative Role of the Female. *Gender roles* are found in every society. There is some room for flexibility and variations, of course, and some individuals refuse to be bound by the roles. Nevertheless, *gender roles specify certain kinds of behaviour as appropriate, and other kinds as inappropriate, for men and women.* What, then, is the *traditional role for the Canadian female,* and how does this role contribute to inequality?

In essence, Canadians have advocated the *traditional homemaker role of females and the parallel traditional breadwinner role of males.* Certainly, not all females conform to the traditional role. Working-class, Aboriginal, and black Canadian women, in particular, have been likely to work outside the home. For the bulk of middle- and upper-class whites, however, the wife has been expected to provide a home for her husband and children, and to find her fulfillment in caring for her family. The role assumes, then, that a woman will marry and have children, and will focus on pleasing her husband and caring for her children. In the 1960s and 1970s women's attitudes toward this traditional role changed considerably. Yet the traditional view still receives considerable support, particularly with respect to the woman's responsibility for the home.

The traditional role obviously discourages women from pursuing higher education or a career. In a social context in which being female means taking care of a home and family, and submitting to one's husband, it may be difficult to secure an advanced degree or to commit oneself to a career. However, as we noted earlier, more women than ever are participating in the Canadian labour force, even though they may experience more work interruptions. Fast and Da Pont (1997) have noted that work interruptions have more serious implications for women than they do for men, especially in terms of earnings, employability, and long-term economic well-being, because women experience more frequent and long work interruptions. Many women do not return to paid work after bearing and raising children or caring for family or friends, and nearly one-quarter of those employed full time before a work interruption returned to only part-time employment after their caregiving experiences.

When women do return to paid work, the role of caregiver does not end. Part-time jobs may be viewed as a way of improving the balance between family and job responsibilities. For many women, part-time work may be the only available option after a lengthy interruption to paid employment. Skills may have deteriorated or job requirements may have increased, making it difficult to find a full-time job.

Even though the federal Liberal government has frequently promised to create full on-site childcare programs for Canadian families, these promises have yet to be met.

The research on women's aspirations suggests that if females are treated the same as males, if parents hold similar expectations for their girls and boys and encourage them equally, women will achieve the same levels of education and probably the same levels of work and careers. A great many women would like to work or pursue a career but do not because it conflicts with other role obligations. A *New York Times* poll found that 55 percent of women age 18 to 44 express a preference for combining marriage, children, and a career (Belkin 1989). Only a minority of women prefer either a career without marriage or marriage and children without a career.

The ability to opt for multiple roles is crucial, because a *restrictive role for women can lead to illness.* For both men and women, both marriage and employment increase well-being (Crosby 1991; Burke 1995). Multiple roles not only promote well-being, including physical health, but also tend to lengthen a woman's life (Moen, Dempster-McClain, and Williams 1989, 1992). Even when employed, women are still largely responsible for looking after their homes and families. According to Statistics Canada (2000), in 1998 women employed full-time with a spouse and at least one child under the age of 19 at home spent 4.9 hours per day on unpaid work activities, an hour and a half more than their male counterparts.

In 1999, Statistics Canada found that 2.1 million Canadians cared for elderly, ill, and dying family members. Six out of ten caregivers are women. Hochschild (1997) refers to this additional caregiving task as the "double shift" in which so many women find themselves.

There is in Canadian culture a general expectation that care of the elderly, the sick, and the dying is "women's work." The assumption is that women are better suited for this activity than men, and there is also the notion that somehow such caring abilities are genetic or biological. In this sense, then, such work is seen as natural for women. However, there is in fact no caring gene; rather, these are societal and cultural expectations of women. Men are as capable and as genetically endowed to perform this necessary and important cultural work (Auger and Tedford Little 2002).

Even though women who go to work have better physical and mental health, working does not solve all their problems. Such women are still likely to have more health problems than their male counterparts. A woman who breaks out of the traditional constraints and goes to work may experience overload. Traditional obligations are not easily cast off, even when nontraditional ones are assumed. When women work outside the home, get low pay, and continue to assume the major responsibility for the home, some of the benefits of working are lost (Carrier and Davies 1999; Gaszo-Windle and McMullin 2003).

For many women, in other words, having jobs outside the home means "in addition to" rather than "instead of" taking care of their homes. There has been a trend toward greater sharing of household responsibilities, but employed women still spend substantially more hours than their husbands doing housework, as tables 6.8 and 6.9 show.

Another problem the working woman faces is the effect her work has on her marital relationship. Husbands of working wives have a tendency to feel less adequate as family breadwinners, and this feeling may lower their satisfaction with their own jobs and with their lives generally (Staines, Pottick, and Fudge 1986). This outcome, of course, is more likely when the husband still clings to traditional notions of male and female roles. However, if both husband and wife prefer her to work, both spouses benefit psychologically from the arrangement, particularly if the husband shares the housework (Ross, Mirowsky, and Huber 1983). When women perceive inequity in the division of household tasks, on the other hand, they are prone to be distressed and depressed (Bird 1999). Thus, working can be a kind of psychological salvation for many women, but only when both spouses have cast off traditional notions about sex roles. When the man is willing to assume some traditional female responsibilities and the woman assumes some traditional male responsibilities, both are likely to benefit.

Socialization: Home, School, and the Mass Media.   To understand why women would accept the traditional role, you must look at their *socialization*. At home and at school (and, for that matter, throughout the culture) women are taught the traditional meaning of their role. They learn it at an early age. For instance, parents tend to treat their sons and daughters differently from the beginning. They are likely to speak softly to their daughters and firmly to their sons. One researcher estimates that by the age of 32 months, little girls hear twice as many diminutives (affectionate words like "kitty" and "dollie") as do boys (Mehren 1992). As a result of differential treatment, children become aware of gender-role differences as early as two years of age (Witt 1997).

The differential treatment continues as children grow. Parents tend to define certain toys as appropriate for boys and others as appropriate for girls, and boys in particular are discouraged from playing with "girls'" toys (Campenni 1999). Similarly, children learn that various occupations may be more or less appropriate for them depending upon their sex. By the time they are in elementary school, boys tend to choose "male" occupations and girls tend to choose "female" occupations for their future (Helwig 1998).

In almost all aspects of childrearing, differences tend to occur between the ways boys and girls are raised. Mothers and fathers are likely to talk about emotional aspects of events in similar ways, but both tend to use a greater number and variety of emotion words with their daughters than their sons, and to mention a greater number of sad aspects of the events with their daughters than their sons (Kuebli and Fivush 1992). Mothers tend to give sons more verbal stimulation of the type that facilitates cognitive development (Weitzman, Birns, and Friend 1985).

Finally, parents tend to have lower educational aspirations for their daughters than for their sons (Adelman 1991), and they are not prone to provide the encouragement and family resources for their daughters to enter more traditional male fields such as science (Hanson 1996). Rather, women who are encouraged to pursue the highest levels of education and career report that their parents tried to direct them into traditional female fields like teaching.

In Canadian schools there is a growing concern about issues of gender and the inequalities between girls and boys. Sanford and Blair (1999) examined the effect of popular media, especially magazines and television programs, to ascertain the types of popular images portrayed of each gender and young people's reactions to them. They concluded that both genders were portrayed in stereotypical ways in that boys were shown (and perceived by the students) as being interested in "action and adventure shows and televised sports, [and] they read magazines that focus on activity and sport. Their role models are adult men who are strong and in control" (1999:103). On the other hand, girls "watch shows focusing on friends and relationships; they read fashion magazines. Their role models, often female adolescents, show them how to look good, how to belong to the 'right' crowd and how to please their peers" (ibid). As the authors point out, these two sets of sex roles for women and men are in opposition to one another, so rather than recognize the similarities between the genders, they reinforce the differences. This is problematic when creating school curricula that address the different

TABLE 6.8 ■ ■ ▪

Average Time Spent on Activities, by Sex (Male), 1998

Note: Averaged over a seven-day week.

1. The average number of hours per day spent on the activity for the entire population aged 15 years and over (whether or not the person reported the activity).

2. The average number of hours per day spent on the activity for the population that reported the activity.

3. The proportion of the population that reported spending some time on the activity.

	Total Population[1]	Participants[2]	Participation Rate[3]
	Hours per Day		%
Activity group, total	24.0	24.0	100
Total work	**7.8**	**8.0**	**97**
Paid work and education	**5.0**	**8.8**	**58**
Paid work and related activities	4.5	8.8	51
Paid work	4.1	8.2	50
Activities related to paid work	0.1	0.7	9
Commuting	0.4	0.9	45
Education and related activities	**0.5**	**6.0**	**9**
Unpaid work	**2.7**	**3.2**	**87**
Household work and related activities	2.4	2.8	85
Cooking and washing up	0.4	0.7	63
Housekeeping	0.3	1.5	22
Maintenance and repair	0.2	2.7	9
Other household work	0.4	1.6	27
Shopping for goods and services	0.7	1.8	38
Childcare	0.3	1.8	16
Civic and voluntary work	0.3	2.0	17
Personal care	10.2	10.2	100
Night sleep	8.0	8.0	100
Meals (excluding restaurant meals)	1.1	1.2	92
Other personal activities	1.1	1.2	94
Free time	**6.0**	**6.1**	**97**
Socializing including restaurant meals	1.9	3.0	62
Restaurant meals	0.3	1.6	20
Socializing in homes	1.2	2.5	49
Other socializing	0.3	2.7	12
Television, reading, and other passive leisure	2.9	3.3	87
Watching television	2.4	3.0	80
Reading books, magazines, newspapers	0.4	1.3	30
Other passive leisure	0.1	1.1	9
Sports, movies, and other entertainment events	0.2	2.6	6
Active leisure	1.1	2.6	41
Active sports	0.6	2.3	26
Other active leisure	0.5	2.4	21

Source: Statistics Canada, CANSIM, table 113-0001.

needs of *all* students, especially those who choose to break down such rigid stereotypes in their own lives. As well, because the sexual scripts rely heavily on heterosexual role models, they do little to recognize the needs of students who choose other sexualities. This may reflect the fact that many parents believe their sons are more intelligent than their daughters (Furnham, Reeves, and Budhani 2002). In other words, many women achieve far beyond what their parents expected or encouraged. Yet it is important to

TABLE 6.9 ■ ■ ■

Average Time Spent on Activities, by Sex (Female), 1998

Note: Averaged over a seven-day week.

1. The average number of hours per day spent on the activity for the entire population aged 15 years and over (whether or not the person reported the activity).
2. The average number of hours per day spent on the activity for the population that reported the activity.
3. The proportion of the population that reported spending some time on the activity.

	Total Population[1]	Participants[2]	Participation Rate[3]
	Hours per Day		%
Activity group, total	24.0	24.0	100
Total work	7.8	7.9	99
Paid work and education	3.4	7.7	44
Paid work and related activities	2.8	7.7	36
Paid work	2.5	7.1	35
Activities related to paid work	0.0	0.5	6
Commuting	0.3	0.8	32
Education and related activities	0.6	6.3	9
Unpaid work	4.4	4.6	96
Household work and related activities	4.1	4.3	95
Cooking and washing up	1.1	1.3	85
Housekeeping	1.0	1.8	59
Maintenance and repair	0.1	2.0	4
Other household work	0.4	1.1	33
Shopping for goods and services	0.9	1.9	47
Childcare	0.6	2.4	24
Civic and voluntary work	0.4	1.9	19
Personal care	10.6	10.6	100
Night sleep	8.2	8.2	100
Meals (excluding restaurant meals)	1.1	1.2	91
Other personal activities	1.4	1.4	96
Free time	5.6	5.7	97
Socializing including restaurant meals	2.0	2.8	70
Restaurant meals	0.3	1.5	18
Socializing in homes	1.4	2.3	61
Other socializing	0.3	2.6	12
Television, reading, and other passive leisure	2.6	3.1	84
Watching television	2.0	2.7	75
Reading books, magazines, newspapers	0.5	1.4	34
Other passive leisure	0.1	1.1	9
Sports, movies, and other entertainment events	0.2	2.8	6
Active leisure	0.8	2.2	39
Active sports	0.4	1.7	22
Other active leisure	0.5	2.1	22

Source: Statistics Canada, CANSIM, table 113-0001.

remember that the *aspirations of the children are likely to reflect the aspirations of the parents* (Bourque and Cosand 1989).

The school may reinforce the parental pattern. Observations of classrooms show that girls in some classes receive less attention and less helpful feedback than boys (Sadker and Sadker 1994). Teachers are usually unaware of the fact that they are discriminating by such conduct as giving girls direct answers to their questions while encouraging

Gender stereotyping by the mass media can affect the way people think and behave.

boys to figure out the answers for themselves. The net effect of such practices is to give girls the sense that they are less capable than boys and to deprive them of opportunities for developing problem-solving skills.

Last, the mass media may reinforce the patterns of parents and teachers. For example, children's picture books and elementary reading books portray males and females in more egalitarian ways than in the past, but they are still more likely to appear in traditional roles (Evans and Davies 2000; Gooden and Gooden 2001).

In the school bureaucracy there is also systemic gender discrimination. Stephen Jull, writing in the *Alberta Journal of Education Research* (2002), examined the Canadian teaching profession in terms of the number of women and men who were involved in the administrative and bureaucratic functions of such organizations. He found that women were underrepresented at all levels of the bureaucracy and concluded that the "imbalanced gender distribution in the teaching profession, and the continuation of the role of women as the teachers (and as the volunteers in schools where personnel resources are limited) and not as principals and school board administrators," may contribute to the "reinforcement of patriarchal structures and a social order that is consistent with the status quo views and expectations of women as un(der) paid caregivers and caretakers of children" (2002:47).

Jull went on further to note that if men continue to occupy the positions of power in the school administrative hierarchies, with all the incumbent exclusive economic and social rewards, then "male educators are more likely to focus their attention on supporting traditional schooling agendas in order to advance their own careers and secure their place in the hierarchy" (ibid).

Who runs our schools, and the role models they present to the students who attend them, is also about the presentation of particular types of role models to young people who at some point decide what they want to be when they grow up. It is clearly important that girls and boys be provided with a selection of role models of both genders from which to choose their own careers.

Even college and university textbooks reinforce traditional stereotypes. An examination of more than 1,000 photographs of women in college-level human sexuality and marriage and family textbooks in the U.S. found more egalitarianism in the 1990s than in the 1970s. However, photographs with traditional messages about women still dominated the 1990s texts (Low and Sherrard 1999).

Studies of television shows have consistently found considerable gender stereotyping. An analysis of the 2001–2002 prime-time schedule reported that white, male characters dominated; only 36 percent of all characters on prime time were female (Children Now 2002). Gender stereotyping is found in television commercials as well as in the programs (Coltrane 2000).

YOU ARE WHAT YOU READ AND VIEW

Someone has said, "You are what you read." As noted in this chapter, one factor in perpetuating gender-role inequality is the books that you read as a child and the television programs (especially cartoons) that you watch. Conduct your own research into children's literature and cartoons. The librarian at a local public library can help you make a selection. Decide on what age level you want to investigate first. Then find five books written for this age level before 1975 and five of the most recent, and watch two television cartoons.

Compare the books and cartoons in terms of the number of male and female characters and the gender roles portrayed. How do the earlier books and cartoons differ from the more recent ones? To what extent do you believe that the later books and cartoons overcome gender inequality? Identify two or three aspects of traditional gender roles in the earlier books that are either maintained or eliminated in the later ones.

The question is, does this stereotyping affect the way that people think and behave? Is there any practical significance to the fact that books, newspapers, and other mass media contain pictures that reflect traditional stereotypes?

In an experiment with 96 undergraduates, MacKay and Covell (1997) found evidence that mass media stereotyping does have practical consequences. They had the students evaluate ads from current popular magazines. Half of the students saw ads in which women were portrayed as sex objects, while the other half viewed ads that portrayed women in other ways. Afterward, both male and female students who saw the ads in which women were portrayed as sex objects scored higher than those who saw the other ads on measures of gender stereotypes and acceptance of rape myths. The students who saw the sex-object ads also showed less support for feminism than those who saw the other ads.

Another practical consequence of media portrayal of the sexes is that people who engage in the *fallacy of circular reasoning* find support for their arguments. Consider the following exchange two of the authors once had with an older man, who made the statement: "Everyone knows that men are rational and women are emotional." They asked the man how he knew that. "Everyone knows that. Look around you. Look at television." When the man was told that television is fiction, he replied: "But it is based on fact, on what is real about people. And men are really rational and women are really emotional."

In sum, children learn that they live in a male-dominated world where men are engaged in demanding, exciting activities and women are keepers of the home and family. What they learn from an early age at home and school legitimates the restricted role traditionally assigned females, which, in turn, creates difficulties for women who attempt to carve out a nontraditional life.

The Economics of Gender Inequality.   Situations that continue in the country are *likely profitable* for someone, and gender inequality is no exception. The kind of gender inequalities we have discussed are beneficial for men in a variety of ways. They increase men's job opportunities, incomes, and power. It has been said the hand that rocks the cradle rocks the world (which suggests that real power belongs to women). In most people's experience, however, the hand that holds the biggest purse holds the most power—and this hand typically belongs to a man.

Furthermore, the present amount of income inequality between men and women means that men benefit by having to work less to earn the same amount of money. In essence, a woman might work seven days or more to earn what a man makes in five days. Some of the changes in the Canadian labour force are reflected in changes to the family as more women enter the workforce and more men are expected to engage in household work and childrearing activities. Much has changed in the North American perception of what constitutes "women's work." In March of 1945, CBC Radio aired a program dealing with what was then the burning question of "What Is Women's Work?" The questions that the panel of men in an army barracks discussed included Are working women losing their femininity? Should married women be allowed to hold jobs, even if they put returning soldiers out of work? and Should they receive equal pay? Another topic that was discussed in this forum—held aboard the *HMS Stadacona*, docked in Halifax, Nova Scotia—was whether women should be university educated. If you are interested in some historical viewpoints on this topic from a male perspective, you can hear this broadcast at http://archives.cbc.ca/IDD-1-71-855/conflict_war/women_ww2/ (click on clip #11, "What Is Women's Work?").

When the war ended and the men returned home, public opinion again turned against employment of women, particularly of married women. Fear of another economic recession and persisting hostility toward the notion of women competing with men in the economy were two important factors, according to Chafe (1972). Many women were fired to create more jobs for the vast numbers of returning servicemen, but many women who did not want to return to their traditional roles continued to work. Obviously, women preferred to participate in the economy to a greater extent than many men considered appropriate and desirable.

Since the end of the Second World War, women and men have been engaged in an ongoing struggle over the extent of women's participation in the workplace. That the struggle is one for the better positions is illustrated by the relative ease with which women can secure menial and low-paying jobs. Such jobs must be done by someone if other jobs are to be highly paid and employers are to maintain high levels of profit. Who will take such jobs?

sexism
prejudice or discrimination against someone because of his or her sex

Szymanski (1976) showed that **sexism** and *racism* are *functional substitutes* with respect to such jobs. That is, women and racial and ethnic minorities tend to cluster in the low-paying, menial jobs. Where racial or ethnic minorities are available, they provide that labour. Where they are not available, women provide it. This does not mean that where racial or ethnic minorities are available for low-paying jobs, women are equal to men in the labour market. Women are merely the next-to-the-lowest group on the totem pole, rather than the lowest.

There are two other pressing social issues that have an impact on the lives of women, especially in the larger provinces of Canada. These are a) the role of migrant sex workers who come to this country to provide their services, and b) e-brides.

Migrant Sex Workers   As Brock, Gilles, Oliver, and Mook (2000) have noted, there is currently discussion among Canadian politicians, immigrant settlement associations, academics, and those involved in the immigrant sex trade in Canada, especially in Toronto, around whether such work is a form of paid labour or is exploitative of the women who supply the services—in that they are often underpaid, without employment benefits or adequate health care subsidies, and subject to deportation if found to be in the country illegally. The authors conclude that Canadian immigration law enforcement agencies need to consider how sex-trade workers are assessed and treated when applying to come to Canada to ensure that they are not exploited or victimized.

E-Brides   As we have noted elsewhere, the Internet provides yet another forum for the exploitation of women, children, and men. Mail-order-bride services have now moved to the Internet, where potential husbands can see photographs of their brides to be, read about their experiences, and—for a price—receive the bride of their choice. For many poor families in less developed parts of the world, the opportunity to sell a daughter or sister can provide much-needed funds to purchase basic necessities of life, or to purchase goods and services not otherwise financially available (Clark 2002).

A recent (February 2005) Internet search using the search term Mail Order Bride retrieved more than 3,000 sites offering brides from around the world at different prices. As Pehar (2003) has noted, the lack of regulation of the Internet has enabled sexual exploiters to become the commercial champions of the cyber world, normalizing the buying and selling of women (and sometimes their children) as a simple matter of supply and demand. In our efforts to obtain equality for women and men at all levels of life, it is important to factor in the role that the Internet plays in the exploitation and victimization of women.

The Religious Justification.   Justification of gender inequality is found in both the teachings and the practices of the world's religions (Deckard 1975). Religious leaders assert or imply that men are superior to women and/or that women should be subservient.

In recent decades, a number of Christian theologians, both male and female, have argued that biblical teachings have been misinterpreted by generations of people who used them to justify and maintain patriarchal systems (Meyers 1988; Clifford 2001). Nevertheless, many religious people, but particularly the most conservative ones (known as fundamentalists), justify sexism on religious grounds (Peek, Lowe, and Williams 1991; Bendroth 1994). Religious conservatism and social conservatism tend to go hand in hand. Thus, 85 percent of religious liberals, but only 59.6 percent of religious conservatives in the U.S., disagree that men are better suited emotionally to politics than are women (McConkey 2001); and 81.2 percent of the liberals, but only 68.1 percent of the conservatives, disagree that it's more important for wives to help their husband's careers than to have careers themselves.

▪▪ Social Psychological Factors

Attitudes and Values.   The structural factors we have identified that perpetuate gender inequality are themselves perpetuated by attitudes and values of both men and women. Attitudes toward gender roles have become more *egalitarian* over the past few decades, but there are contradictory attitudes among Canadians and contradictions between attitudes and behaviour.

In the past, attitudes favoured traditional roles, the differential treatment of men and women, and acceptance of the notion that in many ways women are less competent than are men. In more recent decades, a different set of attitudes has developed among some people. These attitudes, however, are no less detrimental to the progress of women, for they assert that there is no more discrimination; that women who continue to make demands and complain of discrimination are troublemakers or "radical feminists"; and that policies designed to help women are unnecessary (Swim 1995).

Yet the belief that negative or condescending attitudes toward women no longer exist is contradicted by research. A survey of 2,500 women reported that one out of four felt "talked down to" or treated like a child by a physician, and nearly one out of five had been told that a medical condition was "all in your head" (Laurence and Weinhouse 1995). In an experiment in which students were given names of famous and nonfamous men and women, the students attributed fame to more male than female names (Banaji and Greenwald 1995).

Negative attitudes also affect women in the workplace. Many women feel compelled to perform better than men in order to prove themselves and be accepted. For example, there is evidence that women must work harder to prove that they have the ability because men expect women—including women in supervisory and managerial positions—to be less competent than men and this bias enters into the evaluation of women (Biernat and Kobrynowicz 1997; Martell, Parker, and Emrich 1998; Heilman 2001).

In male-dominated occupations, the attitudes may be particularly detrimental. McIlwee and Robinson (1992) argue that an "engineering culture" affects the career prospects of female engineers. The culture is a kind of locker-room macho display, in which men compete with each other by showing off their technical virtuosity; at the same time, they intimidate women who lack the experience that brings self-confidence.

As we noted earlier, many women also fear that they will be penalized in their careers if they become mothers. In fact, some employers do place women into two categories: achievers and mothers. A management expert has even proposed that the notion be formalized (Schwartz 1989) by allowing most working mothers to pursue a more moderate career path. Only those women who put aside family considerations would be allowed to pursue the fast lane to executive status. Critics called the moderated career line the "mommy track." Again the question arises, why should women be penalized for something that has always been allowed for men?

Ideology and Inequality.

In the 19th century, numerous writers stressed two "facts" about women. First, women were said to have a "higher nature" than men, in the sense that they were more virtuous. Second, women were said to have a higher calling than men, a nobler work to perform, because they were the guardians of the nation's morality through their example and influence on children. When women failed in this role, the consequences were disastrous. As Philip Wylie, one of the more severe writers of recent times, expressed it:

> Mom got herself out of the nursery and the kitchen. She then got out of the house. . . .
> She also got herself the vote, and, although politics never interested her (unless she was
> exceptionally naive, a hairy foghorn, or a size 40 scorpion) the damage she forthwith did
> to society was so enormous and so rapid that the best men lost track of things . . .
> political scurviness, hoodlumism, gangsterism, labor strife, monopolistic thuggery, moral
> degeneration, civil corruption, smuggling, bribery, theft, murder, homosexuality,
> drunkenness, financial depression, chaos, and war. (Deckard 1975:3–4)

Most North Americans would not go to such extremes in attributing moral and social decay to women's abdication of their domestic role. However, many still believe that a woman's place is in the home; and when she leaves the home to pursue higher education or a career, she leaves her post as one of the guardians of the social order. The ideology that *women's abdication of the home* can result only in *social disorganization* was expressed by those who insisted that women return to their homes after the Second World War. They identified working women as a primary cause of delinquency, and argued that for women to continue in the labour force would mean instability in the social institutions of the nation. More recently, in the surveys of religious people noted earlier, 81.2 percent of religious liberals, but only 44.2 percent of conservatives, disagreed that everyone is better off if the man is the achiever outside the home and the woman cares for her home and family (McConkey 2001:162).

Legal change can be effective in reducing inequality. In Canada, federal human rights legislation has improved the status of women drastically; however, in 2003–4 the United Nations Development Program (UNDP) ranked Canada third among the 162 nations surveyed for a series of programs such as health education, life expectancy, and standard of living. But when the UNDP employed the Gender Empowerment Measure, which measures the advancement of women in terms of political, economic, and professional life, our ranking declined from third to fifth place (behind Norway, Iceland, Sweden, and Finland) (UNDP Annual Report 2003–4:214). Among other things, discrimination in official policies and practices and admissions quotas have been abolished. Accordingly, students are to be treated equally in terms of rules and services; married women, for instance, are no longer excluded from financial aid because they are married—and sexual harassment is explicitly forbidden. As we noted earlier, covert discrimination still occurs, and the problems of women on the campus are by no means fully resolved; but gains have been made as a result of legal change.

Finally, business and industry can take the important step of *ensuring women equal career opportunities*. In particular, the business world can reject the "mommy track" notion and allow women to be mothers without sacrificing a professional career. An example is the "family plan" implemented by Johnson & Johnson to help its employees cope with family responsibilities (Deutsch 1990). Included in the plan are a nationwide resource and referral system for childcare and elder care; a year's family care leave, with full benefits for an employee who has to care for a child, a spouse, or a parent; training of supervisors to make them aware of the needs and problems involved in balancing work and family demands; and benefits that pay some of the costs of adopting a child. Some companies offer reduced work hours or other kinds of help for those with family responsibilities. But such programs are available to only a small minority of women employees.

It is important to recognize that women are not a homogenous group (neither are men); there are varied and unique social problems facing women who are Aboriginals, women of colour, disabled, lesbians, elderly, immigrants, and so on. These women face what is called a "double jeopardy" in that they may be discriminated against on the basis of not only their gender, but also their race, ability, sexual orientation, age, class, and citizenship status.

When we speak of gender inequality, then, we need to recognize that the extent of the inequality depends upon any particular women's status, role, geographic location, and the particular time in her life. There is a great deal of diversity among women and their experiences that we need to be aware of.

 ## ▪▪ From Social Problems to Solutions

The social problem of gender inequality, especially systemic discrimination against women on a worldwide basis, is being addressed at every level of society. Governments at all levels have Status of Women committees and organizations, and these committees work with and for community-based groups that have concerns for women's (and men's) issues. Most Canadian universities and colleges, and even some high schools, have women's centres on their campuses.

Most Canadian provinces have Status of Women committees that advise them on issues of concern to women, such as violence, labour standards and salary differences, childcare services, poverty concerns, and minority women such as lesbians, immigrants, women of colour, and disabled women.

In Canada, a vast array of groups exist to promote the equality of women with men; these groups of individuals range from Media Watch (info@mediawatch.ca)—whose main focus is to eradicate the sexism found in advertising and television programming and that harms women and girls—to the Metropolis Project of the Status of Women Canada, which works with immigrant women who come to Canada to work as domestics or in other work-related positions to ensure that they have the same legal protection and rights as women born in Canada regarding employment standards.

In every community in Canada, woman and men are working together to bring about the equality of women in every sphere of social life. These individuals range from academics to housewives to young girls to men who are concerned with equality for all.

▪▪ SUMMARY

Because they have suffered some of the same problems as minorities, women have been called Canada's "largest minority." In fact, they comprise a slight majority of the population. Until recently, much of professional and popular opinion viewed the disadvantages of women as rooted in biology rather than in society. In other words, many Canadians have accepted the ideas that women are less capable than men and that feminine and masculine traits result from biological differences. Freud argued that differences between men and women have a biological basis and that the differences are justification for women's subordinate position—but the bulk of evidence shows that sociocultural rather than biological factors account for most differences between men and women.

The effects of gender inequality have in some ways been similar to the effects of racial inequalities. Women have been denied the right to equal economic opportunities. Women comprise an increasing proportion of the labour force, but there is considerable evidence of discrimination in career entry, advancement, and salary in all occupational categories. Women are less likely than men to hold desirable political positions. And various beliefs and patterns of interaction between men and women violate women's dignity as human beings.

The normative role of the female in Canadian society is an important structural factor perpetuating women's problems. This is also the case for the societal expectations of men. Parents who hold to a traditional, home-centred role for women are less likely to encourage their daughters to follow a career. Norms about the female role are so strong that women who go to work tend to continue to have major responsibility for the home.

Women and men accept the traditional role because of their socialization at home and school. They learn the traditional role at a very early age, and most aspects of the culture reinforce that learning. Men can easily accept the traditional role for women because it maximizes their economic advantages. Some religious groups also help maintain the subordination of women.

Among social psychological factors involved in gender inequalities, certain attitudes and values reflect the traditional stereotypes of the sexes. Both men and women have tended to believe that women are more emotional, less logical, more passive, more dependent, more fragile, and more interested in domestic affairs. Such attitudes justify discrimination against women in education and work.

Inequality also is perpetuated by the ideology that says women are more virtuous than men and therefore their high calling is to act as guardians of the nation's morality and social order. Women who choose to focus their activities outside the home are said to abdicate this responsibility, leading to inevitable damage to society. The evidence contradicts the ideology, showing that neither children nor the social order is damaged by working women; but the ideology inhibits women who accept it from participating in the economy and other outside activities.

▪▪ KEY TERMS

Gender 158	Innate 158	Sex 158	Sexual Harassment 172
Gender Role 158	Pay Equity 165	Sexism 180	

▪▪ STUDY QUESTIONS

1. What are some of the arguments and evidence given in the chapter to support the priority of either biology or society as the basis for sex differences?

2. To what extent do women have equal economic opportunities with men?

3. Discuss the achievements and frustrations of women in political life in Canada.

4. In what ways are women's rights to dignity as human beings violated?

5. Discuss the ways in which the traditional female role affects the problem of gender inequality.

6. How are females socialized differently from males?

7. What kinds of economic considerations enter into the problem of gender inequality?

8. What is the division of labour in your household? If your household is a same-sex one, discuss who does what.

9. Identify the attitudes, values, and ideologies that tend to perpetuate gender inequality.

10. Show the error in some common myths about female workers.

11. What steps can be taken to reduce gender inequality?

12. Find out if there is a women's centre on your campus. What kinds of services and programs are offered there? Who organizes them? Who funds them?

13. What does equal pay for work of equal value mean? How should we measure and compare the value of

The McGraw·Hill Companies

SEND SERVICE INQUIRIES TO: ENVOYEZ VOS DEMANDES DE RENSEIGNEMENT À:		SEND RETURNS TO: ENVOYEZ VOS RETOURS À:
MCGRAW-HILL RYERSON P.O. BOX 635 STN. MAIN WHITBY, ON L1N 9Z9 **PHONE:** **TÉLÉPHONE:** 1-800-565-5758	 **McGraw-Hill Ryerson**	MCGRAW-HILL RYERSON 300 WATER ST WHITBY ONTARIO L1N 9B6 **PHONE:** **TÉLÉPHONE:**

THIS IS NOT AN INVOICE / CECI N'EST PAS UNE FACTURE

** Shipping charges and tax, if applicable, are not reflected on this document.** ** Please see your invoice for final pricing information.**	*** Frais de transport et taxes, si applicables, ne sont pas inclus dans ce document** ** S.V.P. Veuillez vous référer à votre facture pour le montant exact.**

Parcel ID:
N. D'EXPÉDITION: **25100948**

PACKING LIST
BORDEREAU D'EXPEDITION

Ship To Account: Compte de Livraison: 105335	Bill To Account: Compte de Facturation: 105335
KORBLA (PETER) PUPLAMPU SOCIOLOGY GRANT MACEWAN COLLEGE 10700-104 AVE EDMONTON AB T5J 4S2	KORBLA (PETER) PUPLAMPU SOCIOLOGY GRANT MACEWAN COLLEGE 10700-104 AVE EDMONTON AB T5J 4S2

Purchase Order No: N. De Commande:		TOTAL CARTONS for this PO#:	SHIP METHOD: MÉTHODE D'ENVOI: CANADA POST EXPRESS
MH Order No: MH N. de commande: 7960220	DATE: 09/07/06	TOTAL BOÎTES pour ce PO#: **1**	ORDER TYPE: TYPE DE COMMANDE: COMPLIMENTARY COPY
Delivery ID: Numéro de livraison: 24376884			INVOICE: FACTURE: 24376884

ISBN	DESCRIPTION TITRE	QUANTITY QUANTITÉ	UNIT PRICE PRIX UNITAIRE	DISC ESC	EXTENDED PRICE PRIX NET
0070939918	SOCIAL PROBLEMS	1			
TOTAL FOR / TOTAL POUR PO#		**1**			

** COMPLIMENTS OF / CE VOLUME VOUS EST OFFERT PAR VOTRE REPRESENTANT(E) **
SETH CROOK

different activities that make us happy and content in our work and home lives? Should women be paid to do housework? If so, by who?

14. Find out how sports teams based on gender are funded on your campus. Which teams receive the most money? Which win the most often?

15. Find out which, if any, men's groups exist in your province or territory. What are their goals and objectives? Do you agree with them?

16. On the Internet, find out how many mail-order bride sites exist. What does it cost to buy a wife from a range of selected countries? What sorts of women are for sale, and from which countries? Are some more expensive than others? What are your thoughts on this practice?

17. Find out the types of projects in your local community that are geared toward achieving equality for women.

18. What are some of the areas of concern that you feel are relevant to the women you know?

19. Do you think that men can be feminists? Why or why not?

■■ FOR FURTHER READING

Almey, Maria, et al. Women in Canada 2000: A Gender-Based Statistical Report. Ottawa: Statistics Canada, 2000.

Bordo, Susan. *Unbearable Weight: Feminism, Western Culture and the Body.* Berkeley, CA: University of California Press, 1993. An examination of eating disorders and other aspects of women's care of their bodies in terms of a disorder in American culture. The net result for women, Bordo argues, is an undermining of their ability to achieve their full potential.

Crosby, Faye. *Juggling: The Unexpected Advantages of Balancing Career and Home for Women and Their Families.* New York: Free Press, 1991. Confronts the myths about working and motherhood, and shows that women actually benefit from juggling numerous roles.

Day, Shelagh, and Gwen Bradley. Women and Equity Deficit: The Impact of Restructuring Canada's Social Programs. Ottawa: Status of Women Canada, 1998.

Dinnerstein, Myra. *Women between Two Worlds: Midlife Reflections on Work and Family.* Philadelphia: Temple University Press, 1992. An in-depth examination of 22 middle-class women who began their adult lives as mothers but eventually pursued professional careers. Shows the conflicts and adjustments they were required to make.

Flexner, Eleanor. *Century of Struggle: The Woman's Rights Movement in the United States.* New York: Atheneum, 1972. An excellent and thorough history of the struggle of American women—both white and black—from colonial times to 1920.

Harding, Sophie. Our Voices, Our Revolutions: Di/Verse Voices of Black Women, First Nations Women and Women of Colour in Canada. Toronto: Inanna Press, 2000. This book is a collection of works of short stories, poetry, essays, and fiction written by women whose voices are not normally heard in Canadian writing.

Hooks, Bell. *Feminism Is for Everybody: Passionate Politics.* Cambridge, MA: South End Press, 2000. An examination of a range of issues facing women, including the meaning of feminist politics, consciousness raising, education, abortion rights, work, and the beauty myth.

Johnson, Holly. Danger Domains: Violence Against Women in Canada. Scarborough, Ontario: Nelson, 1996.

Kaufman, M. Cracking the Armour: Power, Pain and the Lives of Men. Toronto: Penguin Books, 1993.

Kaufman, M. 1997. Working with Young Men to End Sexism. Orbit, 28(1): 16–18.

McKenna, Katherine M.J., and June Larkin (Eds). Violence Against Women: New Perspectives. Toronto: Inanna Press, 2002. This book represents a comprehensive collection of articles documenting 30 years of activism against violence against women in Canada. It also contains statistical information about the prevalence and types of violence.

Schwalbe, Michael. Unlocking the Iron Gage: The Men's Movement, Gender, Politics and American Culture. New York: Oxford University Press, 1996.

United Nations. Development Fund Report. New York: Oxford University Press, 2003–4.

Valian, Virginia. *Why So Slow? The Advancement of Women.* Cambridge, MA.: MIT Press, 1998. Argues that "gender schemas," a set of implicit beliefs about sex differences, play a central role in shaping the behaviour of men and women in the workplace.

Williams, Joan. *Unbending Gender: Why Family and Work Conflict and What to Do about It.* New York: Oxford University Press, 2000. A discussion of the contradictions between the economy and family life, and policy suggestions for resolving the problems. Williams advocates what she calls "reconstructive feminism."

RACE, ETHNIC GROUPS, AND RACISM

LEARNING OBJECTIVES

1. Discuss the meanings of the terms *race, ethnic group, visible minorities, racism,* and *multiculturalism.*

2. Understand the extent and origin of the problems of minorities.

3. Identify the ways in which the problems of minorities negatively affect the quality of life for them.

4. Know the social structural factors that contribute to the problems of minorities.

5. Show some ways to address the problems of minorities.

THINGS ARE NOT WHAT THEY APPEAR TO BE

Pearl is a 59-year-old woman who immigrated to Canada from Jamaica. She has lived in Canada for more than 30 years.

I worked in a variety of jobs, mostly service-industry jobs such as serving food in cafeterias and homemaking work, helping new mothers and elderly people. I have always worked. If I lost a job, within days I would be working again. That is, up until five years ago, when the company I was working for moved out of the country. So, when I was laid off, I was not too worried. I did what I always did. I heard about jobs, filled out applications, and figured I would start working within days. But this time there were no phone calls saying that I had the job. My guess is that it is my age—I was 54 then—because they might think that you would be retiring earlier or you might be slower or something. I don't know.

I do hear people say the reason why I am not working is because of my colour. But I always say to my kids, "don't think that." Gloria, my daughter, insists that it is colour. She tells me she was looking for a job. She saw an ad for a good office job. They called her to come in for an interview and all that. She speaks very well when she's on the phone; she speaks with a Canadian accent. When she went in for the interview, the woman came out to greet her, and her face just went funny. She saw she was black, and she said, "Are you Gloria?" And she said, "Yes, I am." She filled out the application and whatever. She never called Gloria. So Gloria said "I'm sure that it's because of my colour that I didn't get that job. She couldn't pick up colour on the phone."

It's all confusing for me. My daughter, she picked up race and she explained how she saw it. I try to look away from that. It's not a good thing to look at because it can really bring you down.... If we could be more positive in the world I think that could help us. Pick the best person. Don't look for the colour. I don't make it an issue.

But just maybe I was wrong. After all, the jobs I had when I was younger were jobs where coloured people worked. So, race? Maybe, I don't know. It could be. ■

■■ INTRODUCTION

Are people with white skin biologically inferior? Are they inherently less capable, less deserving, or less willing to work to get ahead than others? These questions may sound absurd to some of you, but millions of Canadians who are minorities confront such questions about themselves. Throughout Canadian history, minorities have been treated as if they were somehow inferior human beings; but racial inequalities are rooted in sociocultural rather than biological factors. We are all one species—human.

Before discussing the race problem (which is a shorthand phrase for the problem of relationships between people of diverse racial and ethnic backgrounds), we explore the meaning of race. Then we look at the origin and distribution of Canada's minorities, what the "race problem" means for them, what factors contribute to the problem, and how the problem can be attacked.

■■ THE MEANING OF RACE, ETHNIC GROUPS, AND RACISM

race
a group of people distinguished from other groups on the basis of certain biological characteristics

biological characteristic
an inherited, rather than learned, characteristic

We define **race** as a group of people who are distinguished from other groups on the basis of certain **biological characteristics.** But which biological characteristics? At the popular level, "different races" refers to people of different *skin colours.* But skin colouring varies enormously. There are people whose parents are of one "race" but who could easily be classified as members of a different "race" on the basis of skin colour. Because there are so many shades of skin colour, classifying a person as a member of one or another race on that basis is arbitrary.

There are other biological characteristics by which people could be classified: blood type, the presence or absence of the Rh factor in the blood, or the ability to taste the chemical phenylthiocarbamide. In each case the groups would be composed of different people. For instance, people who can taste the chemical (as opposed to those who cannot taste it) include large numbers of Europeans, Canadians, First Nations people, and Chinese. The point is that any biological basis for distinguishing among people is arbitrary and results in different groupings, which is why geneticists view race as more of a sociological than a biological phenomenon (Lewis 2002).

morphological
pertaining to form and structure

All human beings belong to one biological species—*Homo sapiens.* The breakdown of that species into subcategories is arbitrary. A frequently used system of classification, devised by Coon, Garn, and Birdsell (1950), used geographical distributions, **morphological** characteristics, and population size to identify six major "stocks" comprising 30 races. The six stocks are Mongoloid, White, Negroid, Australoid, American Indian, and Polynesian. Each represents a group of races that share certain characteristics. For example, the Mongoloid category includes all races that have adapted to very severe winters and the Negroid category includes all races that have achieved special adaptation to extreme light and heat.

Although this scheme is more elaborate than some others, it is also arbitrary. As Jefferson Fish (1995:55) sums it up: "The short answer to the question 'What is race?' is: There is no such thing. Race is a myth. And our racial classification scheme is loaded with pure fantasy." Nevertheless, people continue to identify different races primarily on the basis of skin colour and the inequalities people experience follow directly from that identification. We follow the categories of the Canadian Census, which uses people's self-identification as visible minorities. The Census uses the *Employment Equity Act's* definition of visible minority as "persons other than Aboriginal peoples, who are non-Caucasian in race or non-white in colour." According to the 2001 Census, more than 4 million individuals self-defined as visible minorities. Visible minority groups include Chinese, South Asians, Blacks, Filipinos, Arabs, West Asians, Latin Americans, Southeast Asians, Koreans, and Japanese.

ethnic group

people who have a shared historical and cultural background that leads them to identify with each other

The term **ethnic group** refers to people who have a shared historical or cultural background that leads them to identify with each other. The 2001 Census listed more than 200 different ethnic origins, including Canada's First Nations people and individuals whose origins are French, British, or European (see table 7.1). New ethnic origins come "from Eastern Europe, Central Asia, the Middle East, Africa, and Central and South America. This host of new groups includes: Kosovars from Yugoslavia; Azerbaijani and Georgians from Central Asia; Pashtun from Afghanistan; Yemeni and Saudi Arabians from the Middle East; Khmer from Southeast Asia; Nepali and Kashmiri from South Asia; Congolese, Yoruba and Ashanti from Africa; and Bolivians, Maya and Carib Indians from Central and South America" (Statistics Canada 2004:12).

racism

the belief that some racial groups are inherently inferior to others

Keep in mind that *all people have more shared than different characteristics, and no group is biologically superior to another.* Nevertheless, **racism,** the belief that some racial groups are inherently inferior to others, has been common and is used to *justify discrimination and inequality.* Essed (1991) has identified three forms of "everyday" racism: *marginalization* is making people of other races feel excluded and unimportant; *problematization* is imputing racial problems to those of other races rather than to one's own race; and *containment* refers to efforts to deny the existence of racism. We discuss various other forms of racism throughout this chapter.

Although we look primarily at white racism (because whites have been the dominant power in Canadian society and racism has hurt minorities more than it has whites), all groups have racists. Among others, we have seen conflict in recent years between blacks and Asians, and between subgroups of the various races (e.g., Chinese and Vietnamese).

TABLE 7.1 ■ ■ ▨

Top 10 Ethnic Origins Based on Total Responses, Canada, 2001 and 1996

(1) Table shows total responses. Because some respondents reported more than one ethnic origin, the sum is greater than the total population or 100 percent.

	2001			1996	
	Number	%		Number	%
Total Population	**29,639,030**	**100.0**	**Total Population**	**28,528,125**	**100.0**
Canadian	11,682,680	39.4	Canadian	8,806,275	30.9
English	5,978,875	20.2	English	6,832,095	23.9
French	4,668,410	15.8	French	5,597,845	19.6
Scottish	4,157,215	14.0	Scottish	4,260,840	14.9
Irish	3,822,660	12.9	Irish	3,767,610	13.2
German	2,742,765	9.3	German	2,757,140	9.7
Italian	1,270,369	4.3	Italian	1,207,475	4.2
Chinese	1,094,700	3.7	Ukrainian	1,026,475	3.6
Ukrainian	1,071,055	3.6	Chinese	921,585	3.2
North American Indian	1,000,890	3.4	Dutch (Netherlands)	916,215	3.2

Source: Statistics Canada, 2004.

▪▪ EXTENT AND ORIGIN OF RACES AND RACISM IN CANADA

As table 7.2 and figure 7.1 show, the composition of the Canadian population is changing. The visible minority population is growing at a much faster rate than the Canadian population at large. For example, since 1996 the Canadian population has grown by 6 percent, while the visible minority population has grown by 25 percent. The population growth of visible minorities is largely due to patterns of immigration from non-European countries (see table 7.3). For example, the largest visible minority group is Chinese, comprising 3.7 percent of the population and more than 25 percent of all visible minority groups. The growth in Chinese population between 1996 and 2001 was 20 percent, but this was second only to the South Asians (second largest visible minority group), whose population increased by 37 percent during the same time period.

The third largest visible minority group is blacks (17 percent), who comprise 2.2 percent of the Canadian population. The black population in Canada dates back many centuries. Black Canadians account for the largest visible minority group in the Maritimes.

TABLE 7.2 ▪ ▪ ▪

Proportion of Visible Minorities in Canada, 1981–2001

Census Year	Total Population	Visible Minorities	
		Number	Percentage of Total Population
1981	24,083,495	1,131,825	4.7
1986	25,021,915	1,577,715	6.3
1991	26,994,040	2,525,480	9.4
1996	28,528,125	3,197,480	11.2
2001	29,639,030	3,983,845	13.4

Source: Adapted from Statistics Canada, 2004

FIGURE 7.1 ▪ ▪ ▪

Visible minority groups, Canada, 1991 and 2001.

Source: Adapted from Statistics Canada.

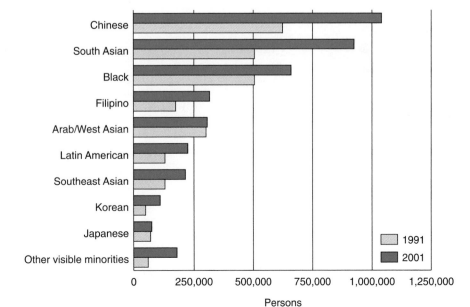

TABLE 7.3 ■ ■ ■

Top 10 Countries of Birth, Canada, 2001

(1) Includes data up to May 15, 2001.

Immigrated before 1961			Immigrated 1991–2001(1)		
	Number	%		Number	%
Total Immigrants	**894,465**	**100.0**	**Total Immigrants**	**1,830,680**	**100.0**
United Kingdom	217,175	24.3	China, People's Republic of	197,360	10.8
Italy	147,320	16.5	India	156,120	8.5
Germany	96,770	10.8	Philippines	122,010	6.7
Netherlands	79,170	8.9	Hong Kong, Special Administrative Region	118,385	6.5
Poland	44,340	5.0	Sri Lanka	62,590	3.4
United States	34,810	3.9	Pakistan	57,990	3.2
Hungary	27,425	3.1	Taiwan	53,755	2.9
Ukraine	21,240	2.4	United States	51,440	2.8
Greece	20,755	2.3	Iran	47,080	2.6
China, People's Republic of	15,850	1.8	Poland	43,370	2.4

Source: Statistics Canada, 2004.

The Canadian Aboriginal population has steadily been increasing; between 1901 and 2001, there has been a tenfold increase (see figure 7.2). Aboriginals accounted for 4.6 percent of the Canadian population (1.3 million people) in 2001, compared to 3.8 percent in 1996.

As we discuss the quality of life of the racial and ethnic groups, it is important to keep in mind the diversity within groups in such matters as economic status, occupational level, immigration status, and ability to speak English (Aponte 1991). Similarly, while Asians as a group are among the more educated and higher-income groups in the nation (including whites), some of the immigrants from Southeast Asia, such as the Vietnamese, have lower education levels and higher unemployment and poverty rates.

FIGURE 7.2 ■ ■ ■

Population reporting Aboriginal ancestry (origin), Canada, 1901–2001.

Source: Statistics Canada, 2004.

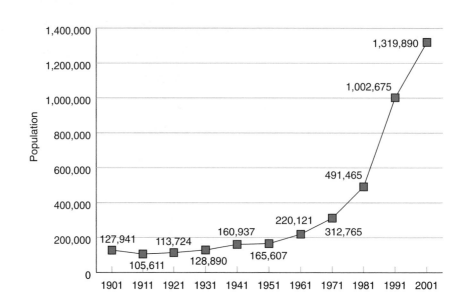

First Nations groups have brought attention to social problems for Native peoples in recent years.

assimilation
the integration of minority groups into the dominant culture

Why are there problems between the various races and ethnic groups in Canada? The fact is that no nation in the world is able to contain diverse groups without some degree of tension between them. *Dividing people into "us" and "them" occurs routinely.* Combined with competition for jobs, power, and prestige, the potential for intergroup conflict is high. Once groups enter into conflict, the animosity can linger for generations or centuries. Thus, when the former Soviet Union and Yugoslavia broke up in the early 1990s, old ethnic rivalries surfaced again, and vicious wars erupted between groups that had been seemingly united.

The United States has embraced a "melting pot" policy, where different ethnic groups **assimilate** into the dominant culture. In Canada we are committed to a multicultural society, acknowledging and accepting groups that are culturally diverse (*Canadian Multiculturalism Act* 1988). For this reason, Canadian culture is often viewed as a "mosaic." But the notion of multiculturalism is not universally supported. Critics have argued that multiculturalism in fact promotes the "politics of difference"—meaning that minority groups identify with their own groups rather than with Canadians in general. Furthermore, multiculturalism leads to ethno-racial segregation, which Canadians do not support (in Macionis and Gerber 2005:69–70). Other critics have argued that multiculturalism does not address historical and structural inequalities (in Bolaria 2000). Minority groups whose members are, for example, well-educated can take advantage of government programs and support, while other groups do not possess the necessary skills to take advantage of these programs or grants; and, if they do, they have a greater likelihood of rejection, "a classic case of a relationship in which one group defines the rules of the game to which the other group, in this case the ethnic minority, must comply" (Peter 1981 in Bolaria 2000:240).

■■ RACE, ETHNICITY, AND THE QUALITY OF LIFE

What does it mean to be a minority in Canada? How does being a minority affect the *quality of life?* We will look at four areas in which all Canadians are supposed to have equal rights:

1. Certain rights as citizens.
2. Equal economic opportunities.
3. The right to happiness.
4. The right to dignity as a human being.

In each of the four areas, being white is a distinct advantage, although the advantage is not as great as it was in the past.

▪▪ The Rights of Citizenship

The mass media often remind you of the *rights and privileges attached to your citizenship:*

1. This is a nation governed by laws rather than by individuals.
2. As a citizen, you have both the privilege and the responsibility of participating in the political process to ensure that laws reflect the will of the people.
3. The people do not exist to serve the government; the government exists to serve the people, and to serve all equally.

All these statements break down when we consider minority groups.

The Right to Vote. If you don't like the way things are going, it is said that you can express your disapproval at the polls. Indeed, voting is the responsibility of every citizen because one way Canadians are presumably able to change things is by exercising their right to vote. However, this right and privilege, basic as it is to our notions of government, has often eluded certain ethno-racial groups and was long withheld from First Nations people.

All Canadians, regardless of ethno-racial background, health status, or incarceration, have the right to vote. However, universal voting is a fairly recent phenomenon. Shortly after Confederation, a small percentage of the male population was allowed to vote. Immigrants from Japan, China, and India were disfranchised. After the First World War the vote was extended to all women over the age of 21, and in the 1921 election only 50 percent of the Canadian population had the right to vote. Canadians of Asian origin were given the vote only in 1948. The *Canada Elections Act* of 1960 gave voting rights to registered Indians on reserves. Persons with mental disabilities were not allowed to vote until 1988. And finally, on October 31, 2002 all inmates got the right to vote in federal elections. The road to universal suffrage has not been straightforward: "[t]he adoption of the Charter has been the single most effective trigger for the removal of the last vestiges of discrimination" (Elections Canada 2003).

The right to vote does not necessarily translate into voting. Most Aboriginal people do not vote in federal elections (Walker 2004). Three possible theories have been posited to explain the low voting turnout among Aboriginal people: history, socioeconomic factors, and language accessibility. According to Walker, many "aboriginal people are still smarting" from the fact that they were not given the right to vote until 1960 and "that even when [the vote] was granted it was being used 'as a tool of assimilation.'" Also, First Nations people are highly represented among the poor, they have comparatively less education, and they are on average younger than the general population; these are all factors that explain low voting turnout. Finally, campaign material is seldom translated into Aboriginal languages. For the Aboriginal communities this signifies "a general feeling that their concerns are excluded from the political mainstage" (Walker 2004).

The Law. Another right and privilege of citizenship is to live in a land governed by laws rather than by individuals. The laws, however, have failed to fully protect minority rights in the areas of *housing, public accommodations, and school desegregation.*

With regard to housing, the laws forbid discrimination in the sale, rental, or financing of any housing. Legally, a home that is for rent or sale should be available to anyone who can afford it. However, minorities may be at a disadvantage even in finding low-income housing. For example, in 2002 in Toronto the Centre for Equality Rights in Accommodation (CERA), an organization that "ensure[s] that human rights protections in housing would be effective for low income households and to address systemic barriers to accessing affordable accommodation," brought a case to the Ontario Human Rights Board (OHRB) that challenged landlords who selected tenants on the basis of landlord references, credit history, minimum income, and job security (for more, see box 7.1 on housing discrimination). The OHRB found that new immigrants to Canada were indeed discriminated against by these policies, which are now illegal under Ontario's *Human Rights Code* (CERA Webpage 2004).

Box 7.1

Housing Discrimination

Many impoverished ethnic communities have sprung from immigrants and refugees abandoning strife-torn countries over the past decade, arriving traumatized and nearly penniless on the tarmac in Toronto. But others, such as Jamaicans and Vietnamese, have inhabited the city for decades, speak fluent English, and endure the same low-wage jobs and marginal housing as newcomers fumbling for a foothold in a strange new country.

"Partly, it has to do with discrimination, but in a subtle way," Prof. Ornstein said. "The exclusion has primarily to do with things that are not that conscious, not with people saying, 'I hate those coloured people and they shouldn't be around,' but with assumptions about behaviour, assumptions about which people are like you and who you can work with."

Whether conscious or not, poor blacks and south Asians are winding up clustered in some of the most rundown buildings in Toronto, the closest the city comes to ghettoes. To be sure, new immigrants will drift to buildings where others speak their language and share their culture. But no one would settle in some of these slum-like buildings unless there was little choice.

Places like the building just around the corner from the high-rise that shuns Ms. Ahmed's clients. Just metres away from the roaring Don Valley Parkway, it is a building where the urine-soaked rug has been pulled up from the elevator floor, where slabs of plywood stand in for the occasional window pane, and where each apartment door is equipped with a series of heavy-duty locks. Here, Ms. Ahmed says, "100 per cent of the tenants are people of colour" -- mostly poor Sri Lankans.

...Landlords have long discriminated against visible minorities based on their race and low income, in blatant violation of Ontario's human-rights code. But the province's repeal of rent-control protections a few years ago has allowed landlords to raise rents to a level that shuts out poor immigrants from all but the shabbiest of buildings. And with long waiting lists for social housing and none being constructed, most poor immigrants are left to the devices of the private rental market.

All this, says M. S. Mwarigha, program director with the Centre for Equality Rights in Accommodation, is working to segregate poor racial minorities into concentrated pockets of disadvantage across Toronto.

"I've identified buildings with concentrations of immigrants and people of colour and other buildings with foundations that are white and middle-class, and they happen to be close to one another," he said.

"What we're ending up with is a rental market cut into layers: the top, middle-class white; the middle, middle-class other colour; and at the bottom we have immigrants in poorly maintained buildings paying rent not necessarily that much lower."

Several blocks to the southeast of Flemingdon, in the Thorncliffe Park neighbourhood of Toronto, sits a prime example. On Thorncliffe Park Road are three bleached-white apartment high-rises, sorry-looking buildings with scrubby lawns, no sign of landscaping and, on one, a wide-open rear door that makes a mockery of the security locks installed in the front lobby.

> There are few English-sounding names in the building directories and no sign of a white face on the grounds. A two-bedroom apartment in these buildings rents for $963 a month. Only a few doors down the street is an apartment building of a different calibre. The foyer walls are marble. Maintenance workers walk around the building. The preponderance of names on the building directory are English and the people milling about the building are white.
>
> When Ms. Ahmed asks the building superintendent about vacancies, she is informed that she would require a note from her employer. No one on welfare is welcome here—even with a letter from a guarantor—though to refuse such people contravenes Ontario's human-rights laws. Here, a two-bedroom apartment goes for $1,100 a month—not much higher than at the down-at-heel buildings a few doors away.
>
> "You see walking proof [of racial discrimination]," Ms. Ahmed says, "but you don't have any tangible proof."
>
> Source: Excerpt from Margaret Philp, "Poor? Coloured? Then It's No Vacancy: Housing Discrimination Rampant, Says Poverty Report, Despite Fact That Visible Minorities Are Poised to Become City's Majority," *The Globe and Mail*, Tuesday, July 18, 2000.

All Canadians are supposed to stand as *equals before the law*. Most people, of course, quickly recognize that not all Canadians are treated equally. The wealthy are rarely accorded the harsh treatment endured by the poor. Probably few people are aware of the extent to which minorities receive unequal treatment in virtually every aspect of civil and criminal proceedings (Butterfield 2000).

There is some evidence that police are more likely to harass visible minorities (Cruz 1995; Shapiro 1997). According to an investigative series on race and crime run by the Toronto Star (October 2002):

> black people charged with simple drug possession are taken to police stations more often than whites … [and] are held overnight for a bail hearing at twice the rate of whites.
>
> It also shows a disproportionate number of black motorists are ticketed for violations that only surface after a traffic stop.
>
> In addition, the report suggests that in situations where officers have discretion, whites are often treated more leniently than blacks.

In January 2005, the Montreal police force openly admitted that blacks are stopped more often than non-blacks because of racial profiling. In Montreal, black people are often stopped by police for just driving their car; they call this DWB, or "driving while black" (The Link 2005).

Courts mete out harsher penalties for visible minorities than for white perpetrators (Steffensmeier and Demuth 2000). Minorities are more likely than whites to be imprisoned, even for the same offence, so there is a disproportionate number of blacks and Aboriginals in jails and prisons (Hsia and Hamparian 1998; Oliver 2001). First Nations people represent only 3.3 percent of the general population, yet they comprise 17 percent of all prisoners. Black Canadians, who represent 2 percent of the population, account for 6 percent of the federal prison population. Further, they are five times more likely to be incarcerated than their white counterparts (Gartner and Dawson 2004).

■■ The Right to Equal Economic Opportunities

Among other things, racial and ethnic discrimination means that minorities are more likely to be poor, unemployed, or, if they work, underemployed. Minorities also receive, on the average, less income than whites.

Employment. A group might have *unequal access to employment* in at least four ways. First, the group might have a higher rate of unemployment than other groups. Second, a greater proportion of the group might be *underemployed.* Third, members of the group might be clustered at the lower levels of occupational categories (i.e., even if the proportion of minorities in a catetory is the same as that of whites, the minorities cluster at the lower levels). Fourth, a disproportionate number of the group might become disillusioned and drop out of the labour market.

All four kinds of inequality apply to minorities in Canada. The following examples, although based on American research, capture the experiences of minority groups in Canada. As a survey of 4,078 employers showed, *the inequality is maintained by practices at the job candidate, job entry, and job promotion stages* (Braddock and McPartland 1987). At the job candidate stage, many of the better jobs are still discovered through informal methods such as friends as much as through a formal recruitment process. A survey of 185 firms found that employers focus their efforts on white neighbourhoods and avoid recruitment strategies that could bring them a disproportionately inner-city, black labour force (Neckerman and Kirschenman 1991). A study of professionals of Asian origin concluded that they face a "glass ceiling" similar to that women encounter if they aspire to the higher positions (Woo 2000).

Immigrants may be particularly disadvantaged by this process. For example, Asian immigrant women wind up in garment sweatshops on the West Coast (Kim et al. 1992). The nature of the jobs is described by Helen Wong, who came with her husband and five children from Hong Kong in 1988 and found work in a small shop (Louie 1992). She worked on women's dresses and pantsuits for piece rates, which means that any breaks and other time off were unpaid. She worked Monday through Saturday, and came in on Sundays when there was a special rush order. The pay was the same regardless of how many hours or days she worked. On the average, she made between $1 and $2 an hour.

Among the most accessible data on inequality in employment are unemployment rates. The visible-minority community has increased fourfold since 1981, when foreign-born visible-minority men had higher employment rates and lower unemployment rates than Canadian-born non–visible minority men (Tran 2004). With the downturn in the economy in the 1980s, unemployment rates rose for both visible and non-visible minorities. However, visible minority men's rates of unemployment increased at a faster rate than Canadian-born non–visible minority men. The gap was widest in 1996 and decreased to some extent in 2001 (figure 7.3). Furthermore, the rate of unemployment recovery is slower for visible minority men compared to non–visible minority men (Harvey and Reil 2002).

It is interesting to note that that this gap occurred even though visible minorities had higher rates of university education (figure 7.4). Tran (2004:9) points out that "this pattern contradicts the widely-held view that workers benefit from more skills, education and experience and are in greater demand."

Differences in income also exist between visible minority and non–visible minority immigrants. The early 1990s recession saw slight increases in income for non–visible minorities, yet for visible minorities income actually decreased between 1991 and 1996 (Harvey and Reil 2002):

> In Canada, the average employment income for visible minority immigrants decreased by $1,082, yet increased by $909 for immigrants who are not visible minorities. In Ontario, the average employment incomes for visible minority immigrants in Ontario decreased by $783, yet increased by $1,992 for immigrants who are not visible minorities. The pattern is repeated in the Toronto CMA, where average employment incomes of visible minority immigrants decreased by $1,313, yet increased by $3,013 for immigrants who are not visible minorities.

FIGURE 7.3 ■ ▩ ▨

Employment by visible minority.

Source: Statistics Canada, censuses of population.

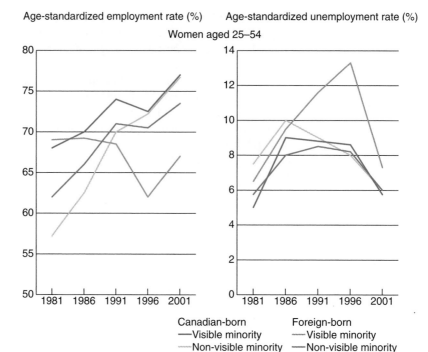

Age-standardized employment rate (%)   Age-standardized unemployment rate (%)

Women aged 25–54

Canadian-born
——Visible minority
······Non-visible minority

Foreign-born
——Visible minority
——Non-visible minority

FIGURE 7.4 ■ ▩ ▨

Education by visible minority.

Source: Statistics Canada, censuses of population.

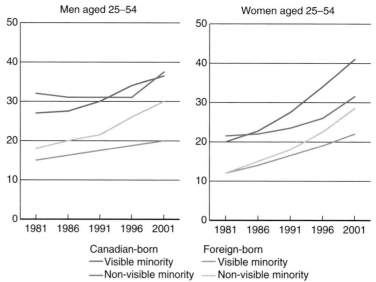

% with a university education

Men aged 25–54   Women aged 25–54

Canadian-born
——Visible minority
——Non-visible minority

Foreign-born
——Visible minority
······Non-visible minority

To be a minority, then, means to suffer *discrimination in job opportunities.* Minorities also encounter obstacles in business and the professions. Overall, visible minorities work in jobs that are lower in status and earn less income. The differences are greater for Canada's First Nations people (table 7.4). For example, 15.4 percent of white Canadians hold professional jobs, compared to 8.4 percent of Aboriginals; Caribbean blacks and South Asians fare better, at 13.5 and 13.2 percent, respectively. First Nations people also proportionately account for more than twice as many manual

TABLE 7.4 ■ ■ ■

Employed Persons by Selected Ethno-racial Groups and Occupation

Occupation	ETHNIC ORIGIN				
	Chinese	South Asian	Caribbean	Aboriginal	Total
Senior managers	1.0	0.5	0.2	1.8	1.3
Middle and other managers	10.2	6.0	5.5	4.2	8.9
Professionals	23.4	13.2	13.5	8.4	15.4
Semi-professionals and technicians	7.9	6.0	7.6	8.4	7.7
Clerical	10.1	11.2	13.7	8.1	9.6
Semi-skilled manual workers	9.5	20.0	14.9	13.8	10.8
Sales and service	7.8	14.4	10.4	15.0	9.4
Manual workers	2.9	6.5	4.9	8.3	3.8

Source: Adapted from the Census 2001.

workers than whites. Thus, according to Kunz (2000), "the higher you go in the workplace, the whiter it becomes." Data from the 2001 Census show that university academics tend to be largely white (82.4 percent), a small change from the 1996 Census (83.9 percent were white). South Asian and Chinese Canadians, respectively, comprise 3.6 percent of university teachers, Arab or West Asians 2 percent, and blacks only 1.6 percent (CAUT 2004). The 2001 Census also reveals that 60 percent of new immigrants work in different occupations than in their country of origin. Many of these immigrants have degrees but work in sales and service or manufacturing jobs. They are "dismally" underrepresented in senior-level jobs and on boards of directors (Conference Board of Canada 2004:3):

> Certainly, there is a strong feeling among visible minorities that a "sticky floor" limits their opportunities for initial advancement and a "glass (or cement) ceiling" stops them from attaining top positions in organizations.

Clearly, the nation has not yet resolved the problem of discrimination in job opportunities.

Income and Wealth. Wealth includes all the assets of a family—housing equity, investments, insurance, and so on. Great disparity exists between ethno-racial groups in wealth, with blacks and First Nations people having substancially fewer assets than white families (Conley 2000; Flippen 2001).

An important component of wealth is income. Figure 7.5 shows the extent to which blacks and First Nations people are concentrated more heavily than whites in the lower income brackets. The opposite is true as well. Proportionately few black and First Nations people have household incomes greater than $100,000. The incidence of low income is particularly prevalent among visible-minority immigrants. This pattern has been consistently observed since 1961, which only leads to disturbing conclusions:

> The "race" factor appears to have implications on how severe, extensive and persistent immigrants' socioeconomic disadvantages are. Visible minority groups experience economic disadvantages more, deeper and longer than most European groups.

> The persistence of economic disadvantages for some ethnocultural groups (e.g. Asian, Black, East European and Latin American) over thirty years demands more research and

FIGURE 7.5 ■ ■ ■

Household income by
selected ethno-racial
groups.

Source: Adapted from The Census,
1996.

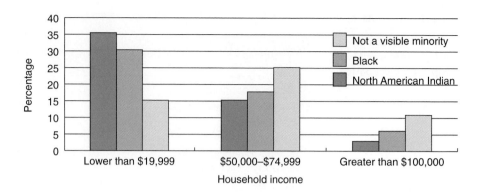

> attention from policy makers. Is this a reflection of the incongruity between immigration
> and settlement policies? Is it an issue of public education and resource allocation? Is it a
> function of deep-rooted institutional barriers? (Harvey et al. 1999:8)

In general, income inequality is widespread across occupations and is certainly a consequence of discrimination. Incomes for black Canadians and First Nations people are lower than those of whites even for those workers with the same education, occupation, experience, authority, and number of hours worked (Smith 1997). The gap actually increases in the higher-income occupational categories (Grodsky and Pager 2001). Moreover, because of the type of assets and pension plans available, the disadvantage is even greater in retirement than it was during their working years (Hogan and Perrucci 1998).

■■ The Right to Life and Happiness

The right to a life of freedom and happiness is important to Canadians. However, those rights are not distributed equally in Canada. Surveys report *less happiness and less satisfaction among blacks* than among whites (Aldous and Ganey 1999; Saad and Newport 2001). Blacks score lower than whites on life satisfaction, happiness, marital happiness, and perceived health, and they score higher on mistrust.

Like most other minority groups, blacks have not had ample access to those things important to happiness and life satisfaction: work, recognition and success, financial well-being, health, and good housing. For example, blacks and First Nations people are far more likely than whites to live in low-quality housing and to report dissatisfaction with that housing (Philp 2000; Ornstein 2000; Cook and Bruin 1994; Golant and La Greca 1994). In this section, we look at two other areas crucial to happiness: life chances and freedom from fear.

life chances

the probability of gaining
certain advantages defined
as desirable, such as long
life and health

Life Chances. Insurance companies and government agencies compile large amounts of information on **life chances,** which include probability of divorce, disease, suicide, mental illness, and premature death. The life chances of whites are generally better than those of minorities (Hayward and Heron 1999; McLaughlin and Stokes 2002; Smedley, Stith, and Nelson 2002). For example, compared to whites, minorities tend to have (1) a higher rate of infant deaths and deaths from tuberculosis, AIDS, and homicide; (2) a lower median family income; (3) lower-level jobs; (4) proportionately fewer full-time and white-collar jobs; and (5) fewer people receiving old age and survivor insurance benefits. Many of the differences are striking. First Nations women have high infant mortality rates (8 per 1,000 live births) compared to that of the general population (5.5 per 1,000 live births) (Statistical Profile on the Health of First

First Nations and Inuit people are the poorest minority groups in Canada.

Nations in Canada 2003). Further, the average life expectancy for First Nations people is lower than that of the average Canadian population. In 2000, the life expectancy of First Nations males was 68.9 years, and for females it was 76.6, compared to 75.7 years for the average Canadian male and 81.4 years for the average female.

Disadvantages with respect to life chances are rooted in a number of factors. Racism is a major contributor to problems of both physical and mental health (Byrd and Clayton 2001; Dana 2002). Minorities are more likely to live near hazardous waste facilities and be exposed to toxic materials (Stretesky and Hogan 1998). Because of such things as pressure to perform and a sense of isolation, being the "token" minority in a work organization is more likely to lead to depression and anxiety than to a sense of having "made it" (Jackson, Thoits, and Taylor 1995). Finally, minorities are disadvantaged in life chances because of their lower economic levels (Meckler 1998; McLaughlin and Stokes 2002).

People who live in poverty or who try to survive at low income levels have higher rates of physical and emotional problems. Impoverishment combined with racism take a dreadful toll in high rates of such things as cirrhosis of the liver, homicide, accidents, and drug and alcohol abuse. Blacks are about twice as likely to have high blood pressure as whites. Some observers thought that a genetic factor was involved in the higher rates for blacks, but research suggests that the *stress of living in a race-conscious society* and possibly some dietary factors are more likely than genetic factors to be responsible (Whittle et al. 1991).

Minorities are also more likely to be crime victims (Parker 1991). Asian Canadians, who in other ways are better off than any other group in terms of life chances, are more likely to be killed by outgroup (non-Asian) members than are whites or blacks (Jan, Messner, and South 1991). Part of the difference in the life expectancy of whites and blacks is the result of the high rate of black murder victims (Potter 2001).

First Nations people are the poorest of all the minorities, with a family income that averages less than half that of whites. Mortality rates from homicide, suicide, and accidents are disproportionately high, with suicide rates higher than the national average—

especially for women, with rates of eight times higher for women aged 15 to 24, and five times higher for those aged 25 to 39 (Statistical Profile on the Health of First Nations in Canada 2003).

First Nations people are also more likely to be crime victims than are other Canadians (see Chapter 4). Aboriginal people represent 20 percent of inmates in provincial and territorial correction facilities, and 17 percent of inmates in federal facilities (Carriere 2003).

First Nations people also have serious problems of abuse, neglect, alcoholism, fetal alcohol syndrome, mental and physical disabilities, depression, school problems, and delinquency (Statistical Profile on the Health of First Nations 2003). Death rates from alcoholism are considerably higher than those of the general population.

Freedom from Fear. One of the basic freedoms for Canadians is freedom from fear. No one should have to live in constant fear of offending someone who claims to be superior. Yet, for decades black mothers and fathers taught their children to fear offending white people. Richard Wright related an incident from his own childhood that illustrates the point (Bernard 1966). A group of white boys threw broken bottles at him and some of his friends, and the two groups fought. Wright was badly cut. He went home and sat on his steps to wait for his mother to come home from work. He felt that she would understand both the pain of the cut and the hurt that was inside him. Rather than sympathy, he received a severe beating. Had a white mother treated her son in this way, you might have questioned her love; but Wright's mother was teaching him what she regarded as a most important lesson—to avoid such encounters at all costs. She was teaching him what it meant to be black: that he would always be the loser in battles with whites. Her method was severe, but so was the reality in which she knew he would exist.

Throughout their history in Canada, minorities have feared being *victims of violence.* Violence and threats of violence against people because of their group membership are now called *hate crimes.* Such crimes remind minorities that some people despise them and are willing to use violent means to intimidate them. You need only read the daily papers to realize that the victims of hate crimes include blacks, Muslims, Jews, Asians, and Indians. The crimes range from verbal abuse to physical violence and even murder. Those who survive them are likely to suffer severe emotional problems (McDevitt et al. 2001). In recent years, the incidents have included such things as chaining a black man to the rear of a truck and dragging him to his death, bombing of a Jewish day school, and harassing Muslim women who wear the traditional jihab.

Many hate crimes are committed by members of the numerous racist and neo-Nazi groups (Padilla 1999). The groups have somewhat varied ideologies, but all of them proclaim the superiority of the white race and the threats to whites posed by various racial minorities. Stimulated by such ideology, their members commit thousands of hate crimes every year (CRRF 2004).

The cherished rights of Canadians to move about as they please, to live according to their means, and to enjoy the use of all public facilities has not yet been fully extended to minorities. Minorities who try to break down old barriers are still subject to threats of violence and efforts at intimidation. Freedom from fear is an unmet promise rather than a reality.

■■ The Right to Dignity as a Human Being

Most of the material already discussed in this chapter illustrates how minorities are directly *deprived of their dignity as human beings.* Even those who achieve some degree of success are not immune from having their dignity violated. Feagin (1991) did in-depth interviews with 37 middle-class blacks. They reported a variety of incidents that reveal racial bias and hostility: white couples who cross the street when a black male approaches them; poor service in public accommodations; and verbal attacks, including people who shout racial epithets in the streets. Similar incidents were uncovered by a reporter for a national U.S. news magazine, who called them evidence of a "stealth racism" that is *"poisoning black–white relations"* (Eddings 1995). **Stealth racism** involves hidden or subtle acts of prejudice and discrimination, acts that may be apparent only to the victim. Examples of stealth racism include taxis that never stop for minorities; suspicious stares from clerks in stores; the assumption that the minority individual is in a subordinate role (like the couple who came out of an expensive restaurant and asked a black man to get their car, not realizing he was a senior editor at a national magazine); the sense of being unwelcome (such as when looking for a new home in a well-to-do neighbourhood); and the surprise expressed when the minority person is articulate and sophisticated.

stealth racism
hidden or subtle acts of prejudice and discrimination that may be apparent only to the victim

Some of the incidents are irritating and demeaning. For instance, a black woman returning a rented video is ignored by the clerks until she speaks up and asks for help (St. Jean and Feagin 1998). Or consider the problem of "DWB"—driving while black—as mentioned earlier in this chapter. There is evidence that black drivers are far more likely to be stopped by police than are white drivers; they are also more likely to have their cars searched (Stetz 1999). Stealth racism also can be hazardous for the victims, such as when physicians are less likely to order sophisticated cardiac tests for blacks who complain of chest pains than for whites with the same symptoms (Schulman et al. 1999). At that point, the right to dignity may mean the right to life-saving measures.

The right to dignity also includes the right to truthful representation of one's group. Two often-heard myths violate this right.

The Myth of Success around the Corner.

A common Canadian myth is that *success is "just around the corner" for anyone who is willing to work for it.* The implication is that the minorities can end their impoverishment merely by being willing to work as hard as other people. "If they want to get ahead," it is said, "let them work for it and earn it." The point, of course, is that if they do not get ahead, it is their own fault. The *fallacy of personal attack* is used to defend an unjust social order. The reasoning is that if the minorities have as many opportunities as anyone else and yet remain in the lower levels of society, something is wrong with the minorities.

Unfortunately, many people do believe that minorities have the same opportunities as whites. According to an American Gallup poll, 79 percent of whites but only 46 percent of blacks believe that the chances for getting a job are equal for the two races (Gallup Organization 1997). Another poll found that 71 percent of whites but only 42 percent of blacks believe that the white–black income gap will eventually be closed (Polling Report 2002).

Many whites believe not just that minorities have an equal opportunity, but that minorities now possess an advantage. They see themselves as victims of *reverse discrimination,* with their own opportunities becoming restricted as minority opportunities have opened. They cite cases where minorities (including women) have been given preference over white males even when the white males have seniority or somewhat better qualifications. According to such beliefs, if minorities do not achieve success, it is clearly their own fault.

Associated with the myth that success is readily available to those willing to work for it is the notion that blacks prefer welfare to hard work. This is also a distortion of the truth. Blacks did not appear on welfare rolls in large numbers until the late 1940s. Furthermore, few able-bodied men of any race are receiving welfare. Poor blacks are, like anyone else, eager to escape their poverty. There is no evidence that minorities prefer welfare to work or that they are failing to take advantage of work opportunities available to them. Quite simply, the notion that success is just around the corner for anyone willing to work for it is a myth.

The Myth of Inferiority.

The insidious myth that minorities are *inherently inferior* is far from dead. Polls in the U.S. show that about one of seven non-black Americans believe that African Americans have less native intelligence than whites, and the majority believe that African Americans are lazier or at least less hardworking than whites.[1] The argument about inferiority takes a number of different forms. One argument is that minorities are, and always have been, biologically inferior. This argument can take the form of the *fallacy of circular reasoning.* An individual argues that blacks are inferior because their IQs are lower than those of whites. "But," one could reply, "they are only lower for those who live in deprived conditions." "No," is the response, "they are lower because they are inferior people."

The theory of biological inferiority also has appeared in respectable scientific sources. A few social scientists and others have argued that blacks are intellectually inferior to whites for genetic reasons. Intense controversy over the issue began after educational psychologist Arthur Jensen published an article in 1969 that attributed the gap between black and white IQ scores to *genetic differences* and not merely to environmental deprivation of blacks. According to Jensen (1972, 1980), environmental differences such as poverty and deprivation cannot explain the consistent differences in IQ scores between blacks and whites or between the poor and nonpoor.

The most recent attempt to argue for innate inferiority is *The Bell Curve,* by Herrnstein and Murray (1994). Herrnstein, a psychologist, and Murray, a political scientist, claim that about 60 percent of IQ is genetic, and the rest is due to the individual's environment (Jensen claimed that 80 percent was genetic). Since the majority of our intelligence capacity is inherited, differences in achievement are both inevitable and unchangeable.

Like its predecessors, *The Bell Curve* has been severely criticized by scientists. They point out, for example, that the authors used only data from other people's sources, and at least some of those sources are organizations and researchers who believe in the superiority of the white race. Data from other research that contradicts their findings are either discounted or ignored altogether (Goldberger and Manski 1995).

It is probable that some people will continue to argue for innate white superiority. Two points should be kept in mind. First, most social scientists agree that IQ tests are culturally biased and, at the most, reflect *mental achievement* rather than *mental capacity.* Second, geneticists reject claims of racial superiority. In fact, geneticists agree with the point made earlier, that "race" as we use it is virtually meaningless from a scientific point of view. Three geneticists who synthesized a half-century of research in population genetics concluded that apart from such minor traits as skin colour and size, the so-called races are remarkably alike (Cavalli-Sforza, Menozzi, and Piazza 1994). For any given human characteristic, there is more intragroup variation than there is intergroup variation, so that there is no scientific basis for arguing for the genetic superiority of any population over any other.

Note also that some evidence exists that *contradicts the argument of genetic superiority.* Studies of identical twins (genetically the same) who have been separated and reared in different environments show that the children grow up to be quite different individuals and may have IQ scores as much as 14 points apart. Other studies have found that African Americans score better on IQ tests when the tests are administered by blacks rather than by whites. Also, there is evidence that IQ scores can be altered dramatically by specific programs.

The argument of a second form of the inferiority myth is that minorities are *culturally inferior.* Whatever may or may not be true biologically, it is argued, the culture of a particular people is obviously inferior and the people therefore are unfit to rise above their low status.

However, Canadians overall do not share the same attitudes toward diverse groups shown by their American neighbours. A CRIC–*Globe and Mail* survey examined the attitudes of Canadians toward diversity (Parkins and Mendelsohn 2003). According to Parkins and Mendelsohn, "Canadians like to think of themselves as welcoming new arrivals from all corners of the earth, and opposing all forms of discrimination." Indeed, the survey confirmed this view. For example, most Canadians—especially younger ones—believe that ethnic background is not a factor when it comes to friendships or marriage. Only 12 percent of Canadians state that ethno-racial relations are problematic, "compared with 30 to 50 percent who feel this way in the U.S., the UK, France, and Italy." Overall, young Canadians appear to support and "are comfortable with diversity, adamant about equality, and supportive of further change, such as recognition of same-sex marriage." The one exception is First Nations people; Canadians are not as accepting of First Nations people as they are of other minority groups.

The reality, however, for many (but not all) visible-minority groups is that they continue to struggle economically and do not hold the same types of "good jobs" as their Canadian counterparts. We simply cannot discount discrimination as an explanation (for more, see chapter 9, "Work and the Economy").

▪▪ CONTRIBUTING FACTORS

Canadians believe in the primacy of individual dignity, equality, and the right of all citizens to the same justice and the same opportunities, but the racial behaviour systematically denies minorities the same rights and benefits accorded to whites.

▪▪ Social Structural Factors

The tables in this chapter show that minorities occupy a *low position in the stratification system.* This raises the question of whether the main problems facing minorities are due to social class, ethno-racial identity, or both. The answer seems to be both. Minorities share some characteristics with lower-class whites, but, as you have seen, even those who achieve higher socioeconomic levels still face various disadvantages and assaults on their dignity.

institutional racism policies and practices of social institutions that tend to perpetuate racial discrimination

The disadvantages are not always due to biased individuals. The term **institutional racism** was coined to refer to the fact that established policies and practices of social institutions tend to perpetuate racial discrimination. In other words, whether or not the people involved are prejudiced or deliberate in their discriminatory behaviour, the normal practices and policies themselves guarantee that minorities will be short-changed. The reason for this is that policies and practices are set by those in power, and minorities typically have lacked the power necessary to control institutional processes. We examine institutional racism in four important areas: the media, education, the economy, and government.

Mass Media. *The portrayal of minorities in the media has tended to perpetuate various negative stereotypes.* The problem was particularly severe in the past when movies and radio and TV programs—such as the *Amos 'n Andy* radio show—portrayed blacks as lazy, inferior, stupid, and dishonest. After the mid-1960s the portrayals changed, and various racial minorities appeared more frequently and in more positive roles.

DISAPPEARING DIFFERENCE

Recently, a group of Jewish and Muslim students on a campus decided to meet and share their views on issues related to peace in the Middle East. After a few meetings, members from each group remarked that "the more often we meet, the less we think about each other as Jew or Muslim." It was their way of saying that the contact had broken down some of the prejudices they harboured.

Social scientists have long known that interracial contact is one way to deal with prejudice. Arrange for a visit with an ethno-racialized group other than your own. It might be a student organization on campus, or some kind of community organization. Talk with some of the members and explore how they feel about the current ethno-racial situation. Ask them about their aspirations for themselves and their children. Discuss their outlook on the future. Do they feel that the situation for their race has improved or worsened in the 2000s? Why?

What insights into the life of the other race did you gain from the visit? Do they have any needs and aspirations that are fundamentally different from your own? How does Canada's race problem look from their point of view? Can you see the basis for their point of view?

If possible, you might arrange some kind of exchange visit with the group. As the people from the different ethno-racial groups mingle with each other, note any changes in prejudicial attitudes and any increases in mutual understanding.

Racial and ethnic minorities still do not receive equitable treatment in the media, however. An examination of television commercials concluded that white men tended to be portrayed as powerful and white women as sex objects, while black men were more likely to be aggressive and black women were inconsequential (Coltrane 2000). A study of prime-time television programs for the 2001–2002 season found (Children Now 2002):

- Most white youth interacted with their parents, but only a fourth of Hispanic youth did.
- A homogenous and segregated world was portrayed in the eight P.M. programs.
- Virtually all service workers and unskilled labourers were people of colour.

Other media also contribute to the problem of negative stereotypes. A study of children's books drew a number of conclusions (Pescosolido, Grauerholz, and Milkie 1997). First, the number of black characters varied over time: The number declined from the late 1930s through the late 1950s, was almost nonexistent through 1964, increased considerably to the early 1970s, then levelled off. Second, there is an absence of intimate, egalitarian interracial relationships. Third, there are few books that have a black adult as a central character. Even American college textbooks can be misleading. In her examination of economics textbooks, Clawson (2002) found black faces "overwhelmingly portrayed" among the poor (recall that, in terms of numbers, there are far more poor whites than poor blacks).

In sum, some progress has been made, but the mass media as a whole continue to either neglect minorities or reinforce negative stereotypes.

Education. Four primary and secondary educational practices that perpetuate discrimination are *spending cuts to schools, so-called IQ testing, so-called ability-grouping of children, and differential treatment of children based on ethno-racial identity.* All these practices discriminate against people in the lower socioeconomic strata, and because most minorities are disproportionately in the lower strata they suffer disproportionately from such practices.

Throughout the 1990s, provincial governments increasingly cut funding to schools. The onus was placed on individual schools, namely parents, to fundraise. According to

People For Education, a grassroots group committed to saving public education in Toronto, "[s]chool councils in Ontario's elementary schools currently fundraise approximately $39 million per year, over half of which pays for textbooks, computers and classroom supplies. Secondary schools report raising approximately $20 million annually" (People for Education 2004). Clearly, schools in middle-class or better neighbourhoods are supported by families who are involved and have the resources and means to be effective fundraisers. Schools in less advantaged neighbourhoods are limited in their fundraising abilities and consequently these schools are lower in quality in every way, including fewer resources and less technology (such as multimedia computers) than are available at other schools (Trotter 1997).

IQ testing also works to the disadvantage of minorities. A child may do poorly on an IQ test, for example, because little in his or her home environment has served as preparation for tests constructed by middle-class educators. Then, when placed in a group of lower ability, a child may accept the label of mediocrity or even inferiority.

At the post-secondary level, efforts are made to recruit more minority students than have attended in the past. Some of the efforts are successful. But those who begin their educational journey from a deprived, minority base will face many built-in hurdles, such as rising admission standards, decreasing financial aid, and a hostile campus climate (Halcon and Reyes 1991).

Finally, minority students may be treated differently from white students. A researcher who looked at the discipline patterns of 11,000 middle-school students found that black students were more than twice as likely as whites to be sent to the principal's office or suspended, and more than four times as likely as whites to be expelled (Morse 2002b). It is difficult to learn if you are in a school where you feel more vulnerable to disciplinary action simply because of your race.

Schools in higher-income neighbourhoods are advantaged in all ways.

exploitation
use or manipulation of
people for one's own
advantage or profit

The Economy. Institutional racism has pervaded the economy in at least three ways: **exploitation** *of minority labour, exclusion of minorities from full participation in the economy, and exploitation of minority consumers.* We noted earlier that minorities tend to secure the lower paying jobs. This tendency is reinforced by the shift from an industry- to a service-based economy (Jaret 1991; Woody 1991). Even in the same occupational categories, however, a gap exists between minority and white income (McCall 2001). Minorities also tend to have the worst jobs in terms of health hazards. For instance, blacks have a 37-percent greater chance than do whites of suffering an occupational injury or illness (Wright and Bullard 1990).

As for participation in the economy, minorities come out best during economic booms and worst when the economy falters. Thus, black–white inequality in employment is greater in those regions of the country where the economy is not as strong (Cohn and Fossett 1995). When restructuring or downsizing occurs, minorities are likely to suffer more job loss than are whites, particularly the black minority (Singh 1991). For example, as noted in chapter 5, the clothing industry, with the advent of the North American Free Trade Agreement (NAFTA), has been particularly unstable over the past decade (Pierson and Cohen, 1995). More than three-quarters of all Canadian garment workers are women. Of those, 50 percent are immigrants, and about 30 percent are visible minorities (Yanz et al. 1999), mostly of Asian origin[2] (Das Gupta, 1996). Das Gupta believes that, forced into difficult and unstable working conditions, "working class women of colour and Black women are subordinated by an interplay of racist, sexist and classist ideologies" (1996:10).

Minorities also fail to participate fully in the economy as entrepreneurs, a fact that is closely related to credit practices and policies. Lending institutions traditionally demand credit history, some kind of collateral, and some evidence of potential success before they lend money to prospective businesspersons, whether or not they are white. These are standard practices, defined as necessary and practical when giving credit; but applying them to minorities, who may have poor credit records because of exploitation and who may have nothing to use as collateral because of poverty, means that the standard practices only ensure continued white domination of the economy.

Insisting on comparable "sound" business practices when the prospective customers are minorities results in exploitation of the minority consumer. It is true that the poor are greater credit risks and that businesses in ghetto areas must pay higher insurance premiums because of the greater probability of theft and property damage; yet it is also true that these higher costs of doing business exploit the minority consumer, who must then pay more than others for the same quality of goods.

The most serious exploitation may be in housing, however. Blacks are often forced to pay more than whites for the same quality of housing. In fact, housing in poor neighbourhoods is sometimes costlier in terms of square footage and is frequently costlier in terms of *quality* square footage than is housing in suburban areas. When minorities attempt to find better housing in the suburbs, they may find themselves steered into some areas and kept away from other areas by real estate agents.

Economic deprivation of minorities has meant economic gains for whites. When minorities are kept in a subordinate position, whites are able to secure a higher occupational status, lower rates of unemployment, and higher family income (Tomaskovic-Devey and Roscigno 1996). At least some of those who resist equal opportunities are not unaware of such implications.

Government. The government is supposed to protect and help all citizens equally. Yet minorities do not always benefit from the government as much as whites do, and the law may work strongly against minorities. Recall from chapter 4 that visible minorities are disproportionately represented in the criminal justice system. In part this may be due to racial profiling, where police target minorities for crimes, or to the fact that minorities do not have the financial means to hire lawyers who can work the system so that conviction and/or incarceration does not occur. Whether the law is intentionally racist, it is in effect a racist law, punishing blacks more severely than whites for an equivalent crime.

Minorities have not benefited from government employment practices, particularly at the federal level. Visible minorities in 1995 represented only 4.1 percent of the public service (table 7.5) even though they comprised 11 percent of the population (refer to table 7.2). Job promotions were equally unimpressive (table 7.6). Most disconcerting, however, was that visible-minority hires decreased in the middle 1990s (below the 1988 rate), at a time when Canada's visible minority population was increasing (table 7.7). Visible minorities fared substantially better in the federally regulated private sector, especially vis-à-vis promotions (11.6 percent) (see table 7.6).

If minorities are to make headway in their efforts to achieve equality of opportunity, they must be able to secure *political power* and find help in the courts. However, minorities have barely begun to infiltrate positions of political power. In 1993, only 4.4 percent of elected members of parliament represented visible minorities, while in 2000 the percentage had risen marginally to 5.6 (table 7.8).

Thus, the social structure has tended to create and perpetuate superior/inferior patterns of interaction because of the clustering of minorities in low-status, low-power roles in institutions. The minorities have lacked the power to exercise control over the institutions and have, therefore, failed to receive the full benefits of *participation* in those institutions. The policies and practices of economic institutions, like government bodies, tend to maximize and perpetuate the well-being of those who are dominant. Institutions thereby work to the detriment of minorities independent of any individual prejudice among institutional leaders.

TABLE 7.5 ▪ ▪ ▪

Representation of Visible Minorities in the Public Service and the Federally Regulated Private Sector

Sector	1987	1988	1989	1990	1991	1992	1993	1994	1995
Public service	2.7%	2.9%	3.1%	3.5%	3.6%	3.8%	3.8%	3.8%	4.1%
Private sector	5.0%	5.7%	6.7%	7.1%	7.6%	7.9%	8.1%	8.3%	8.8%

Sources: Treasury Board Secretariat: Annual and Special Reports; HRDC: Annual Reports on Employment Equity.

TABLE 7.6 ▪ ▪ ▪

Promotions of Visible Minorities in the Public Service and the Federally Regulated Private Sector

Sector	1987	1988	1989	1990	1991	1992	1993	1994	1995
Public service	N/A	N/A	N/A	N/A	3.9%	N/A	4.0%	3.9%	4.1%
Private sector	6.9%	7.6%	9.4%	10.9%	10.8%	11.1%	10.7%	11.1%	11.6%

N/A: Not Available

Sources: Treasury Board Secretariat: Annual and Special Reports and Canadian Human Rights Commission Reports.

TABLE 7.7 ▪ ▪ ▪

Percentage of Visible Minority Hires in the Public Service

Sector	1988	1989	1990	1991	1992	1993	1994	1995
Public-service hires	3.3%	4.0%	4.6%	5.0%	5.5%	5.2%	2.7%	2.9%

Sources: Treasury Board Secretariat: Annual and Special Reports and Canadian Human Rights Commission Reports.

TABLE 7.8

Ethno-racial Origins of Canadian MPs Elected in 1993, 1997, and 2000

Ethno-racial Origin	1993 #	1993 %	1997 #	1997 %	2000 #	2000 %
Majority[a]	193	65.4	194	64.5	190	63.1
Majority–Minority[b]	27	9.2	24	8	34	11.3
Minority	71	24.1	75	24.9	71	23.6
European	53	18.0	52	17.3	49	16.3
Jewish[c]	4	1.4	4	1.3	5	1.7
Visible Minorities[d]	13	4.4	19	6.3	17	5.6
Other[e]	1	0.3	—	—	—	—
Aboriginal[f]	4	1.4	7	2.3	5	1.7
Other[g]	—	—	1	0.3	1	0.3
(N)		295		301		301

a) Includes single British origins and British-only multiples, all French origins, and British-French multiples.
b) Includes British and/or French *and* European multiples.
c) For 1997 and 2000, one Jewish visible minority individual is counted once in the visible minority category only.
d) Follows Statistics Canada origins classifications: Chinese, South Asians, Blacks, Arabs and West Asians, Filipinos, Southeast Asians, Latin American (except Chileans and Argentinians), Japanese, Korean, and Pacific Islanders.
e) Chilean.
f) Includes Aboriginal and Aboriginal–nonaboriginal references.
g) No further classification possible beyond British *or* German

Source: Jerome H. Black, "Ethnoracial Minorities in the House of Commons," *Canadian Parliamentary Review*, Vol 25, No.1, Spring 2002.

▪▪ Social Psychological Factors

We said previously that ideology affects social interaction. Why does the ideology of equal opportunity not alter the superior/inferior kind of interaction between whites and minorities that results from the social structure? It might, except for the many ideologies in any society. Some of the ideologies of Canada have helped to shape and sustain the traditional interaction patterns between ethno-racial groups. In fact, some values, attitudes, and ideologies among both whites and minorities tend to perpetuate the race problem. We examine those of the whites first.

Majority Perspectives. The initial low position of minorities in Canada stems from the circumstances of their arrival—as servants or unskilled labourers. The *ideology necessary to legitimate the subordination of minorities was already present.* The first white settlers in North America believed in their own racial superiority and certainly considered themselves superior to the "savages" who were native to North America. Similarly, the English, on first making contact with Africans, considered them very "puzzling" creatures, and tried to determine why the people were black. In one explanation, blacks were said to be the descendants of Ham, whom the Bible says God had cursed. Actually, as stated in the ninth chapter of Genesis, the curse was pronounced by Noah, not God, and it was against Ham's son, Canaan. The fact that many people have accepted the argument underscores the power of the *fallacy of the appeal to prejudice,* for those who accepted the argument undoubtedly acted out of prejudice rather than knowledge of the Bible. In any case, Africans were a different kind of people, and the difference was seen to be undesirable.

A number of white groups entered the country in low-status, low-power positions (and were to some extent the objects of prejudice), but none of them were so looked down upon as the visible minorities. A number of additional factors worked against visible minorities but not against whites: (1) the economy needed less and less unskilled labour, (2) their skin colour was a visible disability, (3) the political system no longer offered jobs for votes so freely, and (4) their smaller households probably did not have several wage earners.

prejudice

a rigid, emotional attitude that legitimates discriminatory behaviour toward people in a group

Prejudice, a "rigid, emotional attitude toward a human group" (Simpson and Yinger 1965:15), is an attitude widely held among the white majority. Prejudice legitimates different treatment of group members and helps to perpetuate white dominance. Prejudice is an individual characteristic, but its causes lie outside the individual—no one is born with prejudice. Simpson and Yinger (1965:49–51) identified a number of sources of prejudice. The sources included personality needs; the usefulness of prejudice for certain groups (low-status whites, for instance, who have been better off than blacks); group tradition (children learn to hate without knowing precisely why); and certain attributes possessed by the minority group. "Group attributes" are questionable as a source, however. They may serve as a useful rationalization for prejudice, but they do not generally cause that prejudice.

Prejudice does not necessarily have so rational a basis as a consistent set of beliefs about or a well-defined image of the target group. Social psychologists have known for a long time that certain groups can be defined as undesirable even when the attributes of those groups are vague. This insight is expressed in an old poem:

> I do not love thee, Dr. Fell,
> the reason why I cannot tell.
> But this I know and know quite well,
> I do not love thee, Dr. Fell.

One consequence of prejudice is that it facilitates fallacious thinking. To the prejudiced person, certain *fallacies of non sequiturs* come easily: They are on welfare, therefore they don't want to work; they have more children than they can properly care for, therefore they show themselves to be immoral; they don't speak proper English, therefore they are intellectually inferior; and so forth. The "they" of course is whichever minority group the speaker wants to castigate. The same arguments have been used about many different groups.

Prejudice continues to exist, in spite of decades of efforts to combat it. Most whites believe that minorities have equal opportunities now, but minorities assert that they encounter prejudice frequently or even daily.[3] Studies of interracial behaviour in everything from classrooms to stores to street encounters to choice of housing location confirm the existence of a great deal of prejudice (Delpit 1995; Deyhle 1995; Feagin and Vera 1995; Emerson, Yancey, and Chai 2001).

Stereotypes that reinforce prejudice and discriminatory behaviour also continue (Jackson and Reeves 1994, Jackson et al. 1997). An example of stereotypical thinking is provided by two researchers who asked a group of white post secondary students to select from a list of words those that seemed to them to be typical of the communicative behaviour of black students (Leonard and Locke 1993). The 10 most frequently chosen terms were, in order, loud, ostentatious, aggressive, active, boastful, talkative, friendly, noisy, straightforward, and emotional. Another study asked about images of black women (Weitz and Gordon 1993). The students characterized black women as loud, talkative, aggressive, intelligent, straightforward, and argumentative.

No group is free of prejudice or of being victims of prejudice.

The insidious nature of prejudice is illustrated by the way it legitimates and helps to perpetuate the interaction patterns occurring in institutions. In the schools, for instance, a black child may perform poorly because, in part, he or she senses a teacher's hostility, born of prejudice. The teacher labels the child as having mediocre ability and places him or her in an appropriate group. The child may accept the teacher's definition of his or her ability, and that definition may be further reinforced through IQ tests and subsequent teachers' reactions. Thus, prejudice further reduces the chances of academic success for a poorly prepared child, and the normal policies and practices of the school, such as IQ testing and grouping by ability, reinforce an official definition of the child's ability. If a child rebels against this hostile and repressive environment and becomes a "behaviour problem," the teacher will conclude that his or her initial hostility is fully justified.

Disparaging Attitudes. In the face of disparaging attitudes and ideologies, minorities can get trapped in a vicious circle. By experiencing disparagement, deprivation, and powerlessness, members of a minority group may develop attitudes of alienation and cynicism about society. For example, there is sufficient evidence since the early 1990s that police are racially biased. Consider these figures from the Canadian Race Relations Foundation (Racial Profiling Fact Sheet #1):

- A 1993 Canadian Civil Liberties Association survey found that 71 percent of visible minorities compared to 50 percent of whites had a negative experience with the police, including racial slurs when questioned.
- A 1995 survey of 1,200 people found that 44 percent of black males, compared to 25 percent of whites, had been stopped and questioned at least once in a two-year period. Further, blacks who earn high incomes were more likely to be stopped than working-class blacks.
- Police swore at blacks more often than at whites (58.8 and 38.3 percent, respectively).
- Police drew their weapons more often at black than at white people (12.5 and 6.7 percent, respectively) when responding to "minor offences."

Some of these attitudes may lead minorities to accept their low position rather than to struggle against it. In turn, remaining deprived and powerless maintains them in subordinate positions where they see a pervasive hopelessness, and as such, live in a climate of low expectations. Many social psychologists argue that these expectations are crucial, virtually guaranteeing continued deprivation unless the expectations are somehow changed.

PREJUDICE IN EUROPE

Prejudice is found everywhere. It varies from one country to another as well as within countries. In the United States, the fear of economic competition (for jobs and income) has often fanned the flames of prejudice and led to racial tensions and riots. The threat—real or not—of economic competition is also a factor in prejudice in other nations.

Quillian (1995) studied prejudice in a number of European countries. He found that the average prejudice scores varied from one country to another (figure 7.6). He also looked at the extent to which the people in each nation defined the threat from those of other races and nationalities as being due to such things as adding to problems of delinquency and

violence, leading to lower educational quality, and creating a drain on social security benefits.

Quillian's analysis showed that perceived threat explained most of the variations in average prejudice scores in the 12 European nations. He found that such individual characteristics as education, age, and social class had little impact on prejudice and explained none of the variations between countries. Rather, the economic conditions in each country and the size of the racial or immigrant group and the more problematic the economy, the more the minorities are perceived to be an economic threat and the higher level of prejudice.

SOURCE
  Quillian 1995.

FIGURE 7.6

Racial prejudice in
Europe.

Source: Adapted from Quillian
1995.

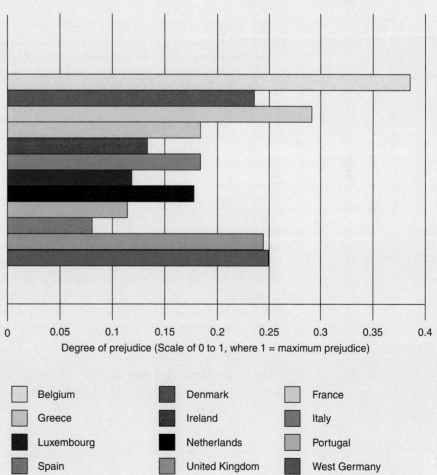

▪▪▪ From Social Problems to Solutions

Minority groups themselves have launched attacks on the forces that discriminate against them to the detriment of their desired quality of life. The result has been *inter-group conflict* as minorities strive to alter values, attitudes, ideologies, and social structural arrangements.

Resolution of the problem requires more than the actions of the minorities, however. What kind of actions may be taken, keeping in mind that any action will probably involve some conflict (verbal debate at the very least)?

First, attitudes and ideologies can be changed through a policy of persistent education in schools and the mass media. Many efforts have already been initiated, of course, but throughout the country there still are extensive prejudice and adherence to ideologies that disparage minorities. Educational efforts, incidentally, should attack not only the negative attitudes and ideologies about minorities but also the unrealistic ideas that many whites have about the consequences of an integrated society (Scherer and Slawski 1981; Mickelson 2001). Private initiatives that bring whites and minorities together in community settings also can reduce prejudice (Vora and Vora 2002).

Second, minorities need to continue to mobilize for political action that will shape public policy. It is imperative to exercise expanded influence in the government at all levels. For example, in the United States, an analysis of black employment in the civil service in 43 cities showed that not only the size of the black population but also the presence of a black mayor increased the levels of black employment (Eisinger 1980).

Third, legislation must be continually introduced, backed up by the commitment of the federal government to enforce the law. Many beneficial changes have occurred in the wake of such legislation and commitment. Laws can change attitudes and alter behaviour, but only by increments. A law is passed, people find ways to circumvent it, and a new law is passed to address the contradiction between the intended and the actual results of the first law. Over time the intent of the law is increasingly realized.

Programs must attack institutional racism directly. Visible minorities in Canada experience lower rates of labour force activity and less income than those of white Canadians even though they have reached higher levels of education (Kunz et al. 2001). For this reason, it is necessary to implement *affirmative-action programs* to increase minority participation in business, industry, education, and service agencies. In essence, affirmative action is a preemptive policy, preventing discrimination before it ever occurred (Reskin 1998). There is evidence that such programs can be effective (Fosu 1992; Davidson and Lewis 1997). For example, the Canadian Anti-Racism Education and Research Society (CAERS) is a "frontline, grass roots anti-racist organization that tracks, monitors and fights racism and hate crime" (www.antiracist.com). The organization works with local communities, schools and businesses and lobbies governments in matters of human rights. Workshops offered include "Anti-racism and the workplace," which provides information to new immigrants and minority groups on issues of equality at work; "Combating hate on the Net," for parents and helping professionals to identify and prevent hate and bias activities on the Internet; and "Anti-racist youth leadership," which develops leadership skills, builds coalition, and works at finding solutions.

▪▪ SUMMARY

Visible minorities comprise a substantial and growing proportion of the population. Inequalities between the majority white race and minority races are primarily the result of sociocultural factors. Skin colour is a minor biological characteristic, but it is a major sociocultural factor.

The meaning of the problem and the diminished quality of life it imposes on minorities may be summed up in terms of citizenship rights and economic opportunities; in each of these areas, it is a distinct advantage to be white. Minorities have been deprived of basic citizenship rights, such as the right to vote and the right to be governed by, and be equal before, the law. Economically, minorities have suffered discrimination in employment opportunities and income. This is particularly true for Canada's First Nations people.

An important social structural factor that contributes to the problem is institutional racism. Minorities are kept clustered in the lower levels of the stratification system and are exploited by the normal policies and practices of institutions, including the mass media, education, the economy, and government. Social psychological factors of attitudes, values, and ideologies of both the white majority and the minorities compound the structural discrimination. While the social structural factors lead to devaluation of minorities, the social psychological factors can lead, in addition, to self-defeating behaviour on the part of minorities.

▪▪ KEY TERMS

Assimilation 191	Ethnic Group 188	Life Chances 198	Race 187
Biological Characteristic 187	Exploitation 206	Morphological 187	Racism 188
	Institutional Racism 203	Prejudice 209	Stealth Racism 201

▪▪ STUDY QUESTIONS

1. What do social scientists mean by "race"?

2. Discuss the extent and origin of races, ethnic groups, and racism in Canada.

3. How do prejudice and discrimination affect minorities' rights of citizenship?

4. Do minorities have equal economic opportunities?

5. In what sense do prejudice and discrimination violate minorities' rights to life and happiness and to dignity as human beings?

6. How is their position in the stratification system a factor in the problems of minorities?

7. Discuss the ways in which social institutions diminish minorities' quality of life.

8. What kinds of attitudes on the part of minorities exacerbate the race problem in Canada?

9. Discuss some of the institutional changes that are needed to address the problems of Canada's minorities.

10. Think about relationships you have had with people who are from a different ethno-racial group. What factors make these relationships more positive than others?

▪▪ FOR FURTHER READING

Das Gupta, T. *Racism and Paid Work*. Toronto: Garamond Press, 1996. Discusses the relation between exploitive work, racism, and gender.

Dobratz, Betty A., and Stephanie L. Shanks-Meile. *"White Power, White Pride!": The White Separatist Movement in the United States*. New York: Twayne Publishers, 1997. A useful review of extremist groups such as the Ku Klux Klan and American Nazis, including their ideologies and political efforts.

Frideres J., and R. Gadacz. *Aboriginal People in Canada: Contemporary Conflicts*. Toronto: Prentice Hall, 2001. This book examines historical and present-day contexts of Aboriginal people, including the Métis.

Graves, Joseph L., Jr. *The Emperor's New Clothes: Biological Theories of Race at the Millenium*. Brunswick, NJ: Rutgers University Press, 2001. A biologist gives a history of the idea of race and shows how race is a social rather than a biological construct.

Loury, Glenn C. *The Anatomy of Racial Inequality.* Cambridge, MA: Harvard University Press, 2002. Details the continued deprivation of African Americans and shows how structural and social psychological factors interact to continue the problem.

Nelson C.A., and C.A. Nelson (Eds.). *Racism, Eh? A Critical Inter-Disciplinary Anthology of Race and Racism in Canada.* Concord, ON: Captus Press, 2004. A historical and contemporary analysis of racism situated within the Canadian social context.

■■ NOTES

1. Reported in *U.S. News and World Report,* October 23, 1995.

2. There are virtually no black women working in the clothing industry, as black women are stereotyped as "rebellious," a characteristic that is not suited to "the meticulous, precise and repetitive work garment making entails" (Das Gupta 1996:57).

3. *Ibid.,* p. 100. See also Feagin and Sikes (1994); Kiang and Kaplan (1994); and Tan (1994).

Problems of Social Institutions

Social institutions exist in every society to solve the problems and meet the needs of people. The government should protect people, secure social order, and maintain an equitable society. The economy should provide the basic necessities of life. Education should fulfill people and train them to function well in society. The family should nurture its members and provide them with emotional stability and security. The health care system should maintain emotional and physical well-being.

Unfortunately, social institutions create as well as solve problems. In this section, you'll learn how the government and the political system fail in some of their functions; how the economy, including work, is detrimental to the quality of life for some people; how education fails to fulfill its functions for some individuals; how family life can detract from, rather than enhance, well-being; and how the health care system does not adequately meet the physical and emotional needs of some Canadians.

Society cannot exist without social institutions, but not everyone benefits equally from those institutions. Some even become victims. Institutions need reshaping in order to maximize the well-being of all Canadians.

GOVERNMENT AND POLITICS

"WHY ISN'T THERE HELP FOR PEOPLE LIKE ME?"

Jacquelyn is the single mother of two preschool children. Shortly before her second child was born, her husband, Ed, lost his job. He was unable to find another one. About the time they had exhausted their savings, he announced that he couldn't take it anymore and disappeared. Jacquelyn, who has only a high-school education, is struggling to survive:

> We lost our home. The kids and I are living in a cheap apartment. We're barely getting by. I don't have enough money to even buy my kids any new toys. And when I go to the grocery store, I see other mothers putting all kinds of good food into their baskets that I can't afford. My parents give us a little, but my dad is on disability and they have a hard time meeting their own bills. I married Ed right out of high school. So I've never worked, and I don't have any skills. I can't even use a computer.
>
> I remember that we were promised the government would give us a safety net. Well, where is it? I'm in a job training program now, but who's going to take care of my kids while I work? And how am I going to pay for someone to take care of my kids? How much do they think I'm going to make from the kinds of jobs they're training me for?
>
> What I'd like to know is, why isn't there some real help for people like me? Why doesn't the government find Ed and make him help support his kids? For all I know, he's found work somewhere else and has plenty of money. Or why doesn't the government make sure that I get a job that will pay me enough so I can give my kids a decent life? Our country goes all over the world helping people in need, and forgets about people like me. I'd like to see some of those politicians take my place for a while. Maybe then they would realize how some of us die a little bit every day from worrying about what's going to happen to us and our kids and how we're going to survive. ∎

▪▪ INTRODUCTION

What adjectives would you use to describe Canadian government? How about Canadian politics? If you are like many students we have taught, you probably came up with such adjectives as "huge," "inefficient," "corrupt," and "self-serving." However, we have also had students who described government and politics as "effective" and "helpful."

Let's follow up with another question: What role does government play in social problems? Some students see government as a major contributor to social problems. Others see it as the only hope for resolving them. Most students agree that the government should take a leading role in attacking various problems.

Each of these responses has some validity. Throughout this book, we note various ways in which the government and politics enter into both the causes and the resolution of social problems. In this chapter, we concentrate on the ways in which government and politics are themselves problems. We begin by examining the functions of government—what people believe they can legitimately expect from government. We then look at four specific ways in which government and politics are problems, how those problems affect people's quality of life, and various structural and social psychological factors that contribute to the problems. Finally, we explore possible ways to attack the problems of government and politics.

▪▪ WHY GOVERNMENT?

anarchism
the philosophy that advocates the abolition of government in order to secure true freedom for people

Can you imagine a society without any government? Some people can. **Anarchism** is a philosophy that advocates the abolition of government in order to secure true freedom for people. According to anarchists, people are free only when they can cooperate with each other to achieve their ends without the restraints of government and law. To be sure, history provides abundant examples of governments that have deprived people of freedom. Nevertheless, we agree with the student who said: "When I look at the way that governments have exploited and oppressed people throughout history, I am sympathetic to the idea of anarchism. But I still think we need government."

The question is, why do we need government? What do people expect from their government? What functions does it fulfill?

▪▪ Protect the Citizenry

The first function of government is to protect the citizenry. Canadians expect the government to protect them from various threats to their well-being, *threats that come from sources more powerful than any individual* (Sypnowich 2000). For example, people look to government for protection from environmental hazards, unsafe or unfair business practices, and corporate exploitation of consumers.

regulatory agency
an organization established by the government to enforce statutes that apply to a particular activity

This protection comes in the form of laws and regulatory agencies. A **regulatory agency** is an organization established by the government to enforce statutes that apply to a particular activity. For instance, the Canadian Industrial Relations Board (CIRB) monitors employer–employee relations, while the trading of stocks and bonds is monitored by provincial agencies (e.g., the Ontario Securities Commission, the British Columbia Securities Commission, and the Alberta Securities Commission). Although many people complain about the irrational and autocratic procedures of the regulatory agencies, they were established mainly in response to demands from citizens who felt the need for protection.

An example of the way the protective function works is seen in the *Food and Drug Act*, which monitors the safety of prescription drugs, food, and cosmetics manufactured not only in Canada but also abroad. In the early 1960s, the world was shocked at the news of babies being born without arms or legs. The tragedy took place, for the most part, in Europe and Australia and was linked to mothers' ingestion of the drug thalidomide. Thalidomide had been used as a tranquilizer and to treat nausea in pregnant women (Colburn, Dumanoski, and Myers 1997), but it was eventually shown that the drug also caused terrible deformities in children who were exposed to it while in the womb. Thalidomide was first available in West Germany in October 1957. It was not licensed in Canada until April 1961. In December 1961, Thalidomide was removed from many European markets but continued to be legally available in Canada until March 1962 (Thalidomide Victims Association of Canada 2003). The delayed removal of thalidomide from the Canadian market exposed many children to serious disabilities.

▪▪ Secure Order

A second function of government is to *secure order*. In contrast to anarchists, many observers argue that government is necessary to control individuals so that society does not degenerate into chaos and violence. By regulating people's behaviour in the economy and other areas of social life, government helps prevent the destructive disorder that would result from a situation in which individuals acted to benefit themselves (Durkheim 1933).

While there may be disagreement about whether government is necessary for social order, there is no disagreement about the importance of that order. Imagine what it would be like to live in a society in which there were no consensual rules about such matters as traffic, education of the young, or the right to private property. *Order is essential to both our emotional and our physical well-being.*

▪▪ Distribute Power Equitably

A third function of government is to distribute power equitably so that a person's freedom and aspirations are not constricted because of his or her sex, race, age, religion, or socioeconomic background. A person should not have more power than others simply because he is male rather than female, white rather than nonwhite, and so on.

We have shown in previous chapters that such factors have and do affect people's life chances. We have also noted the role of the government in redressing these inequities. A good example is the right to vote (Burns, Peterson, and Cronin 1984; Prentice et al. 1988). In the early years of the nation, the right to vote was limited to white, male adults who were property owners and taxpayers. After confederation, a very small minority of Canada's population (about 16 percent) could vote. There were only four provinces and 181 members of parliament (compared to 308 members in 2004). The provincial laws determined who was allowed to vote. Universal suffrage did not come quickly. Women gained the right to vote in both provincial and federal elections between 1916 and 1925. In Quebec, however, women did not have a legal right to vote until 1940. Many Canadians of Asian origin could not vote until 1948. The Inuit were legal-

A statue of two of the "Famous Five," Nellie McClung and Irene Parlby, who fought for the recognition of women as persons in the 1920s.

ly able to vote in 1950, and First Nations people in 1960. Today, most adult Canadians over the age of 18 can vote, the exception being inmates in British Columbia, Alberta, Saskatchewan, Nova Scotia, and New Brunswick, who can not legally vote provincially but are able to vote federally.

▪▪ Provide a Safety Net

Finally, government functions *to provide a safety net, a minimum standard of living below which it will not allow citizens to fall.* Even if opportunities abound, some people—because of such things as the economy and life circumstances—are not able to achieve what most Canadians define as a minimal standard of living. In addition, as Canadians discovered in the Great Depression that followed the stock-market crash in 1929, there are times when opportunities are severely limited. It was in response to the hardships of the Depression that in the 1930s the government was pressured to become more involved in the economy and the social well-being of Canadians. Canadians wanted a social safety net that would include such programs as medicare, unemployment insurance, old-age security, and social welfare for single mothers and persons with disabilities. Since that time, Canadians have come to expect government actions to provide a safety net that secures a minimum standard of living.

Differences exist over what should be included in the safety net. Currently, safety-net benefits include such things as pensions and medicare for the retired, short-term financial aid for the unemployed, subsidized lunches for poor school children, and health insurance (Long and Marquis 1999).

▪▪ PROBLEMS OF GOVERNMENT AND POLITICS

The problems discussed in this section reflect the fact that *political parties and government bureaucracy play a central role in the way representative democracy functions in Canada.* **Political parties** are organized groups that attempt to control the government through the electoral process. A **bureaucracy** is an organization in which there are specific areas of authority and responsibility, a hierarchy of authority, management based on written documents, worker expertise, management based on rules, and full-time workers. The government bureaucracy includes those government employees whose jobs do not depend on elections or political appointment.

▪▪ Inequalities in Power

The actual distribution of power in Canadian society contradicts the expectation that the government should ensure equity. But exactly how is power distributed? This is not an easy question to answer.

Pluralism or Power Elites?

Who holds the most power in Canada? Many social scientists believe that Canada is a *pluralistic society* in terms of the distribution of power. **Pluralism** means that power is distributed more or less equally among **interest groups,** which are groups that attempt to influence public opinion and political decisions in accord with the particular interests of their members. Thus, an interest group such as the National Firearms Association (NFA) exercises power in the political sphere to protect its members' insistence on the right to own firearms. The National Action Committee on the Status of Women (NAC) exercises power to protect and advance the rights of women.

---

political party
an organized group that attempts to control the government through the electoral process

bureaucracy
an organization in which there are specific areas of authority and responsibility, a hierarchy of authority, management based on written documents, worker expertise, management based on rules, and full-time workers

pluralism
the more or less equal distribution of power among interest groups

interest group
a group that attempts to influence public opinion and political decisions in accord with the particular interests of its members

power elite model
a model of politics in which power is concentrated in political, economic, and military leaders

In contrast to the pluralist view, the **power elite model** asserts that power is concentrated in a small group of political, economic, and military leaders (Mills 1956). In essence, the top leaders in government, in business, and in the military determine the major policies and programs of the nation—and they do this in a way that furthers their own interests and solidifies their power. A variation, held by Marxists and some others, is that capitalists wield the power, including power over the government (Barry 2002). Most who hold to the power elite view argue that interest groups have some limited power (unions being an example), while the great bulk of individuals is an unorganized, powerless mass controlled by the power elite. Domhoff's (1990) analysis of decision making, for example, concludes that the upper class generally rules the nation.

Power and Inequality.   While there is some validity to both the pluralist and the power elite positions, neither seems to capture fully the realities of power distribution. *People are not powerless, particularly when they organize.* For example, the Coalition for Gun Control is a lobby, research, and education group founded following the Montreal massacre (when 14 female engineering students were killed in class by a gunman who shouted "I hate feminists!" as he opened fire) "to reduce gun death, injury and crime." Mothers Against Drunk Driving (MADD) has influenced the passage of new legislation on drinking and driving, helping to reduce the number of deaths caused by drunk drivers.

At the same time, *there clearly are power inequities;* otherwise the poor, women, and minorities, among others, would not have had to struggle for so long against their various disadvantages. In spite of efforts by many women's groups, even though women's levels of education today are approaching those of men (Wilson 1996) their job profiles continue to parallel those of 40 years ago (clerical, sales and service, and teaching and nursing professions) (Pierson and Cohen 1995). Further, women continue to receive less pay than men for work of equal value. Other minorities have made only modest headway in their efforts to achieve equity in the economy. In other words, regardless of which model of power distribution most accurately reflects the realities of social life, the government clearly has not maintained an equitable distribution of power.

■■ The Failure of Trust

An important part of the task of securing order is the building of trust (Levi 1998). Trust in this context means having confidence that others will fulfill their responsibilities. Citizens need to trust each other and they need to trust the government. Trust is essential if people are to cooperate and work together in maintaining the norms and the laws of society. If citizens distrust their government, they are more apt to resist and even ignore governmental policies and laws.

How much do Canadians trust their government? Since 1981, overall trust in federal government has declined. According to the World Values Survey, 37 percent of Canadians in 1981 were very supportive of public institutions. By 1990, the percentage dropped to 29 percent, and to 22 percent in 1998. Roese (2002) points out that this trend can have a positive interpretation. Being distrustful may mean that Canadians are more involved with and have a better understanding of politics. Thus, questioning government can be viewed as part of healthy skepticism. But, according to an Ekos Research Survey (March 2002), 37 percent of respondents believe that "quite a few" of Canadian politicians are "crooked," and 27 percent of Canadians are trustful that the government will "do what is right." It should be noted that in the 1960s an overwhelming 80 percent of Canadians trusted the government to do what is right.

Trusting government is not only a Canadian phenomenon; this trend is also observed among Western nations. In the United States, for example, events in the 1960s and 1970s—including the growing disillusionment with the Vietnam War and with the truth of official reports about the war—contributed to the decline in confidence. During the same time period, Canada witnessed its own political crises, but public opinion supported government action. In October 1970 Prime Minister Pierre Trudeau proclaimed the *War Measures Act* in response to two kidnappings—of John Cross, a British diplomat, and Pierre Laporte, a Quebec Member of Parliament—by a Québécois terrorist group that called itself the Front de Libération du Québec, or the FLQ (for more, see box 8.1):

> If a democratic society is to continue to exist, it must be able to root out the cancer of an armed, revolutionary movement that is bent on destroying the very basis of our freedom. For that reason the government, following an analysis of the facts, including requests of the government of Quebec and the city of Montreal for urgent action, decided to proclaim the *War Measures Act*. (Trudeau 1970)

Although the press was critical of the Act, which "suspends civil liberties" (Newman 2001), the public did not share this view; they felt that the government was acting responsibly by protecting its citizens by defeating terrorism. The public's support for the *War Measures Act* notwithstanding, public confidence in government began to decline slowly thereafter.

So, why do Canadians view government with more skepticism than they do other social institutions? Unfortunately, researchers who survey people on their level of confidence do not probe into the reasons for their responses. It is probably true, as Levi (1998) asserts, that such things as the breaking of campaign promises, incompetence, and the lack of responsiveness to people's interests and needs lead to distrust. Scandals and corruption, which have never been absent from Canadian political life, also contribute to distrust.

The *War Measures Act* was first enacted in 1914, at the beginning of the First World War, and gives the government powers of censorship, arrest, detention without trial, and deportation.

Since the 1990s we have witnessed much global unrest—more specifically, the 1994 Gulf War followed by the invasion of Iraq less than a decade later. Both President George W. Bush of the United States and Prime Minister Tony Blair of Britain justified the war on Iraq by claiming the Iraqi government possessed weapons of mass destruction. We now know these allegations are false; such acts of deception, according to Donolo (2003:A15), "will have long-term and corrosive effects on politics and public opinion both in their own nations and internationally." Donolo adds that, now, "[i]n our own society, cynicism and distrust of 'the official line' runs deep."

Whatever the reasons for the growing lack of trust, a number of consequences follow from it. Below, we discuss lack of citizen participation, voting and young people, voting and education, and political alienation.

Box 8.1

The October Crisis

In the early 1960s, Quebec underwent what was called the "Quiet Revolution." Throughout the mid twentieth century, French Canadians grew increasingly concerned about their exclusion from political and social systems in Canada. This struggle took many forms, ranging from lobby groups demanding increased protection and funding for French programs and politics, to the formation of nationalist groups that argued the only way for Quebec to develop was if it became a sovereign country. In October 1970, one such nationalist group, the FLQ, kidnapped James Cross (the British Trade Minister) and Pierre Laporte (Quebec's minister of Labour and Immigration). They demanded that their manifesto, which called for independence and a francophone-workers' revolution, be broadcast on CBC Radio Canada, and also asked for $500,000 in gold, an aircraft to take the kidnappers to Cuba or Algeria, and the release of 23 political prisoners. (To read the full manifesto, go to www.ola.bc.ca/online/cf/documents/1970FLQManifesto.html.) These kidnappings deeply divided the loyalties of the province, as many students, unions, newspapers, and political parties endorsed the goals of the FLQ as outlined in their manifesto (Moore 1996).

On October 16 the Quebec government headed by Premier Bourassa requested that Prime Minister Pierre Trudeau declare a state of "apprehended insurrection" and impose martial law under the *War Measures Act*. The next day, Pierre Laporte's strangled body was found in a car trunk. However, it is unclear whether his death was intentional.

Under the *War Measures Act* the FLQ was banned, and almost 500 Québécois were summarily arrested; all but four were released without charges. The FLQ Liberation Cell—Jacques Cossette-Trudel, Louise Cossette-Trudel, Jacques Lanctôt, Marc Carbonneau, and Yves Langlois—who were responsible for the kidnapping of James Cross, were granted safe passage to Cuba in exchange for Cross's release.

On December 24, 1970, the army pulled out of Quebec and the government withdrew the *War Measures Act*.

Lack of Citizen Participation.   Why participate in the political process if you lack confidence in the government? Why vote if you believe that no matter who is elected the government will not function as it ought?

Although it is not the only reason for not voting, *the failure of trust is certainly one reason* for the relatively low proportion of voters (Jamieson, Shin, and Day 2002). According to Elections Canada, voter percentage rates from the Second World War until the 1980s held at about 75 percent. Since the 1980s voter rates have steadily declined: to 70 percent in 1993; 67 percent in 1997; just over 61 percent in 2000; and an all-time low of 60.5 percent in the 2004 federal election. The question plaguing Canadian policy analysts is how to explain this declining trend. Let's explore who is or is not voting, and why voting rates have decreased across the country.

Who Votes?   Voting is related to age, education, and household income (see figures 8.1 through 8.3). If you are younger, less educated, and have a relatively low household income, you are less likely to vote. In general, the older one is the more likely

FIGURE 8.1

Did not vote, by age group, 2000 election.

Source: Adapted from 2000 Canadian National Election Study.

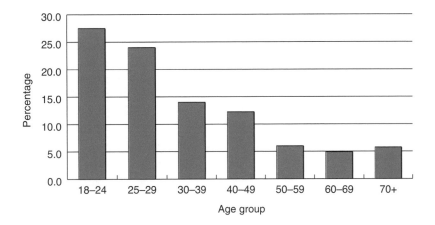

FIGURE 8.2

Did not vote, by education, 2000 election.

Source: Adapted from 2000 Canadian National Election Study.

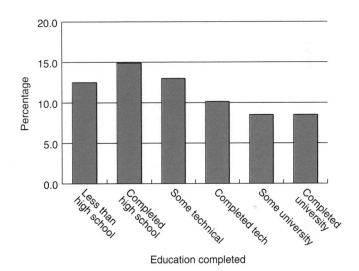

FIGURE 8.3

Did not vote, by income, 2000 election.

Source: Adapted from 2000 Canadian National Election Study.

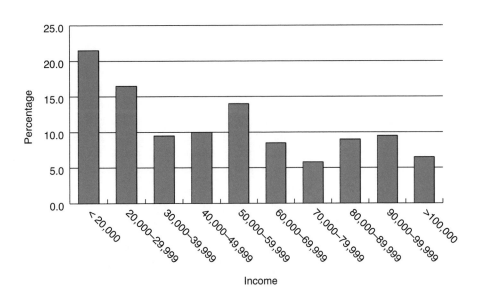

she or he is to vote, up to a point; after the age of 70, voting rates slightly decline. Analysts are careful to classify people in terms of age *cohorts*, or generations. For example, Elections Canada noticed that two-thirds of Canadians who became eligible for voting during the Trudeau years (referred to as the Trudeau cohort) voted in the 2000 election, compared to 54.2 percent of Canadians during the Mulroney years and only 22.4 percent of the 2000 cohort (Pammett 2003). According to these rates, even if voting rates rise according to life cycles the overall percentage of Canadians who vote will decline.

Voting and Young People.   In response to the low voter turnout for the 2000 federal elections, researchers examined why fewer Canadians were voting and found that age was the most important factor (Pammett 2003). Primary reasons offered by youth for not voting were "lack of interest" and "apathy" (see table 8.1). Researchers following voting patterns among young Canadians in the 2004 federal election also found that low turnout is attributed to apathy (Gidengil et al. 2004).

Political scientist Brenda O'Neil (2001) carried out a "Success of Canadian Democracy" (SCD) survey, asking the same questions from a 1990 survey to assess not only trends in Canadians' political opinions and actions, but also whether the opinions and actions were generational, life cycle, or period-based. The study concluded that with age Canadians tend to develop a greater interest in politics. However, younger Canadians today, although more satisfied with the democratic process, have less faith in our electoral system and the political parties. Further, there is a generational effect whereby younger voters today are participating at lower rates than those in previous generations.

O'Neil offers two explanations. The first and more optimistic view is that younger people today, who have grown up with relative financial and global security, have adopted "post-material" concerns. This means it is not political interest that has decreased, but rather interest in traditional political forms. This interest is being expressed in alternative ways, examples being grassroots organizing, anti-globalization, and protest work. The second possibility is that "technological and social change over the last 30 years has led to a significant decline in **social capital**—consisting of levels of civic engagement, trust in traditional institutions and exchange among members of communities and neighbourhoods—which is most evident among younger generations in advanced industrial states" (2001:9).

social capital
the degree of participation and involvement within a community between its citizens and institutions—characterized by trust, reciprocity, identity—to achieve mutual benefits

Voting and Education.   Education is a "classic and powerful determinant of voting" (Blais et al. forthcoming:7). Overall, levels of education have increased in Canada. It is, then, reasonable to assume that proportionately more Canadians would vote. But, this is not the case; instead, the propensity to vote in all groups has slightly declined. A research project that examined Canadian election studies from 1968 to 2000 found that voting patterns today among the better educated continue to be the same as in times past (Blais et al. forthcoming). However, whereas the majority of people with lesser education voted in earlier time periods, fewer than one-third cast a vote in the most recent elections. What this means is that "the educational gap has considerably widened," and, according to the researchers, "education remains a powerful determinant of voting, more powerful than it used to be at least in Canada" (8).

political alienation
a feeling of political disillusionment, powerlessness, and estrangement

Political Alienation.   Another consequence of the failure of trust is **political alienation,** *a feeling of political disillusionment, powerlessness, and estrangement.* Alienated people lose interest in political life (Dennis and Owen 2001). They may believe that the political process is pointless. Low voting participation is an indication of alienation. So is the fact that in a 2004 survey only 60 percent of Canadians in their 20s were able to name Paul Martin as leader of the Liberal Party, only 47 percent could name Stephen Harper as the Conservative Party leader, and only 34 percent could name

Main Reason for Not Voting	Age						Total
	65+	55–64	45–54	35–44	25–34	18–24	
Lack of interest							
Not interested; didn't care; apathy	14.8	29.0	18.3	19.7	27.3	28.0	25.0
Vote meaningless; doesn't count; election foregone conclusion	6.4	8.4	9.6	10.0	11.4	6.5	9.0
Forgot; unaware	4.2	0.0	0.0	1.2	2.0	3.9	2.3
Too complicated; confusing	0.0	0.0	2.3	2.5	0.7	0.0	0.9
Total—Lack of interest	25.4	37.4	30.2	33.4	41.4	38.4	37.2
Negativity							
No appealing candidates/parties/issues	9.9	13.4	22.7	21.2	14.1	13.9	15.9
Lack of faith/confidence in candidates/ parties/leaders	17.7	13.5	21.3	16.7	14.0	6.3	12.8
Lack of information about candidates/parties/ issues	0.0	3.0	3.0	2.8	0.5	0.8	1.4
Regional discontent	0.03	3.0	3.0	2.8	0.5	0.8	1.4
Total—Negativity	27.6	31.5	50.3	45.7	31.7	27.3	34.4
Personal/Administrative							
Too busy with work/school/family	5.0	3.4	3.1	11.9	13.7	22.6	14.3
Away from riding/province/country	20.3	23.0	9.3	8.0	10.9	7.9	10.4
Registration problems	4.0	3.0	6.7	2.7	5.2	7.4	5.5
Illness; health issues	19.5	5.8	7.7	1.9	2.0	4.2	2.9
Didn't know where or when; polling station problems; transportation	5.7	5.1	2.7	2.5	2.2	4.2	3.3
Moving-related problems	0.0	0.0	2.5	1.1	1.2	0.5	0.9
Total—Personal/Administrative	54.5	40.3	32.0	28.1	35.2	43.0	37.3
Other							
Religious reason	5.5	3.0	1.5	2.0	1.1	0.9	1.5
Other; unclassifiable; unclear; none	0.0	0.9	0.8	3.1	1.8	3.6	2.4
Total—Other	5.5	3.9	2.3	5.1	2.9	4.5	3.9
TOTAL	100.0	100.0	100.0	100.0	100.0	100.0	100.0
N	43	58	109	171	331	347	1,059

TABLE 8.1 ■ ■ ■

Main Reasons for Not Voting, 2000 (Open-ended; multiple responses; percentage of respondents)

Source: Elections Canada (2003) http://www.elections.ca/content.asp?section=loi&document=index&dir=tur/tud&lang=e&textonly=false

Jack Layton as the NDP leader. Further, 35 percent of respondents said they did not know which party would be best to deal with their number-one issue of concern: health care (Gidengil et al. 2004). In spite of the increasing levels of education (see chapter 10) and the increasing amount of information available through the various media, the public's political knowledge has decreased since the 1960s and is low compared to that in other Western democracies (Milner 2001).

Alienated people do not blame individual politicians for the sorry state of affairs in political life. They are not merely turned off by the mudslinging and broken promises and endless conflict in the political arena. Rather, they are *disillusioned with the entire system.* They believe that the system itself is fundamentally flawed (Scher 1997). For such people, it will take more than appeals to civic duty to involve them once again in the nation's political life.

■■ Waste, Corruption, and Scandals

Canadians believe they have a right to expect effectiveness, efficiency, and honesty from the politicians who are running their government. Unfortunately, Canadians believe they observe contrary qualities—waste, corruption, and scandals—in those politicians. "Government waste" refers to such things as *excessive paperwork, excessive costs, and unnecessary expenditures.* We are all familiar with the *existence of corruption and scandals.*

Even today, ridings that elect members of parliament are thanked with infrastructure programs and government contracts. For example, an internal audit of Human Resources Development Canada (HRDC) in 1998 found that $1 billion in funding for job creation programs was unmonitored and unaccounted for. It was later revealed that HRDC Minister Jane Stewart between 1996 and 1998 assigned $19 million in job-creation money to her own riding. To make matters worse, the public also learned that Prime Minster Jean Chrétien's riding received $200,000 for a fountain project from Canada Economic Development, an independent government agency.

Indeed, Jean Chrétien's 20-year tenure as prime minister was rocked with scandals of patronage—but none as big as what we now refer to as the "sponsorship scandal." A

Prime Minister Paul Martin responds to a question concerning the sponsorship scandal during Question Period in the House of Commons on Parliament Hill in Ottawa.

sponsorship program was established by Chrétien to counter separatism in Quebec. On October 30, 1995—after the No side narrowly won the referendum on the issue of Quebec's separation from Canada—the Liberal government launched a pro-Canada advertisement campaign. The sponsorship program received $250 million over a four-year period. Communications consultants with close ties to the Liberal party received more than $100 million. As well, five Crown corporations—the RCMP, Via Rail, Canada Post, the Business Development Bank of Canada, and the Old Port of Montreal—were accused of funnelling money.

In February 2004, federal Auditor General Sheila Fraser released a detailed report that outlined the government corruption. Chrétien had already resigned as prime minister, and responsibility for the scandal fell on the new chosen leader of the Liberal Party, Paul Martin. Highlights of the report include:

* The government donated $3 million to the RCMP's 125th birthday party. Three advertising agencies—Lafleur, Media/I.D.A. Vision, and Gosselin—deducted $1.3 million in commissions before passing the money on to the RCMP. At the same time, the bank records of the RCMP were destroyed.

* Communications Canada gave $1.5 million to the Old Port of Montreal to buy a new screen for its science centre—Lafleur and Media/I.D.A. Vision were once again responsible for delivering the money and this time collected $225,000 in commissions.

* The government paid $5 million to fund a TV show about hockey hero Maurice Richard: Lafleur, Media/I.D.A. Vision, Gosselin, and Groupaction received $440,000 in commissions not having signed any contracts or having done any work.

Members of the opposition claimed that the source of funding was hidden, the money was used as income for private companies, and there was no known public benefit. Legally, the sponsorship scandal is in breach of the *Federal Administration Act*, which attempts to promote transparency and fairness in the government's financial dealings.

patronage
giving government jobs to people who are members of the winning party

A corrupt practice that is less common today than earlier in the nation's history is **patronage,** giving government jobs to people who are members of the winning party. Recall that one of the fundamental characteristics of a bureaucracy is the expertise of workers. Yet politicians have often hired, or used their influence to obtain employment for, relatives, friends, and party workers no matter their level of expertise. This practice is less common than it once was, since the bulk of government jobs now come under civil service. Nevertheless, officeholders still have a number of positions to fill, and their selections may be based on things other than the expertise of those hired.

Corruption may also take the form of "stuffing the ballot box" or other methods of rigging elections. Frizzell and Westell (1984:144) discuss corrupt voting practices in Quebec during the 1984 general election. Hired cars drove voters to the polls; certain individuals, known as "telegraphers," were paid to vote more than once; and violence and intimidation was used on opposing supporters. Although such practices are less common today, various types of voting irregularities still exist. For example, Sheila Copps, the former 20-year cabinet minister for Jean Chrétien's government, lost the nomination for her riding for the 2004 federal election to Tony Valeri, who was hand-picked by Paul Martin. Boundary ridings were redrawn and voting rules were changed. She told the CBC (2004) that she had been "drummed out as if I've done something wrong."

Sex scandals in Canada have been less common. The first and perhaps most famous sex scandal occurred in 1966, when a number of senior ministers in the ruling Conservative government under Prime Minister John Diefenbaker—including the associate minister of national defence—had sexual relations with a German playgirl, Gerda Munsinger. Ms. Munsinger was thought to be a spy for the KGB (Soviet Union). Remember that the 1960s was in the middle of the Cold War (a period between the 1940s and 1980s that was marked by political conflict and a nuclear arms race between Western nations and the Soviet Union), and because of this Canada was in a frenzy over the possible security risk.

▪▪ Gridlock

gridlock
the inability of the government to legislate significant new policies

Frequently, the government seems *mired in inaction,* unable to legislate new policies because of ideological conflict, party differences, or a standoff between the executive and legislative branches of the government. Such a situation is known as **gridlock** (Brady and Volden 1998). Gridlock may reflect the fact that politicians are taking stands in accord with contradictory values and are unable to reach a compromise. However, gridlock also occurs when politicians are engaged in power struggles in which who is in control is more important than what gets done. Gridlock can occur at any level of government. It is likely to maintain or even intensify the failure of trust. A government mired in inaction appears weak to the public it supposedly serves.

A filibuster is a delay tactic used by members of the opposition in Parliament to stop a bill from passing. One way this is done is that amendments—and amendments to the amendments (referred to as "sub-amendments")—to every clause can be suggested. In theory, this debate can last until a new election is called. Perhaps the most famous filibuster in Canada's history took place in 1963, when the newly elected Liberal Prime Minister Lester B. Pearson proposed a new flag for Canada. (Canada did not have an official flag; the Red Ensign, with the Union Jack in the upper left corner and the Canadian coat of arms in the lower right corner, represented Canada.) John Diefenbaker, the Progressive Conservative leader of the opposition, was incensed that the proposed new flag, with three maple leafs and a blue stripe on each end on a white background, in no way captured "Canada's majestic traditions, its British and Christian past" (Hilmer 2004). A filibuster was mounted by Diefenbaker and other members of the opposition; parliament was forced to sit throughout the summer. In the end, the flag we know today, with one maple leaf in the centre and two red stripes on each end, replaced Pearson's original proposal.

▪▪ GOVERNMENT, POLITICS, AND THE QUALITY OF LIFE

As with all the problems we are examining, government and politics affect the quality of life of great numbers of people. We consider here the way government action or inaction leads to three problem areas that affect quality of life: unequal opportunities for a high quality of life, inadequate protection of individual rights, and the lack of responsiveness to needs.

▪▪ Unequal Opportunities for a High Quality of Life

Today, Canadians generally expect government to maintain an equitable distribution of power so that they have an equal opportunity to secure a high quality of life. Politicians themselves acknowledge their role in this quest for a high quality of life.

Clearly, *politicians and citizens alike expect government at all levels to have a role in those matters that affect the quality of life.* Yet government has not measured up to these expectations and maintained a system in which all Canadians have an equal opportunity to reap the benefits deemed necessary for a high quality of life. We noted in the previous two chapters various ways in which some groups benefit to the detriment of others: how, for instance, the wealthy benefit more than the poor from tax laws and other government policies and practices, and how white males have more opportunities than women or people of either sex from racial and ethnic minorities.

These disadvantages mean a lower quality of life for whole groups of people. For example, visible minorities and those in the lower socioeconomic strata have higher rates of negative mood, such as feelings of sadness, than do whites and those in the higher strata (Blackwell, Collins, and Coles 2002).

The relationship between advantages and quality of life holds true in other nations as well. Surveys of people's sense of their well-being in 55 nations, representing three-quarters of the earth's population, found that the higher the income and the greater the amount of equality in the nation, the higher the people's sense of well-being (Diener, Diener, and Diener 1995).

In essence, then, *the government has failed to maintain a social system in which all individuals, regardless of their social origins, have equal opportunities.* Note that this does not mean that people expect equal outcomes. The nation's ideology is that anyone can succeed, but no one expects the government to ensure that every individual achieves the highest quality of life. However, Canadians do expect the government to ensure a system in which no one's quality of life is diminished automatically because of his or her sex or social origins.

▪▪ Inadequate Protection of Individual Rights

There is also *a contradiction between the value of individual rights and the way government functions to protect them.* As we noted in the last two chapters, government has not always protected the rights of women and of racial and ethnic minorities. In addition, government has threatened or violated certain basic rights that every citizen ideally possesses. For example, for many years the RCMP and Canadian Security Intelligence Service (CSIS) secretly gathered information and kept files on thousands of Canadians who openly opposed certain government programs and policies. Some of this information was secured by illegal means, such as breaking and entering or unauthorized taps of telephone lines:

> Would anyone believe that Royal Canadian Mounted Police (RCMP) security operatives—the Canadian version of a secret police—spied on tea and Tupperware parties? During the 1950s and '60s they did. They also monitored high-school students, gays and lesbians, trade unionists, and left-wing political groups, including the New Democratic Party and its forerunner, the CCF, as well as feminists and consumer housewives' associations.

> They watched civil servants, university students and professors, peace activists, immigrants, Canada Council grant recipients, Learned Society meetings, black community activists, First Nations people, and, of course, Quebec sovereignists. (Kinsman et al. 2001)

Since 1995 CSIS has been given the power to wiretap freely (that is, without a warrant) under the guise of securing our nation.

It is important to acknowledge that at least a part of the problem of inadequate protection of individual rights lies in *the dilemma faced by government—how can individual rights and social order both be preserved?* A classic instance of the dilemma is the clash between individual rights and national security. During the Second World War, the clash was decided in favour of national security, resulting in the internment of around 22,000 Japanese Canadians. Even though they were Canadian citizens, they were viewed as a threat because of the war with Japan. Some observers still believe that the internment was the appropriate course of action (Rehnquist 1998). Others, however, have concluded that Japanese Canadian citizens were deprived of their rights; in fact, lawsuits were instituted in the 1990s to obtain reparations for the injustice.

Individual rights versus national security remains a prominent issue, especially since the events of September 11, 2001. In its attempt to fight terrorism, the Canadian government and CSIS drastically reformed legislation that increased their unaccountable powers. Legislative changes include (ICLMG 2004; Canadian Border Service Agency 2004):

- Bill C-36, which grants police expanded investigative and surveillance power, the pre-emptive arrests of suspected terrorists, the de-registration of charities with suspected links to terrorist organizations, and the creation of a data bank that holds information for up to six years on the foreign air travel of all Canadians.
- Bill C-18, which allows the revocation of naturalized citizens in the name of security interests without disclosure of evidence or a right to appeal.
- Smart Border Legislation, a non-legislated, bilateral agreement with the U.S. that allows for intelligence sharing and hopes to harmonize U.S. and Canadian immigration and visa policies.
- The proposal by the Minister of Citizenship and Immigration to introduce a national ID card
- The 2002 *Immigration and Refugee Protection Act*, which allowed for the "streamlining" of security certificates. The Minister of Public Safety and Emergency Preparedness can issue security certificates to quickly remove foreign nationals or permanent residents deemed a threat to national security. Once signed, the case is turned over to a judge and the defendant is placed in custody. There are no appeals.

These measures eliminate public accountability or monitoring, and place expansive powers in the hands of very few ministers.

Another issue is the potential "criminalization of dissent." What this means is that without public accountability and debate, radical social action groups that are critical of the government become vulnerable to de-legitimization or even to being labelled terrorists. Native groups, environmental lobbyists, and anti-globalization activists have all been targeted under the new legislation. Community leaders of Muslim and Arab groups have been increasingly harassed by the police, and live in fear of arrest or deportation. For example:

- In November 2002, U.S. Attorney General John Ashcroft created a National Security Entry–Exit Registry System, allowing border guards to arbitrarily detain, photograph, fingerprint, and interrogate suspicious persons. By February, there had been 59 complaints of wrongful treatment from Canadians, almost all of Arabic or Muslim origin.
- Immediately following September 11, Maher Arar stopped over in New York on a flight from Tunisia to Canada; he was detained and deported back to Syria, his birth country, even though he was travelling with a Canadian passport. An inquiry is currently being conducted into the Canadian government's handling of the situation.

• As of August 2004, five Muslim men had been held in jail without charges laid, bail, and disclosure of evidence for a collective total of 154 months.

The issue of the protection of individual rights continues to be a nettlesome one.

■■ Lack of Responsiveness to Needs

Any satisfying relationship, including the relationship individuals have with organizations, *requires give and take.* If you find school a satisfying experience, for example, it is because you have given your time, money, and energy to complying with the school's requirements and have gained from your classes the knowledge and credentials needed to pursue your goals. People expect the same sort of give and take from government. Yet some Canadians perceive the government to be all "take"—in the form of taxes and the demand for compliance with laws and regulations—and no "give"—in the sense of being unresponsive to the needs of the citizenry (see "Why Isn't There Help for People Like Me?" at the beginning of the chapter). Many perceive the government to be more "take" than is legitimate and less "give" than is responsible.

It is probably true that, in the computer age, people expect more from the government than service; they expect government service to be as speedy and efficient as the service they may encounter in the private sector (Dawes et al. 1999). In many cases, government service seems torturously slow; in some cases, it never occurs.

Eventually, the appearance of responsiveness is no better than the lack of responsiveness. Both lead to cynicism. People begin to *view government not as their protector and safety net, but as their competitor for the good things of life, or even as their enemy.* The citizens lose an important source of security and confidence, and the government loses a substantial amount of commitment to civic duty as people ignore or subvert laws and regulations whenever they feel they can do so with impunity.

■■ CONTRIBUTING FACTORS

While many Canadians blame inept or self-serving politicians, the problems of government cannot be reduced to defects in elected officials. You don't want to engage in the *fallacy of personal attack* and claim that the problems of government will be solved when present officials are replaced with better ones. Rather, you must recognize and deal with the varied social structural and social psychological factors that create and help perpetuate the problems of government.

■■ Social Structural Factors

Size.   As figures 8.4 and 8.5 show, the rate of increase in the number of government employees was much higher than the rate of increase in the population during the 20th century. For example, whereas the population of Canada in 2001 (just over 31,000,000) is four times greater than in 1911 (8,788,000), the growth of the public sector is more than eight times greater in 2001 (350,252) than in 1911 (41,957). (It is also noteworthy that the public sector has sharply declined over the last decade.)

The growth of government reflects both a growing population and a growing number of functions and services assumed by government. Government was smaller and simpler in the early years of the nation. There were far fewer people and a more homogeneous population. There were also no income taxes to collect, no services to the poor to regulate, no monitoring and regulating of the conduct of businesses, no governmental health care obligations, no elaborate defence system to support, and so on. Whether

FIGURE 8.4 ■ ■ ▨

Growth of federal
government employees,
1911–2001.

Source: Adapted from Statistics
Canada, 2004.

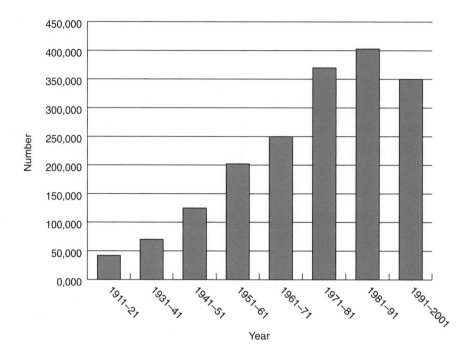

FIGURE 8.5 ■ ■ ▨

Growth of census
population, 1911–2001.

Source: Adapted from Statistics
Canada, 2004.

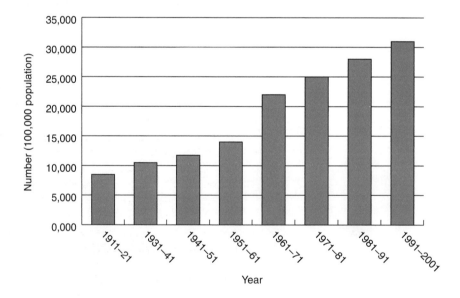

the size of government today is necessary may be debatable, but a substantial amount of the growth was either inevitable because of the growing population or a response to public demand for protection or assistance.

Still, *size—both the size of government and the size of the population—has consequences for functioning.* Consider the size of government. It is more difficult for large organizations to be efficient and responsive to the needs of people. Questions must be addressed and procedures must be followed that are not necessary when individuals help each other or small community organizations help people locally. When an individual seeks assistance from the federal government, for example, such questions as the following arise: What agency is responsible for helping? Who in the agency should handle the situation? What procedures (including filling out necessary paperwork) must be followed to meet the requirement of accountability? Who in the agency and/or other government organizations must approve the assistance? And so on. In the case of entire groups who need help (the poor, those suffering discrimination, etc.), the questions and answers become even more complicated and demanding.

The size of the governed population also affects function. It is more difficult to gain compliance and enforce rules when regulating a large number of people. For example, in any large city there are hundreds of thousands of outstanding housing-code violations. The City of Toronto has excellent by-laws to protect tenants, but there are very few charges as the only 152 inspectors can not possibly enforce every housing-code violation. According to Ehrenhalt (1997), the municipal government's failure to respond to these violations is rooted in neither indifference nor ineptness. Rather, there are simply more citizens violating the law "than even the most efficient government can possibly keep track of."

The Structure of Government.   There are two aspects of the structure of government that contribute to the problems. The first is the extent to which a government is a political democracy. Frey and Al-Roumi (1999), who define democracy as the extent to which a nation maintains political rights and civil liberties for the citizenry, gathered data on the quality of life from 87 countries of the world. Quality of life was measured by infant mortality rate, literacy rate, and life expectancy. They found *a strong relationship between the level of political democracy and the quality of life in the nations.* It seems that such things as competitive elections, the opportunity for all citizens to participate in the political process, and a free press contribute to the government's being more responsive to people's needs and implementing policies that enhance their well-being. To the extent that political democracy is maintained, the government is more of a solution than a problem.

The other aspect of structure is *the way the government is organized to fulfill its functions.* In Canada, the federal system provides a constitutional separation of powers between the federal and provincial governments. In addition, there are municipal governments. All have direct authority over individuals. This arrangement has the advantages of creating unity without enforcing uniformity, encouraging experimentation, and keeping government close to the people (Burns, Peterson, and Cronin 1984).

However, there are disadvantages as well. What level of government is best equipped to provide efficient and effective service? What level of government is responsible for dealing with various social problems? Consider, for example, the following questions: Is a safety net for the poor the primary responsibility of the federal government or of provincial and local governments? Who is going to handle problems of discrimination based on race/ethnicity, gender, age, or sexual orientation? Should there be national standards for education, or should education be completely under the control of local school boards?

An ongoing struggle among various levels of government over responsibility, or the efforts of government at one level to shift responsibility for a problem to government at another level, can result in an inadequate response to people's needs. As we discussed in chapter 6, the current transfer of major responsibility for poverty from the federal to the provincial and local level is having a negative impact on the quality of life for many of Canada's poor.

Finally, *the government is organized along bureaucratic lines in order to fulfill its various functions.* Look back at the characteristics of a bureaucracy that we discussed earlier, and you will see that it should be a highly efficient and effective form of large-scale administration. If those in a bureaucracy function according to the criteria we listed, the organization should help people expertly and impartially.

In practice, however, bureaucracies never measure up to the ideal. As a result, and in spite of many positive achievements, the very term *bureaucrat* has become a term of disparagement, and a wide variety of government problems are blamed on the bureaucrats. To blame bureaucrats, however, is to substitute the *fallacy of personal attack* for a realistic appraisal.

There are various reasons for the disparity between the ideal and the reality. Middle-class bureaucrats may not treat lower-class citizens with the same respect and concern as they do those in higher classes. Bureaucrats who try to be impartial in their dealings with people face severe pressure and potential reprisals from individuals who want special consideration. Some government bureaucrats may be in positions for which they have not been properly trained, lacking needed expertise.

Other bureaucrats may rigidly follow the rules of the organization even if the rules don't apply well to particular cases. Two business writers call such bureaucrats the "white-collar gestapo," arguing that they mindlessly enforce a growing number of arbitrary rules and regulations (McMenamin and Novack 1999). Indeed, even though the bureaucratic rules and regulations are supposed to cover all circumstances, you can raise the question of whether this is possible when dealing with a large, heterogeneous population. Perhaps bureaucrats need the flexibility to exercise more discretion.

Furthermore, in spite of the highly bureaucratic nature of government, *the government is not organized in a way to deal effectively with waste and corruption.* One way to stop waste and corruption would be to encourage employees to act as internal watchdogs and report such practices (to be "whistleblowers," in contemporary terminology). From time to time, this happens; but most government employees fear reprisals if they blow the whistle on corrupt or wasteful practices (Maier 1998).

The Economics of Campaigning.   How much would it cost you to become a Member of Parliament (MP)? If you were to have run as a candidate for the 2000 federal election, it would have cost you, on average, $23,000 (Elections Canada 2004). Visit the Online Learning Centre at **www.mcgrawhill.ca/college/lauer** for a table that breaks down election expenses by political party. A contender for office may get money from varied sources, including individuals, groups and organizations, and the contender's political party.

In light of the costs of running a campaign, *it is evident that people without access to considerable sums of money or money-raising skills are unlikely to win an election.* In order to gain and remain in office, whether they are personally rich or not, politicians need massive amounts of money. This makes politicians beholden to the wealthy and to various interest groups. Legislation that dictates limits on campaign spending for political parties and their candidates in many ways stems from the famous televised election debate for president of the U.S. between Democrat John F. Kennedy and Republican Richard Nixon. In fact, this debate was pivotal for the ways later politicians organized their election campaigns both in the United States and in Canada. Television became an effective medium to reach millions of people, but a very costly one where smaller parties were at a clear disadvantage (Mapleleaf.com 2003).

Throughout the 1960s and early 1970s campaign costs were quickly becoming exorbitant, and the advantage was clearly to individuals and political parties who had either personal wealth or corporate donations (or more often both). The NDP and other grassroots parties were not able to compete fairly. Consequently, in 1974 the minority Liberal government with NDP support enacted legislation—the 1974 *Election Expenses Act*—that controlled monetary spending on an election campaign:

BUREAUCRACY IN INDONESIA

As noted in the text, bureaucrats are supposed to have expertise and act impartially in accord with written rules—but they do not always function that way. Dwight King (1998a, 1998b) studied the Indonesian civil service and found a number of reasons why the bureaucracy fell short of the ideal.

The Indonesian civil service is organized in 17 ranks. Each employee has a grade and a step ranking within the grade that is based on education and seniority. Employees who perform their duties well advance one step every four years and eventually can qualify for a higher grade. At a certain level, however, the employees must acquire additional education or pass a test in order to continue their advancement.

In spite of this apparently well-organized arrangement, there is often a disparity between an individual's qualifications and the requirements of the position that he or she holds. For instance, an individual who has a graduate degree in liberal arts might be promoted to the head of the agency on public works because no one with an engineering degree is in as high a grade at the time as is the liberal arts graduate. Bureaucrats' educational attainment and civil service grade are more important in determining where they work in the government than is their educational specialization.

In addition, a substantial number of civil servants are promoted even when they have not reached the required grade. Two practices are at work here. One is to promote someone to an "acting" position. The other is to utilize an exception clause in the regulations that allows those who have performed in an "extraordinary" way for two years to be promoted even when they are not in the necessary grade.

For some functions, the Indonesian government bureaucracy is also hampered by the lack of clearly defined areas of responsibility. For example, three different agencies have responsibility for education: the Ministry of Education and Culture (MOEC), the Ministry of Home Affairs (MOHA), and the Ministry of Religious Affairs (MORA). MOEC is responsible for secondary and higher education, but shares responsibility for primary education with MOHA. MORA is responsible for the Islamic schools, which are mainly at the post-primary level.

This dispersion of responsibility has negative consequences for Indonesian education. First, little effort is made to improve primary education because neither MOEC nor MOHA seeks the resources needed. MOHA secures funding for primary education, but has not sought additional funds because it is responsible for funding, not for quality. MOEC is aware of the need for improvement, but funding is not part of its responsibility.

Second, some schools do not receive the resources they need. For example, MOEC publishes textbooks and sends them to regional warehouses. From there, the regional government is supposed to distribute them to the schools. But the regional governments complain that they do not have the necessary funds to distribute books. Thus, some schools, particularly those in relatively isolated areas, may not receive needed texts and materials.

Third, career advancement for primary school teachers occurs in the context of the contrary decisions of MOEC and regional governments. MOEC evaluates the teachers' performance. Regional governments, however, make promotion and transfer decisions—often independently of MOEC evaluations.

In sum, government bureaucracy in Indonesia is similar to that in other nations: It falls short of the bureaucratic ideal. Yet it does no good to simply complain of "bureaucrats." A different set of people in the same system would make little or no difference in the outcome. It is the way the bureaucracy is organized, not the kind of people in it, that is primarily responsible for the problems.

A candidate who is elected or receives at least 15 percent of the valid votes cast at the election is entitled to a reimbursement of 50 percent of the actual paid election expenses and the paid personal expenses to a maximum of 50 percent of the election expenses limit. [464(1), 465(2)]

The government was also interested in promoting financial support from the public, and introduced a tax credit for political donations. An individual received a tax credit of 75 percent on the first $100, to a maximum credit of $550.

Although government spending on election campaigns is regulated, legislation loopholes do exist and "soft money" donations are not uncommon:

> … parties have become increasingly dependent on big business and/or unions for funding. For example, in 2001, 95 of the top 100 donors to the Liberal Party were businesses. The same figure holds true for the Canadian Alliance Party. Even the NDP depends heavily on union funding.
>
> While these groups may not directly affect government policy, they are perceived as having a stake in government decisions. Often, corporations expect that a large contribution will give them access to a minister or government official. (Mapleleaf.com 2003)

Public cries for transparency were increasing as scandalous relationships between business donations and government contracts were publicized. In 2003, Prime Minister Chrétien's Liberal government introduced Bill C-24, an act to amend the *Canada Elections Act* and the *Income Tax Act* to limit individual and corporate donations. For a summary on limits on contributions by individuals, please visit the text's Online Learning Centre at **www.mcgrawhill.ca/college/lauer**.

The Media.   In the aforementioned televised presidential debate in 1960, Richard Nixon looked unkempt and nervous in contrast to John F. Kennedy, who appeared crisp and confident. Although Nixon won the debate among those listening on radio, Kennedy came out ahead among those who watched on television. This began a new era in the relationship between media coverage and election results in both the United States and Canada.

The media have always played a role in Canadian politics, but *both the nature of the coverage and the influence of the media have changed as radio, network television, cable television, and now the Internet have been added to the print media as factors in the political process.* Let's explore the impact of the media on three aspects of political life: elections; political agendas and action; and public trust.

First, the media are important in political campaigns. For one thing, advertising by candidates accounts for a substantial proportion of the enormous costs of campaigns. Television advertising is particularly expensive, but it is necessary because *the majority of Canadians rely on television for their political news*, and television ads affect the outcome of elections (Kryzanek 1999:95; Shaw 1999). Yet relying on television means that voters get far less information than is provided by the print media or even by radio. Voters depend heavily on "sound bites"—those brief excerpts from the campaign trail that, in the opinion of television editors, capture something informative about the candidate's position or newsworthy and sensational about the candidate's activities. Interestingly, the length of sound bites decreased from 42.3 seconds in the late 1960s to 7.3 seconds in the 1990s (Kryzanek 1999:95). How much accurate information can a 7.3-second excerpt from a speech give about a candidate's position?

The point is, voters' knowledge of candidates and their positions are derived from decisions by those who control the media. What appears in the media, therefore, affects how people vote. The way that the media interpret an incumbent politi-

Campaigning for elective office is expensive, and critics argue that the wealthy are at an advantage.

cian's performance, for example, strongly influences his or her chances for re-election (Dover 1998). Research by political scientist David Barker (1999) shows that listening to the right-wing program of U.S. radio personality Rush Limbaugh increased voter preference for Republican candidates. Similar effects of the media have been found in other nations as well (Forrest and Marks 1999).

The Internet offers another outlet for campaigning with as yet unknown consequences for the electoral process. All the political parties have Websites with links to Web pages for each candidate running for member of parliament. The Websites are used to present party issues and events, and to provide information about the candidate's qualifications and positions on various issues. Second, the media affect political agendas and governmental actions. The influence of the media is not limited to elections. As Cook (1998) has argued, *the media are an integral part of the governing of the nation.* Government officials use the media to shape public opinion and gain support for decisions and programs. In turn, officials are influenced in their decision-making process by the information they glean from the media (Edwards and Wood 1999). To a considerable extent, the media help decide what are the issues, problems, and crises to which political leaders must respond (Dye 1995).

If the media were impartial and accurate, their influence would not be a cause for concern. *However, control of the media lies in the hands of a small number of corporations* (Dye 1995). In the United States, the two largest are the Walt Disney Company and AOL Time Warner—which is the largest multimedia corporation in the world and includes Netscape, Warner movies, CNN, and *Time* magazine. Only two Canadian corporations, Rogers and CanWest Global, are on the global top 50 (Brym 2004:131). Daily newspapers have followed a similar path, and ownership is concentrated in three corporations: CanWest Global, Quebecor Media Inc., and Torstar.

In other words, the public's knowledge of the issues, problems, and crises facing the nation is provided by media that are controlled by the rich and powerful. This doesn't mean that the information is always biased or distorted. It does mean, however, that people must be careful not to engage in the *fallacy of authority* and assume that what comes to them through the media is *ipso facto* accurate and impartial. It also means that serious problems, affecting considerable numbers of citizens, may be largely invisible because they are ignored by the media.

Finally, the media have contributed to the failure of trust. Is government more corrupt, unreliable, and unresponsive now than it was in the past? On the one hand, such things as the civil service, term limits, and extension of the right to vote are evidence that government and political life are more democratic and more effective now than in the past. On the other hand, all too frequent scandals and deceptions at the various levels of government raise questions about the integrity of government and undoubtedly contribute to the failure of trust. Still, such scandals are not new.

What is new is *the way in which the media give so much coverage to scandals, including matters that would have been glossed over as private affairs in past decades.* The mainline media play up stories of scandals and potential scandals in ways similar to those of the tabloids. Many Canadians indicated a weariness with this extensive coverage, noting its negative impact on their trust in government. At the same time, there is an almost *insatiable curiosity about the scandals* (Ricchiardi 1998). As long as this public demand exists, the media will continue to provide in-depth reports that may expose problems in politics but may also contribute to the growing distrust in government.

Interest Groups.   The most effective way to influence a massive organization like government is through other organizations. The lone individual has little chance of bringing about change, but an organization can put considerable pressure on politicians.

For that reason, *interest groups have become an increasingly important factor in Canadian political life.*

There are more than 20,000 special-interest groups in Canada, differing in mandate, organizational structure, and funding (Valentine 2003). According to Valentine, special-interest groups fall into two categories. The first category is represented by *economic and professional association groups*. These groups focus on strategies to gain economic benefits for businesses and professions, examples being the Canadian Bankers Association (CBA) and the Canadian Manufacturers Association (CMA). The second category is *public interest groups*. These groups do not seek personal benefits but instead advocate for social policy changes that benefit all Canadians. Examples of public interest groups include the Council of Canadians with Disabilities (CCD), the National Action Committee on the Status of Women (NAC), the Assembly of First Nations (AFN), AIDS Action Now!, Greenpeace, and Amnesty International.

lobbyist
an individual who tries to influence legislation in accord with the preferences of an interest group

Interest groups also hire **lobbyists,** individuals who try to influence legislation in accord with the preferences of the interest groups. *Lobbyists use various means to influence politicians.* They may provide a politician with information that supports the interest group's position on a given issue. They may try to cultivate personal friendships with particular politicians. They may treat a politician to expensive dinners and trips. In addition, there is always the promise of support through votes and contributions by members of the interest groups.

Understandably, interest groups wield power. Many represent a considerable number of citizens (hundreds of thousands of members), have large staffs (hundreds), and huge operating budgets (millions of dollars). One example of the power of interest groups is CropLife Canada, a group of pesticide manufacturers, developers, and distributors who believe that "Pesticides used properly constitute no unacceptable risk to people's health or to the environment" (Mitchell 2004:A1). Pesticides are highly regulated by both federal and provincial laws. CropLife is currently appealing a 2004 ruling by the Ontario Superior Court that stated the City of Toronto had the right to enact a by-law restricting pesticide use on public and private property.

This by-law is supported by a growing literature that argues that lifelong exposure to minute amounts of environmental carcinogens are contributing significantly to our risk of cancer (Steingraber 1998:273). Environmentalists such as Steingraber believe that governments have failed to adequately protect the health of their citizens and the environment; those who have benefited, according to McKinlay (1994), are the "manufacturers of illness," such as the pesticide and drug industries (see chapter 14, "The Environment").

Clearly, *interest groups are able to affect the legislative process in a way that protects particular interests to the detriment of the general well-being.* But not all interest groups work against the welfare of the Canadian people. Democracy Watch is a watchdog citizen group that promotes democratic reform, government accountability, and corporate responsibility. Since its first campaign in 1994 the group has been influential in implementing changes to key laws. Here are some of its achievements:

- Together with a coalition of 100 citizen groups stopped a proposed merger of two banks in 1998.
- Influenced legislation that promotes more transparency, specifically lobbying disclosure laws.
- Influenced legislation in 2000 that "limits paid advertising spending during election campaign periods by so-called 'third parties' (non-political parties or interest groups)."
- Influenced legislation in March 2004 that "changed the *Criminal Code* to make it easier to hold corporations accountable for crime."

■■ Social Psychological Factors

Public Attitudes. We are all familiar with the American ideal that government is of the people, by the people, and for the people. This means that government originates in the people, involves the people, and effectively represents them. This ideal is also shared by Canadians. However, when Canadians were surveyed to see what effect government has on most Canadians' lives, 37 percent stated that government had a negative impact, 28 percent said there was not much impact, and only 28 percent believed there was a positive impact. Furthermore, when the survey asked, "Which level of government do you trust more to protect the programs you care about?" 14 percent said the federal government, 23 percent said the provincial government, 27 percent claimed both levels of government, and 34 percent said they trusted neither federal nor provincial government (Portraits of Canada 2002).

Such attitudes reflect the failure of trust. They also help perpetuate the failure of trust. Instead of stimulating people to get involved in government and make necessary reforms, *negative attitudes lead to alienation and withdrawal from political life.*

In addition to negative attitudes about government and politics, a set of *contrary attitudes* contribute to the problem. Cronin and Genovese (1998) have identified a number of these contrary attitudes in their discussion of the "nine paradoxes" of the American presidency. These contrary attitudes can easily be applied to Canadians and include:

- the desire for strong leaders, but also fear of the abuse of power that a strong leader might bring to the office.
- favourable attitudes toward ordinary people holding political office (thus, the traditional appeal of the candidate who was born in a log cabin), but also value for charisma in their leaders.
- the desire for leaders who will unify the people, but also the need not to compromise their own positions in order to forge the unity.
- admiration for leaders with vision, but also the belief that leaders should be responsive to public opinion.

Moreover, Canadians tend to approve of such things as lower taxes, reduced government spending, and less government interference in daily life. Yet they also resist proposals to reduce government or government spending in those areas from which they benefit or which they support for ideological reasons (Young 1998). For example, many Canadians believe that, in general, the government has too much power and does too much. Yet, when asked in a survey "Would you say you favour a smaller government with fewer services, or a larger government with more services?" 42 percent answered they would prefer a smaller government with fewer services and 45 percent said a larger government with more services (Portrait of Canada 2002). The majority of Canadians, for example, believe that government should increase health care spending to cover rising costs. Fewer than 10 percent feel that costs should be limited.

Such contrary attitudes pose *a dilemma for politicians.* In essence, no matter what a politician does, some segment of the population will be disappointed and frustrated. The course of action often taken is to follow his or her conscience when possible and, at other times, follow the desires of those who contribute the funds necessary to stay in office.

Ideologies. Canadians, for the most part, are suspicious of extreme ideologues and value compromise in resolving political conflicts. According to political scientist Sylvia Bashevkin, Canadians have historically preferred the political centre, regardless of party affiliations:

> It's a long-standing cluster.... Most Canadians also think they're middle class whether they are or not. Canada is an extremely consensual society. This country is built on consensus and people finding common ground. (in Cobb 2002)

Her comment was made in response to a 2002 Southam News and Global Television poll that examined Canadians' knowledge of basic politics. The findings were disconcerting—most Canadians were unable to differentiate between the political right and the left. Just under half of the respondents (47 percent) answered correctly that the NDP was to the left of the Alliance; 18 percent believed that the Alliance was to the left, and one-third claimed they did not know the political leanings of these two parties.

The misunderstanding of political differences between the right and the left can be explained in part by "the fact … that party leaders often try to cover their tracks to attract voters who might otherwise be offended if they knew how right-wing some of their policies really are" (Bashevkin in Cobb 2002). Further, Bashevkin points out that Canadians are not boxed into ideological platforms. Their views on taxation tend to lean toward the right because the personal preference is to pay lower taxes. When it comes to social programs such as health care and education, Canadians prefer a more progressive stance that, as stated earlier, supports increased spending. Overall, Canadians prefer balance. That is why the federal Liberals have been Canada's dominant ruling or governing party, holding power for 62 of the past 75 years.

 ## ■■ From Social Problems to Solutions

Many of the factors that contribute to the problems of government pose an ongoing dilemma. For example, you cannot reduce the size of the population served. It is also not a good idea to reduce the overall size of government, as this often translates into serious cuts to social programs.

The most recent federal election in June 2004 is a case in point that our political system is in need of a makeover. Voter apathy could not be ignored, as this election proved to have the lowest turnout since Confederation (60.4 percent). This may mean that Canadians are increasingly distrustful of a political process that fails to represent their views.

In Canada, it is possible for the ruling party to have a majority government without a majority vote. For example, the Liberals in the 1997 federal election received only 38 percent of the popular vote, yet they were able to form a majority government. Once there is a majority government the governing party has the power to do what it wants, as politicians do not necessarily have to be accountable to their constituents—that is, at least until the next election is called (MacDonald 2001).

The problem of electoral representation was highlighted again in the 2004 election. The Liberal Party, with 36.7 percent of the popular vote, now holds 135 out of the 308 seats in Parliament. This time, however, they were able to form only a minority government. The Conservative Party, with 99 seats, had 29.6 percent of the popular vote; the Bloc Québécois, with 54 seats, had 12.4 of the popular support; and the NDP, with 19 seats, ended up with 15.7 percent of the popular vote (there is one independent seat). The Green Party, representing 4.4 percent of the Canadian population, does not have a voice in Parliament.

Fair Vote Canada (FVC), a group of Canadians representing all political parties and all regions throughout Canada, "demand[s] a fair voting system—a fundamental requirement for healthy representative democracy and government accountability" (Fair Vote Canada 2004). Their solution is to have a voting system based on proportional representation. This system is not a new idea but one that is in use in many democracies throughout the world, including Indonesia, Italy, New Zealand, Panama, Peru, Uruguay, Venezuela, and most European countries.

The way this system works is quite straightforward. Should a party receive 35 percent of the vote, then in turn it would represent 35 percent of the seats in Parliament. Simply put, the party would receive the same proportionate number of seats as the popular vote. Let us refer back to the 2004 federal election and see how seats in Parliament would be distributed, approximately, under a proportional representation system (actual seats are shown in brackets):

Liberals	113 (135)
Conservatives	91 (99)
Bloc Québecois	38 (54)
NDP	48 (19)
Green Party	14 (0)
Other	3 (1)

You can see why political parties such as the NDP and the Green Party support proportional representation. This type of system could not only eliminate the large differential between popular support and seat division but also discourage regionalism and force regional parties (like the Bloc) to try to gain more mass appeal. But how would such a system work? How would we choose our members of parliament?

One possible solution, as used in many European countries, is the notion of "party lists." At the time of an election, each political party produces a list of candidates or hopeful members of parliament. After the election, each party receives the percentage of candidates that can go to Parliament. In some countries, the party ranks the candidates; in others, the candidate lists are also printed on the election ballot. Voters not only vote for the party but also rank-order the candidates, thus ensuring that the voters rather than the party leadership determine who represents the respective party in Parliament (Fair Vote Canada 2004).

■■ SUMMARY

Government is necessary because it fulfills a number of important social functions, functions that reflect people's expectations of their government. First, government is expected to protect the citizenry from foreign aggressors and from threats to individual well-being. Regulatory agencies were established to protect citizens from threats to their well-being. Second, government is expected to secure social order. Third, government is expected to distribute power equitably so that citizens have an equal opportunity in all areas of their lives. Fourth, government is expected to provide a safety net, a minimum standard of living below which it will not allow citizens to fall.

A number of problems of government and politics exist in Canada. There are inequalities in the distribution of power. Social scientists disagree about whether power is distributed in accord with a pluralistic or a power elite model. The failure of trust is a second problem. Canadians trust most other institutions far more than they trust the government. This has a number of consequences: it leads to a lack of citizen participation in the political process; it alters people's voting patterns; and it leads to political alienation, a feeling of political disillusionment, powerlessness, and estrangement.

A third problem involves waste, corruption, and scandals in government. Waste refers to such things as excessive paperwork, excessive costs, and unnecessary expenditures. Corruption and scandals usually involve a politician acting in terms of self-interest or particular interest to the detriment of the politician's constituency or the general public.

Gridlock is a fourth problem. Gridlock means that the government is mired in inaction, unable to legislate significant new policies because of ideological conflict, party differences, or a standoff between the executive and legislative branches. Gridlock is likely to intensify the failure of trust.

Problems in government and politics affect the quality of life in a number of ways. Such problems mean that people have unequal opportunities for a high quality of life. They mean that the freedoms and rights of citizens are not always adequately protected and that the government is not adequately responsive to people's needs.

Various factors contribute to the problems of government and politics. The size of the population served and the size of the government itself both affect how well the government can function. The way the government is organized to fulfill its functions—the separation of powers between the federal and provincial governments and the bureaucratic nature of government agencies—also creates some difficulties in effective functioning. On the other hand, the government is *not* organized so as to deal effectively with waste and corruption.

The costs and financing methods of campaigning have particularly adverse effects. Many social scientists believe they threaten the democratic process itself, and virtually ensure politicians' unresponsiveness to people's needs.

The media also contribute to the problems. They are a substantial part of the cost of campaigns and determine the information and perspectives voters get about the candidates. They affect political agendas and actions of those in office, acting as an integral part of the governing of the nation. They also contribute to the failure of trust.

Interest groups have become an increasingly important part of Canadian political life through contributions, lobbyists, and influence on voting behaviour. Interest groups can affect legislation in a way that protects particular interests to the detriment of the general well-being as well as promoting positive changes.

Social psychological factors that contribute to the problems include the attitudes of the public and the ideologies of politicians. Negative attitudes of the public lead to alienation and withdrawal from political life; contrary attitudes pose a dilemma for politicians. Canada, in general, is a consensual society. Canadians seek balance among their politicians: they prefer cuts to taxes yet they want the government to spend more money on social programs such as health care.

■■ KEY TERMS

Anarchism 217	Interest Group 219	Pluralism 219	Power Elite Model 220
Bureaucracy 219	Lobbyist 238	Political Alienation 224	Regulatory Agency 217
Gridlock 228	Patronage 227	Political Party 219	Social Capital 224

▪▪ STUDY QUESTIONS

1. What is meant by anarchism and why does it appeal to some people?
2. What are the functions of government?
3. Explain the different views on the distribution of power in Canada.
4. What is meant by the "failure of trust," and what are the consequences of this failure?
5. Give some examples of waste, corruption, and scandals in government.
6. How can legislative gridlock occur?
7. In what ways do problems of government and politics affect Canadians' quality of life?
8. What social structural factors contribute to the problems of government and politics?
9. How do public attitudes affect the political life of the nation?
10. Explain why many Canadians have difficulties differentiating between the right and the left.
11. What are some of the important steps to be taken in order to deal with the problems of government and politics?

▪▪ FOR FURTHER READING

Cook, Timothy E. *Governing with the News: The News Media as a Political Institution.* Chicago: University of Chicago Press, 1998. Examination of the relationship between the media and political life both historically and in the present, showing how the news sets political agendas and stimulates action.

Janoski, Thomas. *Citizenship and Civil Society: A Framework of Rights and Obligations in Liberal, Traditional, and Social Democratic Regimes.* Cambridge: Cambridge University Press, 1998. Examines two topics of prime interest in the social sciences—citizenship and civil society—and discusses how rights and obligations work out in different kinds of political systems.

Lipset, Seymour Martin. *American Exceptionalism: A Double-Edged Sword.* New York: W. W. Norton, 1996. An analysis of the American political system and how it functions in the light of systems in other cultures.

Katz, Richard S. *Democracy and Elections.* New York: Oxford University Press, 1997. Discusses various matters related to elections in a democratic society, including a history of voting and elections and how tensions develop in a democratic society.

Scott, James C. *Seeing Like a State: How Certain Schemes to Improve the Human Condition Have Failed.* New Haven, CT: Yale University Press, 1998. Offers a number of case studies of efforts by governments in various nations to address a national problem, and analyzes why some of them disastrously failed.

Wiesberg, Herb F., and Samuel C. Patterson. *Great Theater: The American Congress in the 1990s.* New York: Cambridge University Press, 1998. An analysis of the U.S. Congress in the 1990s, showing the consequences of the ideological conflict and the partisan divisions.

Wilensky, Harold L. *Rich Democracies: Political Economy, Public Policy, and Performance.* Berkeley, CA: University of California Press, 2002. Uses a variety of data, including hundreds of interviews, to analyze differing styles of the conflict resolution and the common social, economic, and labour problems of modern governments.

WORK AND THE ECONOMY

1. Identify various ways in which the economy is changing.

2. Know how work and the workforce are changing, and how problems of work detract from people's quality of life.

3. Understand the ways in which the economic system is detrimental to the well-being of many Canadians.

4. Identify the ways in which the government and social roles contribute to the problems of work.

5. Discuss attitudes toward work and workers, including the ideology of the Protestant work ethic, as aspects of the work problem in Canada.

6. Suggest steps that can be taken to reduce the problems and make work more meaningful.

"I'M NOT A WORRIER, BUT . . ."

Some people are optimistic by nature. They tend not to worry even when they are struggling with problems. But, as Ted points out, unemployment can strain even the most optimistic of outlooks. Ted is in his mid 30s. He has been out of work for more than a year, a situation that was inconceivable to him only a few months before he lost his job:

I'm a sales supervisor. This was my first "real" job where I made a decent wage. In fact, I loved my job, the people, the company. I was beginning to feel settled in all areas of my life: a good job, recently married, and some savings in the bank for a down payment on a house. A group of us were laid off at the same time. We were all completely taken by surprise. We knew things were slack, but there was no talk of any layoffs. They just called us each in one day and told us they didn't have a job for us anymore.

At first, I was kind of cocky about it. I was hurt, because I really liked working there. But I was also sure that they would call me back—because, after all, I was "indispensable." I fantasized about writing them a letter and thanking them for giving me the opportunity to advance myself.

That was over a year ago. In the meantime, I have sent out about a hundred résumés and applications. I'm not a worrier. But I'm really worried now. And every month when the rent comes due, I worry a little more. My wife's job keeps us afloat, but we've about exhausted our savings, and our dream of buying a house is just that, a dream.

But you know what the worst part of it is? Just waiting and waiting and not hearing, and feeling more and more useless and more and more helpless. I've lost the chance at jobs for which I'm a perfect fit but I do not have the education credentials. It's really depressing. I'll keep trying, but it gets harder all the time to make yourself go through the application process, and it gets harder all the time to feel hopeful, to really believe that this could be the place that will finally hire me. Everyone tells me that maybe I should go back to school, but I feel that I am just too old to do so. ■

▪▪ INTRODUCTION

Many Canadians fantasize about becoming independently wealthy so that they can do whatever they please. Moreover, they believe that the Canadian economy offers that possibility. Think about this fantasy for a moment. Do you believe that the economy offers you the possibility of becoming independently wealthy? If so, what are your chances? If it happens, what will you do? Will you continue to work?

When we pose such questions to social problems in classes, virtually everyone agrees that he or she could become independently wealthy. Many do not think the chances of this are very good, however, and nearly all the students say they would continue to work.

In general, the students believe that the Canadian economy is the best and are committed to it and to the work ethic. The **work ethic** involves the notion that *your sense of worth and the satisfaction of your needs are intricately related to the kind of* work you do.

In this chapter we explore evidence related to these beliefs about work and the economy. We look at the changing nature of the economy, work, and the workforce as well as the diverse meanings people attach to their work. We consider the kinds of problems associated with work, discuss how they affect the quality of life, and note the factors that contribute to and help to perpetuate those problems. Finally, we outline a few approaches to resolving the problems.

▪▪ THE ECONOMY, WORK, AND THE WORKFORCE IN CANADA

All things change. The Canadian economy, the nature of work, and the nature of the workforce are vastly different today from what they were at various times in the past.

▪▪ The Changing Economy

Initially, Canada was *an agrarian society;* that is, a society in which agriculture is the dominant form of work and people and animals are the major sources of energy. It has been estimated that as late as 1850, 65 percent of the energy used in work was supplied by people and animals (Lenski 1966). After the middle of the 19th century, the nation industrialized rapidly. In simple terms, *industrialization is economic development through a transformation of the sources and quantities of energy employed.*

Canadian industrialization, like that of most nations, occurred in the context of **capitalism,** an economic system in which there is private, rather than state, ownership of wealth and control of the production and distribution of goods. In a capitalist system, people are motivated by profit and they compete with each other to maximize their share of the profits. The premise is that the combination of private ownership and the pursuit of profit benefits everyone, because it motivates capitalists to be efficient and to provide the best goods and services at the lowest possible prices.

In a pure capitalist system, government involvement in the economy is minimal. In Canada, the government role in the economy has grown over the past century. In addition, our economy is affected by various other factors such as the global economy, weather, wars, and so on. *The global economy has become particularly important.* In simplest terms, globalization of the economy means a significant increase in the amount of international trade and investment (Weisbrot 2000). In Canada, for example, trade as a percentage of the gross domestic product is now nearly double what it was in the early 1970s. As an American economist has put it: "The business enterprise is

work ethic
the notion that our sense of worth and the satisfaction of our needs are intricately related to the kind of *work* we do

capitalism
an economic system in which there is private, rather than state, ownership of wealth and control of the production and distribution of goods; people are motivated by profit and compete with each other for maximum shares of profit

now the major actor on the world stage and the global marketplace is a key driver of the U.S. economy" (Weidenbaum 1999:506). Supermarkets have become more important than superpowers for key economic decisions. When governments try to impose restrictions to protect or enhance the national economy, enterprises simply shift the work to another setting. For instance, when Japan raised postage rates, direct mailers sent their mailings to Hong Kong, which mailed them back to Japan at considerably less cost to the mailers.

Technology has driven down the cost of international communication and travel. Thus, there has been a growth in trade, the flow of capital across national borders, foreign investment, shared research and development, and movement of personnel (including students attending universities in foreign countries). Business enterprises maximize their profits by locating the best markets and the least expensive places for operations. As a result, a particular product may have components made in various parts of the world.

In other words, the economy is now truly global. According to Weidenbaum (1999), about US$1 trillion moves across national borders every hour! Many large firms, including Exxon, Colgate-Palmolive, and Coca-Cola, get the majority of their income from overseas markets.

Combined with new technologies, globalization presents the Canadian economy and the Canadian worker with new challenges. *Globalization means that businesses find low-skilled workers in other nations who work for lower pay than Canadians.* Well-paid, lower-skilled jobs in Canada, therefore, are increasingly difficult to find. In fact, there has been a growing gap in the earnings between the top and the bottom wage earners:

> For example, between 1973 and 1997, the share of total earnings in Canada going to the bottom 20 percent of families with children fell steeply from a paltry 5.3 percent to 2.6 percent, which represents several billion dollars in total. In contrast, the share of earnings going to the top 20 percent increased from an already generous 38.4 percent to 42.8 percent. This is income redistribution in reverse. (Ross et al. 2000)

Although, as you shall see, unemployment is down considerably, many Canadian workers have experienced job loss or less job security. (For an example of job loss through outsourcing, visit the text's Online Learning Centre at **www.mcgrawhill.ca/college/lauer**.) Moreover, unions lose their bargaining power when companies can simply shift operations to a different nation.

In the competitive context of the global economy, then, *a number of changes have occurred that are detrimental to the well-being of many Canadian workers* (Krahn and Lowe 2002; Statistics Canada 2004):

downsizing
reduction of the labour force in a company or corporation

- Businesses and corporations have used **downsizing** (reduction of the labour force) to become "lean and mean."
- An increasing number of jobs are temporary or part-time, with no fringe benefits such as health insurance.
- Unions continue to decline in membership and power.
- Corporate tax obligations have been reduced, cutting back on revenues necessary to support social programs.
- When corrected for inflation, the income of many Canadian families has declined.

As a result of such changes, many Canadians are not only unable to fare as well as their parents, but are finding themselves worse off than their parents. In sum, the nature of the changes in the economy means that many Canadian families are worse off financially in the early 2000s than they were in the 1970s.

▪▪ The Changing Workforce

labour force
all civilians who are employed or unemployed but able and desirous of work

The **labour force** (defined as all civilians who are employed or unemployed but able and wanting to work) has increased enormously over time (see figure 9.1). It was this rapid increase since the beginning of the 19th century that made the nation's swift industrial growth possible. The workforce was low in 1800 because all but a small proportion of Canadians lived on farms, and the family farmer along with his wife and children are not counted—only those who work for pay outside the home are included in the workforce. Since 1940 the labour force has been growing faster than the population.

division of labour
the separation of work into specialized tasks

The *occupational structure* also has changed with an increasing **division of labour** or *specialization*. There are now more than 30,000 different occupations. This is not due to growth in all job categories, however. If you look at categories of occupations, you will find that since the beginning of the 20th century the proportion of workers in professional, technical, managerial, clerical, and service jobs has increased greatly. The proportion of workers classified as farm workers (less than 3 percent of the Canadian labour force), on the other hand, has declined dramatically. Jobs requiring more skill and training have tended to increase at a faster rate than others. In other words, there has been a general upgrading of the occupational structure. With increased industrialization and technological development, the need for farmers and unskilled workers has diminished and the need for skilled workers and clerical and other white-collar workers has increased. Canada has moved into a service and, some would argue, an informational society, in which growing numbers of workers are needed outside the manufacturing areas. It is increasingly likely that workers will engage in tasks involving *substantive complexity* such as verbal and math skills and abstract thinking rather than motor skills such as lifting, stooping, coordination, or finger dexterity. More than 2.5 million of the 15.6 million people active in the Canadian labour force worked in highly skilled jobs that generally require a university education, a one-third increase from 1991 (Census 2001).

Unfortunately, many new jobs, particularly those in the service area, do not pay well and are part time (Krahn and Lowe 2002). Many workers supplement their income with second jobs. Thus, many Canadian workers either work longer hours or face a lower standard of living.

FIGURE 9.1 ▪ ▪ ▪

Canadian labour force participation, by sex, 1901–2003.

Source: Adapted from Statistics Canada CANSIM II SERIES V2461462; and Krahn and Lowe 2002.

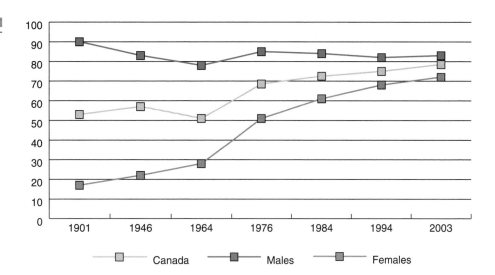

▪▪ The Changing Composition of the Labour Force

As the general skill level increases, *the educational level of the workforce also increases.* For example, in 1951 only 2 percent of Canadians had post-secondary education; in 2001 more than half continued schooling after high school (table 9.1). The 1990s marked the impressive growth in the number of Canadians who had post-secondary education. According to the Statistics Canada Census 2001 report on labour force activity, three factors explain the increased levels of education attainment: "first, a labour market preference for skilled workers to compete in a global and technologically advanced economy; second, immigration rules designed to attract highly skilled immigrants; third, the recession of the early 90s that was particularly difficult for Canadian youth" (Statistics Canada 2004).

Another substantial change in the labour force involves the *proportion of workers who are female* (figure 9.1). Since the early 1960s women's participation in the labour force has doubled, with the largest increase occurring between 1971 and 1981. In 1991, women made up 45 percent of the labour force. Ghalam's (1996) study of women in the workplace found that "women accounted for almost three quarters (72 percent) of all growth in employment between 1975 and 1991." Growth in women's employment rate is due to increases in married women's continued participation in the labour force. In contrast to 1951, when fewer than 10 percent of married women worked outside the home, in 1991 63 percent of women with children were employed. During periods of economic growth women's employment rate has increased substantially, while men's rate has been stable. In times of recession (1981–83 and the early 1990s) women's employment has slightly decreased, in contrast to significant drops in men's rates.

TABLE 9.1 ▪ ▪ ▪

Highest Level of Schooling, 1951 to 2001

	High School or Less	Some Post-Secondary	University
1951	98.1	0.0	1.9
1961	97.1	0.0	2.9
1971	78.2	17.1	4.8
1981	64.3	27.7	8.0
1991	56.9	31.7	11.4
2001	49.0	35.6	15.4

Source: The Census 2001.

FIGURE 9.2 ▪ ▪ ▪

Union membership in Canada, 1911–2004.

Source: 1911–1981 Graham and Lowe 2002; 1991–2004 Workplace Gazette, Vol. 7, No. 3, http://www.hrsdc.gc.ca/en/lp/wid/pdf/16UnionMembership2004.pdf.

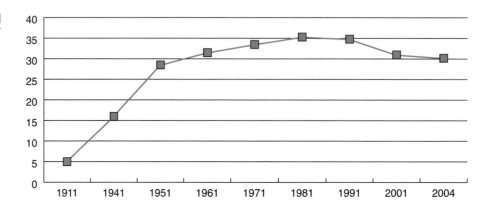

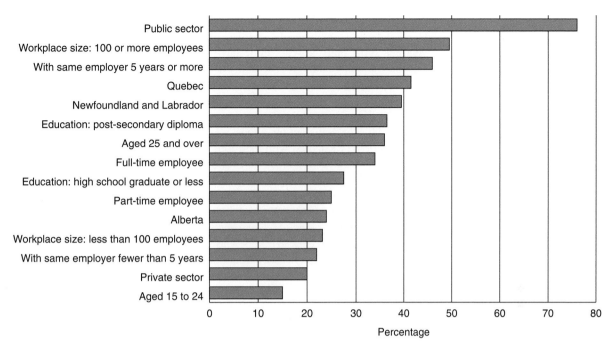

FIGURE 9.3 ■ ■ ■

Characteristics of union membership, 2003.

Source: Statistics Canada, Labour Force Survey.

The labour force also became more *unionized* until the 1980s. Since the 1980s, however, the proportion of workers who are members of unions has declined (see figure 9.2). Declining rates in unionization are seen among men, people between the ages of 25 and 54, and people who work in the private sector. Higher rates of unionization occur in public-sector jobs such as education, utilities, public administration, health care, and social assistance; among people with higher education; and with long-term employment (see figure 9.3). Unionized jobs are generally associated with better working conditions and higher wages. Unionized workers in 2003 on average received $21 per hour, while non-unionized workers received $16.65. Finally, unionization rates vary from province to province, with Quebec having the highest rate and Alberta the lowest (Statistics Canada 2003).

■■ The Changing Meaning of Work

When we try to determine the *meaning of work* for Canadians, we find ourselves in a morass of contradictions. Some people argue that work is one of the most important activities in an individual's life. They maintain that those who do not have a satisfying job do not have a fully satisfying life. Others insist that work is purely instrumental, a way to attain the goal of *maximum consumption.* There is also disagreement about whether Canadians enjoy their work, with some observers claiming that most Canadians hate their jobs and others asserting that there is a high rate of *job satisfaction.*

What about the *work ethic,* the notion that work is intrinsically good and useful and that people should therefore continue to work even if they are financially independent? Do Canadians still believe this? Or would they gladly abandon work for leisure pursuits if they had the means to do so?

While it is difficult to resolve these contradictions, surveys taken over the last three decades do indicate something of Canadians' feelings about their work. For example, these surveys show that the work ethic has remained strong among both males and females, the various racial groups, and differing occupational categories (Weaver 1997). In a survey that asked people how important it is to teach children that "with hard work and perseverance, anyone can succeed," 83 percent of the respondents agreed that the theme is essential or very important.[1]

With regard to work satisfaction, almost 90 percent of Canadians report that they are either satisfied or very satisfied with their jobs (Statistics Canada 2001). Overall, there is very little difference between men and women. With age, job satisfaction increases. For example, 14.1 percent of employees under age 25 are not satisfied with their jobs, compared to 9.8 percent between the ages of 25 and 44, and 8.7 percent 45 years and older. Occupation is directly related to job satisfaction. Managers and professionals are more likely to be very satisfied (44.1 percent and 38.5 percent, respectively) than production workers (22.1 percent). Workers who are satisfied with their jobs are not necessarily satisfied with their pay: 76.2 percent of employees reported that they were dissatisfied with their pay (76.2 percent). Women tend to be less satisfied with pay than men, but this makes sense as women's salaries overall are less than those of men.

Curiously, there appears to be little relationship between job satisfaction and workplace stress. When Canadians were asked about workplace stress, just over 60 percent claimed that their jobs were stressful (Changing Employee Relationships Survey 2000). Further, other scholars argue that results of job satisfaction surveys should be challenged (Krahn and Lowe 2002; Rhinehart 1978). Workers' behaviour such as strikes, job absenteeism, and job quitting is a better indicator of job satisfaction than surveys. Workers in blue-collar jobs see their time at work belonging to the employer, and the job is viewed "simply as that—'just a job'" (Rhinehart 2001:133). Krahn and Lowe (2002:430) point out that "general job satisfaction questions may be similar to replies to the question, 'How are you today?' Most of us would say 'fine.'" As such, better survey questions are needed that can specifically probe feelings of satisfaction or dissatisfaction.

An increasing number of Canadians no longer accept the notion that their self-worth is tied in with their work or that they have a moral duty to work. On the contrary, Canadians increasingly expect their work to have *meaning,* to be emotionally and intellectually *stimulating,* and to offer an opportunity to feel *good about themselves and the products of their labour.* Income is no longer the most important facet of an individual's work.

In evaluating job quality, an individual is likely to consider not just income, but such nonincome factors as job duties and working conditions, job satisfaction, period of work, job status, and job security (Rosenthal 1989; Moen and Yu 2000). The term *job duties and working conditions* refers to such matters as whether the job is hazardous, repetitive, stressful, closely supervised, and isolated (versus working with a team). *Job satisfaction* increases when the worker engages in problem solving, has the opportunity to be creative, gains recognition, can fully utilize skills and learn new skills, and has the chance for advancement.

Period of work is the extent to which the job involves weekend or shift work, overtime, or flexible work hours. *Job status* includes both social status (being recognized by outsiders as having a more prestigious or less prestigious job) and status within the organization. *Job security* is closely related to how positively the worker evaluates his job; workers are less comfortable with seasonal jobs and with those that have a high risk of layoff.

Canadians, then, are not rejecting work. They are rejecting meaningless work and low-quality jobs. To say, as we have heard from some students and employers, that

Canadians today "just don't want to work anymore" is the *fallacy of personal attack*. In a national U.S. survey, for example, only 5.1 percent of those not working said it was because they were "not interested in working" (Weismantle 2001). The great majority wants to work, but at work that is important and that fosters a sense of achievement.

▪▪ WORK AS A SOCIAL PROBLEM

Because most Canadians want to work and expect their work to provide some degree of personal fulfillment, there are three basic problems associated with work in Canada today. First, there is the problem of *unemployment and* **underemployment.** People are underemployed if they work full time for poverty wages, work part time when they desire full-time work, or work at jobs that are temporary or below their skill levels. Second, there is the problem of *dissatisfaction and alienation*. Finally, there is the problem of various kinds of *work hazards*.

underemployment
working full time for poverty wages, working part time when full-time work is desired, or working at a job below the worker's skill level

▪▪ Unemployment and Underemployment

Underemployment is perhaps as serious as unemployment for those who look to work for meaningful activity. There are no precise figures on underemployment, but women and blacks have higher rates than do white males (De Jong and Madamba 2001). A large number of the underemployed are in temporary jobs. Businesspeople claim that temporary work serves the interests of those who want something other than a permanent work situation. However, *temporary workers are underemployed because most of them are looking for full-time permanent employment* and most dislike the lack of stability and the degradation of being a temporary worker (Parker 1994).

unemployment rate
the proportion of the labour force that is not working but is available for work and has made specific efforts to find work

There are reliable data on the **unemployment rate.** This rate is the proportion of the labour force that is not working but is available for work and has made specific efforts to find work. The unemployment rate fluctuates considerably. During times of recession, unemployment rates increase. For example, unemployment rates jumped from 7.6 percent in 1981 to 11.9 percent in 1983, the highest rate in more than 30 years (see figure 9.4). The recession in the early 1990s also saw high unemployment rates, although marginally lower (11.4 percent) than those in 1983. The strong economy at the end of the 1990s saw many new jobs introduced into the labour market and unemployment rates dropped, reaching the lowest rate—6.8 percent—in 30 years. Groups of people who are at greater risk for long-term unemployment include men, workers over age 45, people with lower education, and people living in Quebec and British Columbia (Dubé 2004). By 2003, the overall rate was 7.6 percent, or 1.3 million workers (Statistics Canada 2004). This does not mean, however, that only 1.3 million workers were affected by unemployment in that year. Many people are unemployed for only a portion of the year. Thus, while the official number of unemployed was 1.3 million, the actual number who experienced some unemployment during that year was substantially greater.

In addition, there are millions of Canadians who are not in the labour force. This means that they are not actively looking for work. The number of people who are not in the labour force is substantially higher, six times, than those who are unemployed (figure 9.5). In 2003, more than 8 million Canadians were not in the labour force. Fewer than 1 percent of people who are not in the labour force are referred to as "discouraged searchers," those who did not look for work because they believed there was no work available. The largest group of people not in the labour force (44 percent) is people over age 65. There has been a steady decline in the percentage of people not in the labour force (from 38 percent in 1976 to 32 percent in 2003), but given that the future trend is

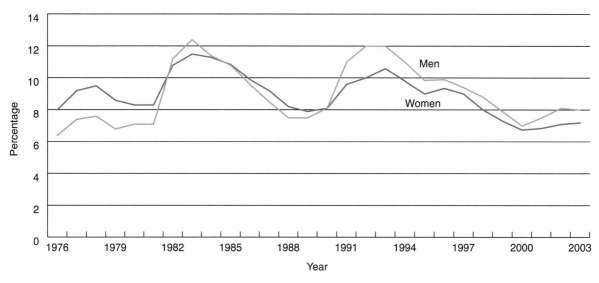

FIGURE 9.4 ■ ■ ■

Unemployment rates, by sex, Canada, 1976–2003.

Source: Statistics Canada, Labour Force Survey, CANSIM table 282-0002.

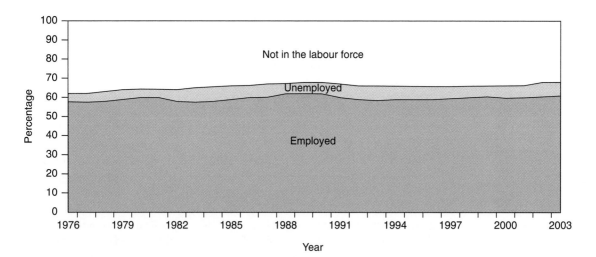

FIGURE 9.5 ■ ■ ■

Labour force status rates, Canada, 1976–2003.

Source: Statistics Canada, Labour Force Survey, CANSIM table 282-0002.

toward an aging population, the percentage of the population not in the labour force is expected to rise (Statistics Canada 2004).

Those who want work but are not actively looking are not counted in the unemployment rate. When you take into account those unemployed for a part of the year and those not in the labour force, the number of people affected by unemployment is far higher than the official figures.

Unemployment does not strike all groups the same, and changes over time. For example, in the 1970s and 1980s the men's unemployment rate was typically lower than the women's (refer to figure 9.4). Since 1990 there has been a reversal, and women's unemployment rate is now lower than men's. Statistics Canada (2004) explains the shift as due to the growth of service-industry jobs, where the overwhelming majority (87 percent) of women work, compared to 64 percent of employed men. Unemployment rates among young people have always been higher than for adults, but the gap has been decreasing. Whereas in 1976 young people comprised almost half of all the unemployed, in 2003 they represented close to one-third. Finally, recall from chapter 7 that visible minorities have higher unemployment rates than non–visible minorities (Tran 2004). Typically, the rates are higher for women than for men, higher for minorities than for whites, and higher for younger than for older workers.

Unemployment also varies by occupational category, with rates tending to be higher among blue-collar workers. In 2004, for example, manufacturing jobs steadily decreased throughout the year, along with jobs in accommodation and food services. Job growth occurred in finance, insurance, real estate, and leasing (The Daily, December 3, 2004). Overall, occupations in information technology, followed by accounting and financial analysis, have low unemployment rates (Census 2001).

▪▪ Dissatisfaction and Alienation

We previously defined *alienation* as a sense of estrangement that is usually measured by an individual's feelings of powerlessness, normlessness, isolation, and meaninglessness. This is a subjective approach to alienation. Alienation is an objective phenomenon, according to Karl Marx. In a capitalist society the worker is *estranged from his or her own labour* (because work is something that is coerced and external to the worker rather than a fulfillment of the worker's needs), from other people, and from his or her own humanity. The worker sinks to the level of a commodity and becomes the most wretched of commodities. Because capitalism wrenches the means of production from the control of those intimately involved in production, workers are necessarily alienated whether or not they feel any sense of alienation.

The amount of alienation in the workplace, therefore, depends on whether a Marxist or a social psychological approach to the question is taken. For Marxists, all workers in a capitalist society are alienated by definition. For social psychologists, workers are alienated to the extent that they perceive themselves as powerless and isolated. Social psychological studies indicate that some workers, but by no means the majority, are alienated. In fact, some researchers have found that many workers say they would rather continue their jobs than to get the same wages for not working.

Nevertheless, there are indications that dissatisfaction is still a problem. First, no matter which polls are used to measure job dissatisfaction, there is evidence of various troublesome issues among those who say they are satisfied. Those who work in companies that have cut the workforce tend to rate their employer lower on everything from management practices to ethics (Stoneman 1999), and workers in demanding, fast-paced jobs in the high-tech world experience family and personal problems that lead to unscheduled absences from work (Stone 1999).

▪▪ Work Hazards and Stress

While most Canadians report job satisfaction at their work, they also claim that work is stressful. High stress levels at a job are indeed worrisome, as they can lead to injuries.

UNEMPLOYMENT RATES IN INDUSTRIAL NATIONS

Unemployment is a huge and ongoing problem in many underdeveloped nations. For one thing, economic growth lags behind population growth, so that even a robust economy cannot absorb all the new workers coming into the labour force each year. In the developed nations, unemployment tends to be smaller but is still an enduring problem. The unemployment rate varies considerably, however, depending on how the economy is structured. Note in table 9.2 that some nations have lower rates than Canada, while others typically have higher rates.

Although the rates are strikingly low in some cases, every nation confronts the problem in which a segment of its population wants but is unable to obtain employment—and in every nation, those who are unemployed face some of the same problems of stress and self-worth as do Canadians. One major difference is that in countries such as Sweden there are more benefits available for the unemployed, so that unemployment is not as likely to be associated with abject poverty.

TABLE 9.2 ■ ■ ■

Unemployment Rates, by Country, 1980–2003

	1980	1990	2003
United States	7.1	5.5	6.0
Australia	6.1	6.9	6.1
Canada	7.5	8.1	7.6
France	6.5	9.1	9.5
Germany	2.8	5.0	9.1
Italy	4.4	7.0	8.5
Netherlands	6.0	7.5	4.7
Sweden	2.0	1.7	6.3
United Kingdom	7.0	6.9	5.0

Source: U.S. Census Bureau 2001:847 and OECD March 2005.

According to the Statistical Report on the Health of Canadians (1999:246), Canadians in 1996 reported more than 377,000 time-loss work injuries, a rate of 27.6 injuries for every 1,000 workers. Injury rates have steadily declined since 1987, when they were highest at 48.5 per 1,000. Men reported more than two times more injuries than women, and young men (between ages 15 and 29) have the highest rate (43.3 per 1,000) for all age groups and sexes. There is wide variation in injuries reported by provinces; Prince Edward Island and British Columbia have the highest rates, at 40.6 per 1,000 and 39.7 per 1,000, respectively. Finally, between 1994 and 1998 there was a threefold greater likelihood of having a motor vehicle accident than having a work-related injury. During this period the number of traffic accidents and occupational accidents decreased, but the rate of decrease for traffic accidents was 11 percent compared to 3 percent for occupational accidents (see figure 9.6). Because these figures are based on reports from business and industry, it is likely that the actual numbers are higher. Moreover, a multitude of minor accidents and work-related illnesses are not included in the figures.

We use the term *work hazards* broadly to include *work-induced stress* as well as *work-related injuries and illnesses.* For example, a spot welder on an auto assembly line told about some of the daily hazards to which he is exposed:

FIGURE 9.6 ■ ■ ▨

Work injuries and
traffic accidents,
1994–1998.

Source: HRSDC 1994:
http://www.hrsdc.gc.ca/asp/
gateway.asp?hr=/en/lp/lo/ohs/
statistics/naosh/4.shtml&hs=oxs.

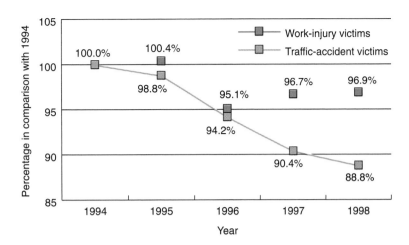

I pulled a muscle in my neck, straining. This gun, when you grab this thing from the ceiling, cable, weight, I mean you're pulling everything. . . . This whole edge here is sharp. I go through a shirt every two weeks, it just goes right through. My overalls catch on fire. I've had gloves catch on fire. (Indicates arms.) See them little holes? That's what sparks do. I've got burns across here from last night. (Terkel 1972:224)

For some workers, the hazards are physical. They may be exposed to toxic chemicals or a work environment that is conducive to accidents. Workers employed in logging and forestry have the highest rate at 82.4 per 1,000, followed by transportation (53.6 per 1,000), manufacturing (51.9 per 1,000), and construction (41.4 per 1,000) (Statistical Report on the Health of Canadians 1999). These workers are exposed to unsafe conditions as well as pollutants such as toxic gases, radioactive materials, and mineral dusts (Rinehart 2001:131). Such exposures are directly linked to cancer, emphysema, black lung disease, and silicosis, to name a few.

Psychological as well as physical hazards occur in the workplace. Some occupations are particularly likely to expose workers to stress. For instance, many taxi drivers work under the continual threat of robbery. Salespeople often endure harassment from customers. Many high-tech workers feel ongoing pressure to produce and to make their work the consuming focus of their lives. Psychiatrists and psychotherapists often find their work to be emotionally draining. In other jobs, stress is associated with such conditions as lack of communication and delegation of authority by management, fast-paced work in poor environmental conditions, frequent overtime, conflict between workers, recent reduction of employee benefits, and downsizing (Koretz 1997; Grunberg, Anderson-Connolly, and Greenberg 2000).

■■ WORK AND THE QUALITY OF LIFE

Many people thoroughly enjoy their work. They find it meaningful and satisfying, thus providing them with a higher quality of life. They are more likely to enjoy their work when they perceive themselves to be included in the information network and the decision-making processes of their workplace (Barak and Levin 2002).

There are also many people for whom the effect of working is a kind of *emotional and spiritual malaise.* They do not despise their work, but neither are they excited by it. At best, they are apathetic or resigned. At worst, they sense an uneasiness or mild but chronic frustration. One important area that work affects is the mental and physical health of the worker.

■■ Work, Unemployment, and Health

Ironically, both working and not working can adversely affect your health. What are the risks?

Work and Health.   Work can have a *negative impact on both the emotional and the physical well-being of workers* (Spector 2002). Feelings of alienation or high levels of job dissatisfaction may lead to heavy drinking in an effort to cope (Greenberg and Grunberg 1995; Martin and Roman 1996) or to burnout (Powell 1994). Those whose work provides relatively low rewards (including low job security or advancement possibilities) for high levels of effort may increase their risk of cardiovascular disease three- to fourfold (Siegrist 1995). Independently of their level of effort, job insecurity puts workers under continual stress and can produce various kinds of health problems (Heaney, Israel, and House 1994). In some high-stress occupations, such as physicians and law enforcement officers, suicide rates are high (Boxer, Burnett, and Swanson 1995). A study of death rates across various occupations found that high-risk occupations (those associated with higher death rates at earlier ages) include taxi drivers, cooks, longshoremen, and transportation operatives (Johnson, Sorlie, and Backlund 1999).

Underemployment also poses health risks. Those who are underemployed, in the sense of being overeducated and overqualified for their jobs, are likely to lack job satisfaction and to leave their jobs sooner than others (Tsang, Rumberger, and Levin 1991). Further, they are more likely than others to become depressed (Dooley, Ham-Rowbottom, and Prause 2001).

Overall, workplace stress is increasing in Canada. A 2001 study of 6,000 workers from an array of occupations found that 55 percent of workers reported a high level of stress, compared to 47 percent in 1991 (Duxbury and Higgins 2001). To what extent, then, does job satisfaction affect a person's well-being? According to Health Canada, "increased pressure for competitiveness in a global market and changes in the nature of work has led to high levels of workplace stress and related health problems linked to long working hours, job insecurity, physical injuries such as repetitive strain, decreases in worker participation and control, and problems related to work–family balance" (Health Canada 2004:3). An American study concluded that more than 71,000 Americans died in one year from diseases like cancer and cardiovascular and neurological problems induced by work conditions (Scott 1990a). The study called job-related illnesses an "invisible killer." Finally, the General Social Surveys of 1994 and 2000 examined workplace stressors (triggers) among Canadian workers. Here are some findings to consider (Williams 2003):

- About one-third of Canadians (in 1994 and 2000) who worked claimed that the most common workplace stressors were too many demands or too many hours.
- About 15 percent reported poor interpersonal relations.
- Risk or accident injury and threat of layoff or job loss each accounted for 13 percent of workplace stressors.
- Just over 10 percent of Canadians cited having to learn computer skills.
- Men were 14 percent less likely than women to feel that too many demands or too many hours are a stress trigger at work.
- Workers in health-related occupations were seven times more likely to worry about accidents or injuries compared to those in management, business, finance, or science.

There is, in sum, a strong relationship between stressful working conditions and physical and emotional illness. And the stress occurs in all kinds of work. A Protestant minister described his own health problems caused by stress at work. The stresses he experienced could occur in virtually any kind of job, and his story shows that no one is immune.[2]

> I arrived at my new church with an intense anticipation of a rewarding and fruitful ministry. I brought the enthusiasm and recklessness of youth to a job that demanded the caution and wisdom of age. For about a year, the enthusiasm was sufficient. It carried me through some discouragements and minimized any overt criticism. Then I made the mistake of criticizing an older member of the church. The criticism was neither harsh nor malicious, but the member was quite sensitive and quite influential. I also plunged ahead and pushed programs and began projects without first consulting the officers. At the beginning of my second year, criticism erupted and quickly mushroomed.
>
> For about the next five years, I had problems with various people in the church. And I had a series of things go wrong with myself, both emotionally and physically. At one point, it seemed that everything was coming to a head and there would be a final all-out struggle to see whose way would prevail—mine or those that felt I was taking the church down the wrong road. Just before this culminating battle, I lost about 20 pounds from my slender physique. One week I broke out in a rash. I had severe sinus problems. Worst of all, I nearly developed a phobia about being in an enclosed area with a lot of people. I found it torturous to go to a crowded restaurant. One day I had to leave a church conference because my heart was pounding and I felt intense panic. Sometimes I even felt serious anxiety when I led the worship service.
>
> As it turned out, the "final" battle was not really the final one after all. It had only served to trigger the various physical and mental ailments that I endured for the next few years. Ultimately, we were able to work out the differences we had. I think I gained some in wisdom and lost some of my recklessness. The church began to stabilize and then grow, and some of those with whom I had fought became my best friends. After about eight years or so, I finally lost my fear of crowded places. In a way, I suppose you could say it all had a happy ending. But I wouldn't go through that again for anything. It was the only time of my life when the thought of suicide entered my mind as an appealing option.

Unemployment and Health. The stress of being forcibly unemployed can be as serious as the stress of working in undesirable conditions or in an unfulfilling job. For most people, *unemployment* is a traumatic experience. As we discussed earlier, although unemployment rates were low during the 1990s, millions of Canadians are still affected by unemployment every year. Some are unemployed for only a portion of the year. Some find employment, but the work is not meaningful to them. Some have dropped out of the labour force, discouraged by their inability to find employment in their line of work. Some are the victims of downsizing that eliminated their jobs (Uchitelle and Kleinfield 1996).

Whatever the reason for being out of work, *unemployment is detrimental to both physical and emotional well-being.* Unemployment is associated with high levels of stress and lowered life satisfaction (Fenwick and Tausig 1994). It can lead to such things as depression, lowered self-esteem, anger and resentment, shame and embarrassment, social isolation, serious mental illness, physical health problems, alcohol abuse, criminal behaviour, and suicide (Dooley and Prause 1998; Crutchfield, Glusker, and Bridges 1999; Fergusson, Horwood and Woodward 2001). The negative consequences are likely to be more severe for workers who experience a second job loss (or who lose three or more jobs) than for those who experience their first loss (Chen, Marks, and Bersani 1994).

Three researchers found an association between unemployment and rates of illness (including cardiovascular disease), mortality, and suicide (Jin, Shah, and Svoboda 1995). The detrimental physical and emotional consequences of unemployment also are seen world-wide. A Swedish study reported higher tobacco and drug use, increased crime rates, and higher mortality rates (especially by suicide and accidents) among unemployed youth (Hammarstrom 1994). In Australia, researchers found youth unemployment to be associated with such psychological symptoms as depression and loss of confidence, and with suicide (Morrell, Taylor, and Kerr 1998). A comparison of unemployed with employed people in Spain reported that the unemployed had higher rates of respiratory illness (Kogevinas et al. 1998).

■■ Interpersonal Relationships

A number of studies support the notion that both work-related stress and unemployment *can adversely affect interpersonal relationships.* Work in stressful conditions can lead to conflict at home (Kopacsi 1991; Menaghan 1991). The stress can be rooted in multiple factors, including the general conditions under which the work is performed. For example, *shift work tends to create both personal stress and interpersonal problems.* In a study of work and marital quality using a random national sample, U.S. researchers found that shift work tends to depress marital happiness and interaction, and to increase disagreements and problems, including sexual and childrearing problems (White and Keith 1990).

Underemployment is also stressful, and those who are underemployed may be less satisfied than others with their marriages (Zvonkovic 1988). The strains and frustrations of stressful work conditions or of underemployment often carry over into family life, increasing tension and conflict and decreasing satisfaction.

Unemployment tends to place even more strain on an individual's relationships, including relationships within the family. During the Great Depression, when the unemployment rate went as high as one-quarter of the labour force, many workers blamed themselves for their unemployment, became disillusioned with themselves, and began to have trouble within their homes (Komarovsky 1940). Even in less serious economic recessions, workers are embarrassed by being unemployed, may begin to withdraw from social contacts, and may direct some of their hostility toward members of their families. It is, of course, not merely the embarrassment and stress of being unemployed, but the strain of trying to meet the expenses of food, clothing, housing, and health care that contributes to the conflict between spouses and between parents and children (Dail 1988).

Not all the problems are due to either unemployment or job dissatisfaction. In some cases there is simply a *conflict between work and family life* (Hugick and Leonard 1991). For men, the conflict generally focuses on excessive work time—they are spending too much of their time and energy on their work. For women, the conflict is more likely to be one of scheduling problems or fatigue and irritability. In any case, the outcome is a certain amount of conflict between family members.

■■ CONTRIBUTING FACTORS

The factors that contribute to unemployment are generally different from the factors involved in work dissatisfaction, alienation, and work hazards. Although we focus on the latter factors, we also examine the political economy of unemployment.

■■ Social Structural Factors

The Capitalist Economy.
We noted earlier that people in a capitalist economy are motivated by profit. *In business and corporations, profit tends to be the "bottom line."* That is, the goal is profit, and managers do whatever is necessary to maximize profits. This "bottom-line" approach has led owners, executives, and managers to act in

Unions continue to challenge government policies.

ways that have adverse consequences for large numbers of people. One type of action is longstanding: the subservience of workers' needs to organizational needs. Three other actions changed in nature or increased greatly after 1980: union busting (the practice of dealing with strikes by hiring permanent replacements rather than by negotiating with the union), downsizing, and the use of temporary workers.

The *subservience of workers' needs to organizational needs* is illustrated by the other three actions. Workers need well-paying and meaningful jobs, but downsizing and the use of temporary workers are ways to meet the organization's need for profits at the expense of the workers' needs. In addition, workers may be abused and exploited by tyrannical managers and supervisors who focus on efficiency and productivity rather than the workers' needs for self-esteem, encouragement, and fulfillment (Ashforth 1994).

Downsizing, as noted above, also has taken on a different character, for it occurs independently of whether the economy is booming or in recession. It even occurs in companies that are doing well (Uchitelle and Kleinfield 1996). Ironically, executives are rewarded for downsizing, for to the extent that profits increase as a result of the lower costs of a smaller workforce, executive bonuses go up.

Finally, *there is increasing use of temporary and part-time workers.* The use of temporary employment as a category monitoring labour force activity trends was introduced by Statistics Canada only in 1997, even though temporary work has been around for many years. At that time, 11 percent of Canadians held temporary jobs, compared to 13 percent in 2000. Almost half of temporary jobs are contractually based, 23 percent are seasonal, and 27 percent are casual. Men and women are equally likely to hold temporary jobs, and Canadians between the ages of 15 and 24 are disproportionately represented in temporary work (Krahn and Lowe 2002). Interviews with managers of temporary employment firms show that the higher demand for temporaries does not reflect workers' preference but rather employers' desire for flexibility and lower costs (Parker 1994). Some temporary workers are former employees who return as "rentals" to the company for which they formerly worked (Uchitelle 1996). Not surprisingly, they often struggle with resentment over now doing the same work at lower pay and with few or no fringe benefits.

Part-time work has dramatically increased over the last half century. In 1950, fewer than 4 percent of Canadians were employed in part-time jobs. In 2003, the part-time rate was four and a half times greater, at 18.3 percent. Many people also work part time who would prefer to work full time. In 2000, 2.7 million or 25 percent of part-timers who usually worked full time were working part time because they were unable to find full-time work (Statistics Canada 2001).

The Political Economy of Work. The traditional notion of man as the breadwinner assumed that a man's work would allow him to support his family. One of the problems of work today is that *a large number of jobs provide inadequate support and*

FIGURE 9.7   ■ ■ ■

Multiple jobholders in
Canada, 1976–2004.

Source: Labour Force Survey 2004,
CANSIM V2054036.

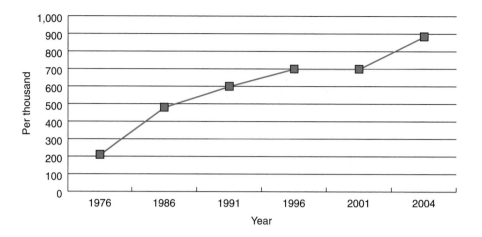

benefits to enable a family to live well. A substantial number of Canadians have to work longer hours or hold more than one job in order to provide sufficient income for their families. Since 1976, the number of Canadians who hold multiple jobs has increased fourfold (see figure 9.7).

Many workers also struggle with wages that have not kept pace with inflation or with reduced employee benefits. The average earnings stagnated between 1980 and 1990 (Census 2001). In the late 1990s, they began to rise again, but the workers were far behind others whose income continued to increase during these two decades (Census 2001). The reality is that in 2000 more than 6.5 million Canadians earned less than $20,000 (Census 2001). Just over 20 percent, or 1,482,000 people, worked full time, and more than half of them (54 percent) were women.

Unfortunately, even as earnings began to rise, fringe benefits were cut back. Employers increasingly opted to provide less expensive types of health coverage and pension plans. About half of the private-sector workforce is not covered by any employer-sponsored retirement plan.

The result of these various trends is that many jobs offer workers low pay, and in 1999 only 27 percent of non-unionized employees were covered by a pension plan, compared to 80 percent of unionized workers (Akyeampong 2002). The notion of a single breadwinner in a family—one person who has one job and provides all the family's needs—is increasingly unrealistic.

The Political Economy of Unemployment.   It is important to distinguish between *structural and discriminatory unemployment.* Discriminatory unemployment involves high unemployment rates for particular groups, such as women and minorities, and is discussed in the chapters that deal with those groups. Structural unemployment is the result of the *functioning of the political–economic system itself.*

Structural unemployment takes various forms. Since the Great Depression, the economy has been regulated basically in accord with the theories of the English economist John Maynard Keynes. In Keynes's view, governments can *control the swings of the economy,* greatly moderating the inflationary and deflationary trends, by means such as spending programs and taxation. There is *an inverse relationship between employment and inflation.* When the rate of inflation is high, the government may take steps that will result in an increase in unemployment. Some unemployment is necessary, and some fluctuations are inevitable. Yet because of the moderating impact of government intervention, fluctuations need not be as severe as they have been over the last two decades.

The unemployment rates shown in figure 9.4 reflect in large part the government's efforts to regulate the economy. There will always be some unemployment in a capitalist economy. The amount can be controlled and perhaps lessened by government intervention, but unemployment cannot be eliminated.

In addition to the overall rate of unemployment, the functioning of the political–economic system contributes to the high rates of unemployment in particular areas or in particular occupations at certain times. *Government spending* can create many jobs and then eliminate those jobs when the priorities change. For example, massive federal funding of the space program in the 1960s created many jobs, some of which vanished when the priorities changed in the 1970s.

Technological Changes and Women's Work. The effects of economic restructuring and advances in technology have particularly targeted clerical positions, which historically have been filled by close to 25 percent of all women in the labour force (Phillips and Phillips 1993). The introduction of computer and electronic technology into offices has not only reduced the time needed to perform tasks, but also contributed to the restructuring of the office.

Another example of fallout due to office restructuring is the increasing trend to downshift clerical work from full time to part time (de Wolff 1995:7). Rates of part-time employment in the financial industry are steadily increasing to fill the gaps left by "daily break periods." However, part-time employment is more a factor of "bank automation and the growing dependence on new forms of technology" (Duffy and Pupo 1992:208). In addition to increases in part-time jobs, there is the push for part-time shift work (de Wolff, 1995; Duffy and Pupo 1992).

The introduction of microelectronic technology into offices has led not only to restructuring and downsizing of the workplace, but also to the "de-skilling" of jobs. The goal in many offices is to replace labour and skills with machinery and computer technology (Phillips and Phillips 1993). The workplace, consequently, has been restructured, and many full-time jobs have disappeared. In retail, for example, computers organize much of the store inventory once managed by employees. Subsequently, fewer employees are needed and the workforce can be organized "by scheduling part-timers to match consumer demand" (Duffy et al. 1997:174).

Job de-skilling is a phenomenon found not just in offices; its effects are felt in women-dominated blue-collar jobs where human labour is being replaced by computer technology. In hindsight, it can be said that the automation of the fish packing industry in New Brunswick in 1980 "to reduce workforce needs" (McFarland 1980:99) was a foreshadowing of what was to come. Today, automated cutting machines and highly technical sewing machines in the clothing manufacturing industry are affecting an already vulnerable population of women employees, who mostly are immigrants and of colour (Phillips and Phillips 1993).

The Organizational Context of Work: Unions. The union movement has been instrumental in bringing about higher wages, fringe benefits, and safer conditions for workers (Krahn and Lowe 2002; Rinehart 2001). However, as we noted earlier, union membership over the last five years has decreased somewhat. This is in part explained by two recessions and industrial restructuring that "cut deeply into the traditional membership strength of unions in manufacturing and other blue-collar occupations" (Krahn and Lowe 2002:355). The public sector has also undergone restructuring, meaning downsizing and budget cuts. Finally, governments and courts have weakened collective bargaining rights, producing challenging labour relations (Krahn and Lowe 2002). Notwithstanding these challenges, Canadian unions have not been affected in the ways American unions have. Union membership in the United States has been whittled to 13.5 percent of employed workers (U.S. Census 2001). American unions have faced adverse rulings by conservative federal judges and the National Labor Relations Board (NLRB) regarding the right of unions to organize and strike. Meanwhile, management often has been supported by the legal system in efforts to keep unions out or to break existing unions. The obstacles faced by unions are illustrated by a study of an Arizona miners' strike (Rosenblum 1995). The miners, who were largely Mexican Americans, went on strike against one of the world's largest copper producers. The strike was a reaction to the company's demand that cost-of-living adjustments and some other benefits be eliminated. The company replaced all the workers, and the replacements voted to decertify the union. The National Labor Relations Board ruled in favour of the company when the union protested. The globalization of the economy also has weakened the bargaining power of unions by allowing employers to opt for foreign locations for a part or all of the work.

Contemporary Work Roles and Environments.   Job dissatisfaction and alienation reflect the *nature of work roles and work environments* in contemporary society. Workers suffer when they lack such things as positive relationships at the workplace, clear definitions of their work, and physical comfort in the work environment (Turnipseed 1992). They particularly suffer when they feel they have no control over their work lives and no security in their jobs, a situation that is exacerbated by what has been called the "disposable worker," a growing tendency to use part-time and temporary workers.

Work roles in Canadian society result from a combination of factors, including *technological developments, efforts to maximize profits, and the bureaucratization of work.* The disposable worker is one consequence of the effort to maximize profits. At least three consequences of the technological developments bear upon the meaningfulness of work. First, technology brought with it *highly specialized tasks,* with the result that many workers focus on a narrow range of tasks and may have little or no sense of the overall project.

Second, and associated with the intense specialization, many jobs are stressful. A considerable number of *extremely repetitious, routine tasks* have been created. In some cases, workers may choose to spend their work time on these tasks. Molstad (1986) studied a brewery and observed that some workers opt for the boring work because it relieves them of work situations in which they have responsibility for, but not control over, outcomes. Rather than face the frustration and stress of that dilemma, they accept the boring jobs (ironically, as we show below, the boring jobs also subject them to stress). Even though they have chosen the routine task, they must *come to terms with the boredom of their work.* Thus, they develop a number of mental tactics such as daydreaming, playing, singing, and talking. These tactics do not disrupt the work routine, but they do reinforce the workers' alienation from the work.

Barbara Garson (1975) described the *coping mechanisms* utilized by people who work in routine jobs ranging from typists, to key-punchers, to workers who stack Ping-Pong paddles all day, to tuna cleaners in a seafood plant. The deadly routine of many jobs is portrayed in the account of Cindy, a girl who worked for a time in the Ping-Pong factory.

> My job was stacking the Ping-Pong paddles into piles of fifty. Actually I didn't have to count all the way up to fifty. To make it a little easier they told me to stack them in circles of four with the first handle facing me. When there got to be thirteen handles on the second one from the front, then I'd know I had fifty. . . . As soon as I'd stack 'em, they'd unstack 'em. Maybe it wouldn't have been so bad if I could have seen all the piles I stacked at the end of the day. But they were taking them down as fast as I was piling them up. That was the worst part of the job. (Garson 1975:1–2)

Such jobs are stressful. They may also be physically and emotionally harmful. For example, women in general are segregated into clerical and service industry jobs (Pierson and Cohen 1995). These jobs tend to be low-paying and have harsh working conditions (Messing 1998). *Repetitive strain injuries* are "commonplace among workers who constantly perform the same muscle movements during the course of their work" (Pierson and Cohen 1995:109). Women who work as data processors, in supermarket checkouts, and in fish plants are particularly vulnerable to repetitive strain injuries. Interviews with 52 women with *repetitive strain injuries* found the women to report reduced capacity for housework, troubled family relationships, mental distress, and lowered self-esteem (Ewan, Lowy, and Reid 1991).

Third, technological developments are associated with *depersonalization* within the workplace. Workers tend to be *isolated* in certain kinds of jobs. For instance, isolation may occur when the work is computerized or automated. In such cases, the workers may have to pay closer attention to their work, have less interaction with people, and engage in fewer tasks that require teamwork.

Work roles also are affected by *bureaucratization of work*. Perhaps the majority of Canadians work in bureaucratic organizations, which tend to be *authoritarian*. A defining characteristic of a bureaucracy is the hierarchy of authority. Workers in an authoritarian organization are likely to experience negative emotions and attitudes ranging from job dissatisfaction to alienation. People prefer to be *involved in decisions that affect them and their work*. Their satisfaction with their work, their motivation, and their effectiveness all can be enhanced by participation in the decision-making process (Schnake, Bushardt, and Spottswood 1984; Barak and Levin 2002).

Participation gives the worker some control over his or her work. The more control the worker has, the more likely he or she is to be satisfied and the more likely the work is to enhance his or her health (Tetrick and LaRocco 1987; Spector 2002). Indeed, people with little control over their jobs have rates of heart disease that are two to three times greater than those with a high amount of control (Adler 1989). Low-control jobs are apt to be lower prestige as well. Assembly-line workers, waiters, and cooks have jobs with high demand and low control, and their rates of heart disease are about three times the average for all workers.

Unfortunately, workers are unlikely to have the opportunity for participation and a sense of control in many bureaucratic organizations. Lacking that opportunity, they are likely to have lower levels of job satisfaction, lower morale, and lower levels of motivation.

In addition to the frustrations of working in an authoritarian organization, workers must deal with a certain amount of *built-in conflict* that bureaucracies tend to generate. In theory, such conflict is unnecessary because the chain of command is clear: All workers are experts in their own jobs, and there are rules to cover all tasks and any problems. In reality, a certain amount of conflict is invariably found in work roles. There may be *role ambiguity* (a lack of clear information about a particular work role) that results in lower job satisfaction and higher stress levels (Revicki and May 1989). There may be *role conflict* because different groups in the workplace have different expectations for a particular work role or because the role expectations are excessive. Role conflict, like role ambiguity, leads to lower satisfaction and higher stress levels. The important point is that these problems are not the result of the individual worker's cantankerous nature but of contradictions that are part of the work role itself. The individual falls victim to the role and suffers the consequences of lowered satisfaction and higher stress levels.

The Political Economy of Work Hazards.
Some jobs necessarily entail more risk than others, and others entail more risk than necessary. Many work-related illnesses and injuries could be prevented or at least minimized if the health and well-being of

Despite efforts to protect the health and lives of workers, on-the-job accidents and deaths continue to be a problem, especially in high-risk occupations.

workers took priority over profit. Historically, untold numbers of Canadian workers have died in the name of profit and with the approval or apathy of the government.

Employers historically have been resistant to setting health and safety standards because of the associated reduction in profits. Through the hard work of unions, there has been a greater push through collective bargaining to improve work conditions and to promote health and safety in the workplace. In the 1920s, a no-fault compensation system was introduced where, in the event of an accident, workers would receive financial compensation regardless of fault. But if the accident were due to the employer's negligence, the worker was not able to sue. The no-fault compensation system is funded by employers; the amount varies by the individual company's safety record. The idea here is that employers would voluntarily promote health and safety practices, thus paying less compensation. The no-fault compensation system still exists today (Krahn and Lowe 2002).

Workers became directly involved with health and safety matters through the internal responsibility system (IRS), which establishes a labour–management health and

TABLE 9.3 ■ ■ ■

Number of Injuries and Injury Incidence Rates, 1994–1998

Source: Adapted from HRSDC 2004: http://www.hrsdc.gc.ca/asp/gateway.asp?hr=/en/lp/lo/ohs/statistics/naosh/1.shtml&hs=oxs.

Year	Number of Fatalities	Number of Time-Loss Injuries	Injury Incident Rate per 100 Workers	Time-Loss Injury Incident Rate per 100 Workers
1994	725	430,756	6.16	3.24
1995	748	410,464	6.08	3.04
1996	703	377,885	5.69	2.76
1997	833	379,851	5.68	2.72
1998	798	375,360	5.54	2.62

safety committee—called Joint Health & Safety Committees (JHSC)—to improve health and safety in the workplace. The IRS underpins the occupational health and safety legislation in all Canadian jurisdictions, and was first enacted in Saskatchewan in 1972. (Of note here is that although workers can influence health and safety matters they have no decision making-powers.)

Today in Canada, each province, territory, and the federal government has its own Occupational Health and Safety (OH&S) legislation (CCOHS 2004). In addition, there is a "right to know" legislation—the Workplace Hazardous Materials Information System (WHMIS)—that specifically addresses hazardous products. Information is made available through "product labels, material safety data sheets (MSDS) and worker education programs" (CCOHS 2004).

Since the introduction of the IRS, worker safety has improved. According to Gordon (1994:548, in Krahn and Lowe 2002:312), workers' recommendations to management are taken seriously and time-loss injury rates have steadily decreased (see table 9.3). That said, numbers of accidental deaths continue to be high, and work hazards continue to put many workers at risk (see box 9.1 on workplace accidents).

Box 9.1

Workplace Accidents

Occupational health and safety legislation ... imposes a duty on the employer to provide a reasonably safe workplace, to provide workers with information to help themselves, and allows workers to refuse dangerous work on an individual basis. Workers are provided with elaborate processes (through joint health and safety committees, certified workers representatives, etc.) which allow them to be consulted and to make recommendations but not, of course, to impose conditions. That right is left with employers.

It is in this context that governments set minimum standards. New standards are generated as evidence mounts that a particular kind of injury or disease is repetitively inflicted on workers. In fact, although this is never explicitly acknowledged, the standards which do exist are a direct reflection of the body counts which workers have provided. As long as occupational health and safety harms continue to be seen as arising from the technical problems of production rather than from the politics of production, the most significant way in which workers will continue to contribute to the improvement of conditions is by offering their bodies and minds to their employers for exploitation.

...Unlike soldiers, workers cannot console themselves with the argument that they are maimed and killed for a worthwhile cause. They do not die fighting for a worthwhile cause. They die to help employers satisfy their greed. They help them because they have no choice: their economic position forces them to accept this role. They die in a war, a class war. Only one class of people dies on the battlefield known as the workplace. Risk is created by the pursuit of profit by private wealth owners, but those profiting employers do not get injured or killed at work.

...Only two things reduce the-injury and death rate in the workplace. The first is unemployment. There is already too much of that and, as it goes up, the only other useful weapon in the fight against death at work—inspection and enforcement—is detoothed. This is part of the current intensification of class warfare as capitalists feel their oats. Study after study shows that the greater the number of inspections, the greater the willingness to enforce compliance with regulations, the lower the serious injury and fatality rates are. At the very least we owe it to our fallen brothers and sisters to make sure that the minimal safeguards they helped fight for are monitored stringently and enforced vigorously. This struggle can be usefully linked to the fight of the besieged government inspectors to retain both their self-respect and their jobs.

Other strategies suggest themselves. Workers must continuously argue that, as they take all of the physical risk and bear most of the financial costs (workers' compensation, unemployment insurance, social welfare and health care premiums come mainly from workers' wages and taxes), basic democratic principles require that they be given most of the decision-making power. They must demand the right to shut down operations when they think them dangerous, a right which is possessed by workers in Australia and Scandinavian countries. But, because of their dependence on continued production, this right is not easily exercisable. It is a symbolic minimum. Workers also must demand that they have a majority on joint health and safety commit tees and that these committees be given decision-making, rather than mere recommendation-making, power. Complementary symbolic fights should be waged.

Source: Excerpted from H. J. Glasbeek. "End the slaughter (workplace accidents)." *Canadian Dimension*, May–June 1996 vol. 30 no. 3, p. 31(3).

■■ Social Psychological Factors

Attitudes.   We noted in chapter 7 that, overall, Canadians support and are comfortable with diversity and oppose all forms of discrimination. However, according to the 2001 Census, the average earnings of visible minorities are 15 percent less than the national average. Visible minorities are employed in lower-paying jobs, and also have on average higher rates of unemployment, notwithstanding higher levels of education, than those of non–visible minority Canadian workers. Further, they are underrepresented in senior management and supervisory jobs.

The role of racism as an explanation for these differences "is often denied, but the existence of racial barriers to employment has been well-documented in hundreds if not thousands of complaints to employment equity and human rights tribunals" (Jackson 2002:13). Earlier studies found that Canadians' prejudicial attitudes toward visible minorities are rooted in a fear of perceived or real competition from immigrants (Filson 1983, in Li 1996). Even earlier, in 1965, research showed that Canadians were resistant to using "services of immigrants in prestigious jobs" (Li 1996). Do these attitudes linger today? Although the majority of Canadians strongly support and are committed to diversity, this fact is juxtaposed with the real working conditions and experiences of visible minorities: lower incomes, higher unemployment rates, fewer "better" jobs. Public opinion vacillates, of course, and may shift again in a more favourable direction. However, the decline in public approval of labour unions is an unwelcome sign to those who strive to improve the lot of workers.

Another attitude that enters into work problems is the sense of superiority people might have toward certain workers. The attitudes of many Canadians toward service workers, manual labourers, and clerical workers range from patronizing to contemptuous. If some workers are dissatisfied or alienated, it is in part because others *treat them with little or no respect because of their jobs.* For example, we have seen many instances of secretaries and clerks being treated with contempt by their superiors or by customers who feel they should quickly respond to demands from those who "pay your salary."

FUN AND GAMES AT WORK

As various studies in this chapter indicate, many Canadians find little pleasure in their jobs, though most expect their work to be enjoyable and fulfilling. By young adulthood, most people have worked at some job. Consider how much enjoyment and fulfillment you have received from your own work experiences. With respect to any job (or jobs) you have had, think about your feelings toward the work, the impact that the work had on your life, and the problems and satisfactions connected to the work. Imagine that someone is interviewing you about your experiences. Write out your answers to the following questions about a job you have had or now have.

What did you most like about the job?

What did you most dislike about the job?

How would you feel about working at the job for all or the major portion of your life? Why?

How were you treated by others in your work role?

Did the job make any difference in the way you feel about yourself? Why or why not?

How could the job be made more meaningful to workers?

Gather with other class members working on this project and summarize the results. What do the results say about the amount of worker dissatisfaction and alienation in Canada? If the only jobs available were the kinds discussed by the class, would most Canadians prefer not to work? Could all the jobs be made into meaningful and fulfilling experiences?

Socialization.   One of the more important reasons why Canadians desire interesting work that makes full use of their skills and abilities is that they have been socialized to expect it. *The socialization process in Canada involves an emphasis on achievement,* and that achievement involves a job that will enable you to do better than your parents and to fulfill yourself. Work—the right kind of work—is an integral part of the Canadian dream. That is why parents will forgo some of their own pleasures in order to send their children through university, and why professionals frequently prefer for their children to follow them in some kind of professional career.

In other words, you learn at an early age that if you are going to be happy, you must secure the kind of work that is conducive to the pursuit. As long as work is an integral part of individual fulfillment, and as long as the economy does not yield sufficient numbers of jobs that facilitate fulfillment, Canadians will continue to have the quality of their lives diminished by the contradiction between socialized expectations and the realities of society.

■■ The Ideology and Reality of Work

A final factor in work problems is the incongruity between the ideology about work and the reality of work. One line of thought, which dates back to the first Protestants, insists on the *value of all work.* The classic devotional writer William Law (1906:32) said that, "Worldly business is to be made holy unto the Lord, by being done as a service to Him, and in conformity to His Divine will." This ideology regards work as a sacred obligation and implies that all work is equally good.

Although Canadian ideology emphasizes the value of work and the equal value of all work, in practice not all work is given equal value. As noted earlier, some kinds of work are looked down upon by people who have jobs with higher prestige. Many Canadians accept the ideology that work of any kind is intrinsically superior to nonwork, only to find themselves disparaged by other Canadians who have "better" jobs. This ideology compounds the problems of the unemployed, who tend to define a social problem as personal and blame themselves for their plight. In addition, the work ideology may make the unemployed feel guilty about not working, even though they are the victims of a political–economic system rather than blame-worthy promoters of unemployment.

■■ From Social Problems to Solutions

The problems of work can be attacked in a number of different ways. First, with regard to unemployment, it is unlikely that the rate can go much lower than it was from the late 1990s through 2001. The challenge is not to bring the unemployment rate down to zero; this won't happen (even economists do not mean zero unemployment when they use the term "full employment"). The challenge is to keep the rate low by maintaining a strong economy while supporting those who are unemployed.

Government programs to train, or reschool, and find jobs for the unemployed are one form of support. Although such programs often benefit people, they also are usually controversial in terms of cost and effectiveness. Finding an effective job-training program is as much a political as a technical matter and, thus, requires a strong commitment from politicians.

Employment Insurance (EI) benefits are another form of support. Such benefits depend on action by both federal and state governments. Contrary to what some people believe, EI benefits are not automatically available to anyone who loses a job. In 2003, for example, just more than half (57.3 percent) of unemployed persons were "potentially eligible" to receive EI benefits (The Daily, June 22, 2004). Those who are ineligible to receive EI are no longer counted as being in the labour force. Thus, the unemployment rate does not capture how many Canadians are truly unemployed.

Being employed does not necessarily translate into a decent standard of living. Minimum wage in Canada varies from province to province (HRSDC 2004). British Columbia has the highest minimum wage of all Canadian provinces ($8.00 per hour), and Alberta and Newfoundland have the lowest ($5.90 and $6.00, respectively). Not all work sectors are covered by minimum wage—examples are certain groups of salespersons, farm workers, commercial fishers, oilfield workers, loggers, home-care givers, and home-based workers. Full-time workers who receive minimum wage have incomes well below the poverty line. Further, these jobs generally are not unionized, and do not offer benefits. This means that these workers get no pension, dental, and extended health benefits (such as drug plans), and no sick days.

Regarding the problem of work hazards, governmental and union actions have significantly reduced the incidence of occupational injuries and illnesses. The Occupational Health and Safety (OHS) legislation acts to enforce safety regulations. Since workers and management together have been actively involved in workplace health and safety committees, numbers of time-loss injuries have decreased. The IRS system is viewed as a success, and is being considered in the United States. That said, we need to be cautious in our praise of the IRS, as workplace mortality numbers have changed little over the last decades. When push comes to shove, the underlying goals of workers and management are fundamentally different, and consensus often works against the workers (Glasbeek and Tucker 1992). A health and safety program that is truly successful must at minimum reduce mortality rates. The only way to move forward is to give workers decision-making powers, and to implement a system that promotes inspections and enforcements (Glasbeek 1996).

There are various measures that can help address the problems of job dissatisfaction and alienation. From the earlier discussion about the causes of the problems, you can see that more challenging work, greater worker participation and control, and more worker autonomy are needed. In addition, the quality of the relationship between bosses and co-workers is closely related to job satisfaction. Workers who are on good terms with and feel supported by others at the workplace have higher levels of satisfaction than do others (Ting 1997; El-Bassel et al. 1998). Thus, programs that engage in team-building and conflict-resolution skills can enhance the quality of workplace relationships.

Job enrichment efforts also can reduce dissatisfaction and alienation. Job enrichment involves such things as more worker responsibility and less direct control over the worker. It also includes the upgrading of skills required for a job and enlargement of the job so that the worker is not confined to a single, highly specialized task. Some job enrichment programs have resulted in higher job satisfaction, higher levels of worker morale, fewer grievances, and less absenteeism and turnover.

Still another measure for dealing with dissatisfaction and alienation is *flextime*, which made its debut in North America in 1970 after being used successfully in Europe. There are at least three different types of flextime systems, varying by the amount of choice given to the worker. In one type, the employer lets the workers choose from a range of times to start their eight-hour workdays. A second type allows employees to choose their own schedules. Once chosen and approved, the schedules must be followed for a specified length of time. In a third type, employees can vary their own schedules on a daily basis without prior approval of supervisors. All types have limits within which employees must function. One in four Canadians now work under flextime, and the results include greater satisfaction, higher morale, increased productivity, and less stress driving to work (Worklife Compendium 2001).

Dissatisfaction and alienation also can be addressed through *participatory management or organizational democracy, which involves worker participation in the decision-making process.* Marshall Sashkin (1984) has called this measure an "ethical imperative." He notes that employees may participate in the decision-making process in four areas: setting organizational goals, solving problems, selecting from among alternative courses of action, and making changes in the organization. In more extreme forms of involvement, employees participate in decisions about hiring and firing and about their own wages and benefits.

Employees may participate in the decisions as individuals, as part of manager–employee pairs, or as members of a group of managers and employees. Such participation fulfills the needs of employees for some degree of control over their lives, for more meaningful work, and for the kind of involvement that attacks the problem of alienation. Participation programs can be costly to implement and conflict with the traditional management–worker relationship. However, they can improve productivity, quality control, and a company's market share of the product (Tausky and Chelte 1988).

A final measure is *employee ownership*, including the more radical form of *employee takeover of a company*. Thousands of companies now offer workers an employee share ownership plan (ESOP). There are four types of employee ownership plans in Canada (ESOP 2004).

- ESOPs started by employers to reward employees for their effort in making the company successful.
- ESOPs started by public companies to reward key employees for their efforts, and then expanded to include all employees through matching share purchase programs.
- ESOPs started due to financial crisis, utilizing provincial ESOP legislation; used mainly to save jobs.
- ESOPs started by employers and/or employees utilizing current tax laws and provincial legislation; some are for companies in crisis as well as healthy companies.

The results tend to be uniformly positive: higher productivity, lower costs, and greater worker satisfaction and morale.

▪▪ SUMMARY

The Canadian economy, the nature of work, and the nature of the workforce all have changed over time in Canada. Some recent changes in the economy that are detrimental to many Canadians are corporate downsizing, increased use of temporary workers, declining union strength, reduced corporate tax obligations, and decline in income for some families. The labour force and the division of labour have increased substantially. The educational level and the proportion of females in the labour force are also increasing. The work ethic remains strong, but workers now insist that their jobs be a source of fulfillment and not solely a source of income.

Work is a social problem because of unemployment and underemployment, work hazards, and dissatisfaction and alienation. Each year millions of Canadians are unemployed, though the rate varies for different groups and different occupations. Many Canadians are not deeply dissatisfied with or alienated from work, but many also desire a job different from the one they have. Among the hazards of work are work-induced stress and work-related injuries and illnesses.

Work is intimately related to the quality of life because it involves the worker's health. Work-induced stress, injuries and illnesses, and job dissatisfaction can all adversely affect the worker's health. Unemployment tends to be a traumatic, stressful experience that adverse-ly affects the worker's interpersonal relationships and health.

Capitalism, with its emphasis on profit, is one of the factors that contributes to problems in the Canadian economy. Subservience of workers' needs to organizational needs, union-busting, downsizing, and increased numbers of temporary jobs all reflect the drive for profit. Structural unemployment is also a product of the capitalistic system, which includes the natural swings of the economy, technological change, government spending priorities, and the growth of multinational corporations. The nature of work roles in the Canadian technological, bureaucratic society produces much dissatisfaction, stress, and conflict. Work hazards are frequently more common than necessary because companies give priority to profit, not to worker health and safety.

Among social psychological factors that add to the problems of work are the attitudes of Canadians toward visible minorities and toward other Canadians whose jobs they regard as inferior to their own. The contradiction between the ideology and reality of work is another contributing factor. The ideology glorifies work and working and places an equal value on all work. The reality is disparagement of some work and a political–economic system that guarantees a certain amount of unemployment.

▪▪ KEY TERMS

Capitalism 245
Division of Labour 247
Downsizing 246
Labour Force 247
Underemployment 251
Unemployment Rate 251
Work Ethic 245

▪▪ STUDY QUESTIONS

1. How have the economy, work, and the workforce been changing in Canada?
2. What are some consequences for workers of the globalization of the economy?
3. Discuss whether the meaning of work is changing.
4. How much and what kinds of unemployment are there in Canada?
5. How serious are the problems of work dissatisfaction and of hazards at work?
6. How do work problems affect people's health and interpersonal relationships?
7. How do state and work policies alter Canadians' labour force activity?
8. How have technological changes in the workplace affected women's work?
9. In what ways do contemporary work roles increase job dissatisfaction and alienation?
10. How has union membership in Canada changed over the last decade?
11. Discuss the contradiction between the ideology and the reality of work in Canada.
12. What can Canadians do to reduce unemployment, job hazards, and job dissatisfaction?

▪▪ FOR FURTHER READING

Duffy, A. and N. Pupo. *Part-time Paradox: Connecting Gender, Work & Family*. Toronto: McClelland and Stewart, 1992. Although published in 1992, the theoretical concepts on part-time work and family continue to be applicable.

Galenson, Walter. *Trade Union Growth and Decline: An International Study*. Westport, CT: Praeger, 1994. Looks at the situation of unions in 25 nations and shows that unions are declining in most of them. Discusses how union growth and decline are related to economic growth.

Messing, K. *One-Eyed Science: Occupational Health and Women Workers*. Philadelphia: Temple University Press, 1984. Messing argues convincingly that women's health problems largely are rendered invisible because of gender biases in the workers' compensation systems that recognize only health problems associated with men's traditional jobs.

Milkman, Ruth. *Farewell to the Factory: Auto Workers in the Late Twentieth Century*. Berkeley: University of California Press, 1997. A case study of an automobile plant that experienced downsizing and transformation. Describes in detail the experience of workers both before and after the change.

Rinehart, J.W. *The Tyranny of Work: Alienation and Labour Process*. 4th edition. Toronto: Thomson Nelson, 2001. A Canadian text that examines work as a social problem.

Rogers, Jackie Krasas. *Temps: The Many Faces of the Changing Workplace*. Ithaca, NY: Cornell University Press, 2000. A critique of the temporary worker trend, dispelling some of the myths about why people work part time and showing the stress experienced by those unwillingly caught up in temp work.

Schaeffer, Robert K. *Understanding Globalization: The Social Consequences of Political, Economic, and Environmental Change*. Lanham, MD: Rowman & Littlefield, 1997. Shows the pervasive effects of the globalization of the economy on social life and human well-being.

▪▪ NOTES

1. Reported in *The Public Perspective*, April–May 1999, p. 16.

2. The minister supplied the authors with this account.

EDUCATION

"I KEPT MY MOUTH SHUT"

In theory, all Canadians have an equal chance to prove themselves in school. In practice, you are disadvantaged if you come from a poor or minority-group family. Marcia is an undergraduate student who comes from a middle-class family. She remembers with some regret about the time she learned how others are disadvantaged:

> I was in Grade 1 when I learned that we weren't all really equal at school. It was recess and I was playing on the monkey bars. One of my classmates was playing beside me. Her name was Ramona. She came from a poor family. I didn't think about it at the time, but she was very ill-kept. Neither she nor her clothes were very clean. But I liked her. I enjoyed playing with her at recess.

> As we were playing, and Ramona was turning around on the bars, some of the other girls began to make fun of her and talk about her dirty underwear. I felt sorry for her and mad at the other girls for saying such mean things to her. I hollered to them: "She can't help it if her underwear is dirty." No sooner had I said it than the strong voice of our teacher came booming at us: "Yes, she can."

> I could see the embarrassment on Ramona's face. She got off the monkey bars and went over and sat by herself on a bench for the rest of the recess. I'm ashamed to say that the teacher really intimidated me. I felt really bad about Ramona, but I was very careful to keep my mouth shut about it after that. I didn't want to incur the teacher's wrath, and I didn't want all the other girls to reject me.

> I think it was about Grade 4 when I no longer saw Ramona. I don't know if she dropped out or her family moved or what. I do know that she never did well in school. But I don't think it was because she wasn't smart. Ramona just never had much of a chance. ■

■■ INTRODUCTION

If you are reading this book, it is probably because you are one of the almost one million students currently enrolled in a Canadian university (The Daily, July 30, 2004). As such, you are one of the privileged few who can a) afford university tuition, b) have high enough grades to obtain admittance into university (and perhaps a tuition scholarship to assist with paying your fees and living expenses), or c) come from a family background and cultural group that recognizes and supports education as a valuable tool to gaining employment opportunities in the future. Or, you may have none of these advantages but do possess the determination, in spite of great challenges, to acquire the Canadian dream of a "good education."

In a recent *Maclean's* magazine poll leading up to the 2004 federal election, Canadians ranked education (along with health care and social services) as the number-one priority for government interv0on and the need for increased expenditure (*Maclean's* 2004). In a previous online poll (Dec. 29, 2003), *Maclean's* asked readers what they considered the most important issue facing Canada today. Education was ranked the sixth cause of concern among those who responded (*Maclean's* 2003).

Over the past ten years, an author of this textbook has asked hundreds of Social Problems students to provide a list of what they deem the top five social problems facing Canadians. They have always placed education in the top three. When questioned further, they speak about education as a social problem for the following reasons:

1. Increased tuition costs.
2. Increased student loan debt.
3. Lack of inclusivity in core curriculums so that the experiences of non-white, disabled, lesbian, gay, bisexual, and transgendered persons and immigrants are not included.
4. Lack of student engagement in their courses and in the willingness of instructors to solicit their opinions and experiences.
5. Decreased access to university due to higher costs, more competitive grading systems, and more international students being encouraged to attend Canadian universities. (International students often pay a differential, higher fee than Canadian students and they complain about that, plus the lack of services to accommodate their needs socially, culturally, and in a religious context).
6. Lack of teachers in non-university/college classrooms.
7. Inadequate training of teachers at all levels.
8. Lack of adequate facilities in schools, especially as regards recreation, language, and science laboratories and access to computers.
9. Overly large class sizes with less access to instructors on a one-to-one basis.
10. Lack of practical experiences and information that is related to potential jobs. (Many universities provide practicum placements for some disciplines, usually in the sciences, but seldom for arts or other programs.)
11. Too many school buildings in need of repair and/or maintenance; "sick building" syndrome.
12. Not enough government support of education at any level.

As you can see, these particular students—who are, after all, the consumers of the educational system in Canada—are able to produce a long list of what they see as social problems when it comes to education. These opinions, although derived from students at just one Canadian university, are nonetheless shared with their colleagues elsewhere, including those in organizations such as the Canadian Union of Students. When education is in trouble it is a very serious matter, because education is the foundation of Canadian life.

In what sense has education become a problem? In this chapter we first look at the functions of education and the high value typically placed on education. We also show how the high value is reflected in the continually "higher" amount of education attained by Canadians.

In light of the functions and value of education, we look at how certain problems such as unequal opportunities bear upon the quality of life of Canadians. We then examine some structural and social psychological factors that contribute to the problems and conclude with some examples of efforts to resolve the problems.

▪▪ WHY EDUCATION?

What do Canadians expect their educational system to achieve for them personally and for their society? There are many functions of the educational system. Some are obvious, such as a) socializing young people to learn the expected behaviours, rules, and values of their culture, b) training individuals for general and specific careers and work opportunities, c) providing the opportunity for personal growth and development and meeting like-minded others with whom to socialize and learn, and d) enabling students to meet, read, and hear about the experiences of others from cultures that are vastly different from (and similar to) their own.

In contrast, there are also some less obvious functions of the educational system, such as the reproduction and maintenance of a particular white, middle-class, heterosexual, able-bodied social order. Smith (1992) has noted that there is a "hidden curriculum" of education that centres on cultural indoctrination and social control "which … helps control meaning. It preserves and distributes what is previewed to be 'legitimate knowledge'—the knowledge that 'we' must all have. Thus schools confer cultural legitimacy on the knowledge of specific groups at the expense of others" (76).

In this sense, education can be seen as a means to assimilate diverse members of society into a group that reflects not the diversity the individuals represent, but rather the sameness or assimilation that those who control culture wish to achieve.

If you are an "average" Canadian student (whoever she or he may be), you are probably sitting in a classroom built (or renovated) more than 50 to 100 years ago, with desks arranged in rows facing the front of the room, where a teacher sits or stands and lectures at you (with or without a computer console or some other technological aid). This physical setting and its layout is more than just a particular configuration of items and people in space. It also represents a graphic representation of the ideological assumption about what learning is, and "should be."

Thus, one function of education is to create *good and effective citizens.* There is some dispute about what it means to be a good citizen, however. Some believe that education should produce citizens who will accept traditional values and protect the "Canadian way of life" (which obviously means different things to different people). Education does this as it transmits the **culture** from one generation to the next; that is, as it *socializes the young into the basic values, beliefs, and customs of the society.* Others believe that education should equip the citizenry to reshape their society so that the flaws and inequities are eliminated. In any case, education has been held to be essential in the process of creating effective citizens in the republic.

A second function of education is to provide the individual with the *possibility for upward mobility.* For a long time Canadians have associated education with good jobs. Most students in colleges and universities are there to prepare for the better-paying and more prestigious jobs, not for the love of learning. Education achieves this function as it *instructs the young in knowledge and skills.*

culture
the way of life of a people, including both material products (such as technology) and nonmaterial characteristics (such as values, norms, language, and beliefs)

The third function of education is personal development. Education does this by *liberating people from the bonds of ignorance and preparing them to maximize their intellectual, emotional, and social development.* This function is important to educators, but few people set educational goals with personal development in mind. Many researchers of education in Canada also refer to the functions of education as "credentialing" students, not only in terms of the previous tasks, but also with regards to preparing them for employment after graduation.

Whatever their views of the primary aim of education, most Canadians would probably agree that all three functions are legitimate. The schools should produce good citizens. They should help the individual to better himself or herself, and they should prepare the individual to maximize his or her own development. Since all three functions are related to the *quality of life* of the individual, if any person or group is not given the opportunity to secure an education that fulfills the functions, education becomes a social problem. Quality of life is diminished when the individual lacks the tools necessary to participate effectively in political processes, to achieve some measure of success in work or a career, or to develop his or her potential to its fullest.

■■ EDUCATIONAL ATTAINMENT AND PAYOFF

Because of its importance to quality of life, you would expect Canadians to secure an increasing amount of education over time. Most do aspire to a high level, but what about the **attainment**? Once attained, does education yield the expected payoff? Is the high value on education reflected in concrete results?

■■ Levels of Attainment

attainment
as distinguished from educational "achievement," the number of years of education completed by a student

Educational attainment varies globally. According to the World Bank, an average universal basic or even primary education has not been achieved in many countries. Moreover, enrollment rates do not fit into a single neat pattern: countries and groups within countries display a variety of profiles in educational attainment. For example, in Brazil nearly all children aged 15 to 19 have completed at least one year of schooling, while only 56 percent have completed Grade 6—the implied dropout rate is high and constant over time. In contrast, in India 56 percent have completed Grade 6 but this is the result of only 70 percent completing Grade 1 and a relatively low dropout rate. In Indonesia, virtually all have completed Grade 1 and 85 percent have completed Grade 6, but only 53 percent have completed Grade 7. In Mali, only 12 percent of the poor have completed Grade 1, whereas 60 percent of the rich have done so (World Bank 2004).

Another way to look at the increasing education attainment is to note the diminishing *dropout rate.* Students begin to drop out of school after Grade 5. Since the 1920s, the proportion dropping out, especially before completing elementary school, has decreased greatly. The likelihood of dropping out, however, varies among different groups. Males are more likely to drop out than are females. Those in the lower socioeconomic strata are more likely than those in higher strata to drop out. Except for Asian Canadians, minority groups have higher dropout rates than whites. The rate is particularly high among Aboriginal Canadians, who are 2.6 times more likely to drop out of school than non-Aboriginals (Gilbert and Ork 1993:3). According to a report by Maria Spergel (2004), each year in Canada 18 percent of high school students drop out. Reasons provided by the students range from poverty in the family that requires the student to find work; to having parents who also dropped out of school and so don't provide support in the home for school-related activities such as homework; to bullying in

FIGURE 10.1 ■ ■ ■

Proportion of the population aged 25–64 with college or university qualifications, top ten OECD countries, 2001.

Source: OECD, http://www.oecd.org/home

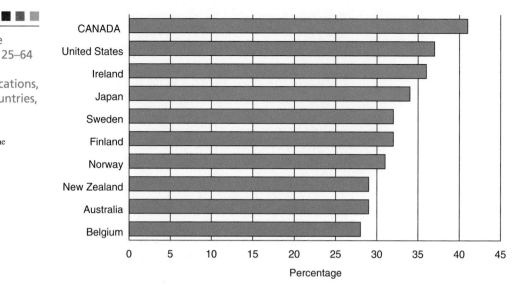

the schools; to low self-esteem that hinders academic achievement for many of the previously stated reasons.

In another report, compiled by Social Development Canada (1997), the authors noted that a quarter of all school dropouts do return to complete high school because they recognize the importance of a high school diploma when looking for work.

Overall, then, the level of educational attainment has been steadily increasing in Canada, a reflection in part of the changing occupational structure and the consequent need for increased education. As figure 10.1 shows, Canada is a world leader in university attendance. In 2001–2 a record number of students enrolled in Canadian universities, exceeding the peak recorded in 1992–3. In its strongest increase in ten years, university enrollment rose by 4.3 percent, reaching the record number of 886,800.

Not only did the number of Canadian students increase in that year, so too did the rate of foreign students attending Canadian universities. In 2001–2 the number of 52,000 was up 60 percent compared with 1997–8. In total, international students comprise approximately 6 percent of the student population in Canada, coming mainly from European countries, North and Central America, and the Caribbean (The Daily, July 30, 2004).

The minimum amount of education considered appropriate today is completion of high school, and the majority of Canadians have reached that level. The dropout rate, which once increased steadily from Grade 5 on, now tends to remain minimal until after Grade 8. Canadians are getting more and more education. Is it yielding the expected payoff?

■■ Attainment and Payoff

In some ways you cannot talk about the *payoff of education*. You cannot, for instance, measure the personal development of individuals and correlate that with education. However, there is a positive relationship between happiness and educational level; that is, the higher the level of education, the higher the reported happiness and satisfaction with life (Jonas and Wilson 1997). Of course, happiness and life satisfaction are not measures of personal development—the fulfillment of an individual's potential. At best, you can say that the greater happiness and satisfaction reported by the better educated may reflect a tendency toward greater fulfillment of potential.

More educated people are also more likely to hold democratic values and to support democratic practices. While such relationships indicate positive contributions of education to citizenship, they do not tell us whether education helps people to detect and reject demagoguery and to participate meaningfully in the defence of freedom and the shaping of a just social order. Education does increase political participation and understanding. However, the more educated usually are the political and corporate heads who accept and maintain the institutional policies and practices that can contribute to the various social problems of the nation.

There is more evidence with respect to the third function of education—providing a means of upward mobility. We know that there is a strong relationship between levels of education and income. According to Statistics Canada (2003), those who completed a university degree were likely to earn as much as 20 to 30 percent more annually than those who did not. Individuals with degrees at the master and doctoral levels were also more likely to earn higher overall salaries, as figure 10.2 shows.

The majority of the close to half a million people who were making $100,000 or more in 2000 were university-educated men in their prime working years. While men accounted for about 84 percent, or 373,000, of the 447,000 people in this earnings bracket, this figure was lower than in 1990, when men accounted for 89 percent of this same group.

The majority of female high earners working full-year, full-time were in only 15 occupational categories. The top two categories for women were lawyers and general practitioners/family physicians. Combined, they accounted for more than 10 percent of high-earning women (The Daily, March 11, 2003).

Does this mean that an individual can maximize his or her income by maximizing education? In general, yes. But to assume that *anyone* can reach the highest levels of income by maximizing education is the *fallacy of non sequitur*. Your background, including your racial or ethnic identity, and the economy are among the factors that affect your chances. We discuss this in some detail later, but the point here is that the high correlation between education and income does not mean that education is the open road to success. Those who attain high levels of education are likely to be those

FIGURE 10.2 ■ ■ ■

Relative earnings by level of educational attainment, 25- to 64-year-olds.

Source: Table E 2.4. OECD, http://www.oecd.org/home

Notes: Countries are ranked in descending order of relative earnings for the population with university education.

This figure was last updated on June 23, 2004.

Statistics Canada. 2003. *Education indicators in Canada: Report of the Pan-Canadian Education Indicators Program.*

Catalogue no. 81-582-XIE. Ottawa

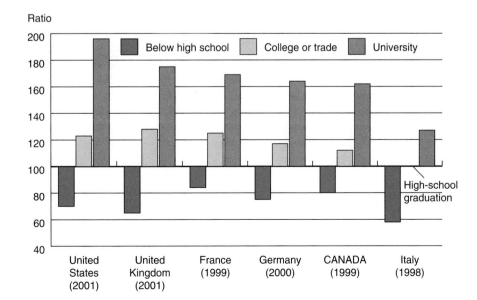

EDUCATIONAL ATTAINMENT, BY COUNTRY

A nation cannot successfully modernize or implement a political democracy without an educated populace. People must be educated in order to function effectively in the kinds of jobs associated with an industrial economy, and they must be educated in order to participate meaningfully in a democratic political process.

An economist argued that economic growth cannot begin in a country until at least 6 percent of the population is enrolled in primary school (Peaslee 1969). As the country continues to modernize, increasing educational levels are required. Thus, nations like the United States that are the most economically and technologically developed typically have the highest average levels of educational attainment.

Political leaders are aware of the crucial importance of education and in most nations are attempting to provide expanded educational opportunities. Table 10.1 shows the educational attainment of a number of nations throughout the world. Note that the richer countries tend to have a much lower proportion of the population at the lowest level of education. More than 80 percent of adults ages 25 to 64 have attained more than an elementary school education in the United States, Germany, and Switzerland.

In contrast, in nations like Turkey, Greece, and Spain, nations that are far better off economically than the poorer of the world, two-thirds or more of the population lack a high school education. With such disparities in educational attainment, it is unlikely that the inequalities between nations in such things as income, employment, and standard of living will lessen in the near future.

Country	Percentage of Persons 25 to 64 Years Old With			
	Early Childhood, Primary, and Lower Secondary Education	Upper Secondary Education	Nonuniversity Tertiary Education	University Education
Australia	44	31	9	17
Belgium	43	31	13	12
Canada	20	28	33	19
Finland	32	39	17	13
Germany	16	56	13	14
Greece	54	25	8	11
Ireland	49	30	10	11
Norway	17	57	3	24
Spain	67	13	6	14
Switzerland	19	56	9	14
Turkey	82	11	1	6
United Kingdom	19	57	8	15
United States	14	52	8	27

Source: U.S. Census Bureau 2001:839.

TABLE 10.1 ■ ■ ■

Educational Attainment, by Country

It is important to recognize that there are dramatic differences in educational attainment depending on where one lives in the world.

whose parents had a relatively high level of education. There is mobility in Canada, but education is more useful to the privileged as a means of passing on their privileges to their children than as a means for the underdog to be upwardly mobile.

Some people have argued that education is of no use in reducing inequality in Canada, that schools do virtually nothing to help the poor be upwardly mobile, and that education has little effect on the future incomes of people. Rather, they feel that economic opportunities depend upon the state of the economy; one's family background; and various other noneducational factors, such as the contacts one is able to make.

It is true that education alone is not sufficient to deal with economic inequality, and it is true that the best way to "get ahead" is to start from a high socioeconomic position (obviously something over which the individual has no control). This argument overstates the case, however. The advantaged child will not maintain his or her advantage without an education, and at least some people gain new advantages through education. Education is not a cure-all, but it is not useless in the struggle for new advantages. Thus, in their study of how people achieve positions in top corporate management, Useem and Karabel (1986) found that

1. Those who achieve such positions tend to have a bachelor's degree from a top-ranked college or university, an MBA from a prestigious program, or a law degree from a top-ranked university.
2. Given the same amount of education, an upper-class background improves one's chances of reaching the top.

You may conclude, then, that while many people are upwardly mobile through educational attainment, those most likely to benefit from education are already in the middle and upper strata. In terms of mobility, the payoff from education is not equally likely for all groups.

■■ EDUCATION AND THE QUALITY OF LIFE

Ideally, as we have shown, education performs a number of valued functions that enhance the quality of life. It prepares you to be a good, effective citizen. It is the pathway to your social and economic betterment. It is the tool by which you develop your full potential as an individual. To perform such functions, education would have to be of high quality, be equally available to all, and consistently yield the expected payoff. Education is a problem because there are inequalities, and the expected payoff does not always occur.

■■ Inequality of Opportunity and Attainment

Besides the inequality of attainment we have touched on, there is *inequality of opportunity*—a debatable and ambiguous notion, as you will see. Such inequalities contradict *the Canadian value of education and the ideology of equal opportunities* for all. Ideally, every Canadian ought to have equal opportunity to maximize his or her education. However, minorities and the poor do not attain the same educational levels as white males. Is this inequality of attainment a reflection of unequal opportunities or of some characteristics of the groups themselves? You have seen in previous chapters that the answer is both, but that the characteristics of the groups do not include an inferior level of intelligence. Part of the reason a son of a poor white farmer does not go to university may be his own lack of motivation, but even that lack must be seen as a social phenomenon that is rooted in a complex situation in which multiple factors work together. In other words, unequal educational attainment does not mean that those groups with lower levels of attainment are incapable of extending their education. It is important to keep this in mind as we explore the ways in which educational opportunities and attainment are distributed in society.

The Meaning of Unequal Opportunities.

There is debate over the meaning of inequality of opportunity. Most Canadians, including most social scientists, would affirm the *ideal of equal educational opportunity* for all. But what does that mean? Does it mean that all children should be schooled with equal amounts of money? Does it mean that the proportion of people of various kinds (minorities and those from different socioeconomic strata) in the differing educational levels should be the same as their proportion in the total population? Does it mean that each child should have access to the same quality and the same amount of education? Does it mean that the same amount of education should yield the same payoff in terms of income or personal development?

Or are all these matters important? If, for instance, you define equality as equal funds per student, children could still attend segregated schools or be less likely to attend university if they are black, Aboriginal, or poor.

Since the meaning of unequal opportunities is debated, it is unlikely that we can settle upon a definition that will be acceptable to everyone. Nevertheless, it is important to select a meaning so that we can explore the extent of inequality in Canada. For our purposes, equality of educational opportunity means that every child has access to quality education and is not deterred from maximizing that education by social background or economic factors. Social background factors include race, ethnic origin, sex, and socioeconomic status. Economic factors include the funding of education and the cost to the student. In brief, equality means that all Canadians, whatever their background, have the opportunity to attain fairly equal amounts of education. It also means that students attend schools that are equally funded and that the cost of post-secondary education does not force some students to drop out before they have reached their goal. In these terms, how much inequality is there?

Inequality of Attainment.

We have given figures in previous chapters on *differences in educational attainment*. A measure of inequality may be the proportion of various groups that has attained different levels of education. In a recent *Maclean's* magazine article, Bergman noted that more than half of the country's 800,000-plus Aboriginal population is under the age of 25. The number of Aboriginal people of working age will double in the next ten years, growing at a rate three to five times faster than that of other Canadians. According to the latest available Canadian Census figures, only 3 percent of status Indians 15 years and older hold university degrees, compared to 14 percent of other Canadians. Of those who made it to university, only 36 percent of status Indians completed a degree; the comparable figure for non-natives is 64 percent (Bergman 2002).

However, in *The Daily* on September 24, 2003, Statistics Canada noted that educational levels for Aboriginal people across the country were increasing as many more were completing post-secondary studies. However, many obstacles still exist that hinder Aboriginal youth from attending educational establishments. Among those aged 25 to 44, family responsibilities topped the list of reasons for not finishing post-secondary studies. Although most governmental departments of education are now providing additional funds in the form of scholarships to encourage Aboriginal Canadians to improve their educational status, there are still obstacles to overcome before they are able to do so.

The reasons for these variations are unclear, but they do caution us against the assumption that ethnicity per se is the only important variable in understanding attainment levels of Canada's minorities.

Funding and Costs. The second aspect of unequal opportunities is the *funding and cost of education.* Children do not have equal educational opportunities if they attend schools with unequal resources or if they are forced to drop out at some point because they cannot pay for the cost of their education.

There are considerable inequalities of resources, both among the provinces and among school boards within a province. According to the Statistics Canada publication "Report of the Pan-Canadian Education Indicators Program 2003," between 1997–8 and 2001–2 the total governmental expenditure on education rose 6 percent; the average cost per student for all educational levels combined rose 5.6 percent, while the expenditure per capita increased by 2 percent.

In the years 1999–2000, expenditure on education represented 6.6 percent of the Canadian gross domestic product (GDP), with Canada ranking first among the G-7 countries with funds allocated to education. The United States was second. The territories and smaller provinces allocated a higher percentage of their GDP to education than did larger provinces.

In 2001, all governments—federal, provincial, and territorial—spent 15 percent of their total expenditure on education, compared to 17 percent for health.

Private funding also helps to pay for education in Canada. In 2001–2, private sources provided 7 percent of all monies spent on education at the elementary level, and 27 percent at the post-secondary level. In 2002, 43 percent of households incurred educational expenses, spending an average of $1,946. Tuition fees at all universities in Canada also increased during the 1990s. They almost doubled for undergraduate programs between 1990–1 and 2001–2, rising from an average of $1,806 to $3,585. Between 1990–1 and 1999–2000, student tuition and other non-governmental revenues increased from 32 percent to 45 percent of total university revenue. Most of the expenditures at the elementary–secondary level are on teachers' salaries, which accounted for three-quarters of all expenditures in 1999–2000 (Pan-Canadian Education Indicators Program 2003).

Some provinces, such as New Brunswick, Manitoba, and Saskatchewan, spent more money on education over the past ten years, while other provinces spent less. The provincial breakdown of costs for post-secondary education is shown in table 10.2.

The province of Nova Scotia, which decreased spending on post-secondary education over the past ten years, also has the highest tuition costs in Canada at approximately $6,000 per student. Overall, undergraduate students paid an average of $4,025 in tuition fees for the 2004 academic year. The only areas of the country in which tuition fees either declined or remained constant were in Newfoundland and Labrador—the average undergraduate fees in this province dropped 4.5 percent to $2,606 in 2003–4.

Year	NL	PEI	NS	NB	QC	ON	MB	SK	AB	BC	Canada
1992–3	6.4%	5.1%	7.5%	5.6%	7.6%	5.8%	4.4%	5.1%	6.4%	5.9%	6.3%
2002–3	5.6%	4.7%	5.5%	6.1%	6.2%	5.4%	6.7%	6.5%	5.2%	5.5%	5.7%

TABLE 10.2 ■ ■ ■

Breakdown of Post-Secondary Education Costs by Province

Source: Canadian Association of University Teachers, *Almanac of Post-Secondary Education*: Ottawa: 2004:34.

The biggest increases in university tuition were in the faculties of dentistry, medicine, and law, which also continue to be the most expensive programs. Average tuition fees in dentistry rose 20.9 percent to $11,733 in 2004; medical students paid an average of $9,406 (up by 16.7 percent); and law students paid $5,995 on average, a 19.4-percent increase over previous years (*The Daily*, August 12, 2004).

Graduate students enrolled in Canadian universities were also paying higher tuition fees across the country, with the average tuition rising by 6.8 percent to $51,999. International students, who already pay a differential fee to attend Canadian universities, saw an increase in their tuition by 7.5 percent, to an average of $11,256 (ibid).

The figures provided above refer to university tuition costs only and do not reflect the additional compulsory fees, such as those for accommodations, meals, recreation and athletics, student health services, and student associations, which have also increased over the past ten years. It is clearly becoming more expensive to achieve the Canadian ideal of post-secondary education. Moreover, there are provincial and regional differences in the cost of maintaining schools. Still, children in one of those regions below the national average in school expenditures will have to go to a school that is less well funded.

We are cautious about our conclusions. A particular school in a region with lower-than-average funding may offer an immeasurably better education than another region, but to conclude from this example that the lower-than-average region offers a better education is the *fallacy of dramatic instance*. The point is not that every school in the better-funded region is better than every school in the more poorly funded one. Rather, overall, the schools in the better-funded region have an advantage in resources for educating students, so that the typical student is likely to experience an education backed by greater resources.

Funding also varies considerably within provinces. Schools have been funded by the property tax (discussed in more detail later). This means that a school board populated largely by people from lower-income groups who live in cheaper homes will have a low tax base. School boards that encompass affluent areas, on the other hand, may actually have a lower rate of taxation (number of dollars of school tax per assessed value of the property) but a much higher per-pupil income. An affluent school district may have double, triple, or quadruple the funds per pupil that an adjacent poor school district has. Should the funds available for a child's schooling be considerably less because of the neighbourhood in which he or she happens to be born?

Similarly, you may ask whether an individual should drop out of university because of inadequate financial resources even though he or she is quite capable of doing the work. In a recent *Maclean's* magazine article, readers were asked to respond to the following question: Is rising tuition deterring Canadians from pursuing a post-secondary education? Thousands of Canadians responded to the poll: the answers were Yes = 80%, No = 20% (*Maclean's*, November 24, 2003).

In 2000, about half of all college graduates and those who graduated with bachelor's degrees left school owing money for their education, mostly in the form of government student loans. On average, these students owed $20,000. One in seven graduates, about 14 percent, owed $25,000 or more in student loan debts upon graduating (The Daily, April 26, 2004).

Many students who graduate with large student loan debts cannot afford to wait for work in their chosen field and take jobs that cause them to be underemployed in terms of their skill levels and interests. Students who choose to advance their education and enroll in graduate education obviously increase their debt load considerably, but some choose this option with the hope of increased earnings after graduation rather than entering the job market for a low salary. This means that millions of Canadian families have annual incomes less than the cost of room, board, and tuition at an average university. Moreover, the disparity between those who can and those who cannot afford university is expected to grow. There are no signs yet that the spiralling costs of higher education will stop.

In sum, the quality of life for many Canadians is depressed because of unequal opportunities at all levels of education. Many children cannot afford to go to university. Their level of attainment will be less than their abilities warrant and often less than they desire. Those same children probably attended elementary and secondary schools that spent less on them than other schools could spend. Inequality in education exists from kindergarten to university.

■■ The Atmosphere: Learning or Surviving?

atmosphere
the general mood and social influences in a situation or place

Another kind of inequality that contradicts the Canadian ideology of equal opportunity involves the **atmosphere** of the school. Some atmospheres are conducive to learning, some inhibit learning, and some require the student to focus on surviving—merely getting through the institution with body and sanity intact.

Education as Boring.   One frequently heard criticism is that education is boring (Gallagher et al. 1997; Kastelic and McLinn 1997; Babbage 1998). For example, boredom often results when students are required to memorize large amounts of data that are not integrated with each other and not linked to important principles or ideas. Thus, history students may be required to memorize names, dates, and events without discussing their significance for understanding the processes of social life.

Boredom can afflict students at any level. The slowest students may be bored because they cannot grasp the materials. Others may be bored because they see no point to what they are doing. Gifted children may also suffer from boredom. Boredom may lead them to behave as if they lack interest or are unable to focus their attention (Webb 2000).

The Atmosphere of Fear.   Perhaps even worse than boredom is the *atmosphere of fear* in which some students must function. Some students are afraid to attend school as the result of bullying behaviours that occur there. Paula Buchanan of the Red Deer School District and Margret Winzer of the University of Lethbridge in Alberta conducted research into the effects of bullying on children's self-perception (2004). In reviewing the literature on school bullying the authors found that this behaviour occurs in every school district in Canada. Some studies in larger cities reported that up to 49 percent of students experience some form of bullying on a regular basis.

Children most often bullied included those from poorer families, immigrants, those assumed to be lesbian or gay, and those with physical disabilities. Children who came from homes in which violence was present were more likely to bully others.

There are no studies that accurately reflect the total number of students who experience bullying in schools across the county, and school boards are naturally disinclined to research this social problem fully. However, a review of the literature from various sources would indicate that school bullying is on the increase in Canada.

cyberbullying
bullying through e-mail, cell phones, and instant messaging

Cyberbullying is a new source of bullying prevalent on the Internet, where young teens in particular turn to the World Wide Web as a source of support and companionship when they feel rejected at school. As Snider and Borel note, "cyberbullies' weapons of choice are e-mail, cell phones that can send text messages, and instant messaging programs that allow users to chat electronically in real time … sites have emerged where students vote on their school's biggest geek or sluttiest girl" (2004).

To keep the situation in perspective, it is important to point out that *students are safer at school than away from school.* They are more likely to be victimized in settings other than the school building, but this does not erase the fear they experience in school.

▪▪ The Payoff: A Great Training Robbery?

One of the Canadian expectations about education is that it will pay off in terms of upward mobility. Historically, the correlation between education and income has been strong, but in the early 1970s a *contradiction developed between education and the economy.* Educational attainment outstripped the capacity of the economy to absorb the graduates into jobs commensurate with their training. Even when the unemployment rate is very low, many workers cannot find employment that utilizes the skills and training they have (Livingstone 1998). *The disparity between educational attainment and the skill demands of the workplace means that some workers are underemployed.* Canada entered the 21st century with a better educated population than ever, according to the 2001 Census. The hallmark of the 1990s was the tremendous growth in the number of Canadians with a college or university education, a trend that began at the end of the Second World War.

According to the Census, 28 percent of all individuals aged 25 to 34 had university qualifications, and 21 percent held a college diploma. Another 12 percent had trade credentials. In all, 61 percent of people in this age group had qualifications beyond high school.

Average annual earnings surpassed $30,000 for the first time in 2001; this was a 7.3-percent gain from the previous Census in 1996. As well, high income earners—those who make $80,000 or more a year—also increased significantly in 2001. These results are seen to be directly attributed to the rising number of Canadians with increased education (The Daily, March 11, 2003).

Another part of the problem is the assumption that greater educational attainment guarantees career advancement. In fact, employers do not routinely reward educational attainment; rather, they reward it only when they believe it will contribute to the employee's productivity (Spilerman and Lunde 1991).

However, keep in mind that there is still a strong correlation between education, occupation, and income. Over a lifetime, average income will range from $1.2 million for high school graduates, to $2.1 million for those with a bachelor's degree, to $3.4 million for those with a doctoral degree and $4.4 million for those with professional degrees (Bergman 2002). It is a minority of workers who are affected by a contradiction between their training and the economy.

You also should keep in mind that the diminished payoff refers strictly to employment and income. Unfortunately, Canadians have focused so strongly on the economic payoff that many consider their post-secondary education useless if it does not yield a desirable, well-paying job. Only in this sense can we speak of an "oversupply" of university graduates. We could argue that all or at least the majority of Canadians would profit by some university, because higher education can enable the individual to think more deeply, explore more widely, and enjoy a greater range of experiences; but as long as education is valued only for its economic payoff, any failure to yield that payoff will depress the quality of life of those involved.

▪▪ Canadian Education: A Challenging Time?

Periodically, observers make severe criticisms of Canadian education. Benjamin Levin of the University of Manitoba (1998) compared the literature indicating that educators have been facing intense and elevated levels of criticism since the 1950s in Canada. He set out to compare the levels of criticism from 1957 to the present and found that very little has changed in either the severity of the criticism or its content.

Levin noted that the list of criticisms continues to include the following:

In 1957:

1. Public schools are controlled or dominated by professional educationists of schools of education, school superintendents, "experts" in the fields of education, and governmental offices of education.
2. John Dewey and "progressive education" have taken over the public schools, and this philosophy is the chief cause of the crisis in education.
3. The life adjustment education movement is replacing intellectual training with soft social programs in most public school systems.
4. The spirit of competition, an important incentive for learning, has been eliminated by the 100-percent annual promotion policy and the multiple-standard report cards.
5. Lax discipline in the public school system is contributing to the increase in juvenile delinquency.
6. The teaching of classical and modern foreign languages is disappearing from the secondary schools.
7. High school students, even the bright ones, are avoiding science and mathematics; fewer students are taking these courses now than 30 years ago.
8. Public school is neglecting the gifted children because they are geared to teaching the average child.
9. Public schools are neglecting the training of children in moral and spiritual values.
10. The academic standards of schools of education are low; their programs of study are of questionable value, and the intellectual qualities of their students are the poorest in the universities.

In 1997:

The above still apply, with the addition of:

11. Declining test scores.
12. Poor performance on international achievement comparisons.
13. A supposed increase in funding without positive results.
14. High school dropout rates increasing.
15. The need for a stronger link between school and work.

As a result of his study, Levin concludes that schools will always be the subject of intense criticism for at least two reasons. First, society's goals for schools are extremely ambitious. As he notes, "In an important sense, schooling is about perfection. We want our schools to do everything—shape young people who are thoughtful, productive, and articulate, considerate, knowledgeable, patriotic, worldly, idealistic, challenging, accepting, critical, loyal. We expect our schools to teach children knowledge, skills, and values and to overcome the same social problems that adults have been unable to solve, to reduce poverty, to build the economy, to save the environment, to include the excluded, to look after oneself and care for others, to overcome materialism." Second, Levin argues that much of the criticism of schooling is based on the fact that people do not agree about which of the previous goals are most important or about how any given goal is best accomplished. Some want to stress individual excellence, and others social equity. Schools cannot satisfy all of the expectations all Canadians have of them. However, Levin's work does point out that Canadians do care about their educational establishments, that we want to improve them, and that education is a key component of the value structure of our citizens (Levin 1998).

All the reports suggested that the educational system is marred by mediocrity. This means a *contradiction between the Canadian value of and expectations about education,* on the one hand, and *the functioning of the educational system,* on the other hand.

▪▪ CONTRIBUTING FACTORS

Why are there inequalities in educational opportunities and attainment? Why hasn't education yielded the expected payoff for some people? As you will see, part of the answer does lie in the structure and processes of the educational system. A greater part of the answer lies in nonschool factors. The problems of education are only partially a problem of the schools.

▪▪ Social Structural Factors

Social Class, Family Background, and Educational Inequality. In our discussion of poverty, we pointed out that *families in the lower strata* of society are different in a number of respects from those in the middle and upper strata. Certain characteristics of the lower-strata family tend to depress **cognitive development.** This suggests that children who come from such families enter school with an intellectual disadvantage, and various studies confirm this (Guo 1998). Large numbers of children are coming to school with a background that includes poor health care, parents who are minimally involved with them, few preschool opportunities, unsafe neighbourhoods, and some degree of malnourishment (Chira 1991). As a result, a third or more of the students who come to kindergarten are *not prepared to learn,* lacking the vocabulary and sentence structure skills that are necessary for success in school. Even if they attend equally good schools and receive equal treatment from teachers, children from such a disadvantaged background cannot have educational opportunity equal to that of others.

Thus, *the position of the family in the stratification system has a close relationship to the educational attainment of the children.* Parental educational attainment and parental influence and expectations for children strongly affect children's educational aspirations and achievement (Bourque and Cosand 1989; Goyette and Xie 1999). In turn, the parental behaviour is related to social class; the higher the social class, the more likely parents are to have high attainment, hold high expectations, and positively influence the child to attain a high degree of education. The greater the parental income and the fewer children in the family (both of which tend to characterize the higher strata), the more willing the parents are to pay for higher education (Steelman and Powell 1991).

Socioeconomic background affects a child at every point in his or her academic career. Those from low-income backgrounds are less likely to graduate from high school, less likely to go to university even if they do graduate (in part because they are more likely to marry at an early age), less likely to complete university if they enroll, and less likely to go to a prestigious school regardless of their ability or aspirations (Hearn 1991; Davies and Guppy 1997; Zucker and Dawson 2001).

Socioeconomic status is also one of the prime factors in unequal educational **achievement** at all levels of education, from elementary school through high school and university (Betts and Morell 1999; Hossler, Schmit, and Vesper 1999). This is not to say that those from a lower socioeconomic background can never succeed. Some poor youths who have had strong parenting and sufficient opportunities have risen above their circumstances and carved out a better life for themselves (Furstenberg et al. 1999).

cognitive development
growth in the ability to perform increasingly complex intellectual activities, particularly abstract relationships

achievement
as distinguished from educational "attainment," the level the student has reached as measured by scores on various verbal and nonverbal tests

WHAT IS THE PURPOSE OF EDUCATION?

In recent decades, the proportion of majors in such areas as English, philosophy, history, and modern languages has dropped considerably. In many Canadian high schools and universities, students can be graduated without studying such subjects as European history, Canadian literature, or the civilizations of ancient Greece and Rome. What do these facts say about the purpose of education? To what extent do colleges and universities help Canadians fulfill the functions of education noted at the beginning of this chapter?

Interview a number of students and faculty members at your school. Ask them what they believe to be the purposes of education. Then ask them to what extent your school has goals that fulfill those purposes. Ask them to identify both their personal educational goals (in the case of faculty, their goals in teaching) and what they believe to be the true goals of the school. If your school is one of those that supports the points noted in the previous paragraph, ask your respondents how they feel about the place of history, literature, and philosophy in the education of people.

What is education for, according to your respondents? Do you agree or disagree? Would you affirm or modify the three purposes of education discussed in this chapter?

Yet the poor will always have a greater struggle. Among other things, those from the lower strata are more likely to find school an alien setting. They and their teachers from the middle strata of society may be totally unprepared to deal with each other. The teachers may react to the children's range of experiences with astonishment and perplexity. The children may not even be able to distinguish the various colours when they enter school, and they may appear to have little grasp of abstract qualities such as shape and length. They may be unfamiliar with such cultural phenomena as Frosty the Snowman, phenomena that teachers may take for granted are known to all students. Most teachers' training does not prepare them for these kinds of students.

As these children progress through school, their academic problems become more rather than less serious. Learning depends increasingly on the ability to deal with abstractions. What is a society? What is a nation? What happened in the past? Children from a deprived background may even have difficulty with such fundamental distinctions as bigger and smaller, higher and lower, round and square.

Such children could be looked upon as a challenge, but teachers may be more likely to react to them with despair or contempt. Indeed, one of the reasons why children from poor families do not achieve in school is that their *teachers may not like them.* Poor children have, if anything, a greater need for acceptance and warmth but are less likely to receive it than are middle-class children.

In addition to socioeconomic level, a number of other family background factors are important in achievement. One is the extent to which parents are involved in the process of education (e.g., meeting with teachers, volunteering at school, monitoring their children's progress, ensuring that homework is done, etc.). Children whose parents are highly involved tend to show high levels of achievement, while dropouts are more likely to have parents who are uninvolved (Marcon 1999; Jimerson et al. 2000).

What about families where the mother works outside the home? Although it might appear that a job or career allows little or no time for involvement in the children's education, it seems that a working mother does not mean a more uninvolved mother. In fact, working mothers, particularly those who work in high-status occupations, seem to encourage higher levels of educational attainment and achievement in their children (Kalmijn 1994).

The Organization of Education.   The gap between children from the lower socioeconomic strata and those from the middle and upper strata tends to increase with the level of school. This suggests that the schools *may somehow contribute to educational inequality—children who are disadvantaged by their social background when they enter school become even more disadvantaged as they progress through school.*

At least two factors contribute to the disadvantage. One is the quality of teaching. Many instructors are teaching subjects for which they are not trained (*Education Week* 2000). Thousands of teachers have been hired with emergency or substandard certification (Applebome 1996). These teachers are more likely to be in schools serving the lower strata. Even when the teachers are competent, they are likely to come from middle-class backgrounds and find it difficult to understand, relate to, and help children from disadvantaged backgrounds (Potterfield and Pace 1992).

A second factor is the *evaluation and labelling of ability.* This grouping by ability, or *tracking,* of students has been common in public schools, beginning in the first grade. It is a controversial practice. Proponents point out that tracking is necessary for dealing with the boredom and lack of adequate progress among bright students when course work proceeds too slowly in order to accommodate slower students. Tracking allows students to proceed at their own pace. "Detracking," they argue, not only hurts the brighter students but also can harm the self-confidence of low achievers when they are forced to compete with the bright students (Loveless 1999).

Opponents of tracking argue that high achievers do not benefit that much and that low achievers are stigmatized and deprived of opportunities for success (Romo 1999). Tracking also puts minorities at a disadvantage (Ansalone 2000). It is true that once placed in a particular track, it is difficult for students to escape it. In fact, they tend to take classes that ensure they will remain in the same track (Kershaw 1992).

Tracking, then, helps perpetuate the status quo. Because the students from a disadvantaged background are more likely to come to school unprepared to learn, they will be placed in a slower track. Once in the slow track, everything works to maintain the situation, including the fact that slower students cannot benefit from the stimulation of interacting with more advanced students.

As Shanker (1993) has noted, then, both the advocates and the critics of tracking make valid claims, so that the question should not be one of tracking or no tracking. Rather, the real question is how to organize schools and classrooms in light of the fact that children learn differently and at different rates. The important point to keep in mind is that inequality of achievement during the first years of school does not mean that the low achievers lack the capacity to attain high educational levels. Low achievement, as we have shown, tends to follow from a particular kind of social and family background. We also have shown, in previous chapters, the effects of labelling. If the low achiever is labelled as one with a low capacity, both the reaction of the teacher and the self-expectations of the child are negatively affected. In effect, labelling becomes a form of the *fallacy of personal attack,* blaming the students rather than the system for their lack of achievement.

The effects of labelling on children's achievement are dramatized in an elementary school experiment which showed that teachers' expectations about the intellectual abilities of their students were reflected in the students' IQ scores (Rosenthal and Jacobson 1968). A student whom the teacher expected to do poorly tended to get lower scores, and a student whom the teacher expected to do well got higher scores. The performance of people, whether children or adults, can be significantly influenced by the expectations of others and can reflect those expectations more than any innate abilities.

Thus, labels can become *self-fulfilling prophecies,* retarding or stifling the achievement of able students. Is there any evidence that the labels are inaccurate? Can't teachers detect and encourage children who are bright but who perform poorly on achievement tests? No doubt some teachers can and do. However, children from lower socioeconomic backgrounds may have a capacity that is masked by their initial disadvantage and by their subsequent experiences and performance in the school. The evidence is scattered and, in some cases, indirect. We will furnish some evidence when we discuss the effects of desegregation in the last section of this chapter.

The Politics of School Financing.   If fiscal resources prevent some school boards from having an adequate or high-quality staff, one way to deal with educational inequality would be to *equalize the money available* to various boards. Currently, as noted earlier, a wide discrepancy exists between the money allocated per child in various districts.

The reason for the discrepancy is that public education is financed largely by the federal government to the provinces through tax transfers to the provinces. Municipal school budgets are managed by school boards across the county or region with financial assistance from the provinces. As a result, pupils in wealthier regions with more expensive homes have more money available for their education. Throughout the country, children in more advantaged areas are likely to have clean, well-staffed schools with good facilities and up-to-date books and technological aids, whereas children in more disadvantaged areas are likely to attend class in dilapidated school buildings staffed by less than fully qualified teachers and supplied with outdated textbooks and few, if any, technological aids. The differences in resources are illustrated by the availability of computers. A child today whose early education is devoid of computer use lacks an important resource and has a serious deficiency in his or her education. Yet schools in poorer areas are likely to have far fewer computers available to the students than schools in more advantaged districts. Government statistics show that schools appear to play a vital role in bridging the "digital divide" between rural and urban high school students in terms of access to computers and frequency of their use. Canadian students rank among the highest in the world in terms of access to computers both at home and at school.

The vast majority of urban and rural youth, around 96 percent in both cases, reported using a computer during the previous 12-month period, according to the 2000 General Social Survey conducted by Statistics Canada.

Differences in gender and socioeconomic status did materialize in this survey, with only 45 percent of female students having access to home computers daily compared with 57 percent of males. As well, one-third of youth whose parents had little or no formal education reported that they had no computers in their home, compared to 13 percent of those whose parents had completed high school (The Daily, June 23, 2003).

In 2002–3, virtually all elementary and secondary schools in Canada had computers and were connected to the Internet during the school year. However, a survey conducted by Statistics Canada also found that most teachers could use this technology for preparing report cards, taking attendance, or recording grades, but less than half of school principals felt that the majority of their teachers were adequately prepared to engage their students effectively in the use of information and communications technologies (ICTs).

As well, many school computers are aging and so did not have the necessary specifications or speed required for students to use up-to-date software programs. Further, many school principals also noted that their school districts did not have the necessary funds available to purchase up-to-date computers for their students and staff, even though nine out of ten surveyed agreed that ICTs enabled the curriculum to be more challenging and enriching for students and teachers alike (The Daily, June 10, 2004).

Poorer school boards cannot provide the resources enjoyed by wealthier boards.

The point is that *even if the student in a lower socio-economic area overcomes the handicaps of a disadvantaged family, he or she faces obstacles to educational attainment in the school itself.*

In principle, many Canadians support the idea of equalizing the funds available to school districts—but how would that be done? Some have argued that it can be accomplished only by eliminating the property tax as the basis for funding. They point out that no child should be denied a quality education simply because his or her parents happen to live in a poorer area.

There is another aspect to the politics of financing—the extent to which political leaders give high priority to education. School districts get revenues from local, provincial, and federal sources. When support at one of the levels declines for whatever reason, education is likely to suffer.

The Economics of Education. The politics of school financing interact closely with the economics of education. As with so many important areas of Canadian life, *education is affected by the ups and downs of the economy,* and political and economic factors are intertwined as they affect the educational process. Educational decisions may be made on the basis of economic considerations.

Economic factors can become even more powerful in times of recessions, when political leaders look with jaundiced eyes at the costs of education and resist any changes that involve more money. Inflation also can be troublesome. Inflation may rapidly outstrip the fiscal resources of schools and result in problems regarding salaries and the purchase of supplies.

As pointed out above, *economic problems are also political problems.* Not everyone and not everything suffers equally in times of economic difficulty—political leaders make decisions that bear upon the resources available. The minister of education and government members of a province must decide whether education, mental health, highway maintenance, or a number of other areas will receive priority consideration when budgets must be cut.

Obviously, the problems of education cannot be separated from other problems in a time of national economic difficulty. When resources are scarce, the decision to more fully fund one area—such as education—is a decision not to adequately fund another area—such as health programs. A faltering economy, therefore, inevitably means an intensification of at least some social problems.

■■ Social Psychological Factors

Attitudes. We have already noted some *attitudes that contribute to educational problems.* The attitudes of children in the lower strata, for example, tend to inhibit them from aspiring to higher levels of attainment. Even if such children have aspirations, they may not expect to be able to realize those aspirations (Hanson 1994). Their attitudes reflect those of their parents, who neither expect high educational attainment from their children nor behave in ways to encourage such attainment (Crosnoe, Mistry, and Elder 2002). When the lower expectations of the parents and children are combined with the low expectations and negative attitudes of their teachers, the impediments to achievement are enormous.

The attitudes of students toward school and schoolwork also affect their achievement. When asked what can be done about student apathy, sociology students agree that for some it does exist but argue that if courses were more interesting, and if there were more connection between what they learn in school to their private lives and work aspirations, then students would be more engaged and interested in what takes place in classrooms across the country.

As well, they argue that much of what they learn in the classroom is outdated and not necessarily related to their experiences in the present. They contend that if some of these problems were addressed then they would be more interested in their academic lives and more willing to do homework and other school activities.

Older students in these classes often say that they feel they are more committed to their education than younger ones because they are clearer as to their future goals (often, to upgrade their credentials for employment). They also argue that they have already had the opportunity to experience more in the world and so feel more ready for the academic experience than their younger peers.

The attitudes of teachers also contribute to educational problems. The attitudes of teachers are rooted in the conditions under which they must work. Low salaries, inadequate resources, and other poor working conditions may lead teachers to change professions. Others remain in teaching, but they develop jaded attitudes about their work and education generally; and sinking teacher morale usually is accompanied by lower student achievement (Black 2001).

■■ A Concluding Note on Inequality in Education

We have suggested that if the various factors we identified are all taken into account, then children of different racial, ethnic, and socioeconomic backgrounds should be able to show about the same levels of achievement.

The importance of education to the employment of Aboriginal persons is obvious. In 1996 the unemployment rate for young Native adults without high school was 40 percent; for those with a university degree it was 9 percent. Clearly, then, more government involvement in providing higher education for Aboriginal persons is crucial, as is the investment of Aboriginal band councils and employers (Macionis and Gerber 2004:517).

Thus, unequal educational achievement in Canada is a sociocultural, not a racial-genetic, matter (Myerson et al. 1998). In the U.S., gaps in reading and math and science scores also narrowed in response to programs designed to aid minorities (National Center for Educational Statistics 2001). Such results underscore both the social nature of the problem and the importance of social action for addressing it.

■■ From Social Problems to Solutions

Our analysis suggests a variety of ways to attack the various problems of education. Clearly, it must be a multifaceted attack. Undoubtedly, parental involvement is one of the crucial factors in children's educational attainment. Among other things, having high expectations for the children's education, creating an educationally rich environment in the home, and helping with homework will make a difference in how much children achieve academically (Bibby 2001).

Another obvious need is reform of school financing. The inequities between school boards must be addressed. In addition, a variety of other efforts and proposals exist that hold promise: quality enhancement measures, efforts to reduce racial and ethnic inequality, and compensatory and other innovative programs. Some are quite controversial.

Quality Enhancement Measures

A variety of suggestions exist for enhancing the quality of education, including the following:

- Emphasize multicultural education, which will promote more understanding and tolerance and, therefore, a better learning climate for minority groups (Banks 1991).
- Institute a curriculum audit, which is a way to use outside evaluators to determine whether school personnel know whether the content of their curriculum is appropriate for their students (Vertiz 1992).
- Establish strong national standards for what students should know and be able to do, along with a system for evaluating schools in terms of whether they meet those standards (Shanker 1994b).
- Improve school atmosphere by ensuring the safety of students, fostering parent involvement, and making the schools drug- and gun-free environments (Ingersoll and LeBoeuf 1997).
- Give all children the opportunity to attend preschool, which is particularly helpful to students from disadvantaged backgrounds (Walsh 1999).
- Put all children into small classes, for those in small classes from kindergarten on do far better academically than those in large classes (Finn et al. 2001).

Some analysts believe that all such efforts are only a "tinkering" with the system, and that *what is needed is a complete restructuring* (Shanker 1990). There is no consensus on exactly what is meant by restructuring, but advocates agree that it requires decentralization (whether in the form of school-site management, a choice plan, or some variation on privatization).

Restructuring through decentralization gives parents and local schools greater control over the educational process. At first glance, this sounds like a positive step. Why should all schools have to conform to a uniform set of policies and procedures? Who knows the needs of a particular school and its students better than the principal and teachers? In sum, restructuring seems to work well in some situations, but there is no single form of restructuring that will work well everywhere.

private school
a nonreligious public school approved by the local school district but free of many regulations and policies that apply to other public schools

A different way to enhance quality is to start from scratch with a school—namely, establish a **private school**. *Private schools are nonreligious public schools that are approved by the local school district but free of many regulations and policies that apply to other public schools.* Private schools can be converted public schools or entirely new facilities. They are operated by educators, parents, and/or community members. In essence, the district and the school negotiate a contract or "charter" that covers a specified number of years and that spells out the school's mission, program, goals, type of student body, and method of accountability.

compensatory programs
programs designed to give intensive help to disadvantaged pupils and increase their academic skills

In 1998–9, 5.6 percent (298,000) of all children in elementary and secondary schools in Canada were enrolled in private schools, up from 4.6 percent in 1987–8 and expected to increase substantially as social problems related to schooling persist. Five million attended public schools. Just fewer than 9 percent of children who attend private school are from families with incomes below $50,000, while 26 percent are from families with at least twice as much income. Clearly, private schooling is seen as a necessary option for families that wish to enroll their children in smaller classes with more resources available for enhanced learning (The Daily, July 4, 2001).

Reducing Racial and Ethnic Inequality

Racial and ethnic inequalities in education must be reduced in order to create a society of equal opportunity.

Mentoring programs are provided throughout school systems in Canada (most notably by Big Brothers and Big Sisters of Canada) as well as on university and college campuses, whereby students are provided with mentors who assist them with their school work and also provide sources of support and encouragement intended to help them get through the school years. The role of the mentor is to help the student develop learning skills and habits that will ensure they complete their schoolwork and by so doing increase their self-esteem and ability to achieve goals.

The Deschooling or Home Schooling Movement

The *deschooling movement* aims at providing students with a situation in which they will maximize their learning. The movement emphasizes the necessity of a break with the existing educational structure and the creation of new schools where the children can be free to learn. The most radical advocate of deschooling was Ivan Illich (1975), who argued that learning has become a commodity and that the existing schools monopolize the market. If educational institutions are needed at all, they should "ideally take the form of facility centers where one can get a roof of the right size over his head, access to a piano or a kiln, and to records, books, or slides" (Illich 1975:89).

The most common manifestation of deschooling today is *home schooling*. People decide for various reasons to teach their children at home rather than send them to the schools. Initially, most home schooling was done by conservative Christians who felt that their children were not given sufficient moral guidance in the schools (Hawkins 1996). As a five-year-old girl explained to the author, she would not go to public school because "they don't teach about God there." The second wave of home schoolers, however, includes more people who are dissatisfied either with the quality of teaching in the schools or with the potential for emotional or physical harm to their children in the schools (Cloud and Morse 2001).

Estimates of the number of children home schooled from kindergarten through high school vary. How well are home-schooled children educated? The evidence suggests that, on the whole, they receive a competent education. Home schooling and home

Some parents have sought to maximize their children's education by removing them from traditional schools, opting instead to home school.

study programs are legally recognized and accepted forms of education in Canada. According to Smith (1996), in 1996 there were some 10,000 registered home-school students.

It is thought that the increase in home schooling in Canada—which, according to the Canadian Alliance of Home Schoolers, has increased 15 times since 1996—is due to the fact that parents want more parental involvement in their children's education, especially those with specific religious backgrounds who do not feel that their children receive adequate religious and moral training. Violence in schools also was often cited as a reason for parents to teach their children at home. Other parents express concern at the quality of education their children receive and feel that they can experience a richer and more diverse education within their own homes (Home Schooling 2004). Still others argue that they want more control over their children's education in terms not only of content, but also of the techniques used to teach and involve their children in meaningful education interaction (Bruce 2000:204).

A national survey conducted in the U.S. of a random sample of 1,516 families from one organization's membership found that home-schooled students, on the average, scored at or above the 80th percentile on standardized achievement tests (the national average is the 50th percentile) (Ray 1999). Another survey of 11,930 families reported that the home-schooled students typically scored in the 70th to 80th percentile on the standardized tests and that a fourth of them were being taught at a grade level higher than their age-level peers in private and public schools (Rudner 1999).

Home-schooled students also appear to exhibit sound social and emotional adjustment (Ray 1999). They are involved in extracurricular activities of various kinds. They have healthy self-concepts, and they tend to be more independent of peer pressure than are their public and private school peers.

Undoubtedly, some children receive an inadequate education through home schooling; but, on average, those who are home schooled appear to be benefiting. Parents who opt for it, however, need to recognize the extent to which they are committing themselves to their children's lives. Parenting is a consuming task as it is; when home schooling is added, parenting becomes more than a full-time job.

Two other pressing social problems currently being encountered in Canadian educational facilities, especially at the elementary and high school levels, are bullying and racism. There are many ways in which these social problems are interconnected in that immigrants and non-white students experience bullying at much higher rates than do white students (Alladin 1996:76). Various community-based organizations, schools, teachers' federations, parent–teacher alliances, on-campus student groups, corporations, and governments are attempting to create programs and services to deal with these issues.

Bullying The Internet site www.nomorebullies.com defines bullying as "repeated, harmful behaviour against a victim," and suggests that it is a combination of one or more of the following: intimidation, gossip, spreading rumours, humiliation, rejection, name-calling, extortion, violence, exclusion, threats, putdowns, stealing, and teasing. Various studies on bullying (see, for example, Ahmad and Smith 1994; Batsche and Knoff 1994; Charach, Peplar, and Ziegler 1995, among others) note that it is a worldwide social problem and that approximately 15 percent of Canadian students are either bullied regularly or are initiators of bullying behaviour.

A British Columbia study of high school students across the province found that 10 to 15 percent are bullying, while 8 to 10 percent are victims (Craig and Peplar 1997:60). In this study, only 25 percent of students reported that teachers intervened in bullying situations, whereas 71 percent of teachers reported that they believed they always intervened (Ibid:42). Clearly, there is a lack of communication about bullying between teachers and students. In a similar study conducted in Toronto high schools it was found that a bullying act occurred every seven seconds, but teachers were aware of only 4 percent of the incidents (Safety Council 2004).

According to Canadian researchers Charach, Peplar, and Zeigler (1995), boys are more likely to bully than girls, with 23 percent of young males self-reporting that they have bullied and only 8 percent of girls making the same claim. While boys are more likely to engage in direct bullying methods, girls who bully are more likely to use more subtle, indirect strategies such as spreading rumours and enforcing social isolation (Ahmed and Smith 1994).

Bullying has social consequences not only for victims—such as low self-esteem, anxiety, fear of going to school, suicide attempts (some which are successful), psychological trauma, and so on—but also for perpetrators. The Evergreen site for prevention of bullying notes that "By age 24, up to 60 percent of people identified as childhood bullies have at least one criminal conviction" (Evergreen 2004) .

Students who engage in bullying behaviours seem to have a need to feel powerful and in control. They appear to derive satisfaction from inflicting injury and suffering, whether physical or emotional, on others whom they see as weaker than they. Charach, Peplar, and Ziegler (1995) found that bullies considered their victims to be "weak," "nerds," and "afraid to fight back" (17). These researchers also note that bullies often expressed the notion that bullying "taught" victims to become "tougher" and to "fight back" (ibid). As well, bullies often claim that their victims provoked them in some way. Studies show that bullies often come from homes where physical punishment and domestic violence is prevalent (Batsche and Knoff 1994; Olweus 1993). Batsche and Knoff (1994) suggest that direct bullying increases during the elementary years, peaks in the middle school/junior high years, and declines during the high school years. While direct physical assault seems to decrease with age, verbal abuse remains constant throughout the school years (1994:172).

Regional police in almost every province in Canada are also setting up anti-bullying hotline programs to eradicate school bullying and to provide students, their families, and schools with supportive educational and information programs. As well, many schools have initiated zero-tolerance programs for bullying. In Alberta in 2003, the Edmonton city council passed a bylaw enabling the police department to fine $250 to anyone found guilty of bullying an individual under the age of 18 in a public place. Edmonton was the first Canadian city to bring in such legislation, and other provinces such as Ontario and British Columbia are considering similar action (CBC News 2003).

Racism We said earlier in this section that bullying and racism are often interconnected social problems, especially when the victims of such abuses are immigrants, refugees, or members of racial minority groups. Enid Lee (1998) defines racism as "the use of institutional power to deny or grant people and groups of people rights, respect, representation and resources based on their skin color. Racism in action makes Whiteness a preferred way of being human" (1998:27).

The typical Canadian school has undergone significant transformation over the last decade; as of May 2001, the visible-minority population comprised 5.4 million people, or 18.4 percent of the total population who were born outside the country. This was the highest proportion since 1931, when foreign-born people made up 22.2 percent of the population. In 1996, the proportion was 17.4 percent. Of those who immigrated in the 1990s, 58 percent were born in Asia, including the Middle East; 20 percent in Europe; 11 percent in the Caribbean and Central and South America; 8 percent in Africa; and 3 percent in the United States.

Canada was home to almost 4 million individuals who identified themselves as members of visible minority groups in 2001, accounting for 13.4 percent of the total population. Visible minorities are defined by the *Employment Equity Act* as "persons, other than Aboriginal peoples, who are non-Caucasian in race or non-white in colour." This proportion has increased steadily over the past 20 years. In 1981, 1.1 million members of visible-minority groups accounted for 4.7 percent of the total population; by 1996, 3.2 million accounted for 11.2 percent.

Combined, the three largest visible minority groups in 2001—Chinese, South Asians, and blacks—accounted for two-thirds of the visible-minority population. They were followed by Filipinos, Arabs and West Asians, Latin Americans, Southeast Asians, Koreans, and Japanese (The Daily, September 29, 2003).

As well as immigrants, in 2001 a total of 976,300 people identified themselves as members of at least one of three Aboriginal groups: North American Indian, Métis, or Inuit. This was 22 percent higher than the 1996 figure of 799,000. In contrast, the total non-Aboriginal population grew only 3.4 percent between 1996 and 2001. People who identified themselves as Aboriginal accounted for 3.3 percent of the nation's total population in 2001, compared with 2.8 percent in 1996 (ibid).

With the ever-increasing number of non-white students attending Canadian schools, it is imperative that educators at all levels provide all students with inclusive educational materials that speak to the cultural, social, and religious practices of those in the classrooms, and that racism in schools is eradicated.

Clearly, when assessing the social problem of racism in Canadian schools it is necessary to examine the historical and social backgrounds in which this behaviour occurs, and to separate out which components of the problem are based purely on racist attitudes and which are the result of systemic discrimination against people on the basis of race in any community.

▪▪ SUMMARY

Education is a problem when it fails to fulfill its expected functions: creating good and effective citizens, providing the possibility for upward mobility, and facilitating individual development. For these purposes education is highly valued by Canadians. Lack of education is frequently associated with failure to achieve one's ambitions in life.

Canada has become an increasingly educated society. Whether this education has yielded the expected payoffs is not always clear. The greater degree of happiness reported by the highly educated may reflect a tendency toward greater fulfillment of individual potential. Education increases political participation and understanding. There is a strong relationship between education and income, but those most likely to benefit from education are already in the middle and upper strata.

Education is a problem because there are inequalities, and the expected payoff does not always occur. Educational attainment is unequally distributed among various groups. Educational funding is unequally distributed among provinces and school boards within them. The cost of education prices many Canadians out of the better colleges and universities. The learning atmosphere of some schools (critics would say nearly all schools) is rigid and joyless and precludes individual schedules of learning; sometimes students suffer an atmosphere of fear and threat or ritualized deprivation.

Among the social structural factors that contribute to the problems of education, social class and family background are particularly important. The organization of education also makes a difference in students' achievement and attainment. Particularly important are the distribution of funds, the assignment of teachers, the socio-economic composition of the student body, and the evaluation and labelling of ability. The inequitable distribution of funds is a political issue that must be resolved by political action. Finally, the quality of education varies with the economy. Both recessions and inflation drain the resources available to schools.

Attitudes of parents, students, and teachers are important social psychological factors that contribute to the problems of education. The attitudes of parents and students toward school and intellectual activities and toward the educational potential of the students are strongly related to achievement. Teacher attitudes can inhibit or facilitate student achievement.

Our analysis implies that when the various contributing factors are taken into account, children of different social backgrounds have the same capacity for achievement. Given the same socioeconomic background, family background, attitudes, and the like, there is only about a 1-percent difference in the achievement scores of the various racial and ethnic groups.

▪▪ KEY TERMS

Achievement 286	Cognitive Development	Compensatory Programs	Cyberbullying 283
Atmosphere 283	286	292	Private School 292
Attainment 275		Culture 274	

▪▪ STUDY QUESTIONS

1. What are three functions of education?

2. Discuss the levels of educational attainment in Canada and the varied payoffs from that attainment.

3. How much inequality of opportunity is there in Canada, and how does it affect attainment?

4. What kinds of school atmosphere contribute to the problems of education?

5. What could the educational system do to have better prepared you for university?

6. In what ways is family background important for education?

7. What are the political and economic factors involved in educational problems?

8. Discuss the attitudes and values involved in education problems.

9. What are ways to resolve educational problems?

■■ FOR FURTHER READING

Bevie, Arai A. "Reasons for Home Schooling in Canada." *Canadian Journal of Education*. Issue 2, 2000:204.

Bryk, Anthony S., Valerie E. Lee, and Peter B. Holland. *Catholic Schools and the Common Good.* Cambridge, MA: Harvard University Press, 1993. The authors set forth the Catholic school as a model, describe ways in which it is superior to the public school, and identify various organizational features that help explain that superiority.

Dougherty, Kevin J. *The Contradictory College: The Conflicting Origins, Impacts, and Futures of the Community College.* Albany State University of New York Press, 1994. An examination of community colleges over time, showing how they affect educational attainment and occupational success. Also explains why community colleges have political support.

Erwin, Lorna, and David MacLennan. *Sociology of Education in Canada: Critical Perspectives on Theory, Research and Practice.* Toronto: Copp, Clark Longman, 1994.

Fiske, Edward B. *Smart Schools, Smart Kids: Why Do Some Schools Work?* New York: Simon & Schuster, 1992. Describes schools in various parts of the nation that "work" in the sense of turning out students who can function as effective workers and citizens. Among other things, such schools are managed from within rather than by a board of education, stress cooperative rather than competitive learning, and have flexible scheduling.

Gittell, Marilyn J. *Strategies for School Equity: Creating Productive Schools in a Just Society.* New Haven, CT: Yale University Press, 1998. A discussion of how school financing creates inequities and a suggested way for the federal government to resolve the inequities and create a just system of education.

Guppy, Neil, and Scott Davies. *Education in Canada: Recent Trends and Future Challenges.* Ottawa: Statistics Canada, 1998.

Kozol, Jonathan. *Savage Inequalities: Children in America's Schools.* New York: Crown Publishers, 1992. A comparison of schools in some poor areas in the nation with others in well-to-do districts, dramatizing the way in which students who come from a disadvantaged background continue to struggle in a deprived educational setting.

Pope, Denise Clark. *Doing School: How We Are Creating a Generation of Stressed Out, Materialistic, and Miseducated Students.* New Haven, CT: Yale University Press, 2001. An in-depth study of five high-school students who represent the "best and brightest," and who illustrate the shortcomings and problems of education today.

Taylor, Arson. Credentialing the High School. Paper Presented to the Annual Meeting of the American Educational Research Association (April 2002), New Orleans.

Wotherspoon, Terry. *The Sociology of Education in Canada: Critical Perspective.* Toronto: Oxford University Press, 1998.

FAMILY PROBLEMS

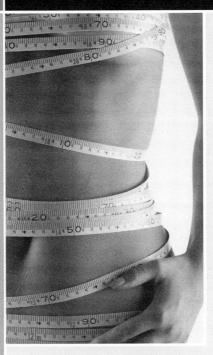

"I SURVIVED THE ABUSE"

Patricia is a self-confident university student who is about to graduate. Yet she could have turned out quite differently, for she grew up in a home where she suffered ongoing criticism from her father and brothers, which led in part to her becoming anorexic:

> My father loves thin, stick-like models (probably because my mother has a weight problem), and he really loved to show me off when I was little and did ballet lessons. He always told me not to eat junk food, and was always on my case about not overeating. His nickname for me was Twiglet and he joked with his friends about how one day I was going to be a famous model and make him rich—as long as I kept my "svelte" figure. My brothers also liked me to be thin and said that they preferred to go out with girls who had less "meat" on them. I know my Dad loved me and was really proud of the way I looked, and I felt a lot of pressure to be "right" for him and my brothers. Things started to change when I left high school for university and I started to gain weight and had less time for exercise. Suddenly I wasn't daddy's little girl anymore, and he started being really judgmental about the way I looked. My brothers started getting on my case too and calling me names, it was like I couldn't please any of them anymore. At the time my dad was being so critical, so was the guy I was dating—he was always pointing out other girls and how nice they looked, and of course they were all thin girls! My dad would buy me new clothes and stuff, always two sizes too small, and offer me rewards (like a new CD player, money, trips) if I would lose weight. My dad, my boyfriend, and my brothers would make all these jokes about fat girls, and how they were stupid and stuff like that. I felt like I was just letting them all down, and no matter what I did I kept gaining weight. I was on every diet there was. I really cut down on eating, maybe to only one meal a day, and then I got thin and started getting all the compliments again so that

was great. Then it got to be that no matter how little I ate the fatter I thought I was, and I was so worried about making them not like the way I looked again. My dad was buying me all sorts of new clothes, and my boyfriend stopped comparing me with other girls and seemed to really like the way I looked. But I was feeling really weak, I had these huge headaches and I felt sick all the time. Eventually I collapsed at school and one of my roommates found me and called an ambulance.

The doctors diagnosed me as anorexic and suggested I see a therapist. She was really great and helped me a lot. That was three years ago. I had to have family therapy sessions, especially with my dad. I got rid of that boyfriend, and now I am just about to graduate and am trying to deal with my weight issues. You know, your family can be the most wonderful part of your life, or it can really mess you up—like mine did back then. ■

■■ INTRODUCTION

Is the family a dying institution? Some observers say yes, arguing that the family is doomed. Others go further, maintaining that the family *should* be doomed because it no longer functions in a useful way. The family, according to this argument, contributes more misery than benefit because it is ill adapted to modern social life.

Still others argue that the family is essential and ineradicable. What is needed, they argue, is help for troubled families, not radical changes or the abolition of family life. In this chapter we consider the argument that the family is doomed. Then, taking the position that it is not doomed, we look at the family as a problem. In previous chapters we asked how the family contributed to other problems. Now we examine the nature and extent of family problems. We also describe how those problems affect the quality of life. Finally, we identify the structural and social psychological factors that contribute to family problems and inquire into ways to resolve the problems.

■■ IS THE FAMILY DOOMED?

In Canada today there are several types of family, which include (Auger 1990):

- **Nuclear family:** Two parents with one or more children, who may or may not be biologically related to one another.
- **Extended family:** Parents and their children and other relatives such as grandparents, aunts, uncles, cousins, etc., either living together or within close proximity.
- **Lone (solo) parent family:** One parent with child(ren), by choice (e.g., through the use of artificial insemination, surrogacy, foster care, or adoption).
- **Single-parent family:** One parent with child(ren), not by choice but due to divorce or separation. Single-parent families may also result from the death of a partner.
- **Childless family:** Married (legally, common-law, or same-sex) who choose not to or are unable to have children.
- **Blended family:** Parents and child(ren) from previous marriages or other unions who now live together.

- **Common-law family:** Adults with or without children who are not formally married but have common-law status, either heterosexual or lesbian/gay.
- **Same-sex family:** Two partners of the same sex, who may or may not be legally married or have registered domestic partnerships, either without children or with children from previous marriages or heterosexual unions or through fostering, adoption, sperm/egg donation, or some other form of reproductive technology.
- **Family of choice (affinity):** Groups of individuals, with or without children, who choose to live communally as a family.

The family, thus, is a crucial factor in both individual well-being and social life. Nevertheless, if prophecies could kill, the family would have died long ago. The popular and the professional literature continue to forecast the *death of the family,* at least the death of the **nuclear family** consisting of a husband, a wife, and their children, if any. The evidence used to support the notion that the nuclear family is dying typically includes things such as **divorce rates,** birthrates, runaway children, people who abandon their spouses and/or children, the growing number of youth communes, **cohabitation,** or common-law relationships as well as **same-sex** ones. The increasing rate of family disruption, combined with various other changes going on in the society, makes family life appear to be in peril to some observers. At the same time, the fact that communes and cohabitation have proliferated suggests that *intimate relationships* must and will continue. Some people are merely finding alternate ways to express their intimacy needs.

nuclear family
husband, wife, and children, if any

divorce rate
typically, the number of divorces per 1,000 marriages

cohabitation
living together without being married (also called common-law family)

same-sex family
two persons of the same sex living together, with or without children

▪▪ Alternative Forms of the Family

There are many alternatives to the traditional nuclear family, a number of which have been explored by researchers (Lauer and Lauer 1983). One alternative is group marriage, which has been tried in some communes. In this arrangement, all males and females have access to each other for sex and companionship. Other proposed alternatives include trial marriages with renewable contracts for specified periods of time, and "open marriages" in which each partner has the right to sexual and companionate relationships with someone other than the spouse.

Another arrangement, which has increased enormously since the 1970s, is common-law relationships. The 2001 Census showed than an increasing proportion of couples are living common-law. Married couples accounted for 70 percent of all families in 2001 (5,901 persons), down from 83 percent in 1981. At the same time, the proportion of common-law couples rose from 6 percent to 14 percent (1,311 persons).

The number of common-law couples in Canada with children under the age of 25 is also increasing. In 2001, they accounted for 7 percent of all couples in Canada, compared with only 2 percent two decades earlier. Thirteen percent of the children (732,900) lived with common-law parents in 2001; this is more than four times the proportion of 3 percent two decades ago. Younger children were more likely to live with common-law parents. (The Daily, October 22, 2002). Table 11.1 provides an overview of the marital arrangements of Canadian families.

▪▪ Family Portraits

Statistics Canada's 2001 Census includes three main components in its definition of a "Census family"—married couples, common-law couples (including same-sex couples), and single parents.

The *reasons for cohabiting* are varied: as an alternative to marriage, as a preparation for marriage and family living, or as a way to deal with loneliness (Popenoe and

TABLE 11.1 ■ ■ ■

Marital Arrangement of Canadian Families, 2001

Families Composed Of	Total of Families	Percentage
Married couples	5,901,425	70.5
With children at home	3,469,700	41.5
Without children at home	2,431,725	29.0
Common-law couples	1,158,405	13.8
With children at home	530,900	6.3
Without children at home	627,505	7.5
Single parents	1,311,190	15.7

Source: Statistics Canada: *Family Portraits 2001*: Ottawa: Government of Canada. Charts and tables prepared by Chief of Research Patricia Treble.

Whitehead 1999). Those who view cohabitation as a preparation for marriage may be cautious because of the high divorce rate or because they have been previously married and divorced. A substantial number of cohabiting couples have children in the home.

To return to the initial question: Is the family doomed? Clearly, the Canadian family is changing in important ways. Yet, as we discuss later, most Canadians retain some traditional values about the family. We take the position that, despite the critics and the changes, the family remains strong and crucial to the well-being of people. At the same time, it is clear that fewer people opt for the traditional form of the family in which there is a breadwinner husband, a housewife, and children. Precisely how, then, is the Canadian family changing?

■■ The Changing Canadian Family

Among the important changes in Canadian families in recent times are *increases* in (1) age at first marriage, (2) proportion of young adults remaining single, (3) divorced adults, (4) adults living alone, (5) unmarried couples, (6) families maintained by adults with no spouse present, (7) children living with only one parent, (8) wives and mothers working, (9) dual-career families (in which both husband and wife pursue careers, with minimal, if any, interruption of the wife's career for childbearing), and (10) same-sex relationships. At the same time, there has been a *decrease* in the number of children couples have. The effect of the various changes has been, among other things, to dramatically alter the typical composition of Canadian households over the past decades. Consider the specific data in the following paragraphs:

The 2001 Census is the first to provide data on same-sex partnerships. A total of 34,200 couples identified themselves as same-sex common-law couples, accounting for 0.5 percent of all couples in the country. However, as we have noted before, it is unlikely that the majority of lesbian and gay couples would have identified themselves as such as Canada is still a homophobic country, and to self-identify in this way could cause harm to some.

The 2001 Census counted almost 11,563 households in that year, up from 6.5 percent in 1996. In that year there were as many one-person households as there were those with four or more people, so that more Canadians are choosing to live alone. Between 1981 and 2001 the average size of households declined from 2.9 to 2.6 people.

There is little variation in average family size across the country. In 2001, families in Prince Edward Island, Ontario, Manitoba, Saskatchewan, and Alberta were slightly larger than average, while the remaining provinces were right around the national figure (Profile of Families and Households 2004).

In addition to the large number of Canadians who live with their immediate family, a substantial number live with other relatives in an extended family, such as the family of a son or daughter. This is especially true for seniors. In 2001, 9 percent of all Canadians aged 65 and over lived in this type of family arrangement. Women are more likely than older men to live with other family members, especially those aged 85 and over. In 2001, 24 percent of such women had this type of family situation (Census of Canada 2001).

While such changes may be interpreted as threatening to the traditional nuclear family, you also must consider other evidence. First, a number of the most recent figures reflect a reversal rather than a continuation of a trend. For example, the divorce rate has tended to decrease since 1980. Second, most Canadians marry at some time in their lives. Only a minority of those who are single are so by choice. Third, the bulk of Canadians rate a good marriage and family life as extremely important to them (Whitehead and Popenoe 2001). Fourth, most are satisfied with their own family life. A 2001 poll of adults reported that 96 percent felt good about relations with their family and 61 percent felt good about their marriage (Polling Report 2002).

Indeed, married people generally are happier and healthier than the nonmarried. More than 130 studies have reported that both married men and married women are happier and less stressed (as measured by such things as alcoholism rates, suicide rates, and physical and emotional health) than are the unmarried (Lauer and Lauer 1986, 2003).

Clearly, then, Canadians still value the traditional nuclear family. Just as clearly, there is an increasing tendency to prefer nontraditional roles, particularly an egalitarian arrangement (in which both partners work and share responsibility for home and children).

▪▪ Functions of the Family

Whether Canadians opt for a traditional or a nontraditional family arrangement, they face certain problems. The problems reflect not only the expectations and values about family life but also the *functions of the family*. Those functions, like other aspects of the family, have changed over time. At one time the family was primarily responsible for matters such as education, religious training, recreation, and providing the necessities of life. Those functions have been largely assumed by other institutions. However, the family continues to be an important factor in *regulating sexual behaviour, reproduction, and rearing of children*.

Another important function of the family is to provide a *primary group* for individuals. The **primary group,** consisting of the people with whom you have intimate, face-to-face interaction on a recurring basis, is of enormous importance. In a classic study, a children's home created "artificial" families after it was noted that the children were having developmental problems (Stanton and Schwartz 1961). Previously, all the children had been cared for by all the attendants, who carefully avoided too much involvement with any one child so as not to appear to have favourites. However, when this arrangement was abandoned and the home was divided into family groups of about four children and a "mother," the results were "astonishing."

> The need for individual attachment for the feelings which had been lying dormant came out in a rush. In the course of the one week all six families were completely and firmly established . . . the children began to develop in leaps and bounds. The most gratifying effect was that several children who had seemed hopeless as far as the training for cleanliness was concerned suddenly started to use the pot regularly and effectively. (Stanton and Schwartz 1961:236)

Primary groups are important for adults as well as children. You have a personal status in primary groups. You gain an understanding of the kind of person you are and

primary group
the people with whom one has intimate, face-to-face interaction on a recurring basis, such as parents, spouse, children, and close friends

learn the kind of norms by which you are to live. Primary groups, in other words, are crucial to your well-being as a functioning human. For most Canadians, the family is a primary group *par excellence.*

When problems arise in the family, they arise in the group that is important to your well-being, that provides you with important emotional support, and that is of central importance to your life satisfaction and happiness (Lauer and Lauer 2003). That is not to say that the family is always a solution; it is also a problem, as we will further explain. The point is that the family is a central aspect of your well-being; thus, when family life becomes problematic, you are threatened at the very foundation of the quality of your life.

■■ THE EXTENT OF FAMILY PROBLEMS

The family becomes a problem when it does not fulfill its purposes, particularly its purpose as a primary group. The Canadian ideal is that the family should be *structurally complete.* Children should have two parents in the home. The family should be a *supportive group,* providing emotional support for each member. "Ideal" in this context does not mean "perfect" (and therefore unrealistic). Rather, the ideal is defined as realistic and expected. When the actual situation falls short of the ideal, the *quality of life* is diminished. Expectations are thwarted, the most important primary group is disrupted, and family members experience stress.

For many people today, the expectations are thwarted more than once. In your lifetime, you might live in five, six, or more different families, each of which could fail in some way to fulfill your needs for structure and support. If your parents were divorced when you were young, and you lived with one parent for a while, then a stepparent for some years, you would have had three different family experiences before adulthood. As an adult, if you cohabited, married, divorced, and remarried one or more times your family experiences would rise to six or more.

Consider next the extent of structural and supportive problems. *Structural problems* relate to the breaking up of husband and wife and/or parent and child. *Supportive problems* involve the lack of emotional support.

■■ Disrupted and Reconstituted Families

Divorce rates, one measure of structural problems, have fluctuated in Canada, but the *general trend has been upward.* The rates are affected by business cycles and special circumstances such as war. Since 1860 there has been a general increase in the number of divorces per 1,000 population. Since 1965 the rate has increased dramatically.

■■ Divorce Rates

Fewer Canadian couples are getting divorced, and those who do are doing so at a later age. After three consecutive years of growth, the number of divorces has dropped for two years in a row. In 2002, a total of 70,155 couples had a divorce finalized, down 1.3 percent from 2001 and 1.4 percent from 2000. The divorce rate is now 11.2 percent.

In 2002, the number of divorces fell in nine provinces and territories from 2000, particularly in New Brunswick, where the decline was 14.9 percent, and in Saskatchewan, where it was 10.7 percent. However, divorces were up in Alberta, British Columbia, Ontario, and the Yukon. The provincial variation in divorce rates is shown in Table 11.2.

It appears that the length of marriage has some bearing on divorce rates, so that those who have been married for one year have a 4.3-percent divorce rate (per 1,000 mar-

TABLE 11.2 ■ ■ ■

Provincial Variations in Divorce Rates

	2000	2001	2002	2000–2002
				Percentage Change
	Number of Divorces			
Canada	71,144	71,110	70,155	–1.4
Newfoundland and Labrador	913	755	842	–7.8
Prince Edward Island	272	246	258	–5.1
Nova Scotia	2,054	1,945	1,990	–3.1
New Brunswick	1,717	1,570	1,461	–14.9
Quebec	17,054	17,094	16,499	–3.3
Ontario	26,148	26,516	26,170	0.1
Manitoba	2,430	2,480	2,396	–1.4
Saskatchewan	2,194	1,955	1,959	–10.7
Alberta	8,176	8,252	8,291	1.4
British Columbia	10,017	10,115	10,125	1.1
Yukon	68	91	90	32.4
Northwest Territories	94	83	68	–27.7
Nunavut	7	8	6	–14.3

Source: The Daily, Tuesday May 4, 2004, http://www.statcan/Daily/English/040504/d040504a.htm.

riages), for two years 18 percent, for three years 25 percent, and a peak is reached with a divorce rate of 25.7 percent for those married for four years. The risk of divorce decreases slowly for each year after the fourth. In 2001, the majority of divorces (60 percent) were among those married for fewer than 15 years.

In 2001, 29 percent of custody arrangements after divorce (mainly for children under 18) were granted through the courts rather than outside the legal divorce proceedings. In 49.5 percent of these cases custody was awarded to the wife—the first time in Canadian history that custody was awarded to the wife for fewer than half of the dependants. In 1988, the wife was awarded 75.8 percent of dependants, and this number has been declining ever since.

Increasingly, the courts are ruling in favour of joint custody of children, so that in 2001 41.8 percent of dependants were awarded to the husband and wife jointly (The Daily, May 4, 2004).

■■ Birth Rates

One of the most dramatic changes to Canadian family life has been the steady decrease in birth rates over the past 50 years. In 1997 there were just 43 births for every 1,000 women in Canada aged 15 to 49, less than half the figure in 1959 when there were 116 births per 1,000 women in this age range.

Most of the long-term decline in the birth rate occurred in the 1960s, when the number of births per 1,000 women aged 15 to 44 fell from 116 in 1959 to just over 70 in 1969. However, after a fairly stable two decades, birth rates are falling again. The birth rate of 43 to every 1,000 women in 1997 was 26 percent lower than the 1990 rate. In total, there were 341,000 births in Canada in 1999, down 1.4 percent from the total just a year earlier and 15 percent fewer than in 1992.

Because a variety of birth control methods are more readily available than they were 50 years ago, and as more women seek careers outside of the home, more couples choose to be childless, and there is less pressure to raise children, so do we see that Canadians are having fewer and fewer children.

Whether the rates remain relatively stable, increase, or decline, the number of Canadians affected by divorce will continue to be in the millions. Children as well as adults are affected; both the number and the proportion of children affected are increasing. In 1970, 85 percent of children lived with both parents. By the late 1990s, only 68 percent of children lived with both parents (Snyder and Sickmund 1999:8).

During the 1960s and 1970s, divorce was the major cause of single-parent families. Since then, however, delayed marriage and out-of-wedlock births are responsible for more mother–child families than is divorce (Bianchi 1995). As noted earlier, three out of 10 children are born to unmarried mothers. A parent also may be lost through death, separation, or abandonment. The combination of all these factors has meant a dramatic increase in the number of single-parent families since 1970. The proportion of families with both parents present has decreased. We show below some of the consequences of living in a single-parent family.

One-third or more of marriages in Canada involve at least one partner who has been married before (Milan 2000). If the remarriage includes children from a previous marriage of one or both partners, a **blended family** is formed. Demographers estimate that the blended family will be the main type of Canadian family by 2010.

Conflict with or about stepchildren may be common in blended families, putting a strain on the marriage. As a result, the divorce rate among second marriages is even higher than that among first marriages. White and Booth (1985) found that the percentage who divorced over a four-year period was slightly higher for remarried (8 percent) than for first-married (6 percent) couples if one of the partners in the remarriage was previously unmarried. The chances of divorce went up (to 10 percent) if both partners were previously married (with no children), and went up considerably (to 17 percent) if both were previously married and one or both brought stepchildren into the marriage.

At the beginning of the 21st century, the 2001 Census shows that the makeup of the Canadian family has declined from the traditional one of mother, father, and two or more children living at home to one in which there are no children living in the family home.

Many Canadian families do not include children living at home—the rate was 39 percent of married couples in 2001, up from 35 percent in 1991, 32 percent in 1981, and just 27 percent in 1971. Because many couples are now marrying for the first time, or remarrying later in life, it may be that their children are now too old to live at home, or that the couple can no longer have them.

As of May 15, 2001, married or common-law couples (whether heterosexual or lesbian/gay) with children aged 24 and under and living at home represented only 44 percent of all families. These accounted for 49 percent of all families in 1991 and more than one-half in 1981 (The Daily, October 22, 2002).

In 2001, 15 percent of all Canadians over the age of 15 lived alone. This was especially the case for those aged 65 and over. In 1996 (the date for which most recent figures are available), 29 percent of Canadian seniors lived alone, compared to 9 percent of individuals aged 15 to 64.

Senior women were more likely to live alone than senior men; in 1996, the rate was 58 percent of women aged 85 and over. That year, 49 percent of senior women aged 75 to 84 lived alone, compared with 30 percent of both women and men aged 65 to 74 and men aged 85 and over, 19 percent of men aged 75 to 84, and 14 percent of men aged 65 to 74 (Statistics Canada 1996 Census).

blended family
a family formed by marriage that includes one or more children from a previous marriage

▪▪ Family Violence

Information on the amount of *violence in families* shows that it is not a rare phenomenon. Violence, of course, represents an alarming example of the failure of supportiveness. It is found in every kind of family and can reach extreme levels. For example, family fights are one of the most frequent reasons for police calls. In fact, in the U.S. domestic violence is one of the leading causes of death among women and is the most common cause of nonfatal injury (Kyriacou et al. 1999).

Studies of *spouse abuse* and *child abuse* were rare until the 1960s. Since then, numerous studies, including some national surveys, have been undertaken. In 2001, the Canadian Incidence Study of Child Abuse and Neglect reported that 135,573 child maltreatment investigations were carried out across Canada by provincial child and family service agencies. Of this total, 61,201 (45 percent) were substantiated, 29,668 remained suspect (22 percent), and 44,704 (33 percent) were unsubstantiated. The types of abuse most often perpetrated against children were as follows: physical abuse, 31 percent; sexual abuse, 10 percent; emotional abuse, 19 percent; and neglect, most prevalent at 40 percent (National Clearinghouse on Family Violence 2001:37).

One of the most contentious issues currently being debated by Canadians is with respect to the issue of corporal punishment and the extent to which parents can discipline their children. On January 30, 2004, the Supreme Court of Canada ruled that parents have a limited right to use physical punishment to discipline children. Section 43 of the *Criminal Code* states that "every school teacher, parent or person standing in the place of a parent is justified in using force by way of correction towards a pupil or child, as the case may be, who is under his care, if the force does not exceed what is reasonable under the circumstances."

One-quarter of all violent crimes reported to a sample of police services in Canada in 2001 involved cases of spousal/family violence. Two-thirds of these cases were violence committed by a spouse or an ex-spouse, and 85 percent of the victims were women. Spousal violence is defined by Statistics Canada (2003) as cases of murder, attempted murder, sexual and physical assault, threats, criminal harassment, and other violent offences in which the accused person is a spouse, ex-spouse, or common-law partner of the victim.

Severe violence occurs in some families.

From 1996 to 2001, the rate of incidence of spousal violence reported by police increased, and did so for both women and men. One of the social solutions to family violence in Canadian communities has been the creation of shelters for abused women and their children. From 1992 to 2002, the number of shelters in Canada increased from 376 to 524; shelters exist in every province and territory in Canada. Table 11.3 shows that the number of women and children using such shelters across the country is very high. Table 11.4 shows the reasons why women and children utilize shelter facilities.

Every year, the Transition House survey takes a one-day statistical snapshot of the activity in shelters in Canada. On April 15, 2002, a total of 3,287 women and 2,999 children were residing in shelters in Canada. The majority of women (73 percent) and of children (84 percent) were there to escape abuse in the family home. On that day, 115 shelters referred 295 women and 257 children elsewhere; in three-quarters of these cases, the shelters were full.

Abuse takes many forms: sexual and physical assault; threats and harassment; and financial, emotional, and psychological abuse. One-

TABLE 11.3 ▪ ▪ ▪

Annual Admissions to Shelters, by Province and Territory, 2001/02

	Admissions[1]		
	Total	Women	Children
Canada	**101,248**	**55,901**	**45,347**
Newfoundland and Labrador	1,162	693	469
Prince Edward Island	232	113	119
Nova Scotia	1,897	1,117	780
New Brunswick	2,131	1,224	907
Quebec	21,148	14,379	6,769
Ontario	34,588	18,066	16,522
Manitoba	6,565	2,911	3,654
Saskatchewan	4,572	2,088	2,484
Alberta	10,642	5,086	5,556
British Columbia	15,909	9,168	6,741
Yukon	754	417	337
Northwest Territories	1,030	397	633
Nunavut	618	242	376

[1]A person may be admitted more than once during the reporting period.
Source: Family Violence in Canada: A Statistical Profile. 85-224-XIE. http://www.statcan.ca.

	Women				Dependent Children			
	Abuse[1]		Non-Abuse[2]		Abuse[1]		Non-Abuse[2]	
	Number	%	Number	%	Number	%	Number	%
Total	**2,401**	**73**	**886**	**27**	**2,513**	**84**	**486**	**16**
Transition house	1,219	84	238	16	1,094	94	64	5
Second-stage housing	542	95	28	5	760	98	17	2
Safe home network	16	94	0	0	12	100	0	0
Women's emergency centre/shelter	230	42	311	57	260	55	215	45
Emergency shelter	253	65	134	35	328	94	20	6
Family resource centre	23	40	34	60	15	22	52	78
Other[3]	117	45	139	54	44	30	105	70

TABLE 11.4 ▪ ▪ ▪

Number of Women and Children Residing in Shelters and the Reasons for Admission, by Facility Type, April 2002

[1]Abuse includes physical and sexual abuse, threats, harassment, and financial and psychological abuse.
[2]Non-abuse includes housing problems, mental health problems, drug and alcohol addiction, and other reasons.
[3]Includes rural family violence prevention centres, interim housing, and other facility types.
Source: *Juristat*: Canada's Shelters for Abused Women. 2001/2, Vol. 23, No. 4. p. 17.

quarter of women and 16 percent of children were in shelters for other reasons, including housing problems, mental health problems, and drug and alcohol addiction. Among the women who left shelters on April 15, 2002, only 12 percent were known to have returned to their spouse. One-quarter left the shelter to go to alternate housing, 19 percent went to other accommodations, 12 percent went to stay with relatives or friends, and the remainder returned to their homes without their spouse.

Even though the majority of individuals who are abused within family relationships are women and children, in 2001/2 there were no shelters in Canada specifically for the needs of adult males; however, some shelters provided services to men abused by family members. In the year ending March 31, 2002, 18 men were admitted to shelters for reasons related to family violence (The Daily, June 23, 2003).

Family violence may take the form of spouse abuse, child abuse, or abuse of parents (including the abuse of elderly parents by adult children). Abuse of parents is probably less common than the others. Still, in a survey of 469 university students, Browne and Hamilton (1998) found that 14.5 percent acknowledged using violent tactics with a mother and/or father, and 3.8 percent admitted that they were severely violent. A substantial number of the violent students, it should be noted, also reported being maltreated by their parents in earlier years.

Spouse abuse involves wives beating husbands as well as husbands beating wives. According to Statistics Canada, family members convicted of most forms of violent crime against spouses, children, and seniors are less likely than other violent offenders to be given prison terms (The Daily, July 6, 2004). The one exception was in regard to criminal harassment or stalking. In these cases, one-third of spouses convicted of this crime received a prison term, compared with one-quarter of offenders who were not convicted of spousal violence. Table 11.5 provides additional information.

The violence of women against their husbands is frequently a case of self-defence or, at least, a response to prior abuse by the husband. The probability of severe injury

TABLE 11.5 ■ ■ ■

Sentencing in Single-Conviction Cases of Spousal Violence and Non-Spousal Violence[1]

Note: Percentages may not equal 100 percent due to rounding.

[1]This demonstration study excludes all cases with multiple victims.

| Spousal Violence | Percentage of Total Cases | | | |
	Prison Term	Conditional Sentence	Probation	Other
Sexual assault	28	24	48	0
Major assault	32	5	61	3
Common assault	17	1	74	8
Uttering threats	18	2	76	4
Criminal harassment	32	8	58	3
Other violent offences	46	10	41	2
Total	**19**	**2**	**72**	**7**
Non-Spousal Violence				
Sexual assault	36	15	43	6
Major assault	36	5	47	12
Common assault	21	1	58	19
Uttering threats	25	1	64	9
Criminal harassment	26	5	67	1
Other violent offences	72	7	18	2
Total	**29**	**4**	**53**	**14**

Source: *The Daily*, Tuesday July 6, 2004. Family Violence: Demonstration Study of Sentencing Outcomes, Statistics Canada, Catalogue No. 85-224-XIE.

MARITAL QUALITY AND WELL-BEING OF CHILDREN

As noted in the text, the family is a central element for individual well-being. In nations throughout the world, the more stable and harmonious family life, the higher the life satisfaction of family members. Four researchers surveyed 2,625 male and 4,118 female college students from 39 nations on six continents (Gohm et al. 1998). They categorized the nations by whether they have a collectivist or individualist culture. In individualist cultures (such as the United States, Canada, Germany, Australia, Japan, and Spain), people perceive their lives as depending largely on their own actions. They see society as a collection of individuals rather than as a highly integrated group. They believe that the course of their individual lives has no necessary relationship to the course of social life. Thus, they see possibilities for individual success and happiness even if the society as a whole is deteriorating.

In collectivist cultures (such as China, Brazil, India, and Tanzania), people perceive their lives as inextricably bound up with what happens in groups and in the nation as a whole. They cannot conceive of individual success that is independent of the groups to which they belong. Individual happiness, for them, is not as important as group well-being.

The researchers thought that the well-being of the college students in their survey might vary not only by the kind of family in which they grew up but also by the kind of culture in which they lived. Some of their results are shown in figure 11.1.

Clearly, there were both cultural and state-of-marriage differences in student well-being. Generally, students in individualist cultures scored higher on a life satisfaction test than students in collectivist cultures. But regardless of the type of culture, students from intact homes (with two natural parents or a remarriage) in which there was low interparental conflict tended to score higher than those from homes with a single parent or with high interparental conflict. The highest scores of all were those in homes headed by a married couple with low conflict.

In sum, for people everywhere, the family is important for individual well-being. If the family is functioning well, the well-being of each member is maximized. If the family is functioning poorly, all members are adversely affected.

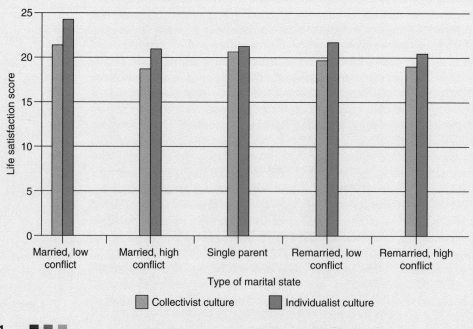

FIGURE 11.1 ■ ■ ■

Marital status and child well-being in 39 nations.

Source: Gohm et al. 1998.

is also greater in the case of wife beating than husband beating. However, interviews with 90 women and 10 men who filed assault charges against an intimate partner found that the adverse emotional effects on the victimized women and men were about the same (McFarlane et al. 2000).

Child abuse, another form of family violence, is more likely when one of the natural parents is missing. Children in a single-parent home, or those with a stepparent, are much more likely to be victims of abuse (Snyder and Sickmund 1999). According to a Statistics Canada report conducted in 2004, crimes by parents against their children continued to increase in Canada in the previous five years. In a subset of 18 urban centres, police records and court files showed that between 1997–8 and 2001–2 there were more than 4,000 convicted cases of assault against children and youth under age 18; 84 percent of those charged with these criminal offences were men. Family members convicted of physical violence against children received less harsh sentences, compared with cases that did not involve family members. However, those who committed sexual assaults against their children were given harsher penalties than those against children to whom they were unrelated.

The same study determined that there were more than 700 convicted cases of assaults against seniors. The convicted perpetrators of these crimes were just as likely to be family members as non–family members.

In terms of murder-suicides, the study concluded that between 1993 and 2002, 31 percent of males who killed their spouses also committed suicide, compared with 3 percent of females. In 61 percent of chargeable cases the murder of a female spouse resulted in the most serious charge of first-degree murder; in comparison, in the case of murders of a male spouse this charge resulted 32 percent of the time, with charges lowered to second-degree murder. In these cases, the female spouse was found to have killed her husband in self-defence, whereas in the cases where husbands killed wives the murders were seen as planned and deliberate. Between 1993 and 2003, women were four times as likely as men to be killed by their spouse. The risk was higher among younger women and common-law spouses (Statistics Canada 2004). Clearly, as these statistics and many others show, for some women, and for children in particular, family is the least supportive and safe place in which to live!

Indeed, one way to get a more accurate indication of the amount of abuse is to ask the victims themselves. In a study of juniors and seniors in a midwestern U.S. high school, Roscoe and Callahan (1985) reported that 43 percent of the adolescents said they had experienced some physical violence in their homes. Fathers were more likely than anyone else to be the perpetrators of the violence. The most common form of abuse was slapping, but 18 percent (21.1 percent of the boys and 14.8 percent of the girls) said they had been hit with a fist, and 16 percent said that an object had been thrown at them or they had been kicked.

Incest, which we discussed briefly in chapter 4, is more likely to victimize girls than boys. About 4.5 percent of the abusers are fathers of the girls (Russell 1986). Father–daughter incest usually begins when the girl is between six and 11 years of age, and lasts an average of two years (Stark 1984). The father may initiate the sexual relationship by force or by intimidation. The mother may collude by refusing to acknowledge the incestuous relationship.

Besides the observable and measurable supportive problems in family violence, there is a considerable amount of supportive failure that we cannot measure—intense conflict or alienation within families. In addition, there is the problem of neglect. Neglectful parents abuse their children psychologically through lack of feeling and caring. They are emotionally distant from their children. They may be struggling to retain their own sanity or totally absorbed in their own pleasures. For whatever reason, they provide none of the support that parents typically give. Neglected children may never learn to trust adults. They may suffer various physical ailments because of inadequate nutrition, clothing, and sleep. They are likely to have retarded intellectual development and be insecure, withdrawn, and unable to express emotions.

▪▪ FAMILY PROBLEMS AND THE QUALITY OF LIFE

The effect of family problems on the *quality of life* is sometimes obvious and sometimes not. Physical violence against a person by someone in his or her primary group produces emotional trauma as well as physical pain. *Alienation from those in one's primary group is emotionally traumatic.*

Parenting is demanding and stressful even when there are two parents in the home. Not surprisingly, both single parents and their children face a broad range of stresses, including feelings of responsibility, task, and emotional overload on the part of the parent; and emotional, interpersonal, and school problems on the part of the children (Goldberg et al. 1992; McLanahan and Sandefur 1994; Gringlas and Weinraub 1995; Dunifon and Kowaleski-Jones 2002).

Supportive problems mean, by definition, that family members endure some degree of stress. But the consequences of structural problems are less clear. Much of this section will be an examination of structural problems. You will discover that supportive problems also have some not-so-obvious consequences for the quality of life.

Most of the effects that we discuss later in this section involve a *contradiction between interaction patterns and Canadian values.* Supportive problems mean that interaction patterns within the family contradict the value of emotional and physical health. Structural problems result in interaction patterns that contradict the value of social adjustment. Because children who grow up in homes where parental relationships have ended lack experience with either a mother or a father, they often have various problems of adjustment and have to cope with such things as illness, poverty, and deviant behaviour more than others do.

The structural characteristics peculiar to the blended family, on the other hand, can lead to different types of problems (Lauer and Lauer 1999). Each member of a blended family may have lost an important primary relationship. Children may be angry about the loss and focus that anger on the stepparent. The noncustodial parent may interfere with the blended family's adjustment. The children and the stepparent also might compete for the custodial parent's attention and affection; the stepparent, after all, is entering an ongoing relationship as an "extra" member. The stepparent and children may even have difficulty because the role of stepparent is still somewhat ambiguous. Is the stepparent to be like a parent, a friend, or a teacher? Finally, the children may try to work their biological parents one against the other to gain various ends. Thus, in both single-parent and blended families, interaction patterns may diminish the quality of life.

▪▪ Physical and Emotional Difficulties

Physical and mental illnesses are rooted, in part, in family arrangements. National data show that children growing up with both biological parents receive more social, emotional, and material support than children in any other kind of family (Marks 1995). In contrast, broken homes (structural failure) and homes in which parents frequently quarrel (supportive failure) have been linked to stress in children, often resulting in physical or emotional illness.

For adults, adjustment to divorce has *striking similarities to the bereavement process.* Contrary to a popular notion that divorce may be an avenue to freedom and therefore an exhilarating experience (at least once the legal procedure has been com-

An increasing number of Canadians struggle in their role of single parent.

pleted), divorced people typically face a painful process of adjustment not unlike that which occurs after a death in the family. In both death and divorce, a *primary relationship has been disrupted,* and the disruption of a primary relationship is always traumatic. A sense of loss, bewilderment, uncertainty, and deprivation is likely to follow.

Particularly in the first months, divorce is more likely to bring emotional and physical disturbances than the anticipated sense of freedom. In fact, various studies have shown that those who are divorced have higher rates of suicide, death from various other causes, accidents, physical and mental ailments, and alcoholism (Kitson, Babri, and Roach 1985; Kurdek 1990; Richards, Hardy, and Wadsworth 1997). Of course, these problems are not always the result of a divorce. In some cases, they existed prior to, and helped bring about, the divorce, but they also can result from the divorce. In addition, there can be longlasting as well as short-term consequences. A U.S. study of divorced women found that anger, loneliness, and depression can continue for 10 years or more after a divorce (Wallerstein 1986). While some people can turn a divorce into a positive experience of growth, even they suffer short-term negative consequences (Lauer and Lauer 1988). Unfortunately, others experience long-term trauma.

These consequences together with its high rate make divorce a major health problem. The problem is likely to become more severe as fathers play a more nurturing role in the family and thereby suffer greater loss if the relationships with their children change (Jacobs 1982). Incidentally, in assessing the amount of trauma involved in divorce, one should not overlook those in the larger family group, such as the parents of the divorcing couple. They may be sufficiently distressed by the divorce to require supportive help (Johnson and Vinick 1981).

While parents, grandparents, and other relatives may endure varying degrees of distress, children suffer the most in divorce. The negative consequences for young children and adolescents whose families are disrupted by divorce include the following:

- Children in divorced families are more likely to be anxious, depressed, and withdrawn than those in intact families, and their mental health problems tend to persist when they become adults (Peterson and Zill 1986; Dawson 1991; Amato 2001).
- Children in divorced families are more likely to have eating problems and disorders (Wynn and Bowering 1990).
- Young women from divorced families rate themselves as less attractive and report more dissatisfaction with their bodies than do women from intact families (Billingham and Abrahams 1998).
- Children in divorced families tend to receive less maternal warmth and empathy (the conflict and pain of most divorces leave little energy for nurturance of children), which contributes to various emotional and behaviour problems (Kline, Johnston, and Tschann 1991).

- Children in divorced families rate themselves lower in social competence, and, in fact, are likely to be less sociable and less responsive at home, school, and play (Peretti and di Vitorrio 1993).
- Children in divorced families have lower levels of emotional well-being when they become adults (Amato and Sobolewski 2001).

Children also face *problems of adjustment.* They confront questions from peers, particularly when they are in elementary school, about why they have only one parent at home. They have to adjust to a change in primary relationships and possibly to restricted interaction with one of the parents (generally the father). They may have to cope with parental conflict, which often continues after the divorce, and with attempts by each parent to gain the child's loyalty and affection at the expense of the other. It is not surprising, then, that children whose parents are divorced are prone to both emotional and physical problems.

However, in a re-examination and analysis of 92 relevant and related studies on the effects of divorce on children, researchers Amato and Keith (1991) found that on average the overall effect of divorce on children's well-being is not strong and is declining over time. This may be in part because divorce is becoming a more common cultural reality and fewer stigmas are associated with it; further, many support groups for the children of divorced parents now exist in schools and on the Internet, making it easier for them to share their experiences with others.

Most of the studies conducted with children whose parents have divorced, or who are in the process of obtaining a divorce, use as data providers families that have sought psychological and therapeutic counselling because they are unable to cope with the consequences of the family breakdown. Those who are able to adjust—and even to celebrate the divorce as a positive experience—do not become part of the database. Therefore, our knowledge of those who successfully divorce, both children and parents, is scant.

Other researchers (Nielsen 1999; Pasley and Minton 2001; Thompson and Amato 1999) have observed and documented the fact that many behavioural and adjustment problems experienced by the children of divorced parents existed prior to the divorce and therefore cannot be attributed to it.

Nevertheless, the discord that leads to divorce is probably more stressful for the child than is divorce itself (Kelly 1998). Parents who stay together "for the children's sake" may actually harm the children more than if they were to separate. A home with continual conflict or emotional coldness can be more damaging to the children than a home where the parental relationship has ended. Children from divorce-disrupted families have higher rates of depression and withdrawal than others, but the rates are even higher for those who live in a home with persistent conflict than for those who live in a single-parent home (Peterson and Zill 1986). Self-esteem also may suffer; primary school girls and adolescent girls and boys in conflict-ridden homes tend to have lower self-esteem than others (Amato 1986). In addition, a longitudinal study reported that high levels of family conflict were associated with increased levels of depression, anxiety, and physical symptoms among adolescents over time (Mechanic and Hansell 1989). There were no such longitudinal changes in health outcomes among those whose parents had divorced.

Thus, the intact home may have supportive problems that are far more damaging to the child or to the spouses than a structural problem would be. In other words, while structural problems of broken homes are associated with various kinds of physical and emotional problems, this does not mean that the intact home is free of such problems.

What about the blended family? Does remarriage mitigate the negative health effects of divorce? As noted earlier, the blended family has its own peculiar set of problems.

In the long run, stepchildren seem to do as well as those who grow up with both biological and adoptive parents. However, in the short run, children in blended families do exhibit more behaviour problems of various kinds (Hetherington 1993; Thomson, Hanson, and McLanahan 1994); but they are not lower than those in intact families in self-esteem, psychological functioning, or academic achievement—although the outcome may vary by type of stepfamily. One U.S. study found that sixth- and seventh-grade students living with stepfathers had higher self-esteem and reported fewer problems than those living with stepmothers (Fine and Kurdek 1992).

As far as the effects of abuse are concerned, there tends to be both *short-term and long-term trauma*. Abused children may become withdrawn and isolated; feel shame, guilt, or unworthiness; and become anxious and depressed (Cole 1995). They are likely to exhibit, to a greater degree than nonabused children, a variety of problem behaviours, such as quick anger, frequent fighting, resisting of parental authority, school problems, and violence (Markward 1997). Abuse at an early age can also lead to impaired brain functioning (Teicher 2002).

The problems of abused children tend to persist into adulthood. Physical or sexual abuse during childhood is associated with a wide assortment of problems among adults: physical ailments, emotional problems, substance abuse, post-traumatic stress disorder, and attempted suicide (McCauley et al. 1997; Rudd and Herzberger 1999; McGruder-Johnson et al. 2000; Dube et al. 2001). Some of these problems appear in those who observed violence in their families as well as those who were the victims of family violence (Julian et al. 1999).

Thus, the damage from abuse can be severe. The physical harm ranges from bruises and broken bones to permanent brain damage and even death. The emotional harm is more difficult to measure. Yet some indication may be seen in both the high rates of mental disorders and attempted suicide (deWilde et al. 1992).

▪▪ Poverty

We previously noted that *female-headed families* are more likely to experience *poverty* than male-headed families. Since most single-parent families have a female head, they have a higher probability of being in poverty than do other homes. Moreover, the never-married single mother is even more likely than the divorced single mother to be in poverty. Because of low welfare payments and low wages in available jobs, the single mother may be caught in a bind: Whether she works or stays home and receives welfare, she may find herself and her family living in poverty (Tilly and Albelda 1994). In recent years, the rate of poverty among families headed by a female with no husband present has been more than twice that of the general population. In 2001, Canadian women were about 20 percent more likely to live in poverty than Canadian men (Swift, Davies, Clarke, and Czesny 2004:179). Some 56 percent of all single mothers in Canada live below the Statistics Canada Low Income Cutoff (ibid).

Because there is a correlation between the *absence of the father and lower academic achievement* (recall that education is vital to upward mobility), poverty tends to be perpetuated by the absence of the father from the home. Children in single-parent homes tend to have lower academic self-concepts. Compared with those who grow up with both parents, teenagers who spend part of their childhood apart from their natural father are twice as likely to drop out of high school (McLanahan and Sandefur 1994). They are, therefore, less likely to achieve higher levels of education, occupation, and income (Caspi et al. 1998). They are more likely than those who grew up with both natural parents to be both out of school and out of work into their early 20s (McLanahan and Sandefur 1994; Caspi et al. 1998).

▪▪ Deviant Behaviour

Sexual variance, drug and alcohol abuse, and juvenile delinquency have been associated with disturbed family life. We pointed out in earlier chapters that prostitutes and drug and alcohol abusers often have a background of disturbed relationships with their parents. There is also a higher rate of deviant behaviour among children in single-parent homes (Pfiffner, McBurnett, and Rathouz 2001). Using a representative national sample of adolescents in the U.S., Dornbusch et al. (1985) found that children in mother-only homes are more likely than those in two-parent homes to have two or more contacts with the law, to have been arrested, to be truants, to have problems at school, to be runaways, and to smoke regularly (see also Thornberry et al. 1999).

Additional research underscores the negative impact of disturbed family life. Thus, intact-family children have fewer absences at school; higher popularity ratings; higher IQ, reading, spelling, and math scores; and fewer behavioural problems at school than do children from divorced families (Guidubaldi, Perry, and Nastasi 1987; Dawson 1991). Adolescents from divorced families tend to have higher rates of drug use (including alcohol) and premarital sexual activity, poorer academic performance, and higher rates of dropout from school (Flewelling and Bauman 1990; Needle, Su, and Doherty 1990; Zimiles and Lee 1991; McLanahan and Sandefur 1994). Even when the child in a single-parent home is strongly attached to the custodial parent, the child is still more likely than those in an intact home who are strongly attached to both parents to engage in delinquent activity (Rankin and Kern 1994).

▪▪ Maladjustment

maladjustment
poor adjustment to one's
social environment

People who come from disturbed families tend to have various difficulties that we subsume under the category of **maladjustment:** antisocial behaviour (such as aggression and bullying), insecurity, overconformity to one's peers, a tendency to withdraw from relationships, difficulties in relating to others, problems with one's personal identity, and various problems as adults. For example, those who grow up in a single-parent home are, as adults, more likely to be fitfully employed and more likely to have marital problems, including divorce (McLanahan and Sandefur 1994).

The maladjustment affects all areas of a child's life. Divorce, severe parental conflict, and abuse all are associated with higher rates of conduct disorder and problems with both adults and peers (Fendrich, Warner, and Weissman 1990; Gringlas and Weinraub 1995; Flisher et al. 1997). Such children have problems with trusting others and, therefore, it is difficult for them to establish effective relationships.

These problems of maladjustment continue to afflict the children as they grow into adulthood. A significant number of abused children, for example, will become abusers themselves when they grow up. They are far more likely than those not abused to be aggressive and abusive in intimate relationships, including relationships with their own children.

From the point of view of the child, *abuse is a form of rejection.* It is, however, not the only way in which parents can reject and distress a child. Parental hostility is a form of supportive failure that can result in maladjustment as the child attempts to relate to others. Inconsistency—including inconsistency in discipline—in how the parent treats the child is another form of supportive failure. Inconsistency means the child lives in a capricious environment, and no one functions well with chronic uncertainty. Consequently, parents who are inconsistent in the way in which they relate to and discipline their children foster various kinds of maladjustment, including hostility and difficulties in relating to peers and to adults (Gross, Sambrook, and Fogg 1999).

The *child's sense of self-esteem,* so important in his or her social functioning, is crucially related to family experiences. Self-esteem tends to be high when a child has nurturing parents and a harmonious family environment (Scott, Scott, and McCabe 1991). Parents build self-esteem through such things as affirming and supporting their children, showing their children how to constructively express their feelings, taking an interest in their children's activities, showing respect for their children's point of view, and teaching their children how to exercise self-control and handle responsibility. In contrast, supportive failure, including abuse, is related to low self-esteem (Gelles and Straus 1988), and low self-esteem tends to lead to emotional and interpersonal problems.

■■ Same-Sex Families

Canada is among the world leaders (along with the Netherlands, Belgium, and Spain) in our attempts to grant same-sex marriage equality to lesbians and gay men. In the summer of 2005, members of Parliament voted to pass Bill C-38, "An Act respecting certain aspects of legal capacity for marriage for civil purposes." The Act amended the Charter of Rights and Freedoms to ensure that same-sex couples have equal access to the civil effects of marriage and divorce.

Statistics on same-sex families in Canada are very difficult to acquire for a variety of reasons. Lesbians and gay men may have children from previous heterosexual marriages; they may adopt; and they may have children through artificial insemination or egg donation, either through fertility clinics or as a private arrangement with friends or relatives. They may bring children into relationships from previous ones, or as lone parents. Whereas some same-sex families may have parents who are legally married or who have domestic registered partnerships (or the equivalent), and who would therefore be part of a statistical database, others choose not to formally register their relationship.

In the 2001 Census, of the 34,200 same-sex common-law couples who identified as families, 15 percent of the females had children, as compared to only 3 percent of the males. It is important to reiterate the fact as noted elsewhere in this book that the 2001 Census did not ask questions about sexual orientation; rather, the question raised was whether or not persons were living with a partner of the same sex (Wichmann 2005).

Even though no official demographics exist for lesbian and gay families with or without children, it has been estimated that three million lesbian and gay couples in the United States are raising one or more children (Gabb 2004). In Canada, it has been estimated that approximately half a million gay and lesbian parents are raising children (Arnup 1995:167).

■■ CONTRIBUTING FACTORS

The factors we examine in this section contribute to both structural and supportive problems. Some families suffer from both types of problems. The two types can be independent, but more often are interdependent. Structural problems, for instance, may either make supportive failure more likely or reflect supportive failure in the past.

■■ Social Structural Factors

Social Norms. An important factor in the divorce rate is that divorce is more "respectable" now than it was in the past. In other words, the *norms about divorce have changed.* In the past, religion and the law both said in effect, "You should not get a divorce. You should make every effort to work it out and stay together." Today the norms about divorce reflect a loosening of the laws ("no-fault" divorce) and greater tolerance among religious groups. In contrast to the *stigma* formerly attached to divorce and the divorcee, most Canadians now agree that divorce is an acceptable option if the marriage isn't working out. This is based on the norm of happiness, the notion that each individual has the right, if not the obligation, to be happy. The *fallacy of non sequitur* may be involved in the process: "I have a right to be happy; therefore, I must get a divorce." Even if you agree to the individual's right to happiness, it doesn't follow that divorce is necessary. All marriages have troubled times. Those who have achieved long-term, satisfying marriages point out that happiness comes by working through problems, not by avoiding or leaving them (Lauer and Lauer 1986). Of course, some marriages may be hopeless, but many break up too quickly because people believe the marriage is infringing on their right to happiness.

Divorce is more likely if people marry at a young age and there is a short or no engagement period. In particular, those who marry as adolescents have higher rates of divorce than those who marry as adults (Amato and Rogers 1997). Age at marriage is one of the more important factors in marital instability.

Both structural and supportive problems are more common among the very young. In fact, adolescent marriage and parenthood have been called a case of "children raising children." Not only is the marriage more likely to break up, but problems of child-rearing are likely to be serious, including a greater probability of child abuse. A study of infanticide reported that while young women under the age of 17 have 2 percent of all births, their babies are 7 percent of all infant homicide victims (Overpeck et al. 1998). The study also reported that having more than one child before the age of 19 involves a ninefold increase in the risk of an infant homicide compared to those who have children after the age of 25.

Why do adolescents marry at a young age? Social norms define the appropriate time for marriage. For most Canadians, that time has been soon after high school graduation or, at the latest, soon after post-secondary education. In the 1950s, people lowered the

Intact families are likely to give more support and facilitate a healthier life for their members.

ideal age for getting married. Females who were not married by the time they were 20 could develop a sense of panic that they would become old maids. Males who waited until their late 20s or after to get married might be suspected of having homosexual tendencies or an inadequate sex drive (which was an affront to their manhood). Subsequently, however, the norm about marital age has reverted to earlier notions. It is now acceptable for an individual to be and to remain single. Yet the average age for marriage is still relatively young, and the single individual may not be wholly acceptable to many businesses and corporations that still prefer their young executives to be married. As long as this is the case, structural and supportive problems due to marriage at a young age will continue.

Norms also contribute to the amount of family violence in the nation. A common norm in families is that it is proper to hit someone who is misbehaving and who does not respond to reason.

Role Problems.   A number of *role problems* contribute to both structural and supportive problems. Indeed, whatever else may be true of modern marital roles, they place an *emotional burden on people that is probably unprecedented in human history*. Modern couples often do not have the proximate interpersonal resources available to those in extended families or to those in small, preindustrial communities. Instead, they rely heavily on each other for advice, intimacy, and emotional support in times of difficulty or crisis.

Moreover, the marital role is ambiguous as well as demanding. *Role obligations* in a changing society are not as clear-cut as those in more traditional settings. Couples who disagree on role obligations of husband and wife are more prone to divorce than those who agree. The nature of these obligations is not as important as whether the couple agrees on them and on whether each feels that the other is fulfilling them. A gap between expectations and perceived behaviour increases dissatisfaction.

The majority of heterosexual Canadian couples are willing to participate in activities once regarded as the domain of the opposite sex, but they do not want to give up their own traditional gender roles (Robinson and Godbey 1997). A husband's expectations still carry more weight than a wife's in determining the division of labour. Wives are more accepting of noncompliance with expectations than husbands are. Again, however, the crucial factor is not whether the couple is traditional or nontraditional, but whether they agree on their arrangement of role obligations.

For women, *role flexibility* is important for well-being. That is, women need to be free to choose whether to work outside the home. The number who make that choice will probably continue to increase inasmuch as those who work full time outside the home have greater work satisfaction than those engaged in full-time housekeeping (Weaver and Matthews 1990).

The divorce rate is higher among women who work outside the home (South 2001). Financial independence allows women to escape from unhappy unions, such as those in which they perceive severe inequity in the relationship. When wives work outside the home, then, negotiation over role obligations may be required to effect a more equal sharing of both responsibilities and privileges. A study of 42 dual-career couples found that those most satisfied with their marriages perceived equality and reciprocity in the sense that each spouse both gave support to and received support from the other, the partners were involved in each other's careers and had equal commitment to their relationship, and they were equally involved in making decisions about work and home (Ray 1990).

Finally, role problems can be critical in the reconstituted family. Exactly what is the relationship between stepparent and stepchild? People often bring unrealistic expectations to stepfamilies. Women who become stepmothers, for example, tend to expect themselves to:

- Somehow compensate the children for the distress caused by the death or divorce.
- Create a happy and close-knit family unit.
- Maintain happiness and contentedness in all family members.
- Demonstrate through appropriate behaviour that the notion of the wicked stepmother is just a myth.
- Love, and be loved by, the stepchildren almost immediately as if the stepchildren were her own natural children. (Lauer and Lauer 1999)

People who impose such role obligations on themselves, or who have them imposed by others, are certain to encounter problems.

Family Continuity. There is a tendency for those who are reared in problem families to perpetuate the problems in their own families. Those who come from families in which one or more parents died tend to have rates of disruption similar to those who come from intact families. But those who come from families in which the parents were divorced or separated have higher marital disruption rates than those coming from intact families (Amato and DeBoer 2001).

Similarly, family violence tends to be continued from one generation to the next (Stith et al. 2000). Parents who abuse their children were often abused by their own parents. Marital abuse also is transmitted from one generation to another. The husband who abuses his wife is likely to be a man predisposed to violence because he learned such behaviour from his parents. He may have been abused, or he simply may have witnessed violence between his parents (Kalmuss 1984; Carlson 1990). Unfortunately, some children learn from watching their parents that those who love you also hit you, and that this is an appropriate means to get your own way and deal with stress. Such children are *modelling their behaviour* after that of their parents, although that behaviour may be considered undesirable or immoral by most others.

Even if the child does not grow up to be an abuser, *the mere fact of witnessing violence between one's parents tends to lead to problems of adjustment*—problems that can continue into adulthood (Henning et al. 1996). Witnessing violence in the home is associated with such maladies as depression and other emotional ills, delinquency, and behaviour problems (O'Keefe 1994; Graham-Bermann and Levendosky 1998).

A family can perpetuate its problems into the next generation simply because it is such an important factor in the *socialization* of the child. The family is an important place for learning what it means to be a male or a female, how to function as a parent, and generally how to relate to others. Thus, there is some continuity in parent–child relationships and husband–wife relationships from generation to generation.

Stratification and Family Problems. As with all problems, there are social-class differences among families. For one, *divorce is more common in the lower strata than in the middle and upper strata* (Orbuch et al. 2002). This may seem contrary to common sense, for the well-to-do can afford the costs of divorce more easily than the poor; but financial problems put enormous strains on marital and family relationships. In fact, income is one of the best predictors of family stability. The increasing rates of structural failure as you go down the socioeconomic ladder reflect the greater potential for financial difficulties, which, in turn, produce interpersonal problems that lead to marital disruption.

Another factor that bears on the divorce rate is jointly owned property and financial investments, both of which are more likely to be held by people in the middle- and upper-income levels. Divorce is more difficult and expensive when it involves a division of assets. Middle- and upper-income people are also more likely to have a network of friends and relations who will resist their divorce and who may support them as they try to work through their problems.

Finally, the combination of the higher rates of unmarried mothers and higher divorce rates means that fewer children in the lower socioeconomic strata live with both parents. Thus, the undesirable consequences of living in a disrupted or single-parent home are more prevalent in the lower socioeconomic strata.

Supportive failure is suggested by data on abuse and neglect. A certain amount of abuse occurs in middle- and upper-class families, but both neglect and abuse seem to be more prevalent in the lower than in the middle or upper strata (Gelles and Straus 1988; Whipple and Webster-Stratton 1991; Kruttschnitt, McLeod, and Domfeld 1994).

The Family in a Changing Structure.   Rapid change of the social structure creates its own problems, including problems for families. Certain kinds of change can affect the divorce rate. If roles are in a state of flux, the potential for conflict within the family is increased and the probability of divorce becomes greater. If rapid change involves confusion and ambiguity about what it means to be a husband, a wife, or a parent, then you would expect more stress, more conflict, and more structural and supportive problems.

Most observers agree that this is a time of rapid change. Any family can put down an anchor somewhere and suddenly find that there is nothing solid to hold it in place. A family moves into a neighbourhood in the hope of having a better life, only to find the neighbourhood deteriorating. A family moves to a new city because one parent is offered a better job, only to face unemployment when an economic reversal occurs. To compound the problem, the family has no roots in the area and the family members are wholly dependent on each other for emotional support. Moreover, even if the new job opportunity works out well, the family still may be strained by the lack of a social support system. Thus, the divorce rate in America is positively related to urbanity, population change, and lack of church membership (Breault and Kposowa 1987; Amato and Rogers 1997), all of which are indicators of a lack of integration into a local community.

▪▪ Social Psychological Factors

Attitudes.   Some Canadians have negative attitudes toward the single-parent family. These attitudes contribute to the problems of the single-parent family. For example, female-headed households are found in many different societies, but they are not viewed as inherently inferior or pathological, nor do their children suffer disproportionately from economic or psychological deprivation (Bilge and Kaufman 1983). Even in Canadian society, children in single-parent, female-headed families tend to be emotionally well adjusted as long as they are not impoverished or hampered by being socially stigmatized (Olson and Haynes 1993).

Attitudes are also a factor in problems of abuse. Men who sexually abuse their children come up with a variety of rationales that minimize or even justify the incest (Hartley 1998). In cases where there is no intercourse, they may dismiss the seriousness of the relationship on the grounds that it "wasn't really sex." Where intercourse occurs, they may define it as an adult-to-adult rather than an adult-to-child relationship or maintain that the child was a willing participant who gave permission for the incest.

Values and Homogamy.   When you marry, you undoubtedly hope that the relationship will last and be rewarding to both you and your spouse. Is that more likely to happen if you and your spouse have similar or dissimilar backgrounds? The answer to this question has been debated by social scientists. Some have argued that those with

ONE BIG HAPPY FAMILY

Some utopian communities have considered traditional family arrangements detrimental to human well-being. The 19th-century Oneida community, for instance, was founded on the notion of "Bible communism." Private property was abolished, including the private property of a spouse or child. The entire community was a family. Every adult was expected to have sex relations with a great variety of others. Women who bore children cared for them for the first 15 months and then placed them in the "children's house," where they were raised communally and taught to regard all adults in the community as their parents.

Secure literature about utopian communities of the present or past (see Lauer and Lauer 1983). For example, you might investigate Bethel, Brook Farm, Oneida, Ephrata, the Icarians, the Rappites, the Shakers, or any one of numerous contemporary communes. Consider what kinds of family arrangements they have created. Do any of these arrangements solve the kinds of problems discussed in this chapter? Why or why not? Do the utopian arrangements appear to create other kinds of problems? Would the utopian arrangement be practical for an entire society? What is your own ideal after reading about the utopians and the alternatives mentioned earlier in this chapter?

heterogamy
marriage between those with diverse values and backgrounds

homogamy
marriage between those with similar values and backgrounds

dissimilar backgrounds (**heterogamy**) will be attracted to each other and will *complement* each other so that the marriage is more rewarding and successful. Others have argued that *similar backgrounds and shared rather than different values* (**homogamy**) are more likely to produce a rewarding and lasting marriage.

Research generally supports the view that homogamy is more conducive to a lasting marriage. While homogamy does not mean that the couple must have similar backgrounds in every respect, it appears that the greater the similarity, the greater the likelihood of a satisfactory marriage (Whyte 1990). This kind of relationship is more likely to result when there is similarity in family background, socioeconomic background, cultural background, personality traits, and religion. Homogamy tends to correlate with marital happiness. Perhaps the more similarity between spouses, the fewer areas of conflict. In any case, shared rather than dissimilar values are important in securing a satisfactory marriage. Structural and supportive problems are more likely to occur when the couple come from dissimilar backgrounds and hold diverse values.

The Value of Success. The Canadian *value of success* can lead to supportive failure in the family. Merton (1957:136 ff.) showed how the "goal of monetary success" pervades society so that Canadians "are bombarded on every side by precepts which affirm the right or, often, the duty of retaining the goal even in the face of repeated frustration." In families, schools, and the mass media, they are urged to pursue the goal with unrelenting diligence. Most Canadians share this value of success. Even in the lower socioeconomic strata, where people often do not *expect* success, they still *wish* for it.

Monetary success often requires long hours at work and minimal contact with family. What are the consequences? Many Canadians believe that lack of time together is one of the greatest threats to the family today (Mellman, Lazarus, and Rivlin 1990). Sixty-one percent of those in a national survey said they find it difficult to enjoy life because of the time consumed in earning a living (Castro 1991). It seems clear that a strong emphasis on success can result in supportive failure in the family. Those who are attaining such success may be neglecting their families. Those severely frustrated in their attempts may react with violence in the family setting. In either case, the family members are the victims of a value that is deeply ingrained in Canadian society.

Ideology of the Family. Unfulfilled or conflicting expectations about role obligations can lead to marital dissatisfaction and dissolution (Pasley, Kerpelman, and

Many Canadians believe that lack of time together is the family's greatest threat.

Builbert 2001). *The Canadian ideology of the "good" family generates a set of expectations* that may create problems if the expectations are not met. Two versions of this ideology exist, each of which can give rise to unrealistic or conflicting expectations.

One version asserts that *a good family is a happy family* and that *happy families are harmonious* and free of conflict. Further, the family is a kind of miniature society in which all important human relationships and feelings can be experienced. Each person can find within the family a complete range of experiences in the context of harmony and happiness. This view of family life is unrealistic, and the result is a higher rate of emotional stress when conflict is suppressed because of the ideology.

A different version of the ideology of the good family stresses the need to express feelings and engage in creative conflict. This ideology has grown out of small-group work and says, in effect, that the good family maintains *healthy relationships* and that healthy relations can be obtained only when people give *free expression to their feelings*. People should "level" with each other and accept each other.

If the first ideology errs by condemning conflict in the family, the second one errs by encouraging too much *anger and aggression* in the home. Giving free expression to feelings may provide you with a sense of release and relief, but it does not enhance the quality of your interpersonal relationships. The free expression of anger is likely to lead to verbal and even physical aggression. In marriage, the higher and more severe the level of aggression, the lower your satisfaction and the more likely you are to experience disruption (Rogge and Bradbury 1999).

Finally, the *ideology of nonintervention* also affects family problems. According to this ideology, there is a strong reluctance on the part of outsiders to interfere in family affairs. People who might aid a woman being beaten by a man would not interfere if that same man were beating his wife. People who might stop a woman from abusing a child would not intervene if that child were her own.

The ideology of nonintervention affects the police as well. As Ferraro (1989) found, the police may use their ideologies about battered women and family fights to evaluate specific incidents. The police officers with whom Ferraro worked believed that if battered women opted to stay in their situations, it was not the responsibility of the police to control the violent behaviour. One male officer even insisted that since a man's home is his castle, he should be able to do whatever he wants there. Furthermore, the officer asserted, most wife abuse is provoked by the woman herself. Thus, in spite of a presumptive arrest policy (arrests are required when there is probable cause and the offender is present), the police frequently did not arrest the offender. Rather, they would reassure the woman and tell her to call them if anything further happened.

Such negative experiences with law enforcement authorities are less common now, but they still exist and lead some women to be hesitant about trying to get help from the police. Research with victims who came to a battered women's shelter found that two-thirds of the women had had contact with the police some time during the previous six months, but most did not have as much contact as they had needed (Fleury et al. 1998). The women gave various reasons for not calling the police, including *fear of even greater violence* and *previous negative experiences with the police themselves.*

▪▪ From Social Problems to Solutions

As with all problems, *both therapeutic and preventive measures* can be applied. Therapeutic measures include the more traditional counselling services as well as newer efforts involving discussion and interaction in small-group settings. Public policy could require intervention, counselling, and needed protection in cases of abuse and divorce. Such measures, of course, attempt to resolve problems after they have already begun.

What kind of preventive measures could be taken? That is, what measures might minimize the number of family problems? New approaches could be tried; for instance, the legalization of a system of trial marriage. Couples would contract to marry for a specific period of time and then have the option of renewing the contract. However, you need to be aware of the nature of experiments. They are searches—often blind gropings—for answers, and not firm guidelines. That means that some experiments may work, but others may not (and perhaps may even make a problem worse). A contrary approach would be to make it harder to divorce.

Beneficial *family life education*, at all stages of the life cycle, through the schools and the mass media, could change negative attitudes about single-parent families and the legitimacy of violent behaviour, as well as break down harmful ideologies about the "good" family. Family life education might change some norms. The way in which changed norms could affect family well-being is illustrated by the norm of family size. As Blake (1989) has shown, children from small families do better than those from large families in numerous ways, including educational attainment and social and cultural activities. Of course, the norms for family size have changed over time. Many families are reaping the advantages of fewer children, but those in the lower socioeconomic strata are more likely to have larger families than those in the middle and upper strata, thus perpetuating their disadvantaged situation.

The point is that changing norms is not a trivial matter. New norms can affect family life in crucial ways. Norms needing to be changed include those about young marriages (again, this is mainly true for those in the lower socioeconomic strata) and those about roles and the division of labour in the home. Husbands today are more willing than in the past to agree with greater role freedom for their wives. Yet even women who have careers still tend to take major responsibility for home and children. Canadians are egalitarian in theory but not yet in practice.

A great many false or counterproductive ideas can be attacked through educational programs. There are a variety of *marriage enrichment programs* that can help couples confront and work through the common issues in marriage and family life. Such programs teach couples how, among other things, to create and maintain good communication patterns, handle conflict constructively, work out an equitable division of labour in the home, and manage their finances.

The problem of family violence needs to be addressed through the law, education, and practical aids like shelters for battered women. These efforts need to be buttressed by bringing about ideological changes in the culture. Religious groups can help in this, for there is a lower amount of domestic violence among those who report regular attendance at religious services than among those who are not regular or who are nonattenders (Ellison, Bartkowski, and Anderson 1999; Cunradi, Caetano, and Schafer 2002).

Ideologies of the family where authorities and others (such as neighbours or relatives) regard domestic violence as a private matter need to be changed. If domestic violence is a private matter, then, people will be hesitant to intervene and offer help to the victim, particularly when the ideology is combined with the *fallacy of personal attack*. The fallacy of personal attack is the argument that the woman has done something to deserve the violence. A former victim of abuse told two of the authors that she stayed in her marriage for many years because everyone she knew, including her priest and her own family, kept telling her that she must be doing something wrong to make her husband act so violently! Hopefully, education through schools and the mass media can change people's understanding of family violence, get rid of the old ideologies, and lead to an open confrontation of the problem. Spouse and child abuse must be seen for what they are: crimes of violence and not justifiable acts within the confines of a group—the family—that is off limits to outsiders.

Finally, shelters for battered women also address the problem of violence. They provide many services, including emergency shelter, crisis counselling, support groups, child care, and assistance with housing, employment, and education. These shelters help reduce the amount of domestic violence. The very existence of shelters warns batterers that their wives have an alternative to remaining in an abusive relationship. Although the number of shelters has increased over the past few decades, there are still too few to meet the demand (Goodyear 2001). Even when the shelters have room, they may require women to find alternative housing within weeks; and the waiting lists for public or subsidized housing can be anywhere from seven months to years. The lack of alternatives ultimately forces many of the women to return to the men who battered them. Additional shelters would allow more women to escape abusive relationships, and the shelters also would stand as a visible reminder to men that violence against women is no longer tolerable.

As indicated above, family problems, like others we have examined, are more intense in the lower socioeconomic strata. At least some of the problems of family life are intertwined with the problem of poverty. Solving the poverty problem will not completely resolve family problems but it will alleviate some of the difficulties.

■■ SUMMARY

Family problems are so common that some observers have argued that the family, as we know it, is doomed. Those who predict the end of the present type of family suggest a number of alternatives, such as group marriages, trial marriages, open marriages, or cohabitation. But most Canadians continue to marry and establish homes, and to prefer that over alternatives.

The problems of the family stem from the fact that it is one of the most important primary groups. Canadians believe the family to be the cornerstone of society and that an ideal family provides stability, support, and continuity for Canadian values. We can identify two basic types of problems: structural (disruption and reconstitution of families) and supportive (lack of emotional support).

Several kinds of data suggest the extent and seriousness of family problems. Structural problems may be measured by the divorce rate, by the number of single-parent families, and by the number of reconstituted families in which there is a stepparent–stepchild relationship. Supportive problems are evident in the amount of family violence, including child abuse.

All family problems diminish the quality of life. Physical and emotional difficulties may result from family conflict. Additional problems of adjusting to a broken home result from separation or divorce. And problems of adjustment to new and ambiguous roles must be confronted in the stepfamily. Poverty is more frequently associated with a female-headed than with a two-parent family, and the poverty tends to be perpetuated because the child from a single-headed family does not perform as well academically as others. Several kinds of deviant behaviour have been associated with disturbed family life: sexual deviance, drug and alcohol abuse, and juvenile delinquency. People who come from families with problems tend to develop various kinds of maladjustment: antisocial behaviour, interpersonal problems, and low self-esteem.

Norms that are permissive about divorce and that encourage young marriages are two social structural factors that contribute to family problems. Role problems contribute to marital dissatisfaction and thereby lead to both structural and supportive failure. Family problems are especially likely to occur when there is disagreement on role obligations, and when expectations are in conflict

and unfulfilled for one or both spouses. The stepfamily has its own peculiar set of problems, stemming from the difficulties of the stepparent–stepchild relationship. The family itself also contributes to future family problems. Because parents act as role models for their children, the children may learn patterns of behaviour that will create future problems.

Family problems are generally more prevalent in the lower social strata, partly because of financial strains and partly because of different norms and roles. Rapid social change is yet another structural cause of family problems.

Among the social psychological factors, attitudes are important. Social attitudes tend to stigmatize the single-parent family. Attitudes are important for those victims of abuse who develop attitudes that justify the abuse, thereby perpetuating it—and attitudes of the abusers toward themselves (such as low self-esteem) are part of the reason for the violent behaviour. Values are also a significant factor in family problems. A couple with similar values based on similar backgrounds is more likely to have a satisfactory marriage. The value of success in Canadian culture, on the other hand, puts a strain on marriages and family life because certain occupations can consume those who are striving for that success.

Two "good family" ideologies generate expectations and behaviour that strain marriage and family relationships. One says the good family is happy and free of conflict, which can lead to a suppression of conflict and guilt. The other claims that in the good family people can freely express their feelings, including aggression; this ideology can perpetuate debilitating conflict. Both ideologies tend to result in supportive problems. Families need a balance between excessive openness and free expression of feelings, on the one hand, and suppression and guilt, on the other hand. Finally, the ideology of nonintervention worsens the problem of abuse within the family.

As we noted at the beginning of this chapter and elsewhere, the only constant in the makeup of the Canadian family is the element of change. Now that lesbians and gay men are allowed to marry in Canada, we will see an increase in the numbers of same-sex families, thus pushing the boundaries of the Canadian family structure into even further challenges.

■■ KEY TERMS

Blended Family 300, 306
Childless Family 300
Cohabitation 301
Common-Law Family
  301

Divorce Rate 301
Extended Family 300
Family of Choice
  (Affinity) 301
Heterogamy 322

Homogamy 322
Lone (Solo) Parent Family
  300
Maladjustment 316
Nuclear Family 300, 301

Primary Group 303
Same-Sex Family 301
Single-Parent Family 300

■■ STUDY QUESTIONS

1. What are some alternative forms of the family?

2. In what ways is the Canadian family changing?

3. What are the important functions of the modern family?

4. What are the various kinds of problems that afflict families, and how extensive are those problems?

5. How does family disruption affect the physical and emotional well-being of people?

6. How do family problems relate to deviant behaviour and maladjustment in families?

7. What norms contribute to family problems?

8. Explain the role problems that can result in both structural and supportive difficulties in families.

9. What are the relationships between the stratification system and family problems?

10. Name and explain the kinds of attitudes, values, and ideologies that contribute to family problems.

11. What are the therapeutic and preventive measures that can address family problems in Canada?

12. Where do you think Canada would fit on the chart on page 310 (figure 11.1) and why?

13. Would you like to live in an Oneida community as discussed on page 322? Why or why not?

■■ FOR FURTHER READING

Booth, Alan, and Ann C. Crouter, eds. *Just Living Together: Implications of Cohabitation on Families, Children, and Social Policy.* Mahwah, NJ: Lawrence Erlbaum Associates, 2002. An exploration, by a variety of experts, of individual, familial, and social causes and consequences of cohabitation.

Casper, Lynne M., and Suzanne M. Bianchi. *Continuity and Change in the American Family.* Thousand Oaks, CA: Sage, 2002. An examination of various facets of change and continuity in family life in America in the last half of the 20th century, including cohabitation, work, parenting, and single-mother families.

Daniels, Cynthia R., ed. *Lost Fathers: The Politics of Fatherlessness in America.* New York: St. Martin's Press, 2000. A collection of diverse perspectives on how the lack of a father in the home intersects with such issues as welfare, poverty, sexuality, family values, children's well-being, and the race problem.

Furstenberg, Frank F., Jr. Thomas D. Cook, Jacquelynne Eccles, Glen H. Elder, Jr., and Arnold J. Sameroff. *Managing to Make It: Urban Families and Adolescent Success.* Chicago: University of Chicago Press, 1998. Shows how some disadvantaged families managed to help their children achieve success in spite of their impoverished situations.

Lauer, Robert H., and Jeanette C. Lauer. *'Til Death Do Us Part: How Couples Stay Together.* New York: Haworth Press, 1986. A study of 362 couples who have been married 15 years or more, showing how they keep their marriage intact. Compares happy, long-term marriages to those in which one or both partners are unhappy.

McLanahan, Sara, and Gary Sandefur. *Growing Up with a Single Parent: What Hurts, What Helps.* Cambridge, MA: Harvard University Press, 1994. Details how children growing up in one-parent homes are more likely to suffer various adverse outcomes, and shows how inadequate resources can explain much of the disadvantage of such children.

Thompson, Ross A., and Paul R. Amato. *The Postdivorce Family: Children, Parenting, and Society.* Thousand Oaks, CA: Sage, 1999. An examination of the consequences of divorce for children and for parents, including custody and parenting after divorce and the social consequences of a high divorce rate.

HEALTH CARE AND ILLNESS: PHYSICAL AND MENTAL

LEARNING OBJECTIVES

1. Understand the meaning and extent of physical and mental illness.

2. Know the kinds of undesirable consequences of illness, including suffering, disrupted interpersonal relationships, constraints on personal freedom, and economic costs.

3. Discuss the ways in which Canadians receive inadequate health care, including deinstitutionalization.

4. Show how roles and social institutions affect health care problems.

5. Describe the attitudes, values, and ideologies that contribute to the health care problem.

6. Identify some ways to address Canada's health care problems.

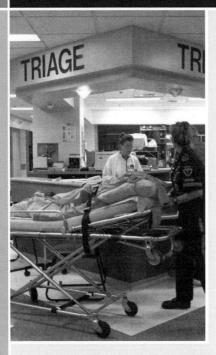

"IF YOU WANT TO LIVE A LONG LIFE"

Tami, in her 40s, has what she calls a "bizarre, cruel disease." She also says the disease may be helping her live a long life: "If you want to live a long life, get a chronic disease and take care of it." Tami's story illustrates both the trauma of chronic illness and the ability of some people to triumph over the trauma and live a reasonably normal life:

> I have lupus. It is intermittent and recurrent, and I know it can destroy my life, my will to live, and my ability to cope. In lupus, your body and soul are enmeshed in a web of pain and desperation. When the symptoms first appeared, people thought I was a hypochondriac. Doctors said nothing was wrong with me. They labelled me a neurotic, and I began to think of myself that way. Friends and family saw me looking well one moment and distressed the next. My internist finally turned me over to a psychiatrist. Nothing helped.

> Then I got a new physician, and I had the shock of learning that I had a complicated, chronic illness that would alter all my plans and dreams for my life. I was both relieved and in panic. It was a relief to finally identify the problem. It was panic to know what the problem was. I suddenly had to confront the possibility of my own death. A feeling of emptiness spread throughout my body.

> Before I got sick, I was full of life. Now I was physically, emotionally, and spiritually exhausted. At times, I could barely raise my arms to attend to personal needs. My husband remained optimistic. My daughter was angry. But as time passed, I was forced to make a decision: I had to try to take charge of my life, or waste away into nothing. I began a program of educating myself. Slowly, I got stronger. I went into remission. No one knows if it was the treatment or my changed attitudes or just a natural process.

> I harbour no false hopes. I know I'm not cured. Sometimes, when the sun is shining I feel sad. I want to go out and bask in it. I want to forget that the

sun is my enemy, that it can kill someone with lupus. But I get over the sadness. I can't make the lupus disappear by an act of my will, but I can refuse to let it destroy my spirit. I don't know what the future holds. For now, I just focus my energy on what I can control, and live moment to moment. ■

■■ INTRODUCTION

If you were living before 1910, were sick, and randomly chose a doctor, your chances of benefiting from that doctor's ministrations were less than 50 percent. Your chances today are much better, but they vary according to such things as whether you are physically or mentally ill, live in the city or a rural area, and are poor or well-to-do. The unequal probabilities of all Canadians having good health and good health care contradict the *value of equality*. Inequality of care, then, is one reason why health care is a social problem.

Another reason why health care and illness are social problems is that both physical and mental illness may be induced by social factors. For instance, poverty may force an individual to live in an unhealthy physical environment. Rapid social change may generate anxiety, depression, or other mental disorders.

Adverse effects on health are serious because Canadians place a *high value on good health*. Indeed, this high value is reflected in the fact that North Americans say good health contributes substantially to their happiness and life (Pilcher 1998; Michalos, Zumbo, and Hubley 2000). It is also seen in the use of health and health care to measure the quality of life in communities, as well as in the enormous amounts of money Canadians spend to secure good health.

prevalence
the number of cases of an illness that exist at any particular time

incidence
the number of new cases of an illness that occur during a particular period of time

epidemiology
the study of factors that affect the incidence, prevalence, and distribution of illnesses

In this chapter, we examine health care and illness by first drawing the distinction between physical and mental illnesses and then discussing their **prevalence** in Canadian society. (Prevalence is the number of cases of a disease that exist at any particular time, while **incidence** is the number of new cases that occur during a particular period of time.) Next, we show how the problem affects the quality of life. Then we consider the **epidemiology** of physical and mental illness—the factors that affect the incidence, prevalence, and distribution of illnesses. Finally, we discuss ways to deal with the problem.

■■ NATURE OF THE PROBLEM: HEALTH CARE AND ILLNESS

Are Canadians unnecessarily concerned about their health and health care system? Doesn't Canada have some of the world's best medical care? Whatever the facts may be about the health of Canadians and the adequacy of the health care system, *people's attitudes reflect deep concerns*. A poll taken in 2001 showed that health ranked as the highest pressing social issue for Canadians (69 percent), followed by child poverty (58 percent) and education (52 percent) (Perspectives Canada 2001).

As we examine the nature and extent of physical and mental illness, keep in mind that the two are not really separable (Ziegelstein 2001; Jacobsen et al. 2002). Physical illness can cause emotional problems. Mental illness can be manifested in physical distress. Both physical and mental illness have social causes. However, the methods used to assess the extent of physical and mental illnesses are different and must be discussed separately.

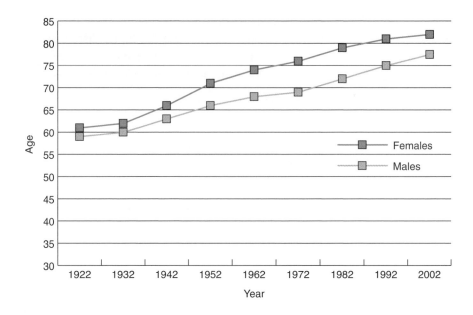

FIGURE 12.1 ■ ■ ■

Life expectancy at birth, 1992–2002.

Source: Adapted from Statistics Canada 2004.

■■ Physical Illness

life expectancy

the average number of years a newborn can be expected to live

Important indicators show that Canadians have made important advances in health matters. For instance, **life expectancy,** the average number of years a person can expect to live, has increased dramatically (see figure 12.1). In 2002, Canadians are expected to live one-third longer than Canadians born in 1920. In large part, this increase in life expectancy *reflects reduced infant mortality and lower rates of infectious diseases.* It isn't that the majority of people lived only until their late 50s in the early 1900s. Rather, the large number of infant deaths combined with the high rate of infectious diseases among the middle-aged severely depressed the average length of life. Sanitation, better diet, reduced fertility, and advancing medical knowledge and technology greatly reduced both the prevalence and the seriousness of infectious diseases.

Despite the progress, physical illness is a major problem. It is even a problem for the young, with close to one-third of young Canadians aged 12 to 17 believing their health is "no better than 'good'" (The Daily, Oct. 31, 2003).

Table 12.1 shows the diseases primarily responsible for death. Cardiovascular diseases, including high blood pressure, coronary heart disease, rheumatic heart disease, and strokes, afflict millions of Canadians and have been at the top of the list since the beginning of the 20th century.

Chronic diseases are the major cause of death in Canada (table 12.1). Chronic diseases are those of long duration. They may be classified along a number of dimensions (Rolland 1987). They may be *progressive* (worsening over time) or *constant.* Lung cancer is progressive, whereas stroke is constant. Their onset may be *acute* (short-term) or *gradual* (occurring over an extended period of time). Stroke is acute, whereas lung cancer is gradual. They may be *fatal* (lung cancer), *possibly fatal or life-shortening* (stroke), or *nonfatal* (kidney stones). Although heart disease and cancer are the leading causes of death, the most common chronic conditions are arthritis and sinusitis. Dementia, including Alzheimer's disease, afflicts one-third or more of those who live to age 85 (St. George–Hyslop 2000). Increasing concern has developed over health problems created by obesity. One measure of obesity is one's score on the body mass index (BMI): 14.9 percent of Canadians between ages 20 and 64 have a BMI of 30 or

TABLE 12.1   ■ ■ ■

**Selected Leading Causes
of Death, by Sex, 1997**

[1]Age-standardized mortality rate
per 100,000 population.

	%	Males Rate[1]	Females Rate[1]
All causes	**100**	**844**	**521.6**
Cancers	27.2	229.7	148.5
Diseases of the heart	26.6	230.8	129.7
Cerebrovascular diseases	7.4	52.8	43.9
Chronic obstructive pulmonary diseases and allied conditions	4.5	44.5	20.1
Unintentional injuries	4	37.8	17.9
Pneumonia and influenza	3.7	31.5	19.2
Diabetes mellitus	2.6	20.6	14.8
Hereditary and degenerative diseases of the central nervous system	2.3	16.7	13.9
Diseases of arteries, arterioles, and capillaries	2.2	19.5	10.6
Psychoses	2.2	13.3	13.4
Suicide	1.7	19.5	4.9
Nephritis, nephrotic syndrome, and nephrosis	1.2	11	6.1
Chronic liver diseases and cirrhosis	0.9	8.9	4.2
Neurotic disorders, personality disorders, other nonpsychotic mental disorders	0.5	4.8	2.5
HIV infection	0.3	3.6	0.5

Source: Adapted from Statistics Canada 2004.

higher. According to the World Health Organization, a BMI of greater than 30 is considered obese (Health Indicators 2003). Diabetes is another growing concern. For example, in 1997 only 2.7 percent of Canadians had diabetes (see table 12.1); in 2001, 4.5 percent of Canadians—approximately 1.1 million—were diagnosed with diabetes (Millar and Young 2003). Explanations to account for the increase include aging, family history, inactivity, and being overweight.

There is also concern about a *resurgence of infectious diseases.* Infectious disease mortality declined during the first eight decades of the 20th century (Armstrong, Conn, and Pinner 1999). However, the rates began to increase in the 1980s and 1990s. Today, infectious diseases are a serious problem throughout the world (see the Global Comparisons box later in this chapter). Infectious diseases cause more deaths worldwide than heart disease and cancer combined. In addition to increasing rates of such diseases as tuberculosis, at least 30 previously unknown diseases have emerged in recent decades, including Lyme disease (caused by a tick bite), AIDS (discussed next), legionnaires' disease (spread via air-conditioning systems), toxic shock syndrome (caused by ultra-absorbent tampons), and SARS. New infections whose source may be obscure and for which there is no known treatment continue to appear. These include bacteria and new strains of diseases like tuberculosis that are resistant to the most powerful antibiotics and other drugs now available (Stolberg 1998; Reichman and Tanne 2001).

As table 12.1 shows, *the health problems you are likely to face vary according to your sex.* In general, women have higher rates of acute diseases (such as respiratory ailments and viral infections), short-term disabilities, and nonfatal chronic diseases. Men have more injuries, more visual and hearing problems, and higher rates of life-threatening chronic diseases such as emphysema and the major cardiovascular diseases.

Health problems also vary according to racial or ethnic origin. This may be due as much to socioeconomic differences as to racial factors per se (Hayward et al. 2000). For example, in the United States strokes (which may be related to diet) are a leading cause of death, but the mortality rates are higher among African Americans, American Indians, and Asian Americans than among whites (Centers for Disease Control 2000). Rates also vary within ethnic groups. According to the National Center for Health Statistics (2000), Puerto Ricans have more health problems than other Hispanics. For instance, more Puerto Ricans report limiting activities, having fair or poor health, and spending time in hospital. In Canada, health status among First Nations people is poorer than that of the general Canadian population. First Nations people have higher rates of chronic and respiratory diseases, infectious and parasitic diseases, accidents, HIV/AIDS, and alcoholism (Segall and Chappell 2000; Picard 2004). Factors that explain these differences include poorer housing conditions, greater exposure to untreated water, higher unemployment rates, and lower education. Life expectancy of First Nations people is lower than that of the general population, but the gap is decreasing (see figure 12.2)—in part, according to Health Canada, because the government is "working to continue to address health inequalities among First Nations and Inuit communities by providing access to health care programs and services, and by focusing on prevention of illness and promotion of good health" (Health Canada Performance Report 2003).

Finally, *health problems vary by age and tend to intensify with age.* But, according to the National Public Health Survey, older people, up until 75 years old, report that they are generally in good health, and need little assistance with activities of daily living (see figure 12.3). After age 75, health problems do have an adverse effect on their quality of life (see table 12.2). Research has shown that chronic health problems are more prevalent among those with low income, and women (Moore et al. 1997).

AIDS. **AIDS** is caused by a virus that attacks certain white blood cells, eventually *causing the individual's immune system to stop functioning.* The individual then falls prey to one infection after another. Even normally mild diseases can prove fatal. Many AIDS patients develop rare cancers or suffer serious brain damage.

There is no cure for AIDS. Drugs can prolong the lives of some AIDS victims, but each infection takes its toll, and the immune system continues to collapse. In the

AIDS

acquired immune deficiency syndrome, a disease in which a viral infection causes the immune system to stop functioning, inevitably resulting in death

FIGURE 12.2 ■ ■ ■

Life expectancy of First Nations people, 1980–2000.

Source: Indian and Northern Affairs Canada 2001, Basic Departmental Data 2001. Ottawa: Minister of Indian Affairs and Northern Development Catalogue No: R12-7/2000E.

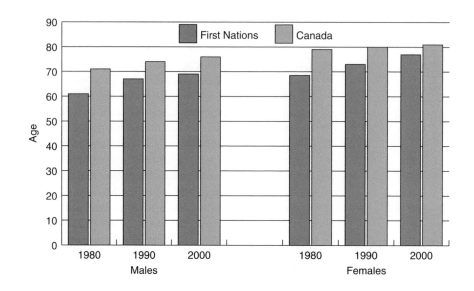

FIGURE 12.3 ▪ ▪ ▪

Self-assessed health status of Canadian women and men, age 55 and older, 1995.

Source: National Population Health Survey (http://collection.nlc-bnc. ca/100/201/300/cdn_medical_ association/cmaj/vol-157/issue-8/ 1025fla.gifPHS).

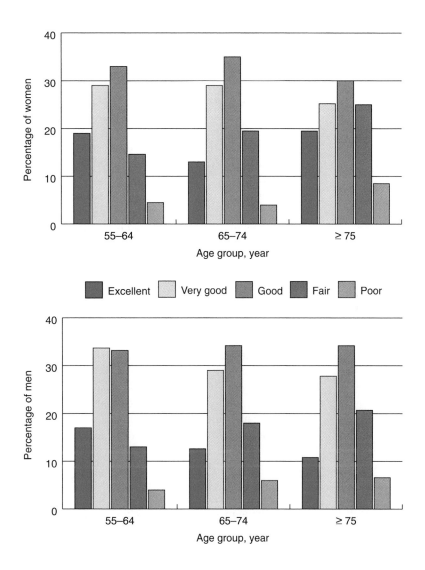

TABLE 12.2 ▪ ▪ ▪

Percentage of Elderly Canadians with a Physical Limitation, 1995

| Age | Physical Limitation; Percentage of Elderly Population | | | | |
	Vision	Hearing	Speech	Mobility	Agility
Women					
55–64	3.8	2	1.1	3.4	0.8
65–74	5.8	5.9	2.3	6.9	1.2
75	16	8.7	0.8	23.5	1.3
Men					
55–64	2.7	4.3	1	2.6	0.3
65–74	3.8	6.1	2.3	6.3	0.9
75	7.1	11.7	3.2	14.8	1.4

Source: NPHS. Adapted, with permission, from Health Reports 1996;8(3):10–1 (Statistics Canada, cat no 82-003. http://collection.nlc-bnc.ca/100/201/300/cdn_medical_association/cmaj/vol-157/issue-8/1025tab2.htm).

advanced stages of HIV infection, 15 to 20 percent of patients develop a type of dementia that involves slow mental functioning (Portegies and Rosenberg 1998). Eventually, the individual succumbs and dies.

How is AIDS spread? The two primary ways are through sex (oral, anal, or vaginal) with someone infected with the AIDS virus, and by sharing drug needles and syringes with an infected person. Some people were infected through blood transfusions before blood was tested for the virus. Infected mothers can transmit the disease to their babies before or during birth or while breastfeeding (Schwarez and Rutherford 1989). Primarily, then, the *virus is spread through blood or semen.* Females who get the disease are either intravenous drug users or sex partners of an infected male (Cohen, Hauer, and Wofsy 1989). In fact, a woman is 12 times as likely as a man to be infected with the AIDS virus during heterosexual intercourse, and, once infected, is likely to die more quickly (Ickovics and Rodin 1992).

Who is most likely to be infected? In Sub-Saharan Africa, where more than half of all AIDS victims reside, the infection is spread mainly by heterosexual intercourse (Sills 1994). In other nations, including the United States, the main causes are homosexual relationships and intravenous drug use. Worldwide, at least 40 million people are infected with the AIDS virus, 28 million of them in Africa (Ezzell 2002). The disease has cut life expectancy in Nigeria by four years, in Kenya by 18 years, and in Zimbabwe by 26 years (Stanecki 1999).

In Canada, the number of new AIDS cases peaked in the early 1990s, then declined. By 2000, the total number of AIDS cases in Canada was estimated at 49,800. Overall, people with AIDS are living healthier and longer lives. But this does not mean that AIDS is no longer the urgent problem it was in the mid-1980s. Even though most Canadians "[understand the] modes of HIV transmission, risk factors and prevention options, the virus continues to spread" (Canada's Report on HIV/AIDS 2002:2). Each year, there are more than 4,000 new cases. As mentioned above, First Nations people are proportionately more likely to become infected with HIV/AIDS (approximately 370 a year) than are the general population. Furthermore, while the number of Canadians with AIDS is decreasing, the opposite is true for First Nations people.

Although AIDS continues to be most prevalent among gay men and drug users, transmission is more often occurring through heterosexual relationships. Of concern is the increasing number of young women between ages 15 and 29 who are being diagnosed with HIV and AIDS.

The reaction to AIDS has varied from skepticism about its importance to near-panic. Some have warned of an AIDS epidemic sweeping over the nation and over the world. The extent to which Canadians are concerned is seen in a number of ways. In the early 1990s, more money was spent on research on AIDS than on any other disease except cancer (Pear 1993). There has been some increase in bias against gay men, because of their role in spreading the disease. New dating services have appeared that test people regularly and issue them cards showing that they are free of sexually transmitted diseases. Many people are afraid even to be around those with AIDS.

Some people believe that the concern over AIDS is overdrawn. Certainly, it seems an exaggeration to say that AIDS is an *epidemic.* The incidence is low compared to other diseases. Death rates are down. Moreover, there are ways to minimize the risks. Health experts advise the use of condoms as one of the best preventive measures (condoms are not foolproof, however). Others argue that only changed sexual and drug-use behaviour can eliminate the disease. Unfortunately, too many people ignore the preventive measures. People continue to share drug needles, and to have unprotected sex (in some cases, even those who know they are HIV-positive) (Diaz et al. 2002; Semple, Patterson, and Grant 2002). It is likely that AIDS will be a matter of great concern for some time to come.

THE WORLDWIDE CHALLENGE OF INFECTIOUS DISEASES

Most research money in Canada is devoted to the study of chronic diseases, the primary cause of death for Canadians. Worldwide, infectious diseases are far more prevalent and far more likely to be the cause of death. Some diseases that afflict millions of people are unknown to many Canadians and are relatively rare in Canada (see figure 12.4).

Although diarrheal diseases are the most prevalent, acute respiratory infections, such as pneumonia, kill more people annually. AIDS, tuberculosis, malaria, and measles are also responsible for millions of deaths worldwide.

In Africa, mosquito-killing insecticide reduced the number of deaths from malaria for a time, but the insects could not be effectively controlled, and the incidence of malaria increased again in the 1990s. Malaria is once again one of Africa's most serious health problems, causing approximately a million deaths a year. Children account for a majority of the deaths.

An even greater killer worldwide is tuberculosis. In 2003, for example, an estimated 1.7 million people died from tuberculosis and nearly 8.8 million new cases were added to the 15.4 million existing cases (WHO 2005).

Although the Canadian death rate from tuberculosis is now quite low, the disease presents a challenge to Canada as well as to other nations, for new strains have appeared that are resistant to formerly effective drugs. Tuberculosis is also more likely to develop in people who are infected with HIV (the virus that causes AIDS). As a result, tuberculosis could once again become the leading cause of death in the world (as it was in the early years of the 20th century). In any case, it is clear that, in looking at the world as a whole, infectious rather than chronic diseases are still the major problem. In all likelihood, they will continue to be so, as health officials grapple with both the resurgence of old diseases and the appearance of new ones.

SOURCE:
WHO Report 2005

FIGURE 12.4 ■ ■ ▨

Worldwide incidence of infectious diseases, in millions, 2004.

Source: Adapted from World Health Report 2004 and http://www.globalhealth.org/view_top.php3?id=228.

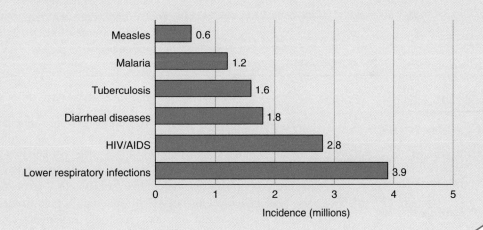

▪▪ Mental Illness

Types of Mental Illness.
Some sociologists prefer the term *mental disorder* to mental illness. "Illness" suggests to them a medical model, a problem deeply rooted in an individual that may also have an organic basis. "Disorder" suggests to them a problem that is more social in its origin and resolution. We believe that both perspectives are valid in part. A particular individual's problem may be a biologically based illness, or it may be behaviour that results from the actions and reactions of others (see the discussion of labelling below). Or it may be a combination of both. Thus, we use the terms "mental illness" and "mental disorder" interchangeably to avoid any simplistic assumptions about the problems.

EXCEPT ME AND THEE?

There is an old saying that all of the world is crazy except "me and thee, and sometimes I am not too sure of thee." As pointed out in this chapter, it is probable that only a minority of the population is free of any psychiatric symptoms. To say that someone has symptoms, of course, does not mean that the individual requires psychiatric care or has problems functioning in his or her responsibilities. Nevertheless, the ideal for Canadians would be the very best health—freedom from all symptoms.

How do you stack up? You can test yourself on a set of symptoms suggested by Walter Gove and Michael Geerken (1977). For the symptoms listed, write "often," "sometimes," or "never" beside each to indicate how often you have experienced them during the past few weeks.

1. I felt anxious about something or someone.
2. I was bothered by special fears.
3. I felt that people were saying things behind my back.
4. I felt it was safer not to trust anyone.
5. I couldn't take care of things because I couldn't get going.
6. I was so blue or depressed that it interfered with my daily activities.
7. I was bothered by nervousness.
8. I was in low spirits.
9. I was bothered by special thoughts.
10. I was so restless I couldn't sit for long in a chair.
11. I felt that nothing turned out the way I wanted it to.
12. I felt alone even when I was among friends.
13. I felt that personal worries were getting me down, making me physically ill.
14. I felt that nothing was worthwhile anymore.

Give yourself two points for each "often," one point for each "sometimes," and no points for each "never."

Your total score can range between 0 and 28. A score of 0 would mean that you are completely free of psychiatric symptoms. A score of 28 would mean that you have serious levels of those symptoms. If the entire class participates in this exercise, each score can be given anonymously to the instructor, who can give you the range and compute the average for the entire class. What do you think the results say about the prevalence of psychiatric symptoms in the population? Do you think students' scores would be higher or lower than those of the population at large? Why? Finally, do you think that a questionnaire such as this is a good measure of depression?

psychosis
a disorder in which the individual fails to distinguish between internal and external stimuli

neurosis
a mental disorder involving anxiety that impairs functioning

psychosomatic disorder
an impairment in physiological functioning that results from the individual's emotional state

Before 1980, mental disorders were separated into three broad categories: psychoses, neuroses, and psychosomatic disorders. This is still a useful way to get a general sense of the kinds of disorders that afflict people. In a **psychosis,** the individual is unable to distinguish between internal and external stimuli. The individual's thinking and perceptions are disordered. In everyday terms, he or she has "lost touch with reality." The individual may have hallucinations or fantasize in a way that has no relationship to the real world. The individual may experience chronic perplexity and uncertainty. Emotions may vacillate between extreme elation and depression, and behaviour may involve either hyperactivity or extreme inactivity.

Neurosis refers to a disorder with symptoms that are distressing and are defined as unacceptable or alien. Neuroses involve anxiety sufficiently intense to impair the individual's functioning in some way.

Psychosomatic disorders are *impairments in physiological functioning that result from the individual's emotional state.* Certain phrases express the reality of psychosomatic disorders, such as he "is a pain in the neck" or she "gives me a headache." Such expressions can be literally true. *Your emotional reactions to others* can result in aches and pains of various kinds.

Rather than a simple division of mental illness into psychoses, neuroses, and psychosomatic disorders, multiple categories are now used (DSM-IV, American Psychiatric Association 2000). The major categories (with some illustrative, specific disorders) are:

- Disorders usually first evident in infancy, childhood, or adolescence (mental retardation, conduct disorders, eating disorders).
- Organic mental disorders (alcohol-induced amnesia).
- Substance-use disorders (alcohol or drug abuse).
- Schizophrenic disorders (various forms of **schizophrenia,** a psychosis that involves a thinking disorder, particularly hallucinations and fantasies).
- Paranoid disorders (various forms of paranoia).
- Affective disorders (**manic-depressive reaction,** in which the individual fluctuates between emotional extremes).
- Anxiety disorders (phobias, obsessive-compulsive disorder).
- Somatoform disorders (the conversion of emotional into physical problems, as in hysteria).
- Dissociative disorders (multiple personality).
- Psychosexual disorders (transsexualism).
- Disorders of impulse control (pathological gambling, kleptomania).
- Personality disorders (narcissism, an absorbing preoccupation with one's own needs, desires, and image).

schizophrenia
a psychosis that involves a thinking disorder, particularly hallucinations and fantasies

manic-depressive reaction
a disorder involving fluctuation between emotional extremes

Extent of Mental Illness. *Mental illness is a problem in all societies.* It is found among preindustrial people and in small, relatively isolated communities as well as in modernized societies. How many Canadians suffer from mental disorders? Some researchers believe that about one in five Canadians in any one-year period will be affected by mental illness (Offord et al. 1996). That said, it is difficult to estimate the prevalence of mental illness. According to "A Report on Mental Illness in Canada" (2002), hospitalization data provide the best available source of information. However, hospitalization data must be interpreted cautiously because they reflect changing styles of treatment as well as changing levels of prevalence. Therapy with new drugs became common in the late 1950s. In the 1960s, **deinstitutionalization**—a movement to change the setting of treatment from the state mental hospital to the community—began. (We discuss deinstitutionalization later.) The hospitalization data (see figure 12.5) indicate that mental illness is prevalent in all age groups. Mental illness is most common in the 25 to 44 age group, and rates decrease in every subsequent age group. Of note are the high rates of mental illness in individuals between the ages of 15 and 24, signifying the emotional struggles that young adults confront. In every age group, mental illness is more prevalent among women than men. Finally, mental illness is experienced across all occupations, educational and income levels, and ethno-racial groups (A Report on Mental Illness in Canada 2002).

deinstitutionalization
a movement to change the setting of treatment of mental disorders from hospitals to the community through rapid discharge of patients

A comprehensive American survey that involved a structured psychiatric interview with a national probability sample of 8,098 Americans ages 15 to 54 years (Kessler et al. 1994) found some differing results. Among the conclusions:

- Nearly half reported at least one lifetime disorder and nearly 30 percent reported a disorder in the previous 12 months.
- At any given time, however, only 3 to 5 percent of individuals were in serious need of psychiatric help.
- The most common disorders are major depressive episodes, alcohol dependence, and phobias.
- More than half of all lifetime disorders occurred in the 14 percent of the population with a history of three or more disorders.

The study found not only *variations in prevalence of the different disorders but also variations in at-risk background factors.* Women have more affective and anxiety

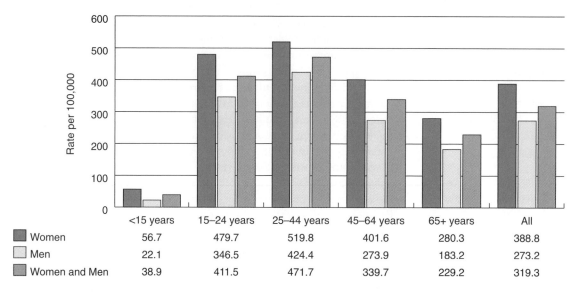

Most responsible diagnosis is one of anxiety disorders, bipolar disorders, schizophrenia, major depression, personality disorders, eating disorders, and attempted suicide.

Source: Centre for Chronic Disease Prevention and Control, Health Canada using data from Hospital Morbidity File, Canadian Institute for Health Information

FIGURE 12.5　■ ■ ■

Rates of patients in general hospital, by age and sex, Canada, 1999–2000.

Source: http://www.phac-aspc.gc.ca/publicat/miic-mmac/images/fig_1-1_e.gif.

disorders, including depression; men have more problems with substance abuse and higher rates of antisocial personality disorder. Rates of most disorders are higher in the younger age groups and lower socioeconomic strata (for a summary of the relationship between poverty and mental illness, please go to this text's Online Learning Centre at **www.mcgrawhill.ca/college/lauer**).

■■ HEALTH CARE, ILLNESS, AND THE QUALITY OF LIFE

One effect illness has on the quality of life is this: People must endure considerable stress and suffering because of illness, which is a contradiction to Canadians' value of good health. In addition, illness impacts interpersonal relationships, involves people in inadequate health care, is compounded by deinstitutionalization, interferes with individual freedom, and costs the individual and the nation economically.

■■ Stress and Suffering

The obvious impact of illness on the quality of life is the *stress and suffering* that illness imposes on people. Consider Anton Boisen's (1936:3) account of his psychotic episode:

> [T]here came surging in upon me with overpowering force a terrifying idea about a coming world catastrophe. Although I had never before given serious thought to such a subject, there came flashing into my mind, as though from a source without myself, the

idea that this little planet of ours, which has existed for we know not how many millions of years, was about to undergo some sort of metamorphosis. It was like a seed or an egg. In it were stored up a quantity of food materials, represented by our natural resources. But now we were like a seed in the process of germinating or an egg that had just been fertilized. We were starting to grow. Just within the short space of a hundred years we had begun to draw upon our resources to such an extent that the timber and the gas and the oil were likely soon to be exhausted. In the wake of this idea followed others. I myself was more important than I had ever dreamed of being; I was also a zero quantity. Strange and mysterious forces of evil of which before I had not had the slightest suspicion were also revealed. I was terrified beyond measure and in terror I talked. . . . I soon found myself in a psychopathic hospital. There followed three weeks of violent delirium which remain indelibly burned into my memory. . . . It seemed as if I were living thousands of years within that time. Then I came out of it much as one awakens out of a bad dream.

Physical illness also involves *stressful disruptions* in a person's life. If the person's work is disrupted, he or she may experience economic anxiety. If the illness is chronic, the individual may struggle with his or her identity (what kind of person am I?) and with alterations in lifestyle (Charmaz 1995). Protracted or chronic illness also affects the rest of the family (Lundwall 2002). Taking care of a chronically ill individual is demanding and stressful (Adams et al. 2002). The marital relationship may suffer (Woods and Lewis 1995). Family patterns may be altered and highly constrained by the sick member.

Because physical and mental health are intertwined, physical health problems can generate *long-term fears* and even *serious emotional problems*. A substantial number of people experience high levels of psychological distress before or after surgery (Glosser et al. 2000). People diagnosed with serious diseases such as AIDS may develop high levels of anxiety and depression, problems with their work and social lives, and thoughts of suicide (Griffin et al. 1998).

Heart attack victims and cancer patients may have problems readjusting to normal routines. They often experience depression and anxiety even when the prognosis for the future is good, and they may have serious reservations about returning to a normal routine (Peleg-Oren and Sherer 2001).

Serious *emotional problems* often are involved in cases of *organ transplants* (Dew et al. 2001). Severe depression and even psychosis have been reported. Men who receive organs from women may fear that their characters will be altered or that they will be feminized. Some patients develop fantasies about the transplanted organ and think of it almost in human terms as a living being within them. Some develop an image of the organ as a malevolent or hostile being; others conceive of it as life-giving. Not every patient has such serious problems, of course, but some long-term fears are probably common.

The *disabled* also endure stress and suffering because they are often *socially disvalued*. Social devaluation is particularly acute when the disability is visible. The visibly disabled individual may be treated as inferior and may be subject to serious disadvantages in job opportunities. Such experiences result in insecurity and anxiety.

The close relationship of physical and mental illness works both ways, because emotional problems can lead to physical illness. A physician has shown how high levels of cynicism and hostility cause bodily responses that lead to heart attacks (Williams 1989). To some extent, the problem can become a vicious circle for the individual, who may become entangled in the interaction between physical and mental disorders.

■■ Interpersonal Relationships

There is a contradiction between the *sick role* and Canadians' attitudes and values about desirable behaviour; this can result in disrupted interpersonal relationships. Although

stigma
that which symbolizes
disrepute or disgrace

people realize that illness is inevitable, they are reluctant to allow the illnesses of others to disturb their routines. Furthermore, there are some illnesses, such as cancer and various kinds of mental illness, that carry a social **stigma** (Mechanic et al. 1994; Report on Mental Illness in Canada 2002). A study of cancer survivors found discriminatory treatment at the workplace and a lower likelihood of marriage than for those without cancer (Christian 1991). A survey of parents and spouses of 156 first-admission psychiatric patients found that half of them concealed the hospitalization to some degree (Phelan, Bromet, and Link 1998). They did not want people to know that someone in their immediate family had a mental disorder.

The *strain on interpersonal relationships* when one of the interactants is ill is also seen in patterns of family relationships. Both physical and mental illness can lead to disruption in the family. In families with a chronically ill member, the ill member can become a focal point of family life. If the mother is ill, the husband and children may experience an emotional void in their lives. If the father is ill, there is a likelihood of economic problems and a lowered standard of living. Moreover, the father may tend to monopolize the attention of his wife, leaving the children feeling neglected. If the family develops a subculture of illness, they withdraw into themselves, isolated from outsiders.

Not all families respond to serious illness in this way, of course. Some families become more integrated, and the members experience a greater richness of family life. Others experience a temporary breakdown but recover and return to normal. Still others disintegrate in the face of the challenge, especially if the family was already weakly integrated. In every case, however, illness presents a serious challenge to the family.

One reason serious illness tends to disrupt family life is that it *precludes proper role functioning*. The physically or emotionally ill may be incapable of adequately fulfilling the role of spouse, parent, or breadwinner (Peleg-Oren and Sherer 2001). The normal functioning of family life may give way to a focus on the ill person. In extreme cases, most activities of family members reflect the ill person's needs and limitations.

As with the interplay between mental and physical illness, the relationship between interpersonal relations and illness can become a vicious circle. Poor interpersonal relationships can be a factor in the onset of a mental disorder, and mental disorders adversely affect interpersonal relationships. On the other hand, *good interpersonal relationships are associated with better health* (Berkman 2000). Two psychologists found that people with a strong desire and ability to engage in intimate relations have better mental health than others (McAdams and Bryant 1987). Women who scored high said they are generally happy and satisfied with work, family, and leisure. Men who scored high reported fewer problems of mental and physical health, less drug and alcohol abuse, and less uncertainty about the future.

In sum, there is a relationship between patterns of interaction and health. Illness, whether physical or mental, tends to be associated with disturbed interpersonal relationships. The relation between interaction and illness may be a vicious circle: bad interpersonal relationships being a factor in the onset of illness, and illness being a factor in causing disturbed relationships.

■■ Inadequate Care

iatrogenic problems
problems caused by the
physician in the course of
his or her treatment of a
patient

The value of good health is contradicted by the *inadequate care* that many Canadians receive. Inadequate care may be the result of **iatrogenic problems,** those caused by the physician in the course of a patient's treatment. Among other things, physicians may misdiagnose a case, prescribe the wrong medication, and even order unnecessary surgery (Weinberg and Stason 1998; Pilippo et al. 1999). In their study of an American hospital's admissions over a 14-month period, Weinberg and Stason (1998) found problems in 6 percent of all admissions, including missed or delayed diagnoses, inappropriate treatments, and complications caused by physicians. The behaviour of physicians was central to three-quarters of the problems. But, according to the Canadian Institute for Health Information (Millar 2001:80), "errors in healthcare whether they are caused by physicians, nurses or other personnel, occur in the context of the 'system' and often can be prevented through system solutions." Millar notes that in Canada there is little research that examines medical error. Extrapolating data from United States, Britain, and Australia, Millar estimates "approximately 10,000 deaths per year and hundreds of thousands of cases experiencing injury and prolonged hospital stays as a consequence of health system errors" (80).

medicalization
the expansion of day-to-day life/behaviour into the practice of medicine

Hospital personnel, including medical lab technicians, also make mistakes. A study of an intensive care unit found an average of 178 activities per patient per day and about 1.7 errors per patient per day (Donchin et al. 1995). Physicians and nurses contributed about equally to the number of errors. A survey of medication in 36 hospitals reported that nearly one of five doses were in error—given at the wrong time, not given, the wrong amount, or an unauthorized drug (Barker et al. 2002).

Women's health seems to be particularly prone to iatrogenic problems and **medicalization** (the expansion of day to day life/behaviour into the practice of medicine). One example is the unnecessary medical interventions that occur in childbirth, specifically the high rates of caesarean sections. According to the World Health Organization (WHO), a caesarean rate over 15 percent is "inappropriate usage." In Canada, the caesarean rate in 2002 was 19.9 percent, up from 18.7 percent in 2000 (CIHI 2005). However, rates vary among and within provinces; in some hospitals, up to 50 percent of caesareans may be performed unnecessarily (1993). In 2002–3, the caesarean rate in New Brunswick was 28 percent (Carr 2004), almost twice the appropriate rate determined by the WHO.

With age, women are particularly vulnerable to unnecessary medical procedures. Hysterectomy (the surgical removal of the uterus) is a case in point. Close to 60,000 hysterectomies are performed in Canada each year; approximately 90 percent are for non-cancerous reasons. An estimated 25 percent of Canadian women have had hysterectomies, compared to 30 percent of American women. The rate in Canada is twice that in Europe (Abramson 1994; Women's Health Matters 1992). Rates also vary among and within provinces. Women in Newfoundland and Labrador are more than twice as likely to have a hysterectomy than are women living in Ontario. It is estimated that half the hysterectomies performed in Canada are medically unnecessary.

Overall, medical errors probably cause more deaths than car accidents, breast cancer, suicide, homicide, or AIDS. A study by the Institute of Medicine estimated that nearly 100,000 people a year die in hospitals alone from mistakes like wrong medication, misdiagnoses, and surgical errors (Stolberg 1999).

The value of good health is also contradicted by the actual state of the science of medicine. Contrary to the expectations and attitudes of many Canadians, *medicine is an inexact science.* Many symptoms, such as extreme fatigue or a pain in the back, are difficult to diagnose. Diagnosing mental disorders is even more problematic. Psychiatry is a field of *competing ideologies* rather than a science of mental therapy. There are various schools of therapy with different ideologies of health and illness and different views about diagnostic categories. A psychiatrist's diagnosis of a case will depend partly on *which school of therapy* he or she follows, but even within a particular ideology, diagnosis of mental disorders is difficult.

A psychiatric diagnosis also may be influenced by stereotyped thinking. That is, the diagnosis may be a perfect illustration of the *fallacy of non sequitur:* "because this is a woman, her symptoms show her to be hysterical," and so forth. It isn't that the therapist consciously thinks in those terms, of course, but the diagnosis does reflect stereotypes, whether the stereotype involves gender, race, or social class (Dixon, Gordon, and Khomusi 1995; Wang et al. 2002).

For example, 209 psychiatrists evaluated two cases of patients with a schizophrenic disorder (Loring and Powell 1988). All of the symptoms were presented, but the researchers varied the race and gender of the patients. Some of the psychiatrists thought they were evaluating two white males, while others evaluated two white females, two black males, two black females, or two clients with unnamed sex and race. A majority correctly identified the disorder as schizophrenia when no sex or race was listed. For the other cases, less than a majority made the correct diagnosis. Only 21 percent diagnosed the white females correctly. The race and gender of both the psychiatrist and the patient tended to affect the diagnosis. In general, when the race and sex of psychiatrist and patient were the same, the diagnosis tended to be the same as if there were no information about the patient's sex and race. In other cases, however, the psychiatrists were affected by stereotypical thinking.

In addition to incompetence, errors, and the fact that medicine is an art as well as a science, many people do not receive the quality of care they desire because of the *maldistribution of medical care*. Both economic and geographic factors enter into the maldistribution. *Maldistribution of doctors* means that people in certain areas have less access to doctors than those in other areas. There are a disproportionate number of doctors and nurses in cities and in the more well-to-do areas of the cities, leaving many rural areas and impoverished urban neighbourhoods with inadequate care. For example, in 2000 the number of physicians per 100,000 population varied among the provinces from a low of 128 in P.E.I. to a high of 214 in Quebec (Southam Medical Database 2004). For a link to more data on this, please go to the text's Online Learning Centre at **www.mcgrawhill.ca/college/lauer**.

■■ Deinstitutionalization

The inadequate care of the mentally ill has been compounded by the deinstitutionalization movement that began in the mid-1950s (Lamb 1998). Partly because of newly available drugs, hospitals began discharging a great many patients, including some with serious mental disorders and some who could not be effectively treated without 24-hour care. The goal was to provide a more humane, more effective, and less costly method of treating the disorders by using a community setting rather than a mental hospital. The drugs would keep the patients from harming others or themselves and enable them to function relatively well while they recovered. Their recovery would be facilitated by more normal living conditions. Further, their civil rights would be respected. In other words, the movement seemed to offer a new and enlightened approach that would transform the care of the mentally ill. Unfortunately, the reality diverged sharply from the ideal, adding to the problem of inadequate care.

One goal was met: A great many patients were released from hospitals. Those who now go into hospitals are likely to stay only a short time compared to those who were institutionalized before 1960. As a result, the hospitals are treating more people than formerly, but they also have fewer patients in residence at any one time.

Nevertheless, deinstitutionalization not only has failed to solve many problems but also has created new ones. In fact, many regard the movement as a total failure because it has basically taken the mentally ill out of the hospitals and put them on the streets or in the jails (Isaac and Armat 1990; Gilligan 2001).

Studies of the homeless illustrate the way in which deinstitutionalization has failed. A majority of the homeless have serious problems of mental illness, including drug addiction (Barrow et al. 1999; Sleegers 2000). Homeless shelters are available, but they are hardly adequate to provide treatment for the mentally ill even if the staff had the time. Thus, large numbers of the deinstitutionalized mentally ill are lost and homeless or in jails. The legal basis for the deinstitutionalization movement is the right of patients to be involved in treatment—including the right to refuse treatment (Dickinson 1994:475). The difficulty, however, is balancing a contradiction that has emerged: "the fact that mental health policy and practice has a dual function: it is intended to provide care and treatment to those in need and it is intended to protect others from mentally disordered individuals who may be dangerous." To remedy this problem, the courts can order a person who is viewed as a danger to himself or herself or the community to take medication. The rationale is to prevent re-hospitalization. But, as Dickinson (1994:476) points out, "a potential contradiction can be seen to exist between the principles of protecting individuals' rights to refuse treatment, particularly if they are not an immediate danger to themselves or others, and the commitment to community care and least cost solutions of tertiary prevention (i.e. the prevention of the need for expensive in-patient treatment)." Unfortunately, most individuals with severe mental disorders require medication, and the disorders are likely to impair their judgment and make it unlikely that they will voluntarily submit to treatment.

Other problems created by deinstitutionalization include economic strain on health care budgets, adverse citizen reactions to the presence of patients in their communities, citizen fears about the dangers and lowered property values that might result if a small-group home for mental patients were set up in their community, and increased stress on those who must care for a chronically mentally ill family member (Wright, Avirappattu, and Lafuze 1999).

▪▪ Individual Freedom

Canadians are complex people. They cherish the *freedom of the individual* and tend to react strongly to anything that threatens that freedom. However, they also value good health and Canada's health care system. Some religious groups, for example, resist medical procedures such as blood transfusions and vaccinations on the grounds that these violate their religious beliefs. If they are forced to undergo such medical treatment, their religious convictions and freedom of choice are violated. However, a counterargument is made that they may jeopardize the health or the lives of others by their refusal; thus, their freedom cannot extend to the point where it affects the well-being of others.

The issue of freedom is also raised by advances in biological engineering. In the U.S., for example, the 1972 National Sickle Cell Anemia Control Act required people to submit to a screening blood test to determine the likelihood of their producing children with sickle cell anemia. Many Canadians would feel that this was a clear invasion of privacy. Many more would probably consider it an invasion of privacy if the next step were taken: preventing people with certain genetic deficiencies from having children or even from marrying. Certain genetic diseases can be controlled only by forbidding certain couples to have children. So, whose individual freedom are we protecting? (See box 12.1.)

The history of medicine is marked by ongoing conflict between the advocates of medical advances and those who defend the freedom of the individual. Greater advances in medicine will intensify the conflict and compound the problems.

▪▪ Economic Costs

It is estimated that in 2004 health care spending will cost the Canadian government $130.3 billion, a 5.9-percent increase since 2003. This is "the lowest annual growth

Box 12.1

Presentation to EU Conference, "Human Genetic Testing, What Implications?"

By Bill Albert, Chair of Bioethics Committee DPI Europe

Brussels, May 6, 2004

"...Despite the fact that the sequencing of the human genome has demonstrated our molecular commonality, its more saleable message has been about individual uniqueness and individual choice. Besides fitting in so well with the ruling ethos of our consumer society, what makes the genetics project appear even more desirable is that the choices promised have been coupled invariably with improved health. A winning and most saleable combination.

So why are disabled people, at least the disabled people who I represent in the disability movement in Europe, not won over. Why instead are we so concerned about the impact of new genetics on our human rights? There is the little issue of our recent history. Although we would not equate new genetics with the Nazi atrocities against disabled people, we can still hear the echoes and feel the icy touch of eugenic elimination in this latest, ostensibly softer, market driven phase.

It also must be remembered that throughout the world, even in those countries with anti-discrimination legislation and where social provision is comprehensive, albeit rarely adequate, disabled people remain an extremely disadvantaged minority. Disability is stigmatised and disabled people are still routinely discriminated against in education, employment, transport, access to all kinds of social and cultural activities as well as health care. We remain the poorest of the poor, in every country in the world....[I]n many countries disabled people find their basic human rights, often their right to life itself, violated as a matter of course. In many countries so called "mercy killing" of disabled people goes either unpunished or lightly punished, with the murderer often being given a sympathetic press. sinister layer of social prejudice to a group which is already socially disadvantaged and excluded.

...Let me give you a couple of examples of what I mean with respect to the current eugenic discourse. One of the main boosters of the genetic project has touted it by saying: "Soon it will be a sin for parents to have a child which carries the heavy burden of genetic disease. We are entering a world where we have to consider the quality of our children."(1) ... More recently, James Watson, made a similar observation. "I strongly favour controlling our children's genetic destinies. Working intelligently and wisely to see that good genes dominate as many lives as possible is the truly moral way for us to proceed." (2) Why do calls for this new form of 'population improvement', this new form of eugenics, seem to be so readily accepted or at least not condemned out of hand for what they are?

Well, aren't we all consumers now? And when we make choices, what do we as consumers want? Products which are not defective, at the very least. So, what is happening now and is likely to become more prevalent as the genetic project becomes stronger and more pervasive is that medical conditions will increasingly be equated with the prospective child. All the many other things which make us who we are will be ignored, lost in these genetically targeted medical conditions. A Downs child, a cystic fibrosis child, a spinabifida child, a deaf child—not a son or daughter, not a brother or sister, not a friend or lover, not a joy to the world or a pain in the ass, all of those rich possibilities too come, sliced away by a cruel genetic logic which leads to such a convenient, socially efficient equation.

Rather more prosaically, remember what one of the first question is when you've heard a friend or relative has had a baby. "And, how's the baby." Too simple? Clearly too simple, but the easy and understandable acceptance of such a loaded question, offers one key to understanding the deep-seated, profound social assumptions about disability. If you think you are immune to such assumptions, then think again. It is the continuing power of these assumptions which allows society to hold at the same time the apparently contradictory views that disabled people should be granted full human and civil rights while at the same time leading to the embrace of a social discourse and clinical genetic structures which mouths individual choice while promoting genetic cleansing.

The popular concept of geneticisation allied to big business and floating on the ethical solvent of individual choice or autonomy has begun to stigmatise and through this threatens to reduce the genuine social acceptance of human genetic diversity. There is a strong tendency in the human genetics project to restrict incrementally the idea of what human life can be. By doing so it will make those of us who are left all the poorer.

No one, least of all a disabled person, should have to defend the right to life of disabled people. No one should have to live that life in a society which values them so little it makes a social and medical virtue out of eliminating people who might be like them.

Variety is not the spice of life. It is life. In the disability movement we believe passionately that rather than promoting genetic search and destroy strategies there is an inherent value in extending our sense of what a human life can be."

(1) *Sunday Times*, July 4, 1999.

(2) *The Independent*, April 16, 2001

Source: Disabled Peoples International, http://www.dpi.org/en/resources/topics/bioethics/05-10-04_balbert.htm.

rate since 1997" (CIHI 2005). Health expenditure as a percentage of the GDP remains the same, at 10.1 percent (see figure 12.6). Compared to other G-8 nations, in 2002 Canada ranked fourth in health care spending (GDP then was 9.6 percent). The United States was the highest ranking, at 14.6 percent (CIHI 2005). The per capita cost is $4,077, a 5-percent increase from 2003. Health care spending also varies by province: Manitoba has the highest per capita cost at $4,275, while PEI has the lowest at $3,926 (CIHI 2005).

Figure 12.7 details health care costs from 1975 to 2004. Hospital costs consistently comprise the largest part of health care spending. In 2004 it is estimated to account for 30 percent of total health expenditure (CIHI 2005). Drug costs since 1997 make up the second largest part of spending, overtaking physician costs.

For the individual, burdensome costs often result from long-term chronic diseases and from diseases requiring the use of *sophisticated medical technology*. Even with Canadian health coverage, an individual or a family *may find the cost of illness oppressive*. Why the dramatic increase in costs? Four factors can account for the increase in

FIGURE 12.6 ■ ■ ■

Health care costs as a percentage of GDP, Canada, 1975–2004.

Source: Adapted from CIHI 2005 http://secure.cihi.ca/cihiweb/dispPage.jsp?cw_page=media_08dec2004_e.

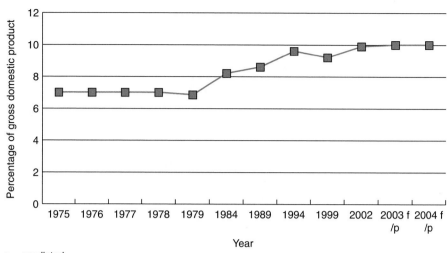

p = predicted

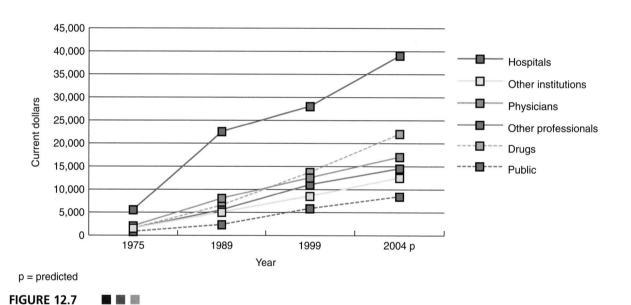

p = predicted

FIGURE 12.7 ■ ■ ■

Total health expenditure in current dollars, Canada, 1975–2004.

Source: Adapted from CIHI 2005 http://secure.cihi.ca/cihiweb/dispPage.jsp?cw_page=media_08dec2004_e.

expenditures on medical care since 1950: inflation, population growth, technological advances and the increasing use of medical services involving these expensive advances (Callahan 1998), and drug costs.

Thus, an increasing portion of the economic resources of individuals, families, and the nation are consumed by medical care (Toner and Stolberg 2002). There are two ways in which mental illness has an impact on the Canadian economy: productivity loss through absences from work, and health care costs (A Report on Mental Illnesses in Canada 2002). It is difficult to measure the exact impact on health care costs. Based on a 1996–7 National Public Health Survey, researchers estimated the cost to be $14.4 billion (ibid). With the costs of both physical and mental health care continuing to rise each year, an interesting question arises. Despite the high value placed on good health, should

Canadians forgo some measure of health care in order to retain more of their economic resources? (For more insight, see box 12.2 on Canada's health care system.)

Box 12.2

Canada's Health Care System—Medicare

Medicare is a cornerstone of contemporary Canadian culture. Canada supports a system of publicly funded, privately delivered health care. Taxes are collected at both the provincial and federal level and are allocated to not-for-profit hospitals and doctors, who essentially operate small, for-profit businesses (Raisa). Currently, there is much public debate regarding whether the system should support large, private for-profit businesses in health care delivery and whether citizens should be able to pay for medical services over and above those offered by medicare.

While medicare is a fundamental aspect of contemporary Canadian society, it has been in existence only for five and a half decades. The development of medicare followed the Second World War, when a high level of support existed for government to develop forms of universal social assistance and welfare (Paul). The growth of medicare began in 1947 in Saskatchewan, championed by then–Premier Tommy Douglas. Douglas, a staunch socialist politician, created universal, public hospital insurance within his province. Over the following 14 years, all of the other remaining provinces developed similar systems of hospital insurance, and the federal government agreed to help support the costs of publicly funded health care through the *Hospital Insurance and Diagnostics Act*. Today, Douglas has been celebrated as "The Greatest Canadian," further underscoring Canadians' belief in the importance of their health care system.

Since the birth of universal hospital services, medicare has expanded to cover more than just hospital costs. In 1968, the *Medical Care Act* ensured an equal provincial/federal sharing of medical costs beyond those generated by hospitals. By 1972, all provincial plans had broadened to cover physician services. In 1984, a critical piece of legislation was passed: the *Canada Health Act* ideologically links all of the provincial plans through a series of five health care criteria. While constitutionally each province has jurisdiction over its own public health insurance plan, the *Canada Health Act* ensures that all the provinces meet certain criteria in order to receive federal health care funding.

The five criteria set out by the *CHA* are:

1. Public administration: the administration of the health insurance plan must be handled by a public (i.e. governmental) authority on a non-profit basis
2. Comprehensiveness: provinces must insure all medically necessary physician and doctor services
3. Universality: Everyone in the province who is insured must receive uniform care
4. Portability: All insured members of the province must be able to take their coverage with them as they move and travel
5. Accessibility: Access to care must not be impeded by obstacles, financial or otherwise.

Beyond these criteria, the *Canada Health Act* also prohibits extra billing by medical practitioners, as well as user fees for insured services.

▪▪ CONTRIBUTING FACTORS

We have pointed out that there are sociocultural factors in illness. In this section we examine some of those factors in detail. We show that sociocultural factors are involved not only in the **etiology** (causes) of diseases, but also in inadequate care and the maldistribution of care.

etiology
the causes of a disease

▪▪ Social Structural Factors

Roles.   Many studies have shown that *stress* leads to a variety of physical and mental health problems, including cardiovascular disease, digestive problems, heightened susceptibility to infection, problems of the skeletal-muscular system, and mental disorders (Mayer, Craske, and Naliboff 2001; House 2002). Stress can be a product of roles that are excessively demanding, contradictory, or overly restrictive. Not everyone who occupies a particular role will experience the same amount of stress, nor will everyone who occupies a particular role get sick. Nonetheless, *certain roles are considered stress-inducing* because they have been associated with a disproportionate amount of illness, particularly the female role and certain occupational roles in Canadian society.

Women seem to have more health problems than men. Health statistics consistently show that women in Canada and other Western nations have higher rates of **morbidity,** health service usage, and certain mental disorders (A Report on Mental Illness in Canada 2002; Kazanjian 1998; Trypuc 1994; Walters 1994). In part, these health problems reflect the fact that women generally suffer more distress (sadness, anger, anxiety, aches, etc.) than men (Mirowsky and Ross 1995, Denton et al. 2004)—and this, in turn, may be rooted in the female role.

morbidity
the prevalence of a specified illness in a specified area

One characteristic of the female role is that *women are more emotionally involved than are men in the lives of those around them* (Kessler and McLeod 1984; Walters 1994). Women are more likely than men to be stressed by "network" events (events in the lives of those they care about) such as the death of a spouse, divorce, and illness of a family member. The cost of this caring is greater vulnerability to stress and illness.

The *traditional role of married women* is another reason for higher rates of illness (DeStafano and Colasanto 1990). Married women have higher rates of mental disorders than married men, but single or widowed women tend to have lower rates than their male counterparts. (Among both sexes, married people have lower rates than unmarried [Robins and Regier 1991].)

We have noted that the majority of married women now work outside the home (see chapter 9). Is it, then, a problem of overload? Interestingly, working tends to enhance rather than diminish the health of women (Hibbard and Pope 1991; Arber and Khlat 2002). In other words, *multiple roles are associated with better health* (Hong and Seltzer 1995). The point is, the restrictions of the traditional role—staying at home and taking care of the house and children—are more stressful for many women than taking on additional responsibilities. To be sure, some find the traditional role fulfilling, but others do not. Those who are confined to, but dissatisfied with, the traditional role of housewife exhibit the higher rates of illness (Shehan, Burg, and Rexroat 1986). This conclusion is supported by research showing that when men and women have equivalent gender roles, the gender differences in health tend to disappear (Bird and Fremont 1991; Gutierrez-Lobos 2000). In sum, for both men and women, role satisfaction is associated with better health (Wickrama et al. 1995).

We noted in chapter 9 that certain occupational roles generate considerable physical and/or mental risks. In some cases, the occupational role may carry intrinsic risks—for example, mining occupations or high-pressure sales jobs. In other cases, the risks reflect the particular shape the role is given by those in the workplace. For example, an engineer told two of the authors of this text:

> I love my work. But I hate this job. My boss terrorizes everyone. If it was just the work I do, I would love going in. But I get a feeling of dread when I go through the gates every morning because I never know from one day to the next what new craziness we'll all have to endure from the boss. His demands are unreasonable, and you can't sit down and discuss things with him. He has managed to turn enjoyable work into a daily grind.

The Family Context of Illness.   Among the institutional arrangements that contribute to illness are family patterns of interaction and **socialization** (the process by which an individual learns to participate in a group). We noted above that married people of both sexes have lower rates of mental illness than the unmarried. The mental health of the married couple depends on the quality of the marriage, however. When the intimate relationship between a man and a woman is defined by both as basically rewarding, the pair is likely to enjoy positive mental health (Wickrama et al. 1995). Infidelity or a conflicted relationship, in contrast, is associated with major depression (Cano and O'Leary 2000).

For children, both physical and mental health are crucially related to the *quality of the relationship between the child and parents* (Feeney 2000). Children who have a good relationship with their parents and who feel themselves to be an integral part of family life are less likely to engage in various kinds of health-risk behaviour, including the use of alcohol, tobacco, and other drugs (Resnick et al. 1997).

Family disruption is stressful for children and typically leads to higher rates of physical and emotional problems. A study of two-year-olds, for example, reported a higher proportion of accidents and higher rates of treatment for physical illnesses among those in single-parent and stepfamilies than those in intact homes (Dunn et al. 2000).

The adverse effects of a troubled family life may continue into adulthood. A long-term study of physicians reported that those who developed cancer or mental illness or who committed suicide had scored significantly lower on tests of family relationships taken when they were medical students (Locke and Colligan 1986). They felt less close to their parents and less emotionally attached to their families than did others.

Siblings as well as parents are important to a child's well-being. Thus, in a community study, researchers found that children who had siblings with a substance abuse problem were more likely both to use drugs themselves and to suffer from depression (Reinherz et al. 2000). They also found more depression among those whose parents were depressed.

The Industrial Economy.   Certain aspects of the Canadian economy, and indeed of the world economy, are involved in the onset of illness. In an increasingly industrial, technological world, people and materials move around the globe in great numbers. As Platt (1996:24) wrote: "The movement of people, plants, animals, and goods—known as biological mixing—serves to increase exposure to disease. Any person, plant, or animal that moves can potentially carry a microbe or organism that will be foreign at its destination." An infectious virus now can travel around the world in a few hours.

In the modern economy, both agricultural workers (because of the use of artificial fertilizers, herbicides, and pesticides) and other workers are exposed to materials that are **carcinogenic** (cancer-causing). Some common carcinogens in nonagricultural occupations are shown in table 12.3. People who work in industries using carcinogenic materials are more likely to get cancer than are others.

An industrial economy also exposes the citizenry to illness through *different kinds of pollution*. Lead poisoning can have disastrous effects on children: mental retardation,

socialization
the process by which an individual learns to participate in a group

carcinogenic
causing cancer

Agent	Organ Affected	Occupation
Wood	Nasal cavity and sinuses	Woodworkers
Leather	Nasal cavity and sinuses; urinary bladder	Leather and shoe workers
Iron oxide	Lung; larynx	Iron ore miners; metal grinders and polishers; silver finishers; iron foundry workers
Nickel	Nasal sinuses; lung	Nickel smelters, mixers, and roasters; electrolysis workers
Arsenic	Skin; lung; liver	Miners; smelters; insecticide makers and sprayers; tanners: chemical workers; oil refiners; vintners
Chromium	Nasal cavity and sinuses; lung; larynx	Chromium producers, processors, and users; acetylene and aniline workers: bleachers, glass, pottery, and linoleum workers; battery makers
Asbestos	Lung (pleural and peritoneal mesothelioma)	Miners; millers; textile and shipyard workers
Petroleum, petroleum coke, wax, creosote, shale, and mineral oils	Nasal cavity; larynx; lung; skin; scrotum	Contact with lubricating, cooling, paraffin or wax fuel oils or coke; rubber fillers; retort workers: textile weavers, diesel jet testers
Mustard gas	Larynx; lung; trachea; bronchi	Mustard gas workers
Vinyl chloride	Liver; brain	Plastic workers
Bis-chloromethyl ether, chloromethyl methyl ether	Lung	Chemical workers
Isopropyl oil	Nasal cavity	Isopropyl oil producers
Coal soot, coal tar, other products of coal combustion	Lung; larynx; skin; scrotum; urinary bladder	Gashouse workers, stokers. and producers; asphalt, coal tar, and pitch workers; coke oven workers; miners; still cleaners
Benzene	Bone marrow	Explosives, benzene, or rubber cement workers; distillers; dye users; painters; shoemakers
Auramine, benzidine, alphaNaphthylamine, magenta, 4-Aminodiphenyl, 4-Nitrodiphenyl	Urinary bladder	Dyestuffs manufacturers and users; rubber workers (pressmen, filtermen, laborers); textile dyers; paint manufacturers

Source: American Public Health Association; *Health and Work in America* (Washington, DC: Government Printing Office, 1975).

TABLE 12.3 ▪ ▪ ▪

Common Occupational Carcinogens

Many workers are exposed to carcinogenic materials in their workplace.

pica
a craving for unnatural substances, such as dirt or clay

behavioural difficulties, perceptual problems, and emotional instability. Lead poisoning is most common among ghetto children, who ingest chips of paint from flaking walls or other substances containing lead (Richardson 2002). Use of lead in paint was discontinued for the most part by 1950, but leaded paint still exists in older buildings. Craving for such unnatural substances—a condition called **pica**—is frequently associated with impoverished living. In rural areas, pica may lead to eating dirt and clay, which is not healthful but is probably less damaging than leaded paint.

The most familiar pollutant to many Canadians is automobile exhaust, which contains carbon monoxide. Carbon monoxide poisoning can lead to apathy, headaches, perceptual problems, retardation, and even psychosis. However, the precise effects of carbon monoxide poisoning are unclear. The amount of carbon monoxide released into the air from automobile exhaust varies considerably from one area to another. We discuss chemical pollutants further in chapter 14.

Noise is another kind of pollution linked to the industrial economy that can have deleterious effects. The noise level endured by some workers can create mental stress, as can the noise associated with living near an airport. Noise combined with other sources of stress generates considerable annoyance and may cause mental disorders.

As we noted in chapter 9, *fluctuations in the state of the economy* also have been identified as having adverse effects on people's health. Unemployment is associated with health problems in all societies (Rodriguez 2001). In fact, a study of 42 nations showed that unemployment lowers well-being even in those countries with high levels of social security (Ouweneel 2002).

The Politics of Illness.   Usually people do not think of illness as a political issue, but *government policy* is a crucial factor in health care. For example, consider the problem noted earlier of the maldistribution of health care. This maldistribution reflects, among other things, the fact that in the early 1990s the federal government substantially decreased health care funding to the provinces in order to eliminate the deficit. Many hospitals have closed; others have been forced to close beds and substantially reduce the length of hospital stays. One disturbing outcome is that there have been many more readmissions due to health complications (Clarke 1996). The more disadvantaged groups are particularly affected, as they do not necessarily have the support in the community (such as personal family physicians) for follow-up care.

Funding for research into causes and cures of diseases also reflects political as well as scientific and humanitarian considerations. We noted that more funds have been spent in recent years on AIDS research than on any disease except cancer. Since cardiovascular diseases are still the major killers, one could argue that they should receive the most funding.

Another example is the controversy about *stem cell research* (Rosenberg 2002). Stem cells are obtained from human embryos, which are destroyed in the process. Stem cells have the potential to become any type of cell. This means that they have the potential to cure a variety of diseases that result from particular cells in the body being disabled or destroyed (diabetes, Parkinson's disease, cirrhosis of the liver, etc.).

In the United States, the topic of stem cell research is particularly contentious. Because the embryos are destroyed, the Bush administration limited federal funding of research to existing stem cell lines in 2001. No new lines could be created by researchers who are federally funded. The scientific community claimed that the restrictions would severely hamper research that could lead to desperately needed cures. Right-to-lifers applauded the decision as one that safeguards human life. A few stem-cell researchers considered going to another nation, such as England, where the research can be freely pursued. The decision to restrict the research was political rather than scientific.

Recall that drugs make up the second largest part of health care spending. Drug companies and the medical profession are highly motivated by the desire to make profits. Consequently, there are numerous examples of incomplete scientific research and premature drug approval. For example, anti-inflammatory drugs to treat arthritis, such as Vioxx (approved in 1999) and Celebrex (which accounted for $2 billion in sales for Pfizer in 2003), recently have been removed from the market because their use was found to be linked to increased risk of heart attack and stroke.

Women have been particularly affected by scientific research that has proven to be flawed and incomplete. Thalidomide in the 1960s, and diethylstilbestrol (DES)[1] between 1940 and 1960, were drugs prescribed to pregnant women and women trying to get pregnant, respectively, that came with promises of effectiveness and safety. Throughout the 1990s, doctors offered menopausal women prescriptions for hormone replacement therapy (HRT) (SOGC 1994). Once again, women were confronted with assurances of safety and even health benefits, though the research established numerous health risks—breast cancer being one—associated with hormone use (Abramson 2002).

Finally, there is the issue of governmental regulations that can reduce exposure to a number of known health threats. Fagin and Lavelle (1999) ask why no regulations exist on such matters as the use of certain toxic weed killers that have been linked with cancer and birth defects in farming communities, the use of a chemical by dry cleaners that pollutes homes, and "dry clean only" labels in clothing that can now be cleaned by cheaper and safer water-based alternatives. Of course, the answer to these and the other examples they cite is that political considerations outweigh public health needs.

The Stratification of Illness.   When we speak of the stratification of illness, we are referring to the *different patterns of illness* and *variations in health care among the socioeconomic strata*. People in the lower strata have more physical health problems (including more chronic diseases) than those in the middle and upper strata; have more days of restricted activity due to illness; are less knowledgeable about and less likely to use health care services (including fewer visits to physicians and dentists); are less knowledgeable about and less likely to engage in good health practices (nonsmoking, proper diet, etc.); and are less likely to have basic preventive health measures like vaccinations (Statistical Report on the Health of Canadians 1999). They are also likely to die at an earlier age even when their health risk behaviour is no different from the behaviour of those in higher strata.

Ironically, then, poor and uneducated Canadians have the fewest resources to meet medical expenses (including, for example, prescription drugs), and the greatest likelihood of discovering that they have a serious, chronic, disabling, or even fatal illness. The pattern of physical illness in Canadian society—more problems and less help as people descend the socioeconomic ladder—is likely to continue because of both the lack of information and resources among the poor and the concentration of medical services outside the areas where they live.

The pattern for mental illness is similar. In general, the rates of psychiatric disorders are higher in the lower strata (Robins and Regier 1991; Williams, Takeuchi, and Adair 1992; Turner and Lloyd 1999; Gilman et al. 2002; A Report on Mental Illnesses in Canada 2002).

The reasons for the higher rates in the lower strata have not been precisely identified. A reasonable assumption, however, is that they relate to factors we have already discussed: more role problems, a greater degree of family disorganization, more economic stress, and less adequate care (Feinstein 1993; Ensminger 1995). In addition, those in the lower strata have more work problems, including higher rates of unemployment and unfulfilling jobs.

Changing Structure: The Future Shock Thesis.   Both the nature of the social structure and the *structure's rate of change* influence health and illness. When norms, roles, institutional arrangements, and the stratification system are in rapid flux, the individual may endure considerable stress, which can result in illness. The individual may be so overwhelmed by the lack of stability in the world that he or she may succumb to *"future shock"* (Toffler 1970).

One effort to determine the effects of change on illness involves the use of the Social Readjustment Rating Scale. A respondent indicates which of the 43 events comprising the scale have happened to him or her within the last year. The events include role changes (such as death of spouse, divorce or marriage, beginning or stopping work) and changes in institutional participation (school, church activities, financial status). Each event is rated in terms of how much adjustment it requires. Scores range from 100 for the most stressful event (death of a spouse) to 11 for the least stressful (a minor violation of the law). The total score reflects the number and kinds of events that have occurred in an individual's life during the previous year. In one study, 79 percent of those scoring 300 or above, 51 percent of those scoring between 200 and 299, and 37 percent of those scoring between 150 and 199 had changes in their health in the following year (Holmes and Masuda 1974).

Considerable research since the early 1970s supports the thesis. For example, a high rate of change in life events can result in more injuries (Lee et al. 1989), panic attacks (Pollard, Pollard, and Corn 1989), a lessening of the body's ability to ward off disease (Zautra et al. 1989), and various other physical and emotional disorders (Turner and Lloyd 1995; McQuaid et al. 2000; Tiet et al. 2001).

Note, however, that while a rapid rate of change does increase stress, the stress may be moderated if the people perceive the changes as desirable (Lauer 1974; Vinokur and Selzer 1975). It is *undesirable life events,* rather than change per se, that are likely to cause illness (Seivewright 1987). People may function in a context of rapid change with minimal effects on their physical and mental health as long as they desire the changes that are occurring (and, perhaps, as long as they have areas of stability in the midst of the change).

▪▪ Social Psychological Factors

Attitudes and Values. Certain attitudes and values of those who are ill, of the public, and of medical personnel affect rates of illness and the nature of health care. Negative attitudes toward one's work can increase the risk of illness. An individual's work is a focal point of his or her existence as well as one of the most time-consuming areas of life. If it is defined in negative terms, the risk of illness is increased (Tetrick and LaRocco 1987).

A particular personality type, identified by a cluster of attitudes and values, has an increased probability of coronary heart disease. Men who are ambitious, highly competitive, and self-driving and who impose frequent deadlines on themselves have a higher incidence of coronary heart disease than do men with opposite characteristics (Ganster 1986; Rosenman 1990). All these characteristics are admired in Canadian society; they are long-held values. Unfortunately, when accepted and followed diligently, they are also the precursors of illness.

The sick person's attitudes about his or her illness and prospects for recovery are another important factor. Some people are skeptical about the ability of medical care to affect their health (Fiscella, Franks, and Clancy 1998). Such skepticism is stronger among young, white males in the lower socioeconomic strata. In contrast, there are those who believe that their prospects for recovery from illness are very good. They rely confidently on medical help and, in some cases, also believe that God or another deity is at work to bring about healing. Such beliefs tend to shorten the illness and add years to people's lives (Phillips, Ruth, and Wagner 1993; Oxman, Freeman, and Manheimer 1995).

The attitudes of others may be as important as the ill person's own attitudes. We have noted the stigma that is associated with certain kinds of physical and mental illness, a stigma that creates adverse reactions in those who are ill. For example, people with Parkinson's disease tend to feel ashamed and want to withdraw from public situations because, among other things, they are unable to control their saliva and have difficulty speaking (Nijhof 1995). They are aware of the embarrassment and unease created in those with whom they interact.

The mentally ill also must deal with negative attitudes and reactions that arise out of the acceptance of certain myths (Socall and Holtgraves 1992; Bower 1998). The myths are a form of the *fallacy of personal attack,* for they stigmatize current and past mental patients. The following are some of the common myths:

A person who has been mentally ill can never be normal.
Persons with mental illness are unpredictable.
Mentally ill persons are dangerous.
Anyone who has had shock treatment must be in a really bad way.
When you learn that a person has been mentally ill, you have learned the most important thing about his or her personality.
A former mental patient will make a second-rate employee. (National Institute of Mental Health 1988)

These statements are myths. Note, however, that while the vast majority of people with serious mental illness are no more dangerous than those in the general population, there is a subgroup of the mentally ill that does pose a risk of acting violently (Torrey 1994; Swanson et al. 2002). Those with a history of violent behaviour, those who do not take their medication, and those with a problem of substance abuse are more likely than others to engage in violent behaviour. Yet for the great majority of the mentally ill, all the above statements, including the statement that they are dangerous, are myths.

The myths illustrate the way in which people who are troubled or different tend to be labelled. Thomas Scheff (1966) made the most thorough use of labelling theory to analyze mental illness. According to Scheff, the mentally ill are *rule breakers,* though the rules they break are different from the rules criminals break. The mentally ill break rules that govern normal social interaction, rules that define "common decency" and indicate an acceptance of social reality as defined by the group. Everyone occasionally breaks such rules with impunity. You may, for example, overreact to an insult, refuse to talk to someone who has angered you, or talk too loudly or too softly. The person who consistently breaks the rules of conventional interaction runs the risk of being labelled mentally ill.

Yet not everyone who breaks the rules is labelled mentally ill. In fact, most rule breaking is "denied and is of transitory significance" (Scheff 1966:51). A certain amount of rule breaking always goes unnoticed or unpunished. Among other things, the response of others varies in accord with the kinds of rules that are broken. Loud speech, for example, is less likely to be negatively sanctioned than the refusal to speak at all.

How do people know when to label someone as mentally ill when there are various kinds of behaviour that break rules? Scheff points out that *stereotyped imagery of mental illness* is learned early in life and that these stereotypes are reinforced in normal interaction. People avoid behaviour that is a stereotype of mental illness and thereby reinforce the image of that behaviour as a symptom of mental illness. Furthermore, they evaluate others according to the stereotype.

If an individual behaves in accord with the stereotype, he or she may be labelled mentally ill and rewarded for playing out the stereotyped role. Moreover, the individual may be punished for any attempt to abandon the role and adopt more conventional behaviour. This occurs because people desire a *predictable social order,* and you have that with mentally ill people because you know how they will behave even if you do not define their behaviour as desirable. Just as criminals who avow they are beginning new, law-abiding lives are likely to be treated with some suspicion (their behaviour is no longer predictable), the mentally ill who seem to be recovering may be told that they are not as well as they think. In other words, once an individual is labelled as ill, the responses of others tend to perpetuate the behaviour involved.

Scheff denied that his is a complete explanation of mental illness. His aim was not to supplant psychiatric approaches but to supplement them and to stimulate new thinking about mental illness.

There is evidence that labels do have a significant impact. In an important study, Link (1987) found that those labelled (former patients and repeat patients), as compared to those unlabelled (first-treatment patients, untreated cases in the community, and people with no severe psychopathology), were more likely to believe that they would be devalued and discriminated against by most people. The results of these beliefs were higher rates of demoralization, unemployment, and income loss. Moreover, patients and former patients may become secretive and withdrawn because of their fears of rejection,

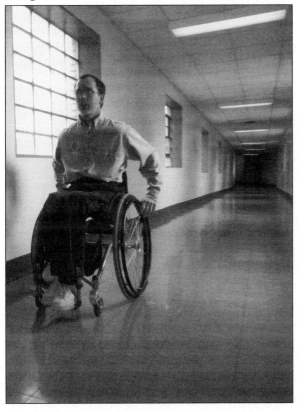

Some mental and physical illnesses are more difficult to cope with because of public stigma.

weakening the social support system that is important to their well-being (Link et al. 1989). Unfortunately, various strategies (like avoidance–withdrawal, secretiveness, and attempts to educate others) for trying to cope with the stigma are ineffective and may do more harm than good (Link, Mirotznik, and Cullen 1991). Labelling is a powerful social factor, and even if it does not directly lead to mental illness, it clearly seems to have negative outcomes (Rosenfield 1997).

Attitudes and values also affect medical care of physical illness. The *distribution of physicians* in Canada does not reflect medical need. Physicians, of course, are attracted to places that have desirable resources, abundant professional opportunities, and an active medical community. They also cluster in areas where they are likely to maximize their income. This pattern has been characteristic for some time, and it implicitly means that many Canadians are receiving inadequate medical care. Since the early 1990s, Canadians have increasingly become frustrated with "a marked deterioration" in the health care system—long waiting lists, a shortage of medical specialists, and the need for more specialized equipment (Matthew 2002:*vii*). In spite of these frustrations, "most Canadians, including the more economically secure, remain deeply committed to a system that guarantees all Canadians access to good quality health care" (*ix*). Canadians have enjoyed the benefits of a nationalized system, boasting long life expectancies and low infant mortality rates. Moreover, Canadians see health care as a human right and are committed to the principle of universal coverage. As such, there has been strong resistance to debates that support privatization and a two-tiered health care system.

■■ From Social Problems to Solutions

As in the case of drug and alcohol abuse, more money and effort have been expended on the treatment of ill health than on its prevention. In order to change this focus, there needs to be an expansion or improvement of existing programs and the development of new innovative programs. An example of an existing program that can be expanded is the community health centre, which addresses the maldistribution of care by bringing medical services to previously neglected groups. Poor people, minority groups, and residents of rural areas have benefited from these government funded centres (AOHC 2004). However, the centres have faced difficulties in maintaining a stable professional staff and receiving adequate funding from the federal government.

The problems of the health care system run deep, and reform must address individual factors such as social and geographic locations, gender, age, and disability; community support, which includes a comprehensive homecare system; and cooperation and collaboration between the provincial and federal governments. In 2001, Prime Minister Jean Chrétien formed the "Commission on the Future of Health Care in Canada," headed by former Premier of Saskatchewan Roy Romanow. The Commission was mandated to explore in-depth the workings of the Canadian health care system; specifically, to determine what works, what needs improvement, and to put forward policy recommendations on what changes are necessary to make medicare work for Canadians. The final report, entitled "Building on Values: The Future of Health Care in Canada," commonly referred to as the Romanow Report, both praises and criticizes medicare (Romanow 2002). Romanow strongly supports a national health care system but recognizes that the concept of medicare needs to be renovated and adapted to today's reality (*xvii*). The report recommended changes to the federal *Health Act*, further investment in health human resources, a restructuring of primary care across Canada, the creation of a national drug strategy (a drug insurance program), and special attention to information technology, homecare, and care for Canada's First Nations people.

Shortly after the Romanow Report was made public, the premiers of the provinces made a commitment to the renewal of the Canadian health care system—more specifically, to ensure that all Canadians have access to health care providers, reduced waiting periods for diagnostic and surgical procedures, better coordination of health care services, and the benefit of a national pharmacare plan (drug coverage). How can quality care be delivered at affordable costs? How can Canadians ensure that no one will lack such care because he or she cannot afford the coverage?

Innovative techniques for addressing health problems are needed. Innovations are also needed in treatment that considers the close relationships between physical and mental health and between mind and body. The mind plays a key role in health, a fact that needs further exploration and exploitation (Jacobs 2001).

Innovations in the treatment of mental disorders also have been developed in an effort to achieve quicker, more effective results. One approach is a *community support system*. In essence, a variety of services, supports, and opportunities are set up within communities to enable people with mental illness to function. Among other things, the support system can include therapy, health and dental care, a crisis-response service, housing, income maintenance, family and community support, and protection and advocacy services. Community support systems can be more effective than hospitalization in dealing with mental illness (Chinman et al. 2001).

Another program offers support to the patient's family when the family is the primary caretaker of the chronically ill person (Ferris and Marshall 1987; Bull and McShane 2002). Family care, which is an alternative to hospitalization, generates various kinds of stress. Groups of families entrusted with the care of a chronically ill member meet for support, skill training, and information. With the aid of a mental health professional, the families are able to form a support group that enables each of them to cope with the difficult task. Some professionals believe that a family-oriented approach offers the highest probability of a positive outcome for mentally ill individuals (Schmidt 1989).

Some innovations aim at *prevention*. Neighbourhood or community health centres attempt to provide checkups for early detection or prevention of physical illness. Similarly, "preventive psychiatry" has emerged as an effort at early detection of mental disorders. Any realistic effort at prevention has to address the sources of stress in society. Stress-inducing roles must be changed. Help must be provided for troubled families. Economic deprivation must be eliminated. Government policy and its agencies must be responsive to health needs rather than to business interests.

One program of prevention that gained momentum in the 1980s is aimed at minimizing or eliminating smoking. Spurred by reports from the surgeon general and anti-smoking groups, the federal government has banned or restricted smoking in all federal facilities. Many provinces and cities have done the same, or have gone even further. Toronto, for example, forbids smoking in all public buildings, including restaurants. Such measures, along with increased education and higher taxes on cigarettes, have resulted in a substantial decline in the number of Canadians who smoke.

Finally, some scholars argue that *lifestyle is a crucial aspect of prevention* (Vita et al. 1998; Kant et al. 2000). What this means is that you have a good deal of control over your own health, and choose to ignore that control at your own peril. Indeed, an unhealthy lifestyle adversely affects physical and mental health. But blaming the individual for poor lifestyle choices is too simplistic. First, not everyone can "control" their lifestyle; and second, lifestyle choices are influenced by a number of upstream factors such as the globalization of markets, media, and advertising (CIHR 2003:4). Take obesity as an example. Williams et al. (2003) believe that obesity in Canada has become epidemic. According to a roundtable discussion on obesity sponsored by the Canadian Institute for Health Information (CIHR 2003), Canadians are *not* overweight by choice. Some causes of obesity include aggressive and successful marketing of high-caloric foods such as fast foods, soft drinks, and candy, which also are much cheaper than healthy foods; the popularity of television, computers, and electronic games, which leads to long periods of sedentary activity; and school policies that have cut physical education programs (CHIR 2003:4). Furthermore, many Canadians living in poverty cannot afford to eat healthy food and partake in recreational activity; in turn, they are more likely to be obese (CHN 2004).

■■ SUMMARY

Good health is a primary value of Canadians. Some advances have been made, as indicated by the increasing life expectancy. The main problem of physical health today is chronic diseases rather than the infectious diseases that plagued society in earlier times. Millions of Canadians are limited in their activities because of chronic conditions. There is general agreement about the classification of mental disorders, which are found in all societies. It is difficult to predict the exact percentage of the Canadian population that suffers from some kind of mental disorder. It has been estimated that approximately 20 percent of Canadians will be affected by mental illness in any year.

Illness affects the quality of life in many ways. The illness itself and the inadequate care that many Canadians receive cause stress and suffering. Interpersonal relationships are adversely affected. Individual freedom is threatened by certain medical advances. Often, heavy economic costs are involved for the nation and for individuals. Both physical and mental illnesses cause fears and anxiety. There is, in fact, a close relationship between physical and mental illness; each can be a factor in bringing about the other, so the individual can be caught in a vicious circle.

Structural factors contribute to the problem. Certain stress-inducing roles have been associated with illness, especially the female role and certain occupational roles. Patterns of interaction and socialization in the family can promote or inhibit good physical and mental health. The industrial economy exposes people to carcinogenic materials and to various pollutants. Fluctuations in the economy generate stress. Political decisions reflect economic interests rather than health needs.

Health care problems are more serious for those in the lower than the higher socioeconomic strata. People in the lower strata suffer higher rates of mental and physical illness and receive less adequate care for both. Also, different kinds of illness characterize the various socioeconomic strata.

Among social psychological factors, attitudes and values are related to illness. The ill person's attitudes about the illness and his or her prospects for recovery are important. Negative attitudes toward one's work and certain attitudes rooted in traditional values increase the probability of illness. Once a person is ill, negative attitudes of others can inhibit recovery—a problem stressed by labelling theory. Finally, the deterioration of Canada's health care system over the last 15 years has contributed to the maldistribution of care. But most Canadians, including the economically secure, value and are committed to a universal health care system.

■■ KEY TERMS

AIDS 332	Incidence 329	Neurosis 336	Schizophrenia 337
Carcinogenic 349	Life Expectancy 330	Pica 351	Socialization 349
Deinstitutionalization 337	Manic-Depressive	Prevalence 329	Stigma 340
Epidemiology 329	Reaction 337	Psychosis 336	
Etiology 348	Medicalization 341	Psychosomatic Disorder	
Iatrogenic Problems 340	Morbidity 348	336	

■■ STUDY QUESTIONS

1. What are the various kinds of physical and mental illness, and how prevalent are they?

2. What kinds of suffering are associated with illness?

3. How does problematic health affect interpersonal relationships?

4. In what sense can it be said that Canadians have inadequate health care? How has deinstitutionalization contributed to this problem?

5. How does illness affect individual freedom?

6. What are the economic costs of health and illness?

7. How do gender and occupational roles contribute to health and illness?

8. In what ways is the health problem affected by the family, the economy, and the polity?

9. What kinds of attitudes and values on the part of those who are ill, the public, and health personnel affect rates of illness and the nature of health care?

10. What innovations could help ameliorate the health problem?

11. Consider the types of food you eat on a daily basis. What factors determine your food choices?

■■ FOR FURTHER READING

Armstrong, P. and H. Armstrong. *Wasting Away: The Undermining of Canadian Health Care.* Toronto: Oxford University Press, 2002. Examines reforms to Canada's health care system that have focused on cost-cutting. The authors argue that these reforms have not addressed Canada's fundamental health care problems.

Charmaz, Kathleen C. *Good Days, Bad Days: The Self in Chronic Illness and Time.* New Brunswick, NJ: Rutgers University Press, 1991. Uses in-depth interviews to show how coping with a chronic illness affects people's lives, including their self-concepts.

Cousins, Norman. *The Healing Heart: Antidotes to Panic and Helplessness.* New York: W. W. Norton, 1983. Shows how one man reacted to a heart problem by actively participating in his own healing process rather than passively accepting the recommended mode of treatment.

Elston, Mary Ann, ed. *The Sociology of Medical Science and Technology.* Malden, MA: Blackwell, 1997. An examination of a wide range of issues and problems in the context of the scientific and highly technological nature of the practice of medicine today.

Evans, R.G., M.L. Barer, and T.R. Marmor. *Why Are Some People Healthy and Others Not? The Determinants of Health of Populations.* New York: A. De Gruyter, 1994.

Kearney, Margaret H. *Understanding Women's Recovery from Illness and Trauma.* Thousand Oaks, CA: Sage, 1999. Explores how women deal with health problems ranging from eating disorders to chronic illnesses of various kinds. Points out how the health and illness of women involve social and political factors.

Steingraber, S. *Living Downstream: A Scientist's Personal Investigation of Cancer and the Environment.* New York: Vintage Books, 1998. The author provides compelling evidence that links cancer to environment contamination.

Weitz, Rose. *Life with AIDS.* New Brunswick, NJ: Rutgers University Press, 1991. An exploration of what it is like to have AIDS, from the point of view of the victims, including a discussion of their inner conflicts, mood swings, self-concepts, sexuality, and social relationships.

Whitaker, Robert. *Mad in America: Bad Science, Bad Medicine, and the Enduring Mistreatment of the Mentally Ill.* Cambridge, MA: Perseus Publishing, 2002. A history of how psychiatrists have treated schizophrenics, underscoring the fact that treatment is a trial-and-error process that changes from generation to generation.

■■ NOTE

1. Thalidomide was prescribed to pregnant women to help combat nausea. The "thalidomide children" were frequently born with either partial limbs or without limbs. Daughters whose mothers took DES are at higher risk for vaginal cancer and other gynecological disorders. The mothers themselves are now at higher risk for breast cancer.

Global Social Problems

Is there hope for civilization? Ever since the invention of gunpowder, pessimists have been predicting that humans will destroy themselves with their own technology. Their pessimism doesn't seem all that far-fetched, particularly since war, terrorism, and environmental problems all pose serious threats to the quality of human life, if not to the very existence of the human race.

In this final part, we examine these problems. We cannot discuss them meaningfully without seeing them in their global context. The threat they pose goes beyond any particular nation and inevitably includes all nations. We examine war and terrorism first. Then we explore the vexing environmental problems that are not only threatening but also involve vexing dilemmas.

PEACE AND CONFLICT

LEARNING OBJECTIVES

1. Distinguish among peace, conflict, war, and terrorism.

2. Understand Canada's role as a peacekeeping country.

3. Discuss the ways in which war and terrorism detract from the quality of life, while peaceful resolutions enhance it.

4. Identify the political and economic factors that contribute to the problems of war and terrorism.

5. Suggest steps that can be taken to address the problems of war and terrorism.

"AN UNJUST WAR"

Canada's Immigration and Refugee Board has been holding hearings over the past two years in which soldiers in the U.S. Army—such as John, age 28—have requested refugee status in Canada. These military personnel have chosen to desert the U.S. Army rather than serve in Iraq in what they believe to be an unjust war, in which they claim there is evidence of a systemic pattern of war crimes, including attacks on civilian population centres and the torture and murder of prisoners. Canada has not granted refugee status to U.S. citizens in the past, but supporters are counting on a precedent in international law to help these Americans. ■

▪▪ INTRODUCTION

Peacekeeping is an important aspect of Canada's national heritage and a reflection of our fundamental beliefs in dealing with conflict situations. Canada has a long tradition of peacekeeping, which is a significant component of our foreign policy and our contribution to multilateral security systems. As of 2005, there are almost 3,500 Canadian Forces personnel stationed abroad on at least 13 missions. They range in size from a one-person commitment to Cyprus and Senegal to the 2,031–strong peacekeeping force on the ground in Kabul, Afghanistan. Canadian peacekeepers are stationed in Haiti, Bosnia-Herzegovina, The Golan Heights, Jerusalem, Sinai, The Congo, Sierra Leone, The Sudan, and the United States (Department of National Defence 2004). Although Canada is committed to continuing its peacekeeping efforts, pressure from the United States to have Canada join its anti-terrorism policies is causing concern.

On September 11, 2001, three American passenger jets were hijacked by terrorists. Two of the planes crashed into the Twin Towers of the World Trade Center and a third slammed into the Pentagon. A fourth plane, headed for the White House, went down in Pennsylvania after passengers tried to stop the hijackers. With more than 3,000 deaths from this terrorist attack, "war" took on a new meaning globally.

In this chapter of conflict and peace, we begin by looking at the nature and extent of the problem. We show the ways war and terrorism detract from the quality of life. We identify the sociocultural factors that contribute to the problem. Finally, we discuss some proposals for minimizing or eliminating war and terrorism.

▪▪ WAR, CIVIL WAR, AND TERRORISM

When you hear the word "war," your first thought may be of armies from two opposing nations clashing with each other. However, this definition doesn't best describe present-day wars, which are more likely to be civil wars or wars of **terrorism.**

▪▪ The New Face of War

terrorism
use of threats or violence against random or symbolic targets in pursuit of political goals

Modern warfare is no longer confined to opposing armies facing each other on the battlefield. Nor is it merely a matter of nuclear powers confronting each other with the threat of mass destruction. Rather, the small armaments that have flooded the world can be used by dissidents to destroy a nation's infrastructure. And:

> Civilians are targets as much as combatants, often more so. . . . Children fight alongside adults. The front line may be someone's bedroom. Hospitals and libraries are fair game. Even humanitarian aid workers become pawns. (Musser and Nemecek 2000:47)

Not only have the struggles spread from the battlefield to the bedroom, but increasingly they have involved civil wars and terrorism. *Civil war* is rebellion by dissident groups within a nation. If the groups are small, they may simply engage in acts of domestic terrorism (discussed in chapter 4). **International terrorism** is politically motivated violence against citizens of political entities different from those of the perpetrators in order to coerce and intimidate others into accepting the perpetrators' goals. Terrorism is not new, but the September 11, 2001, attacks made North Americans painfully aware both of its destructive potential and of their vulnerability to it.

international terrorism
politically motivated violence against citizens of political entities different from those of the perpetrators in order to coerce and intimidate others into accepting the perpetrators' goals

▪▪ The Extent of the Problem

Wars and Civil Wars.
When Canada is not involved in war, Canadians tend to think that the era is one of relative peace. Yet at any point in time the world experiences

war
a major armed conflict
between nations or between
organized groups within a
nation in which a thousand
or more people are killed

a large number of armed conflicts, including both wars and minor armed conflicts. A **war** is defined as a major armed conflict between nations or between organized groups within a nation in which 1,000 or more people are killed (Renner 1997). Minor armed conflicts may involve the same kind of weaponry and fighting, but they result in fewer deaths. In the year 2000, wars or minor armed conflicts occurred in 49 nations in Asia, Africa, and South America, and resulted in seven million deaths (most of them civilians) (Renner 2001).

Most wars in recent decades have involved the developing nations of the world, but Canada, the United States, and other developed nations can be drawn into the conflicts under certain circumstances. One such circumstance occurred in late 1990, when Iraq invaded and took over Kuwait. When Iraq refused to respond to U.N. demands to withdraw, a multinational force began a massive air bombardment in January 1991, thus starting the Gulf War.

Although the war was brief, the damage was massive and it should serve as a reminder that war is always possible. In fact, current events threaten future wars. As of this writing, the United States and Britain are in another war against Iraq. Pakistan and India continue to struggle over Kashmir. Palestinians and Israelis continue to kill each other, and there is continued conflict in the Middle East. The list goes on. The point is that *you live in a world that is never free of war or the threat of war.*

The bloodiest wars in recent years have been civil wars and wars involving just two nations (Renner 1999). More than 1.5 million people died in the civil war in the Sudan (97 percent of them civilians), more than one million died in the Mozambican civil war from 1981 to 1994, and about 1.5 million died in the Soviet intervention in Afghanistan between 1978 and 1992. The incidence of civil wars has been increasing since the end of the Second World War (Fearon and Laitin 2002). They tend to involve ethnic minorities who want political autonomy or insurgents who want to take control of the government. Millions have died in these often protracted wars.

Terrorism. Between 1980 and 2000, the FBI identified 335 incidents or suspected incidents of terrorism in the United States, 247 of which were attributed to domestic terrorists and 88 to international terrorists (Watson 2002). These terrorist acts resulted in far fewer deaths, however, than the more than 3,000 who died on September 11, 2001. (The second highest number occurred in 1998, when 301 were killed in attacks on U.S. embassies in Kenya and Tanzania.) The September 11 attack was the worst single terrorist attack ever in terms of number killed.

The U.S. Department of State (2002) has summarized the extent of international terrorism worldwide between 1981 and 2001. The highest number of incidents occurred in the 1980s. Latin America, followed by western Europe and Asia, was the continent where terrorist acts were most likely to occur. The greatest number of casualties were in Africa, followed by Asia and North America (the latter only because of September 11). Business facilities were more likely to be hit than government, military, or other facilities. Of the 219 anti-U.S. terrorist attacks in 2001, 191 occurred in Latin America, 207 were bombings, and 204 (including the World Trade Center in New York) struck businesses.

Although bombings have been the most common form of terrorism, there is concern that other, possibly even more destructive, forms will emerge, including biological terrorism (Kuhr and Hauer 2001). A vast number of biological, chemical, and radioactive materials are capable of causing mass illness and death, and terrorists are capable of securing many if not most of these materials.

■■ WAR, TERRORISM, AND THE QUALITY OF LIFE

As with violence at the interpersonal and intergroup levels, it is not possible to fully capture in writing the impact of war and terrorism. To give you a sense of what people are doing to each other through such violence, consider a few reported experiences. You will see that war and terrorism destroy and dehumanize.

■■ Human Destruction and Injury

Human destruction reaches a peak in war. The 20th century was the bloodiest in human history (see table 13.1). More than 100 million deaths occurred, compared to 19.4 million in the 19th century and 3.7 million from the 1st to the 15th centuries (Renner 1999:10).

Increasingly, civilians are the victims of war and terrorism through a combination of direct injuries, starvation, and disease; civilians accounted for half of all war-related deaths in the 1950s, three-fourths of deaths in the 1980s, and nearly 90 percent of deaths in 1990 (Renner 1993a:9). Note that in the early part of the 20th century, about nine times as many soldiers as civilians died in war, while in recent wars nine times more civilians than soldiers have died (Mollica et al. 1994). This is a dramatic shift, indeed.

Civilians are the main victims in terrorist attacks. The great majority of individuals killed by terrorists have been civilians, including the thousands of Palestinian and Israeli casualties in the ongoing terrorist attack–retaliation cycle in Israel and the occupied territories.

In addition, *children are increasingly the likely victims of war and terrorism.* Children are victims in a number of ways. First, they are often among those killed. For example, from the mid-1980s to the mid-1990s, at least two million children were killed

Year	>1,000 Dead	>100,000 Dead	Year	>1,000 Dead	>100,000 Dead	Year	>1,000 Dead	>100,000 Dead
1950	11	6	1971	18	9	1983	33	11
1955	10	4	1972	18	9	1984	34	11
1961	11	8	1973	19	7	1985	33	11
1962	16	10	1974	18	7	1986	33	10
1963	13	8	1975	20	8	1987	33	10
1964	12	8	1976	16	6	1988	31	11
1965	17	10	1977	16	6	1989	33	10
1966	15	9	1978	20	8	1990	33	9
1967	16	9	1979	21	5	1991	33	11
1968	15	8	1980	26	7	1992	32	8
1969	17	8	1981	30	10	1993	32	7
1970	17	8	1982	30	10	1994	34	7

Source: World Watch Institute. Global Policy Forum; http://globalpolicy.igc.org/nations/numdead1.htm.

TABLE 13.1   ■ ■ ■

Mortality in Armed Conflicts, 1950–1994, by Number of Armed Conflicts

in wars (Crossette 1995). Second, children suffer severe and sometimes permanent injuries, are left homeless, or fall prey to hunger and disease. From the mid-1980s to the mid-1990s, an estimated four to five million children were disabled and 12 million were left homeless. In Iraq, about 80 percent of those who died from war-related injuries, starvation, or disease after the Gulf War cease-fire were children (Burleigh 1991).

Third, children may be victimized when women who participate in war have babies with birth defects. Women who served in Vietnam, for example, were far more likely to have children with birth defects than were other women (Brooks 1999). Finally, children may be victimized by being forced into combat. Hundreds of thousands of children, some as young as seven years old, have fought in armed conflicts or participated in terrorist attacks around the world.

Following the U.S. invasion of Iraq in 2003, 1,513 members of the U.S. military were killed between 2003 and 2004, along with 86 members of multinational forces, including one Canadian. Civilian deaths, mostly Iraqis, have numbered more than 100,000, according to a recent article in the medical journal *The Lancet* (Roberts 2004:142). As well, 32 journalists have been killed while covering the war, along with 22 United Nations employees. Sixty-six U.S. civilians have also been killed, along with seven Canadians who worked for the Red Cross, Canadian Children's Fund, and contracting firms (CBC News 2005).

Various factors account for the human destruction in war. The obvious factor, of course, is the use of weaponry, including bombs. Even when bombs are aimed at military targets, a certain number will hit civilians. For instance, the 1991 war against Iraq, with its "smart" bombs and missiles that hit military targets with pinpoint accuracy, was heralded as an example of the wonders of modern military technology. However, many hospitals also were hit, including the only hospital in the nation that performed kidney transplants and advanced heart surgery (Burleigh 1991). In addition, the destruction of power plants prevented some hospitals from operating even basic equipment like incubators and refrigerators.

Land mines are also responsible for many civilian deaths and injuries (Renner 1997). At present, an estimated 120 million land mines are planted in more than 70 countries—

Each year, land mines kill or maim more than 25,000 people, many of them children like this young Afghan girl.

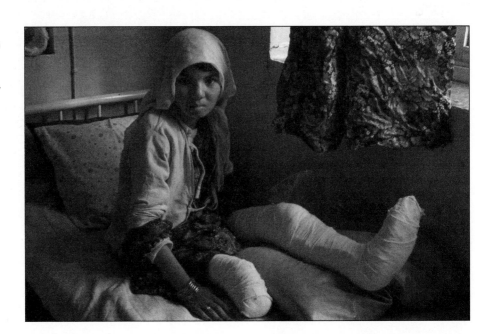

most of which are the poorer nations of the world. These mines, along with unexploded bombs, can remain lethal for decades (Lovering 2001), and millions more are planted every year. Mines kill or maim more than 25,000 people every year, yet an effort to obtain a worldwide ban on the use of land mines was blocked by the United States in 1997 on the grounds that it would jeopardize the safety of American soldiers. The ban was, however, supported by Canada.

Another reason for the destructiveness of war is that, throughout human history, conquering armies have treated the vanquished as undeserving of humane treatment. For girls and women, this means a higher probability of being raped. Rape occurs in all wars, including civil wars. In a survey of households in Sierra Leone, 94 percent reported at least one person having suffered abuse in the previous 10 years of the nation's civil war, and one of eight of the households reported being victimized by some kind of war-related sexual violence (Physicians for Human Rights 2002). Finally, war is destructive because in their quest for military power or military victory, governments may act in ways that harm their own people.

Wars always have been destructive, but they are more destructive now than they were in the past. Clearly, one reason for the increasing number of people killed, as well as the increasing proportion of civilians among those killed, is the *changed nature of war,* which now involves the total population of nations rather than military personnel only.

Another reason for the increased destructiveness of war is the *increasingly sophisticated nature of military technology* compared to past weaponry. It is now possible to kill people in numbers that are staggering. In the First World War, fewer than three people per 100,000 were killed by bombs in England and Germany. In the Second World War, nearly 300 people per 100,000 were killed by bombs (Hart 1957:44). The Second World War also saw the introduction of atomic weapons. Two Japanese cities, Hiroshima and Nagasaki, were each decimated by a single bomb. About 140,000 people in Hiroshima and 70,000 in Nagasaki died immediately or within a few weeks, while another 130,000 died within five years after the attack (Committee for the Compilation of Materials on Damage Caused by the Atomic Bombs in Hiroshima and Nagasaki 1981). It is sobering to realize that while the Hiroshima bomber delivered 25,800 tons of TNT-equivalent explosives, a bomber today can deliver *literally hundreds of times more destructive power,* and that the missiles carried by just one Russian Delta 4 submarine could kill 6.7 million people in the first 30 minutes after detonation and an additional 6 to 12 million would die of radiation sickness in the following weeks (Helfand 1999).

In addition to the destruction of bombs and bullets, there is the horror of biological and chemical warfare. During the Iran–Iraq war from 1980 to 1988 the Iraqis used mustard gas, breaking a 63-year-old international agreement that forbids the use of any chemical weapons.[1] The gas initially causes sneezing and coughing and sometimes nausea and vomiting. Within hours, the victim suffers tightness in the chest and shortness of breath as a result of respiratory inflammation. Painful blisters appear on the body, causing patches of skin to fall off. Some victims recover, but some die and others suffer bone marrow or gastrointestinal problems for years.

The destruction can continue even after a war has officially ended. An examination of 50 nation-wars showed *increased homicide rates in the postwar years.* The increases occurred in both the victorious and the defeated nations and in those with improved as well as those with worsened economic conditions (Archer and Gartner 1979).

A different kind of carryover involves the increased rates of physical problems among veterans. U.S. Veterans of the Vietnam War face a 50-percent greater risk of cancer of the lymph nodes than men who were not in Vietnam.[2] Veterans of the Gulf

War developed a number of persistent physical symptoms: chronic fatigue, skin rashes, muscle and joint pain, shortness of breath, headaches, and diarrhea (Clark 1994; Gray et al. 2002). The causes of such long-term consequences are disputed, ranging from exposure to toxic war materials to the intense stress and anxiety of combat.

Finally, the destruction of human life and well-being is affected by the threat of war as well as war itself. *The production and storage of weapons of war are hazardous even if the weapons are never used.* Radioactive wastes from the production of nuclear weapons contaminate water and soil. Some U.S. government nuclear-production facilities disposed of radioactive waste as though it were harmless; the result was the contamination of some water supplies. Even apart from carelessness, however, no nation has yet solved the problem of safely disposing of the wastes. This results in an increased risk of cancer, including leukemia, and genetic damage.

▪▪ Psychological and Interpersonal Disruption and Dehumanization

Psychological and interpersonal disruption and dehumanization occur during and after war and terrorist attacks—both of which are disruptive for military and civilian personnel. No one escapes the trauma.

The Trauma for Civilians.
Civilian trauma of the severest kind followed the atomic bombings of the Japanese cities of Hiroshima and Nagasaki during the Second World War. Hiroshima was a city accustomed to crises, having experienced periodic disastrous floods. Nevertheless, the social order of the city collapsed after the atomic bomb was dropped. The city was rebuilt mainly through the work of migrants from the hinterland rather than through the efforts of the surviving residents. The survivors

Civilians are the emotional and physical victims of war in massive numbers.

suffered from extreme shock and fatigue that lingered for a year. . . . Demoralization was so extreme that industrial alcohol was sold as a substitute for saki; many citizens died or went blind from drinking it. (Dentler and Cutright 1965:420)

Drugs were used to escape reality. Children who survived developed a fear of becoming attached to others and of having their own children when they became adults. Crimes of violence and thefts of precious water and other scarce goods were common. Four months after the bomb had been dropped, the number of reported crimes for one month was as high as all reported crime throughout the entire war. Years later, the survivors were still not capable of leading normal, happy lives. Most of them carried a *deep sense of guilt,* including the guilt of surviving when so many had died.

Hiroshima became a city of chaos, pain, crime, anxiety, and deep-rooted fear. So many people continued to feel sick a month after the bomb fell that a rumour spread that the bomb had left a poison that would give off deadly fumes for seven years (Hersey 1946:94). Such rumours, of course, intensified the already pervasive anxiety and fear of the people and contributed to an atmosphere that drained people of the necessary psychological strength to function normally and proceed with the work of rebuilding.

The suffering need not be on the scale of Hiroshima for people to experience the emotional trauma of war. Civilians in war zones suffer emotional problems in large numbers (Cardozo et al. 2000), and the problems may continue even after they are out of the war zone. Increased depression and posttraumatic stress disorder were found in a study of 124 Cambodian refugees living in Utah (Blair 2000). A team of researchers interviewed nearly a thousand Cambodians living in a refugee camp on the Thailand–Cambodia border. Many of them had witnessed the murder of a family member, had been raped, or had been physically assaulted during the civil war in their country. More than 80 percent felt depressed (with 55 percent meeting the criteria for clinical depression) and 15 percent had symptoms of posttraumatic stress syndrome (Mollica et al. 1994).

Children as well as adults are traumatized by war. Consider, for example, what it must have been like to have been a Jewish child in a Nazi concentration camp during the Second World War. In Czechoslovakia, the camp at Terezin had 15,000 children. Only 100 of the 15,000 survived, but some of their drawings and writings also survived. Following is part of a poem written by a 15-year-old boy:

> I was once a little child
> Three years ago.
> That child who longed for other worlds.
> But now I am no more a child
> For I have learned to hate.
> I am a grown-up person now,
> I have known fear.
>
> Somewhere, far away out there, childhood sweetly sleeps,
> Along that path among the trees,
> There o'er that house
> Which was once my pride and joy.
> There my mother gave me birth into this world
> So I could weep. . . .[3]

Or consider what life is like for Lebanese children who have grown up in a land racked by war and civil war. Those who experienced the death of a family member or the forced displacement of their family, or saw their home destroyed or someone killed, were about 1.7 times more likely than others to be nervous or depressed and to exhibit aggressive behaviour (Chimienti, Nasr, and Khalifeh 1989). Continued shelling and killing were also responsible for depression among Lebanese mothers, and their depression, in turn, was associated with the illness of their children (Bryce et al. 1989). Among young people injured by shelling in 1996, half suffered some kind of impairment and 29 percent who had been enrolled in school did not continue their education (Mehio Sibai, Shaar Sameer, and el Yassir 2000).

Many children and young people in the Middle East have never experienced an extended time of peace. It is little wonder, then, that children in the Gaza Strip who have been exposed to war conflict have a high rate of emotional and behavioural problems (Thabet and Vostanis 2000). Studies of children in other war situations yield similar results (Zivcic 1993; Ajdukovic 1998).

The Trauma for Combatants.

During the genocide in Rwanda, Major General Romeo Dallaire, who led the Canadian peacekeeping mission, spoke about the horrors he and his troops witnessed while stationed in this small African country in which 800,000 men, women, and children were brutally slaughtered. In his book *Shake Hands with the Devil: The Failure of Humanity in Rwanda* (2003), Dallaire speaks of the lasting effect witnessing such atrocities has had on him and his troops, all of whom are experiencing posttraumatic stress syndrome.

In part because of the horror of battle, there is *a high rate of posttraumatic stress disorder among veterans* (Prigerson, Maciejewski, and Rosenheck 2002). They may re-experience the war trauma in dreams, have recurring images and thoughts related to the trauma, feel a lack of involvement in life, experience guilt about having survived in situations where others died, and struggle with sleep disturbances. The rates are higher among those who experience combat and those taken as prisoners of war (Holmes, Tariot, and Cox 1998; Stuart and Bliese 1998; Ford 1999; Neria et al. 2000).

It is possible that the rate of traumatization among combatants is increasing. Hayman and Scaturo (1993) reported higher rates of posttraumatic stress disorder among American Vietnam veterans than those reported by studies of veterans of other wars. A study of U.S. Gulf War veterans also noted rates of disability compensation two to three times higher than those of the Second World War, the Korean Conflict, or the Vietnam War (Haley, Maddrey, and Gershenfeld 2002). There is as yet no explanation for these increasing rates.

The psychological problems vary in their severity but affect a substantial number of veterans. They tend to generate not only personal distress, but also interpersonal problems, including depressed satisfaction with intimate relationships and troubled marital relationships (Hendrix and Anelli 1993; Gimbel and Booth 1994; Prigerson, Maciejewski, and Rosenheck 2002). Moreover, younger soldiers may be more likely than older ones to develop serious problems. A study of 57 veterans of the Vietnam War found that those who were adolescents (17 to 19 years old) at the time of their tour of duty were more likely than older soldiers to have problems of adjustment (Harmless 1990). The younger soldiers experienced later on a greater number of conflicted relationships and work problems.

As we noted in the previous chapter, there is an integral relationship between physical and emotional health. Continued emotional problems will adversely affect physical health.

Combatant trauma stems from more than battle conditions, however. Military personnel may be traumatized and dehumanized by their own acts. Consider, for example, some of the acts that took place during the Second World War, such as mass extermination of and "medical" experiments on Jews. Some of the worst acts of the war were committed in the infamous *concentration camps,* especially Dachau (Gellhorn 1959:235–42). For example, Nazi Germans wanted to know how long their pilots could survive without oxygen. At Dachau they put prisoners into a car and pumped out the oxygen; some prisoners survived for as long as 15 minutes. They also wanted to see how long pilots could survive in cold water if they were shot down over the English Channel or some other body of water. Thus, prisoners were placed in vats of ice water that reached to their necks; some subjects survived for two and a half hours. Both experiments resulted in painful deaths for all the subjects.

Inhuman punishments were meted out to prisoners at Dachau who violated such rules as standing at attention with their hat off when an SS trooper passed within two metres. Prisoners were lashed with a bullwhip, hung by bound hands from a hook, or placed in a box that prevented them from sitting, kneeling, or lying down.

Perhaps the most disquieting aspect of all was the crematorium. A reporter who was in Dachau after it had been captured by the Allies wrote her reaction on seeing piles of dead bodies:

> They were everywhere. There were piles of them inside the oven room, but the SS had not had time to burn them . . . the bodies were dumped like garbage, rotting in the sun, yellow and nothing but bones, bones grown huge because there was no flesh to cover them, hideous, terrible, agonizing bones, and the unendurable smell of death. . . . Nothing about war was ever as insanely wicked as these starved and outraged, naked, nameless dead. (Gellhorn 1959:240)

Dehumanizing acts are not confined to any one people.

Soldiers who perform such acts may have *serious psychological problems* once they reflect on what they have done. They have treated other human beings as objects, dehumanizing them, and they are appalled at their own actions. Even those who do not participate in such actions may be traumatized. Just being in combat seems to bring some individuals to the point of irrationality if not insanity. Since the time of the ancient Greeks, soldiers have succumbed to madness as a result of the horrors of combat (Gabriel 1987). Anything from fatigue to hysterical paralysis to psychosis may afflict them.

Terrorism and Trauma. *Terrorist acts* also generate emotional trauma (Pfefferbaum 2001, 2002). Indeed, this is a major purpose of terrorism. Terrorists believe that the more they are able to cause fear and panic, the better their chances of gaining their political goals. A number of studies of Americans after the September 11, 2001, attacks reported an increase in emotional distress. Telephone interviews with 1,008 Manhattan residents between one and two months after the attacks found that 7.5 percent reported symptoms consistent with posttraumatic stress syndrome and 9.7 percent reported symptoms of depression (Galea et al. 2002). Some of these symptoms existed prior to the attacks, but the researchers were able to determine that the rate of posttraumatic stress syndrome tripled in the weeks following the attacks.

Other research showed an increase in smoking and alcohol and marijuana use after the attacks (Susser, Herman, and Aaron 2002), and a survey of adolescents reported a sharply increased sense of vulnerability to dying than was found among adolescents prior to the attacks (Halpern-Felsher and Millstein 2002).

■■ Environmental Destruction

environmental destruction
alterations in the environment that make it less habitable or useful for people or other living things

As you will see in the next chapter, a precarious balance exists between natural resources and the growing demand for energy. This means that *conservation of natural resources throughout the world is essential;* but there is a *contradiction between this need and the willingness of people to engage in war,* for war always involves a certain amount of **environmental destruction.** Increasing sophistication in weaponry and increasing power of destructiveness have made wars more disastrous for the land.

Before the war, Vietnam was the "rice bowl of Asia." During the war, massive bombing, destruction of land, and disruption of farming meant the nation had to import rice. It continued to be one of the leading importers into the late 1980s. A woman who toured Vietnam noted that the people blamed the war—particularly the spraying of millions of litres of herbicides on forests and fields in an effort to root out guerrillas—for their high rates of spontaneous abortions, malformed fetuses, and other birth defects (Kemf 1990). The woman saw agricultural lands that are still off limits because of unexploded mines and bombs, as well as vast forests still dead from the herbicides.

The Gulf War also turned into an environmental disaster when the Iraqis dumped hundreds of millions of litres of crude oil into the Persian Gulf and set fire to hundreds of wellheads in Kuwait. At one point, Kuwaiti officials estimated that the fires were burning 22 million litres of oil a day, about 9 percent of the total world consumption of petroleum (Renner 1991:28). The smoke caused daytime April temperatures to drop as much as 27 degrees below normal and created severe smog as far as 1,600 kilometres away. Black rain (soot washed out of the air) coated people, animals, buildings, and crops with a black, oily film (Renner 1991:28).

The longer the warfare lasts, the more severe the environmental consequences. In 2001, the United States and other nations launched an attack on Afghanistan to unseat the ruling Taliban because it had harboured terrorists. The Taliban were defeated and a new government was installed within a matter of months; but the nation had already endured 23 years of wars and the warfare of opposing factions. The resulting environmental destruction has been severe (Garcia 2002). Irrigation canals were destroyed, dense forests were decimated, and a number of species of birds and mammals are close to extinction. Without the trees, the ground has eroded. Dust often hangs in the air, blocking sunlight and causing respiratory problems and other diseases. It is estimated that the present war in Iraq will also cause severe environmental damage to that country, especially as regards chemical pollution and its impact on arable land for growing food and other crops, as well as on water sources, depleted uranium that will poison the land, the loss of species due to polluted habitat, and a toxic sea with further loss of fish and other marine animals, thus affecting the food chain (People and the Planet 2003:12).

Although much of the environmental destruction is the result of intensive bombing, the evidence suggests that such bombing contributes little to winning a war. A study of the strategic bombing of Germany during the Second World War concluded that at least 300,000 Germans were killed (including adults and children) and 780,000 injured; 155,546 British, Canadian, and American airmen also died in the assaults. Nevertheless, "the slaughter made little contribution to victory" (Wilensky 1967:25); similarly, although it dropped more bombs there than all the Allied forces dropped in the Second World War, the United States did not win in Vietnam.

As with other effects, it is not only wartime itself that results in environmental destruction; the years of preparation and the years following a war also have deadly consequences for the environment. Thus, it may take decades to repair the damage in nations like Vietnam and Afghanistan. A 2002 report noted that more than half a century after the naval battles of the Second World War, the oil, chemicals, and unexploded ammunition on sunken ships in the Pacific still pose a serious peril to people and fisheries.[4] Land also continues to be contaminated by materials from the Second World War, including land where armaments were made. Each new war adds to the peril.

▪▪ The Economic Costs

War is *one of the greatest devourers of economic resources.* This point is dramatized by the fact that the war between Iran and Iraq, which lasted from 1980 to 1988, cost an estimated US$416 billion just through 1985. This amount is US$52 billion more than the two nations' combined earnings from oil sales since they first started exporting petroleum (Renner 1994:11). In 1999, the United States and its allies in the North Atlantic Treaty Organization (NATO) engaged in a bombing campaign in Serbia in an effort to stop atrocities against ethnic Albanians (Schmitt 1999a). The B-52 bombers used in the attacks cost $8,300 an hour to operate. The Cruise missiles they launched cost US$2 million each. After just six weeks, the total bill for the United States alone approached US$1 billion.

Consider also the cost of stockpiling weaponry and preparing for possible wars. In the last four decades of the 20th century, the global arms trade amounted to at least US$1.5 trillion (Renner 1999:16). The lengthy arms race between the United States and the Soviet Union that lasted until 1996 cost Americans a staggering US$5.5 trillion (Newman 1998). Clearly, an enormous amount of the world's resources is being channeled into paying for past wars and in preparing for future wars.

The Stockholm International Peace Research Institute reported in 2004 that military spending around the world in 2003 increased by 11 percent, up from a 6.5-percent increase in 2002. Over two years, military spending reached $956 billion. High-income countries account for 75 percent of this spending but only 16 percent of the world population. The combined military spending of these countries was slightly higher than the aggregate foreign debt of all low-income countries, and ten times higher than their combined levels of office development assistance in 2001 (www.sipri.org 2004). The main reason for the increase in world military spending was the massive increase by the United States, which accounts for almost half of the world total. During most of 2003, much of the focus on national military spending was as a result of the global threat of terrorism, with countries wanting to safeguard their borders and increase air, land, and sea surveillance. However, clearly it is not going to be possible to continue to maintain current levels of military spending *and* provide the vast array of social services that Canadians in particular have come to depend upon.

One reason for the *high cost of preparedness* is the technological advances made in weaponry. Sophisticated weapons cost considerably more than weapons of the past. As noted above, a single missile can cost up to US$2 million. In the first three weeks of air attacks on Serbia in 1999, the United States launched about US$9 million worth of various missiles *every day* (Milbank 1999). The costs of the airplanes used in the bombing ranged from US$9 million for each A-10 to US$2 billion for each B-2.

If the costs of preparedness are high, then, the costs of actually fighting a high-tech war are staggering. In the late 1990s, it cost US$2.8 million a day to keep a group of aircraft carriers at sea (Milbank 1999). Deploying and sustaining troops in combat cost more than US$11,000 per month per soldier. That translates into about US$1.5 billion per month for a ground war, and that figure doesn't include equipment like Apache helicopters (costing US$18 million each). These figures are hard to grasp. Think of them this way: A family living at the median family income level would have to give everything it made for more than 15 years to pay for just one minute of war.

Some nations allocate more to their military than they do to health and/or education. The frantic effort by most of the nations of the world to gain **military parity,** if not military superiority, consumed trillions of dollars in the second half of the 20th century.

The economic costs are more than the money spent, of course. There are indirect economic costs, such as the money spent to combat the emotional and physical problems resulting from war and preparations for war. There are also indirect costs that result from so much money being funnelled into the military. For example, while military contracts produce jobs, they are one of the least cost-effective ways to create

military parity
equality or equivalence in military strength

Some argue that military spending increases the number of jobs. Others point out that the same expenditure of funds in other sectors would create far more jobs.

jobs: "Government programs for virtually any other purpose produce more jobs, and more less-specialized jobs, than nuclear weapons modernization outlays" (Marullo 1987:138). While military research has yielded many technological advances, some of the technology does not get to the civilian sector because of secrecy requirements. Finally, the growth of some industries has been retarded because of the heavy investment in defence-related industries. By contrast, Japan, which spends comparatively little on its military, has invested heavily in electronic research and development and become a leader in electronic technologies.

What if the United States and Canada invested the billions spent on military preparedness in electronics, education, health, and other sectors that benefit human beings? What if those nations in which substantial numbers of adults are illiterate and chronically hungry invested their resources in health, education, and industrial development? What could be accomplished?

Consider first what needs to be accomplished. Each year:

- Hundreds of thousands of children become partially or totally blind because of vitamin A deficiency.
- Millions of children die of diseases that could have been prevented by relatively inexpensive immunization.
- Millions of children die before they reach the age of five.
- Millions of children are deprived of a primary education.
- Hundreds of millions of women are illiterate.
- Hundreds of millions of people are chronically malnourished.
- More than a billion people lack access to safe drinking water.

If only a relatively small part of the billions of dollars expended every year on the military were diverted to social programs, many of the above needs could be addressed.

Ironically, we live in a world in which there are more soldiers than physicians per capita, a world in which military technology makes the distance between western Europe and Russia a matter of minutes, while poor women in Africa must walk for hours each day just to get the family's water supply. A military mentality results in an enormous waste of resources that could be channelled into the enhancement of the quality of life of people throughout the world.

Terrorism also has economic costs, and it has become particularly costly since September 11, 2001. The most dramatic economic loss was the World Trade Center— about US$40 billion (Friedman 2002). But the costs of terrorism involve far more than the facilities damaged or destroyed. Since September 11, 2001, governments and businesses have invested huge sums of money to increase security (Moritsugu 2001). The U.S. Congress approved US$40 billion for 2002 to fund the global war on terrorism, clean up and reconstruct the World Trade Center site and the Pentagon, and enhance security at various key facilities throughout the nation.

The economic costs of terrorist activities also include such things as loss of business, higher insurance costs, and impeded international trade because of tighter security at borders. September 11, 2001 made the world generally, and the United States in particular, a much different economic environment.

■■ War, Terrorism, and Civil Liberties

The right of free speech is a longstanding Canadian value. However, there is *a contradiction between this value and the perceived need for consensus during a war.*

MILITARISM: "A WORLD GONE INSANE"

We were discussing the problem of war in a social problems class, focusing on the militarism of American society. A student objected: "Let's not make this an American problem. It's a *world* problem. Even the poorest nations are spending their resources on the military. We live in a world gone insane with arms."

He was right. Militarism is not a problem of any single nation, but of the entire world. From the poorest to the richest of nations, military expenditures are consuming resources that could be used to enhance the quality of life of the citizenry. Table 13.2 shows the figures for a number of nations.

To assess the impact of military spending on a nation, it is necessary to know not only the total amount, but also the per capita amount and the proportion of the gross national product (GNP) represented by the expenditures. Look, for example, at the numbers for Bangladesh, Canada, and Israel. While Bangladesh had far smaller total and per capita military expenditures, it spent nearly the same proportion of its GNP as Canada. Israel's total expenditures were about 20 percent more than those of Canada, but the per capita expenditure was 6.6 times more and the proportion of the GNP was 7.5 times more.

Note that some nations, like Bangladesh and Mexico, spend relatively little on the military; but Mexico, with a GNP of US$4,440 per capita, can afford the military expenditure far better than Bangladesh can, with its GNP of US$370 per capita (U.S. Census Bureau 2001:840).

Overall, in 1997, the developing countries of the world—those with the most serious needs for improved services for their citizens—spent US$232 billion for military purposes (U.S. Census Bureau 2001:327). The improvements in health, education, and other benefits to people represented by that sum are one reason the student called ours a "world gone insane with arms."

TABLE 13.2 ■ ■ ■

Military Expenditures, by Country, 1997

Country	Total (In Millions of Dollars)	Per Capita (Dollars)	Percentage of GNP
United States	276,000	1,030	3.3
Algeria	1,750	59	3.9
Bangladesh	592	5	1.4
Canada	7,800	257	1.3
China	74,900	61	2.2
Egypt	2,180	34	2.8
Germany	32,900	401	1.6
Israel	9,340	1,690	9.7
Italy	22,700	395	2.0
Kuwait	2,760	1,510	7.5
Mexico	4,290	44	1.1
Pakistan	3,380	26	5.7
Poland	5,600	145	2.3
Russia	41,700	283	5.8
Sweden	5,550	626	2.5
Taiwan	13,100	602	4.6
United Kingdom	35,300	600	2.7

Source: U.S. Census Bureau 2001:868.

Davenport (1995) examined events in 57 nations over a 34-year period and found that "increasing the resources given to the army enhanced the likelihood that censorship and political restrictions would be applied by governments." This happened in nations with democratic as well as autocratic governments.

In the United States and Canada, both citizens and government officials have participated in the suppression of civil liberties during wartime. During the First World War there was mob violence against dissenters and numerous prosecutions of people who spoke out against involvement in the war. In the later years of the Vietnam War, there were cases of mass protests against the war, mob violence against war protestors, massive arrests of demonstrators, and resultant court cases in which the issue of civil liberties was fought.

Violations of civil liberties were less severe for most North Americans during the Second World War, but some German Americans were imprisoned in the early days of the war, and Japanese Canadians and Americans were almost totally deprived of their civil rights. In 1942, more than 100,000 Japanese Canadians and Americans were relocated from their homes into detention camps in isolated areas. They had committed no crimes. There was no evidence that they supported Japan rather than Canada or the U.S. in the war, but they were defined as potential sources of subversion. Longstanding prejudice against the Japanese and jealousy of their landholdings, especially on the West Coast of Canada and the U.S., played into this decision. The relocations caused serious economic and psychological problems for many of the victims. The wholesale deprivation of civil liberties was upheld as legal by the Canadian and U.S. supreme courts, which ruled that the government did not have to respect traditional rights during a national emergency.

Unfortunately, if a war is considered legitimate by the masses of people, they may passively accept restrictions on their civil liberties. Furthermore, their institutions, including religion and the mass media, may actively help build consensus. During the Gulf War, the mass media facilitated consensus by not informing the public of Middle Eastern history, by "the jingoistic behavior of American reporters and anchorpersons," and by biased reporting (Stires 1991). For example, just before the bombing began in January 1991, polls showed that the American public was evenly divided in terms of using military and economic sanctions against Iraq to try and force it out of Kuwait; but a content analysis of network news programs between August 8, 1990, and January 3, 1991 reported that of 2,855 minutes of coverage of the Gulf crisis, only a little over 1 percent noted grassroots dissents from presidential policies, only one of 878 news sources was a peace organization, and more professional football players than peace activists were asked about their attitudes toward the war (Stires 1991:141–42).

Terrorism poses as severe a threat to civil liberties as does war. Government actions following the September 11, 2001, attacks alarmed civil libertarians (Liptak, Lewis, and Weiser 2002). More than 1,200 people suspected of violating immigration laws or of being material witnesses to terrorism were detained for weeks or months without being charged. The U.S. attorney general altered federal rules to allow the monitoring of communications between inmates and their lawyers if the government believed there was a reasonable suspicion of terrorist information. The government considered trying suspected terrorists by military tribunals rather than in the courts.

U.S. President George Bush initiated action to create a Department of Homeland Security, which would be responsible for preventing terrorist attacks and reducing the nation's vulnerability to terrorism (White House 2002). "Homeland security," of course, is a new and evolving concept, but it has the potential to be used to violate traditional civil rights (Relyea 2002). For example, one of the responsibilities of the Department of Homeland Security would be "Information analysis and infrastructure protection" (White House 2002). To analyze information, you must gather information. To what extent would the government go to fulfill such a responsibility? Invasive surveillance measures by government agents increased immediately after September 11 (Gould 2002). Will the department legitimate and further increase such measures?

For civil libertarians, this is the *fallacy of non sequitur.* To say that Canadians need increased security does not mean that the government must necessarily curb traditional civil liberties. As the American Civil Liberties Union (2002) argued, without civil rights and privacy protections, "What's to stop the Department [of Homeland Security] from abusing the very citizens it is responsible for protecting?"

As a result of September 11 and under pressure from the U.S. government to improve security measures at Canadian airports and other ports of entry, the Canadian federal government introduced an anti-terrorism bill on October 15, 2001. The objectives of the bill were to stop terrorism in Canada and protect Canadians from terrorist acts; provide more effective tools to identify, prosecute, convict, and punish terrorists; prevent damage to the Canadian economy arising from terrorism; and work with the international community to bring terrorists to justice (Proposed Amendments to the National Defence Act 2004).

Many who argue against this bill do so on the grounds that such legislation would enable customs officials, police officers, and others to arrest certain people because they may represent a particular race or ethnic group. The process, which has received a great deal of media attention lately, is called *racial profiling*: "any action undertaken for reasons of safety, security or public protection that relies on stereotypes about race, colour, ethnicity, ancestry, religion, or place of origin rather than on reasonable suspicion, to single out an individual for greater scrutiny or different treatment" (Ontario Human Rights Commission 2004).

Racial profiling has increased since September 11, and the threat of terrorist activities in North America has exacerbated the already existing racism, xenophobia, anti-Semitism, and other forms of racially motivated violence. Racial profiling has also had an impact on the experiences of refugees to this country, who now feel afraid that their ethnicity will cause other Canadians to fear them. As Abigail Bakan, a professor of political studies, noted in 2003: "Canada was once a place identified with welcoming refugees. But since the World Trade Centre attack, the concept of Canada as a refugee haven has been lost. In the name of stopping terror, victims are treated as victimizers" (Queen's Journal 2004).

Whatever the rationale, racial profiling occurs in Canada for reasons other than the threat of terrorism, and this practice in and of itself creates a social problem in that persons of particular races or ethnic groups feel singled out for criminal activities that they are assumed to be involved in but for which no evidence is ever produced. Racial profiling is but another component of the lack of a good quality of life for those who are judged on stereotypes rather than actual behaviour.

■■ CONTRIBUTING FACTORS

Peace, conflict, war, and terrorism are complex phenomena. As with violence, some thinkers have tried to make them a simple outgrowth of a *human need for aggression.* Yet, like aggression and violence, they are linked with *cultural values and patterns.* Some societies, for example, have no notions of organized warfare. The Hopi Indians traditionally had no place for offensive warfare and did not idealize the warrior as did other tribes. Furthermore, the Hopi conceived of the universe as a harmonious whole, with gods, nature, people, animals, and plants all working together for their common well-being.

Why, then, do people support wars? In particular, why do they support wars in view of the consequences we have described? Why do people support terrorism? What makes a terrorist willing to commit suicide in order to hurt or kill civilians? In the following sections, we examine various factors that help answer these vexing questions.

■■ Social Structural Factors

The Economics of War and Terrorism.

The idea that wars have an *economic cause* is an ancient one. The Greek philosophers Plato and Aristotle both argued that economic factors are fundamental in the outbreak of war. Plato believed that the quest for unlimited wealth brings on not only war but also a number of other human problems. Aristotle saw economic competition as the root of wars. In particular, poverty is the "parent" of both revolution and crime. The same economic inequality that leads to revolution within a nation results in wars between nations.

Marxist

pertaining to the system of thought developed by Karl Marx and Friedrich Engels, particularly emphasizing materialism, class struggle, and the progress of humanity toward communism

Marxists also argue that war has an economic basis. The **Marxist** view is that war is a *mechanism for maintaining inequalities* in a struggle for control of raw materials and markets. The inequalities are necessary because capitalism requires an ever-expanding market to endure. Warfare is one way to ensure that a nation will have control over adequate resources and an expanding market. Consequently, war is an inevitable outcome of capitalism.

While the Marxist explanation of war is debatable, economic factors are probably always at work in war and in preparations for war (Renner 1999). High military budgets mean considerable profits to a number of industries. In 1999, American businesses received US$135.2 billion in military prime contract awards (U.S. Census Bureau 2001:326). With such funds at stake, it is not surprising that there are intense lobbying efforts in the U.S. Congress to maintain and even increase military expenditures. One way that members of Congress can pump money into their districts or states is to maintain a military presence (in the form of a base) or secure military contracts for local industries. The military presence may no longer be needed and the military contracts may be wasteful, but the economic benefits to the district or state outweigh such considerations.

Economic factors are also at work in civil wars and terrorism. In some nations there is sharp economic inequality between racial, ethnic, or religious groups. *These racial, ethnic, or religious divisions may form the basis for civil war or terrorist activities* (Bonneuil and Auriat 2000; Reynal-Querol 2002).

A prime example is the Palestinian suicide bombers in Israel (Ratnesar 2002). Between 2000 and 2002, there were more than 70 bomb attacks or suicide bombings that killed or injured hundreds of civilians. Although even some top leaders of the Palestinians have condemned the bombings, the majority of Palestinians defend the killing of Israeli citizens on the grounds that Palestinians are killed by Israeli troops.

Why do the majority of Palestinians defend what many in the world community denounce as terrorism? Because these terrorist activities have developed in a context of what a U.N. human rights official has called daily experiences of discrimination, inequality, and powerlessness. Palestinians have lost land, work opportunities, freedom of movement, and access to water. In 2000, at least one-quarter of Palestinians were living in poverty. The ongoing cycle of violence and retaliation between Palestinians and Israelis has greatly increased their poverty. By 2002, Palestinian unemployment soared to more than one out of two workers, and a survey reported that 4.3 percent of those in the West Bank and 13.2 of those in the Gaza Strip were suffering from severe malnutrition (Brilliant 2002). The cycle of violence and the cycle of increasing inequality have fed on each other.

The Politics of War: Militarism.   From a political point of view, there are advantages to both militarism and war (Marullo 1987). The presence of a foreign threat, whether real or fabricated by politicians, can create cohesion within a society, including support for both domestic and foreign policies that might otherwise be resisted.

In the international arena, a strong military gives a nation higher status and more power. The nuclear arsenal of the United States, for example, is a "big stick" that can be used to facilitate the nation's diplomatic efforts and economic trade relations with its allies as well as its enemies (Marullo 1987). Of course, the more successful a government is in dealing with other nations, the more it tends to solidify its support at home.

Canada currently spends $12.3 billion on military spending, up by 5 percent since the adoption of the new federal budget passed in 2005. Canada is sixth highest in military spending among NATO countries, and sixteenth highest in the world (Department of National Defence 2004).

Perhaps the most dangerous manifestation of a combined military–industrial interest and influence has been the continuing *high expenditures for arms throughout the world* (see figure 13.1). The United States, Britain, France, Russia, and China supply most of the world's weapons. In 1997, the United States sold US$31.8 billion worth of arms to other nations, Britain sold US$6.6 billion, and France sold US$5.9 billion (U.S. Census Bureau 2001:327).

To what extent do you still need to be concerned about an arms buildup or about nations maintaining high levels of arms? As of this writing, world war seems increasingly remote. The fall of communist governments in Eastern Europe and the 1990 agreement between the United States and Russia on arms control (START) seemed to herald a new era of peace. However, a number of things should give you pause. First, we noted earlier that scores of wars continue throughout the world, and such wars always have the potential for drawing in other nations. Second, the START treaty involved significant reductions in weaponry but allowed both the United States and Russia to retain enough warheads to absorb a first strike and still destroy an enemy a hundred times over (Perle 1990).

Third, further reductions in the United States and Russian arsenals appear—again, as of this writing—very difficult to achieve (Schmitt 1999b). In 1999, an agreement for additional reductions was stalled in the Russian parliament, while a global treaty to ban all nuclear testing was bottled up in the U.S. Senate. Moreover, conservative American

FIGURE 13.1 ■ ■ ▪

Worldwide military expenditures in current dollars, 1980–1997.

Source: U.S. Census Bureau 1996b:354, 2001:327.

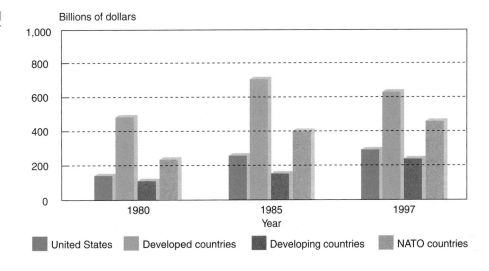

Billions of dollars

Year

■ United States   ▪ Developed countries   ■ Developing countries   ▪ NATO countries

politicians are wary of any drastic reductions in the U.S. arsenal, for they do not want America to lose its nuclear advantage over the rest of the world.

Fourth, even while the United States and Russia are struggling to reduce arms stockpiles, other nations continue to build up their weaponry. Among others, Iran and North Korea are working hard to build new biological, chemical, and nuclear weapons along with long-range missiles (Schmitt 1999b).

Finally, some observers believe that the real threat of nuclear war is not simply the arms race per se, but the reckless behaviour of the developed nations in intervening and supplying the arms used in the ongoing wars around the globe (McLauchlan 1991). The United States justifies the supply of arms on the basis that it protects the nation's own interests. Sometimes, however, it works against those interests. The United States supplied Iraq with arms in its long war with Iran in the 1980s, then faced some of these same weapons in its war against Iraq in 1991.

The Politics of Civil War and Terrorism: Autonomy. Throughout the world, there are groups who both desire and lack political autonomy—the right of people to govern their own affairs. Generally, when people press for autonomy there is a belief that their interests are not adequately represented (or are even ignored) by the current government. Indeed, the United States became a nation under such circumstances.

The lack of political autonomy often results in tension, civil war, and even terrorism. For example, a good deal of bloodshed occurred in the struggle of East Timor to gain independence from Indonesia and the attempt by Yugoslavia to suppress the political autonomy of Kosovo. East Timor was finally granted the right to govern itself and the Yugoslav Republic broke apart when U.N. forces took military action to stop the political oppression of minorities.

The early years of the 21st century are rife with examples of the struggle for political autonomy, including:

- Terrorist acts arising from the dispute between India and Pakistan over Kashmir, and the desire of Kashmir to be independent.
- The Chechnyan revolt against Russia.
- Terrorist acts by Palestinians who want to be free of Israeli control.
- Terrorist acts by the Irish who want Northern Ireland to be free of English control.
- Basque separatists' terrorist acts against Spain.

Political autonomy does not necessarily mean independent nationhood. In the United States, for example, political autonomy is given to the various American Indian nations, the U.S. Virgin Islands, Puerto Rico, Guam, and American Samoa. Hong Kong and Scotland are other places that have autonomy even though they are part of larger nations. In Canada, the Innu and other Aboriginal peoples and the province of Quebec have some political autonomy.

Giving a minority group political autonomy, however, doesn't always put an end to war. In some cases, groups that gain autonomy want to take the next step to full independence—separation from the nation of which they have been a part (Cornell 2002).

▪▪ Social Psychological Factors

Attitudes. Militarism and war are legitimated by a number of attitudes. The concept of a "just war" has a long history in the West. A just war is one that meets a number of tests, such as whether it has a just cause and whether all peaceful alternatives have been exhausted. If the war is just, the people are expected to support it fully. Shortly before the 1991 war against Iraq, some religious leaders questioned whether the notion of a just war is still valid in the face of the awful destructiveness of modern weapons (Anthony Day 1991). Indeed, Stites (1991) called the subsequent war against Iraq a "sanctioned massacre" because of the way in which the U.S. military technology overwhelmed the Iraqi forces. In spite of disparities in the military technology of nations and the incredible destructiveness of modern weapons, most people accept the notion that at least some wars are just.

The attitude that the United States has a mission to be "number one" in the world helps it justify militarism. "We feel a collective strength and confidence that comes from being 'number one' in military power" (Marullo 1987:143). National pride is involved in attaining a place of military superiority. Gibson (1994) has argued that this need for being a "winner" facilitated U.S. involvement in Grenada, Panama, and the Persian Gulf. These military actions reflected the American dream of "redeeming Vietnam and recovering from all the other disappointments and traumas of the late 1960s and 1970s" (Gibson 1994:269). After the Gulf War in particular, Americans purchased a spate of military-type items: commemorative handguns, rifles, knives, and T-shirts and uniforms. Many of those who made the purchases were celebrating the restoration of the nation as the supreme military power of the world.

International misperception is a set of attitudes that legitimate both militarism and war. In a classic analysis, White (1966) identified six forms of misperceptions that recur in cases of international wars:

1. The *diabolical-enemy image* imputes flagrant evil to the enemy, who is conceived to be thoroughly criminal in behaviour. Prior to the 1991 war against Iraq, the nation's political leaders "indulged in personal name-calling, false analogies to past wars and demonic leaders of earlier times" (Mack and Rubin 1991). In 2002, when President Bush urged new action against Iraq, he said the Iraqi regime raped women to intimidate them, tortured dissenters and their children, and that President Saddam Hussein was a "dangerous and brutal man" who sought to acquire the destructive technologies that matched his hatred (Kozaryn 2002).
2. The *virile self-image* implies preoccupation with one's strength and courage and the need to avoid humiliation by determined fighting.
3. The *moral self-image* affirms the nation's goodness; North Americans are the people of God and the enemy is of the devil. This is the *fallacy of personal attack,* ignoring the fact that there are many innocent, decent people among the enemy who also are victims of the struggle between the nations.
4. *Selective inattention* means that only the worst aspects of the enemy are noticed; at the same time we attend to the best aspects of ourselves, reinforcing the idea of the war as a conflict between black and white, good and evil.
5. *Absence of empathy* means inability to understand how the situation looks from the other's viewpoint. A Canadian might wonder, for example, how any German could fight on behalf of Hitler, or how any South Vietnamese could not welcome the American effort to save Vietnam from communism. People on both sides of a war fail to understand how the war could be justified by those on the other side. In the 1991 war against Iraq, Americans denied their contribution to the problem (later reports indicated that the United States had assured the Iraqis it would not interfere if they invaded Kuwait, and it had built up the Iraqi forces during the 1980s) and placed the blame totally on Iraq's shoulders (Mack and Rubin 1991).
6. *Military overconfidence* refers to the conviction that "our side can win." In the case of the 1991 war against Iraq, the Iraqi leaders boasted (and no doubt believed to some extent) that those against them would be soundly and humiliatingly defeated.

INVOLVEMENT

"WHAT A GREAT WAR THAT WAS"

A friend of two of the authors of this text served as a navigator in the Air Force during the Second World War. "Those," he says "were some of the best days of my life." He recalls his days in the military as a time of adventure. He does not desire war, but neither does he think of it in terms of the detrimental consequences discussed in this chapter.

Interview a number of armed forces veterans. If possible, find veterans who served in different wars, and include some who did as well as some who did not have combat experience. How do they describe the experience of war? Do they mention any of the consequences discussed in this chapter? Would they be willing to serve in another war or to have their children serve? Note whether there are differences based on service in different wars or on combat versus noncombat experience. If everyone felt as your respondents did, would the probability of future wars be greater or less?

These attitudes can be found on both sides of a conflict and are encouraged by the opposing leaders. For decades, American leaders portrayed the Soviet Union as an evil empire that threatened the nation's fundamental (and righteous) values. On the other hand, *Pravda,* the Soviet Communist Party's daily newspaper, discussed attempts at arms control with the United States in terms of dealing with "militaristic ambitions," "hotheads in the Pentagon," and "insane anti-logic" (Lichter et al. 1987:12).

In any confrontation between nations, the perceptions on both sides are remarkably similar, and people will support war to the extent that they accept such attitudes. Since both sides have the same attitudes, the attitudes obviously cannot be realistic. Nevertheless, they have typically been defined as valid and have served to legitimate international violence.

With regard to terrorism, we noted earlier that the majority of Palestinians support the suicide bombers and other acts of terror against Israel. Even though most Muslim leaders (both religious and political) condemn terrorism, the people take the attitude that the terrorists are only acting in defence of the Palestinian people and are doing nothing worse than what is being done to them.

Other terrorists also justify their actions on the grounds that they are really defending rights and seeking the well-being of the oppressed. They may also believe that change is nonexistent or too slow and that attention needs to be called to their cause (Jacobs 2001).

War, Terrorism, and Ideology.   *Ideologies* support militarism and the attitudes discussed. There is, for example, the ideology that asserts that Americans are the *police officers of the world.* This ideology says that the U.S. maintains the kind of democratic society that is best for all people and has a duty to protect and extend that kind of society. It may be necessary (even though many would prefer to avoid it) to engage in small wars wherever the American way of life is suppressed or threatened. The nation is thereby protecting people from evil systems, according to this ideology.

This ideology was a part of the rationale for initiating the war against Iraq in 1991. It was necessary, Americans were told, for the United States to take steps to protect the world against dictators like Saddam Hussein. Of course, the ideology is used selectively. In other cases, when dictators and totalitarian governments have initiated action against another country or against a segment of their own country, the U.S. has responded only with moral support or arms. In the case of Iraq, however, the ideology was used to justify a massive assault.

Even though some Canadians felt that we should join the U.S. and its allies in the war on Iraq, a *Globe and Mail* poll conducted in 2004 found that 74 percent of respondents said that the federal government made the right decision by not joining the U.S.–led coalition that invaded Iraq (*Globe and Mail* 2004).

▪▪ From Social Problems to Solutions

Inequalities of wealth and power among nations and between groups within nations, political and ideological conflicts, and economic factors all contribute to the likelihood of war and terrorism. An important step toward solving the problem would be to negotiate treaties that reduced the weaponry and armaments in the world. Current stockpiles, which are more than sufficient to eradicate life on the earth, need to be cut back. Military spending must be reduced. The sale of weapons of mass destruction is not an acceptable way to boost the supplier nation's economy.

The United States has taken the lead in trying to get the world's nations committed to a concerted fight against terrorism. This cooperation is imperative for eliminating terrorists' access to bases of operations and armaments. However, both before and after the September 11 attacks that stimulated the war on terrorism, the government took a number of unilateral actions in the name of the nation's own interests (Cameron 2002). The 1989 Convention on the Rights of the Child was ratified by every nation except Somalia and the United States. The Comprehensive Test Ban Treaty of 1996 to halt nuclear testing and the development of new nuclear weapons was ratified by all the NATO nations and Russia but rejected by the United States. The United States rejected the Ottawa Treaty to Ban Landmines, while 142 other countries approved it. In 2002, the Bush administration gave notice that the United States was pulling out of the 1972 Anti-Ballistic Missile Treaty, which limited the testing and deployment of antimissile weapons. A day later, Russia announced that it was no longer bound by the 1993 START II agreement, which outlawed multiple-warhead missiles and other weapons in the strategic arsenals of the two nations.

In essence, U.S. foreign policy in recent decades reflects more a determination to protect what political leaders define as the nation's self-interest (defined, in part at least, in terms of the international misperception described earlier) than a desire to be a leader in the construction of world peace. It is questionable how long the nation can continue to press for cooperation in fighting terrorism while asserting its right to take unilateral action on other issues whenever it pleases.

The U.S. also needs to stop the ongoing sale of arms to nations throughout the world. As Renner (1993a) has argued, armaments may simply be a symptom of deep conflicts between people, but curbing the availability of arms is still crucial for three reasons. First, arms proliferation tends to gain a momentum of its own, because no nation is satisfied with just being equal to others but wants an advantage over its enemies or potential enemies. Second, if arms are readily available, nations will more likely rely on them than on diplomacy and negotiations to settle their disputes (recall that in chapter 4 we noted that the availability of a weapon makes it more likely that it will be used). Third, when arms are readily available, the ensuing hostilities are likely to be far more devastating than they would be otherwise. For instance, the United States and the Soviet Union both shipped large amounts of arms to Somalia during the Cold War, each trying to lure the country into its sphere of influence. After the Cold War ended, a civil war broke out in Somalia in 1991, decimating the country and turning it into a nightmare of heavily armed, competing factions.

Of course, it is risky for any nation to demilitarize unless its potential adversary does the same, but there is some evidence to suggest that the risk is minimal. In the process called *Graduated Reciprocation in Tension-Reduction* (GRIT), one nation initiates an action that visibly reduces the way it threatens the other nation without at the same time endangering its own security. The action is an invitation to the other side to reciprocate (Elms 1972). Will such reciprocation occur? Following the 1962 Cuban missile crisis, President John F. Kennedy announced that the United States would stop atmospheric nuclear tests, and would resume them only if another country's action compelled it to do so. The next day the Soviet Union agreed to a Western-backed proposal in the United Nations to send observers to Yemen (a proposal the Soviets had been blocking). America reciprocated by agreeing to restore the Hungarian delegation to full status in the United Nations. A few days later Khrushchev announced that Russia would stop producing strategic bombers. Shortly thereafter the "hot line" between the White House and the Kremlin was installed. This series of concessions was the result of each side taking a step that led the other to reciprocate.

Subsequently, Soviet President Gorbachev initiated a number of efforts to reduce tensions and to engage in arms reductions. The United States responded to each effort positively. Neither nation used concessions by the other as an opportunity to attack or even to gain an advantage by further buildup.

In contrast, the reverse process occurred, as noted above, when the United States announced it was breaking the Anti-Ballistic Missile Treaty and Russia responded by disavowing START II. The reverse process also occurred in the Israeli–Palestinian conflict. Each side believed it had the right to—indeed, that it must—retaliate against the other after each attack. Clearly, there is no end to such a process. There can be a graduated reciprocation in tension building as well as in tension reduction.

In addition to reducing arms and taking initiatives in demilitarization, Americans need to work on attitudes and ideologies. More contact between peoples—cultural, educational, and political contact—could alter some of the misperceptions that abound in the world. Education should include an international perspective, so that Americans become increasingly aware of the smallness of the world and of the similarities among human beings everywhere. Instead of viewing other countries as adversaries or as problems, we should view them as partners with whom we need to work on common problems. If the United States strives to be a world leader, let it be a leader in peace and in promoting the well-being of people rather than a leader who uses strength for pursuing self-interest.

The effort to avoid war and terrorism, and to reduce the costs of preparing for war, entails a great deal of work and frustration; but the alternatives to making the effort are grim. A noted man of peace, Martin Luther King, Jr., put it this way:

> In a day when sputniks dash through outer space and guided ballistic missiles are carving highways of death through the stratosphere, nobody can win a war. The choice today is no longer between violence and nonviolence. It is either nonviolence or nonexistence. (quoted in Weinberg and Weinberg 1963:74)

■■ SUMMARY

Canadians are greatly concerned about war and terrorism. Warfare is no longer just a matter of opposing armies on the battlefield, but increasingly involves civil wars and terrorist activities.

War diminishes the quality of life of people and destroys the lives of many. During the 20th century, the bloodiest of all centuries, wars killed more than a hundred million people. War and terrorism cause psychological disruption and dehumanization of everyone involved. As illustrated by the posttraumatic stress disorder, the effects last after the war or terrorist act is over. Much environmental destruction is involved. The economic costs of war, of preparation for possible wars, and of terrorism are staggering. The costs of fighting war and stopping terrorism inevitably mean that certain social needs will be neglected. War and terrorism always pose a threat to civil liberties, as illustrated by sanctions against dissenters and the detention of Japanese Canadians and Americans in isolated camps during the Second World War and measures taken by the government after the September 11, 2001 attacks.

Social structural and social psychological factors help bring about war and terrorist activities and motivate people to support them. Economic factors are involved in wars and terrorism. Military spending is highly profitable to some industries, and people who profit from such spending tend to exercise considerable power in the government. Severe economic inequality between racial, ethnic, or religious groups within nations can give rise to civil war or terrorism.

Militarism is a political factor that can lead to war. The military, the government, and the corporations have some shared interests. This military-industrial-governmental linkage tends to maintain high levels of defence spending. Arms races tend to be self-perpetuating because each side views developments of the other with alarm and responds with its own efforts, which then become the stimuli to the other side to make further advances.

The desire for autonomy is a political factor in civil wars and terrorism. People everywhere want the right to govern themselves and may assert that right through civil war or terrorist activities when they believe their interests are not represented in the government.

A number of attitudes justify war and terrorism, including the notion of a "just" war, the idea that Americans have a mission to be number one in the world, the set of attitudes called "international misperception" held by people on both sides of a potential conflict, and the belief that terrorist acts are a necessary form of self-defence.

Canada is a peacekeeping country, and where possible uses peaceful negotiated strategies for dealing with conflict. With increased pressure from the United States government to become involved in anti-terrorism activities and missile defence strategies such as the North American missile defence shield and NORAD (North American Aerospace Defense Command), it will be an ever-increasing challenge to maintain this stance.

■■ KEY TERMS

Environmental Destruction 371	International Terrorism 363	Marxist 378 Military Parity 373	Terrorism 363 War 364

■■ STUDY QUESTIONS

1. How extensive is the problem of war and terrorism?
2. How has the amount of human destruction and injury during war changed over time?
3. What is meant by "psychological and interpersonal disruption and dehumanization" as a consequence of war and terrorism?
4. What effects does the problem have on the environment?
5. What are the economic costs?
6. How do war and terrorism affect civil liberties?

7. How do economic factors enter into war and terrorism?
8. What kinds of political factors contribute to the problem?
9. What attitudes and ideologies legitimate wars and terrorism?
10. What steps could be taken to diminish the possibility of war and terrorist acts?
11. How did the events of September 11, 2001 affect Canadians?

12. Would you want your child to serve in a peacekeeping mission in Iraq or Afghanistan?

13. Was the invasion of Iraq a "just" war?

■■ FOR FURTHER READING

Cole, David, and James X. Dempsey. *Terrorism and the Constitution: Sacrificing Civil Liberties in the Name of National Security.* 2nd ed. Washington, DC: First Amendment Foundation, 2002. Two constitutional scholars show how the government's response to real or perceived threats, from the communists of the 1950s to the Islamic terrorists of the 21st century, threaten civil liberties.

Dawson, Doyne. *The Origins of Western Warfare: Militarism and Morality in the Ancient World.* Boulder, CO: Westview, 1998. A search for the warlike nature of Western people in the nature of Western civilization itself, focusing on the military traditions in the Greek and Roman cultures.

Harwayne, Shelley. *Messages to Ground Zero: Children Respond to September 11, 2001.* Portsmouth, NH: Heinemann, 2002. A compilation of poems, drawings, and essays that illustrate children's reactions to the terrorist attacks, ranging from admiration for the heroic rescuers to personal feelings of anxiety and grief.

Hiro, Dilip. The *Longest War: The Iran-Iraq Military Conflict.* New York: Routledge, 1991. An examination of the war between two Middle Eastern nations from 1980 to 1988, showing the enormous destruction and, from an external point of view, the total pointlessness of some wars.

Howard, Michael, George J. Andreapoulos, and Mark R. Shulman, eds. *The Laws of War: Constraints on Warfare in the Western World.* New Haven, CT: Yale University Press, 1995. An examination of the formal constraints on war from ancient times to the present, including the role of Christian ethics as set forth by Catholic theologians in the Middle Ages.

Howard, Russell, and Reid Sawyer, eds. *Terrorism and Counterterrorism: Understanding the New Security Environment.* Guilford, CT: McGraw-Hill/Dushkin, 2002. A collection of articles by terrorism experts analyzing terrorism from many perspectives, including suggestions on how to deal with the current terrorist groups.

Welsome, Eileen. *The Plutonium Files: America's Secret Medical Experiments in the Cold War.* New York: Dial Press, 1999. The story of medical experimentation on hundreds of unsuspecting Americans who were injected—without their consent or knowledge—with plutonium in order to study the effects.

■■ NOTES

1. *Time,* August 22, 1988, p. 46.
2. *Science News,* April 14, 1990, p. 236.
3. *I Never Saw Another Butterfly: Children's Drawings and Poems from Terezin Concentration Camp, 1942–1944.* New York: McGraw-Hill, n.d.
4. *Oil Spill Intelligence Report,* April 11, 2002, pp. 1–3.

THE ENVIRONMENT

LEARNING OBJECTIVES

1. Understand the nature of the ecosystem.

2. Identify the types and extent of environmental problems.

3. Discuss the ways in which environmental problems threaten the desired quality of life.

4. Explain the social structural and social psychological factors that underlie environmental problems.

5. Suggest some ways to deal with the problems of environmental pollution and environmental depletion.

"WE'RE NOT SAFE HERE ANYMORE"

Karl lives in Cape Breton, Nova Scotia, right next door to a steel plant. It's the same neighbourhood where his great-grandparents lived, long before the steel plant was built. Yet Karl isn't sure whether his children or his grandchildren will live in this place.

I can't imagine living anywhere else. But I can't imagine my children or grandchildren living here. I don't even want them to. We're not safe here anymore. The hazardous wastes from the steel plant have contaminated our water supply. We can't grow our gardens anymore. We can't drink the water. We don't even feel safe taking a bath in it.

And it's not just the water. When you know that stuff is all around you, you feel like you're living in poison. Of course, I try not to think about it most of the time. But you can't keep it out of your mind altogether. And whenever I do think about it, I can feel myself getting nervous. Or sometimes I just get depressed.

I love this place. It's my home. But sometimes I hate it. At least, I hate what's happened to it. I don't know yet what we're going to do. But I do know that even if my wife and I don't leave, our kids will. And that will be the end of generations of my family on this land. ■

▪▪ INTRODUCTION

"The measure of individuals or nations is whether they respond to the great issues of their time. For our generation, the great issues are environment and poverty. We will be judged by whether we can reverse the environmental degradation of the planet and eradicate the dehumanizing poverty that is now engulfing more and more of the world's people" (Brown 1993:21). Lester Brown, the author of the above, is one of the foremost experts on global environmental problems. He concluded his assessment by arguing that if we do not turn things around, "our children may not have the option of doing so" (Brown 1993:21). In other words, the problems we address in this chapter are both crucial and urgent.

We look first at the ecosystem to set the stage for an understanding of environmental problems. Then we examine various kinds of environmental problems and how extensive these are. We show how these problems affect the quality of life and what structural and social psychological factors contribute to them. Finally, we consider several proposed as well as actual efforts to resolve these problems.

▪▪ THE ECOSYSTEM

ecosystem
a set of living things, their environment, and the interrelationships among and between them

The **ecosystem** refers to the interrelationships among all living things and the environment. The emphasis is on the interdependence of all things: people, land, animals, vegetation, atmosphere, and social processes. Commoner (1971:16–17) called the ecosystem of the earth a "machine" and described some of the crucial interrelationships:

> Without the photosynthetic activity of green plants, there would be no oxygen for our engines, smelters, and furnaces, let alone support for human and animal life. Without the action of the plants, animals, and microorganisms that live in them, we could have no pure water in our lakes and rivers. Without the biological processes that have gone on in the soil for thousands of years, we would have neither food crops, oil, nor coal. This machine is our biological capital, the basic apparatus on which our total productivity depends. If we destroy it, our most advanced technology will become useless and any economic and political system that depends on it will founder. The environmental crisis is a signal of this approaching catastrophe.

Nature is not "out there" to be conquered for human benefit. Rather, people, nature, and the earth form a delicately balanced system. What is done at one place can have serious consequences for the system at other places. Consider, for example, the problems of "acid rain" and the threat to the ozone layer. The problem of acid rain is caused by sulphur dioxide emissions from coal-burning plants and factories and by nitrogen oxides from automobile exhaust and some industries. As they rise, the chemicals mix with water vapour to form sulphuric and nitric acids that then fall to the earth as rain or snow. Acid rain has been responsible for such things as killing fish in lakes, damaging forests, reducing crop yields, contributing to health problems, and damaging buildings and monuments (Lenssen 1993; Bright 2000). Moreover, the damage may occur hundreds or thousands of kilometres away from where the sulphur dioxide emissions occurred.

In recent decades, tougher air pollution regulations have significantly reduced sulphur dioxide emissions. Some damaged lakes and forests are beginning to recover. However, researchers point out that the effects of acid rain are long term and that cutting power plant sulphur dioxide emissions by an additional 80 percent may still bring only partial recovery from the damage by 2050 (Krajick 2001).

The threat to the ozone layer is another example of current environmental problems. Ozone is a rare form of oxygen that is poisonous to human beings at ground level but is necessary in the upper atmosphere to absorb the deadly ultraviolet radiation of the sun. There is a natural balance of ozone distribution from ground level to the stratosphere. However, human activity disturbs that natural balance. High-voltage electrical equipment, including electrostatic air cleaners used to reduce other kinds of air pollution, creates ground level ozone, and higher than normal concentrations at ground level pose health problems to the eyes, throat, and lungs.

The ozone in the upper atmosphere is reduced as a result of a number of human activities, including the use of nitrogen fertilizers, supersonic airplanes, fluorocarbons from aerosol spray cans (now banned in most nations), and nuclear explosions in the atmosphere. The effects of a depleted ozone layer are far reaching, involving changes in the earth's climate, destruction of some plant and animal life, reduced crop yields, increased incidence of skin cancer, possible genetic damage to plants and humans, and an impact on the food chain of the oceans (McGinn 1999).

Environmental problems dramatize the interdependence in the ecosystem. A poet once wrote that one cannot stir a flower without troubling a star. It is imperative that individuals make every effort to evaluate all the implications of human action for their delicately balanced ecosystem.

▪▪ TYPES OF ENVIRONMENTAL PROBLEMS

environmental pollution
harmful alterations in the environment, including air, land, and water

environmental depletion
increasing scarcity of natural resources, including those used for generating energy

pollutant
anything that causes environmental pollution

Environmental problems can be divided into two types: **environmental pollution** and **environmental depletion.** "Pollution" refers to degradation of air, land, water, climate (global warming), aesthetic environment (eye pollution), and sound environment (noise pollution). "Depletion" refers to the diminishing supply of natural resources, illustrated well by the challenge of meeting the ever-increasing demand for energy.

▪▪ Environmental Pollution

"Pollution is the harmful alteration of our environment by our own actions. **Pollutants** are either unwanted by-products of our activities or the obnoxious residues of things we have made, used, and thrown away" (Revelle 1971:382). There are numerous kinds of pollution and pollutants, as we discuss later. It is important to keep in mind that in an ecosystem the overall impact of pollutants is greater than the impact of particular pollutants in particular places.

Pollution can occur in two ways: through catastrophes and through the slower, more insidious poisoning that occurs as a result of various processes and activities. The catastrophes dramatize the problem. In 1984, vapours from a deadly chemical used to manufacture pesticides at a Dow chemical plant escaped through a faulty valve into the air in Bhopal, India. Within a few hours, more than 2,500 people were dead, and thousands were critically ill. It was one of the worst industrial disasters in history. The accident underscored the horrendous consequences of exposure to toxic substances. Yet even more important than the catastrophes are the countless ways in which industries are exposing millions of people to high levels of toxic materials. Many of the victims in Bhopal died quickly. Soil and water in and around Bhopal were tested in 1999 and were revealed to still be contaminated by organochlorines and heavy metals. Others will die more slowly, the result of regular exposure to toxic materials in the air, water, and land. It is estimated that 50,000 people, including children of survivors, continue to suffer with chronic neurological problems: loss of memory, speech, or fine motor skills; and posttraumatic stress disorders that give rise to severe depression and feelings of despair and hopelessness. But cleanup of the site is not about to happen quickly, as allegedly "Dow Chemical has steadfastly refused to clean up the site, provide safe drinking

Survivors of the Bhopal accident wave brooms as they protest outside the Dow Chemicals headquarters. What obligation does Dow have to the people of Bhopal?

water, compensate the victims, or disclose the composition of the gas leak, information that doctors could use to properly treat the victims" (What Happened in Bhopal 2004).

Air Pollution.   Millions of tonnes of pollutants are released into the air every year in North America and are visible in the smog that darkens urban areas. Much other pollution is not visible to the naked eye because it results from the discharge of gases and tiny particulate matter into the air. In some areas, atmospheric conditions tend to concentrate pollutants in the air. Even when winds blow the pollutants away from the populated area where they are generated, damage still occurs.

The U.S. Council on Environmental Quality compiled a list of the major air pollutants and their characteristics, sources, and principal effects, as well as the ways they can be controlled (see figure 14.1). Most air pollution is caused by the burning of fossil fuels—oil, natural gas, and coal (Flavin and Dunn 1999). Air pollution is associated primarily with the production of energy, with industrial processes, and with the exhaust from the internal combustion engines of motor vehicles.

Another kind of air pollution involves contamination of the atmosphere with toxic vapours from manufactured products. For example, formaldehyde, which is used in the manufacture of various products used around the home, gives off toxic vapours that may lead to respiratory ailments and cancer. Formaldehyde is used in a surprising number of products. New bed sheets, permanent-press shirts, fingernail hardeners and polishes, latex paints, some floor finishes, prepasted wallpaper (while wet), plywood and particle-board cabinets, and new plastic-laminated kitchen counters all emit formaldehyde vapours for varying periods of time (Horowitz 1999; Raloff 1999). You might get only a small, short exposure from using fingernail polish. Washing new bed sheets reduces the vapours considerably, but the cabinets and counters may emit vapours for some time. Air pollution, then, is a problem at home as well as outdoors.

Water Pollution.   There are eight different kinds of water pollution (Revelle 1971; Sampat 2000). First is organic sewage, which requires dissolved oxygen in order to be transformed into carbon dioxide, water, phosphates, nitrates, and certain plant

FIGURE 14.1 ■ ■ ■

Major air pollutants for which national ambient air quality standards have been established.

Pollutant	Total suspended particulates (TSP)	Sulphur dioxide (SO$_2$)	Carbon monoxide (CO)
Characteristics	Any solid or liquid particles dispersed in the atmosphere, such as dust, pollen, ash, soot, metals, and various chemicals; the particles are often classified according to size as settleable particles: larger than 50 microns; aerosols: smaller than 50 microns; and fine particulates: smaller than 3 microns	A colourless gas with a pungent odour; SO$_2$ can oxidize to form sulphur trioxide (SO$_3$), which forms sulphuric acid with water.	A colourless, odourless gas with a strong chemical affinity for hemoglobin in blood
Principal sources	Natural events such as forest fires, wind erosion, volcanic eruptions; stationary combustion, especially of solid fuels; construction activities; industrial processes; atmospheric chemical reactions	Combustion of sulphur-containing fossil fuels, smelting of sulphur-bearing metal ores, industrial processes, natural events such as volcanic eruptions	Incomplete combustion of fuels and other carbon-containing substances, such as in motor vehicle exhausts; natural events such as forest fires or decomposition of organic matter
Principal effects	Health: Directly toxic effects or aggravation of the effects of gaseous pollutants; aggravation of asthma or other respiratory or cardiorespiratory symptoms; increased cough and chest discomfort; increased mortality. Other: Soiling and deterioration of building materials and other surfaces, impairment of visibility, cloud formation, interference with plant photosynthesis	Health: Aggravation of respiratory diseases, including asthma, chronic bronchitis, and emphysema; reduced lung function; irritation of eyes and respiratory tract; increased mortality. Other: Corrosion of metals; deterioration of electrical contacts, paper, textiles, leather, finishes and coatings, and building stone; formation of acid rain; leaf injury and reduced growth in plants	Health: Reduced tolerance for exercise, impairment of mental function, impairment of fetal development, aggravation of cardiovascular diseases. Other: unknown
Controls	Cleaning of flue gases with inertial separators, fabric filters, scrubbers, or electrostatic precipitators; alternative means for solid waste reduction; improved control procedures for construction and industrial processes	Use of low-sulphur fuels; removal of sulphur from fuels before use; scrubbing of flue gases with lime or catalytic conversion	Automobile engine modifications (proper tuning, exhaust gas recirculation, redesign of combustion chamber); control of automobile exhaust gases (catalytic or thermal devices); improved design, operation, and maintenance of stationary furnaces (use of finely dispersed fuels, proper mixing with air, high combustion temperature)

nutrients. Less oxygen is needed if the sewage is treated, but the amount of treatment varies and in some places there is no treatment at all.

Eutrophication, a second kind of water pollution, is overfertilization of water from excess nutrients, leading to algae growth and oxygen depletion. Eutrophication threatens aquatic life. It has already killed great numbers of fish in North America.

A third type of water pollution results from infectious agents. Many water-borne bacteria that cause disease have been eliminated in Canada, but there is still danger from infectious viruses such as hepatitis. Organic chemicals such as insecticides, pesticides, and detergents cause a fourth kind of water pollution. These too may be highly toxic to aquatic life.

eutrophication
overfertilization of water due to excess nutrients, leading to algae growth and oxygen depletion

FIGURE 14.1 ■ ■ ■

(Continued)

Pollutant	Photochemical oxidants (Ox)	Nitrogen dioxide (NO$_2$)	Hydrocarbons (HC)
Characteristics	Colourless, gaseous compounds which can comprise photochemical smog, e.g., ozone (O$_3$), peroxyacetyl nitrate (PAN), aldehydes, and other compounds	A brownish red gas with a pungent odour, often formed from oxidation of nitric oxide (NO)	Organic compounds in gaseous or particulate form, e.g., methane, ethylene, and acetylene
Principal sources	Atmospheric reactions of chemical precursors under the influence of sunlight	Motor vehicle exhausts, high-temperature stationary combustion, atmospheric reactions	Incomplete combustion of fuels and other carbon-containing substances, such as in motor vehicles exhausts; processing, distribution, and use of petroleum compounds, such as gasoline and organic solvents; natural events such as forest fires and plant metabolism; atmospheric reactions
Principal effects	Health: Aggravation of respiratory and cardiovascular illness, irritation of eyes and respiratory tract, impairment of cardiopulmonary function Other: Deterioration of rubber, textiles, and paints; impairment of visibility; leaf injury, reduced growth, and premature fruit and leaf drop in plants	Health: Aggravation of respiratory and cardiovascular illnesses and chronic nephritis Other: Fading of paints and dyes, impairment of visibility, reduced growth and premature leaf drop in plants	Health: Suspected contribution to cancer Other: Major precursors in the formation of photochemical oxidants through atmospheric reactions
Controls	Reduced emissions of nitrogen oxides, hydrocarbons, possibly sulphur oxides	Catalytic control of automobile exhaust gases, modification of automobile engines to reduce combustion temperature, scrubbing flue gases with caustic substances or urea	Automobile engine modifications (proper tuning, crankcase ventilation, exhaust gas recirculation, redesign of combustion chamber); control of automobile exhaust gases (catalytic of thermal devices); improved design, operation, and maintenance of stationary furnaces (use of finely dispersed fuels, proper mixing with air, high combustion temperature); improved control procedures in processing and handling petroleum compounds

Inorganic and miscellaneous chemicals constitute a fifth category of water pollutants. These can alter the life of a body of water, kill fish, and create unpleasant tastes when the water is used as a drinking supply. Sixth, sediments from land erosion may cause pollution. These sediments can diminish the water's capacity to assimilate oxygen-demanding wastes and block the sunlight needed by aquatic plants.

Radioactive substances, a seventh kind of pollutant, are likely to become more serious if nuclear power plants to generate electricity become more common. The eighth kind of water pollution is waste heat from power plants and industry. Overheated water holds less oxygen, and fish and other aquatic life are generally very sensitive to temperature changes.

Not only are lakes and rivers being polluted, but the oceans are as well. Oil spills and the dumping of waste into the oceans have made many beaches unsafe for swimming. Millions of barrels of oil are poured into the ocean each year from the cleaning of the bilges of tankers. In addition, there are thousands of oil-polluting incidents every year from such things as tanker accidents. In 2003, 102 illegal spills (e.g., ammonia, arsenic, and carcinogenic solvents) into water have been reported in Ontario. In addition, between 2002 and 2003, violations of water-pollution laws numbered more than 2,000 (Perkel 2005:A10). There have been only one or two charges laid, and many of the violators are repeat offenders:

> The ongoing problem comes despite tougher enforcement by the environment ministry that followed the May 2000 disaster in Walkerton, in which E. coli bacteria in drinking water killed seven people and sickened 2,300 others.
> The tragedy sparked a policy shift away from voluntary adherence to the rules to more stringent ministry action.
> As a result, violations have fallen about 30 per cent since their peak in the late 1990s under the Conservative government of premier Mike Harris.
> Still, the new data highlight the need for even tougher enforcement, far stiffer penalties for polluters, and more transparency. (p. A10)

Land Pollution. **Pesticides, herbicides,** chemical wastes, radioactive fallout, acid rain, and garbage all infect the soil. Some chemicals used in pesticides, herbicides, and a number of manufactured products are hazardous to human health and are highly stable, remaining in the soil for decades (McGinn 2000).

pesticide
a chemical used to kill insects defined as pests

herbicide
a chemical used to kill plant life, particularly weeds

The pesticide DDT, for example, has been banned in Canada since the mid-1970s (CEC 2004). DDT was found to interfere with the formation of normal eggshells in certain birds, adding to the potential extinction of some species. It is incredibly stable, having been detected in Antarctic penguins, in the blood and fat of most Canadians, and in carrots and spinach sold in supermarkets more than a decade after the substance was banned.

The problem of pesticides is compounded by the fact that the pests tend to develop a resistance to them; thus, increasing quantities are required over time. And if the natural enemies of a particular pest disappear, a pest-control program may require monstrous increases in dosage of the pesticide.

Global Warming. Air pollution from gases such as carbon dioxide is a major factor in the so-called greenhouse effect (Dunn 2002). The gases trap solar energy in the atmosphere which, in turn, leads to global warming. Without appropriate action, a warming of 10 degrees or more could occur. This would melt the polar ice caps, raise sea levels, flood low-lying lands, alter the earth's climate, and cause economic and political chaos as people attempt to deal with the severe disruptions (Fisher 1990).

Global warming is a controversial issue. Critics argue that the world may simply be in a warm phase of long-term cyclic temperature variations. Most scientists, however, accept the greenhouse effect as a process demanding action. They note with concern the increasing average temperatures already taking place. Temperatures by and large have been above normal since 1950. The dashed line in figure 14.2 "represents a warming linear trend of 1.1°C over the last 57 years" (Environment Canada 2004).

Noise Pollution. Prolonged exposure to noise of sufficient intensity can not only damage hearing, it may also increase stress and lead to harmful physiological changes such as an increased heart rate (Vera, Vila, and Godoy 1994). At lower levels, noise can increase irritability, prevent sleep, and impair performance on tasks (Persson et al. 2001). Some sources of noise are shown in figure 14.3. It shows that a noise level of

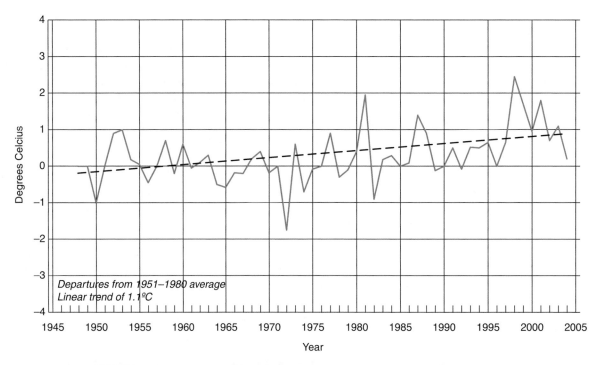

FIGURE 14.2 ■ ■ ■

Annual national temperature departures and long-term trend, 1948–2004.

Source: Environment Canada 2004; http://www.msc-smc.ec.gc.ca/ccrm/bulletin/images/tchttrnd.gif.

80 decibels is "annoying." The noise environment is worsening for most of us; hundreds of millions of people all over the world are exposed to unacceptable noise levels at work and at home (Organisation for Economic Co-operation and Development 1991; Skanberg and Ohrstrom 2002).

Aesthetic Damage. An aesthetically pleasing environment is one component of a high quality of life (Sirgy et al. 2001). An attractive environment can affect mood and influence health-promoting behaviour like exercise (Craig et al. 2002). It is no minor point, then, that pollution involves *deterioration of the beauty of the environment* as well as actual physical damage.

Air pollution, for instance, leads to the deterioration of buildings, statues, and paintings. It can inhibit visibility, obscure scenic views, and produce noxious odours. This kind of aesthetic damage—whether from air and water pollution or from litter—is the effect on the environment that most people first recognize. Whatever the source, it signals that your environment is less pleasing, that the beauty of the natural world has been scarred by human activity.

■■ Environmental Depletion

Natural Resources and Energy Production and Consumption. Air, water, and land can be restored, but the problem of dwindling resources is another matter. If the air is cleaned, it may become just as useful as before it was polluted. But once a mine has been exhausted, an oil well pumped dry, or a patch of soil ruined for farming, you have lost a resource that cannot be reclaimed easily or quickly, if at all.

FIGURE 14.3 ■ ■ ■

Sound levels and human responses.

Source: *Sixth Annual Report of the Council on Environmental Quality* (Washington, DC: Government Printing Office, 1975), p. 85.

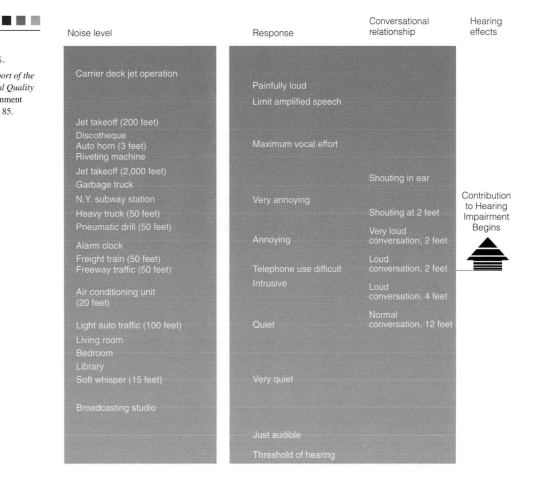

Canada is rich in natural resources. According to the 2004 edition of "Human Activity and the Environment," a statistical report on Canada and its environment, Canada's energy production in 2002 was 45 percent greater than its energy consumption. Since 1958, with very few exceptions, Canadians' use of primary energy on a national and per capita basis continues to rise (see figure 14.4). In 2001 Canadians used 1.6 times more energy than in 1967. What this means is that Canada has now become a net producer and is no longer a net consumer. In 2001, Canada exported $55.1 billion (14 percent of all exports) of energy products, mostly to the United States.

Canadians tend to think that the nation has virtually unlimited natural resources, but this is not the case. In 1973 a group of oil-producing nations temporarily suspended the sale of oil to other nations, and Canadians confronted the fact that no nation in the modern world can be self-sufficient by virtue of its own natural resources. No nation, including Canada, is self-sufficient in the modern world.

▪▪ HOW BIG ARE OUR ENVIRONMENTAL PROBLEMS?

How serious are these problems? Using the same two categories of environmental pollution and environmental depletion, consider what the data reveal.

FIGURE 14.4 ■ ■ ■

Energy production and consumption, by terajoule, 1958–2004.

Source: Adapted from Statistics Canada CANSIM table 128-0002.

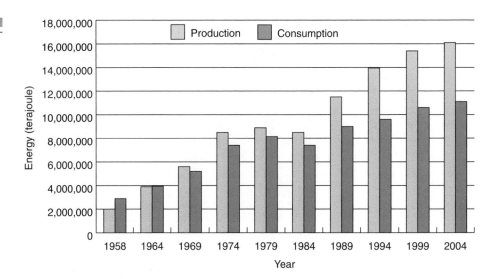

■■ Environmental Pollution

The Canadian federal government in the early 1970s set up the National Ambient Air Quality Objectives (NAAQOs) and established limits for the following air pollutants: carbon monoxide, nitrogen dioxide, ozone, sulphur dioxide, and total suspended particulates (Environment Canada 2004b). These pollutants are measured as either "desirable," "acceptable," or "tolerable" in relationship to environmental damage or possible health effects. In turn, air pollution is rated and reported as either good, fair, poor, or very poor (Environment Canada 2004b).

In general, enforcement of *air pollution standards* has been reducing the amount of the pollutants released into the air (Environment Canada 2004). Although there was a

The Pickering Nuclear Plant. Canadians need to curtail energy use or blackouts, like the one that hit much of Canada and the U.S. in August 2003, will be more common.

WORLD ENERGY PRODUCTION AND CONSUMPTION

As noted in the text, energy production and consumption are an integral part of the problems of pollution and dwindling resources. They also play an integral part in the quality of people's lives. For example, try to imagine a world without electricity and the internal combustion engine. It would still be a livable world, but, as Flavin and Dunn (1999:23) put it:

> Homo sapiens has relied for most of its existence on a virtually limitless flow of renewable energy resources— muscles, plants, sun, wind, and water—to meet its basic needs for shelter, heat, cooking, lighting, and movement. The relatively recent transition to coal that began in Europe in the seventeenth century marked a major shift to dependence on a finite stock of fossilized fuels.

This shift affected every aspect of life—health care, education, leisure activities, and so on. People throughout the world desire the standard of living produced by the shift. As developing nations strive to achieve the standard of living now enjoyed by the developed nations, questions of practicality arise. Does the earth have enough resources for all nations to achieve such a standard? Energy use per capita varies enormously around the world (table 14.1) Note the difference between a developing nation such as India and the developed nations such as Canada.

Notice that even among the developed nations there is a considerable difference in the amount of energy consumed per capita. Some of these differences reflect varying climates (e.g., heating and air conditioning are needed far more in some nations than in others). Yet the figures raise the question of how much energy per capita is needed for a decent standard of living. Is life in Canada, where energy consumed per capita is double or more that of the United Kingdom, Austria, Germany, and Japan, far superior to that of other developed nations? Or is there a good deal of unnecessary energy use in Canada? Could Canadians cut down on their energy use without seriously or even moderately diminishing the quality of their lives?

Look also at the figures on the production of energy. The figures underscore the interdependence of the nations of the world, with some nations clearly far more dependent than others on outside resources.

TABLE 14.1 ■ ■ ■

Energy Production and Consumption of Selected Nations, 2002

Region/Country	Primary Energy Consumption Per Capita (million BTU)	Primary Energy Production (quadrillion BTU)
Canada	417.8	18.198
Mexico	65.0	9.584
United States	339.1	70.793
Brazil	48.7	6.719
Austria	171.9	0.514
Germany	173.1	5.268
United Kingdom	162.2	10.867
Russia	191.1	45.679
Saudi Arabia	218.7	20.122
Nigeria	7.8	0.000
China	33.3	41.852
India	13.3	10.410
Japan	172.3	4.286
New Zealand	228.0	0.722
World Total	**65.9**	**404.981**

Source: Adapted from International Energy Annual 2002, http://www.eia.doe.gov/emeu/iea/wecbtu.html.

decline in the average amount of air pollutants, the problem of air pollution in Canada has not been resolved. For example, although suspended particulates (such as dust and smoke, often from mining and waste incinerators) have declined by half since 1974, they still are a major determinant of local air quality (Environment Canada 2004b). In 2002, more than 7 million kilograms of carcinogenic substances were released into the air, and more than 170,000 kilograms into the water (Pollution Watch 2004). Many areas have not yet achieved desirable levels. Unacceptable smog levels are found "in the Windsor–Quebec City corridor, the Saint John area of the Southern Atlantic region and the Lower Fraser Valley in British Columbia" (Environment Canada 2004b).

Moreover, the problem is even more critical in other parts of the world than it is in Canada (Brown 1998). In cities such as Bangkok, Thailand; Beijing, China; and Mexico City, Mexico, "the air literally is unfit to breathe" (Brown 1998:10). In late 1997, smoke from massive fires in Indonesia and Malaysia, combined with the usual sources of air pollution, closed airports due to lack of visibility and many schools and businesses because workers got sick from the pollution. In India, as many as 2.5 million premature deaths occurred because of air pollution. Worldwide, nearly four million children die each year from respiratory infections associated with air pollution (World Resources Institute 1999).

A more subtle form of air pollution is that which results from toxic vapours. *Indoor air pollution* can cause a building to be "sick," in the sense that a number of people working there suffer from acute physical and/or psychological discomfort that is eased when they leave the building (Thorne et al. 2001). The "sick-building syndrome" includes a variety of symptoms: mucous membrane irritation, eye irritation, headaches, nausea, feelings of lethargy, fatigue, the inability to concentrate, breathing difficulties, and fainting (Soine 1995; Mann 1998). The syndrome is due to such things as inadequately maintained air conditioning and heating systems; pests such as cockroaches and dust mites; mould in ceiling tiles and in carpet, insulation, and furnishings; improper ventilation; and toxic vapours from copy-machine liquids, paint, flooring, and cleaning agents (Mann 1998).

In severe cases, the air quality inside the building may be far worse than the urban air outside the building. It is not known how many buildings are "sick," but up to one-third of indoor work occurs in buildings that have sufficient contaminants and pollutants to cause the syndrome (Mann 1998).

Nor are people's homes necessarily safe. We have noted that formaldehyde is toxic and that a wide range of materials and products used in homes contain formaldehyde. In the 1970s, thousands of homes were insulated with urea formaldehyde. In addition, there are other toxic chemicals in virtually all homes, making them one of the more hazardous places to be.

Another problem in homes came to light in the 1970s when Health Canada studies found that *radon gas, which can cause lung cancer after long periods of exposure,* could leak into homes, posing a risk to the health of the residents. More recent studies from Health Canada show that radon pollution is not a problem today in Canadian homes, as fewer than one-tenth of one percent of Canadian homes exceed the recommended levels (Health Canada). The gas is odourless and colourless and can be detected only by appropriate testing. Radon is produced by the decay of uranium in rocks and soil.

Electromagnetic radiation is another possible form of air pollution. We say "possible" because the issue is controversial. Some scientists argue that such things as power lines, computer terminals, cell phones, and even electric blankets are hazardous to health, causing everything from cancer to miscarriages (Brodeur 1989). However, it is not certain what levels, if any, are unsafe for humans. Researchers have reported such things as increased rates of cancer and increased risk for Alzheimer's disease among those exposed to sustained, high levels of radiation (Gorman 1992; Sobel et al. 1995;

Per capita, Canadians discard almost twice as much garbage as do people in Western Europe or Japan; much of it ends up in landfills.

environmental racism
the poor and visible minorities are more likely to live in neighbourhoods with sites for toxic-waste disposal and polluting industries, and are less likely to be protected by law-makers

Miller et al. 1996). On the other hand, a 16-member committee of the National Research Council in the United States examined more than 500 studies and concluded that there is no convincing evidence that such exposure is related to health problems (Leary 1996). The issue remains unresolved.

With regard to *global warming, the earth's average surface temperature rose about 0.6°C during the 20th century* (Intergovernmental Panel on Climate Change 2001). This was the largest increase in any century during the past 1,000 years. Along with the higher temperatures, snow cover and ice (including glaciers and sea ice) have decreased, average sea level has risen, and a number of changes in climate have occurred (such as rainfall patterns, cloud cover, and temperature ranges).

If the warming trend continues, a number of adverse consequences are likely (Dunn and Flavin 2002). They include reduced crop yields, less availability of water in the subtropics, increased exposure to water-borne diseases (e.g. cholera and malaria), and increased flooding.

Some advances have been made in *water pollution control.* The volume of pollutants discharged into the nation's waterways has decreased, and thousands of hectares of lakes and thousands of kilometres of rivers and streams have been restored and made safe for swimming and fishing. The problem remains serious, however. We noted earlier the problem of oil spills. In addition, serious pollution occurs from various toxic materials dumped into the oceans and waterways and from nitrogen and phosphorus from agricultural runoff. For example, by 1998, 96 percent of the Great Lakes shoreline was polluted (U.S. Census Bureau 2001:215).

Pollution by hazardous wastes has also declined, but the problem is still severe. Millions of tonnes of toxic materials are released into the environment yearly (Pollution Watch 2004). This form of pollution intersects with the problems of racial or ethnic origin and poverty, because chemical plants and toxic wastes tend to be in areas where the poor and minorities live (Krieg 1998; Pine, Marx, and Lakshmanan 2002). This phenomenon is now known as **environmental racism.**

Finally, there is the staggering amount of trash and garbage discarded each year. In 2000, Canadians threw out more than 22 million tonnes of waste: 8.3 million from residential sources; 11.8 million from industrial, commercial, and institutional sources; and 2.8 million from construction and demolition sources (Statistics Canada 2005). North Americans throw out about twice as much garbage per person as do Western Europeans or the Japanese. Trash illustrates the dilemmas of environmental problems. To help clean the air, incinerators, which once burned a good part of the trash, were phased out and "sanitary" landfills became the main method of disposal. Since a good part of the trash is paper, much that is thrown away is supposedly biodegradable. That is, it will eventually break down, decompose, and become a part of the earth.

Unfortunately, this doesn't happen in landfills. Archaeologists have discovered that so-called biodegradable trash and garbage are preserved rather than destroyed in landfills, probably because the materials are tightly packed and covered, with little exposure to light or moisture (Grossman and Shulman 1990). Most of the trash remains essentially unchanged in weight, volume, and form for at least four decades.

It is difficult to estimate the seriousness of all kinds of pollution, partly because measurement techniques have not been developed, and partly because the potential hazards involved have been recognized only recently. Some forms of pollution, such as noise pollution and aesthetic damage, are undesirable or annoying rather than hazardous. How does one assess their seriousness? In spite of such problems, it is clear that pollution in general is one of the serious problems confronting the nation, and it is a problem for which there are no easy answers.

▪▪ Environmental Depletion

Many experts believe that the astounding pace at which people are consuming natural resources threatens the resource capacity of the earth (Gardner and Sampat 1999). We mentioned earlier that Canadians compared to most countries are privileged, as energy production is higher than consumption. But we do need to proceed with caution, because at the same time Canada has one of the highest per capita energy consumptions in the world. In 2003, industry accounted for 30 percent of energy use, transportation 29 percent, residential 18 percent, and commercial 18 percent (Statistics Canada 2005).

The problem of depletion, of course, is international. For example, a major concern for the well-being of the earth is rapid deforestation (Bright 2000). Between 1980 and 1995 at least 490 million acres of forest vanished (Abramovitz 1998). Tropical forests may contain as many as half of the world's plant and animal species, including many plants used for medicine. In addition, they are a major impediment to the buildup of carbon dioxide and, thereby, to global warming. Yet millions of hectares are cut down each year to provide fuel and land for development and agriculture.

Increasing energy use is another major concern. Energy use per capita is increasing in most of the developing nations (U.S. Census Bureau 2001:854). The amount of energy that Canadians consume driving their automobiles is staggering, and the number of kilometres travelled continues to increase in spite of rising gas prices and efforts to encourage car pools. In 2003, 24,665,421 vehicles were registered in Canada.

How can Canadians keep up with their voracious appetite for energy? Some experts believe that nuclear sources are the only hope, but reliance on nuclear power plants poses serious problems. Total reliance on nuclear power is not even feasible because of the number of plants that would have to be built and the problem of storing radioactive wastes. In addition, there is the ever-present possibility of accidents and disasters. This possibility became a reality in April 1986 when two large explosions occurred at the Chernobyl plant in the Soviet Union, "a blast heard round the world" (Flavin 1987). Within days, much of Europe reported the highest levels of radioactive fallout ever. Within two weeks, elevated levels of radioactivity were detected throughout the Northern Hemisphere. For weeks afterward, fresh vegetables in many areas of Europe were contaminated. Cows that grazed on contaminated grass soon produced milk with unhealthy levels of radioactivity. For a number of months, as many as 100 million people had to alter their diets.

The Soviet Union, of course, suffered the worst consequences. Thirty-one people were killed and 1,000 were injured immediately. Another 135,000 were evacuated from their homes. Of the 25,000 workers under the age of 35 who participated in the cleanup, 5,000 to 7,000 died (Chernousenko 1991). As many as four million people in the region are at high risk for cancer and other illnesses. The incidence of these illnesses began to increase within a few years after the accident (Parks 1991). Ten years after the disaster, researchers found a variety of psychosomatic symptoms and high levels of fear and stress (Specter 1996).

The Chernobyl disaster, along with subsequent accidents and near-disasters, has intensified concerns about the utility of nuclear power for generating energy. As a result, a number of nations—including the United States, Great Britain, and Germany—have cut back on the number of reactors in operation.

▪▪ ENVIRONMENTAL PROBLEMS AND THE QUALITY OF LIFE

Environmental problems confront Canadians with *a number of inherent contradictions:* the value of growth and progress versus the value of freedom to choose the size of one's family; the desire for abundant energy versus the value of a clean environment; the preference for reasonably low energy prices versus the value of independence in the world arena. It is impossible to have all these, so it is a matter of *trade-offs.* There will be trade-offs between such things as cost and abundance, national independence and abundance, and abundance and quality of the environment.

▪▪ The Environmental Threat to Life and Health

The *environmental threat to both physical and emotional well-being* occurs from all the environmental problems named thus far.

The Physical Threat.   The physical threat is aptly summarized by the U.S. Public Health Service (1995:80):

> Among the numerous diseases and dysfunctions that have a known or suspected environmental component are cancer, reproductive disorders such as infertility and low birthweight, neurological and immune system impairments, and respiratory conditions such as asthma. Exposure to environmental hazards can be through air, food, or water and covers a broad range of factors such as pesticides, toxic chemicals, and radiation.

An even more dramatic statement of the threat is offered by the World Resources Institute (1999), which asserted that in the poorest regions of the world, environmentally related diseases will kill as many as one in five children under the age of five. This is equivalent to 11 million childhood deaths in the world, equal to the combined populations of Australia and New Zealand.

You are surrounded by hazards of all kinds. Consider some of the things that severe air pollution can cause or contribute to:

- Permanent lung damage in children (Roan 1990).
- Fetal deaths (Pereira et al. 1998).
- Infant mortality (Penna and Duchiade 1991).
- Respiratory illness and death from respiratory infections (Spix et al. 1998; Samet et al. 2000).
- Cardiovascular disease (Samet et al. 2000).
- Skin problems, ulcers, and liver and kidney damage (Organisation for Economic Co-operation and Development 1991).
- Premature deaths (Revkin 2001).
- Asthma attacks (Sarafino, Paterson, and Murphy 1998).
- Lung cancer (Moore 1999).

These adverse consequences may be caused by either outdoor or indoor air pollution. We pointed out earlier that many products and materials in the home give off toxic vapours. A similar situation exists in workplaces. Workers in particular kinds of jobs may be exposed to, or may work with, one of the chemicals known to be a factor in respiratory problems, cancer, and other illnesses (Anderson 1982).

For example, a study of 125 pregnant women who were exposed to organic solvents in their jobs found an increased risk of major fetal malformations; they were thus more likely than women not exposed to give birth to babies with major defects (Khattak et al. 1999). The researchers also found an increased risk of miscarriage among the exposed women.

Some of the chemicals to which workers are exposed are known to be neurotoxic, causing damage to the nervous system, with resulting behavioural and emotional disorders. The problem of neurotoxins came to public attention in the 1970s when workers at a fabrics plant suffered various degrees of nerve damage. The workers had been exposed to a solvent used as an ink thinner and machine cleaner. As a result, they experienced weakness in their hands and feet (so much so that some could barely turn a key or use a screwdriver), loss of weight, and problems with walking (Anderson 1982).

Exposure to toxic materials can also lead to sterility. Male sperm counts have been declining for many decades (Lemonick 1996). The decline may reflect the fact that industries use a number of chemicals that can result in infertility. In Costa Rica, 1,500 banana plantation workers developed permanent sterilization from exposure to a toxic pesticide (Thrupp 1991).

With regard to ozone, the depleted ozone layer raises the risk of skin cancer, while high ozone levels at ground level are harmful to both humans and plant life. Ozone pollution in rural areas has reduced crop yields (Monastersky 1999).

Acid rain is a threat to forests and lakes. Eutrophication in waterways can kill massive numbers of fish, which means less food available for a world in which millions of people are starving. Ironically, some of the eutrophication problems arise from efforts to produce an adequate food supply. More than half of the phosphorus that overfertilizes water comes from municipal wastes, but a substantial minority is due to urban and rural runoff. As farmers continue to apply fertilizer in increasing quantities to improve the yield of needed agricultural products, they also increase the likelihood of eutrophication of waterways and the consequent destruction of needed fish.

Routinely used pesticides and herbicides produce yet another hazard (Misch 1994). There is an increased risk of stillbirth among women exposed to pesticides (Savitz, Whelan, and Kleckner 1989). Women who live in agricultural areas where there are high levels of pesticides have an increased risk of bearing babies with birth defects, including missing and malformed arms and legs (Parachini 1988). Farmers exposed to high levels of pesticides and herbicides risk developing various forms of cancer.

A number of adverse consequences of global warming have already surfaced (Epstein 2000). Disease-causing bacteria, viruses, and fungi are spreading more widely; malaria and other mosquito-associated diseases have begun to appear in areas of the world where they were once absent. The problem will only intensify as the warming continues.

Finally, noise pollution is at best a nuisance and at worst a hazard to personal well-being. Excessive noise levels can result in hearing damage, high blood pressure, increased risk of cardiovascular disorders, sleep disturbance, lower work productivity, and problems in relating to others (Blanchard 1998; Niskar et al. 1998).

The Emotional Threat. The emotional threat is illustrated by the fact that those who work around hazardous materials may suffer from increased anxiety and depression (Roberts 1993). They experience stress over potential health problems—from uncertainty about the seriousness of the exposure and from a sense of powerlessness over the situation (what can an individual do to change the situation?) (Hallman and Wandersman 1992; Matthies, Hoger, and Guski 2000).

Edelstein (1988) interviewed a number of New Jersey residents whose water supply had been contaminated by a municipal landfill. He found that knowledge of the contamination brought with it a radical change in the way the people viewed the world. They began to fear for their own and their families' health. They felt a loss of control over their lives. They viewed their homes as places of danger rather than havens of security. They lost trust in the government.

Another study of psychological consequences involved a survey of 421 people living near a toxic waste landfill in California (Stefanko and Horowitz 1989). The people expressed both negative beliefs and negative feelings. They had little trust in the authorities, and their feelings about their quality of life were fairly low. Those who lived nearest the landfill and/or who had small children expressed the most negative attitudes.

Noise also detracts from emotional well-being. Environmental psychologist Dr. Arline Bronzaft says that noise interferes with daily life, and has linked noise to such health problems as headaches, stress, fatigue, insomnia, high blood pressure, heart and digestive problems, immune system problems, aggressive behaviour, and learning problems in children (CBC Marketplace 2001).

■■ The Threat to the Ecological Balance

Many of the examples given here show that human actions can result in a whole chain of consequences for the environment. One consequence can be an upsetting of the ecological balance. Paul Ehrlich argued that lust for more affluence and unrestrained population growth are ravaging the environment. But don't be deceived, he wrote,

> the imbalance will be redressed. . . . Man is not only running out of food, he is also destroying the life support systems of the Spaceship Earth. The situation was recently summarized very succinctly: "It is the top of the ninth inning. Man, always a threat at the plate, has been hitting Nature hard. It is important to remember, however, that NATURE BATS LAST." (Ehrlich 1971:364)

One way the ecological system has been altered is through the *disappearance of a number of species of animals and plants* as a result of human activity. Hundreds of animals and plants have become extinct and thousands more are threatened. Among animals, for example, 11 percent of birds, 25 percent of mammals, and 34 percent of fish are threatened with extinction (Brown, Gardner, and Halweil 1998). A survey of 242,013 plant species in the U.S. reported that 14 percent are threatened, including 29 percent of plant species (Tuxill 1999). Since a declining number of species means less diversity, this represents a vast biological loss and poses a direct threat to the quality of human life. As Tuxill (1999:7–8) writes:

> In addition to providing the genetic underpinnings of our food supply, plant diversity keeps us healthy—one in every four drugs prescribed in the United States is based on a chemical compound originally discovered in plants. Plants also furnish oils, latexes, gums, fibers, timbers, dyes, essences, and other products that we use to clean, clothe, shelter, and refresh ourselves and that have many industrial uses as well. Health assemblages of native plants renew and enrich soils, regulate our freshwater supplies, prevent soil erosion, and provide the habitat needed by animals and other creatures.

Finally, a diminishing diversity increases the likelihood of pest infestations and outbreaks of disease.

Clearly, *people depend upon biological diversity for the quality of their lives.* Still, we need to exercise caution about the loss of species. Ecosystems are dynamic, not static. Some species would disappear regardless of human activity. On the other hand, we

photosynthesis
a natural process essential to life, resulting in the production of oxygen and organic materials

urbanization
the increasing concentration of people living in cities

need to be careful not to fall into the *fallacy of circular reasoning* by arguing that only those species disappear for which there is no use or importance. Therefore, the argument would run, those that have become extinct are not needed anyway; we're doing just fine without them. This line of reasoning ignores the fact that some species became extinct because of human activity rather than the natural workings of nature. People need to be concerned that the ecological balance is not upset, that they do not start a chain of consequences that will be detrimental to human life.

Perhaps more important than the balance among the species is the possibility that humans will somehow intrude into the major processes of the ecosystem and cause irreversible damage that could threaten life—for the continuation of life demands certain processes, including reproduction, **photosynthesis,** and the recycling of minerals. We know that the reproduction of some species has been affected by certain pollutants. For instance, the use of DDT caused the eggshells of some birds to become thinner and to crack before the young hatched, thus threatening the birds' reproductive capacity. DDT also has affected the reproductive capacity of some fish. Other pesticides and herbicides also may impair reproduction.

Photosynthesis may be adversely affected by air pollution, by pesticides and herbicides, and, above all, by the spread of the human population, which destroys the habitat of other species. Air pollution inhibits the plant life in which photosynthesis occurs, while human activity such as **urbanization** destroys plants by destroying their habitat. It is also possible that the pesticides and herbicides accumulating in the oceans will disrupt the process there as well. Photosynthesis is essential in the production of oxygen; it helps maintain the carbon dioxide balance in the atmosphere and is of fundamental importance in producing the organic material needed for supporting life. It is difficult to imagine that photosynthesis would halt completely. If it did, it would be a catastrophe. But whether or not the process could totally stop, it is clearly adversely affected by certain human activities.

The Economic Costs

It is difficult to place a price tag on ecological problems. To fully assess the cost, we would have to include an enormous number of items: damage to livestock, trees, and crops; the death of wildlife; the expense of pollution-control measures; the cost of medical care for those whose health is adversely affected; the lost work time due to ill health; the expense of maintaining and refurbishing buildings and other structures that deteriorate because of pollution; and the cost of restoring the quality of the air and of waterways. The public is barely aware of the *innumerable ways economic resources are consumed by ecological problems.*

Consider the factors involved in analyzing and estimating these economic costs. First, the pollutants are emitted at a particular time and place. Second, they affect the environmental quality. (For example, the amount of sulphur dioxide in the air at a particular time and place may increase, and may cause an increase in the number of people with respiratory problems.) Finally, a dollar cost must be assigned to the damages.

Every factor in this process is marked by uncertainty. We are not yet aware of all the amounts and kinds of pollutants being emitted. Nor do we yet know how all the pollutants act and interact in the environment. Thus, identifying actual damages is problematic. It is relatively easy to assign a dollar value to some damages, but extremely difficult for others. We can estimate the cost of painting a building marred by air pollution or the cost of replacing damaged crops, but what is the dollar value of a human life; a clear sky; a place for recreation; or a species that contributes to the diversity, complexity, and stability of the ecosystem?

Keeping these difficulties in mind, we can still estimate some of the economic costs of pollution. The costs, in terms of damage to property, materials, health, and vegeta-

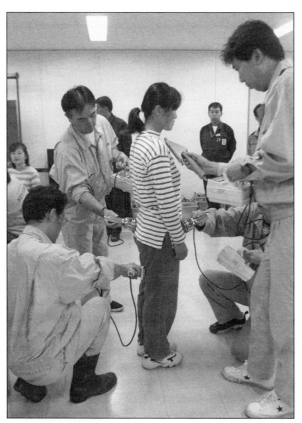

A nuclear reaction at a uranium-reprocessing facility in Japan in 1999 was attributed to human error.

tion, run into many billions of dollars each year for air pollution alone. It is estimated that cleaning up just a small proportion of the hazardous waste sites in the nation will cost billions of dollars (Gardner and Sampat 1999). In other words, eliminating the hazards of pollution will be extremely costly. Environmentalists argue, however, that on balance the economic benefits will be greater than the costs. They point out that while the economic costs of addressing environmental problems are considerable, they are not as great as the cost of allowing the environment to deteriorate.

▪▪ The Threat to World Peace

The contradictions between the demand for energy, the desire for a clean environment, the desire for reasonably low prices for energy, the struggle for natural resources, and the value on political independence are manifested on the international level in the form of a *threat to world peace*. A number of armed conflicts in the world can be traced to the struggle for control of various natural resources (Renner 2002).

In addition, the developing nations of the world are demanding to share in the affluence enjoyed by the West and Japan. Inequality among nations has become a matter of international concern. On May 1, 1974, the General Assembly of the United Nations adopted the "Declaration on the Establishment of a New International Order," which asserted a determination to work for a new and more equitable international economic order. If the widening gap between the developed and the developing nations is not eliminated, many observers fear that the result will be a world war between the relatively few rich nations and the far more numerous poor nations.

Questions arise about whether the earth's resources are sufficient and whether the environmental damage can be adequately contained if the developing nations are to achieve the same standard of living as the developed nations. On the one hand, if the gap between the rich and the poor nations is not narrowed, peace is threatened by those nations or groups of nations that would resort to violence to achieve a higher economic status (Renner 1999). On the other hand, if rich nations help poor nations to achieve a higher standard of living, depleted resources and a damaged environment may drastically lower the quality of life for the entire world. It appears that the contradictions inherent in these ecological problems will continue to plague us in the future.

▪▪ CONTRIBUTING FACTORS

Before looking at the sociocultural factors that contribute to environmental problems, you should note that some of the problems are caused by *ignorance and accidents.* Ignorance is involved because people often do not know and generally cannot anticipate the environmental consequences of their behaviour. DDT, for instance, seemed beneficial because it controlled many pests, including the carriers of malaria. What was not known at the time was that DDT would impair the reproductive capacity of some fish and birds, and would remain in the food chain with such persistence.

Accidents also contribute to environmental problems. It is not possible, for example, to avoid all oil spills. Weather conditions cannot be controlled. Human error cannot be totally eliminated. Thus, it was human error that led to a nuclear reaction in a uranium-reprocessing facility in Tokaimura, Japan, in 1999. The reaction lasted nearly 20 hours and had the potential for creating a Chernobyl-type disaster.

In addition to ignorance and accidents, however, there are a number of sociocultural factors that contribute to environmental problems. As with other social problems, both social structural and social psychological factors are involved.

■■ Social Structural Factors

Population Growth.   *A growing population poses a threat to the environment.* Population growth accelerates the consumption of the earth's natural resources to the point that oil, natural gas, and certain minerals may eventually be exhausted. The population could even reach a number where it would be impossible to produce enough food. The point is, any given area on the earth has a *limited carrying capacity,* that is, a limit to the number of people who can live there without causing a collapse of the biological system. If the biological system collapses, the inhabitants must either be supported by outside resources, move from the area, or face massive deaths.

The problem is illustrated by Brown and Flavin (1999) in their discussion of what is required for 10 billion people to live at the standard now enjoyed by Canadians. They estimate that it would require 360 million barrels of oil a day, more than five times the current production; and it would demand nine billion tons of grain a year, more than four times the current output. These estimates provide an answer to questions about whether the poor nations can achieve the same standard of living as the rich nations. The answer is no, if the population continues to grow as expected in the next half-century.

The problems of population growth are compounded by the fact that the effects of increased population are more than additive. We noted earlier that people generally, and Canadians in particular, are consuming increased amounts of energy and other resources *per capita.* In other words, the impact per person on the environment is far greater today than it was in past years.

A second reason that a growing population has more than an additive impact on the environment is the *threshold effect.* Vegetation in an area may be able to survive a certain size of population and the air pollution created by that population. But further increase in the population might create just enough additional pollution to kill the vegetation. It becomes "the straw that breaks the camel's back."

The threshold effect can occur in all kinds of pollution. A number of cases illustrate this (Brown and Postel 1987). For example, in 1982, about 8 percent of the trees in West Germany were damaged from pollution. The figure jumped to 34 percent one year later, and then to 50 percent by 1984. Something had tipped the balance and caused a sudden surge in deterioration. Several Canadian scientists showed the effects of acid rain by deliberately acidifying a small lake. Over an eight-year period, they gradually increased the concentration of acids in the lake and found a particular point at which a dramatic change occurred in the ability of the various species of fish to reproduce and survive. The effects of population may be additive to a point, and beyond that point *the increasing quantitative changes become a qualitative change.*

The Industrial Economy.   Both pollution and depletion of the environment are rooted in the industrial economy. This is dramatically illustrated by the fact that the United States, with 4.7 percent of the world's population, accounts for 23.1 percent of the world's carbon dioxide emissions (Dunn 2002). Various industrial processes, from the generation of electricity to the production of goods, are responsible for a considerable part of the air pollution problem.

Water pollution is also a by-product of industrial processes. This includes thermal pollution, which occurs when water is taken from a waterway in large quantities and used for cooling. In the cooling process, the water absorbs heat. When this heated water is dumped back into the river or lake, it can then raise the temperature to a point that is dangerous for aquatic life.

A major cause of air pollution in Canada is the *extensive use of the automobile.* The automobile also bears heavy responsibility for the rapid depletion of the world's oil reserves. Canada is involved in a love affair with the automobile. Canadians own more automobiles per capita than air conditioners, clothes washers, microwave ovens, or freezers.

The burgeoning number and use of automobiles creates increasing pollution. Despite the fact that emissions per automobile have been greatly reduced over the past few decades, overall air quality has worsened in many cities because of the increased number of cars. Yet to drastically reduce the use of the automobile not only would be contrary to the Canadian value of freedom and mobility, it also would cause serious economic problems. The automobile, a prime factor in environmental pollution and depletion, is an integral part of our affluent economy. Significant numbers of workers depend on the manufacture, distribution, service, and use of motor vehicles. An attack on the automobile is clearly an attack on the economy. Thus, a way must be found to deal with the environmental problem without ignoring the economic consequences.

As the automobile illustrates, the industrial economy operates at a pace that outstrips the ability to counteract the environmental problems it creates. Consider the chemical industry. Cancer is largely an environmental problem often *caused by carcinogenic chemicals* (Napoli 1998; McGinn 2002). There are approximately two million known chemical compounds, and thousands more are discovered each year. While some of these new compounds will be carcinogenic, there are insufficient facilities to properly test them all.

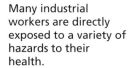

Many industrial workers are directly exposed to a variety of hazards to their health.

These chemical compounds are one example of useful new products. Unfortunately, useful products can have undesirable environmental side effects. Because industrial technology can produce enormous quantities of any single product and an enormous range of products, and because the economy is set up to maximize growth, the whole situation is self-sustaining. Continual expansion is the goal. That goal is facilitated by (1) massive advertising; (2) the proliferation of products, many competing for the same market; (3) the "planned obsolescence" of products; and (4) lobbying at various levels of government to ensure that governmental decisions will be favourable to business and industry. "Planned obsolescence" refers to the fact that many products are specifically designed to last only a limited time. In fact, some are designed and advertised as throw-away products: clothing, pots and pans, and safety razors are to be used once or twice and then discarded. The consequences of planned obsolescence are the production of more trash that must be disposed of, the use of more resources, and the creation of more pollutants from industries that make such products.

Business and industry not only lobby for industrial growth, they vigorously oppose pollution-control proposals and, in some cases, have managed to defeat those proposals either by lobbying or by influencing public opinion. Thus, the industrial economy intersects with the polity in environmental problems.

The Politics of the Environment. Environmental problems have generally not been high-priority items with politicians. This is unfortunate, because one way to get something done about environmental problems is to create positions that have specific responsibility for those problems. For environmental problems, this means governmental positions. Although Canadians dislike the creation of new governmental positions, without them little may be done. There is little incentive for private industry to take the lead in addressing ecological problems.

Pollution is a national problem that requires federal action. In the past, the federal government either ignored the problem or delegated responsibility to the states. This changed with the creation of the *Environmental Protection Act* (see box 14.1). Today, most politicians express interest and concern for environmental issues. Unfortunately, the rhetoric is not always matched by effective action.

Box 14.1

Canada's Environmental Law Regime

Environmental law is a unique area of Canadian law, as it has really only developed over the past 30 years. In the 1970s, the federal and provincial legislatures developed "waste control laws," with an objective to identify sources of waste and to issue permits for them (Lucas 2003:164). This early system of environmental regulation was one of cautious permissions, rather than absolute prohibition of dangerous substances.

Modern environmental law recognizes that waste control is merely one aspect of long-term environmental protection. Canada's current environmental laws strive to achieve broad principles of sustainability, by considering intergenerational effects of environmental damage and by being precautious and anticipatory, even when the environmental effects of certain actions or materials have not been scientifically established. Canada has recognized the international component of environmental law, namely that environmental problems are not contained within provincial or national boundaries. Both federal and provincial laws have developed a wide variety of enforcement mechanisms, ranging from tickets for minor offences to serious criminal offences (Lucas 2003).

Canadian Environmental Protection Act

The *Canadian Environmental Protection Act* (CEPA) is a comprehensive environmental law, as it concerns disposal of substances at sea, standards for fuels, and emissions. Although CEPA is broad in scope, it is criticized for being weak in its implementation. Under CEPA, the minister of the environment has the authority to require specific persons or corporate entities to prepare and implement pollution prevention plans for listed toxic substances or substances likely to cause international air or water pollution. Oddly, once the plans are prepared, CEPA does not require that the plans be reviewed by Environment Canada (Lucas 2003:175).

Provincial Regulatory Regime

Each province has its own environmental protection act, but there is a common legislative scheme. All of the provincial acts are concerned with licensing and controlling contaminant discharges, and breaches of the licensing requirements may result in quasi-criminal offences. In addition to comprehensive environmental protection acts, each province has enacted legislation pertaining to single resources, like Ontario's *Water Resources Act* and Alberta's *Clean Air Act*.

Provinces have recently recognized the importance of public participation in environmental law. Ontario, for example, has instituted an *Environmental Bill of Rights* (EBR), which provides a framework, through an environmental registry, for notifying the public about proposed legislation, policies, or projects that may significantly affect the environment. EBR provides citizens with opportunities to provide their input before the government makes decisions. It also allows citizens to request that the government review specific decisions and policies.

Environmental Assessment

Environmental assessment (EA) is a process of gathering information about the likely environmental effects of a proposed development or activity. The *Canadian Environmental Assessment Act* is the main piece of legislation governing the EA process; each province has its own EA legislation. EA applies only to four types of projects: (1) projects proposed on government lands; (2) projects funded by government; (3) projects requiring government approvals or permits; and (4) projects carried out by government proponents. The EA process has built within it a high capacity for public participation, mainly in the "review panel" type of EA, where the public and project proponent engage in discussions about the project and develop alternatives. The majority of projects are only subject to the "screening" type of EA, which requires the proponent to prepare a report on the likely effects of the proposed project and its alternatives, with very little, if any, public involvement.

Because there are EA processes at both the federal and provincial levels, difficulty arises where a project involves both levels of government. Saskatchewan has been progressive in drafting an agreement with the federal government on "Environmental Assessment Cooperation," which establishes a process for deciding who does what in these situations.

The current status of forest areas graphically illustrates the political failure to deal with environmental problems. As noted earlier, deforestation is a serious problem. Yet even where a government controls a significant proportion of its nation's forests, it may sell the forested land at prices below what the timber is worth (Abramovitz 1998). It also may sell the timber for far less than its worth. In effect, governments pay private enterprise to take public timber. In British Columbia, for example, the government owns more than 95 percent of the timberland. Logging companies pay the Canadian government a fee—called a stumpage fee—for the right to harvest trees on Crown land. The government sets the amount of fees paid, which according to many American logging producers is below market value, thereby subsidizing the forest industry.

Thus, the stance of the federal and provincial governments on environmental issues is crucial. One such example is the Kyoto Accord on global warming (for more, see box 14.2). The federal government ratified the accord without the consultation and approval of the provincial governments. Consequently, there has been much resistance to the Accord spearheaded by Ralph Klein, the Premier of Alberta. The province of Alberta is concerned that because of its oil industry it would have to carry a disproportionate burden of reducing greenhouse gases. Other provinces have resisted ratification because the federal government has not been transparent with its plans for implementation. In response, the federal government claims that implementation will be a gradual process, that businesses will be collaborated, and that Alberta would have no greater burden than any other province. But the federal government has still to implement concrete plans to guarantee compliance with the Kyoto Accord (Stavins 2004:24).

■■ Social Psychological Factors

Attitudes and the Environment.   Many people see the earth as a resource to be mined rather than as a trust to be cared for. "Skyrocketing consumption is the hallmark of our era" (Durning 1991:154). The measure of success is the amount of goods that can be consumed. People are admonished that they could be just as happy with less and warned that they are engaged in a process of self-destruction as they abuse the earth for their own excessive gratification, but these warnings largely seem to fall on deaf ears. Environmentalism is honoured more in theory than in practice. The prevailing attitude is "I must get all that I can out of this life," rather than "I must cherish and sustain the earth that gives us life." However, in Canada, such attitudes are beginning to change. According to the CEO of Pollara, a Canadian public opinion and marketing research firm, "air and water quality issues are now more important to Canadians than at any time" (Marzolini 2001). Furthermore, 90 percent of Canadians are supportive of laws that would offer protection to endangered species. This means that the majority of Canadians support restrictions to mining and logging, and do not support land development that threatens wildlife. Forty-five percent of Canadians would forgo tax cuts if it means protecting wildlife (Jaimet 2001).

The shift in public opinion toward a safer environment is encouraging. However, changes in attitude do not necessarily mean that Canadians would support stricter environmental regulations. The view that regulation is bad often filters in through the United States, where many people believe that stricter environmental regulations will force business closings and bring about a loss of jobs, a belief unsupported by evidence. There may be an occasional closing or the loss of certain jobs, but to generalize from a few cases is to commit the *fallacy of dramatic instance*. In the nation as a whole, there is no conflict between jobs and the environment (Obach 2002).

Racist attitudes contribute to a problem noted earlier: the greater exposure of minorities to hazardous materials both at work and in their homes. *Environmental racism*

Box 14.2

The Kyoto Accord
Background

International recognition of the need to abate the effects of climate change led to the implementation of two international policy instruments. The first was the United Nations Framework Convention on Climate Change (UNFCCC), drafted in 1992. The convention was unsuccessful due to its voluntary nature, where parties were able to set their own emissions targets and were not legally bound to meet those targets. In response to the weaknesses of UNFCCC, a legally binding policy instrument was drafted in Kyoto, Japan, in 1997.

The Kyoto Accord establishes legally binding targets to limit or reduce greenhouse gas emissions in developed countries. It requires parties to the accord to collectively reduce overall net greenhouse gas emissions by at least 5 percent below 1990 levels by the year 2012. Each party to the Accord has agreed to its own net emission target. Although developing countries may be parties to the Accord, there are no obligations imposed upon them. The Accord introduces economic implementation mechanisms to assist countries in reducing their emissions, including tradeable emission permits between developed countries. Because the reduction target is a collective target for all of the involved states, emission permits allow states that are below their allowable emissions levels to trade the excess with countries that are above their allowable limits. The Accord encourages countries to fund emissions-reducing projects in other countries by crediting the emission reduction to the investing country (Bernstein 2002:210).

To date, 127 countries have ratified Kyoto, and at least 40 more are considering ratification. The accord will take effect in February 2005. The effectiveness of implementing Kyoto has already come into question, given that some of the world's largest emitters of greenhouse gases, including the United States, Mexico, and China, are not parties to the Accord (Stavins 2004:24). Kyoto is also criticized for providing only a short-term solution to climate change, as it pertains only to a four-year period, from 2008 to 2012.

Kyoto in the Canadian Context

Contributing about 2 percent of the world's greenhouse gas emissions, Canada is one of the largest emitters per capita (Bernstein 2002:205). Canada ratified the Kyoto Accord in October 2002. As a party to the Accord, it has agreed to reduce its net greenhouse gas emissions by 6 percent of its 1990 levels. Unfortunately, Canada's current levels are 20 percent higher than in 1990, so it will have to reduce emissions by 26 percent to honour its commitment (Stavins 2004:24).

---

means that the worst of the toxic waste sites are in lower-income communities (Maher 1998). It also means that the minorities are more likely to work near such materials. In addition to racial and ethnic minorities, the poor of all races are also more likely to suffer detrimental consequences from environmental problems. The well-to-do, who have more political power than others, have the NIMBY (not-in-my-backyard) attitude that leads them to take action to minimize environmental hazards in their own places of work and housing. Thus, attitudes contribute to the greater exposure of both racial and ethnic minorities and the poor to environmental problems.

"NATURE BATS LAST"

"Of all the problems I've studied," said one student, "the environmental problem is the most frustrating and frightening to me. It seems that no matter what you do, you're trapped. I see what it means to say that nature bats last." In spite of the seriousness of the problems and the dilemmas (such as a new technology that addresses one problem only to create another), this chapter shows that people have made some progress in dealing with environmental problems. Where does your university stand? Make a survey of potential environmental problems. Things you may look for include plastic or Styrofoam material used in the cafeteria, cleaning products, air quality in the classrooms, and asbestos. Check your newspaper, your library, and local officials to get information about their potential harm. Use the materials in this chapter and the data you get from your survey to write an article or a letter to the editor for your local newspaper and/or your school newspaper. Even though nature always bats last, is it possible that both human beings and nature can be winners in the long run?

Values and the Environment.   The value of growth, "the more the better," has been a theme of North American life. Sorokin (1942:255) calls this "quantitative colossalism." It leads to continual expansion of the perception of the "good life," which means ever-increasing goods and services and a concomitant ever-intensifying of environmental problems.

Individualism also contributes to political inaction and thus to the ecological problems. As Hardin (1971) put it, individualism involves us in the *"tragedy of the commons."* In the Middle Ages the "commons" was the pastureland of a village. It was owned by no one person because it was available for use by all the people of the village. The "commons" today are the world's resources, and the "tragedy" is that it is advantageous for individuals to exploit those resources but disadvantageous to all when too many individuals pursue their own advantage. Yet, a focus on individualism (rather than on group well-being), according to Hardin (1971:247), "locks us into a system of 'fouling our own nest,'" by behaving "only as independent, rational, free-enterprisers." The value of individualism also makes citizens reluctant to yield power to government. For many Canadians, political inaction is the soul of good government, but in the realm of ecology, political inaction is the harbinger of disaster.

■■ From Social Problems to Solutions

At the outset, we need to acknowledge that environmental problems pose numerous dilemmas. There are no easy answers. Some of the "solutions" create new problems. For instance, getting the soil to produce more food was a critical problem in the 19th century as the population grew rapidly. The development of nitrogen-based fertilizers enabled farmers to increase production enormously, but those same fertilizers were "also poisoning ecosystems, destroying fisheries, and sickening and killing children throughout the world" (Fisher and Fisher 2001). Thus, the needed additional food is had at the expense of air and water quality.

Still, there are many ways to alleviate the problems. In fact, substantial progress has already been made in a number of areas. Blood lead levels among children have been reduced by such measures as converting to unleaded gasoline, reducing the number of food and soft-drink cans with lead solder, and banning leaded paint in homes. Many lakes and waterways that were once unusable for fishing or swimming are again usable. The Clean Air Agenda is a 10-year plan implemented by the Canadian government in

2000 that is committed to substantively improving the air quality in Canada. Increasing numbers of cities and the provinces have implemented curbside recycling programs.

Yet the problems are still numerous as well as serious. People need to be educated about the seriousness of environmental pollution and depletion in order to change attitudes, values, and behaviour. When they understand what they can do and the benefits of their efforts, they are more likely to engage in the appropriate behaviour (Scott 1999; O'Connor et al. 2002).

Education helps individuals recognize how much each one can do to alleviate the environmental problems. For example, you could stop using throwaway items such as cameras and razors. You could refuse to buy cheese that is sliced and individually wrapped in plastic. Parents could use cloth instead of disposable diapers. MacEachern (1990) offers 750 suggestions for individuals to alleviate environmental problems. In addition, each individual can become a role model and an open advocate of environmental protection. Role modelling (such as picking up your trash at a campsite) and verbal appeals do influence others to behave responsibly (Wagstaff and Wilson 1988).

There are many ways in which you can conserve energy. Minor changes in lifestyle can add up to substantial savings. When millions of people use automobiles that get more kilometres to the litre than older models, when millions participate in recycling efforts, when millions use energy-saving appliances and methods that cut back on electricity, the savings are enormous. People could easily save a million or more barrels of crude oil every day without detracting from their standard of living.

The government could effect savings in resources and simultaneously help the pollution problem by supporting the development of mass transit. Mass transit can carry 70 times the number of people as a highway, generate only 1 percent of the hydrocarbons, and cost one-tenth as much to build per mile as does a highway (Hagerman 1990).

The government can take other important measures. It can diminish or eliminate pollution caused by its own operations and by those supported by federal funds. It can provide direct funding and tax incentives for research into pollution control and alternative energy sources. It can impose tax penalties on businesses and corporations that damage the environment, a measure that has proved to reduce problems in many nations (Roodman 1999). Although Canada has ratified the Kyoto treaty, it still has yet to comply with the standards set out by the treaty to cut emissions of greenhouse gases by 5 percent in order to avert the problem of global warming.

Provincial and local governments also can play a significant role in addressing environmental problems by establishing recycling laws and policies. Consider the advantages:

> Recycling offers communities everywhere the opportunity to trim their waste disposal needs, and thereby reduce disposal costs, while simultaneously combating global environmental problems. Recycling metals, paper, glass, plastics, and organic wastes would lessen the demand for energy and materials. Producing aluminum from scrap instead of bauxite cuts energy usage and air pollution by 95 percent. Making paper from discards instead of virgin timber not only saves valuable forests, it reduces the energy used per ton by up to three quarters and requires less than half as much water. (Pollock 1987:101–02)

The first advantage listed, trimming waste disposal needs, gets into an area that has almost reached crisis proportions in some cities. The volume of discarded material is surpassing the capacity to manage it. Recycling, which can address the problem to a considerable extent, may need to be mandatory. Will people cooperate? Unfortunately, some people will not; but most will, particularly when measures such as curbside pickup of materials are instituted (Domina and Koch 2002).

As for the needed changes in the industrial economy, people must reassess the emphasis on growth. Individuals must learn how to balance growth with ecological considerations and search for *alternative, clean sources of energy* upon which to base the economy. A number of alternatives are already being studied. Some people advocate nuclear power, but you have already seen that a total conversion to nuclear power is not feasible. Furthermore, nuclear power confronts people with the very difficult questions of how to dispose of radioactive waste and how to ensure against leaks and accidents that can release radioactivity into the atmosphere. Other possible alternatives include solar energy (the light and heat from the sun), geothermal energy (the water and hot rock beneath the earth's surface), and the use of wind-driven generators. The advantages and disadvantages of each of these alternatives must be explored carefully but quickly, for the supply of fossil fuels is being rapidly depleted while the demand for energy is increasing throughout the world.

■■ SUMMARY

Environmental problems arise out of the need to maintain a balanced ecosystem—a balance between people and their natural environment. Human activity can disrupt this ecosystem to the point of destruction.

Environmental problems may be broadly classified as environmental pollution and environmental depletion. Pollution includes air pollution, water pollution, land pollution, global warming, noise pollution, and aesthetic damage. Depletion refers to dwindling natural resources, including energy.

It is difficult to measure the extent of these environmental problems. Some progress has been made but the problems remain serious.

Environmental problems involve inherent contradictions among a number of Canadian values. We do not fully understand how these contradictions are being manifested in social life, but we know that they diminish the quality of life in a number of ways. Pollutants threaten the health and life of humans, animals, and plants. The ecological balance is threatened by the potential destruction of certain processes that are necessary to sustain life on earth. The economic costs of both pollution damage and pollution control are enormous, and the contradic-tions between the demand for energy, the need for a clean environment, and the aspirations of the developing world pose a threat to world peace.

Rapid population growth is one of the important threats to the environment. The effects of population growth are more than additive, as evidenced by diminishing returns and the threshold effect. In addition to population growth, the industrial economy is at the root of environmental problems. The products, by-products, and continuing growth in the industrial economy create serious environmental problems. The problems are intensified by the tendency of the government to ignore them or to set up ineffective programs and policies. Federal action is imperative if Canadians are to seriously attack the problems of the environment.

Among social psychological factors, attitudes among Canadians are shifting, placing greater importance on environmental problems. Racist attitudes intensify the problem for minorities by exposing them to more hazards at work and home. Finally, values of growth and individualism have supported the economic and political arrangements that contribute to the problems.

■■ KEY TERMS

Ecosystem 388	Environmental Pollution	Eutrophication 391	Pollutant 389
Environmental Depletion	389	Herbicide 393	Urbanization 404
389	Environmental Racism	Pesticide 393	
	399	Photosynthesis 404	

■■ STUDY QUESTIONS

1. What is the ecosystem? Why is it important to us?

2. Name and explain the three types of environmental problems people face.

3. How extensive are the environmental problems?

4. In what ways do environmental problems pose a threat to life, health, and the ecological balance?

5. Discuss the economic costs of environmental problems.

6. How do environmental problems threaten world peace?

7. What are some of the undesirable effects of population growth?

8. How does the economy and polity affect environmental problems?

9. What kinds of social psychological factors contribute to environmental problems?

10. Do you always recycle? Why or why not?

11. Do you walk or cycle instead of using a car?

12. Does your institution have an active recycling program? If no, why not?

13. What might be done to deal with the problems of environmental pollution and environmental depletion?

▪▪ FOR FURTHER READING

Athanasiou, Tom. *Divided Planet: The Ecology of Rich and Poor.* Athens, GA: University of Georgia Press, 1998. A discussion of global environmental problems that stresses the significance of the gap between the developing and the developed nations for the future of the environment.

Dasgupta, Partha. *Human Well-Being and the Natural Environment.* New York: Oxford University Press, 2001. An economist argues that human well-being depends on the natural environment, including places of beauty, as well as on material goods and knowledge.

Firor, John. *The Changing Atmosphere: A Global Challenge.* New Haven, CT: Yale University Press, 1990. An analysis of the environment that stresses the interdependence in the ecosystem, with the result that no environmental issue can be treated in isolation from others or from social processes.

Gupte, Pranay, Louis Silverstein, and Jack Freeman. *All of Us: Births and a Better Life, Population, Development and Environment in a Globalized World.* New York: Earth Times Books, 1999. A selection of articles from *The Earth Times,* a newspaper devoted to environmental issues. Authors range from noted political leaders to local activists, and topics include the interplay of environment, population growth, and economics.

Harrison, Paul, and Fred Pearce. *AAAS Atlas of Population and Environment.* Berkeley, CA: University of California Press, 2001. Shows how, throughout the world, population growth and density, along with technology, affects the ecosystem. Notes both short-term and long-term effects.

MacEachern, Diane. *Save Our Planet: 750 Everyday Ways You Can Help Clean Up the Earth.* New York: Dell, 1990. Shows how individuals can act to alleviate environmental problems, including what you can do around your home or apartment.

Schnaiberg, Allan, and Kenneth Alan Gould. *Environment and Society: The Enduring Conflict.* New York: St. Martin's Press, 1994. An analysis of the ways in which the interests of labour, business, and government converge at the point of encouraging the kind of growth that is environmentally destructive.

Werbach, Adam. *Act Now, Apologize Later.* New York: HarperCollins, 1997. A call to action, and the rationale for such action, by the president of the Sierra Club. Includes some stories of successful activism.

abuse improper use of drugs or alcohol to the degree that the consequences are defined as detrimental to the user or society

achievement as distinguished from educational "attainment," the level the student has reached as measured by scores on various verbal and nonverbal tests

AIDS acquired immune deficiency syndrome, a disease in which a viral infection causes the immune system to stop functioning, inevitably resulting in death

alienation a sense of estrangement from one's social environment, typically measured by one's feelings of powerlessness, normlessness, isolation, meaninglessness, and self-estrangement

anarchism the philosophy that advocates the abolition of government in order to secure true freedom for people

assimilation the integration of minority groups into the dominant culture

atmosphere the general mood and social influences in a situation or place

attainment as distinguished from educational "achievement," the number of years of education completed by a student

attitude a predisposition about something in one's environment

autonomy the ability or opportunity to govern oneself

biological characteristic an inherited, rather than learned, characteristic

blended family a family formed by a relationship that includes one or more children from a previous relationship

bureaucracy an organization in which there are specific areas of authority and responsibility, a hierarchy of authority, management based on written documents, worker expertise, management based on rules, and full-time workers

capitalism an economic system in which there is private, rather than state, ownership of wealth and control over the production and distribution of goods; people are motivated by profit and compete with each other for maximum shares of profit

carcinogenic causing cancer

cognitive development growth in the ability to perform increasingly complex intellectual activities, particularly abstract relationships

cohabitation living together without being married (also called common-law family)

compensatory programs programs designed to give intensive help to disadvantaged pupils and increase their academic skills

conflict theory a sociological theory that focuses on contradictory interests, inequalities between social groups, and the resulting conflict and change

contradiction opposing phenomena within the same social system

critical thinking the analysis and evaluation of information

culture the way of life of a people, including both material products (such as technology) and nonmaterial characteristics (such as values, norms, language, and beliefs)

cyberbullying bullying through e-mail, cellphones, and instant messaging

dehumanization the process by which an individual is deprived of the qualities or traits of a human being

deinstitutionalization a movement to change the setting of treatment of mental disorders from hospitals to the community through rapid discharge of patients

dependent variable the variable in an experiment that is influenced by an independent variable

detoxification supervised withdrawal from dependence on a drug

differential association theory the theory that illegal behaviour is due to a preponderance of definitions favourable to such behaviour

discrimination arbitrary, unfavourable treatment of the members of some social group

division of labour the separation of work into specialized tasks

divorce rate typically, the number of divorces per 1,000 marriages

downsizing reduction of the labour force in a company or corporation

ecosystem a set of living things, their environment, and the interrelationships among and between them

environmental depletion increasing scarcity of natural resources, including those used for generating energy

environmental destruction alterations in the environment that make it less habitable or useful for people or other living things

environmental pollution harmful alterations in the environment, including air, land, and water

environmental racism the poor and visible minorities are more likely to live in neighbourhoods with sites for toxic-waste disposal and polluting industries, and are less likely to be protected by lawmakers

epidemiology the study of factors that affect the incidence, prevalence, and distribution of illnesses

erotica sexually arousing materials that are not degrading or demeaning to adults or children

ethnic group people who have a shared historical and cultural background that leads them to identify with each other

etiology the causes of a disease

eutrophication overfertilization of water due to excess nutrients, leading to algae growth and oxygen depletion

exploitation use or manipulation of people for one's own advantage or profit

fallacy of appeal to prejudice argument by appealing to popular prejudices or passions

fallacy of authority argument by an illegitimate appeal to authority

fallacy of circular reasoning the practice of assuming something in order to prove the very thing that you assumed

fallacy of composition the assertion that what is true of the part is necessarily true of the whole

fallacy of dramatic instance overgeneralizing

fallacy of misplaced concreteness making something abstract into something concrete

fallacy of non sequitur something that does not follow logically from what has preceded it

fallacy of personal attack argument by attacking the opponent personally rather than dealing with the issue

fallacy of retrospective determinism the argument that things could not have worked out any other way than they did

frequency distribution the organization of data to show the number of times each item occurs

gender the meaning of being male or female in a particular society

gender role the attitudes and behaviour that are expected of men and women in a society; specify certain kinds of behaviour as appropriate, and other kinds as inappropriate, for men and women

ghetto an area in which a certain group is segregated from the rest of society; often used today to refer to the impoverished area of the inner city

gridlock the inability of the government to legislate significant new policies

gross domestic product (GDP) the standard measure of the size of Canada's economy (consumer and government spending, and the difference in the values of exports and imports

gross national income (GNI) the total value, usually in dollars, of all goods and services produced by a nation during a year

herbicide a chemical used to kill plant life, particularly weeds

heterogamy marriage between those with diverse values and backgrounds

heterosexim the erroneous assumption that everyone is heterosexual

homogamy marriage between those with similar values and backgrounds

homophobia an unnatural fear and dislike of lesbians, bisexuals, and gay men

iatrogenic problems problems caused by the physician in the course of his or her treatment of a patient

ideology a set of ideas that explain or justify some aspect of social reality

incidence the number of new cases of an illness that occur during a particular period of time

independent variable the variable in an experiment that is manipulated to see how it effects changes in the dependent variable

innate existing in a person from birth

institution a collective pattern of dealing with a basic social function; typical institutions identified by sociologists are the government, economy, education, family and marriage, and religion

institutional racism policies and practices of social institutions that tend to perpetuate racial discrimination

interaction reciprocally influenced behaviour on the part of two or more people

interest group a group that attempts to influence public opinion and political decisions in accord with the particular interests of its members

international terrorism politically motivated violence against citizens of political entities different from those of the perpetrators in order to coerce and intimidate others into accepting the perpetrators' goals

labour force all civilians who are employed or unemployed but able and desirous of work

life chances the probability of gaining certain advantages defined as desirable, such as long life and health

life expectancy the average number of years a newborn can be expected to live

lobbyist an individual who tries to influence legislation in accord with the preferences of an interest group

maladjustment poor adjustment to one's social environment

malnutrition inadequate food, in amount or type

manic-depressive reaction a disorder involving fluctuation between emotional extremes

Marxist pertaining to the system of thought developed by Karl Marx and Friedrich Engels, particularly emphasizing materialism, class struggle, and the progress of humanity toward communism

mean the average

median the score below which are half of the scores and above which are the other half

medicalization the expansion of day-to-day life/behaviour into the practice of medicine

military parity equality or equivalence in military strength

morbidity the prevalence of a specified illness in a specified area

morphological pertaining to form and structure

neurosis a mental disorder involving anxiety that impairs functioning

norm shared expectations about behaviour

nuclear family husband, wife, and children, if any

obscenity material that is offensive by generally accepted standards of decency

organized crime any group of five or more people engaged in a continuing pattern of serious criminal activity where the primary motive is profit

paraphilia the need for a socially unacceptable stimulus in order to be sexually aroused and satisfied

participant observation a method of research in which one directly participates in and observes the social reality being studied

patronage giving government jobs to people who are members of the winning party

pay equity equal pay for work of equal value

pedophile an adult who depends on children for sexual stimulation

personal problem a problem that can be explained in terms of the qualities of the individual

pesticide a chemical used to kill insects defined as pests

photosynthesis a natural process essential to life, resulting in the production of oxygen and organic materials

pica a craving for unnatural substances, such as dirt or clay

pimp one who earns all or part of his living by acting as a manager or procurer for a prostitute

pluralism the more or less equal distribution of power among interest groups

political alienation a feeling of political disillusionment, powerlessness, and estrangement

political party an organized group that attempts to control the government through the electoral process

pollutant anything that causes environmental pollution

pornography literature, art, Internet materials, or films that are sexually arousing

poverty a state in which income is insufficient to provide the basic necessities such as food, shelter, and clothing

power elite model a model of politics in which power is concentrated in political, economic, and military leaders

prejudice a rigid, emotional attitude that legitimates discriminatory behaviour toward people in a group

prevalence the number of cases of an illness that exist at any particular time

primary group the people with whom one has intimate, face-to-face interaction on a recurring basis, such as parents, spouse, children, and close friends

private school a nonreligious public school approved by the local school board but free of many regulations and policies that apply to other public schools

promiscuity undiscriminating, casual sexual relationships with many people

prostitution having sexual relations for remuneration, usually to provide part or all of one's livelihood

psychosis a disorder in which the individual fails to distinguish between internal and external stimuli

psychosomatic disorder an impairment in physiological functioning that results from the individual's emotional state

qualitiative methods methods of data collection that are used to obtain specific information on individuals and small groups at the micro level

quantitative methods methods of data collection that give a macro perspective on social life

race a group of people distinguished from other groups on the basis of certain biological characteristics

racial profiling police targeting racialized groups

racism the belief that some racial groups are inherently inferior to others

recidivism repeated criminal activity and incarceration

regulatory agency an organization established by the government to enforce statutes that apply to a particular activity

rehabilitation resocializing a criminal and returning him or her to full participation in society

reification defining what is abstract as something concrete

role conflict a person's perception that two or more of his or her roles are contradictory, or that the same role has contradictory expectations, or that the expectations of the role are unacceptable or excessive

role the behaviour associated with a particular position in the social structure

sadomasochism the practice of deriving sexual pleasure from the infliction of pain

same-sex family two persons of the same sex living together, with or without children

sanctions mechanisms of social control for enforcing a society's standards

schizophrenia a psychosis that involves a thinking disorder, particularly hallucinations and fantasies

secondary data analysis analysis of existing research

secondary data sources sources of data not compiled or analyzed personally by the researcher

self-fulfilling prophecy a belief that has consequences (and may become true) simply because it is believed

sex an individual's chromosomal and physiological makeup as male or female

sexism prejudice or discrimination against someone because of his or her sex

sexual harassment unwelcome sexual advances, requests for sexual favours, and other sexual behaviour that either results in punishment when the victim resists or creates a hostile environment or both

social capital the degree of participation and involvement within a community between its citizens and institutions—characterized by trust, reciprocity, identity—to achieve mutual benefits

social problem a condition or pattern of behaviour that contradicts some other condition or pattern of behaviour; is defined as incompatible with the desired quality of life; is caused, facilitated, or prolonged by social factors; involves intergroup conflict; and requires social action for resolution

socialization the process by which an individual learns to participate in a group

socioeconomic status position in the social system based on economic resources, power, education, prestige, and lifestyle

stealth racism hidden or subtle acts of prejudice and discrimination that may be apparent only to the victim

stereotype an image of members of a group that standardizes them and exaggerates certain qualities

stigma that which symbolizes disrepute or disgrace

stratification system arrangement of society into groups that are unequal with regard to such valued resources as wealth, power, and prestige

structural functionalism a sociological theory that focuses on social systems and how their interdependent parts maintain order

subsidy a government grant to a private person or company to assist an enterprise deemed advantageous to the public

survey a method of research in which a sample of people are interviewed or given questionnaires in order to get data on some phenomenon

symbolic interactionism a sociological theory that focuses on the interaction between individuals, the individual's perception of situations, and the ways in which social life is constructed through interaction

terrorism use of threats or violence against random or symbolic targets in pursuit of political goals

test of significance a statistical method for determining the probability that research findings occurred by chance

total institution a place in which the totality of the individual's existence is controlled by external forces

trauma physical or emotional injury

underemployment working full time for poverty wages, working part time when full-time work is desired, or working at a job below the worker's skill level

unemployment rate the proportion of the labour force that is not working but is available for work and has made specific efforts to find work

urbanization the increasing concentration of people living in cities

values things preferred because they are defined as having worth

variable any trait or characteristic that varies in value or magnitude

war a major armed conflict between nations or between organized groups within a nation in which a thousand or more people are killed

white-collar crime crimes committed by respectable citizens in the course of their work

work ethic the notion that our sense of worth and the satisfaction of our needs are intricately related to the kind of work we do

Abbott, Stephanie. 1987. "A new look at treatment trends." *Alcoholism & Addiction* (March–April):44–48.

ABC News. 2001. US–Russia Child Porn Bust. Online at http://www.abc.news.go.com/sections/world.Daily/News/childpornbust_010326.htm.

Aboriginal Healing Foundation. 2003. Fetal Alcohol Syndrome among Aboriginal People in Canada: Review and Analysis of the Intergenerational Links to Residential Schools. Ottawa: Aboriginal Healing Foundation. Online at http://www.ahf.ca/newsite/english/index.shtml.

Abramovitz, Janet N. 1998. *Taking a Stand: Cultivating a New Relationship with the World's Forests.* Washington, DC: Worldwatch Institute.

Abramson, Z. 1994. "Don't ask your gynecologist if you need a hysterectomy." In *On Women Healthsharing*, Dua et al. Eds. Toronto: Women's Press:245–253.

———. 2002 (May). "Losing heart: The estrogen dilemma—Rethinking health research for midlife women." *Women's Health and Urban Life: An International and Interdisciplinary Journal.* Vol. 1, No. 1.

Adam, Barry. 1995. *The Rise of a Gay and Lesbian Movement.* New York: Twayne Publishers.

Adam, Barry. 2002. "Theorizing the globalization of gay and lesbian movements." In *Sociological Views on Political Participation in the 21st Century*, Vol.10:123–137.

Adam, Barry, Jan Willem Duyvendak, and Andrea Kroouwel (Eds). 1999. *The Global Emergence of Gay and Lesbian Politics: National Imprints of a Worldwide Movement.* Philadelphia: Temple University Press.

Adams, B., M. P. Aranda, B. Kemp, and K. Takagi. 2002. "Ethnic and gender differences in distress among Anglo American, African American, Japanese American, and Mexican American spousal caregivers of persons with dementia." *Journal of Clinical Geropsychology* 8:279–301.

Adams, Mary Louise. 1999. *The Trouble with Normal: Postwar Youth and the Making of Heterosexuality.* Toronto: University of Toronto Press.

Addiction Research Foundation. 1994. *Drugs in Ontario.* Ontario: Author.

Adelman, Clifford. 1991. *Women at Thirtysomething: Paradoxes of Attainment.* Washington, DC: U.S. Department of Education.

Adlaf, E. M., and A. Paglia. 2003. Drug Use Among Ontario Students. Online at http://www.camh.net/pdf/OSDUS03_Drug_Report_highlights.pdf.

Adler, Valerie. 1989. "Little control = lots of stress." *Psychology Today* (April): 18–19.

Ajdukovic, Marina. 1998. "Displaced adolescents in Croatia." *Adolescence* 33 (Spring):209–17.

Akerlind, Ingemar, and Jan O. Homquist. 1992. "Loneliness and alcohol abuse: A review of evidences of an interplay." *Social Science and Medicine* 34 (February):405–14.

Akyeampong, E. 2002 (August). "Unionization and fringe benefits." *Perspectives on Labour and Income* 3(8). Ottawa: Statistics Canada. Catalogue No. 75-001-XIE.

Alaimo, Katherine, Christine M. Olson, and Edward A. Frongillo, Jr. 2000. "Food insufficiency and American school–aged children's cognitive, academic, and psychosocial development." *Pediatrics* 108:44–53. Alaimo, Katherine, Christine M. Olson, and Edward A. Frongillo, Jr. 2002. "Family food insufficiency, but not low family income, is positively associated with dysthymia and suicide symptoms in adolescents." *Journal of Nutrition* 132:719–25.

Alaimo, Katherine, Christine M. Olson, Edward A. Frongillo, Jr., and R. R. Briefel. 2001. "Food insufficiency, family income, and health in U.S. preschool and school–aged children." *American Journal of Public Health* 91:781–86.

Aldous, Joan, and Rodney F. Ganey. 1999. "Family life and the pursuit of happiness." *Journal of Family Issues* 20 (March):155–80.

Almey, Maria, et al. 2000. *Women in Canada: A Gender Based Statistical Report.* Ottawa: Statistics Canada.

Amato, Paul R. 2001. "Children of divorce in the 1990s." *Journal of Family Psychology* 15:355–70.

Amato, Paul R., and Bruce Keith. 1991. "Parental divorce and the well-being of children." *Psychological Bulletin* 110:26–46.

Amato, Paul R., and Danelle D. DeBoer. 2001. "The transmission of marital instability across generations." *Journal of Marriage and Family* 63:1038–51.

Amato, Paul R., and Juliana M. Sobolewski. 2001. "The effects of divorce and marital discord on adult children's psychological well–being." *American Sociological Review* 66:900–21.

Amato, Paul R., and Stacy J. Rogers. 1997. "A longitudinal study of marital problems and subsequent divorce." *Journal of Marriage and the Family* 59 (August):612–24.

Ambert, Ann-Marie. 2003. *Same-Sex Couples and Same-Sex Parent Families: Relationships, Parenting, and Issues of Marriage.* Ottawa: Vanier Institute of the Family.

American Civil Liberties Union. 2002. "ACLU says Homeland Security Bill step backward." Press release. American Civil Liberties Union website.

Ames, G. M., J. W. Grube, and R. S. Moore. 2000. "Social control and workplace drinking norms." *Journal of Studies on Alcohol* 61:203–19.

Amnesty International. 1995. *Human Rights Are Women's Rights*. New York: Amnesty International, USA.

Anderson, Alan. 1982. "Neurotoxic follies." *Psychology Today* (July):30–42.

Ansalone, George. 2000. "Keeping on track." *Race, Gender & Class in Education* 7:108–32.

Antecol, H., and D. Cobb–Clark. 2001. "Men, women, and sexual harassment in the U.S. military." *Gender Issues* 19:3–18.

AOHC (Association of Ontario Health Centres). 2004. Online at http://www.aohc.org.

Aponte, Robert. 1991. "Urban Hispanic poverty: Disaggregations and explanations." *Social Problems* 38 (November):516–28.

Applebome, Peter. 1996. "Many new teachers are unprepared, study says." *New York Times*, September 13.

Arber, S. and M. Khlat. 2002. "Introduction to social and economic patterning of women's health in a changing world" *Social Science & Medicine* 54(5):643–647.

Archer, Dane, and Rosemary Gartner. 1979. "Violent acts and violent times: A comparative approach to postwar homicide rates." *American Sociological Review* 41 (December):937–62.

Armstrong P., and H. Armstrong. 1994. *The Double Ghetto: Canadian Women & Their Segregated Work* (3rd ed.). Toronto: McClelland & Stewart Inc.

Armstrong, Gregory L., Laura A. Conn, and Robert W. Pinner. 1999. "Trends in infectious disease mortality in the United States during the 20th century." *Journal of the American Medical Association* 281 (January 6):61–66.

Arnup, Katherine. 1995. *Lesbian Parenting: Living with Pride and Prejudice*. PEI: Gynergy Books.

Aronson, Marita, and Bibbi Hagberg. 1998. "Neuropsychological disorders in children exposed to alcohol during pregnancy." *Alcoholism: Clinical and Experimental Research* 22 (April):321–24.

Asher, Ramona M. 1992. *Women with alcoholic husbands: Ambivalence and the trap of codependency*. Chapel Hill: University of North Carolina Press.

Ashforth, Blake. 1994. "Petty tyranny in organizations." *Human Relations* 47 (July):755–78.

Auger, Jeanette A. 1990. Lecture notes for *The Sociology of the Family*.

———. 2001 and 2003. *Respite Care Needs of Caregivers in Lunenburg County, Nova Scotia*. The Victorian Order of Nurses: Annapolis Valley Branch.

———. 2003. *Passing Through: End of Life Decisions of Lesbians and Gay Men*. Halifax: Fernwood Publishing.

———. 2004. Sociology 1033: Introduction to Social Problems.

Auger, Jeannette A., and Diane Tedford Little. 2002. *From the Inside Looking Out: Competing Ideas About Growing Old*. Halifax: Fernwood Books.

Babbage, Keen J. 1998. *High–Impact Teaching: Overcoming Student Apathy*. Lancaster, PA: Technomic Publishing.

Bachman, R., and R. Peralta. 2002. "The relationship between drinking and violence in an adolescent population." *Deviant Behavior* 23:1–19.

Bagley, C., and P. Tremblay (Eds). 1996. *Suicidal Behaviors in Adolescents and Adults: Taxonomy, Understanding and Prevention*. Vermont: Avebury Books.

Bailey, William C. 1990. "Murder, capital punishment, and television: Execution publicity and homicide rates." *American Sociological Review* 55 (October):628–33.

Baird, Vanessa. 2001. *The No-Nonsense Guide to Sexual Diversity*. Toronto: New Internationalist Publications

Banaji, M. R., and A. G. Greenwald. 1995. "Implicit gender stereotyping in judgments of fame." *Journal of Personality and Social Psychology* 68 (February):181–98.

Banks, James A. 1991. "Multicultural literacy and curriculum reform." *Educational Horizon* 69 (Spring):135–40.

Barak, M. E. M., and A. Levin. 2002. "Outside of the corporate mainstream and excluded from the work community: A study of diversity, job satisfaction and well–being." *Community, Work & Family* 5:133–57.

Barker, David C. 1999. "Rushed decisions: Political talk radio and vote choice, 1994–1996." *Journal of Politics* 61 (May):527–39.

Barker, K. N., E. A. Flynn, G. A. Pepper, D. W. Bates, and R. L. Mikeal. 2002. "Medication errors observed in 36 health care facilities." *Archives of Internal Medicine* 162:1897–903.

Barlow, Hugh D. 1996. *Introduction to Criminology*, 7th ed. New York: HarperCollins.

Barron, Martin, and Martin Kimmel. 2000. "Sexual violence in three pornographic media." *Journal of Sex Research* 37:161–68.

Barrow, S. M., D. B. Herman, P. Cordova, and E. L. Struening. 1999. "Mortality among homeless shelter residents in New York City." *American Journal of Public Health* 89 (April):529–34.

Barry, B. 2002. "Capitalists rule OK? Some puzzles about power." *Politics, Philosophy & Economics* 1:155–84.

B.C. Centre for Excellence in HIV/AIDS. 2004 (September 17). Evaluation of the Supervised Injection Site: One Year Summary. Vancouver: BC Centre for Excellence in HIV/AIDS. Online at www.vandu.org/pdfs/sisyearreport.pdf.

Becker, Howard S. 1952. "Social–class variations in the teacher–pupil relationship." *Journal of Educational Sociology* 25 (April):451–65.

Becker, Judith V., and Robert M. Stein. 1991. "Is sexual erotica associated with sexual deviance in adolescent males?" *International Journal of Law and Psychiatry* 14 (1–2):85–95.

Belkin, Lisa. 1989. "Bars to equality of sexes seen as eroding, slowly." *New York Times*, August 20.

Bell, Alan P., and Martin S. Weinberg. 1978. *Homosexualities: A Study of Diversity among Men and Women*. New York: Simon & Schuster.

Bell, Alan, Martin Weinberg, and Sue Hammersmith. 1981. *Sexual Preference*. Bloomington: Indiana University Press.

Benedek, E. P., and C. F. Brown. 1999. "No excuses: Televised pornography harms children." *Harvard Review of Psychiatry* 7 (November–December):236–40.

Benjamin, D., M. Gunderson, and W. Riddell. 1998. *Labour Market Economics: Theory, Evidence, and Policy in Canada*. (4th ed.). Toronto: McGraw-Hill Ryerson.

Bergen, R. K., and K. A. Bogle. 2000. "Exploring the connection between pornography and sexual violence." *Violence and Victims* 15:227–34.

Berger, Joseph. 1994. "The psychotherapeutic treatment of male homosexuality." *American Journal of Psychotherapy* 48 (Spring):251–61.

Bergman, Brian. 2002 (January 14). "*Chosen peoples: Aboriginals are now being courted by universities across the country*." Macleans.ca: Online at http://www.macleans.ca/topstories/education/article.jsp?content=62247.

Bergman, Mike. 2002. "Census bureau report shows 'big payoff' from educational degrees." Press release. U.S. Census Bureau website.

Bergner, R. M., and A. J. Bridges. 2002. "The significance of heavy pornography involvement for romantic partners." *Journal of Sex and Marital Therapy* 28:193–206.

Berkman, Lisa F. 2000. "From social integration to health." *Social Science & Medicine* 51:843–58.

Bernard, Jessie. 1966. *Marriage and Family among Negroes*. Englewood Cliffs, NJ: Prentice–Hall.

Bernstein, S. 2002. "International institutions and the framing of domestic policies: The Kyoto Protocol and Canada's response to climate change." *Policy Sciences* 35:203–36.

Besserer, S., and C. Trainor. 2000 "Criminal Victimization in Canada, 1999." *Juristat* Volume 20, Number 10.

Besserer, Sandra. 2002 (May). "Criminal Victimization: An International Perspective." *Juristat* 22(4), Catalogue No 85-002-XPE.

Betts, Julian R., and Darlene Morell. 1999. "The determinants of undergraduate grade point average." *Journal of Human Resources* 34 (Spring):268–93.

Bianchi, Suzanne M. 1995. "The changing demographic and socioeconomic characteristics of single parent families." *Marriage and Family Review* 20 (1–2):71–97.

Bibby, Reginald. 1995. *The Bibby Report: Social Trends Canadian Style*. Toronto: Stoddard.

———. 2001. *Canada's Teens: Today, Yesterday and Tomorrow*. Toronto: Stoddard.

Bickel, J. 2000. "Women in academic medicine." *Journal of the American Medical Women's Association* 55 (Winter):10–20.

Biden, Joseph R., Jr. 1990. "They're out there crying for help." *Los Angeles Times*, March 14.

Biernat, Monica, and Diane Kobrynowicz. 1997. "Gender– and race–based standards of competence." *Journal of Personality and Social Psychology* 72 (3):544–57.

Bigner, Jerry J., and R. Brooke Jacobsen. 1992. "Adult responses to child behavior and attitudes toward fathering: Gay and nongay fathers." *Journal of Homosexuality* 23 (3):99–112.

Bilge, Barbara, and Gladis Kaufman. 1983. "Children of divorce and one–parent families: Cross–cultural perspectives." *Family Relations* 32 (January):59–71.

Billingham, Robert, and Taryn Abrahams. 1998. "Parental divorce, body dissatisfaction and physical attractiveness ratings of self and others among college women." *College Student Journal* 32 (March):148–52.

Bird, Chloe E. 1999. "Gender, household labor, and psychological distress." *Journal of Health and Social Behavior* 40:32–45.

Bird, Chloe E., and Allen M. Fremont. 1991. "Gender, time use, and health." *Journal of Health and Social Behavior* 32 (June):114–29.

Bittle, S. 1999. Reconstructing Youth Prostitution. Unpublished masters thesis. British Columbia: School of Criminology, Simon Fraser University.

Bittle, S. 2002 (July). "When protection is punishment: Neoliberalism and secure care approaches to youth prostitution." *Canadian Journal of Criminology* 44(3):317–350.

Black, Susan. 2001. "Morale matters." *American School Board Journal* 188:40–43.

Blackwell, D. L., J. G. Collins, and R. Coles. 2002. *Summary Health Statistics for U.S. Adults*. Washington, DC: Government Printing Office.

Blair, R. G. 2000. "Risk factors associated with PTSD and major depression among Cambodian refugees in Utah." *Health and Social Work* 25 (February): 23–30.

Blais, A., E. Gidengil, N. Nevitte, and R. Nadeau. (forthcoming). "Where does the turnout decline come from?" *European Journal of Political Research*. Online at http://www.ces-eec.umontreal.ca/ces.html.

Blake, Judith. 1989. *Family Size and Achievement*. Berkeley: University of California Press.

Blanchard, Nanette. 1998. "The quietest war." *E*, March–April, pp. 17–22.

Blau, Gary, and Donna Tatum. 2000. "Correlates of perceived gender discrimination for female versus male medical technologists." *Sex Roles* 43:105–18.

Blumberg, Paul. 1989. *The Predatory Society: Deception in the American Marketplace*. New York: Oxford University Press.

Blumstein, Philip, and Pepper Schwartz. 1983. *American Couples: Money, Work, Sex*. New York: William Morrow.

Boeringer, Scot B. 1994. "Pornography and sexual aggression: Associations of violent and nonviolent depictions with rape and rape proclivity." *Deviant Behavior* 15 (3):289–304.

Bohan, J. S. 1996. *Psychology and Sexual Orientation: Coming to Terms*. New York: Rutledge.

Boisen, Anton T. 1936. *The Exploration of the Inner World*. New York: Harper & Bros.

Boles, Jacqueline, and Kirk W. Elifson. 1994. "Sexual identity and HIV: The male prostitute." *Journal of Sex Research* 31 (1):39–46.

Bonner, R., and F. Fessenden. 2000 (Sept. 20). "Absence of Executions." *New York Times*.

Bonneuil, N., and N. Auriat. 2000. "Fifty years of ethnic conflict and cohesion: 1945–94." *Journal of Peace Research* 37:563–81.

Botvin, G. J., et al. 1995. "Long–term follow–up results of a randomized drug abuse prevention trial in a white middle–class population." *Journal of the American Medical Association* 273 (April):1106–12.

Bourque, Linda B., and Beverly J. Cosand. 1989. "Predicting the educational attainment of Los Angeles women." *Sociological Perspectives* 32:137–51.

Bourque, Linda B., Donald P. Tashkin, Virginia A. Clark, and Roberleigh Schuler. 1991 "Demographic and health characteristics of heavy marijuana smokers in Los Angeles county." *International Journal of the Addictions* 26 (July):739–55.

Bower, B. 1998. "Study tracks violence among mentally ill." *Science News* 153 (May 16):309.

Boxer, P. A., C. Burnett, and N. Swanson. 1995. "Suicide and occupation: A review of the literature." *Journal of Occupational and Environmental Medicine* 37 (April):442–52.

Braddock, Jamills Henry II, and James M. McPartland. 1987. "How minorities continue to be excluded from equal employment opportunities." *Journal of Social Issues* 43:5–39.

Bradford, Judith, Caitlin Ryan, and Esther D. Rothblum. 1994. "National lesbian health care survey: Implications for mental health care." *Journal of Consulting and Clinical Psychology* 62 (April):228–42.

Brady, David W., and Craig Volden. 1998. *Resolving Gridlock: Politics and Policy from Carter to Clinton*. Boulder, CO: Westview.

Brannigan, A. and Fleishman. 1998. "Juvenile prostitution and mental health: Policing delinquency or treating pathology." *Canadian Journal of Law and Society* 4:77–98.

Breault, K. D., and Augustine J. Kposowa. 1987. "Explaining divorce in the United States: A study of 3,111 counties, 1980." *Journal of Marriage and the Family* 49 (August):549–58.

Breslau, Naomi, M. Marlyne Kilbey, and Patricia Andreski. 1994. "DSM–III–R nicotine dependence in young adults: prevalence, correlates and associated psychiatric disorders." *Addiction* 89 (June):743–54.

Bright, Chris. 2000. "Anticipating environmental 'surprise.'" In *State of the World 2000*, Lester R. Brown et al., eds., pp. 22–38. New York: W. W. Norton.

Brilliant, Joshua. 2002. "Palestinians suffer malnutrition, poverty." Washington Times website.

Brock, Deborah, and Gary Kinsman. 1986. "Patriarchal relations ignored: An analysis and critique of the Bagley Report on sexual offences against children and youth." In Lowman, Jackman, Palys, and Gavigan, Eds. *Regulating Sex: An Anthology of Commentaries on the Findings of the Bagley and Fraser Reports*. British Columbia: School of Criminology, Simon Fraser University.

Brock, Deborah, Kara Gillies, Chantelle Oliver, and Sutdhibhasilp Mook. 2000. *Canadian Women's Studies*. Vol. 20:84.

Brodeur, Paul. 1989. *Currents of Death: Power Lines, Computer Terminals, and the Attempt to Cover Up Their Threat to Your Health*. New York: Simon & Schuster.

Brooks, Clark. 1999. "Study prompts VA to help ill kids of female Vietnam vets." *San Diego Union–Tribune*, September 4.

Brower, A. M. 2002. "Are College Students Alcoholics?" *Journal of American College Health* 50(5):253–255.

Brown, J. S. 1952. "A comparative study of deviations from sexual mores." *American Sociological Review* 17 (April):135–46.

Brown, Lester R. 1993. "A new era unfolds." In *State of the World 1993*, ed. L. Brown, pp. 3–21. New York: W. W. Norton.

Brown, Lester R., and Sandra Postel. 1987. "Thresholds of change." In *State of the World 1987*, Lester R. Brown, ed., pp. 3–19. New York: W. W. Norton.

Brown, Sandra A., Barbara A. Stetson, and Patricia A. Beatty. 1989. "Cognitive and behavioral features of adolescent coping in high–risk drinking situations." *Addictive Behaviors* 14 (1):43–52.

Brown, T. L., G. S. Parks, R. S. Zimmerman, and C. M. Phillips. 2001. "The role of religion in predicting adolescent alcohol use and problem drinking." *Journal of Studies on Alcohol* 62:696–705.

Brown. 2000. "Challenges of the new century." In *State of the World 2000*, Lester R. Brown et al., eds., pp. 3–21. New York: W. W. Norton.

Browne, Kevin D., and Catherine E. Hamilton. 1998. "Physical violence between young adults and their parents." *Journal of Family Violence* 13 (March):59–79.

Browning, Katharine, and Rolf Loeber. 1999. "Highlights of findings from the Pittsburgh youth study." *OJJDP Fact Sheet #95*. Washington, DC: Government Printing Office.

Bruce, Aria. 2002. "Reasons for Home Schooling in Canada." *Canadian Journal of Education* 25(2):204.

Bryce, Jennifer W., Neff Walker, Francoise Ghorayeb, and Mayada Kanj. 1989. "Life experiences, response styles and mental health among mothers and children in Beirut, Lebanon." *Social Science and Medicine* 28 (7):685–95.

Bryjak, George J. 1999. "Multiple reasons for lower crime rates." *San Diego Union–Tribune*, March 28.

Brym, R. J. 2004. *New Society: Sociology for the 21st Century* (4th ed.). Toronto: Thomson Nelson.

Buchanan, Paula, and Margret Winzer. 2004. "Bullying in schools: Children's voices." *Education Canada* 35:12–18.

Bull, M. J., and R. E. McShane. 2002. "Needs and supports for family caregivers of chronically ill elders." *Home Health Care Management and Practice* 14:92–98.

Burgess, Ann W. 1984. *Child Pornography and Sex Rings*. Lexington, MA: Lexington Books.

Burke, Ronald J. 1995. "Work and career experiences and emotional well–being of managerial and professional women." *Stress Medicine* ll (January):51–60.

Burleigh, Nina. 1991. "Watching children starve to death." *Time*, June 10, pp. 56–58.

Burns, James MacGregor, J. W. Peterson, and Thomas E. Cronin. 1984. *Government by the People*, 12th ed. Englewood Cliffs, NJ: Prentice–Hall.

Burstyn, Varda, Ed. 1985. *Women Against Censorship*. Vancouver, British Columbia: Douglas and McIntyre.

Bush, Patricia J., Kevin P. Weinfurt, and Ronald J. Iannotti. 1994. "Families versus peers: Developmental influences on drug use from grade 4–5 to grade 7–8." *Journal of Applied Developmental Psychology* 15 (July–September):437–56.

Butterfield, Fox. 2000. "Report indicates 'juvenile injustice.'" San Diego Union–Tribune, April 26. Butterfield, Herbert. 1949. *Christianity and History*. London: Fontana Books.

Butterfield, Herbert. 1949. *Christianity and History*. London: Fontana Books.

Byrd, W. Michael, and Linda A. Clayton. 2001. *An American Health Dilemma: Race, Medicine, and Health Care in the United States 1900–2000*. New York: Routledge.

Cameron, F. 2002. "Utilitarian multilateralism." *Politics* 22:68–75.

Campaign 2000. 2002. End Child Poverty in Canada.

Campenni, C. Estelle. 1999. "Gender stereotyping of children's toys." *Sex Roles* 40:212–38.

Canada's Report on HIV/AIDS. 2002. Lessons Learned: Reframing the Response. Ottawa: Health Canada. Online at http://www.phac-aspc.gc.ca/aids-sida/hiv_aids/pdf/report02/aidsrpt02e.pdf.

Canada's Senate Special Committee. 2002. http://www.parl.gc.ca/common/Committee_SenHome.asp?Language=E&Parl=37&Ses=1&comm_id=85.

Canadian Border Services Agency. 2004. Online at http://www.cbsa-asfc.gc.ca/newsroom/factsheets/2004/0311CanadaSafe-e.html.

Canadian Broadcasting Corporation. 2004 (November 5). *Fifth Estate*. Online at http://www.cbc.ca/fifth/landslide/laws_printer.html.

Canadian Centre for Justice Statistics Profile. 2001. Statistics Canada. Catalogue No. 85F0033MIE http://www.statcan.ca/english/freepub/85F0033MIE/85F0033MIE2001001.pdf.

Canadian Community Health Survey. (2000–1). http://www.statcan.ca/english/concepts/health/.

Canadian Council on Social Development. 2001 (October). Defining and Re-Defining Poverty: A CCSD Perspective, Position Paper.

———. 2002. *The Canadian Fact Book on Poverty: 2000*. Ottawa: Canada.

Canadian Paediatric Society. 2002. http://www.cps.ca/english/statements/II/ii02-01.htm.

"Canadians with Low Income." 2001 (June). Canadian Centre for Justice Statistics Profile Series. Ottawa: Statistics Canada. Catalogue No. 85F003MIE.

Cano, Annmarie, and K. Daniel O'Leary. 2000. "Infidelity and separations precipitate major depressive episodes and symptoms of nonspecific depression and anxiety." *Journal of Consulting and Clinical Psychology* 68:774–81.

Cardozo, Barbara Lopes, Alfredo Vergara, Ferid Agani, and Carol A. Golway. 2000. "Mental health, social functioning, and attitudes of Kosovar Albanians following the war in Kosovo." *Journal of the American Medical Association* 284:569–77.

Carlson, Bonnie E. 1990. "Adolescent observers of marital violence." *Journal of Family Violence* 5:285–99.

Carr, T. 2004 (August 16). "Panel to discuss high rate of caesarian sections." *The New Brunswick Telegraph Journal News*:A7.

Carrier, Patricia, and Lorraine Davies. 1999 (Winter). "The importance of power relations for the division of household labour." *Canadian Journal of Sociology*. Vol. 24, No. 1:35.

Carriere, D. 2003. "Adult Correctional Services in Canada 2001–02." Juristat Volume 23, Number 10.

Carter, L. 2000 (November 18). "Canada split over the gun." BBC News. Online at http://news.bbc.co.uk/1/hi/world/americas/1029233.stm.

Caspi, Avshalom, Bradley R. Entner Wright, Terrie E. Moffitt, and Phil A. Silva. 1998. "Early failure in the labor market: Childhood and adolescent predictors of unemployment in the transition to adulthood." *American Sociological Review* 63 (June):424–51.

Castro, Janice. 1991. "The simple life." *Time* (April 8):58–63.

Cato, Jennifer E., and Silvia S. Canetto. 2003. "Attitudes and beliefs about suicidal behavior: When coming out is the precipitant of the suicidal behavior." *Sex Roles*, Vol. 49, No. 9/10:43–57.

CAUT. 2004. "Closing the equity gap: A portrait of Canada's university teachers 1996–2001." *CAUT Education Review* 6(2):1–5. Online at http://www.caut.ca/en/publications/educationreview/educationreview6-2.pdf.

Cavalli–Sforza, Luca, Paolo Menozzi, and Alberto Piazza. 1994. *The History and Geography of Human Genes*. Princeton, NJ: Princeton University Press.

CBC Marketplace. 2001 (November 7). "Noise pollution: How loud is your house? A look at the dangers of noise."

CBC News. 2003 (November 5). See also Indepth: Child Pornography, The Supreme Court and Child Porn.

———. 2004 (Jan. 17). Copps won't rule out move to NDP. Online at http://www.cbc.ca/stories/2004/01/15/copps040115.

———. 2005. Online at www.cbc.ca/story/canada/national/2005/17/03/civiliandeaths.051705.html.

CBC News Online. 2000 (February 25). Top Court Challenges Gun Control Opponents. Online at http://cbc.ca/cgi-bin/templates/view.cgi?/news/2000/02/21/guns000221.

———. 2000 (June 22). Prairie Provinces Refuse to Enforce Gun Law. Online at http://cbc.ca/cgi-bin/templates/view.cgi?ctegory=World&story=/news/2000/06/16/gunlaw_prairies000616.

———. 2004 (June). Online at http://www.cbc.ca/news/background/childporn.

———. 2005 (January 13). Tumultuous Teens. Online at http://www.cbc.ca/news/background/crime/youthcrime.html.

CBC, *The Fifth Estate*. 2004 (March 10). "No Way Home." http://www.cbc.ca/fifth/main_nowayhome.html

CCOHS. 2004. Canadian Centre for Occupational Health and Safety. Government of Canada. http://www.ccohs.ca/legislation/.

CCSA. 1999. "Canadian Profile." Canadian Centre on Substance Abuse. http://www.ccsa.ca/index.asp?menu=Statistics&ID=43.

———. 2004 (November). Canadian Addiction Survey. Ottawa: Canadian Centre on Substance Abuse, and Health Canada. Online at http://www.ccsa.ca/pdf/ccsa-004804-2004.pdf.

Centers for Disease Control. 1995a. "Health–care provider advice on tobacco use to persons aged 10–22

years–United States, 1993." *Morbidity and Mortality Weekly Report*, 44 (November 10).

———. 1995b. "Poverty and infant mortality." *Morbidity and Mortality Weekly Report*, 44 (December 15).

———. 1999. "Decline in cigarette consumption following implementation of a comprehensive tobacco prevention and education program." *Morbidity and Mortality Weekly Report*, 48 (February 26).

———. 2000. "Age-specific excess deaths associated with stroke among racial/ethnic minority populations–United States, 1997." *Morbidity and Mortality Weekly Report*, 49 (February 11).

CERA. 2004. Online at http://www.equalityrights.org/cera/index.cfm.

Chafe, Willian H. 1972. *The American Woman: Her Changing Social, Economic, and Political Roles, 1920–1970*. New York: Oxford University Press.

Changing Employee Relationships Survey. 2000. In G. Lowe and G. Schellenberg. 2001. *What's A Good Job? The Importance of Employment Relationships*. Ottawa: CPRN Study No. W-05. http://www.cprn.com/en/doc.cfm?doc=50.

Chapple, Constance L. 1997. "Dow Corning and the silicone breast implant debacle: A case of corporate crime against women." In *Masculinities and Violence*, Lee H. Bowker, ed., pp. 179–96. Newbury Park, CA: Sage.

Charmaz, Kathy. 1995. "The body, identity, and self: Adapting to impairment." *Sociological Quarterly* 36 (4):657–80.

Chen, Huey–tsyh, Michelle Rose Marks, and Carl A. Bersani. 1994. "Unemployment classifications and subjective well–being." *Sociological Review* 42 (February):62–78.

Chermack, S. T., S. F. Stoltenberg, B. E. Fuller, and F. C. Blow. 2000. "Gender differences in the development of substance–related problems." *Journal of Studies on Alcohol* 61:845–52.

Chernousenko, Vladimir M. 1991. *Chernobyl: Insight from the Inside*. New York: Springer–Verlag.

Children Now. 2002. *Fall Color 2001–2002: Prime–Time Diversity Report*. Oakland, CA: Children Now.

Chimienti, G., J. A. Nasr, and I. Khalifeh. 1989. "Children's reactions to war–related stress." *Social Psychiatry and Psychiatric Epidemiology* 24 (6):282–87.

Chinman, M. J., R. Weingarten, D. Stayner, and L. Davidson. 2001. "Chronicity reconsidered: Improving person–environment fit through a consumer–run service." *Community Mental Health Journal* 37:215–29.

Chira, Susan. 1991. "Report says too many aren't ready for school." *New York Times*, December 8.

Chliwniak, Luba. 1997. "Higher education leadership: Analyzing the gender gap." *ERIC Digest*, 25, p. 4.

CHN (Canadian Health Network). 2004. Healthy Hearts and Healthy Communities. November 15. Public Health

Agency of Canada. Online at http://www.canadian-health-network.ca/servlet/ContentServer?cid=1099486425150& pagename=CHN-RCS/CHNResource/CHNResourcePage Template&c=CHNResource.

Choi, Precilla Y. L., and Harrison G. Pope. 1994. "Violence toward women and illicit androgenicanabolic steroid use." *Annals of Clinical Psychiatry* 6 (March):21–25.

Christenson. 1999. *Substance Use in Popular Movies and Music*. Washington, DC: Government Printing Office.

Christian, Susan. 1991. "Cancer's long shadow." *Los Angeles Times*, August 20.

CIHI (Canadian Institute for Health Information). 2003 (June 23–24). Obesity in Canada: Identifying Policy Priorities, Proceedings of a Round Table. Online at http://secure.cihi .ca/cihiweb/dispPage.jsp?cw_page=download_form_e&cw _sku=OCIPP(PDF)&cw_ctt=2&cw_dform=null.

———. 2005. "Health care spending to reach $130 billion this year; per capita spending to hit $4,000." Online at http://secure.cihi.ca/cihiweb/dispPage.jsp?cw_page= media_08dec2004_e.

CIHI (Canadian Institute for Health Information). 2005. Health System Performance Data Tables. http://www.cihi. ca/hirpt/jsp/HIDispatcher.jsp. Accessed July 24, 2005.

Clark, Cheryl. 1994. "VA secretary vows to find cause of Gulf War syndrome." *San Diego Union–Tribune*, March 30.

Clark, Duncan B., et al. 1998. "Family functioning and adolescent alcohol use disorders." *Journal of Family Psychology* 12 (March):81–92.

Clark, Gary. 2002. The Mail Order Bride Guide. Online at http://www.planet-love.com/gclark/gclark01.

Clarke, Charles, and Deborah Lewis. 1977. *Rape: The Price of Coercive Sexuality*. Toronto: Women's Educational Press.

Clarke, J. N. 1996. *Health, Illness, and Medicine in Canada* 3rd ed. Don Mills, ON: Oxford University Press.

Clawson, Rosalee A. 2002. "Poor people, black faces." *Journal of Black Studies* 32:352–61.

Cloud, John, and Jodie Morse. 2001. "Home sweet school." *Time*, August 27, pp. 47–54.

Coalition for Gun Control. 2004. Online at http://www. guncontrol.ca/Content/default-english.htm.

Cobb, C. 2002 (April 29). "Canadians confused by left and right: 18% put Alliance on wrong side of NDP, 32% haven't a clue." *Ottawa Citizen*. Online at http://www. canada.com/national/features/mandate/story.html?id= 5F5BDF34-59FF-4F8E-9BA4-72C0F483324A.

Cochran, S. D., and V. M. Mays. 2000. "Relation between psychiatric syndromes and behaviorally defined sexual orientation in a sample of the U.S. population." *American Journal of Epidemiology* 151:516–23.

Cohen, Judith B., Laurie B. Hauer, and Constance B. Wofsy. 1989. "Women and IV drugs: Parental and heterosexual transmission of human immunodeficiency virus." *Journal of Drug Issues* 19 (Winter):39–56.

Cohen, Lawrence E., and Marcus Felson. 1979. "Social change and crime rate trends." *American Sociological Review* 44 (August):588–607.

Cohen, Lisa E., Joseph P. Broschak, and Heather A. Haveman. 1998. "And then there were more? The effect of organizational sex composition on the hiring and promotion of managers." *American Sociological Review* 63 (October):711–27.

Cohen, Mark A., and Ted R. Miller. 1998. "The cost of mental health care for victims of crime." *Journal of Interpersonal Violence* 13 (February):93–110.

Cohen, Sidney. 1984. "Cocaine Anonymous." *Drug Abuse & Alcoholism Newsletter* 13 (3).

Cohn, Samuel, and Mark Fossett. 1995. "Why racial employment inequality is greater in northern labor markets: Regional differences in white–black employment differentials." *Social Forces* 74 (December):511–42.

Colburn, Theo, Dianne Dumanoski, and John Peterson Myers. 1997. *Our Stolen Future*. New York: Plume. Cole, Claire Vaught. 1995. "Sexual abuse of middle school students." *School Counselor* 42 (January):239–45.

College Board. 2002. Online at http://www.collegeboard.com.

Collins, Michael D., and James H. Frey. 1992. "Drunken driving and informal social control: The case of peer intervention." *Deviant Behavior* 13 (January–March):73–87.

Coltrane, Scott. 2000. "The perpetuation of subtle prejudice: Race and gender imagery in 1990s television advertising." *Sex Roles* 42:363–89.

Committee for the Compilation of Materials on Damage Caused by the Atomic Bombs in Hiroshima and Nagasaki. 1981. *The Physical, Medical, and Social Effects of the Atomic Bombings*, trans. Eisei Ishikawa and David L. Swain. New York: Basic Books.

Commoner, Barry. 1971. *The Closing Circle*. New York: Alfred A. Knopf.

Compas Opinion and Market Research. 2000 (September 23). "Homosexuality and bisexuality: Third annual Sun/COMPAS sex survey." *Toronto Sun*.

Conference Board of Canada. 2004 (September). The Voices of Visible Minorities Speaking Out on Breaking Down Barriers. Online at http://www.triec.ca/docs/ConfBrdCan VoicesVisibleMinorities.pdf.

Conger, R. and D., Frederick O. Lorenz, Glen H. Elder, Jr., Janet N. Melby, Ronald L. Simons, and Katherine J. Conger. 1991. "A process model of family economic pressure and early adolescent alcohol use." *Journal of Early Adolescence* 11 (November):430–49.

Conley, D. 2000. "The racial wealth gap." *Nonprofit and Voluntary Sector Quarterly* 29:530–40.

Conly, Catherine H., and J. Thomas McEwen. 1990. "Computer Crime." *NIJ Reports*, January–February, pp. 2–7.

Connors, G. J., J. S. Tonigan, and W. R. Miller. 2001. "A longitudinal model of intake symptomatology, AA participation, and outcome." *Journal of Studies on Alcohol* 62:817–25.

Cook, Christine C., and Marilyn J. Bruin. 1994. "Determinants of housing quality: A comparison of white, African–American, and Hispanic single–parent women." *Journal of Family and Economic Issues* 15 (Winter):329–47.

Cook, Timothy E. 1998. *Governing with the News: The News Media as a Political Institution.* Chicago: University of Chicago Press.

Coolbaugh, Kathleen, and Cynthia J. Hansel. 2000. "The comprehensive strategy: Lessons learned from pilot sites." *Juvenile Justice Bulletin.* Washington, DC: Government Printing Office.

Coon, Carleton S., Stanley M. Garn, and Joseph B. Birdsell. 1950. *Races.* Springfield, IL: Charles C Thomas.

Corcoran, Mary. 2000. "Mobility, persistence, and the intergenerational determinants of children's success." *Focus* 21:16–22.

Cornell, Svante E. 2002. "Autonomy as a source of conflict." *World Politics* 54:245–77.

Cotter, David A., Joan M. Hermsen, Seth Ovadia, and Reeve Vanneman. 2001. "The glass ceiling effect." *Social Forces* 80:655–82.

Cozzarelli, C., A. V. Wilkinson, and M. J. Tagler. 2001. "Attitudes toward the poor and attributions for poverty." *Journal of Social Issues* 57:207–27.

Crick, N. R., and J. K. Grotpeter. 1995. "Rational aggression, gender, and social–psychological adjustment." *Child Development* 66 (June):710–22.

Cronin, Thomas E., and Michael A. Genovese. 1998. *The Paradoxes of the American Presidency.* New York: Oxford University Press.

Crosby, Faye J. 1991. *Juggling: The Unexpected Advantages of Balancing Career and Home for Women and Their Families.* New York: Free Press.

Crosnoe, Robert, Rashmita S. Mistry, and Glen H. Elder, Jr. 2002. "Economic disadvantage, family dynamics, and adolescent enrollment in higher education." *Journal of Marriage and Family* 64:690–702.

Crossette, Barbara. 1995. "Children called big losers in small wars." *San Diego Union–Tribune*, December 11.

Crowe, C. 2004 (February 3). The Right to Shelter; Homelessness, Housing and Healthcare. Atkinson Economic Justice Fellow. RNAO Region 6. Toronto: Princess Margaret Hospital. Online at http://www.tdrc.net/Crowe_Speech_04-02-03.htm.

CRRF (Canadian Race Relations Foundation). 2004. Online at http://www.crr.ca/en/default.htm.

Crutchfield, Robert D., Ann Glusker, and George S. Bridges. 1999. "A tale of three cities: Labor markets and homicide." *Sociological Focus* 32 (February):65–83.

Cruz, Wilfredo. 1995. "Police brutality in African American and Latino communities." *Latino Studies Journal* 6 (September):30–47.

CTUMS. 2003. Canadian Tobacco Use Monitoring Survey, February–December 2003. Ottawa: Health Canada. Online at http://www.hc-sc.gc.ca/hecs-sesc/tobacco/research/ctums/#chart2.

Cunningham, R. 1996. *Smoke and Mirrors: The Canadian Tobacco War*, Canada: IDRC. Online at http://web.idrc.ca/en/ev-28829-201-1-DO_TOPIC.html.

Cunradi, C. B., R. Caetano, and J. Schafer. 2002. "Religious affiliation, denominational homogamy, and intimate partner violence among U.S. couples." *Journal for the Scientific Study of Religion* 41:139–51.

Curtis, James, and Lorne Tepperman. 2004. *Social Problems: A Canadian Perspective.* Toronto: Oxford University Press.

D'Allaire, Romeo. 2003. *Shake Hands with the Devil: The Failure of Humanity in Rwanda.* Toronto: Random House Canada.

D'Augelli, A. R., and A. H. Grossman. 2001. "Disclosure of sexual orientation, victimization, and mental health among lesbian, gay, and bisexual older adults." *Journal of Interpersonal Violence* 16:1008–28.

D'Augelli, Anthony R., Scott L. Hershberger, and Neil W. Pilkington. 2001. "Suicidality patterns and sexual orientation-related factors among lesbian, gay and bisexual youth." *Suicide and Life-Threatening Behavior*, Vol. 31, No. 3:250–265.

Dahinten, Susan V. 2003 (June). "Peer sexual harassment in adolescence: The function of gender." *Canadian Journal of Nursing Research*. Vol. 35, No. 2:56.

Dail, Paula W. 1988. "Unemployment and family stress." *Public Welfare* 46 (Winter):30–34.

Daily, The. 2000 (September 14). Women in Canada. Ottawa: Statistics Canada. Online at http://www.statcan.ca/Daily/English/00914/d000914c.htm.

———. 2001 (July 4). Trends in the Use of Private Education. Ottawa: Statistics Canada. Online at http://www.statcan.ca/Daily/English/010704/d010704b.htm.

———. 2001 (June 22). Impact of Smoking on Life Expectancy and Disability. Ottawa: Statistics Canada.

———. 2002 (October 22). Ottawa: Statistics Canada. Online at http://www.statcan.ca/Daily/English/021022/d021022a.htm.

———. 2003 (August 12). University Tuition Fees 2003/04. Ottawa: Statistics Canada.

———. 2003 (March 11). Ottawa: Statistics Canada. Online at http://www.statcan.ca/Daily/English/030311/d030311a.htm.

———. 2003 (June 23a). Digital Divide in Schools: Student Access to and Use of Computers. Ottawa: Statistics Canada. Online at http://www.statcan.ca/Daily/English/030623/d030623b.htm.

———. 2003 (June 23b). Family Violence. Ottawa: Statistics Canada. Online at http:www//statcan.ca/Daily/English/030623/d030623c.htm.

———. 2003 (July 24). Crime Statistics 2002. Ottawa: Statistics Canada.

———. 2003 (September 24). Aboriginal Peoples Survey: Well-Being of the Non-Reserve Aboriginal Population. Ottawa: Statistics Canada.

———. 2003 (October 31). Ottawa: Statistics Canada.

———. 2004 (April 26). Ottawa; Statistics Canada. Online at http://www.statcan.ca/Daily/English/040426/d040426a.htm.

———. 2004 (May 4). Divorces. Statistics Canada. Online at http://www.statcan.ca/Daily/English/040504/d040504a.htm.

———. 2004 (June 10). Information and Communication Technologies in Schools Survey. Ottawa: Statistics Canada. Online at http://www.statcan.ca/Daily/English/040610/d040610b.htm.

———. 2004 (June 22). Ottawa: Statistics Canada.

———. 2004 (July 6). Family Violence: Demonstration Study of Sentencing Outcomes. Ottawa: Statistics Canada. Catalogue No. 85-224-XIE.

———. 2004 (July 30). Ottawa: Statistics Canada. Online at http://www.statscan.ca/Daily/English/040730/d040730b.htm.

———. 2004 (August 12). University Tuition Fees. Ottawa: Statistics Canada. Online at http://www.statcan.ca/Daily/English/030812/d030812a.htm.

———. 2004 (December 3). Labour Force Survey November 2004. Ottawa: Statistics Canada.

Dalla, Rochelle L. 2000. "Exposing the 'Pretty Woman' myth: A qualitative examination of the lives of female streetwalking prostitutes." *Journal of Sex Research* 37:333–43.

———. 2001. "Et tu Brute? A qualitative analysis of streetwalking prostitutes' interpersonal support networks." *Journal of Family Issues* 22:1066–85.

Dana, Richard H. 2002. "Mental health services for African Americans." *Cultural Diversity and Ethnic Minority Psychology* 8:3–18.

Das Gupta, T. 1996. *Racism and Paid Work*. Toronto: Garamond Press.

Davenport, Christian. 1995. "Assessing the miltary's influence on political repression." *Journal of Political and Military Sociology* 23 (Summer):119–44.

Davidson, Robert C., and Ernest L. Lewis. 1997. "Affirmative action and other special consideration admissions at the University of California, Davis, School of Medicine." *Journal of the American Medical Association* 278 (October 8):1153–58.

Davies, Scott, and Neil Guppy. 1997. "Fields of study, college selectivity, and student inequalities in higher education." *Social Forces* 75 (June): 1417–38.

Davis, Nanette J., ed. 1993. *Prostitution: An International Handbook on Trends, Problems, and Policies*. Westport, CT: Greenwood.

Dawes, Sharon S., Peter A. Bloniarz, David R. Connelly, Kristine L. Kelly, and Theresa A. Pardo. 1999. "Four realities of IT innovation in government." *The Public Manager* 28 (Spring):27–32.

Dawson, Deborah A. 1991. "Family structure and children's health and well–being: Data from the 1988 national health interview survey on child health." *Journal of Marriage and the Family* 53 (August):573–84.

Day, Anthony. 1991. "Morality, war: Do they mix?" *Los Angeles Times*, January 15.

De Beauvoir. 1977. *Old Age*. Middlesex, England: Penguin Books.

De Jong, G. F., and A. B. Madamba. 2001. "A double disadvantage? Minority group, immigrant status, and underemployment in the United States." *Social Science Quarterly* 82:117–30.

De Wolff, A. 1995 (September). Job Loss and Entry Level Information Workers: Training and Adjustment Strategies for Clerical Workers in Metropolitan Toronto. Summary Report of the Metro Toronto Clerical Workers Labour Adjustment Committee.

Deckard, Barbara Sinclair. 1975. *The Women's Movement*. New York: Harper & Row.

Delpit, Lisa. 1995. *Other People's Children: Cultural Conflict in the Classroom*. New York: New Press.

Demarest, Jack, and Rita Allen. 2000. "Body image: Gender, ethnic, and age differences." *Journal of Social Psychology* 140:465–72.

Dennis, J., and D. Owen. 2001. "Popular satisfaction with the party system and representative democracy in the United States." *International Political Science Review* 22:399–415.

Denton, M., S. Prus, and V. Walters. 2004. "Gender differences in health: A Canadian study of the psychosocial, structural and behavioural determinants of health." *Social Science and Medicine* 58(12):2585–2600.

Department of Justice Canada. 2000. Backgrounder: Modernization of Benefits and Obligations. Online at http:///canada.justice.gc.ca/en/news/nr/2000/doc_25021.html.

———. 2003a. Stronger Child Pornography Laws Receive Royal Assent. Online at http://canada.justice.gc.ca/en/news/nr/2002/doc_30529.html.

———. 2003b. YCJA Explained. Online at http://canada.justice.gc.ca/en/ps/yj/repository/index.html.

Department of National Defence. 2004. Online at http://www.forces.gc.ca/site/home_asp.

Desjardins, N., and T. Hotton. 2004. "Trends in drug offences and the role of alcohol and drugs in crime." *Juristat: Canadian Centre for Justice Statistics*. Ottawa: Statistics Canada. Catalogue No. 85-002XPE, Vol. 24, No.1.

DeStafano, Linda, and Diane Colasanto. 1990. "Unlike 1975, today most Americans think men have it better." *Gallup Poll Monthly*, February, 293.

Deutsch, Claudia H. 1990. "Saying no to the 'mommy track.'" *New York Times*, January 28.

Devine, Joel A., Mark Plunkett, and James D. Wright. 1992. "The chronicity of poverty: Evidence from the PSID, 1968–1987." *Social Forces* 70 (March):787–812.

Dew, Mary Amanda, et al. 2001. "Prevalence and risk of depression and anxiety–related disorders during the first three years after heart transplantation." *Psychosomatics* 42:300–13.

deWilde, Erik J., Ineke C. W. M. Kienhorst, Rene F. W. Diekstra, and Willem H. G. Wolters. 1992. "The relationship between adolescent suicide behavior and life events in childhood and adolescence." *American Journal of Psychiatry* 149 (January):45–51.

Deyhle, Donna. 1995. "Navajo youth and anglo racism: Cultural integrity and resistance." *Harvard Educational Review* 65 (Fall):403–44.

Diaz, R. M., G. Ayala, E. Bein, J. Henne, and B. V. Marin. 2001. "The impact of homophobia, poverty, and racism on the mental health of gay and bisexual Latino men." *American Journal of Public Health* 91:927–32.

Diaz, T., D. Viahov, V. Edwards, S. Conover, and E. Monterroso. 2002. "Sex–specific differences in circumstances of initiation into injecting–drug use among young adult Latinos in Harlem, New York City." *AIDS and Behavior* 6:117–22.

Dickinson, H. D. 1994. "Mental Health Policy in Canada: What's the Problem?" In *Health, Illness and Health Care in Canada* 2nd ed. Eds. B. Singh Bolaria and H. D. Dickinson:466–481. Toronto: Harcourt Brace and Company.

Diener, Ed, Marissa Diener, and Carol Diener. 1995. "Factors predicting the subjective well–being of nations." *Journal of Personality and Social Psychology* 69 (November):851–64.

Dixon, Jo, Cynthia Gordon, and Tasnim Khomusi. 1995. "Sexual symmetry in psychiatric diagnosis." *Social Problems* 42 (August):429–49.

Dobbin, D. 2004 (June 16). Stephen Harper and the "Corporate Welfare Bums." Online at http://www.rabble.ca/columnists_full.shtml?x=32786.

Doherty, K. T. 1998. "A mind of her own: Effects of need for closure and gender on reactions to nonconformity." *Sex Roles* 38:801–20.

Dolphin, R. 1989 (Jan 30). "Children of crime: A fierce debate over punishing the young." *Maclean's*. Vol. 102, No. 5:43(2).

Domhoff, G. William. 1990. *The Power Elite and the State: How Policy Is Made in America*. New York: Aldine de Gruyter.

Domina, T., and K. Koch. 2002. "Convenience and frequency of recycling." *Environment and Behavior* 34:216–38.

Donchin, Y., et al. 1995. "A look into the nature and causes of human errors in the intensive care unit." *Critical Care Medicine* 23 (February):294–300.

Donnerstein, Edward. 1984. "Pornography: Its effect on violence against women." In *Pornography and Sexual Aggression*, Neil M. Malamuth and Edward Donnerstein, eds. New York: Academic Press.

Donolo, P. 2003 (July 16). "War stories: When politicians cry wolf." *The Globe and Mail*: A15.

Dooley, David, K. A., Ham–Rowbottom, and JoAnn Prause. 2001. "Underemployment and depression." *Journal of Health and Social Behavior* 41:421–36.

Dorfman, Andrea. 1989. "Alcohol's youngest victims." *Time*, August 28, 1989, p. 60.

Dorman, Peter. 2001. *Child Labour in the Developed Countries*. Geneva: International Labour Office.

Dover, E. D. 1998. *The Presidential Election of 1996: Clinton's Incumbency and Television*. Westport, CT: Praeger.

Downs, William R., Brenda A. Miller, Maria Testa, and Denise Panek, 1992. "Long–term effects of parent–tochild violence for women." *Journal of Interpersonal Violence* 7 (September):365–82.

Dube, V. 2004. "Sidelined in the Labour Market." *Perspectives of Labour and Income*. Vol. 5, No. 4. Ottawa: Statistics Canada. Catalogue No. 75-0010X1E.

Duchesne, Doreen. 1999. "Street prostitution in Canada." In Canadian Centre for Justice Statistics, *The Juristat Reader: A Statistical Overview of the Canadian Justice System*. Toronto: Thompson Publishing Inc.:241–252.

Duffy, A. and N. Pupo. 1992. *Part-time Paradox: Connecting Gender, Work & Family*. Toronto: McClelland and Stewart.

Duffy, A., D. Glenday, and N. Pupo. 1997. *Good Jobs, Bad Jobs, No Jobs: The Transformation of Work in the 21st Century*. Toronto: Harcourt Brace.

Dukes, Richard L., and Barbara Day Lorch. 1989. "Concept of self, mediating factors, and adolescent deviance." *Sociological Spectrum* 9 (Fall):301–19.

Duncan, David F. 1991. "Violence and degradation as themes in 'adult' videos." *Psychological Reports* 69 (1):239–40.

Duncan, Greg J., W. Jean Yeung, Jeanne Brooks–Gunn, and Judith R. Smith. 1998. "How much does childhood poverty affect the life chances of children?" *American Sociological Review* 63 (June):406–23.

Dunifon, R., and L. Kowaleski–Jones. 2002. "Who's in the house? Race differences in cohabitation, single parenthood, and child development." *Child Development* 73:1249–64.

Dunlap, David W. 1995. "Homosexuals cite evidence for rights law." *New York Times*, January 15.

Dunn, J., J. Golding, L. Davies, and T. G. O'Connor. 2000. "Distribution of accidents, injuries, and illnesses by family type." *Pediatrics* 106:68–72.

Dunn. 2002. "Exploring the effect of the environment on physical activity." *American Journal of Preventive Medicine* 23:36–43.

Durkheim, Emile. 1933. *The Division of Labor in Society.* Trans. George Simpson. New York: Free Press.

Durkin, Keith F., and Clifton D. Bryant. l995. " 'Log on to sex': Some notes on the carnal computer and erotic cyberspace as an emerging research frontier." *Deviant Behavior* l6 (3):179–200.

Durning, Alan, 1991. "Asking how much is enough." In *State of the World 1991*, L. R. Brown, ed., pp. 153–69. New York: W. W. Norton.

Duxbury, L., and C. Higgins. 2001. Work–Life Balance in the New Millennium: Where Are We? Where Do We Need to Go? Canadian Policy Research Network. Online at http://www.cprn.com/en/doc.cfm?doc=52.

Dye, Thomas R. 1995. *Who's Running America?* Englewood Cliffs, NJ: Prentice–Hall.

Easton. 2004 (June 9). Reported in CTV.ca. "Legalize Marijuana and Tax It, Study Says." http://www.ctv.ca/servlet/ArticleNews/mini/CTVNews/1086779661415_15?s_name=election2004&no_ads=.

Eddings, Jerelyn. l995. "A persistent stealth racism is poisoning black–white relations." *U.S. News and World Report*, October 23.

Edelhertz, Herbert. 1983. "White–collar and professional crime." *American Behavioral Scientist* 27 (October–November):109–28.

Edelstein, Michael E. 1988. *Contaminated Communities: The Social and Psychological Impacts of Residential Toxic Exposure.* Boulder, CO.: Westview.

Edin, Kathryn J. l995. "The myths of dependence and self–sufficiency: Women, welfare, and low–wage work." *Focus* 17 (Fall–Winter):l–9.

Edlin, B. R., et al. 1994. "Intersecting epidemics–Crack cocaine use and HIV infection among inner–city young adults." *New England Journal of Medicine* 331 (November 24):1422–27.

Education Week. 2000. *Quality Counts 2000: Who Should Teach?* Education Week website.

Edwards, George C., III, and B. Dan Wood. 1999. "Who influences whom? The president, Congress, and the media." *American Political Science Review* 93 (June):327–44.

Ehrlich, Paul R. 1971. "Eco–catastrophe!" In *The Survival Equation*, ed. R. Revelle, A. Khosla, and M. Vinovskis, pp. 352–64. Boston: Houghton Mifflin.

Eichenwald, Kurt. 2002. "White–collar defense stance: The criminal–less crime." *New York Times*, March 3.

Eisinger, Peter K. 1980. "Affirmative action in municipal employment: The impact of black political power." *Institute for Research on Poverty* (December):621–80.

El-Bassel, Nabila, Neil Guterman, David Bargal, and Kuo-Hsien Su. 1998. "Main and buffering effects of emotional support on job– and health–related strains." *Employee Assistance Quarterly* 13 (3):1–18.

Elections Canada. 2003 (May). "The evolution of the federal franchise." Online at http://www.elections.ca/content.asp?section=gen&document=ec90785&dir=bkg&lang=e&textonly=false.

Ellison, Christopher G., John P. Bartkowski, and Kristin L. Anderson. 1999. "Are there religious variations in domestic violence?" *Journal of Family Issues* 20 (January):87–113.

Elms, Alan C. 1972. *Social Psychology and Social Relevance.* Boston: Little, Brown.

Emerson, Michael O., George Yancey, and Karen J. Chai. 2001. "Does race matter in residential segregation?" *American Sociological Review* 66:922–35.

Ensminger, Margaret E. l995. "Welfare and psychological distress: A longitudinal study of African American urban mothers." *Journal of Health and Social Behavior* 36 (December):346–59.

Environment Scan on Youth Homelessness. 2003 (December). http://www.hrsdc.gc.ca/asp/gateway.asp?hr=en/on/offices/toronto/worktrav/youthjeun/yes/envscan.shtml&hs=on0.

Epstein, Joan F., and Joseph C. Groerer. 1997. "Heroin abuse in the United States." *OAS Working Paper*. Rockville, Md.: SAMHSA.

Epstein, Paul R. 2000. "Is global warming harmful to health?" *Scientific American*, August, pp. 50–57.

Ericksen, Karen Paige, and Karen F. Trocki. l994. "Sex, alcohol and sexually transmitted diseases: A national survey." *Family Planning Perspectives* 26 (November–December):257–63.

Esbensen, Finn–Aage, and David Huizinga. l993. "Gangs, drugs, and delinquency in a survey of urban youth." *Criminology* 31 (4):565–90.

ESOP. 2004. What Is an ESOP? ESOP Association Canada. Online at http://www.esop-canada.com/esop.html.

Essed, Philomena. 1991. *Understanding Everyday Racism: An Interdisciplinary Theory.* Newbury Park, CA: Sage.

Evans, Lorraine, and Kimberly Davies. 2000. "No sissy boys here: A content analysis of the representation of masculinity in elementary school reading textbooks." *Sex Roles* 42: 255–70.

Evans, N., A. Farkas, E. Gilpin, C. Berry, and J. P. Pierce. l995. "Influence of tobacco marketing and exposure to smokers on adolescent susceptibility to smoking." *Journal of the National Cancer Institute* 87 (October):l538–45.

Ewan, Christine, Eva Lowy, and Janice Reid. 1991. "Falling out of culture: The effects of repetition strain injury on sufferers' roles and identity." *Sociology of Health and Illness* 13 (June):168–92.

Ezzell, Carol. 2002. "Hope in a vial." *Scientific American*, June, pp. 36–45.

Fagan, Jeffrey. 1990. "Social processes of delinquency and drug use among urban gangs." In Gangs in America, C. R. Huff, ed. Newbury Park, CA: Sage.

Fagin, Dan, and Marianne Lavelle. 1999. *Toxic Deception: How the Chemical Industry Manipulates Science, Bends the Law and Endangers Your Health*. Monroe, ME: Common Courage Press.

Fair Vote Canada. 2004. Online at http://www. fairvotecanada.org/fvc.

Family Violence in Canada: A Statistical Profile. 2004. Ottawa: Statistics Canada, Department of Justice. Catalogue No. 85-224-XIE.

Farley, M., and H. Barkan. 1998. "Prostitution, violence, and posttraumatic stress disorder." *Women's Health* 27 (3):37–49.

Fast, Janet, and Carol Da Pont. 1997 (Autumn). "Changes in Women's Work Continuity." *Canadian Social Trends:*2–7

Faulkner, Anne H., and Kevin Cranston. 1998 (February). "Correlates of same-sex sexual behaviour in a random sample of Massachusetts high school students." *Journal of Public Health* 88: 262–266.

Fausto-Sterling, Anne. 1985. *Myths of Gender: Biological Theories about Women and Men*. New York: Basic Books.

FCM. 2002. Youth Violence and Youth Gangs: Responding to Community Concerns. FCM 3503:1–35. Ottawa: Solicitor General Canada. DSS Catalogue No. JSR2-56/1994. Online at http://www.psepc-sppcc.gc.ca/ Publications/Policing/pdf/199456_e.pdf.

Feagin, Joe R. 1991. "The continuing significance of race: Anti–black discrimination in public places." *American Sociological Review* 56 (February):101–16.

Feagin, Joe R., and Hernan Vera. 1995. *White Racism: The Basics*. New York: Routledge.

Fearon, James, and David Laitin. 2002. "A world at war." *Harper's Magazine*, March, p. 84.

Feeney, J. A. 2000. "Implications of attachment style for patterns of health and illness." *Child: Care, Health and Development* 26:277–88.

Feingold, Alan, and Ronald Mazzella. 1998. "Gender differences in body image are increasing." *Psychological Science* 9 (May):190–95.

Feinstein, Jonathan S. 1993. "The relationship between Socioeconomic Status and health." *Milbank Quarterly* 71:279–313.

Fellows, J. L., A. Trosclair, E. K. Adams, and C. C. Rivera. 2002. "Annual smoking–attributable mortality, years of potential life lost, and economic costs–United States, 1995–1999." *Morbidity and Mortality Weekly Report* 51:300–03.

Fendrich, Michael, Virginia Warner, and Myrna M. Weissman. 1990. "Family risk factors, parental depression, and psychopathology in offspring." *Developmental Psychology* 26 (January):40–50.

Fenwick, Rudy, and Mark Tausig. 1994. "The macroeconomic context of job stress." *Journal of Health and Social Behavior* 35 (September):266–82.

Ferber, A. L. 2000. "Racial warriors and the weekend warriors: The construction of masculinity in mythopoetic and white supremacist discourse." *Men and Masculinities* 3:30–56.

Fergusson, David M., L. John Horwood, and Lianne J. Woodward. 2001. "Unemployment and psychosocial adjustment in young adults." *Social Science & Medicine* 53:305–20.

Ferraro, Kathleen J. 1989. "Policing woman battering." *Social Problems* 36 (February):61–74.

Ferris, Patricia A., and Catherine A. Marshall. 1987. "A model project for families of the chronically mentally ill." *Social Work* 32 (March–April):110–14.

Ferriss, Abbott L. 2000. "The quality of life among U.S. states." *Social Indicators Research* 49 (January):1–23.

Filson, Glen. 1983. "Class and ethnic differences in Canadians' attitudes to native peoples' rights and immigrants." *Canadian Review of Sociology and Anthropology* 20(4): 454–482.

Fine, Gary Alan. 2000. "Games and truths: Learning to construct social problems in high school debate." *Sociological Quarterly* 41 (Winter):103–23.

Fine, Mark A., and Lawrence A. Kurdek. 1992. "The adjustment of adolescents in stepfather and stepmother families." *Journal of Marriage and the Family* 54 (November):725–36.

Finn, Jeremy D., Susan B. Gerber, Charles M. Achilles, and Jayne Boyd–Zaharias. 2001. "The enduring effects of small classes." *Teachers College Record* 103:145–83.

Fiscella, Kevin, Peter Franks, and Carolyn M. Clancy. 1998. "Skepticism toward medical care and health care utilization." *Medical Care* 36 (February): 180–89.

Fish, Jefferson M. 1995. "Mixed blood." *Psychology Today*, November–December, pp. 55–61.

Fisher, David E. 1990. *Fire & Ice: The Greenhouse Effect, Ozone Depletion, and Nuclear Winter*. New York: Harper & Row.

Fisher, David E., and Marshall Jon Fisher. 2001. "N: The nitrogen bomb." *Discover*, April, pp. 50–57.

Flaks, David K., Ilda Ficher, Frank Masterpasqua, and Gregory Joseph. 1995. "Lesbians choosing motherhood: A comparative study of lesbian and heterosexual parents and their children." *Developmental Psychology* 31 (January):105–14.

Flannery, Daniel J., Alexander T. Vazsonyi, Julie Torquati, and Angela Fridrich. 1994. "Ethnic and 5 gender differences in risk for early adolescent substance use." *Journal of Youth and Adolescence* 23 (April):195–213.

Flavin, Christopher. 1987. "Reassessing nuclear power." In *State of the World 1987*, Lester R. Brown, ed., pp. 57–80. New York: W. W. Norton.

Flavin, Christopher, and Seth Dunn. 1999. "Reinventing the energy system." In *State of the World 1999*, Lester R. Brown et al., eds., pp. 22–40. New York: W. W. Norton.

Fleury, R. E., C. M. Sullivan, D. I. Bybee, and W. S. Davidson, 2d. 1998. " 'Why don't they just call the cops?' Reasons for differential police contact among women with abusive partners." *Violence and Victims* 13 (Winter):333–46.

Flewelling, Robert L., and Karl E. Bauman. 1990. "Family structure as a predictor of initial substance use and sexual intercourse in early adolescence." *Journal of Marriage and the Family* 52 (February):171–81.

Flippen, Chenoa A. 2001. "Racial and ethnic inequality in home ownership and housing equity." *Sociological Quarterly* 42:121–49.

Flisher, Alan J., et al. 1997. "Psychosocial characteristics of physically abused children and adolescents." *Journal of the American Academy of Child and Adolescent psychiatry* 36 (no. 1):123–31.

Flynn, Cynthia A., and Wayne E. Brown. 1991. "The effects of a mandatory alcohol education program on college student problem drinkers." *Journal of Alcohol and Drug Education* 37 (1):15–24.

Fone, Byrne. 2000. *Homophobia*. Great Britain: Metropolitan Books.

Ford, Clelland S., and Frank A. Beach. 1951. *Patterns of Sexual Behavior*. New York: Harper & Row.

Ford, Julian D. 1999. "Disorders of extreme stress following war–zone military trauma." *Journal of Consulting and Clinical Psychology* 67 (February): 3–12.

Forrest, James, and Gary N. Marks. 1999. "The mass media, election campaigning and voter response." *Party Politics* 5 (1):99–114.

Forster, M. 2002. "Trends and driving factors in income distribution and poverty in the OECD area," *Labour Market and Social Policy Occasional Paper 42*. Paris: OECD. Cited in *The Canadian Fact Book on Poverty: 2000*. Ottawa: Canadian Council on Social Development.

Fosu, Augustin Kwasi. 1992. "Occupational mobility of black women, 1958–1981: The impact of post–1964 antidiscrimination measures." *Industrial and Labor Relations Review* 45 (January):281–94.

Foucault, Michel. 1980. *The History of Sexuality, Volume One: An Introduction*. New York: Vintage.

Francoeur, Robert T. 1991. *Becoming a Sexual Person*, 2d ed. New York: Macmillan.

Franklin, Karen. 2000. "Antigay behaviors among young adults." *Journal of Interpersonal Violence* 15 (April):339–62.

Free, Marvin D., Jr. 1994. "Religiosity, religious conservatism, bonds to school, and juvenile delinquency among three categories of drug users." *Deviant Behavior* 15 (2):151–70.

Freeman, R. C.; K. Collier, and K. M. Parillo. 2002. "Early life sexual abuse as a risk factor for crack cocaine use in a sample of community-recruited women at high risk for illicit drug use." *American Journal of Drug and Alcohol Abuse* 28:109–31.

Freud, Sigmund. 1949. *Three Essays on the Theory of Sexuality*. London: Imago Publishing.

Freund, Kurt, Robin Watson, and Douglas Rienzo. 1989. "Heterosexuality, homosexuality, and erotic age preference." *Journal of Sex Research* 26 (1):107–17.

Freund, Matthew, Nancy Lee, and Terri Leonard. 1991. "Sexual behavior of clients with street prostitutes in Camden, NJ." *Journal of Sex Research* 28 (November):579–91.

Frey, R. Scott, and Ali Al–Roumi. 1999. "Political democracy and the physical quality of life." *Social Indicators Research* 47 (May):73–97.

Friedman, Sam. 2002. "9/11 boosts focus on interruption risks." *National Underwriter Property and Casualty–Risk and Benefits Management* 106:17.

Frizzell, A. and A. Westell, with contributions from Nick Hill, Val Sears, and Jeffrey Simpson. 1985. *The Canadian General Election of 1984: Politicians, Parties, Press and Polls*. Ottawa: Carleton University Press:65, 106.

Furnas, J. C. 1965. *The Life and Times of the Late Demon Rum*. New York: Capricorn.

Furnham, A., E. Reeves, and S. Budhani. 2002. "Parents think their sons are brighter than their daughters." *Journal of Genetic Psychology* 163:24–39.

Furstenberg, Frank F., Jr., Thomas D. Cook, Jacquelynne Eccles, Glenn H. Elder, Jr., and Arnold Sameroff. 1999. *Managing to Make It: Urban Families and Adolescent Success*. Chicago: University of Chicago Press.

Gabb, Jacqui. 2004. "Critical differentials: Querying the incongruities within research on lesbian and gay families." *Sexualities* 7:167–182.

Gabriel, Richard A. 1987. *No More Heroes: Madness and Psychiatry in War*. New York: Farrar, Straus & Giroux.

Galaif, E. R., J. A. Stein, M. D. Newcomb, and D .P. Bernstein. 2001. "Gender differences in the prediction of problem alcohol use in adulthood: Exploring the influence of family factors and childhood maltreatment." *Journal of Studies on Alcohol* 62(4):486–493.

Galea, S., et al. 2002. "Psychological sequelae of the September 11 terrorist attacks in New York City." *New England Journal of Medicine* 346:982–87.

Gallagher, Bernard J., Joseph A. McFalls, and Carolyn N. Vreeland. 1993. "Preliminary results from a national survey of psychiatrists concerning the etiology of male homosexuality." *Psychology: A Journal of Human Behavior* 30 (3–4):1–3.

Gallagher, James, et al. 1997. "Challenge or boredom? Gifted students' views on their schooling." *Roeper Review* 19 (March):132–36.

Galler, Janina R., and Frank Ramsey. 1989. "A follow–up study of the influence of early malnutrition on development: Behavior at home and at school."

Gallivan, Joanne. 1991. "Gender bias in students' rating of essays." *Journal of Social Behavior and Personality* 6 (March):119–24.

Gallup Organization. 1997. *Special Report: Black/White Relations in the U.S.* Gallup Organization website.
Ganster, Daniel C. 1986. "Type A behavior and occupational stress." *Journal of Organizational Behavior Management* 8 (Fall–Winter):61–84.

Ganster, Daniel C. 1986. "Type A behavior and occupational stress." *Journal of Organizational Behavior Management* 8 (Fall–Winter):61–84.

Garcia, Malcolm. 2002. "War–stripped, barren Afghan environment will take years to recover." Knight Ridder/Tribune News Service, February 11. Knight Ridder/Tribune website.

Gardner, Gary, and Brian Halweil. 2000. *Underfed and Overfed: The Global Epidemic of Malnutrition.* Washington, DC: Worldwatch Institute.

Gardner, Gary, and Payal Sampat. 1999. "Forging a sustainable materials economy." In *State of the World 1999*, Lester R. Brown et al., eds., pp. 41–59. New York: W. W. Norton.

Garofalo, R. 1998. "The association between risk behavior and sexual orientation among a school-based sample of adolescents." *Pediatrics* 101:895–902.

Garson, Barbara. 1975. *All the Livelong Day: The Meaning and Demeaning of RoutineWork.* New York: Penguin.
Gastil, John, and James P. Dillard. 1999. "Increasing political sophistication through public deliberation." *Political Communication* 16 (1):3–23.

Gartner, R. and M. Dawson. 2004. *Deviance and Crime. New Society: Sociology for the 21st Century.* R. J. Brym, Ed. Toronto: Thomson-Nelson:492–516.

Gavaler, Judith S. 1991. "Effects of alcohol on female endocrine function." *Alcohol Health & Research World* 15 (12):104–109.

Gazso-Windle, Amber, and Julie Ann McMullin. 2003 (Summer). "Doing domestic labour: Strategizing in a gendered domain." *Canadian Journal of Sociology.* Vol. 28, No. 3:341.

Gelles, Richard J., and Murray A. Straus. 1988. *Intimate Violence.* New York: Simon & Schuster.

Gellhorn, Martha. 1959. *The Face of War.* New York: Simon & Schuster.

Gentry, Cynthia S. 1991. "Pornography and rape: An empirical analysis." *Deviant Behavior* 12 (July–September):277–88.

Ghalam, N. Z. 1996. *Women in the Workplace* (2nd ed.). Ottawa: Statistics Canada. Catalogue No. 71-534.

Gibson, James William. 1994. *Warrior Dreams: Violence and Manhood in Post–Vietnam America.* New York: Hill and Wang.

Gidengil, E., N. Nevitte, A. Blais, P. Fournier, and J. Everitt. 2004 (Aug. 4). "Why Johnny won't vote." *The Globe and Mail.*

Gilbert, Sid, and Bruce Ork. 1993. "School leavers." *Canadian Social Trends* Winter:2–7.

Gilliard, Darrell K. 1999. *Prison and Jail Inmates at Midyear 1998.* Washington, DC: Government Printing Office.

Gilligan, J. 2001. "The last mental hospital." *Psychiatric Quarterly* 72:45–61.

Gilman, S. E., I. Kawachi, G. M. Fitzmaurice, and S. L. Buka. 2002. "Socioeconomic status in childhood and the lifetime risk of major depression." *International Journal of Epidemiology* 31:359–67.

Gimbel, Cynthia, and Alan Booth. 1994. "Why does military combat experience adversely affect marital relations?" *Journal of Marriage and the Family* 56 (August):691–703.

Gips, M. A. 1998. "Where has all the money gone?" *Security Management* 42 (February):32–6.

Glasbeek, H. J. 1996. "End the slaughter." *Canadian Dimension* 30(3)31–3.

Glasbeek, H. J. and E. Tucker. 1992. *Death by Consensus: The Westray Story.* Toronto: The York University Centre for Research on Work and Society.

Glicksman, L., A. Demers, E. Adlaf, B. Newton-Taylor, & K. Schmidt. (2000). *Canadian Campus Survey 1998.* Toronto: Centre for Addiction and Mental Health.

Glosser, G., et al. 2000. "Psychiatric aspects of temporal lobe epilepsy before and after anterior temporal lobectomy." *Journal of Neurological and Neurosurgical Psychiatry* 68 (1):53–8.

Gohm, Carol L., Shigehiro Oishi, Janet Darlington, and Ed Diener. 1998. "Culture, parental conflict, parental marital status, and the subjective well–being of young adults." *Journal of Marriage and the Family* 60 (May):319–34.

Golant, Stephen M., and Anthony J. La Greca. 1994. "Differences in the housing quality of white, black, and Hispanic U.S. elderly households." *Journal of Applied Gerontology* 13 (December):413–37.

Goldberg, Wendy A., Ellen Greenberger, Sharon Hamill, and Robin O'Neil. 1992. "Role demands in the lives of employed single mothers with preschoolers." *Journal of Family Issues* 13 (May):312–33.

Goldberger, Arthur S., and Charles Manski. 1995. "Review article: The Bell Curve by Herrnstein and Murray." *Journal of Economic Literature* 33 (June):762–76.

Golde, J. A., D. S. Strassberg, C. M. Turner, and K. Lowe. 2000. "Attitudinal effects of degrading themes and sexual explicitness in video materials." *Sex Abuse* 12:223–32.

Gomme, Ian. 1993. *The Shadow Line: Deviance and Crime in Canada.* Toronto: Harcourt Brace Jovanovich.

Gooden, Angela M., and Mark A. Gooden. 2001. "Gender representation in notable children's picture books: 1995–1999." *Sex Roles* 45:89–101.

Goodman, Marc. 2001. "Making computer crime count." *Law Enforcement Bulletin* 70:10–17.

Goodyear, Sarah. 2001. "Give me shelter." *Ms. Magazine*, April–May, pp. 38–42.

Gorin, T. 2000 (October). "Rohypnol—How the hype tricks women: A rape crisis centre view." *Canadian Woman Studies.*

Gorman, Christine. 1992. "Danger overhead." *Time* (October 26):70.

Gornick, Janet C., and Jerry A. Jacobs. 1998. "Gender, the welfare state, and public employment: A comparative study of seven industrialized countries." *American Sociological Review* 63 (October):688–710.

Gould, J. B. 2002. "Playing with fire: The civil liberties implications of September 11th" *PAR* 62:74–79.

Gove, Walter R., and Michael P. Geerken. 1977. "The effect of children and employment on the mental health of married men and women." *Social Forces* 56 (September):66–76.

Government of Canada. 1994 (October). Library of Parliament, *Current Issues Review: Prostitution.*

———. 2004. Homelessness. Online at http://www.homelessness.gc.ca/homelessness/index_e.asphttp://www.campaign2000.ca/rc/unsscMAY02/un4.html.

Goyette, Kimberly, and Yu Xie. 1999. "Educational expectations of Asian American youths." *Sociology of Education* 72 (January):22–36.

Graham-Bermann, Sandra A., and Alytia A. Levendosky. 1998. "Traumatic stress symptoms in children of battered women." *Journal of Interpersonal Violence* 13 (March):111–28.

Grant, B. F., and D. A. Dawson. 1998. "Age at onset of alcohol use and its association with DSM–IV alcohol abuse and dependence." *Journal of Substance Abuse* 9 (January):103.

Gray, G. C. et al. 2002. "Self–reported symptoms and medical conditions among 11,868 Gulf War–era veterans." *American Journal of Epidemiology* 155:1033–44.

Gray, Robert T. 1997. "Clamping down on worker crime." *Nation's Business*, April, pp. 44–45.

Green, Frank. 1997. "Rent–to–own stores assailed for interest rates." *San Diego Union–Tribune*, June 13.

Greenberg, Edward S., and Leon Grunberg. 1995. "Work alienation and problem alcohol behavior." *Journal of Health and Social Behavior* 36 (March):83–102.

Greenfeld, Lawrence A. 1998. *Alcohol and Crime.* Washington, DC: Government Printing Office.

Griffin, Kenneth W., Judith G. Rabkin, Robert H. Remien, and Janet B. W. Williams. 1998. "Disease severity, physical limitations, and depression in HIVinfected men." *Journal of Psychosomatic Research* 44 (February):219–27.

Gringlas, Marcy, and Marsha Weinraub. 1995. "The more things change . . . single parenting revisited." *Journal of Family Issues* 16 (January):29–52.

Grodsky, Eric, and Devah Pager. 2001. "The structure of disadvantage: Individual and occupational determinants of the black–white wage gap." *American Sociological Review* 66: 542–67.

Grogan, S., and H. Richards. 2002. "Body image: Focus groups with boys and men." *Men and Masculinities* 4:219–32.

Gross, D., A. Sambrook, and L. Fogg. 1999. "Behavior problems among young children in low–income urban day care centers." *Research in Nursing Health* 22 (February):15–25.

Gross, Jane. 1998. "In quest for the perfect look, more girls choose the scalpel." *New York Times*, November 29.

Grossman, A. 1997. "Growing up with a 'spoiled identity': Lesbian, gay and bisexual youth at risk." *Journal of Gay and Lesbian Social Services* 6(3):45–56.

Grossman, Arnold H., and Matthew S. Kerner. 1998. "Self–esteem and supportiveness as predictors of emotional distress in gay male and lesbian youth." *Journal of Homosexuality* 35 (1):25–39.

Grossman, Dan, and Seth Shulman. 1990. "Down in the dumps." *Discover*, (April):36–41.

Grunberg, Leon, Richard Anderson–Connolly, and Edward S. Greenberg. 2000. "Surviving layoffs." *Work and Occupations* 27 (February):7–31.

Guidubaldi, John, Joseph D. Perry, and Bonnie K. Nastasi. 1987. "Growing up in a divorced family: Initial and long–term perspectives on children's adjustment." In *Family Processes and Problems: Social Psychological Aspects*, S. Oskamp, ed., pp. 202–37. Beverly Hills, CA: Sage.

Gunn, R. A., et al. 1995. "Syphilis in San Diego County 1983–1992: Crack cocaine, prostitution, and the limitations of partner notification." *Sexually Transmitted Diseases* 22 (1):60–6.

Guo, Guang. 1998. "The timing of the influences of cumulative poverty on children's cognitive ability and achievement." *Social Forces* 77 (September):257–88.

Guo, J., J. D. Hawkins, K. G. Hill, and R. D. Abbott. 2001. "Childhood and adolescent predictors of alcohol abuse and dependence in young adulthood." *Journal of Studies on Alcohol* 62:754–62.

Gutierrez-Lobos, K. 2000. "The gender gap in depression reconsidered." *Social Psychiatry and Psychiatric Epidemiology* 35:202–10.

Hagerman, Erik. 1990. "California's drive to mass transit." *World Watch* (September–October):7–8.

Halcon, John J., and Maria de la Luz Reyes. 1991. " 'Trickle–down' reform: Hispanics, higher education, and the excellence movement." *Urban Review* 23 (June):117–35.

Haley, Robert W., Ann Matt Maddrey, and Howard K. Gershenfeld. 2002. "Severely reduced functional status in veterans fitting a case definition of Gulf War syndrome." *American Journal of Public Health* 92:46–47.

Hall, Holly. 1987. "The homeless: A mental–health debate." *Psychology Today* (February):65–66.

Hall, W., N. Solowij, and J. Lemon. The Health and Psychological Consequences of Cannabis Use, Chapter 5. National Drug Strategy Monograph Series No. 25. National Drug and Alcohol Research Centre. Prepared for the National Task Force on Cannabis. Online at http://www.druglibrary.org/schaffer/hemp/medical/ch5.htm.

Hallman, William K., and Abraham Wandersman. 1992. "Attribution of responsibility and individual and collective coping with environmental threats." *Journal of Social Issues* 48 (4):101–18.

Halpern-Felsher, B. L., and S. G. Millstein. 2002. "The effects of terrorism on teens' perceptions of dying." *Journal of Adolescent Health* 30:308–11.

Hammarstrom, Anne. 1994. "Health consequences of youth unemployment." *Social Science and Medicine* 38 (March):699–709.

Hannon, Lance, and James Defronzo. 1998. "The truly disadvantaged, public assistance, and crime." *Social Problems* 45 (August):383–92.

Hansell, Stephen, and Helene Raskin White. 1991. "Adolescent drug use, psychological distress, and physical symptoms." *Journal of Health and Social Behavior* 32 (September):288–301.

Hanson, Sandra L. 1994. "Lost talent: Unrealized educational aspirations and expectations among U.S. youths." *Sociology of Education* 67 (July):159–83.

———. 1996. "Gender, family resources, and success in science." *Journal of Family Issues* 17 (January):83–113.

Hardell, K. 2002 (September). Evicting Tent City: It's About Housing, Silly. Online at http://www.tdrc.net/tc-hardll.htm.

Hardesty, Patrick H., and Kathleen M. Kirby. 1995. "Relation between family religiousness and drug use within adolescent peer groups." *Journal of Social Behavior and Personality* 10 (1):421–30.

Hardin, Garrett. 1971. "The tragedy of the commons." In *Man and the Environment*, W. Jackson, ed., pp. 243–54. Dubuque, IA: Wm. C. Brown.

Harmless, Ann. 1990. "Developmental impact of combat exposure: Comparison of adolescent and adult Vietnam veterans." *Smith College Studies in Social Work* 60 (March):185–95.

Hart, Hornell. 1957. "Acceleration in social change." In *Technology and Social Change*, F. R. Allen et al., eds., pp. 27–55. New York: Appleton–Century–Crofts.

Hartley, Carolyn Copps. 1998. "How incest offenders overcome internal inhibitions through the use of cognitions and cognitive distortions." *Journal of Interpersonal Violence* 13 (February):25–39.

Harvey, E. B., and K. Reil. 2000. "An analysis of socioeconomic situation by ethnocultural groups, periods of immigration and gender for Canada and Toronto CMA, 1986, 1991, and 1996 compared." Online at http://ceris.metropolis.net/Virtual%20Library/economic/harvey2.htm.

Harvey, E. B., B. Siu, and K. D. V. Reil. 1999. "Ethnocultural groups, period of immigration and socioeconomic situation." *Canadian Ethnic Studies Journal.* Vol. 31, No. 3:95–106.

Hawkins, Dana. 1996. "Homeschool battles." *U.S. News and World Report* (February 12):28–29.

Hayman, Peter M., and Douglas J. Scaturo. 1993. "Psychological debriefing of returning military personnel: A protocol for post–combat intervention." *Journal of Social Behavior and Personality* 8 (5):117–30.

Haynie, Dana L., and Bridget K. Gorman. 1999. "A gendered context of opportunity: Determinants of poverty across urban and rural labor markets." *Sociological Quarterly* 40 (2):177–97.

Hayward, Mark D., and Melonie Heron. 1999. "Racial inequality in active life among adult Americans." *Demography* 36 (February):77–91.

He, Jiang, et al. 1999. "Passive smoking and the risk of coronary heart disease." *New England Journal of Medicine* 340 (March 25):920–26.

Health Canada. 2003. Best Practices: Methadone Maintenance Treatment. Online at http://www.hc-sc.gc.ca/hecs-sesc/cds/publications/methadone_treatment_best_practices/toc.htm.

———. 2004. The Social Determinants of Health: An Overview of the Implications for Policy and the Role of the Health Sector. Online at http://www.phac-aspc.gc.ca/ph-sp/phdd/pdf/overview_implications/01_overview_e.pdf.

Health Canada Performance Report. 2003 (March 31). Treasury Board of Canada Secretariat. http://www.tbs-sct.gc.ca/rma/dpr/02-03/HLTH-SANT/HLTH-SANT03DPR_e.asp?printable=True.

Health Indicators. 2003 (November). Vol 2003 No. 2. Statistics Canada: 82-221-XIE.

Heaney, Catherine A., Barbara A. Israel, and James S. House. 1994. "Chronic job insecurity among automobile workers: Effects on job satisfaction and health." *Social Science and Medicine* 38 (May):1431–37.

Hearn, James C. 1991. "Academic and nonacademic influences on the college destinations of 1980 high school graduates." *Sociology of Education* 64 (July):158–71.

Heilman, M. E. 2001. "Description and prescription: How gender stereotypes prevent women's ascent up the organizational ladder." *Journal of Social Issues* 57:657–74.

Heisz, A. and L. McLeod. 2004. Low Income in Census Metropolitan Areas, 1980–2000. Ottawa: Statistics Canada. Catalogue No. 89-613-MIE-No. 001.

Helfand, Ira. 1999. "Moving the world back from nuclear brink." *San Diego Union–Tribune*, October 18.

Helwig, Andrew A. 1998. "Gender-role stereotyping: Testing theory with a longitudinal sample." *Sex Roles* 38 (5–6):403–24.

Hendrix, Charles C., and Lisa M. Anelli. 1993. "Impact of Vietnam War service on veterans' perceptions of family life." *Family Relations* 42 (January):87–92.

Henning, Kris, Harold Leitenberg, Patricia Coffey, Tonia Turner, and Robert T. Bennett. 1996. "Long–term psychological and social impact of witnessing physical conflict between parents." *Journal of Interpersonal Violence* 11 (March):35–51.

Henry, William A., III. 1994. "Pride and prejudice." *Time* (June 17):54–59.

Herek, Gregory M., Roy J. Gillis, Jeanine C. Cogan, and Eric K. Glunt. 1997. "Hate crime victimization among lesbian, gay, and bisexual adults." *Journal of Interpersonal Violence* 12 (April):195–215.

Herlitz, A., and J. E. Yonker. 2002. "Sex differences in episodic memory." *Journal of Clinical and Experimental Neuropsychology* 24:107–14.

Herman, Didi. 1994. *Rights of Passage: Struggles for Lesbian and Gay Legal Equality.* Toronto: University of Toronto Press.

Herrnstein, Richard J., and Charles Murray. 1994. *The Bell Curve: Intelligence and Class Structure in American Life.* New York: Free Press.

Hersey, John. 1946. *Hiroshima.* New York: Alfred A. Knopf.

Hershberger, Scott L., Neil W. Pilkington, and Anthony R. D'Augelli. 1997. "Predictors of suicide attempts among gay, lesbian, and bisexual youth." *Journal of Adolescent Research* 12 (October):477–97.

Hertwig, Kim. 1999 (Spring/Summer). "Pay equity legislation in Canada: A study of the Public Services Alliance of Canada case." *Canadian Women's Studies.* Vol. 19, No. 2:186.

Hesse-Biber, Sharlene. 1996. *Am I Thin Enough Yet? The Cult of Thinness and the Commercialization of Identity.* New York: Oxford University Press.

Hetherington, E. Mavis. 1993. "An overview of the Virginia longitudinal study of divorce and remarriage with a focus on early adolescence." *Journal of Family Psychology* 7:39–56.

Hibbard, Judith H., and Clyde R. Pope. 1991. "Effect of domestic and occupational roles on morbidity and mortality." *Social Science and Medicine* 32 (7):805–11.

Hilmer. 2004. "The flag: Distinctively our own." The Canadian Encyclopaedia, Historical Foundation of Canada. Online at http://www.thecanadianencyclopedia. com/index.cfm?PgNm=ArchivedFeatures&Params=A276.

Hirschman, Robert S., Howard Leventhal, and Kathleen Glynn. 1984. "The development of smoking behavior: Conceptualization and supportive cross–sectional survey data." *Journal of Applied Social Psychology* 14 (May–June):184–206.

Hochschild. 1997. *Census of Canada, 2000.* Ottawa. Minister of Supply and Services.

Hogan, Richard, and Carolyn C. Perrucci. 1998. "Producing and reproducing class and status differences: Racial and gender gaps in U.S. employment and retirement income." *Social Problems* 45 (November):528–49.

Holahan, C. J., R. H. Moos, C. K. Holahan, R. C. Cronkite, and P. K. Randall. 2001. "Drinking to cope: Emotional distress and alcohol use and abuse." *Journal of Studies on Alcohol* 62:190–98.

Hollingshead, August B. 1949. *Elmtown's Youth.* New York: John Wiley & Sons.

Holmes, David T., Pierre N. Tariot, and Christopher Cox. 1998. "Preliminary evidence of psychological distress among reservists in the Persian Gulf war." *Journal of Nervous and Mental Disease* 186 (March):166–73.

Holmes, Thomas H., and Minoru Masuda. 1974. "Life change and illness susceptibility." In *Stressful Life Events,* B. S. Dohrenwend and B. P. Dohrenwend, eds., pp. 45–72. New York: John Wiley & Sons.

"Home Schooling." 2004. Online at http://www.fundy.net/ fplace/hmschl.htm.

Hong, Jinkuk, and Marsha Mailick Seltzer. 1995. "The psychological consequences of multiple roles." *Journal of Health and Social Behavior* 36 (December):386–98.

Horowitz, Janice M. 1999. "Bad news on formaldehyde." *Time,* January 18, p. 94.

Horwitz, Allan V., and Lorraine Davies. 1994. "Are emotional distress and alcohol problems differential outcomes to stress? An exploratory test." *Social Science Quarterly* 75 (September):607–21.

Hossler, Don, Jack Schmit, and Nick Vesper. 1999. *Going to College: How Social, Economic, and Educational Factors Influence the Decisions Students Make.* Baltimore, MD: Johns Hopkins University Press.

House, James S. 2002. "Understanding social factors and inequalities in health." *Journal of Health and Social Behavior* 43:125–42.

Householder, Joanne, Roger P. Hatcher, William J. Burns, and I. Chasnoff. 1982. "Infants born to narcotic–addicted mothers." *Psychological Bulletin* 9 (September):453–68.

Howard, George, et al. 1998. "Cigarette smoking and progression of atherosclerosis." *Journal of the American Medical Association* 279 (January 14):119–24.

Howell, James C. 1998. "Youth gangs: An overview." *Juvenile Justice Bulletin,* August.

HRSDC. 2004. Human Resources and Skills Development Canada. Government of Canada. http://www.hrsdc.gc.ca/ en/home.shtml.

Hsia, Heidi M., and Donna Hamparian. 1998. "Disproportionate minority confinement: 1997 update." *Juvenile Justice Bulletin,* September.

Huber, Joan, and William H. Form. 1973. *Income and Ideology.* New York: Free Press.

Hugick, Larry, and Jennifer Leonard. 1991. "Job dissatisfaction grows: 'Moonlighting' on the rise." *Gallup Poll Monthly*, no. 312 (September):2–15.

Hulchanski, J. D. 2002 (July). Can Canada Afford to Help Cities, Provide Social Housing, and End Homelessness? Why Are Provincial Governments Doing So Little? Notes for Discussion. University of Toronto: Centre for Urban and Community Studies.

Hunt, Geoffrey, Stephanie Riegel, Tomas Morales, and Dan Waldorf. 1993. "Changes in prison culture: Prison gangs and the case of the 'Pepsi generation.'" *Social Problems* 40 (August):398–409.

Hutchinson M. 2001 (November). "Crime Prevention through Healthy Communities and Early Intervention." Aboriginal Times Community. http://www.aboriginaltimes.com/culture/Document.2004-04-25.5146/view.

Hutchinson, Paul. 1962. *The Christian Century Reader*. New York: Association Press.

Hyde, J. S., and E. A. Plant. 1995. "Magnitude of psychological gender differences." *American Psychologist* 50 (March):l59–61.

Hyde, Janet Shibley. 1986. *Understanding Human Sexuality*, 3d ed. New York: McGraw–Hill.

Ickovics, Jeannette R., and Judith Rodin. 1992. "Women and AIDS in the United States: Epidemiology, natural history, and mediating mechanisms." *Health Psychology* 11 (1):1–16.

Illich, Ivan. 1975. "The alternative to schooling." In *Myth and Reality*, 2d ed. G. Smith and C. R. Kniker, eds., pp. 82–94. Boston: Allyn & Bacon.

Ingersoll, Sarah, and Donni LeBoeuf. 1997. "Reaching out to youth out of the educational mainstream." *Juvenile Justice Bulletin* (February).

Intergovernmental Panel on Climate Change. 2001. "Summary for policymakers." IPCC website.

International Civil Liberties Monitoring Group (ICLMG). 2004. In the Shadow of the Law (A report in Response to Justice Canada's 1st annual report on the application of the Anti-Terrorism Act, Bill C-36).

Ipsos-Reid/Globe and Mail/CTV Poll. 2001. http://www.ipsos-na.com/news/pressrelease.cfm?id=1163.

Isaac, Rael Jean, and Virginia C. Armat. 1990. *Madness in the Streets: How Psychiatry and the Law Abandoned the Mentally Ill*. New York: Free Press.

Jackson, A. 2002. "Is work working for workers of colour?" Research Paper #18, Canadian Labour Congress. Online at www.clc-ctc.ca.

Jackson, A. G. 2002 (April 22). The Costs of Drug Abuse and Drug Policy. Prepared for the Senate Special Committee on Illegal Drugs, Library of Parliament.

Jackson, Linda A., Donna A. Lewandowski, Julie M. Ingram, and Carole N. Hodge. 1997. "Group stereotypes: Content, gender specificity, and affect associated with typical group members." *Journal of Social Behavior and Personality* 12 (2):381–96.

Jackson, Pamela Braboy, and S. Mustillo. 2001. "I am woman: The impact of social identities on African American women's mental health." *Women's Health* 32:33–59.

Jackson, Pamela Braboy, Peggy A. Thoits, and Howard F. Taylor. 1995. "Composition of the workplace and psychological well–being: The effects of tokenism on America's black elite." *Social Forces* 74 (December):543–57.

Jackson, Tara, and Keith Reeves. 1994. "Stereotypes and segregation: Neighborhoods in the Detroit area." *American Journal of Sociology* 100 (November):750–80.

Jacobs, G. D. 2001. "The physiology of mind–body interactions." *Journal of Alternative and Complementary Medicine* 7:83–92.

Jacobs, John W. 1982. "The effect of divorce on fathers: An overview of the literature." *American Journal of Psychiatry* 139 (October):1235–41.

Jacobsen, Paul B., et al. 2002. "Predictors of posttraumatic stress disorder symptomatology following bone marrow transplantation for cancer." *Journal of Consulting and Clinical Psychology* 70:235–40.

Jaffe, J. H. 1985. "Drug addiction and drug abuse." In Eds. A. G. Gilman, L. S. Goodman, and F. Murad, *The Pharmacological Basis of Therapeutics* (7th ed.). USA: Macmillan.

Jaimet, K. 2001 (January 30). "90% of public backs protection of species: Pollster says support includes landowners who might be affected." *The Ottawa Citizen*.

Jamieson, Amie, Hyon B. Shin, and Jennifer Day. 2002. *Voting and Registration in the Election of November 2000*. Washington, DC: Government Printing Office.

Jan, Sung Joon, Steven F. Messner, and Scott J. South. 1991. "Predictors of interracial homicide victimization for Asian Americans." *Sociological Perspectives* 34 (Spring):1–19.

Jaret, Charles. 1991. "Recent structural change and US urban ethnic minorities." *Journal of Urban Affairs* 13 (3):307–36.

Jencks, Christopher. 1992. *Rethinking Social Policy: Race, Poverty, and the Underclass*. Cambridge, MA: Harvard University Press.

———. 1994. *The Homeless*. Cambridge, MA: Harvard University Press.

Jennison, Karen M., and Kenneth A. Johnson. 1998. "Alcohol dependence in adult children of alcoholics." *Journal of Drug Education* 28 (1):19–37.

Jensen, Arthur R. 1972. *Genetics and Education*. New York: Harper & Row. Jensen, Arthur R. 1980. *Bias in Mental Testing*. New York: Free Press.

Jimerson, Shane, Byron Egeland, L. Alan Stroufe, and Betty Carlson. 2000. "A prospective longitudinal study of high school dropouts." *Journal of School Psychology* 38:525–49.

Jin, R. L., C. P. Shah, and T. J. Svoboda. 1995. "The impact of unemployment on health." *Canadian Medical Association Journal* 153 (September 1):529–40.

Johal, A. 2004 (July 12). Urban Jungle: Vancouver's Safe Injection Site. Media Monitors Network. Online at http://usa.mediamonitors.net/content/view/full/11829.

John Howard Society. 2002 (August). "Conditions in Ontario Provincial Prisons: A Troubling Picture." Fact Sheet #18. http://www.johnhoward.on.ca/Library/Fctsheet/18/contents.htm.

Johnson, Bruce D., Eric D. Wish, James Schmeidler, and David Huizinga. 1991. "Concentration of delinquent offending: Serious drug involvement and high delinquency rates." *Journal of Drug Issues* 21 (Spring):205–29.

Johnson, Elizabeth S., and Barbara Vinick. 1981. "When an adult son or daughter divorces." *Journal of Divorce* 5 (Fall–Winter):69–77.

Johnson, Holly, and Valerie Pottie Bunge. 2001 (January). "Prevalence and consequences of spousal assault in Canada." *Canadian Journal of Criminology* 43(1): 27–45.

Johnson, Norman J., Paul D. Sorlie, and Eric Backlund. 1999. "The impact of specific occupation on mortality in the U.S. national longitudinal mortality study." *Demography* 36 (August):355–67.

Johnson, Robert A., and Dean R. Gerstein. 1998. "Initiation of use of alcohol, cigarettes, marijuana, cocaine, and other substances in U.S. birth cohorts since 1919." *American Journal of Public Health* 88 (January):27–33.

Jolin, Annette. 1994 (Nov. 2). On the backs of working prostitutes: Feminist theory and prostitution policy. *Crime and Delinquency* 40:69–83.

Jonas, Bruce S., and Ronald W. Wilson. 1997. "Negative mood and urban versus rural residence." National Center for Health Statistics website.

Jones, Diane C., and Renate Houts. 1992. "Parental drinking, parent–child communication, and social skills in young adults." *Journal of Studies on Alcohol* 53 (January):48–56.

Julian, Teresa W., Patrick C. McKenry, Stephen M. Gavazzi, and Julie C. Law. 1999. "Test of family of origin structural models of male verbal and physical aggression." *Journal of Family Issues* 20 (May):397–423.

Jull, Stephen. 2002 (Spring). Locating gender bias and systemic discrimination in public schooling bureaucracy. *Alberta Journal of Educational Research.* Vol.48, No. 1:47

Kalmijn, Matthijs. 1994. "Mothers' occupational status and children's schooling." *American Sociological Review* 59 (April):257–75.

Kalmuss, Debra. 1984. "The intergenerational transmission of marital aggression." *Journal of Marriage and the Family* 46 (February):11–19.

Kandel, Denise, Kevin Chen, and Andrew Gill. 1995. "The impact of drug use on earnings: A life–span perspective." *Social Forces* 74 (September):243–70.

Kang, Sung Yeon, Stephen Magura, and Janet L. Shapiro. 1994. "Correlates of cocaine/crack use among inner–city incarcerated adolescents." *American Journal of Drug and Alcohol Abuse* 20 (4):413–29.

Kant, Ashima K., Arthur Schatzkin, Barry I. Gaubard, and Catherine Schairer. 2000. "A prospective study of diet quality and mortality in women." *Journal of the American Medical Association* 283 (April 26):2109–15.

Kantor, Glenda K., and Murray A. Straus. 1989. "Substance abuse as a precipitant of wife abuse victimization." *American Journal of Drug and Alcohol Abuse* (June):173–89.

Kastelic, Robert L., and Kathleen McLinn. 1997. "Like china in the bull shop: Classroom accidents waiting to happen and downshifting into boredom." *SKOLE* 14 (Spring):15–21.

Kazanijian, Dr. A. 1998. "Understanding women's health through data development and data linkage: Implications for research and policy." *Canadian Medical Association Journal* 159:342.

Keane, Carl. 1998. "Evaluating the influence of fear of crime as an environmental mobility restrictor on women's routine activities." *Environment and Behavior* 30:60–74.

Kehoe, Monika. 1989. "Lesbians over 60 speak for themselves." *Journal of Homosexuality* 16 (3–4):29–78.

Kelly, Joan B. 1998. "Marital conflict, divorce and children's adjustment." *Child and Adolescent Psychiatry* 7 (April):259–71.

Kemf, Elizabeth. 1990. *Month of Pure Light: The Regreening of Vietnam.* London: Women's Press.

Kennedy, Joseph II. 1996. "Keynote address." In *Forced Labor: The Prostitution of Children.* Washington, DC: US Department of Labor—Bureau of International Labor Affairs.

Kershaw, Terry. 1992. "The effects of educational tracking on the social mobility of African Americans." *Journal of Black Studies* 23 (September):152–69.

Kessler, Ronald C., and Jane D. McLeod. 1984. "Sex differences in vulnerability to undesirable life events." *American Sociological Review* 49 (October):620–31.

Kessler, Ronald C., et al. 1994. "Lifetime and 12–month prevalence of DSM–III–R psychiatric disorders in the United States." *Archives of General Psychiatry* 51 (January):8–19.

Khattak, Sohail, et al. 1999. "Pregnancy outcome following gestational exposure to organic solvents." *Journal of the American Medical Association* 281 (March 24–31):1106–09.

Khoo L. 2004 (Nov. 25). "Up in Smoke? Canada's Marijuana Law and the Debate over Decriminalization." http://www.cbc.ca/news/background/marijuana/marijuana_legalize.html.

Kilpatrick, D. G., et al. 2000. "Risk factors for adolescent substance abuse and dependence." *Journal of Consulting and Clinical Psychology* 68:19–30.

Kim, Marlene. 2000. "Women paid low wages: Who they are and where they work." *Monthly Labor Review* 123:26–30.

Kim, Richard, Kane K. Nakamura, Gisele Fong, Ron Cabarloc, Barbara Jung, and Sung Lee. 1992. "Asian immigrant women garment workers in Los Angeles." *Amerasia Journal* 18 (1):69–82.

King, Charles E. 1989. "Homelessness in America." *Humanist* 49 (May–June):8.

King, Dwight Y. 1998a. "Qualifications of Indonesia's civil servants: How appropriate to the dynamic environment?" *Journal of Political and Military Sociology* 26 (Summer):23–38.

———. 1998b. "Reforming basic education and the struggle for decentralized educational administration in Indonesia." *Journal of Political and Military Sociology* 26 (Summer):83–95.

Kinnier, Richard T., Arlene T. Metha, Jeffrey L. Okey, and Jean Marie Keim. 1994. "Adolescent substance abuse and psychological health." *Journal of Alcohol and Drug Education* 40 (Fall):51–56.

Kinsey, A. C., W. B. Pomeroy, and C. E. Martin. 1948. *Sexual Behaviour in the Human Male.* Philadelphia: W.B. Saunders.

Kinsman, G, D. K. Buse, and M. Steedman. 2001 (July/August). Canadian State Surveillance: RCMP and spy on thousands of activists and unionists. *The CCPA.* http://www.policyalternatives.ca.

Kinsman, Gary. 2003. "Queerness is not in our genes: Biological determinism versus social liberation." In Deborah Brock, *Making Normal: Social Regulation in Canada.* Toronto: Thomson-Nelson:262–284.

Kipke, Michele D., et al. 1997. "Homeless youth and their exposure to and involvement in violence while living on the streets." *Journal of Adolescent Health* 20 (May):360–67.

Kitson, Gay C., Karen Benson Babri, and Mary Joan Roach. 1985. "Who divorces and why: A review." *Journal of Family Issues* 6 (September):255–93.

Kline, Marsha, Janet R. Johnston, and Jeanne M. Tschann. 1991. "The long shadow of marital conflict: A model of children's post–divorce adjustment." *Journal of Marriage and the Family* 53 (February):297–309.

Kluegel, James R. 1987. "Macro–economic problems, beliefs about the poor and attitudes toward welfare spending." *Social Problems* 34 (February):82–99.

———. 1990. "Trends in whites' explanations of the black–white gap in socioeconomic status, 1977–1989." *American Sociological Review* 55 (August):512–25.

Knoke, David, and Yoshito Ishio. 1998. "The gender gap in company job training." *Work and Occupations* 25 (May):141–67.

Kogevinas, M., et al. 1998. "Respiratory symptoms, lung function and use of health services among unemployed young adults in Spain." *European Respiratory Journal* 11 (June):1363–68.

Kolata, Gina. 1995. "Man's world, woman's world? Brain studies point to differences." *New York Times*, February 28.

Komarovsky, Mirra. 1940. *The Unemployed Man and His Family.* New York: Dryden Press.

Kopacsi, Rosemarie Capone. 1991. "Limited options for unemployed women." *International Journal of Sociology and Social Policy* 11 (1–3):51–67.

Koretz, Gene. 1997. "The downside of downsizing." *Business Week*, April 28.

Kozaryn, Linda D. 2002. "Bush says Saddam Hussein 'must be stopped.' " U.S. Department of Defense website.

Kozol, Jonathan. 1967. *Death at an Early Age.* New York: Bantam Books.

Krahn, H. J., and G. S. Lowe. 2002. *Work, Industry and Canadian Society* (4th ed.). Toronto: Thomson-Nelson.

Krajick, Kevin. 2001. "Long–term data show lingering effects from acid rain." *Science* 292:195–97.

Kreeger, Karen Young. 2002. "Deciphering how the sexes think." *Scientist*, January 21, pp. 28–33.

Kruks, Gabe. 1991. "Gay and lesbian homeless/street youth: Special issues and concerns." *Journal of Adolescent Health* 12 (November):515–18.

Kruttschnitt, Candace, Jane D. McLeod, and Maude Dornfeld. 1994. "The economic environment of child abuse." *Social Problems* 41 (May):299–315.

Kryzanek, Michael J. 1999. *Angry, Bored, Confused: A Citizen Handbook of American Politics.* Boulder, CO.: Westview.

Kuebli, Janet, and Robyn Fivush. 1992. "Gender differences in parent–child conversations about past emotions." *Sex Roles* 27 (December):683–98.

Kuhr, S., and J. M. Hauer. 2001. "The threat of biological terrorism in the new millenium." *American Behavioral Scientist* 44:1032–41.

Kunz, J. L., A. Milan, and S. Schetagne. 2000. "Unequal access: A Canadian profile of racial differences in education, employment and income." Canadian Council on Social Development. Online at http://www.ccsd.ca.

Kurdek, Lawrence A. 1990. "Divorce history and selfreported psychological distress in husbands and wives." *Journal of Marriage and the Family* 52 :701–08.

Kyriacou, Demetrios N., et al. 1999. "Risk factors for injury to women from domestic violence." *New England Journal of Medicine* 341 (December 16):1892–98.

Lacayo, Richard. 1998. "The new gay struggle." *Time* (October 26):32–44.

LaCroix, Andrea Z., et al. 1991. "Smoking and mortality among older men and women in three communities." *New England Journal of Medicine* 324 (June 6):1619–25.

Lamb, H. R. 1998. "Deinstitutionalization at the beginning of the new millennium." *Harvard Review of Psychiatry* 6 (May–June):1–10.

Lamb, H. R., and L. E. Weinberger. 1998. "Persons with severe mental illness in jails and prisons." *Psychiatric Services* 49 (April):483–92.

Lankoande, Salif, et al. 1998. "Prevalence and risk of HIV infection among female sex workers in Burkina Faso." *International Journal of STD and AIDS 9* (March):146–50.

LaPrairie, C. 1996. *Examining Aboriginal Correction in Canada*. Ottawa: Supply and Services Canada.

Latorre, Ronald A., and Kristina Wendenburg. 1983. "Psychological characteristics of bisexual, heterosexual, and homosexual women." *Journal of Homosexuality* 9 (Fall):87–97.

Lauer, Jeanette C., and Robert H. Lauer. 1986. *'Til Death Do Us Part: How Couples Stay Together*. New York: Haworth.

Lauer, Robert H. 1971. "The middle class looks at poverty." *Urban and Social Change Review* 5 (Fall):8–10.

———. 1974. "Rate of change and stress: A test of the 'future shock' thesis." *Social Forces* 52:510–16.

———. 1976. "Defining social problems: Public opinion and textbook practice." *Social Problems* 24 (October):122–30.

Lauer, Robert H., and Jeanette C. Lauer. 1983. *The Spirit and the Flesh: Sex in Utopian Communities*. Netuchen, NJ: Scarecrow.

———. 1988. *Watersheds: Mastering Life's Unpredictable Crises*. New York: Little, Brown.

Lauer, Robert H., and Jeanette C. Lauer. 1999. *Becoming Family: How to Build a Stepfamily that Really Works*. Minneapolis, MN: Augsburg.

———. 2003. *Marriage and Family: The Quest for Intimacy*. 5th ed. New York: McGraw–Hill.

Laumann, Edward O., Robert T. Michael, John H. Gagnon, and Stuart Michaels. 1994. *The Social Organization of Sexuality*. Chicago: University of Chicago Press.

Laurence, Leslie, and Beth Weinhouse. 1995. "Men get more respect in doctor's office." *San Diego Union– Tribune*, February 9.

Lautt, Ester. 1993. "Prostitution in the Prairie Provinces." In Ian Gomme, Ed. *The Shadow Line: Deviance and Crime in Canada*. Toronto: Harcourt Brace and Jovanovich: 289–299.

Law, William. 1906. *A Serious Call to a Devout and Holy Life*. New York: E. P. Dutton.

Lee, David J., Steve J. Niemcryk, C. David Jenkins, and Robert M. Rose. 1989. "Type A, amicability and injury: A prospective study of air traffic controllers." *Journal of Psychosomatic Research* 33 (2):177–86.

Lee, Matthew R., and Graham C. Ousey. 2001. "Size matters: Examining the link between small manufacturing socioeconomic deprivation and crime rates in nonmetropolitan communities." *Sociological Quarterly* 42:581–602.

Lehman, Wayne E. K., David J. Farabee, Melvin L. Holcom, and D. Dwayne Simpson. 1995. "Prediction of substance use in the workplace: Unique contributions of personal background and work environment variables." *Journal of Drug Issues* 25 (2):253–74.

Lehmann, Joan B., Christoph U. Lehmann, and Patricia J. Kelly. 1998. "Development and health care needs of lesbians." *Journal of Women's Health* 7 (April):379–88.

Leidholdt, Dorchen, and Janice G. Raymond. 1990. *The Sexual Liberals and the Attack of Feminism*. New York: Pergamon.

Lemonick, Michael D. 1996. "What's wrong with our sperm?" *Time*, March 18, pp. 78–79.

Lenski, Gerhard E. 1966. *Power and Privilege*. New York: McGraw–Hill.

Lenssen, Nicholas. 1993. "Providing energy in developing countries." In *State of the World 1993*, ed. L. Brown, pp. 101–19. New York: W. W. Norton.

Leonard, Rebecca, and Don C. Locke. 1993. "Communication steretypes: Is interracial communication possible?" *Journal of Black Studies* 23 (March):332–43.

Lesbian, Gay and Bisexual Youth Project. 2001. *Access Denied: Lesbian, Gay and Bisexual Youth and the Health Care System*. Halifax.

Leshner, Alan I. 1998. "Addiction is a brain disease– and it matters." *National Institute of Justice Journal*, October, pp. 2–6.

Leuchtag, Alice. 1995. "The culture of pornography." *Humanist* 55(3):4–6.

Levi, Margaret. 1998. "A state of trust." In *Trust and Governance*, V. Braithwaite and M. Levi, eds., pp. 77–98. New York: Russell Sage Foundation.

Levin, Benjamin. 1998 (August 20). Criticizing the Schools: Then and Now. *Education Policy Analysis Archives*. Vol. 6, No. 16:1–12

Lewis, Dorothy O., Richard Lovely, Catherine Yeager, and Donna Della–Femina. 1989. "Toward a theory of the genesis of violence: A follow–up study of delinquents." *Journal of the American Academy of Child and Adolescent Psychiatry* 28 (May):431–36.

Lewis, Ricki. 2002. "Race and the clinic: Good science?" *Scientist* 16 (February 18):16.

Li, P. 1996. Literature Review on Immigration: Bibliography on Sociological Perspectives. Prepared for Strategic Policy, Planning and Research, Metropolis Project. Ottawa: Citizenship and Immigration Canada. Online at http://www.yorku.ca/gmcr/race_gender_class/migration_files/Li1996.htm.

Lichter, Daniel T., and David J. Landry. 1991. "Labor force transitions and underemployment: The stratification of male and female workers." *Research in Social Stratification and Mobility* 10:63–87.

Lichter, S. Robert, Linda S. Lichter, Daniel R. Amundson, and Jessica M. Fowler. 1987. "The truth about Pravda: How the Soviets see the United States." *Public Opinion* (March–April):12–13.

Lii, Jane H. 1995. "Week in sweatshop reveals grim conspiracy of the poor." *New York Times*, March 12.

Linda A. Mooney, David Knox, Caroline Schacht, and Adie Nelson. 2001. *Understanding Social Problems: First Canadian Edition*. Toronto: Nelson.

Link, Bruce G. 1987. "Understanding labeling effects in the area of mental disorders: An assessment of the effects of expectations of rejection." *American Sociological Review* 52 (February):96–112.

Link, Bruce G. et al. 1989. "A modified labeling theory approach to mental disorders." *American Sociological Review* 54:400–23.

Link, Bruce G., Jerrold Mirotznik, and Francis T. Cullen. 1991. "The effectiveness of stigma coping orientations: Can negative consequences of mental illness labeling be avoided?" *Journal of Health and Social Behavior* 32 (September):302–20.

Linz, Daniel, and Neil Malamuth. 1993. *Pornography*. Newbury Park, CA: Sage.

Liptak, Adam, Neil A. Lewis, and Benjamin Weiser. 2002. "After Sept. 11, a legal battle on the limits of civil liberty." *New York Times*, August 4.

Liskow, B. I., et al. 2000. "Mortality in male alcoholics after ten to fourteen years." *Journal of Studies on Alcohol* 61:853–61.

Liu, Xiaoru, and Howard B. Kaplan. 1996. "Genderrelated differences in circumstances surrounding initiation and escalation of alcohol and other substance use/abuse." *Deviant Behavior* 17 (1):71–106.

Livingstone, D. W. 1998. *The Education–Jobs Gap: Underemployment or Economic Democracy*. Boulder, CO: Westview Press.

Locke, Steven, and Douglas Colligan. 1986. *The Healer Within: The New Medicine of Mind and Body*. New York: New American Library.

Lockhart, Lettie L., Barbara W. White, Vicki Causby, and Alicia Isaac. 1994. "Letting out the secret: Violence in lesbian relationships." *Journal of Interpersonal Violence* 9 (December):469–92.

Long, J. Scott. 1990. "The origins of sex differences in science." *Social Forces* 68 (June):1297–1315.

Long, Stephen H., and M. Susan Marquis. 1999. "Geographic variation in physician visits for uninsured children: The role of the safety net." *Journal of the American Medical Association* 281 (June 2):2035–41.

Longres, John F. 1991. "An ecological study of parents of adjudicated female teenage prostitutes." *Journal of Social Service Research* 14 (1–2):113–27.

Lopata, Helena Z. 1984. "Social construction of social problems over time." *Social Problems* 31 (February):249–72.

Loring, Marti, and Brian Powell. 1988. "Gender, race, and DSM–III: A study of the objectivity of psychiatric diagnostic behavior." *Journal of Health and Social Behavior* 29 (March):1–22.

Louie, Miriam Ching. 1992. "After sewing, laundry, cleaning and cooking, I have no breath left to sing." *Amerasia Journal* 18 (1):1–26.

Loveless, Tom. 1999. "Will tracking reform promote social equity?" *Educational Leadership* 56 (April):28–32.

Lovering, Daniel. 2001. "Taming the killing fields of Laos." *Scientific American*, August, pp. 67–71.

Low, Jason, and Peter Sherrard. 1999. "Portrayal of women in sexuality and marriage and family textbooks." *Sex Roles* 40 (3–4):309–18.

Lowman, John, Chris Atchison, and Laura Fraser. 1997. *Sexuality in the 1990's: Survey Results*. Vancouver, BC: British Columbia Ministry of the Attorney General.

Lowman, John. 1992. "Street prostitution." In Vincent Sacco, Ed. *Deviance: Conformity and Control in Canadian Society*. Toronto: Nelson.

———. 1995. "Prostitution in Canada." In Margaret Jackson and Curt Griffiths, *Canadian Criminology: Perspectives on Crime and Criminality*. Toronto: Harcourt Brace and Company.

Lucas, A. R. 2003. "Regulatory Legislation." In *Environmental Law and Policy*. 3rd ed. Elaine Hughes, Alastair R. Lucas, and William A. Tilleman, Eds. Toronto: Edmond Montgomery Publications Ltd.:163–213

Lundwall, R. A. 2002. "Parents' perceptions of the impact of their chronic illness or disability on their functioning as parents and on their relationships with their children." *The Family Journal* 10:300–307.

Lynch, John W., George A. Kaplan, and Sarah J. Shema. 1997. "Cumulative impact of sustained economic hardship on physical, cognitive, psychological, and social functioning." *New England Journal of Medicine* 337 (December 25):1889–95.

MacDonald, C. 2001 (May 4). "*This* Is What 'Democracy' Looks Like In Canada: The Case for Voting System Reform." *Context Newsletter*, CAW. Vol. 4, No.2.

MacEachern, Diane. 1990. *Save the Planet: 750 Ways You Can Help Clean Up the Earth*. New York: Dell.

Macionis, J. J., and L. M. Gerber. 2002. *Sociology*. Scarborough, ON: Prentice Hall.

Macionis, J. J., and L. M. Gerber. 2005. *Sociology*. 5th ed. Toronto: Pearson Prentice Hall.

Mack, John E., and Jeffrey Z. Rubin. 1991. "Is this any way to wage peace?" *Los Angeles Times*, January 31.

MacKay, Natalie J., and Katherine Covell. 1997. "The impact of women in advertisements on attitudes toward women." *Sex Roles* 36 (9–10):573–84.

Maclean's. 2003a (November 24). "Canada switchboard." Online at http://www.macleans.ca/switchboard/article.jsp?content=20031113_154913_3704.

————. 2003b. Online at http://www.macleans.ca/shared/print.jsp?content=200318_1302.

————. 2004. Online at http://www.macleans.ca/topstories/article.jsp? content =77548.

MADD. 2004. Mothers Against Drunk Driving. Online at http://www.madd.ca/home.html.

Maher, Timothy. 1998. "Environmental oppression." *Journal of Black Studies* 28 (3):357–67.

Maier, Timothy W. 1998. "Entrapping the whistleblowers." *Insight on the News*, February 2, pp. 8–12.

Malamuth, N. M., T. Addison, and M. Koss. 2000. "Pornography and sexual aggression." *Annual Review of Sex Research* 11:26–91.

Mallon, G. P. 1998. "Lesbian, gay and bisexual orientation in childhood and adolescence." In G. A. Appleby and J. W. Anastas, Eds., *Not Just a Passing Phase: Social Work with Gay, Lesbian and Bisexual People*. New York: Columbia University Press.

Mann, Arnold. 1998. "This place makes me sick." *Time*, December 21, pp. 38–40.

Marcon, Rebecca A. 1999. "Impact of parent involvement on children's development and academic performance." Paper presented at the Southeastern Psychological Association meeting.

Marini, Margaret Mooney, and Pi–Ling Fan. 1997. "The gender gap in earnings at career entry." *American Sociological Review* 62 (August):588–604.

Marks, Nadine F. 1995. "Midlife marital status differences in social support relationships with adult children and psychological well–being." *Journal of Family Issues* 16 (January):5–28.

Markward, Martha J. 1997. "The impact of domestic violence on children." *Families in Society* 78 (January–February):66–71.

Marsch, Lisa A. 1998. "The efficacy of methadone maintenance interventions in reducing illicit opiate use, HIV risk behavior and criminality." *Addiction* 93 (April):515–32.

Martell, Richard F., Christopher Parker, and Cynthia G. Emrich. 1998. "Sex stereotyping in the executive suite." *Journal of Social Behavior and Personality* 13 (1):127–38.

Martin, Christopher S., Patrick R. Clifford, and Rock L. Clapper. 1992. "Patterns and predictors of simultaneous and concurrent use of alcohol, tobacco, marijuana, and hallucinogens in first–year college students." *Journal of Substance Abuse* 4 (3):319–26.

Martin, J. K., A. Tuch-Steven, and P. M. Roman. 2003 (September). "Problem drinking patterns among African Americans: The impacts of reports of discrimination, perceptions of prejudice, and 'risky' coping strategies." *Journal of Health and Social Behavior*. Vol. 44, No. 3:408–25.

Martin, Jack K., and Paul M. Roman. l996. "Job satisfaction, job reward characteristics, and employees' problem drinking behaviors." *Work and Occupations* 23 (February):4–25.

Marullo, Sam. 1987. "The functions and dysfunctions of preparations for fighting nuclear war." *Sociological Focus* 20 (April):135–53.

Marzolini, M. 2001. "What do Canadians want from their government?" *Liberal Times*, http://www.pollara.ca/new/POLLARA_NET.html.

Matthies, E., R. Hoger, and R. Guski. 2000. "Living on polluted soil." *Environment and Behavior* 32:270–86.

Mayall, Alice, and Diana E. Russell. l993. "Racism in pornography." *Feminism and Psychology* 3 (2):275–81.

Mayer, E. A., M. Craske, and B. D. Naliboff. 2001. "Depression, anxiety, and the gastrointestinal system." *Journal of Clinical Psychiatry* 61:28–36.

Mayer, Susan E. 2001. "How did the increase in economic inequality between 1970 and 1990 affect children's educational attainment?" *American Journal of Sociology* 107:1–32.

Mazzeo, Suzanne E. 1999. "Modification of an existing measure of body image preoccupation and its relationship to disordered eating in female college students." *Journal of Counseling Psychology* 46 (January):42–50.

McAdams, Dan P., and Fred B. Bryant. 1987. "Intimacy motivation and subjective mental health in a nationwide sample." *Journal of Personality* 55:395–413.

McBroom, James R. 1992. "Alcohol and drug use by third, fourth, and fifth graders in a town of 20,000." *Sociology and Social Research* 76 (April):156–60.

McCabe, Marita P. 1987. "Desired and experienced levels of premarital affection and sexual intercourse during dating." *Journal of Sex Research* 23:23–33.

McCall, Leslie. 2001. "Sources of racial wage inequality in metropolitan labor markets." *American Sociological Review* 66:520–41.

McCarthy, Bill, and John Hagan. 1992. "Mean streets: The theoretical significance of situational delinquency among homeless youths." *American Journal of Sociology* 98 (November):597–627.

McCauley, Jeanne, et al. 1997. "Clinical characteristics of women with a history of childhood abuse." *Journal of the American Medical Association* 277 (May 7):1362–68.

McConkey, Dale. 2001. "Whither Hunter's culture war? Shifts in evangelical morality, 1988–1998." *Sociology of Religion* 61:149–74.

McDevitt, J., J. Balboni, L. Garcia, and J. Gu. 2001. "Consequences for victims: A comparison of biasand non–bias–motivated assaults." *American Behavioral Scientist* 45:697–713.

McFarland, J. 1980 (Autumn). "Changing Modes of Social Control in a New Brunswick Fishing Packing Town." *Studies in Political Economy*, Vol. 4: 99–113.

McFarlane, Judith, Pamela Willson, Ann Malecha, and Dorothy Lemmey. 2000. "Intimate partner violence." *Journal of Interpersonal Violence* 15 (February):158–69.

McFarlin, S. K., W. Fals–Stewart, D. A. Major, and E. M. Justice. 2001. "Alcohol use and workplace aggression." *Journal of Substance Abuse* 13:303–21.

McGinn, Anne Platt. 1999. "Charting a new course for oceans." In *State of the World 1999*, Lester R. Brown et al., eds., pp. 78–95. New York: W. W. Norton.

McIlwee, Judith S., and J. Gregg Robinson. 1992. *Women in Engineering*. Albany, NY: State University of New York Press.

McKeganey, Neil. l994. "Why do men buy sex and what are their assessments of the HIV–related risks when they do?" *AIDS Care* 6 (3):289–301.

McKenzie, H. 2004. "Taxation: The Martin record." *In Hell and High Water: An Assessment of Paul Martin's Record and Implications for the Future*. Ed. Todd Scarth. Ottawa: Canadian Centre for Policy Alternatives.

McKinlay, J. B. 1994. "The case for refocusing upstream: the political economy of illness." In *The Sociology of Health and Illness: Critical Perspectives*. Ed. P. Conrad. New York: St. Martin's Press: 509–23.

McLanahan, Sara, and Gary Sandefur. l994. *Growing Up with a Single Parent: What Hurts, What Helps*. Cambridge, MA: Harvard University Press.

McLauchlan, Gregory. 1991. "Does the nuclear arms race matter?" *Journal of Peace Research* 28 (August):325–30.

McLaughlin, Diane K., and C. Shannon Stokes. 2002. "Income inequality and mortality in U.S. counties." *American Journal of Public Health* 92:99–104.

McLeod, Jane D., and Kevan Edwards. 1995. "Contextual determinants of children's responses to poverty." *Social Forces* 73 (June):1487–516.

McLoyd, Vonnie C. 1998. "Socioeconomic disadvantage and child development." *American Psychologist* 53 (February):185–204.

McMenamin, Brigid, and Janet Novack. 1999. "The white–collar gestapo." *Forbes*, December 1, pp. 82–91.

McQuaid, J. R., et al. 2000. "Correlates of life stress in an alcohol treatment sample." *Addictive Behaviors* 25 (January–February):131–37.

McWhirter, David P., and Andrew M. Mattison. 1984. *The Male Couple: How Relationships Develop*. Englewood Cliffs, NJ: Prentice-Hall.

Mechanic, D., D. McAlpine, S. Rosenfield, and D. Davis. 1994. "Effects of illness attribution and depression on the quality of life among persons with serious mental illness." *Social Science and Medicine* 39 (July):155–64.

Mechanic, David, and Stephen Hansell. 1989. "Divorce, family conflict, and adolescents' well–being." *Journal of Health and Social Behavior* 30:105–16.

Meckler, Laura. 1998. "Blacks in America get sick more than whites, die sooner." *San Diego Union–Tribune*, November 27.

Mehio Sibai, A., N. Shaar Sameer, and S. el Yassir. 2000. "Impairments, disabilities and needs assessment among

non–fatal war injuries in South Lebanon, Grapes of Wrath, 1996." *Journal of Epidemiology and Community Health* 54 (January):35–39.

Mehren, Elizabeth. 1992. "Cues from the crib." *Los Angeles Times*, May 20.

Mellman, Mark, Edward Lazarus, and Allan Rivlin. 1990. "Family time, family values." In *Rebuilding the Nest: A New Commitment to the American Family*.

Menaghan, Elizabeth G. 1991. "Work experiences and family interaction proceses: The long reach of the job?" *Annual Review of Sociology* 17:419–44.

Mendelsohn, M. 2002 (June). "Canadians' Thoughts on Their Health Care System: Preserving the Canadian Model Through Innovation." A Review of Public Opinion Commission on the Future of Health Care in Canada. http://www.hc-sc.gc.ca/english/pdf/romanow/pdfs/MendelsohnEnglish.pdf.

Menke, E. M., and J. D. Wagner. 1998. "A comparative study of homeless, previously homeless, and never homeless school–aged children's health." *Issues in Comparative Pediatric Nursing* 20 (July–September):153–73.

Merin, Yuval. 2002. *Equality for Same-Sex Couples*. Chicago: University of Chicago Press.

Merton, Robert K. 1957. *Social Theory and Social Structure*. New York: Free Press.

Messing, K. 1984. *One-Eyed Science: Occupational Health and Women Workers*. Philadelphia: Temple University Press.

Michael, Robert, John H. Gagnon, Edward O. Lauman, and Gina Lokata. 1994. *Sex in America: A Definitive Study*. Boston: Little Brown.

Michalos, A. C., B. D. Zumbo, and A. Hubley. 2000. "Health and the quality of life." *Social Indicators Research* 51:245–86.

Mickelson, Roslyn Arlin. 2001. "Subverting Swann: Tracking as second generation segregation in Charlotte, North Carolina." *American Educational Research Journal* 38:215–52.

Milan, Anne. 2000 (Spring). *One Hundred Years of Families: Canadian Social Trends*. Ottawa: Statistics Canada. Catalogue No. 11.008:2–13.

Milbank, Dana. 1999. "The high cost of intervention." *New York Times Magazine*, May 2.

Millar, W. J., and T. K. Young. 2002. "Tracking diabetes: Prevalence, incidence and risk factors." *Health Reports* 14:3.

Miller, A. B., T. To, D. A. Agnew, C. Wall, and L. M. Green. 1996. "Leukemia following occupational exposure to 60–Hz electric and magnetic fields among Ontario electric utility workers." *American Journal of Epidemiology* 144 (July 15):150–60.

Miller, Brenda A., William R. Downs, and Dawn M. Gondoli. 1989. "Spousal violence among alcoholic women as compared to a random household sample of women." *Journal of Studies on Alcohol* 50 (November):533–40.

Miller, Jody, and Martin D. Schwartz. 1995. "Rape myths and violence against street prostitutes." *Deviant Behavior* 16 (January–March):1–23.

Millett, Kate. 1971. "Prostitution: A quartet of female voices." In *Woman in Sexist Society*, V. Gornick and B. K. Moran, eds., pp. 60–125. New York: Mentor Books.

Mills, C. Wright. 1956. *The Power Elite*. New York: Oxford University Press.

———. 1959. *The Sociological Imagination*. New York: Oxford University Press.

Milner, H. 2001 (July). "Civic literacy in comparative context: Why Canadians should be concerned." *Policy Matters*. Vol. 2, No. 2:7.

Mirowsky, John, and Catherine E. Ross. 1995. "Sex differences in distress: Real or artifact?" *American Sociological Review* 60 (June):449–68.

Misch, Ann. 1994. "Assessing environmental health risks." In *State of the World 1994*, Lester R. Brown et al., eds., pp. 117–36. New York: W. W. Norton.

Mitchell, A. 2004 (April 24). "Pesticides too harmful to use in any form, doctorswarn." *The Globe and Mail:*A1.

Mitchell, Arnold. 1983. *The Nine American Lifestyles*. New York: Macmillan.

Moen, Phyllis, and Yan Yu. 2000. "Effective work/life strategies." *Social Problems* 47:291–326.

Moen, Phyllis, Donna Dempster-McClain, and Robin M. Williams, Jr. 1989. "Social integration and longevity: An event history analysis of women's roles and resilience." *American Sociological Review* 54 (August):635–47.

———. 1992. "Successful aging: A life–course perspective on women's multiple roles and health." *American Journal of Sociology* 97 (May):1612–38.

Mollica, R. F., et al. 1994. "The effect of trauma and confinement on functional health and mental health status of Cambodians living in Thailand–Cambodia border camps." *Journal of the American Medical Association* 270 (August 4):581–86.

Molstad, Clark. 1986. "Choosing and coping with boring work." *Urban Life* 15 (July):215–36.

Monastersky, R. 1999. "China's air pollution chokes crop growth." *Science News*, March 27. Science News website.

Money, J. 1998. *Gay, Straight and In-Between: The Sexology of Erotic Orientation*. New York: Oxford University Press.

Montgomery, Mary Beth. 1989. "The decision to have children: Women faculty in social work." *Affilia* 4 (Summer):73–84.

Monto, Martin A. 2001. "Prostitution and fellatio." *Journal of Sex Research* 38:140–45.

Moore, C. 1996 (Oct./Nov.). "October and the historians (October crisis, 1970)." The Beaver. Vol. 76, No. 5:54.

Moore, E. G, M. W. Rosenberg, and D. McGuinness. 1997. Growing Old in Canada: Demographic and Geographic Perspectives. Ottawa: Statistics Canada: Catalogue No. 96-321-MPE, No 1:3.

Moore, John P., and Craig P. Terrett. 1999. "Highlights of the 1997 national youth gang survey." OJJDP Fact Sheet No. 97. Washington, DC: Government Printing Office.

Morissette R., X. Zhung, and M. Drolet. 2002 (February). *The Evolution of Wealth: Inequality in Canada, 1984–1999*. Working Paper No. 187. Business and Labour Market Analysis Division. Ottawa: Statistics Canada.

Moritsugu, Ken. 2001. "U.S. economy struggles to bear brunt of terrorism's costs." Knight Ridder/Tribune News Service, Knight Ridder/Tribune website.

Morrell, S. L., R. J. Taylor, and C. B. Kerr. 1998. "Unemployment and young people's health." *Medical Journal of Australia* 168 (March 2):236–40.

Morris, Joan. 1997. "Chronic homelessness among working–age adults." *Journal of Social Distress and the Homeless* 6 (January):57–69.

Morse, Jodie. 2002b. "Learning while black." *Time*, May 27, pp. 50–52.

Mukamal, K. J., and E. B. Rimm. 2001. "Alcohol's effects on the risk for coronary heart disease." *Alcohol Research and Health* 25:255–61.

Mullahy, John, and Barbara L. Wolfe. 2000. "Health policies for the nonelderly poor." *Focus* 21:32–37.

Myerson, Joel, Mark R. Rank, Fredric Q. Raines, and Mark A. Schnitzler. 1998. "Race and general cognitive ability." *Psychological Science* 9 (March):139–42.

Napoli, Maryann. 1998. "Hormone–disrupting chemicals." *HealthFacts*, November, p. 1.

National Center for Educational Statistics. 2001. *The Condition of Education 2001*. Washington, DC: U.S. Department of Education.

National Center for Health Statistics. 1998. "10 million Americans of all ages do not get enough to eat." Press release. NCHS website.

———. 2000. "Puerto Ricans' health fares worse than other U.S. hispanics." Press release. NCHS website.

National Center on Addiction and Substance Abuse at Columbia University. 1998. *Back to School 1998: The CASA National Survey of American Attitudes on Substance Abuse*. Washington, DC: National Center on Addiction and Substance Abuse.

National Clearinghouse on Family Violence, Ottawa: 2001:37.

———. 2003. Youth and Violence. Online at http://www.hc-sc.gc.ca/hppb/familyviolence/html/nfntsyjviolence_e.html.

National Coalition for the Homeless. 2000. *Welfare to What II?* Washington, DC: NCH.

National Council on Welfare. 2002. *Poverty Profile: 1999*.

National Institute on Alcohol Abuse and Alcoholism. 2001. *Alcohol: Getting the Facts*. Bethesda, MD: NIAAA.

National Institute on Drug Abuse. 1998. *Marijuana: Facts for Teens*. NIDA website.

National Victims Resource Center. 1991. *Juvenile Prostitution: Fact Sheet*. Rockville, MD: Victims Resource Center.

Neal, R. G. 2002 (May). *Voices: Women Poverty and Homelessness in Canada*. National Anti-Poverty Organization Study on Homelessness.

Neckerman, Kathryn M., and Joleen Kirschenman. 1991. "Hiring strategies, racial bias, and inner-city workers." *Social Problems* 38 (November):433–47.

Needle, Richard H., S. Susan Su, and William J. Doherty. 1990. "Divorce, remarriage, and adolescent substance use: A longitudinal study." *Journal of Marriage and the Family* 52:157–69.

Neria, Y., et al. 2000. "Posttraumatic residues of captivity." *Journal of Clinical Psychiatry* 61 (January):39–46.

Ness, Roberta B., et al. 1999. "Cocaine and tobacco use and the risk of spontaneous abortion." *New England Journal of Medicine* 340 (February 4):333–39.

Newman, D. 2001 (April). "Politics and the Press." CBC Newsworld. Online at http://www.cbc.ca/news/indepth/october/newman.html.

Newman, Richard J. 1998. "A U.S. victory, at a cost of $5.5 trillion." *U.S. News & World Report*, July 13.

Newton, Judith. 1998. "White guys: Hegemonic masculinities." *Feminist Studies* 24:11–20.

Nielsen, L. 1999. College aged students with divorced parents: Fact and fiction. *College Student Journal* 33:543–72.

Nijhof, Gerhard. 1995. "Parkinson's disease as a problem of shame in public appearance." *Sociology of Health and Illness* 17 (March):193–205.

Niskar, Amanda Sue, et al. 1998. "Prevalence of hearing loss among children 6 to 19 years of age." *Journal of the American Medical Association* 279 (April 8):1071–76.

Nixon, K., L. Tutty, P. Downe, K. Gorkoff, and J. Ursel. 2002. "The everyday occurrence: Violence in the lives of girls exploited through prostitution." *Violence against Women* 8:1016–43.

Noonberg, Aaron, Gerald Goldstein, and Horace A. Page. 1985. "Premature aging in male alcoholics: 'Accelerated aging' or 'increased vulnerability'?" *Alcoholism: Clinical and Experimental Research* 9 (July–August):334–38.

Norstrom, Thor. 1995. "The impact of alcohol, divorce, and unemployment on suicide: A multilevel analysis." *Social Forces* 74 (September):293–314.

Norstrom, T. 2001. "Per Capita Alcohol Consumption and All-Cause Mortality in 14 European Countries." *Addiction* 96(Supplement 1):S113–S128.

NSACSW 2002. "Family Violence in Canada: A Statistical Profile." Canadian Centre for Justice Statistics: Statistics Canada Catalogue No. 85-224-XIE2004000. http://www.statcan.ca/english/freepub/85-224-XIE/85-224-XIE2004000.pdf

O'Connor, R. E., R. J. Bord, B. Yarnal, and N. Wiefek. 2002. "Who wants to reduce greenhouse gas emissions?" *Social Science Quarterly* 83:1–17.

O'Keefe, Maura. 1994. "Linking marital violence, mother–child/father–child aggression, and child behavior problems." *Journal of Family Violence* 9 (March):63–78.

O'Neil, B. 2001. "Generational patterns in the political opinions and behaviour of Canadians." Montreal: Institute for Research on Public Policy. Vol. 2, No. 5.

Obach, B. K. 2002. "Labor–environmental relations." *Social Science Quarterly* 83:82–100.

Obot, I. S., F. A. Wagner, and J. C. Anthony. 2001. "Early onset and recent drug use among children of parents with alcohol problems." *Drug and Alcohol Dependence* 65:1–8.

Offord, D. R., M. H. Boyle, D. Campbell, P. Goering, E. Lin, M. Wong, and Y. A. Racine. 1996. "One-year prevalence of psychiatric disorder in Ontarians 15 to 64 years of age." *Canadian Journal of Psychiatry* 41:559–563.

Ohshige, K., et al. 2000. "Cross–sectional study on risk factors of HIV among female commercial sex workers in Cambodia." *Epidemiology of Infections* 124 (February):143–52.

Olds, D. L., C. R. Henderson, Jr., and R. Tatelbaum. 1994. "Prevention of intellectual impairment in children of women who smoke during pregnancy." *Pediatrics* 93 (February):228–33.

Olds, R. Scott, and Dennis L. Thombs. 2001. "The relationship of adolescent perceptions of peer norms and parent involvement to cigarette and alcohol use." *Journal of School Health* 71:223–28.

Oliver, Charles. 1995. "Defending pornography: Free speech, sex, and the fight for women's rights." *Reason*, April, pp. 3–6.

Oliver, Pamela. 2001. "Racial disparities in imprisonment." *Focus* 21:28–31.

Olson, Myrna R., and Judith A. Haynes. 1993. "Successful single parents." *Families in Society* 74 (April):259–67.

Ontario Human Rights Commission. 2004. Online at http://www.ohrc.on/english/consultations/racial-profiling-report_3.shtml.

Orbuch, T. L., J. Verogg, H. Hassan, and J. Horrocks. 2002. "Who will divorce: A 14–year longitudinal study of black couples and white couples." *Journal of Social and Personal Relationships* 19:179–202.

Organisation for Economic Co-operation and Development. 1991. *The State of the Environment*. Paris: OECD.

Ornstein, M. 1999. The Differential Effect of Income Criteria on Access to Rental Accommodation on the Basis of Age and Race: 1996 Census Results. CERA. Online at http://www.equalityrights.org/cera/docs/ornstein1999.html.

———. 2000 (May). Ethno-Racial Inequality in Toronto: Analysis of the 1996 Census. City of Toronto Research and Reports.

Ornstein, Michael, and Penni Stewart. 1996 (Fall). "Gender and faculty pay in Canada." *Canadian Journal of Sociology* 21(4):461–481.

Orsagh, Thomas, and Jong–Rong Chen. 1988. "The effect of time served on recidivism: An interdisciplinary theory." *Journal of Quantitative Criminology* 4 (June):155–71.

Ouweneel, P. 2002. "Social security and well–being of the unemployed in 42 nations." *Journal of Happiness Studies* 3:167–92.

Overpeck, Mary D., Ruth A. Brenner, Ann C. Trumble, Lara B. Trifiletti, and Heinz W. Berendes. 1998. "Risk factors for infant homicide in the United States." *New England Journal of Medicine* 339 (October 22):1211–12.

Oxman, Thomas E., Daniel H. Freeman, Jr., and Eric D. Manheimer. 1995. "Lack of social participation or religious strength and comfort as risk factors for death after cardiac surgery in the elderly." *Psychosomatic Medicine* 57 (January–February):5–15.

Padilla, Maria T. 1999. "Race violence leads to rise in anti–racism groups." *Salt Lake Tribune*, August 22.

Paige, Sean. 1998. "Babylon rides high–tech wave." *Insight on the News*, September 28.

Pammett, J. 1991. "Voter turnout in Canada." In *Voter Turnout in Canada*. H. Bakvis, Ed. Vol. 15 of the Research Studies for the Royal Commission on Electoral Reform and Party Financing in Elections Canada. Toronto: Dundurn: 39.

Parachini, Allan. 1988. "Study links women in agricultural counties with severe birth defects." *Los Angeles Times*, July 6.

Parker, Keith D. 1991. "Criminal victimization among black Americans." *Journal of Black Studies* 22 (December):186–95.

Parker, Robert E. 1994. *Flesh Peddlers and Warm Bodies: The Temporary Help Industry and Its Workers*. New Brunswick, NJ: Rutgers University Press.

Parker, S. 1996 (June 17). "Violence with a youthful face: Adolescent criminality explodes in Canada." *Alberta Report*. Vol. 23, No. 27:27–9.

Parkin, A. and M. Mendelsohn. 2003 (October 16). "A new Canada: An identity shaped by diversity." *Opinion Canada* 5(36). Online at http://www.cric.ca/en_html/opinion/opv5n36.html.

Parks, Michael. 1991. "Chernobyl." *Los Angeles Times*, April 23.

Pasley, K., J. Kerpelman, and D. E. Guilbert. 2001. "Gendered conflict, identity disruption, and marital instability." *Journal of Social and Personal Relationships* 18:5–27.

Pasley, Kay, and Carmelle Minton. 2002. "Generative fathering after divorce and remarriage: Beyond the disappearing dad." In T. F. Cohen (Ed.) *Men and Masculinity: A Text Reader*. Belmont, California: Wadsworth:239–48.

Patterson, Charlotte J. 2000. "Family relationships of lesbians and gay men." *Journal of Marriage and the Family* 62:1052–69.

Pear, Robert. 1993. "As AIDS money is parceled out, political questions." *New York Times*, February 7.

Peaslee, Alexander L. 1969. "Education's role in development." *Economic Development and Cultural Change* 17:293–318.

Pehar, Julie. 2003 (Spring/Summer). "E-brides: The mail-order bride industry and the internet." *Canadian Women's Studies*. Vol. 22, No. 3/4:171.

Peleg-Oren, N., and M. Sherer. 2001. "Cancer patients and their spouses." *Journal of Health Psychology* 6:329–38.

"People and the planet." 2003 (January 19). *The Guardian*. London: United Kingdom.

People for Education. 2004. "New funding rule raises many questions." Online at http://www.peopleforeducation.com/releases/2005/nov8_04.html.

Peplau, Letitia Anne. 1981. "What homosexuals want." *Psychology Today* (March):28–37.

Peretti, Peter O., and Anthony di Vitorrio. 1993. "Effect of loss of father through divorce on personality of the preschool child." *Social Behavior and Personality* 21:33–38.

Perkel, C. 2005. "Water Pollution Remains Chronic: More Than 1,000 Violations: Report. Harder Enforcement, Penalties Urged." *Toronto Star:*A10.

Perle, Richard. 1990. "Watching over defense: Cautions in the new climate." *American Enterprise* (May–June):31–34.

Perspectives Canada. 2001, Fall. In "Listening to Canadians: Communication Survey—Communication Canada." Catalogue No. PF4-7/2001-2. http://www.communication.gc.ca/survey_sondage/10/l2c_fall_2001.pdf.

Persson, K., J. Bengtsson, A. Kjeilberg, and S. Benton. 2001. "Low frequency noise 'pollution' interferes with performance." *Noise and Health* 4:33–49.

Pescosolido, Bernice A., Elizabeth Grauerholz, and Melissa A. Milkie. 1997. "Culture and conflict: The portrayal of blacks in U.S. children's picture books through the mid– and late–twentieth century." *American Sociological Review* 62 (June):443–64.

Peters, A. 2003. "Isolation or inclusion: Creating safe spaces for lesbian and gay youth." *Families in Society* 84(3):331–337.

Peterson, James L., and Nicholas Zill. 1986. "Marital disruption, parent–child relationships, and behavior problems in children." *Journal of Marriage and the Family* 48 (May):295–307.

Petoskey, Eva L., Kit R. Van Stelle, and Judith A. De Jong. 1998. "Family variables in substance–misusing male adolescents." *American Journal of Drug and Alcohol Abuse* 24 (1):61–84.

Petry, Nancy M., and Bonnie Martin. 2002. "Low–cost contingency management for treating cocaine– and opioid–abusing methadone patients." *Journal of Consulting and Clinical Psychology* 70:398–405.

Petterson, Stephen M., and Alison Burke Albers. 2001. "Effects of poverty and maternal depression on early child development." *Child Development* 72:1794–813.

Peugh, J., and S. Belenko. 2001. "Alcohol, drugs and sexual function." *Journal of Psychoactive Drugs* 33:223–32.

Pfaff, Donald, ed. 2002. *Hormones, Brain and Behavior*. San Diego, CA: Academic.

Pfefferbaum, B., et al. 2001. "Traumatic grief in a convenience sample of victims seeking support services after a terrorist incident." *Annals of Clinical Psychiatry* 13:19–24. Pfefferbaum, B., et al. 2002. "Exposure and peritraumatic response as predictors of posttraumatic stress in children following the 1995 Oklahoma City bombing." *Journal of Urban Health* 79:354–63.

Pfiffner, L. J., K. McBurnett, and P. J. Rathouz. 2001. "Father absence and familial antisocial characteristics." *Journal of Abnormal Child Psychology* 29:357–67.

Phelan, Jo C., Evelyn J. Bromet, and Bruce G. Link. 1998. "Psychiatric illness and family stigma." *Schizophrenia Bulletin* 24 (1):115–26.

Phillips, D. P., T. E. Ruth, and L. M. Wagner. 1993. "Psychology and survival." *Lancet* 342 (November 6):1142–45.

Phillips, P. and E. Phillips. 1993. *Women & Work: Inequality in the Canadian Labour Market*. Toronto: James Lorimer & Co.

Philp, M. 2000 (July 18). "Poor? Coloured? Then it's no vacancy: Housing discrimination rampant, says poverty report, despite fact that visible minorities are poised to become city's majority." *The Globe and Mail*.

Physicians for Human Rights. 2002. "War–related sexual violence in Sierra Leone." Physicians for Human Rights website.

Picard, A. 2004 (August 12). "We should admit that race matters in health care." *The Globe and Mail:*A15.

Pierce, John P., et al. 1998. "Tobacco industry promotion of cigarettes and adolescent smoking." *Journal of the American Medical Association* 279 (February 18):511–15.

Pierson, R. R. and M. G. Cohen. 1995. *Canadian Women's Issues, Volume II: Bold Visions, Twenty-five Years of Women's Activism in English Canada*. Toronto: James Lorimer & Company.

Pilcher, June J. 1998. "Affective and daily event predictors of life satisfaction in college students." *Social Indicators Research* 43 (March):291–306.

Pilippo, S., L. Mustaniemi, H. Lenko, R. Aine, and J. Maenpaa. 1999. "Surgery for ovarian masses during childhood and adolescence." *Journal of Pediatric and Adolescent Gynecology* 12 (November):223–27.

Pine, J. C., B. D. Marx, and A. Lakshmanan. 2002. "An examination of accidental–release scenarios from chemical–processing sites: The relation of race to distance." *Social Science Quarterly* 83:317–31.

Pinkleton, B. E., Y. Fujioka, and E. W. Austin. 2000. "The role of interpretation processes and parental discussion in the media's effects on adolescents' use of alcohol." *Pediatrics* 105:343–49.

Platt, Anne E. 1996. *Infecting Ourselves: How Environmental and Social Disruptions Trigger Disease*. Washington, DC: Worldwatch Institute.

Pollack, H. A. 2001. "Sudden infant death syndrome, maternal smoking during pregnancy, and the cost-effectiveness of smoking cessation intervention." *American Journal of Public Health* 91:432–36.

Pollard, C. Alec, Heidi J. Pollard, and Kathy J. Corn. 1989. "Panic onset and major events in the lives of agoraphobics: A test of contiguity." *Journal of Abnormal Psychology* 98 (August):318–21.

Polling Report, Inc. 2002. Polls. Polling Report website.

———. 1999. "Important trends in public opinion." Polling Report website.

Pollock, Cynthia. 1987. "Realizing recycling's potential." In *State of the World 1987*, Lester R. Brown, ed., pp. 101–21. New York: W. W. Norton.

Popenoe, David, and Barbara Dafoe Whitehead. 1999. *Should We Live Together?* Rutgers, NJ: National Marriage Project.

Portegies, Peter, and Nathalie R. Rosenberg. 1998. "AIDS dementia complex." *CNS Drugs* 9 (January):31–40.

Portraits of Canada. 2002. Centre for Research and Information on Canada (CRIC) Survey Conducted by Environics Research Group and CROP.

Potter, Lloyd B. 2001. "Influence of homicide on racial disparity in life expectancy–United States, 1998." *Journal of the American Medical Association* 286:1212.

Potterfield, James E., and Marjorie B. Pace. 1992. "Working class children and middle class schools: Teacher training to resolve this volatile combination." *Education* 113 (Fall):149–53.

Powell, William E. 1994. "The relationship between feelings of alienation and burnout in social work." *Families in Society* 75 (April):229–35.

Pratarelli, M. E., and B. J. Steitz. 1995. "Effects of gender on perception of spatial illusions." *Perceptual and Motor Skills* 80 (April):625–26.

Prentice, Alison, Paula Bourre, Gail Cuthbert Brandt, Beth Light, Wendy Mitchinson, and Naomi Black, Eds. 1988. *Canadian Women: A History*. Toronto: Harcourt, Brace, Jovanovich.

Prigerson, Holly G., Paul K. Maciejewski, and Robert A. Rosenheck. 2002. "Population attributable fractions of psychiatric disorders and behavioral outcomes associated with combat exposure among US men." *American Journal of Public Health* 92:59–63.

Prince, Diana A. 1986. "A psychological profile of prostitutes in California and Nevada." Unpublished Ph.D. dissertation, United States International University, San Diego, CA.

Profile of Families and Households: Diversification Continues. Online at www.statcan.ca.

Proposed Amendments to the National Defence Act: Backgrounder: Anti-terrorism Bill. Online at htttp://www.forces.gc.ca/site/newsroom/view_news_e.asp?id=299.

Quadagno, David, Dianne F. Harrison, K. G. Wambach, Philippa Levine, Allen Imershein, Joseph Byers, and Kim Maddox. 1991. "Woman at risk for human immunodeficiency virus." *Journal of Psychology and Human Sexuality* 4 (3):97–110.

Queen's Journal. 2004. "Bakan, Simpson discuss racial profiling." Online at http://www.queensjournal.ca/articlephp/point-vol131/issue21/news/story4.

Quillian, Lincoln. 1995. "Population, perceived threat, and prejudice in Europe." *American Sociological Review* 60 (August):586–611.

Radkowsky, Michael, and Lawrence J. Siegel. 1997. "The gay adolescent: Stressors, adaptations, and psychosocial interventions." *Clinical Psychology Review* 17 (2): 191–216.

Rainwater, L. 1967. "Crisis of the city: Poverty and deprivation." *Washington University Magazine* (Spring):17–21.

Raloff, J. 1999. "Formaldehyde: Some surprises at home." *Science News*, January 9, p. 22.

Ramstedt, M. 2002. "Are Suicide Rates in Canada Related to Changes in Alcohol Consumption? A Time Series Analysis of Postwar Experience." Paper presented at the Seminar: Canadian Alcohol Experiences & Nordic Perspectives. December 12–13, 2002, Voksenasen Hotel, Oslo.

Rank, Mark Robert. 1994. *Living on the Edge: The Realities of Welfare in America*. New York: Columbia University Press.

———. 2001. "The effect of poverty on America's families." *Journal of Family Issues* 22:881–903.

Rankin, Jim, Jennifer Quinn, Michelle Shephard, Scott Simmie, and John Duncanson. 2002 (October 19). "Singled Out: An Investigation into Race and Crime." *Toronto Star:*A1.

Rankin, Joseph H., and Roger M. Kern. 1994. "Parental attachments and delinquency." *Criminology* 32 (November):495–515.

Ranson, G. 2001. "Men at work: Change–or no change?–in the era of the 'new father.'" *Men and Masculinities* 4:3–26.

Ratnesar, Romesh. 2002. "Revenge: Arafat–and why the rage keeps burning." *Time*, April 8.

Ray, Brian D. 1999. *Home Schooling on the Threshold*. Salem, OR: National Home Education Research Institute.

Ray, JoAnn. 1990. "Interactional patterns and marital satisfaction among dual–career couples." *Journal of Independent Social Work* 4:61–73.

RCMP. 2004. http://www.rcmp.ca/scams/index_e.htm.

Rearden, John J., and Becky S. Markwell. 1989. "Self concept and drinking problems of college students raised in alcohol–abused homes." *Addictive Behaviors* 14 (2):225–27.

Rehnquist, William H. 1998. *All the Laws but One: Civil Liberties in Wartime*. New York: Alfred A. Knopf.

Reichman, Lee, and Janice Hopkins Tanne. 2001. *Timebomb: The Global Epidemic of Multi–Drug Resistant Tuberculosis*. New York: McGraw–Hill.

Reid, Jeanne, Peggy Macchetto, and Susan Foster. 1999. *No Safe Haven: Children of Substance–Abusing Parents*. Washington, DC: National Center on Addiction and Substance Abuse.

Reilly, Dennis M. 1984. "Family therapy with adolescent drug abusers and their families: Defying gravity and achieving escape velocity." *Journal of Drug Issues* 14 (Spring):381–91.

Reinhardt, James M., Paul Meadows, and John M. Gillette. 1952. *Social Problems and Social Policy*. New York: American Book.

Reinherz, H. A., R. M. Giaconia, A. M. Hauf, M. S. Wasserman, and A. D. Paradis. 2000. "General and specific childhood risk factors for depression and drug disorders by early adulthood." *Journal of the American Academy of Child Adolescent Psychiatry* 39 (February):223–31.

Relyea, H. C. 2002. "The law: Homeland security." *Presidential Studies Quarterly* 32:397–411.

Renner, Michael. 1991. "Military victory, ecological defeat." *World Watch* July–August):27–34.

———. 1993. *Critical Juncture: The Future of Peacekeeping*. Washington, DC: Worldwatch Institute.

———. 1994. *Budgeting for Disarmament: The Costs of War and Peace*. Washington, DC: Worldwatch Institute.

———. 1997. *Small Arms, Big Impact*. Washington, DC: Worldwatch Institute.

———. 1999. "Ending violent conflict." In *State of the World 1999*, Lester R. Brown et al., eds., pp. 151–68. New York: W. W. Norton.

———. 2001. "Military trends." In *Vital Signs: 2001*, Worldwatch Institute, pp. 81–87. New York: W. W. Norton.

———. 2002. "Breaking the link between resources and repression." In *State of the World 2002*, Linda Starke, ed., pp. 149–73. New York: W. W. Norton.

Report Card on Child Poverty in Canada. 2004. "One Million Too Many: Implementing Solutions to Child Poverty in Canada." Campaign 2000. http://www.campaign2000.ca/rc/rc04/04NationalReportCard.pdf.

Report on Mental Illness in Canada. 2002. Ottawa: Health Canada. Online at http://www.phac-aspc.gc.ca/publicat/miic-mmac/pdf/men_ill_e.pdf.

Reskin, Barbara. 1998. *The Realities of Affirmative Action in Employment*. Washington, DC: American Sociological Association.

Resnick, Michael D., et al. 1997. "Protecting adolescents from harm." *Journal of the American Medical Association* 278 (September 10):823–32.

Revelle, Roger. 1971. "Pollution and cities." In *The Survival Equation: Man, Resources, and His Environment*, R. Revelle, A. Khosla, and M. Vinovskis, eds., pp. 382–414. Boston: Houghton Mifflin.

Revicki, Dennis A., and Harold J. May. 1989. "Organizational characteristics, occupational stress, and mental health in nurses." *Behavioral Medicine* 15 (Spring):30–36.

Revkin, Andrew C. 1989. "Crack in the cradle." Discover (September):62–69.

Reynal-Querol, M. 2002. "Ethnicity, political systems, and civil wars." *Journal of Conflict Resolution* 46:29–54.

Reynolds, John R., and Catherine E. Ross. 1998. "Social stratification and health: Education's benefit beyond economic status and social origins." *Social Problems* 45 (May):221–45.

Ricchiardi, Sherry. 1998. "Double vision." *American Journalism Review* 20 (3):30–36.

Riccucci, Norma M., and Judith R. Saidel. 1997. "The representativeness of state–level bureaucratic leaders." *Public Administration Review* 57 (September–October):423–30.

Rice, Robert W., Michael R. Frone, and Dean B. McFarlin. 1992. "Work–nonwork conflict and the perceived quality of life." *Journal of Organizational Behavior* 13 (March):155–68.

Richards, Marcus, R. Hardy, and M. Wadsworth. 1997. "The effects of divorce and separation on mental health in a national U.K. birth cohort." *Psychological Medicine* 27:1121–28.

Richardson, J. W. 2002. "Poor, powerless and poisoned." *Journal of Children and Poverty* 8: 141–57.

Rinehart, J. W. 1978. "Contradictions of work-related attitudes and behaviour: An Interpretation." *Canadian Review of Sociology and Anthropology* 13:1.

———. 2001. *The Tyranny of Work: Alienation and Labour Process* (4th ed.). Toronto: Thomson-Nelson.

Rivara, and Thomas D. Koepsell. 1997. "State gun safe storage laws and child mortality due to firearms." *Journal of the American Medical Association* 278 (October 1):1084–86.

Roberts, J. Timmons. 1993. "Psychosocial effects of workplace hazardous exposures: Theoretical synthesis and preliminary findings." *Social Problems* 40 (February):74–89.

Roberts, J. V. 2001 (November). Fear of Crime and Attitudes to Criminal Justice in Canada: A Review of Recent Trends 2001–02. Ottawa: Report for the Ministry of the Solicitor General Canada. Online at http://www.psepc-sppcc.gc.ca/publications/corrections/pdf/FearOf Crime_e.pdf.

Roberts, Les, Riy Abhi Afta, Richard Garfield, Jamal Khudhairi, Gilbert Burnham. 2004 (November 20). *Lancet Report on Iraqi Mortality*. Vol. 364:112–148.

Robins, Lee N., and Darrel A. Regier. 1991. *Psychiatric Disorders in America*. New York: Free Press.

Robinson, P. 2003. Adult Criminal Court Statistics, 2001–02. *Juristat* Volume 23, Number 2.

Robinson, John, and Geoffrey Godbey. 1997. *Time for Life: The Surprising Way Americans Use Their Time*. University Park: Pennsylvania State University Press.

Rodgers, Joann Ellison. 1994. "Addiction–A whole new view." *Psychology Today*, September–October, pp. 32–39.

Rodriguez, E. 2001. "Keeping the unemployed healthy." *American Journal of Public Health* 91: 1403–11.

Roese, N. J. 2002. "Canadians' Shrinking Trust in Government: Causes and Consequences." In *Value Change and Governance in Canada*. Neil Nevitte, Ed. Toronto: University of Toronto Press.

Rogers-Dillon, Robin. 1995. "The dynamics of welfare stigma." *Qualitative Sociology* 18 (4):439–56.

Rogge, R. D., and T. N. Bradbury. 1999. "Till violence does us part." *Journal of Consulting and Clinical Psychology* 67 (June):340–51.

Rohrlich, Ted. 1990. "Attorneys report big jump in drinking in ABA survey." *Los Angeles Times*, December 5.

Rolland, John S. 1987. "Chronic illness and the life cycle: A conceptual framework." *Family Process* 26 (2):203–21.

Romanow, R. 2002 (November). Building on Values: The Future of Health Care in Canada. Ottawa: Commission on the Future of Health Care in Canada. Catalogue No. CP32-85/2002E-IN.

Romo, Harriett D. 1999. "Tracking programs derail minority and disadvantaged students' success." *Community College Journal* 69 (January):12–17.

Roodman, David Malin. 1999. "Building a sustainable society." In *State of the World 1999*, ed. Lester R. Brown et al., pp. 169–88. New York: W. W. Norton.

Rorabaugh, W. J. 1979. The Alcoholic Republic: *An American Tradition*. New York: Oxford University Press.

Roscoe, Bruce, and John E. Callahan. 1985. "Adolescents' self–report of violence in families and dating relations." *Adolescence* 20 (Fall):545–53.

Rosenbaum, Emily, and Denise B. Kandel. 1990. "Early onset of adolescent sexual behavior and drug involvement." *Journal of Marriage and the Family* 52 (August):783–98.

Rosenberg, Debra. 2002. "Stem cells: Slow progress." *Newsweek*, August 12.

Rosenblum, Jonathan D. 1995. *Copper Crucible: How the Arizona Miners' Strike of 1983 Recast Labor–Management Relations in America*. Ithaca, NY: ILR Press.

Rosenfeld, Richard. 2002. "Crime decline in context." *Contexts* 1:25–34.

Rosenfield, Sarah. 1997. "Labeling mental illness: The effects of received services and perceived stigma on life satisfaction." *American Sociological Review* 62 (August):660–72.

Rosenman, Ray H. 1990. "Type A behavior pattern: A personal overview." *Journal of Social Behavior and Personality* 5 (1):1–24.

Rosenthal, Neal H. 1989. "More than wages at issue in job quality debate." *Monthly Labor Review* 112 (December):4–8.

Rosenthal, Robert, and Lenore Jacobson. 1968. "Self fulfilling prophecies in the classroom: Teachers' expectations as unintended determinants of pupils' 0 intellectual competence." In *Social Class, Race, and Psychological Development*, M. Deutsch, I. Katz, and A. R. Jensen, eds., pp. 219–53. New York: Holt, Rinehart and Winston.

Ross, Catherine E., John Mirowsky, and Joan Huber. 1983. "Dividing work, sharing work, and in–between: Marriage patterns and depression." *American Sociological Review* 48 (December):809–23.

Ross, D. P., K. J. Scott, and P. J. Smith. 2000. *The Canadian Fact Book on Poverty*. Canadian Council on Social Development. Ottawa: Renouf Books. Excerpt online at http://www.ccsd.ca/pubs/2000/fbpov00/1-intro.htm.

Rossow, I. 2002a. "Alcohol Consumption and Homicides in Canada, 1950–1999." Paper presented at the Seminar: Canadian Alcohol Experiences & Nordic Perspectives. December 12–13, 2002, Voksenasen Hotel, Oslo.

Rossow, I. 2001b. "Alcohol and Homicide: A Cross-Cultural Comparison of the Relationship in 14 European Countries." *Addiction* 96(Supplement 1):S77–S92.

Rudd, J. M., and S. D. Herzberger. 1999. "Brother–sister incest–father–daughter incest: A comparison of characteristics and consequences." *Child Abuse and Neglect* 23 (September):915–28.

Rudner, Lawrence M. 1999. "Scholastic achievement and demographic characteristics of home school students in 1998." *Education Policy Analysis Archives* 7 (8):1–39.

Russell, Diana E. H. 1986. *The Secret Trauma: Incest in the Lives of Girls and Women*. New York: Basic Books.

———. 1998. *Dangerous Relationships: Pornography, Misogyny, and Rape*. Newbury Park, CA: Sage.

Rutter, Peter. 1989. *Sex in the Forbidden Zone: When Men in Power–Therapists, Doctors, Clergy, Teachers and Others–Betray Womens' Trust*. Los Angeles: Jeremy P. Tarcher.

Ryan, C., and D. Futterman. 1997. *Lesbian and Gay Youth: Care and Counseling*. Philadelphia: Hanley and Belfus.

Ryan, William. 1971. *Blaming the Victim*. New York: Pantheon Books.

Saad, Lydia, and Frank Newport. 2001. "Blacks and whites differ about treatment of blacks in America today." *Gallup Poll Monthly*, no. 430, pp. 58–63.

Sacco. 1992. *Crime Counts: A Criminal Events Analysis*. Toronto: Nelson.

Sadker, Myra, and David Sadker. 1994. *Failing at Fairness: How America's Schools Cheat Girls*. New York: Charles Scribner's Sons.

Salamon, E. D. and B. W. Robinson (Eds.). *Gender Roles: Doing What Comes Naturally*. Toronto: Methuen.

Samaan, R. A. 2000. "The influences of race, ethnicity, and poverty on the mental health of children." *Journal of Health Care for the Poor and Underserved* 11 (February):100–10.

Sampat, Payal. 2000. *Deep Trouble: The Hidden Threat of Groundwater Pollution*. Washington, DC: Worldwatch Institute.

Sanford, Kathy, and Heather Blair. 1999 (Spring). "TV and zines: Media and the construction of gender for early adolescents." *Alberta Journal of Educational Research*. Vol. No. 3:103.

Sang, Barbara, Joyce Warshow, and Adrienne J. Smith, eds. 1991. *Lesbians at Midlife: The Creative Transition*. San Francisco: Spinsters.

Sarlo, C. A. 2001. Measuring Poverty in Canada. Critical Issues Bulletin, Fraser Institute.

Sashkin, Marshall. 1984. "Participative management is an ethical imperative." *Organizational Dynamics* 12 (4):5–22.

Satzewcih, V. 1998. *Racism and Social Inequality in Canada: Concepts, Controversies and Strategies of Resistance*. Toronto: Thompson Educational Publishing.

Savitz, David A., Elizabeth A. Whelan, and Robert C. Kleckner. 1989. "Self–reported exposure to pesticides and radiation related to pregnancy outcome– Results from national natality and fetal mortality surveys." *Public Health Reports* 104 (September–October):473–77.

Savoie, J. 2003. "Homicide in Canada, 2002." *Juristat* Volume 23, Number 8.

Scheff, Thomas. 1966. *Being Mentally Ill*. Chicago: Aldine.

Scher, Richard K. 1997. The Modern Political Campaign. New York: M. E. Sharpe.

Scherer, Jacqueline, and Edward Slawski. 1981. "Desegregation: Advantages to whites." *Urban Review* 13 (Winter):217–25.

Schlosser, Eric. 1997. "The business of pornography." *U.S. News and World Report*, February 10.

Schmidt, Gregory L. 1989. "Reversible mental illness: The role of the family in therapeutic context." *Journal of Psychotherapy and the Family* 5 (1–2):89–96.

Schmitt, Eric. 1999a. "It costs a lot more to kill fewer people." *New York Times*, May 2.

———. 1999b. "Arms control is dying. Unless it's reviving." *New York Times*, September 5.

Schnake, Mel E., Stephen C. Bushardt, and Curran Spottswood. 1984. "Internal work motivation and intrinsic job satisfaction: The effects of goal clarity, goal difficulty, participation in goal setting, and task complexity." *Group & Organization Studies* 9 (June):201–19.

Schulman, Kevin A., et al. 1999. "The effect of race and sex on physicians' recommendations for cardiac catheterization." *New England Journal of Medicine* 340 (February 25):618–26.

Schwarez, Sandra K., and George W. Rutherford. 1989. "Acquired immunodeficiency syndrome in infants, children and adolescents." *Journal of Drug Issues* 19 (Winter):79–92.

Schwartz, Felice N. 1989. "Management women and the new facts of life." *Harvard Business Review* 67 (January–February):64–76.

Scott, Daniel. 1999. "Equal opportunity, unequal results." *Environment and Behavior* 31 (March):267–90.

Scott, Janny. 1990a. "Job–related illness called America's invisible killer." *Los Angeles Times*, August 31.

———. 1990b. "Parents' smoking linked to children's lung cancer." *Los Angeles Times*, September 6.

Scott, K. and R. Lessard. 2004. Income Inequality as a Determinant of Health. Online at http://www.hc-sc.gc.ca/hppb/phdd/overview_implications/02_income.html.

Scott, William A., Ruth Scott, and Morag McCabe. 1991. "Family relationships and children's personality: A cross–cultural, cross–source comparison." *British Journal of Social Psychology* 30 (March):1–20.

Seccombe, Karen, Kimberly Battle Walters, and Delores James. 1999. " 'Welfare mothers' welcome reform, urge compassion." *Family Relations* 48 (April):197–206.

Seeman, Melvin, Alice Z. Seeman, and Art Budros. 1988 (September). "Powerlessness, work, and community: A longitudinal study of alienation and alcohol use." *Journal of Health and Social Behavior* 29:185–98.

Segall, A., and N. L. Chappell. 2000. *Health and Health Care in Canada*. Toronto: Prentice Hall.

Seivewright, N. 1987. "Relationship between life events and personality in psychiatric disorder." *Stress Medicine* 3 (July–September):163–68.

Selke, William L., and Harold E. Pepinsky. 1982. "The politics of police reporting in Indianapolis, 1948–1978." *Law & Human Behavior* 6 (3–4):327–42.

Sell, R. L., J. A. Wells, and D. Wypij. 1995. "The prevalence of homosexual behavior and attraction in the United States, the United Kingdom and France: Results of national population–based samples." *Archives of Sexual Behavior* 24 (June):235–48.

Semple, S. J., T. L. Patterson, and I. Grant. 2002. "Gender differences in the sexual risk practices of HIV+ heterosexual men and women." *AIDS and Behavior* 6:45–54.

Senn, Charlene Y., and H. Lorraine Radtke. 1990. "Women's evaluations of and affective reactions to mainstream violent pornography, nonviolent pornography, and erotica." *Violence and Victims* 5 (3):143–55.

Sennett, Richard, and Jonathan Cobb. 1972. *The Hidden Injuries of Class*. New York: Vintage Books.

Shanker, Albert. 1990. "A proposal for using incentives to restructure our public schools." *Phi Kappa Delta* 71 (January):345–57.

———. 1993. "The debate on grouping." *New York Times*, January 31.

———. 1994. "A major accomplishment." *New York Times*, April 24.

Shapiro, Bruce. 1997. "When justice kills." *The Nation*, June 9.

Shaw, Daron R. 1999. "The effect of TV ads and candidate appearances on statewide presidential votes, 1988–96." *American Political Science Review* 93 (June):345–58.

Shehan, Constance L., Mary Ann Burg, and Cynthia A. Rexroat. 1986. "Depression and the social dimensions of the full-time housewife role." *Sociological Quarterly* 27:403–21.

Sherman, Lawrence W., et al. 1998. *Preventing Crime: What Works, What Doesn't, What's Promising*. Washington, DC: Government Printing Office.

Shihadeh, Edward S., and Graham C. Ousey. 1998. "Industrial restructuring and violence: The link between entry–level jobs, economic deprivation, and black and white homicide." *Social Forces* 77 (September):185–206.

Siegrist, Johannes. 1995. "Emotions and health in occupational life." *Patient Education and Counseling* 25 (July):227–36.

Silbert, Mimi, and Ayala M. Pines. 1981. "Occupational hazards of street prostitutes." *Criminal Justice and Behavior* 8 (4):395–99.

Sills, Yole G. 1994. *The AIDS Pandemic: Social Perspectives*. Westport, CT: Greenwood.

Silverstein, Charles. 1981. *Man to Man–Gay couples in America*. New York: William Morrow.

Simon, Thomas, James Mercy, and Craig Perkins. 2001. *Injuries from violent crime, 1992–98*. Washington, DC: Government Printing Office.

Simons, Ronald L., and Les B. Whitbeck. 1991. "Sexual abuse as a precursor to prostitution and victimization among adolescent and adult homeless women." *Journal of Family Issues* 12 (September):361–79.

Simpson, George E., and Milton Yinger. 1965. *Racial and Cultural Minorities*. New York: Harper & Row.

Singer, Lynn T., et al. 2002. "Cognitive and motor outcomes of cocaine–exposed infants." *Journal of the American Medical Association* 287:1952–60.

Singh, Bolaria B. 2000. *Social Issues and Contradictions in Canadian Society*. Toronto: Harcourt Canada.

Singh, Vijai P. 1991. "The underclass in the United States: Some correlates of economic change." *Sociological Inquiry* 61 (Fall):505–21.

Single, E., L. Robson, X. Xie, and J. Rehm, et al. 1996. *The Costs of Substance Abuse in Canada: Highlights*. Ottawa: Canadian Centre on Substance Abuse.

Sirgy, M. Joseph, David Efraty, Phillip Siegel, and Dong Jin Lee. 2001. "A new measure of quality of work life (QWL) based on need satisfaction and spillover theories." *Social Indicators Research* 55:241–302.

Skanberg, A., and E. Ohrstrom. 2002. "Adverse health effects in relation to urban residential soundscapes." *Journal of Sound and Vibration* 250:151–55.

Skog, O-J. 2003. Alcohol consumption and fatal accidents in Canada, 1950–1998. *Addiction* 98(7):883–894.

Sleegers, J. 2000. "Similarities and differences in homelessness in Amsterdam and New York City." *Psychiatric Services* 51 (January):100–04.

Smedley, Brian D., Adrienne Y. Stith, and Alan R. Nelson, eds. 2002 *Unequal Treatment: Confronting Racial and Ethnic Disparities in Health Care*. Washington, DC: Institute of Medicine.

Smith, D. S. 1996 (February). "Parent-generated home study in Canada." *The Canadian School Executive*. Vol. 15, No. 8:1–5.

Smith, Patrick D., P. Clayton Rivers, and Kandy J. Stahl. 1992. "Family cohesion and conflict as predictors of drinking patterns: Beyond demographics and alcohol expectancies." *Family Dynamics of Addiction Quarterly* 2 (2):61–69.

Smith, Ryan A. 1997. "Race, income and authority at work." *Social Problems* 44 (February):19–32.

Snell, Tracy L. 1995. *Correctional Populations in the United States, 1993*. Washington, DC: Bureau of Justice Statistics.

Snider, Michael, and Kathryn Borel. 2004 (May 24). "*Stalked by a cyberbully: Cellphones and the Net are kids' social lifelines—they can also be their social death*." Macleans.ca. Online at http://www.macleans.ca/topstories/technology/article.jsp?.content=2.

Snyder, Howard N., and Melissa Sickmund. 1999. *Juvenile Offenders and Victims: 1999 National Report*. Washington, DC: Office of Juvenile Justice and Delinquency Prevention.

Sobel, E., et al. l995. "Occupations with exposure to electromagnetic fields: A possible risk factor for Alzheimer's disease." *American Journal of Epidemiology* 142 (September 1):515–24.

Socall, Daniel W., and Thomas Holtgraves. 1992. "Attitudes toward the mentally ill: The effects of label and beliefs." *Sociological Quarterly* (3):435–45.

Social Development Canada. 1997. Online at http://www11.sdc.gc.ca/en/cs/sp/arb/publications/bulletins/1997-000.

Soine, L. 1995. "Sick building syndrome and gender bias." *Social Work and Health Care* 20 (3):51–65.

Sontag. 1973 (Sept.). "The Double Standard of Aging." *Saturday Review* 23:29–38.

Sorenson, Jon, Robert Wrinkle, Victoria Brewer, and James Marquart. 1999. "Capital punishment and deterrence: Examining the effect of executions on murder in Texas." *Crime & Delinquency* 45 (October):481–93.

Sorokin, Pitirim A. 1942. *The Crisis of Our Age*. New York: E. P. Dutton.

South, Scott J. 2001. "Time–dependent effects of wives' employment on marital dissolution." *American Sociological Review* 66:226–45.

Specter, Michael. 1996. "10 years later, through fear, Chernobyl still kills in Belarus." *The New York Times*, March 31.

Spector, P. E. 2002. "Employee control and occupational stress." *Current Directions in Psychological Science* 11:133–36.

Spergel, Maria. 2004. Online at www.Hillwatch.com.

Spiess, Michele. 2002. "MDMA (Ecstasy)." Fact sheet. Office of National Drug Control Policy website.

Spilerman, Seymour, and Tormod Lunde, 1991. "Features of educational attainment and job promotion prospects." *American Journal of Sociology* 97 (November):689–720.

St. George-Hyslop, Peter H. 2000. "Piecing together Alzheimer's." *Scientific American*, December, pp. 76–83.

St. Jean, Yannick, and Joe R. Feagin. 1998. *Double Burden: Black Women and Everyday Racism*. Armonk, NY: M. E. Sharpe.

Stack, Steven. 1990. "Execution publicity and homicide in South Carolina: A research note." *Sociological Quarterly* 31 (4):599–611.

Staines, Graham L., Kathleen J. Pottick, and Deborah A. Fudge. 1986. "Wives' employment and husbands' attitudes toward work and life." *Journal of Applied Psychology* 71:118–28.

Stanecki, Karen. 1999. "AIDS cuts life expectancy in many African countries." U.S. Census Bureau press release.

Stanton, Alfred H., and Morris S. Schwartz. 1961. "The mental hospital and the patient." In *Complex Organizations*, A. Etzioni, ed., pp. 234–42. New York: Holt, Rinehart & Winston.

Stark, Elizabeth. 1984. "The unspeakable family secret." *Psychology Today* (May):39–46.

Statistical Profile on the Health of First Nations in Canada. 2003. Online at http://www.hc-sc.gc.ca/fnihb/sppa/hia/publications/statistical_profile.pdf.

Statistical Report on the Health of Canadians. 1999. PEI: Health Canada. Online at http://www.statcan.ca/english/freepub/82-570-XIE/tabc.pdf.

Statistics Canada. 1996. *Census of Canada: Housing and Social Statistics Division*. Ottawa: Government of Canada.

———. 2000. Women in Canada 2000: A Gender-Based Statistical Report. Catalogue No. 89-503 XPE.

———. 2001a. *Census of Canada: Housing and Social Statistics Division*. Ottawa: Government of Canada.

———. 2001b. Workplace and Employee Survey Compendium. Catalogue No. 71-585-XIE/2001001. Online at http://www.statcan.ca/english/freepub/71-585-XIE/71-585-XIE2001001.pdf.

———. 2003a. Report of the Pan-Canadian Education Indicators Program 2003. Online at http://www.statcan/english/freepub/81-582-XIE/2003001/highligh.

———. 2003b. The Canadian Labour Market at a Glance. Catalogue No. 71-222-XWE. Online at http://80-www.statcan.ca.ezproxy.library.yorku.ca/english/freepub/71-222-XIE/71-222-XIE2004000.htm.

———. 2004. The Changing Profile of Canada's Labour Force. Catalogue No. 96F0030XIE2001009. Online at http://www12.statcan.ca/english/census01/Products/Analytic/companion/paid/contents.cfm.

Stavins, R. N. 2004. "Forging a more effective global climate treaty (beyond Kyoto)." *Environment* 46(10):22–30.

Steele, J., J. B. James, and R. C. Barnett. 2002. "Learning in a man's world." *Psychology of Women Quarterly* 26:46–50.

Steelman, Lala Carr, and Brian Powell. 1991. "Sponsoring the next generation: Parental willingness to pay for higher education." *American Journal of Sociology* 96 (May):1505–29.

Stefanko, Michael, and Jordan Horowitz. 1989. "Attitudinal effects associated with an environmental hazard." *Population and Environment* 11 (Fall):43–57.

Steffensmeier, Darrell, and Stephen Demuth. 2000. "Ethnicity and sentencing outcomes in U.S. federal courts." *American Sociological Review* 65:705–29.

Steingraber, Sandra. 1998. *Living Downstream: A Scientist's Personal Investigation of Cancer and the Environment.* New York, Vintage Books.

Stetz, Michael. 1999. " 'Driving while black' no crime, but . . ." *San Diego Union–Tribune*, March 14.

Stice, Eric, and Sarah Kate Bearman. 2001. "Body–image and eating disturbances prospectively predict increases in depressive symptoms in adolescent girls." *Developmental Psychology* 37:597–607.

Stine, Susan M. 1998. "Opiate dependence and current treatments." In *New Treatments for Chemical Addictions*, Elinore F. McCance–Katz, ed., pp. 75–111. Washington, DC: American Psychiatric Association.

Stires, Lloyd K. 1991. "The Gulf 'war' as a sanctioned massacre." *Contemporary Social Psychology* 15 (December):139–43.

Stith, Sandra M., et al. 2000. "The intergenerational transmission of spouse abuse." *Journal of Marriage and Family* 62:640–54.

Stolberg, Sheryl Gay. 1998. "Superbugs." *New York Times Magazine*, August 2.

———. 1999. "Breaking down medicine's culture of silence." *New York Times*, December 5.

Stone, Brad. 1999. "Get a life!" *Newsweek*, June 7.

Stoneman, Bill. 1999. "Un–happy workers." *American Demographics*, May.

Storm, T. 1994. "Social context and aboriginal drinking." In *Aboriginal Substance Use: Research Issues*. Ed. D. McKenzie. Ottawa: Canadian Centre on Substance Use: National Native Alcohol and Drug Abuse Program.

Streissguth, A. P. 1992. "Fetal alcohol syndrome: Early and long–term consequences." In *Problems of Drug Dependence* 1991, L. Harris, ed. Rockville, Md: National Institute on Drug Abuse.

Stretesky, Paul, and Michael J. Hogan. 1998. "Environmental justice: An analysis of superfund sites in Florida." *Social Problems* 45 (May):268–87.

Strickland, Bonnie R. 1995. "Research on sexual orientation and human development." *Developmental Psychology* 31 (January):137–40.

Strossen, Nadine. 1995. "The perils of pornophobia." *Humanist*, May–June, pp. 5–7.

Stuart, John A., and Paul D. Bliese. 1998. "The long–term effects of Operation Desert Storm on the psychological distress of U.S. Army Reserve and National Guard veterans." *Journal of Applied Social Psychology* 28 (January):1–22.

Sturdy, Stephanie. 1997 (Fall). Prostitution in Canada: Criminology 101. Online at http://www.mala.bc.ca/www/crimeweb/Student/Sturdy/htm.

Sui, Jack. 2003 (January 30). *Canada Counts Gay Heads.* Toronto: 365Gay.com/NewscenterContent.

Sullivan, Deborah A. 2001. *Cosmetic Surgery: The Cutting Edge of Commercial Medicine in America.* New Brunswick, NJ: Rutgers University Press.

Susser, Ezra S., Daniel B. Herman, and Barbara Aaron. 2002. "Combating the terror of terrorism." *Scientific American*, August, pp. 70–77.

Sutherland, E. H. 1947. *Principles of Criminology* 4th ed. Philadelphia: J. B. Lippincott.

Sutherland, Edwin H. 1968. "White collar criminality." In *Radical Perspectives on Social Problems*, Frank Lindenfeld, ed., pp. 149–60. New York: Macmillan.

Sutherland, Edwin H., and Donald R. Cressey. 1955. *Principles of Criminology*, 5th ed. Philadelphia: J. B. Lippincott.

Swanson, Jeffrey W., et al. 2002. "The socialenvironmental context of violent behavior in persons treated for severe mental illness." *American Journal of Public Health* 92:1523–31.

Swift, J., J. M. Davies, R. G. Clarke, and M. Czerney. 2003. *Getting Started: On Social Analysis in Canada.* (4th ed.). Toronto: Between the Lines.

Swift, Jamie, Jacqueline M. Davies, Robert Clarke, and Michael Czerny. 2003. *Getting Started on Social Analysis in Canada.* 4th ed. Toronto: Between the Lines.

Swim, Janet K. l995. "Sexism and racism: Old–fashioned and modern prejudices." *Journal of Personality and Social Psychology* 68 (February):199–214.

Symanski, R. 1974. "Prostitution in Nevada." *Annals of the Association of American Geographers* 64 (September):357–77.

Sypnowich, C. 2000. "The culture of citizenship." *Politics & Society* 28:531–55.

Szymanski, A. 1976. "Racism and sexism as functional substitutes in the labor market." *Sociological Quarterly* 17 (Winter):67–73.

Tausky, Curt, and Anthony F. Chelte. 1988. "Workers' participation." *Work and Occupations* 15 (November):363–73.

Tavris, Carol. 1990. "Just another 'disease' to soothe powerlessness." *Los Angeles Times*, March 5.

Teicher, Martin H. 2002. "Scars that won't heal: The neurobiology of child abuse." *Scientific American*, March, pp. 68–75.

Temple, R. J., and M. J. Himmel. 2002. "Safety of newly approved drugs: Implications for prescribing." *Journal of the American Medical Association* 287:2273–2275.

Terkel, Studs. 1972. *Working*. New York: Avon Books.

Tetrick, Lois E., and James M. LaRocco. 1987. "Understanding, prediction, and control as moderators of the relationships between perceived stress, satisfaction, and psychological well–being." *Journal of Applied Psychology* 72 (November):538–43.

Thabet, A. A., and P. Vostanis. 2000. "Posttraumatic stress disorder reactions in children of war." *Child Abuse and Neglect* 24 (February):291–98.

Thalidomide Victims Association of Canada. 2003. Online at http://www.thalidomide.ca/en/index.html.

The Link. 2005 (February 15). "Why are you stopping them?" *The Link, Concordia University*. Online at http://thelink.concordia.ca/article.pl?sid=05/02/15/1019201.

Thomas, H. 1993. "Psychiatric symptoms in cannabis users." *British Journal of Psychiatry* 163:141–149.

Thompson, Ben. 2002 (October 22). *Census Gives Sketch of Canadian Gay Families*. Ottawa: 365Gay.com/NewscenterContent.

Thompson, Ross, and Paul Amato. 1999. *The Post Divorce Family: Children, Parenting and Society*. California, Thousand Oaks: Sage Publishing.

Thomson, Elizabeth, Thomas L. Hanson, and Sara S. McLanahan. 1994. "Family structure and child wellbeing: Economic resources vs. parental behaviors." *Social Forces* 73:221–42.

Thoreau, Henry David. 1968. *Walden and the Essay on Civil Disobedience*. New York: Lancer.

Thornberry, Terence P., Carolyn A. Smith, Craig Rivera, David Huizinga, and Magda Stouthamer–Loeber. 1999.

"Family disruption and delinquency." *Juvenile Justice Bulletin*, September.

Thornberry, Terence P., Marvin D. Krohn, Alan J. Lizotte, and Deborah Chard–Wierschem. 1993. "The role of juvenile gangs in facilitating delinquent behavior." *Journal of Research in Crime and Delinquency* 30 (February):55–87.

Thorne, P. S., et al. 2001. "Indoor environmental quality in six commercial office buildings in the Midwest United States." *Applied Occupational and Environmental Hygiene* 16:1065–77.

Throop, David R. 1997. "What are men's issues?" World Wide Web Virtual Library: Men's Page website.

Thrupp, Lori Ann. 1991. "Sterilization of workers from pesticide exposure: The causes and consequences of DBCP–induced damage in Costa Rica and beyond." *International Journal of Health Services* 21 (4):731–57.

Thun, Michael J., et al. 1997. "Alcohol consumption and mortality among middle–aged and elderly U.S. adults." *New England Journal of Medicine* 337 (December 11):1705–14.

Thurlow, Crispin. 2001. "Naming the 'outsider within': Homophobic pejoratives and the verbal abuse of lesbian, gay and bisexual high–school pupils." *Journal of Adolescence* 24:25–38.

Tickell, Crispin. 1992. "The quality of life: What quality? Whose life?" *Environmental Values* 1 (Spring):65–76.

Tiet, Quyen, et al. 2001. "Relationship between specific adverse life events and psychiatric disorders." *Journal of Abnormal Child Psychology* 29:153–64.

Tilly, Chris, and Randy Albelda. 1994. "It's not working: Why single mothers can't work their way out of poverty." *Dollars and Sense* 196 (November–December):8–10.

Ting, Yuan. 1997. "Determinants of job satisfaction of federal government employees." *Public Personnel Management* 26 (Fall):313–34.

Tjepkema, M. 2004. "Alcohol and illicit drug dependence." Health Reports: How Healthy Are Canadians? Supplement Vol. 15:9–19. Ottawa: Statistics Canada. Catalogue No. 82-003. Online at http://www.statcan.ca/english/freepub/82-003-SIE/2004000/pdf/82-003-SIE2004000.pdf.

Toffler, Alvin. 1970. *Future Shock*. New York: Random House.

Tomaskovic–Devey, Donald, and Vincent J. Roscigno. 1996. "Racial economic subordination and white gain in the U.S. South." *American Sociological Review* 61 (August):565–89.

Tomislava, Cavar. 2002. "The role of male physical educators and administrators in the advancement of female students' physical education. *Canadian Women's Studies*. Vol. 21, No. 3:100.

Toner, Robin, and Sheryl Gay Stolberg. 2002. "Decade after health care crisis, soaring costs bring new strains." *New York Times*, August 11.

Toronto Star. 2002 (October 20). "Police and race." Online at http://www.thestar.com/NASApp/cs/ContentServer? pagename=thestar/Layout/Article_PrintFriendly&c= Article&cid=1026146621495&call_pageid=10349353011 56&DPL=IvsNDS%2f7ChAX&tacodalogin=yes.

Torrey, E. F. 1994. "Violent behavior by individuals with serious mental illness." *Hospital and Community Psychiatry* 45 (July):653–62.

Totten, M. 1999 (February 10). Dispelling Myths about Youth Violence. *The Ottawa Citizen.* Online at http:// www.media-awareness.ca/english/resources/articles/ perceptions_of_crime/myth_youth.cfm.

Toward a Healthy Future: Second Report on the Health of Canadians. 1999 (September). Prepared by the Federal, Provincial and Territorial Advisory Committee on Population Health for the Meeting of Ministers of Health, Charlottetown, P.E.I.

Tracy, Paul E., and James Alan Fox. 1989. "A field experiment on insurance fraud in auto body repair." *Criminology* 27 (August):589–603.

Tran, K. 2004. "Visible Minorities in the Labour Force: 20 Years of Change." *Canadian Social Trends* 73:7–11.

Trotter, Andrew. 1997. "Inequities in access to technology documented." *Education Week*, May 21.

Trudeau, P. 1970. Notes for a National Broadcast by the Prime Minister Pierre Elliott Trudeau. Online at http:// collections.ic.gc.ca/discourspm/anglais/pet/1610970e.html.

Tsang, Mun C., Russell W. Rumberger, and Henry M. Levin. 1991. "The impact of surplus schooling on worker productivity." *Industrial Relations* 30 (Spring):209–28.

Tsui, Lisa. 1998. "The effects of gender, education, and personal skills self–confidence on income in business management." *Sex Roles* 38 (5–6):363–74.

Tubman, Jonathan G. 1993. "Family risk factors, parental alcohol use, and problem behaviors among school–age children." *Family Relations* 42 (January):81–86.

Turner, R. J., and D. A. Lloyd. 1999. "The stress process and the social distribution of depression." *Journal of Health and Social Behavior* 40 (December):374–404.

Turnipseed, David. 1992. "Anxiety and perceptions of the work environment." *Journal of Social Behavior and Personality* 7 (3):375–94.

Tuxill, John. 1999. *Nature's Cornucopia.* Washington, DC: Worldwatch Institute.

Tween, S. H., and C. D. Ryff. 1991. "Adult children of alcoholics: Profiles of wellness amidst distress." *Journal of Studies on Alcohol* 52 (March):133–41.

Tyler, Patrick E. 1995. "China's war zone." *New York Times*, November 16.

U.S. Census Bureau. 2001. *Money Income in the United States: 2000.* Washington, DC: Government Printing Office.

U.S. Department of Justice. 1992. *Drugs, Crime, and the Justice System.* Washington, DC: Government Printing Office.

U.S. Department of State. 2002. *Patterns of Global Terrorism 2001.* Department of State website.

U.S. Public Health Service. 1995. *Healthy People 2000.* Washington DC: Government Printing Office.

Uchitelle, Louis. 1996. "More downsized workers are returning as rentals." *New York Times*, December 8.

Uchitelle, Louis, and N. R. Kleinfield. 1996. "On the battlefields of business, millions of casualties." *New York Times*, March 3.

Uggen, Christopher. 2000. "Work as a turning point in the life course of criminals." *American Sociological Review* 67:529–46.

UNDP Annual Report. 2003. 4:214.

Ungar, Sheldon. 1992. "The rise and (relative) decline of global warming as a social problem." *Sociological Quarterly* 33 (4):483–501.

———. 1998. "Bringing the issue back in: Comparing the marketability of the ozone hole and global warming." *Social Problems* 45 (November):510–27.

United Nations Population Fund. 2001. *Population Issues Briefing Kit 2001.* New York: UNFPA.

Useem, Michael, and Jerome Karabel. 1986. "Pathways to corporate management." *American Sociological Review* 51 (April):184–200.

Vaillant, G. E. 1983. *The Natural History of Alcoholism.* Boston: Harvard University Press.

Valentine, F. 2003. Public Interest Groups: The Canadian Association of Independent Living Centres. Online at http://www.cailc.ca/CAILC/text/illibrary/interestgroups/ public_e.html.

Valera, Roberto J., Robin G. Sawyer, and Glenn R. Schiraldi. 2001. "Perceived health needs of inner–city street prostitutes." *American Journal of Health Behavior* 25:50–59.

Van Koppen, Peter J., and Robert W. J. Jansen. 1999. "The time to rob: Variations in time of number of commercial robberies." *Journal of Research in Crime and Delinquency* 36 (February):7–29.

Vedantam, Shankar, Aaron Epstine, and Bob Geiger. 1997. "Tobacco firm says smoking is addictive." *San Diego Union–Tribune*, March 21.

Vera, Maria Nieves, J. Vila, and J. F. Godoy. 1994. "Cardiovascular effects of traffic noise." *Psychological Medicine* 24 (November):817–27.

Vera-Toscano, E., E. Phimister, and A. Weersink. 2001. "The Dynamics of Income and Employment in Rural Canada: The Risk of Poverty and Exclusion." Ottawa: Statistics Canada, Agriculture Division. Catalogue No. 21-601-MIE01043.

Vertiz, Virginia C. 1992. "The curriculum audit: A quality control vehicle to school reform." *Education* 113 (Winter):165–67.

Vinokur, A., and M. L. Selzer. 1975. "Desirable versus undesirable life events: Their relationship to stress and mental distress." *Journal of Personality and Social Psychology* 32 (August):329–39.

Vita, Anthony J., Richard B. Terry, Helen B. Hubert, and James F. Fries. 1998. "Aging, health risks, and cumulative disability." *New England Journal of Medicine* 338 (April 9):1035–41.

Vora, Erik A., and Jay A. Vora. 2002. "Undoing racism in America." *Journal of Black Studies* 32:389–404.

Wagstaff, Mark C., and Beth E. Wilson. 1988. "The evaluation of litter behavior modification in a river environment." *Journal of Environmental Education* 20 (Fall):39–44.

Walker, K. 2004 (June 21). "Aboriginal vote can matter." CBC, Canada Votes 2004. Online at http://www.cbc.ca/canadavotes/analysiscommentary/katherinewalker.html.

Wallace, M. 2002. "Crime Statistics in Canada, 2002." *Juristat* Volume 23, Number 5.

Wallace, M. 2003. "Canadian crime statistics." *Juristat.* Vol. 24, No. 6. Ottawa: Statistics Canada. Catalogue No. 85-002-XPE-24-06.

Wallerstein, Judith S. 1986. "Women after divorce: Preliminary report from a ten–year follow–up." *American Journal of Orthopsychiatry* 56 (January):65–77.

Walsh, Kenneth T. 1999. "The three R's and the big P." *U.S. News & World Report*, August 30.

Walters, V. 1994. "Women's Perceptions Regarding Health and Illness." In *Health, Illness and Health Care in Canada* 2nd ed. Eds. B. Singh Bolaria and H. D. Dickinson:307–325. Toronto: Harcourt Brace and Company.

Wang, Philip S., Olga Demler, and Ronald C. Kessler. 2002. "Adequacy of treatment for serious mental illness in the United States." *American Journal of Public Health* 92:92–98.

Watson, Dale L. 2002. "The terrorist threat confronting the United States." FBI website.

Watt, Toni Terling. 2002. "Marital and cohabiting relationships of adult children of alcoholics." *Journal of Family Issues* 23:246–65.

Weaver, Charles N. 1997. "Has the work ethic in the USA declined? Evidence from nationwide surveys." *Psychological Reports* 81:491–95.

Weaver, Charles N., and Michael D. Matthews. 1990. "Work satisfaction of females with full–time employment and full–time housekeeping: 15 years later." *Psychological Reports* 66:1248–50.

Webb, James T. 2000. "Mis–diagnosis and dual diagnosis of gifted children." Paper presented at the Annual Conference of the American Psychological Association.

Weeks, Jeffrey. 2000. *Making Sexual History*. London, Polity Press.

Weidenbaum, Murray L. 1999. "A key driver for the U.S. economy: The global economy: Superpowers to supermarkets." *Vital Speeches* 65 (June 1): 506–510.

Weinberg, Arthur, and Lila Weinberg, eds. 1963. *Instead of Violence*. New York: Grossman.

Weinberg, N. S., and W. B. Stason. 1998. "Managing quality in hospital practice." *International Journal of Quality Health Care* 10 (August):295–302.

Weisbrot, Mark. 2000. "Globalism for dummies." *Harper's Magazine*, May, pp. 15–19.

Weisburd, David, and Lorraine Green Mazerolle. 2000. "Crime and disorder in drug hot spots." *Police Quarterly* 3:331–49.

Weisburd, David, Ellen F. Chayet, and Elin J. Waring. 1990. "White–collar crime and criminal careers: Some preliminary findings." *Crime and Delinquency* 36 (July):342–55.

Weismantle, Mai. 2001. "Reasons people do not work." *Current Population Reports*. Washington, DC: Government Printing Office.

Weiss, Robert S. 1990. *Staying the Course: The Emotional and Social Lives of Men Who Do Well at Work*. New York: Free Press.

Weitz, Rose, and Leonard Gordon. 1993. "Images of black women among Anglo college students." *Sex Roles* 28 (January):19–34.

Weitzman, E. R., and I. Kawachi. 2000. "Giving means receiving: the protective effect of social capital on binge drinking on college campuses." *American Journal of Public Health* 90:1936–39.

Weitzman, Nancy, Beverly Birns, and Ronald Friend. 1985. "Traditional and nontraditional mothers' communication with their daughters and sons." *Child Development* 56 (August):894–98.

Welte, John W., and Ernest L. Abel. 1989. "Homicide: Drinking by the victim." *Journal of Studies on Alcohol* 50 (May):197–201.

Werner-Wilson, Ronald Jay, et al. 1997. "Client gender as a process variable in marriage and family therapy." *Journal of Family Psychology* 11 (3):373–77.

West, Candace. 1984. "When the doctor is a 'lady': Power, status and gender in physician–patient encounters." *Symbolic Interaction* 7 (1):87–106.

Whipple, Ellen E., and Carolyn Webster–Stratton. 1991. "The role of parental stress in physically abusive families." *Child Abuse and Neglect* 15 (3):279–91.

Whitam, Frederick L. 1983. "Culturally invariable properties of male homosexuality: Tentative conclusions from cross–cultural research." *Archives of Sexual Behavior* 12 (June):207–26.

White House. 2002. "The Department of Homeland Security." White House website.

White, Lynn K., and Alan Booth. 1985. "Stepchildren in remarriages." *American Sociological Review* 50 (October): 689–98.

White, Lynn, and Bruce Keith. 1990. "The effect of shift work on the quality and stability of marital relations." *Journal of Marriage and the Family* 52 (May):453–62.

White, R. K. 1966. "Misperception and the Vietnam war." *Journal of Social Issues* 22 (July):1–19.

Whitehead, Barbara Dafoe, and David Popenoe. 2001. *The State of Our Unions: The Social Health of Marriage in America*. National Marriage Project website.

Whittle, J. C., P. K. Whelton, A. J. Seidler, and M. J. Klag. 1991. "Does racial variation in risk factors explain black–white differences in the incidence of hypertensive end–stage renal disease?" *Archives of Internal Medicine* 151 (July):1359–64.

Whyte, Martin King. 1990. *Dating, Mating, and Marriage*. New York: Aldine de Gruyter.

Wichmann, Cherami. 2005. Profiles of Families and Children. Ottawa: Department of Justice Canada.

Wickrama, Kas, Rand D. Conger, Fredrick O. Lorenz, and Lisa Matthews. 1995. " Role identity, role satisfaction, and perceived physical health." *Social Psychology Quarterly* 58 (4):270–83.

Widom, Cathy Spatz, and Ashley M. Ames. 1994. "Criminal consequences of childhood sexual victimization." *Child Abuse and Neglect* 18 (April):303–18.

Wilens, Timothy E., et al. 2002. "A family study of the high–risk children of opioid– and alcohol–dependent parents." *American Journal on Addictions* 11:41–51.

Wilensky, Harold L. 1967. *Organizational Intelligence*. New York: Basic Books.

Williams C. 2003. (June). "Sources of workplace stress." *Perspectives of Labour and Income* 4(6):5–12. Ottawa: Statistics Canada. Catalogue No. 75-001-XIE.

Williams, David R., David T. Takeuchi, and Russell K. Adair. 1992. "Socioeconomic status and psychiatric disorder among blacks and whites." *Social Forces* 71 (September):179–94.

Williams, Jr. 1989. "Social integration and longevity: An event history analysis of women's roles and resilience." *American Sociological Review* 54 (August):635–47.

Williams, R. J., F. S. Odaibo, J. M. McGee. 1999. "Incidence of fetal alcohol syndrome in northeastern Manitoba." *Canadian Journal of Public Health*. 90:192–4.

Williams, Terry, and William Kornblum. 1985. *Growing Up Poor*. Lexington, MA: D.C. Heath.

Willms, D. J., M. S. Tremblay, and P. T. Katzmarzyk. 2003. "Geographic and demographic variation in the prevalence of overweight Canadian children." *Obesity Research* 1(5):668–673.

Wilson, Edward O. 2000. *Sociobiology: The New Synthesis*. Cambridge, MA: Harvard University Press.

Wilson, S. J. 1996. *Women, Families & Work* (4th ed.). Toronto: McGraw Hill-Ryerson Limited.

Winick, Charles, and Paul M. Kinsie. 1971. *The Lively Commerce*. Chicago: Quadrangle.

Wintermute, Robert, and Mads Andenaes. 2001. *Legal Recognition of Same-Sex Relationships: A Study of National, European and International Law*. Portland, Oregon: Oxford Hart Publishing.

Wirt, John, et al. 2002. *The Condition of Education 2002*. Washington, DC: National Center for Education Statistics.

Wiseman, Jacqueline P. 1991. *The Other Half: Wives of Alcoholics and Their Social–Psychological Situation*. New York: Aldine de Gruyter.

Witt, Susan D. 1997. "Parental influence on children's socialization to gender roles." *Adolescence* 32 (Summer):253–59.

Wolf, Naomi. 1991. *The Beauty Myth: How Images of Female Beauty Are Used against Women*. New York: William Morrow.

Wolfinger, Nicholas H. 1998. "The effects of parental divorce on adult tobacco and alcohol consumption." *Journal of Health and Social Behavior* 39 (September):254–69.

Women's Health Matters News. 2002 (June 11). "Hysterectomies too frequent in Canada?" Toronto: Sunnybrook & Women's College Health Sciences Centre. Online at http://www.womenshealthmatters.ca/news/news_show.cfm?number=170.

Woo, Deborah. 2000. *Glass Ceilings and Asian Americans*. Walnut Creek, CA: AltaMira Press.

Wood, E., T. Kerr, W. Small, et al. 2004 (September). "Changes in public order after the opening of a medically supervised safer injection facility for illicit injection drug users." *Canadian Medical Association Journal*. Vol. 17, No. 71:731–734. Online at http://www.cmaj.ca/cgi/content/full/171/7/731.

Woodruff, Susan I., and Terry L. Conway. 1992. "A longitudinal assessment of the impact of health/fitness status and health behavior on perceived quality of life." *Perceptual & Motor Skills* 75 (August):3–14.

Woods, N. F., and F. M. Lewis. 1995. "Women with chronic illness: Their views of their families' adaptation." *Nursing Journal* 16 (March–April):135–48.

Woody, Bette. 1991. "Recent employment experience of black women workers in the services economy." *Sociological Practice Review* 2 (July):188–99.

Work–Life Compendium. 2001. 150 Canadian Statistics on Work, Family and Well-Being. University of Guelph: Centre for Families, Work and Well-Being. Women's Bureau Labour Program, Human Resources Development Canada. Online at http://www.hrsdc.gc.ca/en/lp/wid/gaze/spring2003/Spring2003_Compendium.shtml.

World Bank. 2004. Online at http://www.worldbank.org/research/projects/edattain/edattain.htm.

World Resources Institute. 1999. *World Resources 1998–1999*. New York: Oxford University Press.

Wortley, S., and A. McCalla. 2003. "The Debate Continues: Evidence of Bias Against Black People in the Canadian Criminal Justice System." In J. Roberts (Ed.). *Criminal Justice in Canada 2.*

Wren, Christopher S. 1997. "Ex–addicts find methadone more elusive than heroin." *New York Times*, February 2.

Wright, Beverly Hendrix, and Robert D. Bullard. 1990. "Hazards in the workplace and black health." *National Journal of Sociology* 4 (Spring):45–62.

Wright, E. R., G. Avirappattu, and J. E. Lafuze. 1999. "The family experience of deinstitutionalization." *Journal of Behavioral Health Service Research* 26 (August):289–304.

Wright, Harlan I., Judith S. Gavaler, and David Van Thiel. 1991. "Effects of alcohol on the male reproductive system." *Alcohol Health & Research World* 15 (12):110–14.

Wynn, Ruth L., and Jean Bowering. 1990. "Homemaking practices and evening meals in married and separated families with young children." *Journal of Divorce and Remarriage* 14:107–23.

Xie, X., J. Rehm, E. Single, and L. Robson. 1996. *The Economic Costs of Alcohol, Tobacco and Illicit Drug Abuse in Ontario: 1992*. ARF Research Document Series No. 127. Toronto: Addiction Research Foundation.

Xie, X., J. Rehm, E. Single, L. Robson, and J. Paul. 1998. "The Economic Costs of Alcohol Abuse in Ontario." *Pharmacological Research* 37: 241–249.

Yanz, L., B. Jeffcott, D. Ladd, and J. Atlin (Maquila Solidarity Network—Canada). 1999 (January). Policy Options to Improve Standards for Women Garment Workers in Canada and Internationally. Status of Women Canada, Research Directorate Publications.

Yoder, J. D., and L. L. Berendsen. 2001. " 'Outsider within the firehouse." *Psychology of Women* 25:27–36. Young, Michael L. 1998. "A plethora of paradoxes." *USA Today*, March, p. 15.

Young, Michael L. 1998. "A plethora of paradoxes." *USA Today*, March, p. 15.

Youth Suicide Problems. 2004. Online at http://www.virtualcity.com/youthsuicide.

Zautra, Alex J., Morris A. Okun, Sharon E. Robinson, and Douglas Lee. 1989. "Life stress and lymphocyte alterations among patients with rheumatoid arthritis." *Health Psychology* 8 (1):1–14.

Ziegelstein, Roy C. 2001. "Depression in patients recovering from a myocardial infarction." *Journal of the American Medical Association* 286:1621–27.

Zimiles, Herbert, and Valerie E. Lee. 1991. "Adolescent family structure and educational progress." *Developmental Psychology* 27:314–20.

Zivcic, Ivanka. 1993. "War stress in Croatian children." *Journal of the American Academy of Child and Adolescent Psychiatry* 32 (July):709–13.

Zucker, Brian, Royal Dawson, and C. Dennis Carroll. 2001. "Credits and attainment." *Statistical Analysis Report*. National Center for Education Statistics website.

Zuckerbrod, Nancy. 2002. "Number of military ousted for homosexuality rose in '01." *San Diego Union–Tribune*, March 14.

Zuger, Abigail. 1998. "Prostitutes' stress is greater than soldiers'." *San Diego Union–Tribune*, August 19.

Zvonkovic, Anisa M. 1988. "Underemployment: Individual and marital adjustment to income loss." *Lifestyles* 9 (Summer):161–78.

CREDITS

64 Figure 3.1 Adapted from the Statistics Canada publication "Canadian Community Health Survey—Mental health and well-being," 2002, Catalogue 82-617, September 9, 2004; Figure 3.2 Adapted from the Statistics Canada publication "Canadian Community Health Survey—Mental health and well-being," 2002, Catalogue 82-617, September 9, 2004; **65** Box 3.1 Source: Canadian Centre on Substance Abuse (CCSA) http://www.ccsa.ca/CCSA/EN/Topics/Populations/AboriginalPeoplesOverview.htm; **66** Copyright 2003. Centre for Addiction and Mental Health; **76** Adapted from the Canadian Addiction Survey, 2004, Health Canada, published by the Canadian Centre on Substance Abuse; **79** Figure 3.3 Adapted from Physicians for a Smoke-Free Canada (www.smoke-free.ca) and Canadian Tobacco Use Monitoring Survey (December 2003); Figure 3.4 Adapted from the Statistics Canada CANSIM database http://cansim2.statcan.ca, Table 103-0004; **82** Source: The Costs of Drug Abuse and Drug Policy, page 3, Antony Jackson, Economics Division, Parliamentary Information and Research Service, 1992. Reproduced with the permission of the Minister of Public Works and Government Services, 2005; **85** Adapted from the Statistics Canada publications "Canadian Community Health Survey—Mental health and well-being," 2002, Catalogue 82-617, September 9, 2004 and "Health Reports—How Healthy Are Canadians?," Catalogue 82-003, Supplement to Vol. 15, 2004, 2004 Annual Report; **88** Reprinted with permission from News-Medical.Net; **100** Adapted from the Statistics Canada publication "A profile of criminal victimization: results of the 1999 General Social Survey," Catalogue 85-553, August 8, 2001; **101** Adapted from the Statistics Canada publication "A profile of criminal victimization: results of the 1999 General Social Survey," Catalogue 85-553, August 8, 2001; **104** Adapted from the Statistics Canada publication "Juristat," Catalogue 85-002, Vol. 24, No. 6, and Vol. 23, No. 5; **102** Adapted from the Statistics Canada publication "Juristat," Catalogue 85-002, Vol. 24, No. 4, June 2004; **104** Adapted from the Statistics Canada publication "Juristat," Catalogue 85-002, Vol. 24, No. 6, and Vol. 23, No. 5; **105** Table 4.1 Adapted from the Statistics Canada publication "Juristat," Catalogue 85-002, Vol. 23, No. 5, June 2003; Table 4.2; **106** Figure 4.4 Adapted from the Statistics Canada publication "Juristat," Catalogue 85-002, Vol. 23, No. 5, June 2003; Figure 4.5 Adapted from the Statistics Canada publications "Adult correctional services in Canada (data tables)," 2002–2003, Catalogue 85-211, October 27, 2004 and "Juristat," Catalogue 85-002, Vol. 23, No. 11, December 2003; **108** Figure 4.6 Adapted from the Statistics Canada publication "Juristat," Catalogue 85-002, Vol. 23, No. 8, October 2003, page 6; Figure 4.7 Adapted from the Statistics Canada publication "Juristat," Catalogue 85-002, Vol. 23, No. 8, October 2003, page 6; **110** Adapted from the Statistics Canada publication "Juristat," Catalogue 85-002, Vol. 23, No. 2, March 2003, page 5; **113** Adapted from the Statistics Canada publication "Juristat," Catalogue 85-002, Vol. 23, No. 2, March 2003, page 5; **128** Table 5.1 Adapted in part from the Statistics Canada publication "Low income cut offs from 1994–2003 and low income measures 1992–2001," Catalogue 75F0002, 1992–2003, no. 2, March 9, 2004; Table 5.2 Adapted in part from the Statistics Canada publication "Low income cut offs from 1994–2003 and low income measures 1992–2001," Catalogue 75F0002, 1992–2003, no. 2, March 9, 2004; **130** Adapted from the Statistics Canada publication "Income in Canada," 2003, Catalogue 75-202, May 12, 2005 and from the Statistics Canada CANSIM database http://cansim2.statcan.ca, Table 202-0802; **131** Adapted from the Statistics Canada publication "Canadians with low incomes," 1999, Catalogue 85F0033MIE, June 14, 2001; **132** Adapted from the Statistics Canada publication "Survey of Labour and Income Dynamics: public use microdata file," 2002, Catalogue 75M0010XCB, January 12, 2005; **133** Adapted in part from the Statistics Canada website http://www.statcan.ca/english/freepub/71-222-XIE/2004000/chart-i49.htm; **134** Reprinted with permission from the National Anti-Poverty Organization, www.napo-onap.ca; **137** Figure 5.5 Adapted from the Statistics Canada publication "Survey of Labour and Income Dynamics (SLID)—A survey overview," Catalogue 75F0011XIE, May 12, 2005; Table 5.4 Adapted from the Statistics Canada publication "Survey of Labour and Income Dynamics (SLID)—A survey overview," Catalogue 75F0011XIE, May 12, 2005; **140** Lyrics from "Final Notice" reprinted with permission of Eric McIntyre; **141** Adapted from the Statistics Canada publication "A profile of criminal victimization: results of the 1999 General Social Survey," Catalogue 85-553, August 8, 2001; **144** Figure 5.8 Adapted in part from Statistics Canada, National Population Health Survey, 1996–97; **162** Adapted from the Statistics Canada CANSIM database <http://cansim2.statcan.ca>, Table 282-0002; **164** Adapted from the Statistics Canada CANSIM database <http://cansim2.statcan.ca>, Table 282-0008; **166** Adapted from the Statistics Canada CANSIM database <http://cansim2.statcan.ca>, Table 202-0102; **176** Adapted from the Statistics Canada CANSIM database <http://cansim2.statcan.ca>, Table 113-0001; **177** Adapted from the Statistics Canada CANSIM database <http://cansim2.statcan.ca>, Table 113-0001; **188** "Ethnic Diversity Survey: portrait of a multicultural society," 2002, Catalogue 89-593, September 29, 2003; **189** Table 7.2 Adapted from the Statistics Canada website http://142.206.72.67/02/02a/02a_graph/02a_graph_006_1e.htm; Figure 7.1 Adapted from the Statistics Canada publication "Labour Force Activity (8), Immigrant Status and Period of Immigration (10B), Visible Minority Groups (14), Age Groups (11A) and Sex (3) for Population 15 Years and Over, for Canada, Provinces, Territories, Census Metropolitan Areas and Census Agglomerations, 1991 to 2001 Censuses—20% Sample Data," Catalogue 97F0012XIE, February 11, 2005; **190** Table 7.3 Adapted from the Statistics Canada publications "The Nation: 1996 Census of Population," Catalogue 93F0023XDB, November 4, 1997 and "Immigration and Citizenship, 2001 Census," Catalogue 97F0009XIE, October 29, 2003; Figure 7.2 Adapted from the Statistics Canada publication "Canadian Social Trends," Catalogue 11-008, Summer 2004, No. 73; **193** Reprinted with permission from The Globe and Mail; **196** Figure 7.3 Adapted from the Statistics Canada publication "Canadian Social Trends," Catalogue 11-008, Summer 2004, No. 73; Figure 7.4 Adapted from the Statistics Canada publication "Canadian Social Trends," Catalogue 11-008, Summer 2004, No. 73; **197** Adapted from the Statistics Canada publication "Ethnocultural Portrait of Canada: Highlight Tables, 2001 Census," Catalogue 97F0024XIE, January 21, 2003; **198** Adapted from the Statistics Canada publication "The Nation: 1996 Census of Population," Catalogue 93F00340XDB, June 9, 1998; **207** Table 7.5 Source: Annual Report 2003 URL: http://www.chrc-ccdp.ca/publications/annn3-en.asp Author/Organization: Canadian Human Rights Commission. Human Resources Development Canada. Reproduced with the permission of the Ministry of Public Works and Government Services, 2005 and of Her Majesty the Queen in Right of Canada 2005; Table 7.6 Source: Annual Report 2003 URL: http://www.chrc-ccdp.ca/publications/ann3-en.asp Author/Organization: Canadian Human Rights Commission. Human Resources Development Canada. Reproduced with the permission of the Ministry of Public

Works and Government Services, 2005 and of Her Majesty the Queen in Right of Canada 2005; Table 7.7 Source: Annual Report 2003 URL: http://www.chrc-ccdp.ca/publications/annn3-en.asp Author/Organization: Canadian Human Rights Commission. Human Resources Development Canada. Reproduced with the permission of the Ministry of Public Works and Government Services, 2005 and of Her Majesty the Queen in Right of Canada 2005; **208** Reprinted with permission from The Canadian Parliamentary Review; **225** Source: Elections Canada, Explaining the Turnout Decline in Canadian Federal Elections: A New Survey of Non-voters, March 2003, p. 17; **232** Figure 8.4 Adapted from the Statistics Canada website <http://www.statcan.ca/english/freepub/68-213-SIE/2004000/tables/table1.htm; Figure 8.5 Adapted from the Statistics Canada website http://www.statcan.ca/english/freepub/68-213-SIE/2004000/tables/table1.htm and from the Statistics Canada publication "Public Service Employee Survey—Custom tabulations," Catalogue 71C0021, April 1, 2003; **247** Adapted from the Statistics Canada database <http://cansim2.statcan.ca>, Series V2461462; **248** Table 9.1 Adapted from the Statistics Canada publication "Education in Canada: School Attendance and Levels of Schooling, 2001 Census (School attendance, highest level of schooling, age groups and sex for population 15 years and over), Catalogue 95F0418XCB, April 8, 2004; Figure 9.2 Adapted from Union Membership in Canada at, along with: 1911-1981 Graham and Lowe (2002); 1991-2004 Workplace Gazette, Vol. 7, No. 3. Reproduced with the permission of the Ministry of Public Works and Government Services, 2005 and of Her Majesty the Queen in Right of Canada 2005; **249** Adapted from the Statistics Canada publication "The Daily," Catalogue 11-001, Friday, December 3, 2004; **252** Figure 9.4 Adapted from the Statistics Canada CANSIM database <http://cansim2.statcan.ca>, Table 282-002; Figure 9.5 Adapted from the Statistics Canada CANSIM database <http://cansim2.statcan.ca>, Table 282-002; **255** Adapted from the Statistics Canada CANSIM database <http://cansim2.statcan.ca>, Series V2054036 and from the Statistics Canada publication "Labour force historical review," 2004, Catalogue 71F0004XCB, February 18, 2005; **260** Adapted from the Statistics Canada CANSIM database <http://cansim2.statcan.ca>, Series V2054036 and from the Statistics Canada publication "Labour force historical review," 2004, Catalogue 71F0004XCB, February 18, 2005; **277** Adapted in part from Statistics Canada publication "Education indicators in Canada: Report of the Pan-Canadian Education Indicators Program," Catalogue 81-582, 2003, No. 03, November 25, 2003; **302** Adapted from the Statistics Canada publication "The Daily," Catalogue 11-001, Tuesday October 22, 2002; **305** Adapted from the Statistics Canada publication "The Daily," Catalogue 11-001, Tuesday May 4, 2004; **308** Table 11.3 Adapted from the Statistics Canada publication "Family Violence in Canada: a statistical profile," 2004, Catalogue 85-224, July 6, 2004; Table 11.4 Adapted from the Statistics Canada publication "Juristat," Catalogue 85-002, Vol. 23, No. 4, June 2003; **309** Adapted from the Statistics Canada publication "The Daily," Catalogue 11-001, Tuesday July 6, 2004; 330 Adapted from the Statistics Canada publications "New birth cohort life tables for Canada and Quebec, 1801-1991," Catalogue 91F0015MIE, No. 3, October 1, 1997; and from "The Daily," Catalogue 11-001, Monday September 27, 2004, also adapted

from the Statistics Canada website <http://www.statcan.ca/english/freepub/82-401-XIE/2002000/tables/html/dt004_en.htm> and http://www.statcan.ca/english/freepub/84F0211XIE/2002/tables/html/t027_en.htm; 332 Source: "Figure 2.1 Projected Life Expectancy at Birth by Gender, Registered Indian Population and Canadian Population Canada, 1975–2016" In: Basic Departmental Data 2001. Indian and Northern Affairs-2002, URL: http://www.ainc-inac.gc.ca/pr/sts/bdd01/bdd01_e.html. Reproduced with the permission of the Minister of Public Works and Government Services, 2005; **333** Figure 12.3 Adapted from the Statistics Canada publication "Statistical Report on the Health of Canadians," Catalogue 82-570, No. 1, September 16, 1999; Table 12.2 Adapted from the Statistics Canada publication "Statistical Report on the Health of Canadians," Catalogue 82-570, No. 1, September 16, 1999; **338** Source: (A Report on Mental Illnesses in Canada), Public Health Agency of Canada, (October 2002), Adapted and Reproduced with the permission of the Minister of Public Works and Government Services Canada, 2005; **344** Reprinted with permission of Disabled Peoples International, www.dpi.org, and Dr. Abill Albert of the British Council of Disabled People (BCODP); **365** Reproduced with permission from Global Policy Forum. Primary data from World Watch Institute; **394** Reproduced with the permission of Environment Canada, 2005; **396** Adapted from the Statistics Canada CANSIM database, <http://cansim2.statcan.ca>, Table 128-0002.

Photo Credits
1 CP/Larry MacDougal; 2 CP/Ryan Remiorz; 18 Copyright Viviane Moos/Corbis; 31 AP/Wide World Photos; 32 Buccina Studios/Getty Images; 37 Copyright Reporters/eStock Photo; 43 Paul Heim/Unicorn Stock; 48 Bob Daemmrich; 51 CP/Kevin Frayer; **61** Oscar Burriel/Latin Stock/SPL/PR; 67 Spencer Grant/PhotoEdit; 77 James Pickerell/The Image Works; 84 © Digital Vision; 91 AP Photo/Lennox McLenden; 94 CP/Aaron Harris; 98 Patrick Sheandell O'Carroll/PhotoAlto; 117 Toronto Sun/Stan Behal; 125 Andy Levin/Photo Researchers; 126 Anne Marie Rousseau/The Image Works; 143 McGraw-Hill Companies, Inc./Gary He, photographer; **157** Ryan McVay/Getty Images; **158** Alan Carey/The Image Works; 171 Tom McCarthy/PhotoEdit; 178 Copyright Rachel Epstein/The Image Works; 186 Rudi von Briel/PhotoEdit; 191 CP/Joe Bryksa; 199 CP/Ryan Remiorz; 205 AP/Wide World Photos; 210 Halifax Daily News/Scott Dunlop; 215 CP/Tom Hanson; 216 CP/Jonathan Hayward; **218** CP/Adrian Wyld; 221 Montreal Star; 226 CP/Tom Hanson; 236 CP/Adrian Wyld; 244 Bob Daemmrich/Stock Boston; 259 Moncton Times & Transcript; 264 Tom Ballard/EKM Nepenthe; 272 St. Catharines Standard; 290 AP/World Wide Photos; 293 Royalty-Free/CORBIS; 299 Peter Cade/Getty Images; 307 Copyright Claudia Uribe/eStock Photo; 313 Keith Brofsky/Getty Images; 318 Bachmann/The Image Works; 323 Copyright Gary Watts/The Image Works; 328 Toronto Star/Rick Madonik; 351 AP/World Wide Photos; 355 AP/Wide World Photos; 361 Philip James Corwin/Corbis; 362 CP/Adrian Wyld; 366 Corbis; 368 AP/World Wide Photos; 373 Corbis; 387 CP/J P Moczulski; 390 AP/Rajesh Nirgude; 396 CP/Kevin Frayer; 399 Norman R. Rowan/Stock Boston; 405 Reuters NewMedia Inc./Corbis; 407 Tim Jewett/EKM Nepenthe.

NAME INDEX

SUBJECT INDEX